Introduction to Business

SECOND EDITION

RICHARD M. HODGETTS

Florida International University

Introduction to Business

SECOND EDITION

Addison-Wesley Publishing Company

Reading, Massachusetts · Menlo Park, California
London · Amsterdam · Don Mills, Ontario · Sydney

Sponsoring Editor: William H. Hamilton
Production Editor: Marion E. Howe
Designer: Catherine L. Dorin
          Bonnie M. Pauley
Illustrator: Oxford Illustrators Ltd.
          Kristin Kramer
Cover Design: Richard Hannus
Cover Photo: West Stock Inc.
          Ken Stewart

Library of Congress Cataloging in Publication Data

Hodgetts, Richard M
  Introduction to business.

  Includes index.
  1. Business. I. Title.
HF5351.H56 1981   658   80–21284
ISBN 0–201–03894–3

ISBN 0–201–03894–3
ABCDEFGHIJ-MA-8987654321

To Jennifer

The purpose of this book is to introduce you to the world of business, a world that, when we stop to think about it, touches us all. The products we buy and the services we use are all provided by business firms. The alarm clock we turn off in the morning was manufactured by a business firm. So too was the vehicle we use to get to work or school. And much of the equipment we see in business offices and university buildings—from telephones and desks to typewriters and file cabinets—was built by business firms. When we return home at night we are still surrounded by products from the business world, from kitchen appliances and utensils to the couch and television set in the living room. Because of the impact business has on our everyday lives, it is important that we have at least a fundamental understanding of what goes on in this world.

In writing this book I have sought to give you an interesting and informative look at this world and how it operates. This can be quite a chore, of course, because there is much more to the field than one can ever hope to squeeze into a single volume. For this reason, I have sought to maintain a balance between content and readability. Only the most relevant topics have been placed in this book, and they are presented in the form of a model so that you can see how each fits into the overall picture. We will be studying each of the main areas of business both as an entity in itself and as a part of a larger system. In all, there are four major parts to this book.

The first part describes our American business system and provides an introduction to capitalism, the economic environment in which business operates, and the social responsibility of business. The second part of the book examines the operations of business, including (a) how a firm's structure and management are determined, (b) the methods by which companies produce products, (c) the way they manage human assets, (d) how they market their goods and services, (e) the methods used to finance operations, and (f) the techniques used to control their overall operations. Part III deals with business-government relations, addressing such key areas as business law, government regulation of business, and small business. Part IV discusses career opportunities in the business field.

In each chapter I have sought to present the material in an interesting, easy-to-read style. The result is a text that is actually shorter than many others in the field. Approximately 35 percent of this book consists of pictures, cartoons, real-life examples, biographies, and cases designed to supplement the text itself. I think students will find this pedagogical approach very helpful in maintaining their interest and reinforcing the major ideas contained in the book, for in the final analysis it is designed to be a *student* text. This objective has been attained partly through the use of a number of distinguishing features. Nine of them merit particular observation.

DISTINGUISHING FEATURES

First, each chapter contains a list of objectives that tell students what they will be learning in the chapter. Then there are questions at the end of the chapter to help them judge how well they have mastered the material.

Second, tables, charts, figures, real-life examples, cartoons, and photographs, designed to highlight and expand upon the text material, have been included throughout the text.

Third, each chapter contains a biography of a famous person who has performed successfully in the area under discussion. For example, in the chapter on marketing fundamentals there is a biographical sketch of Ray Kroc, the man who made the McDonald's hamburger chain an international organization and a household word; in the chapter on international trade there is a biographical sketch of Abu Su'ud, chief investor for the nation of Kuwait; and the chapter on short-term financing has a biography of America's best-known banker, David Rockefeller, Chairman of the Chase Manhattan Bank.

Fourth, within the chapters there are cases that provide illustrations of the ideas presented in the text. For example, when we discuss entrepreneurship students will learn about Dr. Land, the entrepreneur who developed the Polaroid camera; when sole proprietorships and partnerships are discussed, they will discover how Richard Sears started the Sears, Roebuck Company; and when we discuss organization structure they will learn how Howard Hughes organized his massive $2-billion empire.

Fifth, at the end of each chapter there is a summary of the most important material covered, which should provide a good review of the chapter.

Sixth, also contained at the end of each chapter are key terms that have been mentioned in the material. These terms are those with which business people are very familiar. By studying them, students can build a basic business vocabulary.

Seventh, questions about the text material have been placed at strategic points within the chapters themselves. These help break each chapter into small, self-contained units and make it easy for students to test their progress as they go along.

Eighth, each part or section of the book contains a continuous case that is carried throughout that part. For example, in the section on marketing there are two cases in each of the four chapters on marketing. These eight cases follow the activities of the same firm as it confronts topics and issues similar to those being discussed in the text.

Ninth, at the end of the text there is a comprehensive glossary containing most of the business terms presented in the book. Students looking for a definition can quickly consult the glossary rather than having to leaf through the text trying to identify where they originally saw the term.

SUPPLEMENTARY MATERIALS
Student Study Guide

Prepared by Charles W. Beavin, Karen E. Brinkman (both of Miami-Dade Community College) and myself, the Student Guide reviews the most important ideas presented in each chapter and tests understanding through fill-in-the-blank, true-false, and multiple-choice questions. In addition, each chapter contains an anagram requiring the students to find key business terms. Finally, several interesting projects are included that ask the students to extend their business knowledge in a practical way. A highly unique and useful item is the set of flashcards contained at the back of the book. They are designed to build the students' business vocabulary.

Instructor's Resource Guide

Prepared by Karen E. Brinkman and myself, the Instructor's Resource Guide contains a wealth of information. Included are chapter teaching notes, detailed chapter outlines with commentary, suggested answers to all chapter questions and cases, over thirty-five transparency masters, film guide, contemporary issues, and an extensive test bank with over 800 questions.

ACKNOWLEDGMENTS

There are many people who have helped me write this book. In particular, I would like to thank the staff of Addison-Wesley, who proposed the project and offered me continuing advice and guidance throughout the undertaking, as well as providing many substantive suggestions on how to enliven the text through pictures, cartoons, and real-life examples and to improve the overall readability of the material. Fred Luthans, University of Nebraska, Henry Albers, Western Illinois University, Dean Leonardo Rodriguez, Florida International University, and Charles W. Beavin, Miami-Dade Community College, also contributed helpful suggestions and ideas. In addition, I would like to thank those who read, reviewed, and commented on portions of the text:

Steven Altman, Florida International University
Karen Bessey, Merced College
Robert Bolan, West Los Angeles College

Kent Brigham, Madison Area Technical College
Karen Brinkman, Miami-Dade Community College
James Cox, Lane Community College
William Dickson, Green River Community College
Dee Ezell, Texas Tech University
Marc Paden Golsmith, Thiel College
Martin Gosman, Boston University
Norman Govoni, Babson College
Roy Grundy, College of DuPage
Darvin Hoffman, Texas A & I University
A. Thomas Hollingsworth, University of South Carolina
Peter Irwin, Richland College
Susan Jacobs, LL.D.
Phil Lewis, Walla Walla Community College
Mary E. T. Longstaff, Highline Community College
Louise Luchsinger, Texas Tech University
Richard Metcalf, University of Nebraska
Glenn McEvoy, Loretto Heights College
Cheedle Millard, University of Texas, Dallas
Paul Plescia, American River College
James Snyder, College of Charleston
Timothy Wright, Lakeland Community College

Richard M. Hodgetts
Miami, Florida
October 1980

CONTENTS

PART I
The Nature of American Business

PART II
Business and Its Operations

CHAPTER 23
Data Processing

PART III
Other Critical Dimensions

Careers in Government, Law, and Small Business

PART IV
Business and You

Introduction to Business

The Nature of American Business

How should one begin one's study of the world of business? In this book we are going to start by looking at the firm and its environment. The overriding goal of this part of the text is to give you a general understanding of the American business system.

Chapter 1 will present some of the fundamentals of what makes our American system of business work the way it does. Particular attention will be given to explaining our economic system of capitalism and how it differs from the economic systems of many other countries.

In Chapter 2 the specific environment of American business will be studied. The environmental forces that influence the operations of the firm, such as the government and the economy, will be examined. Particular consideration will also be given to explaining the role and importance of economics and competition.

In Chapter 3 the social responsibility of business will be studied. Companies today know that they need to provide equal opportunity to their employees, take steps to protect the environment, and respond to the needs of their customers by selling safe, quality products at reasonable prices. This chapter will also describe what business is doing to respond to these social challenges.

When you have finished reading this part of the book, you should have an understanding of the nature of the American business firm and its environment. You should also be familiar with a number of key business terms, including *standard of living, capitalism, mixed economies, gross national product, oligopoly, monopolistic competition, pure competition, truth in lending,* and *consumerism.* Finally, you should have gained an appreciation for the dynamic nature of the American business system.

1

Some see private enterprise as a predatory target to be shot, others as a cow to be milked, but few are those who see it as a sturdy horse pulling the wagon.
Winston Churchill

OBJECTIVES OF THIS CHAPTER

The overall purpose of this book is to introduce you to the world of business. The objectives of this chapter are to examine and analyze our own American business system. In particular we will be studying both the purpose of this system and the manner in which business operates. By the end of this chapter you should be able to do the following:

a. define what is meant by the term business;

b. explain what we mean when we talk about standard of living;

c. describe the four major factors of production;

d. tell what capitalism is and describe the three basic foundations upon which it rests;

e. identify the four major groups that exist in a capitalistic economy;

f. describe other economic systems including socialism, communism, and mixed economies; and

g. relate some of the challenges and opportunities that exist in the world of business.

Our American Business System

WHAT IS BUSINESS?

Every day of our lives we have some "business" dealings. Most of the time we are *buyers* or *users* of some good or service. For example, we purchase gasoline for our car or go to the barbershop for a haircut. Everyone in America is a user of some products or services. Sometimes, however, we are *sellers* of goods. Most people who work for a living are either directly or indirectly involved in selling something. As a result, when we really examine what goes on in the business world it becomes obvious that we are all part of it.

In this book we are going to be examining the world of business and how it operates. Before we do that, however, it is important to establish a basic definition of what business is. **Business** *is an organized approach used by individuals for the purpose of providing goods and services to people.* Usually this is done for a profit, although some businesses, as we shall see later in this book, are actually nonprofit in nature. All of them, however, play a key role in improving the society's standard of living.

1. What is the primary goal of business? Explain.

IMPROVING THE STANDARD OF LIVING

Standard of living is a term we use when we talk about how well off the people of a particular nation are. Often it is measured by *dividing total production by population.* The reasoning behind this method of calculation is simply that if production is high and/or population is low, there are more goods and services available to everyone. Today the nations of the world can be divided into two broad categories: those that have a high rate of productivity and those that have a low rate, in relation to their individual populations. As a result, there are "have" and "have-not" nations. We are one of the "have" nations because, when our production is divided by our population, we end up with a lot of the "good things in life." Business, of course, can

do very little to directly increase or decrease a country's population. It can, however, work to increase the production of goods and services by, for example, making available to the consumer more air conditioners, refrigerators, and television sets at prices low enough for people to afford (see Table 1.1). As this happens, the overall standard of living increases. Why do some countries have low standards of living while others have high ones? (see Fig. 1.1). One answer is found in the *factors of production* a country has available and what it does with them.

TABLE 1.1 HOUSEHOLDS IN THE U.S. IN 1977 HAVING SELECTED ELECTRICAL APPLIANCES

ELECTRICAL APPLIANCE		PERCENTAGE
Air conditioners, room		55.3
Clothes dryers		59.3
Clothes washers		73.3
Coffeemakers		99.7
Dishwashers		40.9
Electric blankets		59.9
Food-waste disposers		42.8
Freezers, home		44.8
Mixers		92.4
Radios		99.9
Ranges, electrical		71.9
Refrigerators		99.9
Television	*black and white*	99.9
	color	81.3
Toasters		99.9
Vacuum cleaners		99.9

Sources: Billboard Publications, Inc., and *Merchandising Week*, as reported in *Information Please Almanac*, 1979, p. 74.

Factors of Production

The three primary factors of production, which are basic to the development of a nation's standard of living, are land, labor, and capital. These factors, along with modern technology, to a large degree determine what a country will produce and how well its people will live.

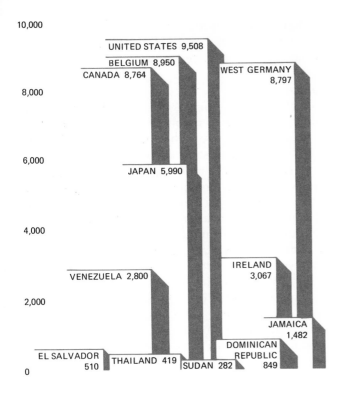

FIG. 1.1 *National income per person in selected countries, in dollars* *(Source:* Reader's Digest 1979 Almanac and Yearbook, *pp. 478–480.)*

Land

The term **land** refers not only to geographic territory but to natural resources as well. The United States is very rich in many natural resources, particularly iron ore. As a result, it has been able to manufacture many iron and steel-type products, including automobiles, airplanes, stoves, refrigerators, and air conditioners. The United States also has an abundant supply of very rich farmland, which has helped it produce more than enough food for its people. In fact, the United States is so successful in raising crops that it exports some of the surplus to other countries to help out their people.

Unfortunately, there is a limit to the amount of raw materials located in any country. The United States has only so much iron ore, coal, and oil beneath its surface. Also, it can produce only a limited

With rich farmland—and modern technology—the United States produces more than enough food for its people and is able to export surplus to countries in need.

7

amount of food. As a result, our standard of living is influenced to a great extent by our natural resources. We must use them wisely, especially if our children are to live as well as we do.

Labor

The term **labor** refers to the people who produce the products or services being consumed. These people consist of workers, supervisors, foremen, clerks, professionals, entrepreneurs, and thousands of others. Some are involved in the manufacture of goods. Some manage their firms' operations. Some serve as the link between the manufacturer and the consumer by, for example, retailing the finished product.

All of these people do something to help improve the nation's standard of living. However, they are more than just "manpower." If they are well trained and can operate or manage complex machinery, they can accomplish far more than those who rely on merely physical strength. Consider, for example, the United States and China. While America has a much smaller work force, it is far more productive in terms of output. One of the reasons is that America has skilled workers.

Capital

Capital is often thought of as another name for money. It is also common to talk about capital in terms of investments, such as raising capital by getting people to invest in a company. Actually, the term **capital** means more than money; it also includes machinery, equipment, tools, and any other physical labor-saving devices that can help people do a job better or faster. Some of the best illustrations of these new, modern techniques are found in our auto assembly plants, where cars can roll off the line every two minutes. Another example is found in our major soft-drink companies, where thousands of cans and bottles of soda pop can be produced every day. And there are thousands of other illustrations throughout American industry. Such new production methods have been very important in helping to raise our overall standard of living.

The term "labor" refers to the people who produce the products or services being consumed.

"Capital" may refer to machinery, equipment, tools, and any other physical labor-saving devices that can help people do a job better or faster.

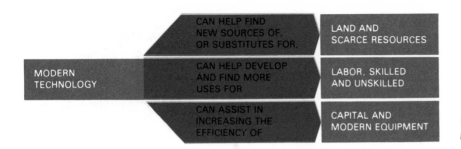

MODERN TECHNOLOGY	CAN HELP FIND NEW SOURCES OF, OR SUBSTITUTES FOR,	LAND AND SCARCE RESOURCES
	CAN HELP DEVELOP AND FIND MORE USES FOR	LABOR, SKILLED AND UNSKILLED
	CAN ASSIST IN INCREASING THE EFFICIENCY OF	CAPITAL AND MODERN EQUIPMENT

FIG. 1.2 *Technology and the three major factors of production*

When these three factors of production are analyzed, it becomes evident that they are **interdependent**—*each relies on the other two.* For example, some of our natural resources can only be extracted economically if we have trained labor and sophisticated equipment. If we do, the resource can be used to further our standard of living. Likewise, with new labor-saving machines we can free manpower for more important jobs, such as thinking up new products that will make life more enjoyable for everyone. Thus a high standard of living is dependent upon all three of these factors. In addition, there is a fourth "new" factor of production that has not yet been discussed but that is also vital to maintaining a high standard of living. This is *modern technology.*

Modern technology

Technology is the application of knowledge to production. Thanks to modern technology, we have been able to increase greatly the efficiency of our work force. New machines and new methods have helped cut down time and expense while increasing overall output. This has meant more production and a higher standard of living.

For most of us in America, modern technology is thought of as the reason why we can have cars and television sets. However, technology has also increased the amount of food available to us, by means of modern farm machinery and animal-breeding techniques, and has extended our life span via medical technology.

Will mankind continue to live longer and have a higher quality of life? In large measure the answer depends on technology and our ability to use it wisely. If we keep making progress as we have over the past fifty years, the answer is definitely yes. The advancement of technology depends upon research and development, and the latest statistics show that the United States is continuing to pump billions of dollars annually into such efforts. So while we are running out of some scarce resources, we may well find technological substitutes for many of them through our research programs.

Therefore, in the final analysis the three major factors of production are all influenced by technology (see Fig. 1.2). For example, as we begin running out of a particular scarce resource, scientists will start looking for a substitute. As we realize that we need new skills or techniques in medicine, people will start developing new technology to meet those needs. As equipment proves to be slow or inefficient, new machines will be invented. Technology responds to our needs in helping us maintain our standard of living.

2. In what way is modern technology a factor of production?

3. Which of the factors of production is most important? Explain. Which is least important? Why?

THE BUSINESS OF AMERICA

The factors of production (land, labor, capital, and technology) all influence the standard of living. In large part, they also help explain the economic differences between "have" and "have-not" nations. For example, the United States has a great quantity of natural resources and skilled labor while Honduras does not. As a consequence, the United States' standard of living is higher than that of Honduras. Likewise, while the Soviet Union also has an abundance of natural resources, it lacks our technology. Thus while Russia may be a "have" nation, its living standards are lower than ours because its production of goods is less.

However, there is another important framework within which to analyze American business. This is the **economic system** within which our country's businesses operate. One simple reason why the United States has become the foremost industrial power in the world is that its economic environment encourages business activity. As Calvin Coolidge noted, "The chief business of the American people is business." This is not so for many other nations, but then they do not operate in a *capitalistic* economic system.

WHAT IS CAPITALISM?

Capitalism is an economic system in which individuals are basically free from government control in determining the kinds of goods and services that will be produced and distributed. In the United States, we live in a capitalistic economic system. Our founding fathers believed that business should be allowed to operate in a laissez-faire environment. **Laissez-faire** is a French term that can be translated to mean that *government should not interfere in the affairs of business*. What the founding fathers had in mind might be called *pure capitalism*. However, over the last ninety years there has been an increase in government control over business. Today we know that many laws at the federal, state, and local

"Nice to meet you, Bascom. Any friend of laissez-faire capitalism is a friend of mine."

Drawing by Lorenz; © 1975. The New Yorker Magazine, Inc.

levels have been passed that are designed to regulate business activities. As a result, we presently live in an economic system that can be termed *modified capitalism*. Nevertheless, the three basic freedoms upon which capitalism rests are still in existence. These are (a) private property, (b) private enterprise, and (c) freedom of choice.

Private Property

Capitalism depends upon the right of **private property.** This right is guaranteed to us in the Constitution. Because of it, people can own their own home, business, factory, machinery, and/or equipment. If they wish to expand their operations, they may increase the size of their factory or buy more machinery and equipment. If they wish to sell their business operations, this is also their right. In addition, they have the right to keep the goods they produce as well as any profits from the sale of these goods.

The Day Profit Finished Second

Every year at State University there is a "Business Day," on which companies throughout the city and state are asked to send a representative to the university to speak to the students. Some of the business representatives talk to classes in the liberal arts, some go to education or engineering departments, others go to the business school. Last year Rodger McHarris of the First National Bank, located in the state's largest city, spoke to a group in the business school. Rodger, the president of the bank, was asked to talk about the bank's role in the community. Part of his talk went as follows:

> The purpose of our bank is to provide the necessary capital and financial assistance for helping out the people and the business community in our city and state. We see our bank as having a key role to play in the future of this state and we are determined to do all we can to fulfill that role.

During the question and answer period that followed the talk, one student asked Rodger if the primary purpose of his bank was to make a profit, just like any other business. Rodger said that profit certainly was important to the bank's future, but that neither he nor any of the other officers really believed that it was the primary goal. "Our job is to provide a service to the people of the community. If we do our job right, the profits will be there. However, we are more concerned with seeing that people have nice homes, a good community, and a little money put aside for sending their kids to college and taking care of any emergencies that might arise. In short, you might say we are in the business of helping people improve their standard of living."

1. What did Rodger mean by his statement that "If we do our job right, the profits will be there"?

2. In what way can a bank help the community raise its standard of living?

3. Which of the factors of production would be most useful to a bank in helping raise the standard of living?

Private Enterprise

Individuals in this country are free to set up and operate their own businesses. These firms are owned by the private citizens who have invested money in them. As such, each is a **private enterprise;** the government has no ownership in them. Most of our large firms are private enterprises, such as General Motors, IBM, General Electric, Standard Oil of New Jersey, and Xerox. Most of our small companies are also private enterprises, including the local barber shop, jewelry store, and pizzeria.

One of the most successful examples of private enterprise has been General Motors, which today is the number-one auto maker in the world. This was not always the case—up until the late 1920s Ford Motor held the top position. However its owner, Henry Ford, believed that autos were a basic necessity and insisted that they all be painted black. General Motors, on the other hand, felt that cars were also a leisure product and should come in all sorts of colors and contain whatever accessories would make driving a pleasure. GM's philosophy won out. By 1930 it had pushed Ford out of the number-one spot in sales. Today General Motors is still the world's leading auto producer, with annual sales of over $50 billion.

The only control the government has over private ownership is that of restricting or regulating some of its activities. For example, in the case of a corporation the state must grant a charter allowing

Walter E. Disney

© Walt Disney Productions

No one understood the nature of American business better than Walt Disney.

Arriving in Hollywood from the Midwest with only $40 in his pocket, he parlayed his holdings into a million-dollar empire. In his early work in the field of cartoons he introduced such universally loved characters as Mickey Mouse, Donald Duck, and Goofy. In his pictures he used the latest technological breakthroughs in sound and color. Then in 1938 he took a great gamble and introduced the first feature-length cartoon: *Snow White and the Seven Dwarfs.* It was a tremendous success and encouraged him to continue along this line. The result was *Fantasia,* in which color, shape, and motion were blended with the classical music of Leopold Stokowski and the Philadelphia Orchestra. Other full-length animated classics included *Pinocchio, Dumbo,* and *Bambi.*

After World War II, Disney pushed on toward other goals. In the 1950s his studio produced both cartoons such as *Cinderella* and *Peter Pan* and live-action movies like *20,000 Leagues under the Sea.* And while Hollywood trembled before the advance of television, Walt Disney plunged right in with his *True-Life Adventure Features.*

Today, years after his death in 1966, Walt Disney's ideas live on in the form of movies, television programs like "The Wonderful World of Disney," Disneyland in California, and Disney World in Florida. And the pattern of his innovation and leadership continues to survive as seen in the firm's financial successes. Disney Productions today gross approximately $500,000,000 annually.

it to come into existence. In the case of a giant conglomerate, the federal government may bring an antitrust suit charging it with attempting to monopolize and thereby restrain fair competition. However, the government does not invest money in these firms nor share in any profits or losses. The businesses are strictly private in nature.

Freedom of Choice

Businesses in America are basically free to choose whatever good or service they wish to provide. There are some restrictions, of course, brought about by government regulation. For example, a firm cannot enter some industries such as electric, telephone, or commercial airline services without government approval. Nor can a business provide an illegal good or service. Aside from these types of restrictions, however, the company has **freedom of choice.**

The customer has the same freedom. He or she can purchase some goods and refuse to buy others. Because this puts the consumer in a commanding position, we often hear the cliché that "the consumer is king." To a large degree this is true. Without the consumer, business would sell nothing. As a result, business must continually gear its product line and services to the needs of the customer.

Workers also have freedom of choice. If they do not like their wages or working conditions, they are free to seek employment elsewhere. As job opportunities in other industries or firms become available, companies paying lower wages or offering less benefits will lose some of their work force. If they improve their wages and working conditions, on the other hand, business firms can attract replacement help from other companies.

In using this freedom of choice, entrepreneurs and managers must consider the goods and services they wish to offer, the employees who will help them attain these objectives, and the customers they all intend to serve. Each of these four groups is very important in a capitalistic economy. For purposes of analysis, we can identify them as (a) entrepreneurs, (b) managers, (c) workers, and (d) consumers.

4. What are three basic freedoms of capitalism?

5. Which of the three do you think is most likely to change over the next two decades? Explain.

6. In what way is the American economic system an illustration of modified capitalism?

THE IMPORTANT GROUPS IN CAPITALISM

Before we examine in depth the four important groups that exist in a capitalistic economy, it is important to realize that each of them is dependent on the others. No one of them can survive by itself. For this reason they are, like the factors of production, *interdependent* groups (see Fig. 1.3).

FIG. 1.3 *Interdependent groups in a capitalistic economy*

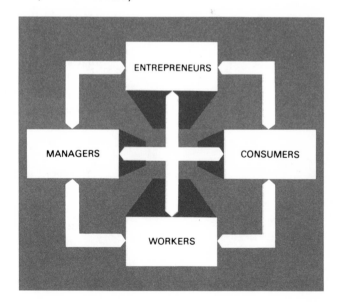

What Ever Happened to Capitalism?

One of the questions Rodger McHarris was asked during his visit to State University was whether he thought the free enterprise system as we know it would survive. Rodger said that he believed it would. However the student who raised the question had her doubts. In particular, the young woman felt that the government was making serious inroads on capitalism and we were well on the road to socialism. Rodger disagreed:

> Sure, the government has been passing a lot of legislation to regulate business. However, this has been in certain areas only. Granted, in our banking industry there are many laws with which we must conform. Overall, though, there is a good deal of freedom to operate in any way we want. For example, the government has no right to tell our stockholders or board of directors what decisions to make. Nor can the government regulate how much dividend we pay on our stock or what services we offer to our depositors. These are things we decide for ourselves. Furthermore, without some type of overall regulation, we might have chaos in the industry. You know, many of the government's laws are designed to help us stay healthy and out of financial difficulty.

The student seemed to accept Rodger's argument. It was evident, however, that a number of the others believed that the bank president had oversimplified the issue. In particular, many seemed to feel that free enterprise as our grandfathers knew it was no longer in existence today. Rodger agreed with this sentiment and said that perhaps we should refer to our economic system today as "modified" capitalism. He called this "capitalism with a little bit of socialism in it." But before closing, Rodger cautioned the students about believing that we were on the road to socialism. "If you look around the world, you will see that there is no stronger supporter of capitalism and free enterprise than the United States. We may have made some minor changes in our basic system, but it's still pretty much what it was one hundred years ago and I think it's going to survive for a long, long time."

1. Exactly what did Rodger mean by "modified" capitalism? Put it in your own words.
2. Which of the basic freedoms of capitalism do you believe have been most eroded by government legislation? Which have been least affected?
3. Do you agree with Rodger's last statement? Explain.

Entrepreneurs

The word **entrepreneur** is French. When translated into English, it means "the organizer or manager of a venture." The term is also used to refer to people who have founded or developed a business of their own that has become a highly successful and profitable organization because of their ingenuity and business skill. Henry Ford, J. Paul Getty, John D. Rockefeller, Ross Perot, and Mary Wells Lawrence are all entrepreneurs.

The entrepreneur is the driving force behind the business. He or she is the one with the ideas about what to produce and to whom it should be sold. This individual also keeps a close eye on revenues, costs, and profits, being constantly ready to take advantage of every opportunity that comes along. In a small business there may be only one entrepreneur, the owner. In larger firms there may be as many as three or four. Without such individuals small firms can never become big, and big ones can never maintain their competitive positions.

Managers

The individuals responsible for operating the business are known as the **managers.** In small firms these people are often the owners as well. In large firms, however, owners and managers are usually separate, with the managers having little, if any, ownership in the company. Instead, the managers tend to be salaried personnel who have chosen a career for themselves in the ranks of management. They are known as **professional managers.** Many of these individuals will remain with one company for their entire business life, serving in a number of managerial positions.

This is not to say that the owners have no control over the managers. If the firm suffers a financial setback, or profits are not up to expectations, the owners may demand a shakeup in the management ranks. Nevertheless, one must not underestimate the importance of these professional managers. Many times they spell the difference between mediocre performance and great success. This is especially

Dr. Land's Polaroid Camera

When Edwin Land was a seventeen-year-old Harvard freshman, he took a leave of absence from his studies to investigate the effect of light-polarizing filters in eliminating automobile headlight glare. He wound up perfecting sheets of polarized material, applied for a patent, and returned to Harvard in 1929.

His interest in research on polarizors continued, however, and in 1937 he founded the Polaroid Corporation. His first big products were Polaroid sunglasses and glare-free study lamps. During World War II his firm worked on military optics and sales rose to almost $17 million. But the best was yet to come. During these years Land had developed something new--a camera that could take a picture and produce a print within sixty seconds! The company had only a small sales organization and a very low advertising budget, but it came up with a unique marketing campaign. It offered exclusive rights to sell the camera for thirty days to one department store in each major city in the country provided the stores did the advertising. Sales were phenomenal. Within ten years the company's revenues were over $59 million, and the corporation had overtaken Bell & Howell and General Aniline & Film in photographic sales. Only giant Eastman Kodak was larger than Polaroid. And it all began with the genius and entrepreneurial ability of Edwin Land.

noticeable in our giant corporations, where professional managers are responsible not only for attaining the objectives desired by the owners but also for directing large numbers of workers and controlling millions of dollars' worth of plant and equipment. No wonder some writers in the field of management claim that *the growth and success of American business is limited only by the talent of its managerial work force.*

Workers

The **workers** are the individuals who perform the physical and mental effort necessary for producing a firm's goods and services. Some are highly skilled, such as die makers, others are semiskilled, such as assembly-line workers, and still others are unskilled, such as common laborers. They are all, however, important assets in a capitalistic system. If they are unhappy with their work situation they will try to find jobs with other firms or, worse, remain with the company but do less work. In either case, they have an impact on the other groups: the entrepreneurs, managers, and consumers.

Consumers

The **consumers** are the individuals who use the goods and services provided by the firm. In one way or another, all of us are consumers. In a capitalistic society we tend to believe that the consumers have the final say about which firms will survive and

FIG. 1.4 *The relationship between business and consumers*

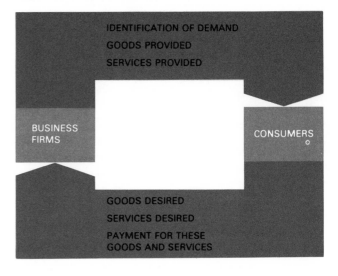

Workers are the individuals who perform the physical and mental effort necessary for producing a firm's goods and services.

which will not. Those companies that can provide the things the consumers want should be profitable and continue to grow. It is all a matter of being able to identify **consumer demand** and then determine how to satisfy that demand. Figure 1.4 illustrates this relationship.

7. Why do we say that the four major groups in capitalism are interdependent?

8. Although the four major groups in capitalism are interdependent, which has the greatest effect on the other three? Explain.

9. Why is the consumer king in a capitalistic economy?

OTHER ECONOMIC SYSTEMS

A country's economic system is tied to its political beliefs. In our country we believe in free enterprise and the right of people to choose what goods and services they want to buy. As a result, capitalism works well for us. Other nations, however, have different political philosophies regarding the proper way to provide goods and services to their people. As a result, there are other economic systems in existence throughout the world. Among these economic systems are (a) socialism, (b) communism, and (c) mixed economies.

Socialism

Countries that operate under **socialism** believe that there are certain goods and services to which everyone is entitled. Such goods are also available in a capitalistic system, but their accessibility is largely dependent upon people's ability to pay for them. In a socialistic country, however, the state believes that these services should be available to everyone, regardless of their ability to pay. It is also common to find socialist countries taking over control of certain *primary* industries—such as steel, utilities, and transportation—and making their services and products available to everyone.

When a firm is **nationalized,** the government usually pays the owners for the company and assumes control of its operations. As you can see, when this happens the government has a large voice in deciding what will be produced and to whom it will be distributed. Most businesses, however, are permitted to continue their operations as before, because they are considered to be *secondary* industries. Thus when we hear that a country such as Great Britain or Sweden has moved toward socialism, we must take care not to believe that they have eliminated free enterprise. What they have done is place restrictions on it.

Communism

Communism as a political doctrine encourages change through revolution. As an economic system it is well entrenched in countries such as the Soviet Union and China. In fact, over one-third of the world's population now live in countries that subscribe to and support the communistic political philosophy, and therefore employ a communistic economic system.

In communist societies everyone is supposed to be treated equally. The poor are given food and clothing; the weak are provided with medical assistance; the elderly are cared for in their old age. Under ideal conditions everyone is supposed to work as hard as they can and, in turn, receive whatever goods and services they require. An old communist cliché says it best: "From each according to his ability; to each according to his need."

The government determines how much of everything will be produced because all the factories and enterprises are owned by the state. The government also decides who will receive the goods and services. As a result, the central government in a communist society has the final say about everything that goes on. The individual's freedom is greatly restricted and there is no free enterprise. If the government does not set production quotas sufficient to satisfy the needs of its people, some will have to do without certain goods. Likewise, if the government orders too much of something to be manufactured, the people will find themselves being urged to buy those goods. Everything depends upon the central government's master plan. An error here will mean problems throughout the economy.

Mixed Economies

So far we have examined three economic systems: capitalism, socialism, and communism. For the most part we have talked about them in "pure" terms. Yet none works quite the way we have described. All are modified in practice; therefore, a particular country might have some features of a capitalistic economy and some of a socialistic economy. For example, in the United States we have a basically capitalistic economy but there are some government restrictions that give us something of a "socialistic" flavor. Likewise, many communist countries have wage systems in which individuals are paid according to ability and profession, giving these countries something of a "capitalistic" flavor.

Yet despite their differences, all economic systems have some common characteristics. One of these is the importance of labor. Without well-trained, highly skilled personnel, no economy can hope to provide an adequate standard of living for its people. Likewise, all of these systems require some type of professional manager to help direct operations. After all, no matter what economic system a country is operating under, it needs competent administrators or managers to see that the correct types of goods and services are produced in the appropriate quantities.

10. In your own words, what is socialism?

11. Does the Soviet Union have a pure or mixed economic system?

12. Why does business operate so well in a capitalistic system?

Now for a Little Capitalism

Mention communist China and everyone immediately conjures up an image of millions of people slaving away all day long just to maintain a mere level of subsistence. However, this is not true. In some places in China, capitalism has begun emerging and families are allowed to supplement their income with side jobs. For example, while 90 percent of the people are agricultural laborers who work in rural communes and get paid according to the amount of work they do and how well they do it, many are also allowed to augment their incomes by cultivating private strips of land and pursuing other legally approved sidelines. As a result, a recent news story out of China reported that one family earned $3,900 in extra income last year, quite a large sum given the fact that annual per capita income is around only $100.

Some Chinese have criticized this capitalistic trend. However, the national newspaper has come to the support of these workers by pointing out that their riches are a result of hard work and not exploitation, theft, or harm to the farm collective. Furthermore, the paper frowned on the idea that the standard of living of everyone should be the same. Conditions vary and so does income, it said. Paying everyone the same wage is egalitarianism, and this has <u>nothing</u> to do with Marxism. So now it looks as if a modified form of capitalism is beginning to grow in China.

There are many opportunities available to those choosing a career in the business world.

THE CHALLENGES AND OPPORTUNITIES OF BUSINESS

The business world faces many challenges. One of these, which we have already examined, is that of helping to maintain a high standard of living for all the people. Others are related to areas we have not yet studied. One is that of producing the needed goods and services at competitive prices. A second is that of making a profit, or breaking even if the organization is nonprofit in nature. A third is the willingness to accept the risks associated with operating the business. A fourth is that of raising the money necessary to keep the firm going. At some time every business will face these challenges.

On the other hand, there are also many opportunities available to those choosing a business career. Helping provide needed goods and services is one of these. A second is the chance to work with other people and experience the rewards and benefits of teamwork. A third is the opportunity to grow with a company. A fourth is the potential for promotion and challenging work. Finally, there is the opportunity to secure a high-paying job.

The purpose of this book is to acquaint you with the world of business. Many of the most important areas will be discussed: choosing a form of ownership, producing goods and services, marketing these goods, and financing overall operations are just a few. As you read each chapter make a note of any areas that particularly interest you. At the end of each section we will discuss future careers in business. This will help you to compare your interests to the careers available, and to decide whether or not you want to spend your life in the world of business.

13. What are some of the challenges faced by the business world?

14. What are some of the opportunities available to those choosing a business career?

15. In your opinion, what are the things an individual should examine in deciding whether or not to take up a business career?

SUMMARY

In this chapter we have examined the nature of American business. We have seen that business is an organized approach used by individuals for the purpose of providing goods and services to other individuals. This process, in turn, helps raise the nation's standard of living. It does so primarily because it leads to increased production. In all, there are four factors of production: land, labor, capital, and technology. Land refers to both geographic territory and natural resources. Labor refers to the people who produce the goods and services. Capital refers to the money and physical labor-saving devices that help people do their work better and faster. Technology refers to the application of knowledge to production.

The success of the United States has come in part from its ability to use these factors of production wisely. It has also resulted from the economic system in which American business operates—capitalism. Capitalism is an economic system in which individuals are basically free to determine the kinds of goods and services that will be produced and distributed. It relies upon three basic freedoms: private property, private enterprise, and freedom of choice. Within the system there are four important groups: entrepreneurs, managers, workers, and consumers.

Capitalism works best in a democratically oriented political environment. Not all countries have this form of government, however, so there are other economic systems in existence. These include socialism, communism, and mixed economies. While some nations might categorize themselves as operating under a "pure" economic system, in reality most use some form of mixed economy. The United States, with its modified capitalistic system, is really an illustration of a mixed economy.

Helping to maintain a high standard of living in a modified capitalistic system is quite a challenge. Yet it is only one of many faced by today's businessperson. At the same time there are numerous opportunities available to those choosing a business career. One of the things you should do as you read this book is to note those areas of business that appeal most to you as possible careers. More will be said on this point throughout the text.

KEY TERMS FOUND IN THIS CHAPTER

QUESTIONS FOR DISCUSSION AND ANALYSIS

1. How can a country improve its standard of living?

2. In terms of factors of production, what is land? Labor? Capital? Technology?

3. In what way are the factors of production interdependent?

4. What did Calvin Coolidge mean when he said that "The chief business of the American people is business"?

5. What is capitalism? Why has American business found it to be such an ideal economic system for private enterprise?

6. Why do we call John D. Rockefeller an entrepreneur?

7. What is socialism? How does it differ from communism?

8. What types of opportunities are available to a person choosing a business career?

Every American enterprise today takes a position in a highly organized world which it did not create, and—necessarily—takes it as it finds it.

Adolf A. Berle, Jr.

OBJECTIVES OF THIS CHAPTER

Business does not exist in a vacuum. It operates in a dynamic world where it must be aware of, and responsive to, many environmental forces. The objectives of this chapter are to examine those forces, especially the economic ones. By the end of the chapter you should be able to do the following:

a. identify and describe the major environments affecting business: historical, natural-physical, political-legal, social-cultural, and economic;

b. define gross national product and explain why it is so well regarded as an economic indicator for the general economy;

c. identify the economic cycles that have occurred over the last fifty years; and

d. describe the four basic types of market models that can exist in an industry: pure monopoly, oligopoly, monopolistic competition, and pure competition.

Business and Its Environment

THE MANY ENVIRONMENTS OF BUSINESS

In the world of business things are always changing. For example, the government passes a new law and some businesses stop doing certain things (or start doing certain things). Or, perhaps, one company lowers its price by $1 and another counters by lowering its price by $1.50. Possibly the price of a raw material goes up and companies start looking for cheaper substitutes. Or workers demand higher wages and the firm announces that it has appointed a committee to look into the matter and report back to the board of directors within a month.

The above are all illustrations of how business adjusts to some of the forces that surround and affect it. We call these forces **the environment of business.** Every business is subject to environmental forces. Successful businesses are those that can respond properly to these forces by "cooperating" with them. This cooperation can take various forms. In the case of the competition lowering its prices, cooperation may require meeting this threat with an identical price reduction. In the case of a demand for higher wages, it may take the form of a 15-percent increase in salary for the workers. In all instances business must interact with environmental forces in order to survive. Failure to do so means bankruptcy (see Fig. 2.1).

The *overall* or total environment in which the firm operates consists of *many smaller environments.* Each of these overlaps and influences the others, yet each is distinct and unique in some way. These smaller environments are the (a) historical environment, (b) natural-physical environment, (c) political-legal environment, (d) social-cultural environment, and (e) economic environment (see Fig. 2.2).

Historical Environment

The **historical environment** provides the *background* for all the other environments. The past is a guide for what to expect in the future. By examining its historical past, business is better able to anticipate new developments and plan for them.

A brief look at the history of American business reveals that there have been some significant changes over the past two hundred years. Very early in our nation's history it was decided that a system of *laissez-faire capitalism*—private ownership free from any government control—would be the best. In the nineteenth century some businesses began to grow larger and larger thanks to new technological developments. Machines began to replace men and America entered the age of *industrialization*. It was during these years that our early giant corporations

FIG. 2.1 *Business and its interaction with the environment*

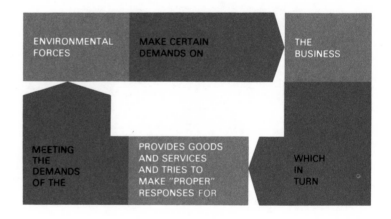

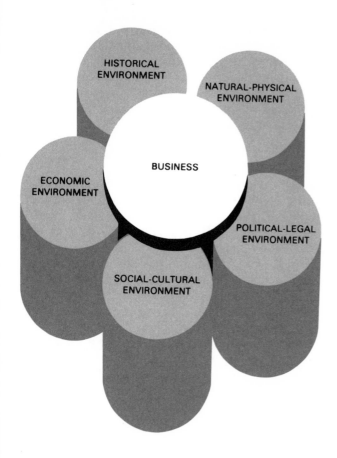

FIG. 2.2 *Environmental forces affecting business*

came into existence. Unfortunately, many of these firms were so big that they began driving out the competition and dictating to society rather than responding to social demands. The result was government legislation to regulate some business activity. This legislation included such well-known laws as the Sherman Antitrust Act and the Clayton Act, and resulted in our historical environment changing to one of *modified capitalism.*

During the present century we have continued to operate under this modified form of capitalism, and the government has continued to regulate business with legislation. The government has also had a greater impact on business because of the increasingly active role it has played in the business arena. This is particularly noticeable in the huge amounts of money it spends every year in buying goods and services from American industry.

In addition, there has been a dynamic growth of labor unions during this century. Since the 1930s their membership has risen from 3.5 million to over 20 million. As a result, labor unions today exert a great deal of influence on business.

When we examine our historical environment we can try to use the lessons of past history to guide us in our future actions. As historians like to say, "the past is prologue." This means that what has already happened helps set the stage for what will occur later on. There are many lessons from the past that can help business decide what to do in the future.

Natural-Physical Environment

The **natural-physical environment** consists of all our natural resources, including air, water, iron ore, silver, and copper. As we noted in the last chapter, these resources become depleted as we produce more and more goods, and in many cases they are nonreplaceable. Oil is an illustration. The United States imports millions of barrels of oil each day to satisfy both consumer and industrial demand. There

The Spindletop

Today the United States imports a great deal of oil from overseas, but the bulk of America's needs are met by domestic production from states like Texas. Before 1900, however, no one knew of the rich oil fields that lay beneath the lone-star state.

A few had suspected that there was oil there. One man, Pattillo Higgins, was convinced that there was oil beneath the fifteen-foot mound known as Spindletop, on the coastal prairie of east Texas. As a result he formed a syndicate to buy up and lease acreage around the mound. Then a mining engineer was brought in and a rotary drill was used to dig deeply into the sandy Texas soil. On January 10, 1901 they struck oil at 1,020 feet. A geyser of oil shot 200 feet into the air. The gusher was so strong that 100,000 barrels of oil a day blew away for ten days before the workers could finally cap the well. Money poured into the area as companies sought to purchase or lease land for thirty miles around. Millionaires were made in minutes as the region became the hub of Texas financial activity. By 1902 there were 440 gushers on Spindletop. Before the field was finally siphoned dry in 1925, it produced 60 million barrels of oil. And by then other fields were discovered in nearby areas, thereby ensuring America a continued supply of a natural resource.

is simply not enough domestic oil to meet our needs. In recent years the price of this foreign oil has increased dramatically. Yet business has little control over the situation because there is no substitute, in most cases, for this raw material. Business is restricted by its natural environment whenever it relies on scarce physical resources.

Political-Legal Environment

A large portion of the **political-legal environment** consists of those laws and regulations that restrict business activity. Over the past one hundred years many important pieces of legislation have been enacted at the federal, state, and local levels. One of the major areas of concern has been that of maintaining competition in the marketplace. Today, for example, it is illegal to monopolize, or attempt to monopolize, a particular market. Companies doing so are subject to antitrust action. For example, IBM is locked in a legal struggle with the Justice Department, which is seeking to break it up on the grounds that the computer giant is so large that it totally dominates the industry. The government currently wants to split IBM up into three smaller companies. Other major areas of legislative concern are related to price fixing, advertising, the minimum wage, and working conditions. In all these cases, business must work within specified guidelines.

Companies are also regulated in regard to their interaction with the environment. Legislation in the last decade has been directed toward improving and maintaining the physical quality of our nation. Examples of such legislation are the Environmental Protection Act, the Water Quality Improvement Act, and the Air Quality Standards Act.

Yet the political-legal environment is more than just a host of laws. The government also interacts with business by serving as a supplier, competitor, and customer. As a *supplier* the government owns a great deal of our natural resources, which it occasionally sells to business. As a *competitor* it provides goods and services in the marketplace. For example, there is the government-owned Tennessee Valley Authority, which provides electricity to people in that area of the country. As a *customer* it buys goods and services from private firms. Some of these transactions are for office machines, computers, and telephone services. Others are for war material for defense purposes. And these expenditures are being made on a daily basis. Thus with a total annual federal budget of around $450 billion, and yearly state expenditures of approximately $200 billion, it is obvious that the government is pumping well over $2 billion into the economy every day of the year!

Social-Cultural Environment

The **social-cultural environment** consists of the beliefs, attitudes, customs, and practices of everyone in the society. Business must coordinate its objectives with the values and beliefs of the society in which it operates. These objectives can take various forms, from helping eliminate high unemployment to improving the safety of consumer products. In all instances, however, the goals are those the society feels will help the world become a better place in which to live. To a large degree business has little control over these desired objectives. Rather, its job is usually that of *responding* to these issues. Some of these issues are found within the firm itself, others are more related to the external environment.

Within the organization, for example, there are employees who have all types of values and attitudes. One of these may be the belief that they would be better off if they unionized. Another may be the feeling that no one should do too much work because someone else may wind up being laid off. A third is that people should be promoted on the basis of merit as well as longevity. All of these beliefs are obtained from the society in which the employees live. The workers bring these attitudes and beliefs to the work place and business must learn to deal with them.

"One pressure group wants us to withdraw sponsorship of our TV show, another pressure group wants us to continue sponsorship of our TV show, and still another pressure group wants us to add more noodles."

From The Wall Street Journal; permission Cartoon Features Syndicate

Other attitudes and beliefs exist among the general community or public and have an impact on business. Some of these can be grouped under the heading of **social responsibility.** In recent years the public has demanded that business assume an active social responsibility role and help fight air, water, and noise pollution. Some of this pollution has been a direct result of business activity, some of it has not. In either case, however, American industry is receiving pressure from the public to clean up the environment. Industry is also being urged to provide equal opportunity for the hard-core unemployed, minority groups, and women. All of these demands are a result of the changing values and beliefs of our society. As these factors continue to change, there will be new demands from the social-cultural environment and business will have to respond appropriately.

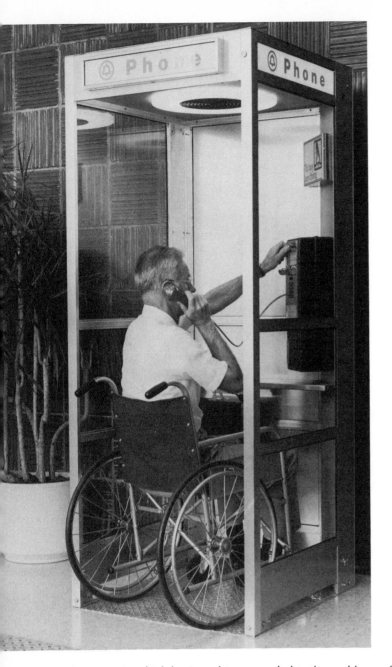

Two ways in which business has responded to the problems of the disadvantaged: Western Electric developed a doorless telephone booth with wide entrance and low telephone; IBM produces a typing unit that "speaks" typed information to help blind typists independently produce error-free copy.

One way in which business is doing so is through the National Alliance of Business, a voluntary group of businesses that are hiring the disadvantaged, Vietnam veterans, and ex-offenders, in addition to providing summer employment for school-aged youngsters. At last report these firms were providing thousands of jobs annually.

Economic Environment

The **economic environment** is the one with which business is more concerned than any other. This environment is characterized by buyers, sellers, and competition. It is in this atmosphere that business sells its goods and services to customers. All the factors of production we discussed in the last chapter (land, labor, capital, and technology) have an impact on the firm's economic environment. So too do the buying habits of the customer. Yet to merely describe in brief terms what goes on in this environment is not enough. It is also important to know a little something about economics and our economy,

including basic market models such as monopoly, oligopoly, monopolistic competition, and pure competition. For this reason, the remainder of the chapter will be devoted to an elaboration of the important aspects of our economic environment.

1. Of what value is a knowledge of the historical environment to business?

2. Over the next decade, will the political-legal environment become more important or less important as an environmental force?

3. In what way has the social-cultural environment changed over the last twenty years?

4. Why do we say that the economic environment is more important to business than any of the other environments?

CASE

Where Service Comes First

When Rodger McHarris of the First National Bank visited the students at State University during Business Day, he found them particularly interested in the bank's overall environment. A number of questions were asked about how much money the bank could lend and whether there was a limit on the amount that could be provided to any one individual. Rodger explained that the federal government required the bank to maintain a certain amount of all deposits in the form of "reserves," which cannot be loaned. The greater the amount of deposits, the larger this total reserve figure will be and vice versa. One of the primary reasons for this total reserve requirement is to regulate the amount of money in circulation. If the government decides to make more money available, all it has to do is lower its reserve requirement. If it wants to pull money out of the economy, it merely raises this requirement and, in many cases, forces the banks to recall some of their loans and put them in reserve. The students found this whole area of increasing and decreasing the money supply to be very interesting.

They were also impressed by the amount of influence that Rodger said the general public has over bank operations. For example, First National had gone to night banking hours one night a week and placed an automatic bank teller in its outer lobby so that people could make deposits or withdraw money any time of the day. The people in the city were demanding more bank services, and First National was trying to comply by introducing these new features. "You know," Rodger told the students, "the best way for a bank to meet its environmental demands is to emphasize service to its customers."

Rodger also felt that the public had a lot to do with the way money was invested in the city. For example, just a week ago members of the mayor's council had come to the bank to ask it to buy some new municipal bonds the city was about to offer. Later that day a group of social action workers came by and asked the bank to look into a project they were sponsoring to build low-cost housing in a slum area. In both cases, Rodger said, it looked as if the bank would get involved. "After all," he said, "we have to help out the local community. They are our customers and we have a responsibility to them."

1. How much influence do you think federal and state laws have in regulating a bank's operations? Give some illustrations.

2. How much of an environmental force is the social-cultural environment for a bank? Explain.

3. In addition to the political-legal and social-cultural environments mentioned in this case, what other environmental factors do you think would have an effect on First National?

ECONOMICS AND BUSINESS

While business must be able to deal with all the environmental forces confronting it, there is a great deal of truth to the statement that "in the final analysis it all comes down to the state of the economy." By this we mean that when economic conditions are good, most businesses do well. When economic conditions are bad, many businesses will do poorly and some will even have to declare bankruptcy. Because business is tied so closely to the economy, it is vital for business people to have at least a fundamental understanding of economics.

The term **economics** means *the allocation of scarce resources for the purpose of fulfilling society's needs.* As we saw in the last chapter, this is

exactly what business does—it takes scarce resources and produces goods and services with them and then sells them to society. One of the big worries for business, however, is that of determining the type of economic conditions that will exist in the future. Should the plant be expanded? Should more people be hired? Should production be increased? Or is the country going into a recession, with the wisest strategy being to either remain at the present size or sell off some of the company's holdings, and to ride out the economic storm before doing any expanding? If business could answer these questions with certainty, the manager could sleep a lot sounder at night. Unfortunately, the best that can be done is to study the economy and make an educated guess.

In so doing business must concern itself with both overall economic conditions and the situation that exists within its particular industry or market.

The Overall Economy

When we talk about the overall economy we are dealing with **macroeconomics.** Much of the economic information we read in our local newspapers or hear about on television is related to macroeconomics. In particular, it is common to hear people talking about gross national product and business cycles.

Gross national product

Gross national product, usually referred to simply as GNP, is the total value of all goods and services produced in the economy in one year. It is generally agreed that the best indicator of an economy's health is the total value of goods and services produced. So everyone, from the United States president to members of Congress, from the businessperson to the homemaker, tends to place a good deal of attention on the GNP each year.

Fortunately for us, the United States has had a tremendous growth in GNP in the last fifty years (see Table 2.1). As you can see, the Great Depression of the 1930s led to a major decline in GNP. However, we have recovered very well.

TABLE 2.1 U.S. GNP FOR SELECTED YEARS

YEAR	GNP (IN BILLIONS)
1929	$103.1
1933	55.6
1938	84.6
1945	211.9
1951	328.4
1961	520.1
1966	749.9
1970	982.4
1975	1528.8
1976	1700.1
1977	1887.2
1978	2141.4*

Source: U.S. Department of Commerce.
* Estimate

TABLE 2.2 AN EXPENDITURES AND INCOME APPROACH TO VIEWING GNP

EXPENDITURES		INCOME
Money spent by households + Money spent by government + Money invested in plant and equipment by business + Money spent by foreigners in the United States	Gross = national = product	Wages received by employees + Rent received by landlords + Interest received on invested money + Profits

One reason why GNP is so highly regarded as an economic indicator is that it gives us an idea of how well people are doing overall. Remember, if $1.88 trillion worth of goods and services were produced in 1977, someone must have bought them. The money spent for these goods and services, therefore, served as income for other people. Yet this is only a general view of this *expenditures-equal-income* equation. Both sides of the identity can then be broken down into smaller parts, as seen in Table 2.2. When this is done it is possible for us to analyze, study, and sometimes predict the economy on the basis of what is happening in each of the parts. For example, if the government starts spending more money, GNP will go up. If business starts investing less in plant and equipment, however, it may offset the government's expenditures. Many of the things you read about the general economy are based on changes taking place on one or both sides of the expenditures-income equation in Table 2.2.

Business cycles

During this century our economy has undergone continuous fluctuations. Usually things go well for a while and then there is a downturn. This may last six months or a year and then things again turn up.

Sometimes, such as during the Great Depression or the 1960s, it may take years for the economy to turn around and go the other way, but usually economic cycles do not last this long.

The 1920s saw a period of prosperity. Except for a sharp but brief depression in 1921 and a few minor problems with unemployment in 1924 and 1927, the Roaring Twenties were good years for America. World War I had created a backlog of demand for goods. To meet these needs new factories were built and new jobs were created. In turn, the stock market boomed and many people lived better than ever before.

The 1930s witnessed a complete reversal. The stock market crash, poor economic policies, and the increasing use of debt to finance expenditures led to the most severe depression of modern times. GNP plummeted from $103.1 billion in 1929 to $55.6 billion in 1933. For the rest of the decade America struggled to right its economic ship.

The 1940s brought both prosperity and inflation. The prosperity was a result of military spending to finance World War II. However, this increased spending also led to inflation. When the war ended many people forecast a postwar depression. Happily this did not occur, although there was continued inflation.

The 1950s were rather mixed. GNP continued to rise, but it was accompanied by inflation. Also, recessions in 1954 and 1958 hurt the economy. Particularly distressing was the fact that during the latter part of this decade the growth in GNP began to slow

Marina Von Neuman Whitman

One of the things that business firms, especially the large ones, need to do is forecast the environment. What is likely to happen during the next 12 to 24 months? At General Motors the individual who is in charge of economic forecasting is Marina von Neuman Whitman, the daughter of John von Neuman. A co-developer of the theory of games, she received her Ph.D. from Columbia University. Her record before coming to General Motors was impressive: she was a winner of innumerable fellowships, awards, and honors; she served on Governor Rockefeller's Commission on Critical Choices. Currently, she is a member of both the Economic Advisory Committee of the U.S. Department of Commerce and the Advisory Committee on the Reform of the International Monetary System of the U.S. Department of the Treasury.

Interestingly, she did not apply for the job at General Motors. She was happy with teaching at the University of Pittsburgh when the company's executive vice-president approached her to fill the vacancy being created by the retirement of their chief economist. Commenting on her job with the corporation she says, "At General Motors I am in a good position to establish a meaningful flow of communication between business, government, and academia. I will be in charge of 'straight-out economic forecasting' which will be used by General Motors' top management to determine how many cars and trucks to produce. I will testify before Congress on public issues. Since General Motors is a world company, I will be responsible for international economics analyses as well. Finally, I will be involved with the economic aspects of industrial organization and anti-trust. To me success means having the kind of job where I can learn, grow, and feel I'm making a contribution." Many people feel that in this current period of stagflation and rising fuel costs, General Motors could not have chosen a better person to direct their economic forecasting efforts.

up; the average annual growth dropped from around 4.5 percent to 2.5 percent.

The 1960s began on a down note. The recession of 1958 and the long steel strike of 1959 were still being felt. In early 1961, however, the economy started a period of expansion that lasted most of the decade. The economic policies of the Kennedy and Johnson administrations played an important part in this upswing. The government enacted a tax credit for investment in new machinery and equipment and an $11-billion tax cut for individual taxpayers. Steps such as these helped push the economy forward. Unfortunately, the latter half of the decade also saw a rise in inflation.

The 1970s saw something of a reversal of this economic prosperity. In particular, the country was faced with stagnation in the growth of real output, coupled with inflation. Economists call this **stagflation.** In an effort to deal with this condition, temporary wage and price controls were instituted. At present, however, this stagflation still continues and some economists feel that the economy is no longer as manageable as was previously believed. The economic theories we relied on during the 1960s and 1970s need to be revised. The economy has changed so dramatically during this time that our present understanding of how to manage recessions and other economic cycles is proving inadequate in many cases. In addition, the energy crisis we now face is a strong indication that as certain raw materials become scarce a nation's economic growth may be placed in jeopardy. The oil crisis, in particular, made this very clear.

Given the ups and downs of the economy, business is faced with quite a challenge when it attempts to deal with its economic environment. Nevertheless, by keeping aware of what is happening on the national economic scene, it is possible to make some predictions and not be caught completely unaware.

5. What is macroeconomics?

6. Why is GNP so popular an economic indicator?

"We can get you away from the prime interest rate and the energy crunch, but I'm afraid there's nothing we can do to get you away from inflation."

7. The overall economy has had many ups and downs over the past fifty years. Explain this statement.

The Economy and the Firm

While business must be concerned with the overall economy, the individual company is more interested in what is happening internally and within its own industry. This is a narrower view of things and is known as **microeconomics.** Microeconomics is concerned with such areas as the cost of producing goods and services, consumer demand, and pricing. It is also concerned with the environment of the industry.

Basic market models

Perhaps the best way to study this area of microeconomics is to examine the types of economic conditions within which companies operate. Most companies do business in a competitive environment. However, the *degree of competitiveness* depends on both the firm and the industry. The local telephone company has no competition, while the

local grocer is fighting for his life against the big food chains. In analyzing the environment of business, we must examine the types of market situations that exist. We call these *basic market models* and there are four of them: (a) pure monopoly, (b) oligopoly, (c) monopolistic competition, and (d) pure competition.

Pure monopoly. A **pure monopoly** is one in which there is only *one* seller or producer and there are *no* substitutes. As a result, we must either do business with this company or forgo the good or service. One of the most common illustrations of a pure monopoly is our local electric company. This company is the only one from whom we can buy our electricity. The same is true for gas, water, and telephones. Only one firm supplies them. Why? Simply because it is cheaper to have one company doing it all. After all, if we had three electric companies in town, each would have to have its own generators, lines, business office, and so forth, and we would have to pay for them in the form of higher rates. One large company can provide cheaper services than many small ones. For this reason, utilities are often given monopoly power through legislation that forbids competition. We call these utilities **natural monopolies.** However this is not the only way to achieve a monopoly position.

Monopolies also exist where one company owns all the *raw materials* for making a particular product. For many years the Aluminum Corporation of America had a monopoly position because of its massive control over the sources of bauxite, the primary ore used in aluminum fabrication. Another illustration is found in the case of the International Nickel Company of Canada, which controls about 90 percent of the world's known nickel reserves. A third example would be the DeBeers Company of South Africa, which owns most of the world's diamond mines.

A third way in which a monopoly is created is through the development of *patents,* which allow a company to exclusively control and use a discovery for seventeen years. The Polaroid Corporation is a

The telephone company has long been one of our most important monopolies. Its logo is instantly recognizable to most Americans.

1889

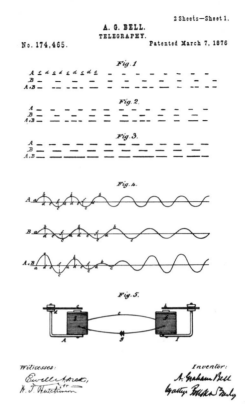

good illustration. The process for their film is patented and has given the firm a monopoly on instant pictures. In recent years both their Square Shooter and SX-70 cameras have helped them maintain their dominant industry position. Many other firms have also been able to use patents to develop monopoly positions for themselves, including General Electric, DuPont, and Xerox. The positions of such firms are often maintained by purchasing patents of others who might offer competition, as well as by the expenditure of increased sums on continued patent research. As a result, some firms can maintain a monopoly position in some area for an indefinite time period.

1900

1921   1939   1964   1969

A fourth way in which a company can create a monopoly is by being *well established*. A firm that is known for high quality and good service can often eliminate its competition *and* prevent new firms from entering the field. In this case the monopoly is brought about by the unwillingness of customers to buy from anyone else. If you will eat at only one particular restaurant in town, it has monopolized your business. If everyone else in town feels the same as you do, the restaurant is an illustration of a pure monopoly.

8. What is meant by the term microeconomics?

9. In what way is the local telephone company an example of a monopoly?

10. Can a company that relies upon patents to secure a monopoly position maintain this position indefinitely? Why or why not?

Oligopoly.   An **oligopoly** is a market in which there are a *few* dominant firms. Often they account for 70 to 80 percent of industry sales, while the remainder of the companies each have very small market shares. One well-known illustration is the auto industry, where the "Big Three" (General Motors, Ford, and Chrysler) hold a major percentage of the market. Another is the tire industry, where the "Big Four" (Goodyear, Firestone, U.S. Rubber, and Goodrich) dominate the market.

One of the characteristics of an oligopoly is that each firm's strategy can affect the others. For example, if any firm lowers its price everyone else will follow. However, if any firm raises its price, no one will follow and the price raiser may lose a considerable number of sales. This ability to influence the others leads each firm to think its strategy through very carefully; the firm must consider a strategy's effect on the competition, as well as how the competition will respond. Because of the effect each can have on the others, we say that there is **mutual interdependence** among the firms in an oligopoly.

Another characteristic of this market structure is that the companies tend to rely heavily on **nonprice competition,** such as advertising and personal selling. One reason is that their goods are all very similar in nature and the firms want to distinguish, at least in the minds of the consumers, their products from those of the competition. For example, many tires are virtually identical to each other, but because of advertising we choose a specific brand name. When firms use nonprice competition we say they are attempting to *differentiate a standardized product*.

A third characteristic of oligopolies is that *entry into the industry is difficult*. The firms already there have patents or own essential raw materials, which often makes it unprofitable for other firms to try to compete. If a company does want to enter the industry, it may have to invest millions of dollars in the venture and wait years before the investment starts to pay off.

Monopolistic competition. Under **monopolistic competition** there are *many* firms in the industry, with each producing only a small share of the total output being demanded. In order to capture as large a share of this market as possible, each firm attempts to *differentiate,* or distinguish, its products from those of the competition. To do this, it relies very heavily on the use of sales representatives, advertisements, credit terms, and company reputation for service. This ability to differentiate products is very important, because with so many competitive producers no one has much control over the price. If a firm has a well-known product it can raise the price modestly and not lose many sales. Consumers may still prefer the good at this new price. However, there is a narrow range between the highest and lowest prices.

The entire market, in fact, is characterized by *vigorous competition,* especially of a *nonprice* nature. As a result, only those firms that believe they can differentiate their products will be willing to enter the industry. Successful differentiation will often require considerable investment in research and development and/or advertising. Common illustrations of monopolistic competition include grocery stores, restaurants, cleaning establishments, shoe stores, and gasoline stations.

Pure competition. In a purely competitive market there are *many independent* sellers, each offering its products in the same basic way. In this market all of the products are standardized, in the sense that they are almost identical and buyers are indifferent to which one they purchase. In addition, no individual firm is capable of exerting any significant control over the product's price because no one of them is supplying more than a small fraction of the total output being demanded. Firms are free to enter or

---

In the city where First National is located there are over fifty banks. Each of them offers a number of similar services. For example, they all pay the same rate on passbook savings, charge the same amount for maintaining a checking account, and offer safe-deposit facilities to those who want them.

In the past, in order to obtain a competitive advantage over the others, First National found that it needed to differentiate its bank from theirs. This it tried to do by offering certain special things. For example, every six months the bank had a drive for new deposits. Every individual opening a new account at the bank for $100 or more, or increasing a current savings account by this amount, was eligible for a gift. In addition, individuals putting $500, $1,000, or $5,000 in new or old savings accounts were entitled to even more expensive gifts. There was, of course, the risk that the depositors would draw out their funds after a few days, but First National found that enough of them left their money in the accounts to make the program pay for itself. First National would have done even better, of course, if the other banks had not also instituted similar programs for getting new accounts. When they did it was common to find some of First National's depositors withdrawing their money and taking it to these banks.

CASE

A Personal Banker for Everyone

This upset the officers at First National because they felt that they never really obtained as much money from these deposits as they could. As a result, six months ago the bank instituted a new program called "personal bankers." Under this program each depositor at the bank was assigned a personal banker. This individual was charged with helping the customer in any way possible. Common examples included getting the paper work done for a small loan (less than $500) before the individual entered the bank, thereby saving the person time; transferring funds from checking to savings or vice versa rather than demanding a written authorization asking for this service; and following up on any problems that might arise due to overdrawn accounts, to see if the bank was in error or the customer. To obtain these services, all the individual had to do was call his or her personal banker, who took the matter from there.

Many of the banks around the city believed that this new program would not work because it involved too much time and effort on the part of the bank. However, after six months First National reported a 20-percent increase in its total number of depositors despite all types of new gift-related programs set up by the competition. Many of the new accounts reported that they had moved their money to First National after hearing about the personal bankers program. A survey of all other depositors indicated that they too thought the new program was an excellent idea.

✿✿✿

1. In what kind of a basic market structure does First National operate: pure monopoly, oligopoly, monopolistic competition, or pure competition? Explain.

2. In what way is this new personal bankers program an illustration of nonprice competition?

3. If First National wants to be even more successful in its economic environment, what other types of programs might it initiate? Explain.

leave the industry with no significant obstacles. A final characteristic of pure competition is that there is *no use of* **nonprice competition,** such as on the basis of advertising, sales promotion, or product quality.

There are very few illustrations of pure competition. One of the best is agriculture. If Farmer Jones raises corn, this is a standardized product. No farmer dominates the corn market and no one seller has any control over the price. As a result, none do any advertising or sales promoting. This same situation holds for wheat, barley, oats, or other farm staples.

A summary of the four basic market models is given in Table 2.3.

11. In what way are firms in an oligopoly mutually interdependent?

12. Why is nonprice competition so important to firms in an oligopoly?

13. How vigorous is the competition between firms in a monopolistically competitive industry?

14. Why are individual firms in a purely competitive environment unable to influence the price of their goods? Also, why do they not use nonprice competition?

SURVIVAL OF THE FITTEST

The successful business is the one that understands its overall and specific environments. Any one of the environmental forces—natural-physical, political-legal, economic, and so forth—could spell trouble for the firm. However, by being aware of developments in each area the company is able to adapt appropriately. In many ways business firms are like all living creatures. If they cannot adapt to their environment they will not survive.

Some environments do not change much. The natural environment is an illustration. Business must work with the raw materials available to it. When they are exhausted, there will be no more. Other environments, such as the economic environment, are more dynamic. Changes in production methods, consumer buying habits, and economic cycles sometimes spell new opportunities, and sometimes bring on new problems for the company. Thus in the environment of business it is necessary to realize that at any given moment some forces will be more important than others. Overall, however, none of them can be ignored.

15. In what way does "survival of the fittest" apply to a business?

TABLE 2.3 CHARACTERISTICS OF THE FOUR BASIC MODELS

| | MARKET MODEL | | | |
CHARACTERISTIC	PURE MONOPOLY	OLIGOPOLY	MONOPOLISTIC COMPETITION	PURE COMPETITION
Number of firms	One	A few	Many	Very, very large number
Control over price	A great deal	Depends on what the others do	Some	None
Type of product	Unique	Can be standardized or differentiated	Differentiated	Standardized
Ability to enter the industry	None	Quite difficult	Fairly easy	Very easy
Use of nonprice competition	Mostly public relations advertising	Quite a bit	Quite a bit	None

SUMMARY

In this chapter we have examined the total environment in which business operates. This environment is made up of many smaller environments. There is the historical environment, in which business has existed in the past. By studying what has already happened, business is in a better position to forecast and prepare for the future. There is the natural-physical environment, which consists of all our physical resources. These resources are often irreplaceable and must be used wisely. There is the political-legal environment, which consists heavily of the laws the government has enacted over the past hundred years to regulate business. It is also made up of the relationship that exists between business and government. There is the social-cultural environment, which is made up of the beliefs, attitudes, and customs of everyone in the society. Over the past twenty years these have changed dramatically and resulted in completely new challenges to business. Finally, there is the economic environment, which consists of the firm's customers and competitors. This environment is of more concern to business than any other. For this reason the manager needs a working knowledge of economics.

Economics is the allocation of scarce resources for the purpose of fulfilling society's needs. For every business firm the greatest concern is how economic conditions will affect it directly. This interest can only be satisfied through an analysis of the overall economy as well as a review of the specific situation that exists within the particular industry or market where the firm does business.

The most common indicator in judging the overall economy is gross national product (GNP). GNP is the total value of all goods and services produced in the economy in one year. In arriving at this total value, it is common to use an expenditures-equal-income approach. All money spent on goods and services must have been received by others as income. Since this GNP equation is made up of a number of different parts, it is possible to analyze and sometimes predict the overall economy on the basis of what is happening in each part. Yet these estimates can be wrong, for the economy tends to run in cycles. During the current decade, for example, we have had quite a time with stagnant economic growth and inflation, known as stagflation. This is a big change from the solid economic growth we witnessed in the early 1960s.

While business is concerned with the overall economy, it is more interested in what is happening internally and within its own industry. This knowledge requires an analysis of consumer demand, production costs, and pricing. It calls for an understanding of specific industry conditions and competitiveness. In all, there are four basic types of industry market models: pure monopoly, oligopoly, monopolistic competition, and pure competition. Each has its own characteristics.

In order to survive, a business must be able to adapt to the environmental forces that surround it. Some of these forces are more important than others but none can be ignored. By keeping itself aware of these forces, business puts itself in the best position to deal with them.

KEY TERMS FOUND IN THIS CHAPTER

QUESTIONS FOR DISCUSSION AND ANALYSIS

1. In what way does the natural-physical environment have an influence on business?

2. At the present time, which of the environmental forces is most important to business? Explain.

3. What is meant by the term economics?

4. How does the expenditures-equal-income approach to computing GNP work?

5. What are some of the factors that can result in a pure monopoly? How can a company secure a pure monopoly position for itself?

6. In your own words, what is an oligopoly? Explain, incorporating into your answer some of the major characteristics of an oligopoly.

7. The local gasoline station is an example of a firm in a monopolistically competitive environment. Support or oppose this statement.

8. How difficult is it to enter or leave a purely competitive market? Can businesses move in or out with much ease? How does this differ from a monopoly? An oligopoly? A monopolistically competitive environment?

3

As volunteers from this private sector, we're doing what we know best: Applying America's business expertise to America's social problems, and seeking solutions with the energy and intelligence that is characteristic of America's greatness.

William F. Rockwell, Jr.

OBJECTIVES OF THIS CHAPTER

As seen in the last chapter, there are many environments with which business needs to be concerned. One of these, which has gained in importance during the last decade, is the social environment. Business is currently facing three major areas of social responsibility: (1) equal opportunity, (2) ecology, and (3) consumerism. In this chapter we will examine business's social obligations and study how companies are responding to them. By the end of this chapter, you should be able to do the following:

a. define what is meant by the term social responsibility;

b. identify the major groups to whom business has social obligations;

c. describe the three major social challenges currently facing business;

d. explain why business is involved in helping to solve social problems;

e. relate some of the things business is doing to meet its social obligations.

The Social Responsibility of Business

WHAT IS SOCIAL RESPONSIBILITY ALL ABOUT?

In recent years we have all heard a great deal about social responsibility. **Social responsibility** is the moral obligation business has to assume concern for the welfare of the society in which it operates. Naturally this responsibility will differ from company to company. For example, the manner in which a bank helps society may be totally different from the approach used by a manufacturing firm. In addition, there are different groups to whom business has *specific* social obligations. Some of the major ones include (a) the stockholders or owners, (b) the customers, (c) the creditors, (d) the employees, (e) the government, and (f) the community (see Fig. 3.1).

Owners

The basic responsibility business has to its owners is that of protecting their investment. This usually takes the form of profit and growth. The owners want to earn a reasonable return on their investment and

they often want the firm to grow and expand. There are two reasons for this. First, by expanding the company is able to take advantage of the opportunity to enter new markets and provide greater goods and services to more people. Second, with growth often comes increased profit. Thus, speaking research that business feels a greater obligation to the owners than to any other group.[1] Thus, speaking very realistically, the social responsibility of business is greatly influenced by its own profit picture and the desires of the owners.

Customers

The ultimate success or failure of every business rests with the customers. If they buy the business's goods or services, the company will do well. If they do not, the firm will have to close its doors. One of the best ways of keeping the customers happy is to remain alert to their changing needs. For example, in the past decade fast-food franchises have sprung up all across America to meet a growing need for quick food service. Similarly, today many banks have installed automatic bank teller machines to provide twenty-four-hour service to customers who do not want to be restricted by regular banking hours.

Creditors

Creditors are all those individuals to whom the business owes money. Some have provided the company with supplies or material. Others have loaned funds to the firm. Business's responsibility to these people is to repay these debts as they come due. If it is unable to do this, its ability to obtain credit in the future will be affected. Thus, by meeting this responsibility business also helps itself.

Employees

Employees produce the goods and services sold by business. The social obligation of the firm to these individuals is to provide good salaries, good working conditions, job security, and satisfying work. Achieving these goals can be quite a chore because they are always changing. A good salary today may not be a good salary tomorrow. Terms that made the union happy at the last contract negotiation may be

FIG. 3.1 *The social responsibility of business*

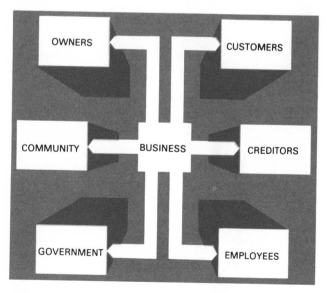

How do you rise to the top of a large organization? Ask Joan Manley and she will tell you that starting out as a secretary really helped her out. "Being a secretary is a darn good entry job," she says. "It plugs you in at a higher level than most entry-level jobs. In effect, you can eavesdrop and learn a lot." And she ought to know. Currently one of the most important women in American business, she is a power in the world of publishing. As a director of Time, Inc., and one of only five group vice-presidents, she is in charge of Time's "Books Group," one of the largest publishing entities anywhere. Currently this group accounts for over $400 million in sales annually. The biggest part of these revenues are accounted for by Time-Life Books, which are sold mostly through direct mail. However, bypassing the typical book retailer has certainly not hurt sales. Time-Life Books can be found in one-out-of-seven homes in the U.S. and rarely are these series unprofitable for the firm.

Graduating from the University of California with a degree in history and English, Mrs. Manley had a de-sire to get into publishing. So off she went to New York and joined Dou-bleday & Company, Inc. It was not long before her boss found that Mrs. Manley had an uncanny knowledge of people. Sitting in during meetings on various business proposals, she was often able to accurately evaluate the people who were making these proposals. When her boss moved to Time Inc., he took her along, and she eventually succeeded him as pub-lisher.

Although she is not a writer her-self, Mrs. Manley can often pick winning projects and recommend that the Books Group support them. As one of her colleagues put it, "The people getting ahead now are people with a reputation as producers. And Mrs. Manley is a producer of profits." How does she do it? By being tough when necessary and exercising good business judgment all of the time. This is why, while still in her forties, she is earning over $200,000 annually. Her ability to succeed in a competi-tive environment where talent and judgment play key roles illustrates that there certainly is room at the top for qualified people—regardless of sex.

Joan Manley

totally unacceptable when the current contract ex-pires. Because management depends so heavily on the employees, it cannot afford to overlook its responsibility to them.

Government

Business has a social responsibility to adhere to both the letter and the spirit of the law. Business has to be more than just a good employer; it has to be a good citizen. While there are laws forbidding dis-crimination on the basis of race, sex, or age, business firms must do more than "token hiring." For exam-ple, if 10 percent of the local area residents are Mexican-American, some firms try to hire 10 percent of their work force from this group. However, they will hire no more than this percentage. This same approach is used in the recruitment of other minori-ties and of women as well. Business's obligation to society requires more than just adhering to some quota system.

Community

Business has a social obligation to make the community a better place in which to live. In so doing the company must join with the community in trying to solve the social problems facing them all. Business is expected to provide jobs and good working conditions. It is also expected to get involved in local community organizations and charities. At the same time, business has an obligation to keep the environment clean. If some of its production processes are leading to pollution of the environment, the company must take steps to minimize, and if possible eliminate, these ecological dangers. It must also provide adequate goods and services at a fair price to both the local community and, if it has national distribution, the country at large.

1. The first responsibility of business is to survive and make a profit. After this it can worry about social responsibility. Comment on these statements.

2. To which group does business have its greatest social responsibility? Rank them in order from first to sixth and explain the obligation to each.

TABLE 3.1 SOCIAL RESPONSIBILITIES OF BUSINESS

| SPECIFIC INTEREST GROUP | TYPE OF SOCIAL RESPONSIBILITY | | |
	EQUAL EMPLOYMENT OPPORTUNITY	ECOLOGY	CONSUMERISM
Owners	X	X	X
Creditors			X
Employees	X	X	
Customers			X
Government	X	X	X
Community	X	X	X

THE CURRENT SOCIAL CHALLENGE

The social challenge facing business today can be reduced to three specific areas. These are (a) equal opportunity in employment, (b) protection of the environment, and (c) better and safer products. For purposes of simplification, these three areas are often referred to as **equal employment opportunity, ecology,** and **consumerism.** Depending upon the specific interest group, the firm's social responsibility will vary. For example, in order to achieve the profit and growth desired by the owners, business has to meet all three responsibilities. However, when it comes to the employees, equal opportunity and ecology (such as the reduction of excessive noise on the job) are most important. Meanwhile, in the case of customers, consumerism is the overriding issue (see Table 3.1).

Equal Employment Opportunity

In America today we talk a lot about being a "land of opportunity," where everyone has an equal chance for success. The truth of the matter, however, is that many people do not have equal opportunity. Some are discriminated against because of their race or color; others are handicapped because of their sex or national origin.

Race and color

There are three major minority groups in America that can be singled out as representative. These consist of the Native American, the black American, and the Mexican-American.

The Native Americans today number less than a million and are more discriminated against than any other group. Most of these individuals live on reservations in substandard housing. Their life expectancy rate is about two thirds that of the average American, and their median family income is far below the current poverty level. By the end of 1979 the rate of unemployment among Native Americans was nearly three times that of the general population. These statistics undoubtedly help account for the

Together, Blacks and Chicanos constitute approximately 18% of the U.S. population, yet they hold very few professional, high-paying jobs. Most hold either semiskilled positions, such as assembly line workers, or unskilled positions.

fact that the suicide rate among Native Americans is higher than that of any other minority group.

The black Americans are the largest minority group in America, constituting approximately 11 percent of the population. However, they too suffer discrimination. For example, the median income for black families in recent years has been only about two thirds that of white families. In addition, the unemployment rate among blacks has always been higher than that of whites. One reason for this is undoubtedly education. Less blacks go on to college and graduate and so fewer of them end up with professional, high-paying jobs. Others who do are sometimes given positions with less advancement potential or are hired as "token" employees to conform with federal laws forbidding discrimination. Fortunately, in recent years black Americans have made some economic gains. However, there is still quite a ways to go in terms of equal employment opportunity.

The Mexican-American, or Chicano, is the second largest minority group in America, constituting around 6.7 percent of the population. Of the three groups mentioned here, Chicanos seem to fare better than the others. Nevertheless, current statistics show that many of these Mexican-Americans live in Southwestern states where they work as common laborers. Their salaries are not very high and their living conditions are poor. In recent years many of them have banded together into a union under the leadership of César Chavez and are members of the AFL-CIO. This move has helped somewhat in bettering conditions, but the basic problems of poverty and discrimination still remain.

Sex

Another major group that is not provided equal opportunity is the American woman. Today, approximately 48 percent of the work force are women. Yet a much smaller percentage are found in managerial and/or high-paying jobs. In fact, recent research shows that although over the last twenty

Realizing the importance of ecological balance, ITT, Rayonier, a major harvester of forests, grows replacement tree seedlings for future planting.

years the number of women managers has increased, the *proportion* of male to female managers has *remained the same.*

Other employment statistics are also bleak. For example, in 1977 the median male salary was $12,465 while that for women was $6,828. Nor was the picture any brighter when it came to unemployment. In 1974, 7.1 percent of women were unemployed as compared to 5.5 percent of men. Statistics such as these indicate that women are definitely not receiving the opportunities available to men.

3. In addition to race and color, what are some other likely reasons for discrimination against Native Americans, blacks, and Mexican-Americans?

4. How can business help in providing equal opportunity to the above groups?

5. Why are women in business discriminated against? Explain.

Ecology

Ecology is a scientific term that refers to the relationship between an organism and its environment. In a biological sense, we know that if an organism is taken out of its normal surroundings and put somewhere else, it will either adapt to this new environment or die. In the last fifty years, America has begun facing ecological problems of its own. All over our country there have been increases in air pollution, water pollution, and noise pollution, to name but a few.

Air pollution

Air pollution can be found everywhere in America. The primary causes are the automobile and industry. Between them they hurl millions of tons of pollution into the air every year. As a result, whenever we find large numbers of cars and factories in one area, we are likely to find a great deal of air pollution. Any one of our major cities would be an illustration. In Los Angeles, for example, the residents are sometimes asked to stay indoors because the level of pollution is so great. In New York City there is evidence to prove that air pollution is actually eating away buildings and monuments! Slowly but surely, air pollution is eroding some structures.

Water pollution

Water pollution has been brought about principally through industrial waste and city sewage. In an attempt to get rid of this waste and sewage, it is dumped into rivers, lakes, and streams. Unfortunately, some of this material is not properly treated before being discarded and has proved to be harmful to the fish and other aquatic life in the water. The result can be catastrophic. Many people today claim that the Great Lakes have already been damaged beyond hope. Certainly over the last fifty years a large amount of industrial waste has been dumped into these lakes, and a great deal of restoration work will have to be undertaken to get them back to their original condition. The same is true for the many other hundreds of rivers and lakes throughout the country.

Noise pollution

A third form of pollution, and one which most of us accept as part of our day-to-day lives, is **noise pollution.** No matter where we go, there is noise. As we walk down the street we hear car horns honking, people calling to one another, a radio playing too loudly, and a commercial aircraft roaring overhead. In our work environment things are similar. Typewriters clatter, telephones ring, people talk, and machines make all sorts of noise. For a long time no one paid much attention to the issue of noise. Today, however, we know that noise pollution is dangerous. It not only can injure a person's hearing but also lead to heart disease, mental disorder, and sexual impotency. There is a great deal of truth in the cliché that "silence is golden."

Consumerism

Consumerism is a catchword used to identify a movement currently under way in America in which buyers are demanding more and better goods and services for their dollar. Every day we see examples of the consumerism movement in action. Illustrations include a boycott of meat by housewives until the price of beef comes down, and a lawsuit brought by a consumer who purchased a defective product and was injured while using it. Today the consumerism movement seems to have taken two interdependent paths. Consumers want (a) to be informed about what they are buying and how much it is going to cost, and (b) product quality and safety in these goods. Just about every complaint raised by consumers fits into one or both of these two categories.

6. If we insist on cleaner air and water, might this not result in some firms going bankrupt? Could not the expenses associated with "cleaning up" be too high for some firms?

7. What is consumerism all about? Put it in your own words.

WHY IS BUSINESS INVOLVED?

While we can all agree that the above social problems need to be solved, why should business get involved? There are a number of important reasons. These include (a) changing personal values of businesspeople, (b) enlightened self-interest, (c) managerial "know-how," and (d) government legislation.

Changing Personal Values

Over the last one hundred years there has been a tremendous change in the behavior of businesspeople. Perhaps they once believed in William Vanderbilt's statement that "the public be damned" —but no longer. Today the business world realizes that it must work *with* society, not against it. What

Equal Opportunity for All

The First National Bank recently made an analysis of its work force and found that less than 3 percent of its employees were minorities. The analysis had been requested by the bank president, Rodger McHarris, who had, in recent months, become more and more concerned with the bank's social image. It seems that he was at a conference of bank presidents not too long ago and heard many of the other participants talking about steps their banks were taking to ensure employment and equal opportunity for all Americans. This involved, in many cases, a concerted effort to go out and hire blacks, Puerto Ricans, Chicanos, and, if they lived in the local area, Native Americans. This idea made a great deal of sense to the president of First National and he decided to follow through with a plan of action.

A few days after he returned from the conference, Rodger ordered an analysis of the work force. A week later he contacted the department vice-presidents and had them come to a meeting. At this meeting Rodger outlined why he felt the bank should put a greater emphasis on minority hiring. Basically, his argument came down to one of "equal opportunity for all Americans." He said that he wanted to increase the number of minority employees in the bank and its branches from the current average of 3 percent to 10 percent by the end of the year.

A few days later a national newspaper got hold of the meeting and ran a special story on First National's new plan for minorities. The results were very rewarding. By the end of the year the bank not only had

has accounted for this new attitude? The answer lies in the fact that many of the things we used to believe in have changed. We have *new values* today. Businesspeople used to think that *any* government interference was wrong. Today they realize that many of these laws are actually helpful. Likewise, businesspeople in the past subscribed to the old cliché, **caveat emptor**—a Latin term that means "let the buyer beware." If someone bought a defective good or paid too much for a product, that was their problem. Modern businesspeople have different attitudes. Today most business executives are no different from you or me. They believe in many of the things we do; they feel business's goals should be to help society, not "rip it off." Their personal values have led to an increase in their willingness to become socially responsible.

Enlightened Self-Interest

Another reason why business is becoming involved in helping solve social problems can be explained by the doctrine of **enlightened self-interest.** This doctrine holds that *by helping society business actually helps itself.* After all, if the business community assists people in finding jobs, the money these workers earn can be used to buy the goods businesses produce. If business makes a safer product, it will find more people willing to buy it. If business replaces old machines that can injure the workers with new, safer ones the employees are not only

achieved its goal but was being pointed to as one of the model employers in its geographic area. Furthermore, the newspaper story had alerted minorities to the bank's plan and the firm found that it was able to obtain a large number of applicants for jobs. Finally, the amount of business First National did with minority groups increased dramatically. Individuals and small minority businesses both began to frequent the bank. One Puerto Rican woman put it this way: "My son works at this bank so everyone in our neighborhood banks here. Why not? If the bank is good to us, we want to be good to the bank."

1. Is minority hiring really a social responsibility of a company like First National? Should this activity not be left up to the giant firms like IBM and General Motors?

2. Did First National start hiring minorities because it wanted to be a good citizen or because it saw a profit in the program? Explain.

3. What kinds of responsibilities does First National have to its stockholders? Is the hiring of minorities part of that responsibility? Explain.

happier but can be more efficient. Thus, an interest in society can be a two-way street for business.

8. In what way is the thinking of today's businesspeople different from that of businesspeople fifty years ago?

9. Enlightened self-interest is just another term for long-run profit. Give your opinion of this statement.

Managerial "Know-How"

A third reason why business has become more active in helping solve our social ills is increased managerial "know-how." Many of our current social problems can be solved only if we call upon the talents of individuals with management expertise. Who are these people? In large degree they are our businesspeople. Every day these people are concerned with setting objectives, drawing up plans, evaluating investment decisions, and choosing courses of action designed to achieve desired goals most efficiently. If the talents of these people were directed to helping solve some of our social problems, we could make a great deal of headway. In addition, argue some people, business has the financial resources for helping out so therefore it ought to get involved.

Many successful businesspeople agree. They believe there must be a balance between profit and

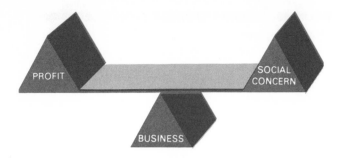

FIG. 3.2 *The social responsibility seesaw*

service to the community. This is not to imply that business intends to bankrupt itself to help out the local community. It is, however, willing to sacrifice more of its short-run profit than before and content to take a longer-run view of things. In a manner of speaking, modern business is trying to balance a social responsibility seesaw by giving both sides their just due (see Fig. 3.2).

Government Legislation

A fourth reason for business concern with social responsibility is government legislation. Laws have been passed in all three main areas of social concern: equal opportunity, ecology, and consumerism.

Equal opportunity laws

There are two major laws that have been enacted to guarantee equal opportunity in the work place. The first is the **Equal Pay Act of 1963.** The purpose of this act is to forbid salary discrimination on the basis of sex, for jobs that require equal skill, effort, and responsibility and are performed under similar working conditions. The term given to these rules is "equal pay for equal work."

In recent years employees have been sued by women who complained that they were doing the same work as men but being paid less. The result has been a number of court rulings declaring that business must pay back wages to its female employees. Some of the biggest awards to date have run into several million dollars.

A second equal opportunity law is the **Civil Rights Act of 1964.** This act forbids discrimination in employment on the basis of race, color, creed, sex, or national origin. To ensure that everyone is given these rights, the act established an Equal Opportunity Commission (EEOC) to investigate complaints. Anyone who feels he or she is being discriminated against can go to the local EEOC office and have the matter looked into.

Ecological laws

Many laws have been passed to protect the environment. Two of the best known are the Environmental Policy Act of 1969 and the National Air Quality Standards Act of 1970. However, there are hundreds of others at the federal and state levels. All are designed to do one thing—help clean up the environment and keep it that way. In addition, many of them permit the government to levy stiff fines against those firms that do not comply with the law.

Consumerism laws

Consumerism has also seen a flood of legislation. In general, however, there are two basic types of laws that have been enacted. The first are designed to provide *information* to consumers. One example is the **Truth in Packaging Act,** which requires that the consumer be told *what* is in the package being purchased and *how much* there is inside. This type of information is very useful in judging competitive products because the buyer now has an opportunity to compare the quantity, as well as the price, of each. Another illustration is the **Truth in Lending Act.** This law requires banks and other lending agencies to tell the borrower *exactly* how much money is being loaned and what the interest rate is on the entire loan. Thus the borrower is made aware of all direct and indirect costs associated with the loan and is in a better position to shop around for the lowest possible rates.

The other kinds of consumerism laws are those designed to provide **product safety.** Some of these laws deal with one product specifically, such as those relating to auto safety. Others are designed to regulate general consumer products such as toys, television sets, washing machines, and bicycles. All of these laws have helped make products safer for general use.

✺✺✺

10. Does business have a responsibility to help with social problems just because it has the "know-how"?

11. Can equal opportunity be assured for everyone through federal and state legislation?

12. How is the Truth in Packaging Act useful to consumers?

So far we have talked about the social issues facing business and why companies should be involved in the social arena. However, we have not yet said anything about business's response to these responsibilities. What is business doing? The answer is—a great deal.

Providing Equal Opportunity

The business community has attacked the issue of equal opportunity on a number of different fronts. Perhaps the biggest emphasis has been given to minority hiring programs, minority capitalism, and women in business.

On to the Supreme Court

Business is currently trying to turn the tables on the government regulators. Specifically, there is a campaign (which is headed for the U. S. Supreme Court) aimed at the Equal Employment Opportunity Commission (EEOC). The firm involved, the West Coast subsidiary of General Telephone & Electronics (GT&E) Corp., if successful, could make federal regulations easier to live with for other businesses.

At issue is the way to proceed when the EEOC expands a complaint from a single worker to a suit on behalf of a large group of workers (for example, all blacks or women) at a particular plant. GT&E is arguing that these are class-action suits and if they are unsuccessful, employers cannot follow-on with individual suits of their own. Otherwise the firm could be bogged down in legal action for an extended period of time.

The EEOC disagrees, arguing that these are not class-action suits, do not have to follow the precise rules laid down by federal courts for such suits, and should not prevent people from following up with individual action of their own.

The first time a U.S. Court of Appeals ruled on the question, it told the EEOC that it had to follow class-action procedures. Then a federal appeals court ruled the other way. Now the case is headed to the Supreme Court and business hopes it will win. In addition to restricting people's right to sue, it will limit the amount of information that has to be given to the federal government to that related to the class-action suit and, in those cases where the firm can persuade the judge not to certify the suit as a class-action, the government will be left representing only the employee who first complained.

Minority hiring programs

In 1968 some of the nation's top business leaders founded an organization known as the **National Alliance of Businessmen** (NAB). The purpose of NAB has been to hire, train, and retain the hard-core unemployed. These are individuals who are considered to be the most difficult to employ because either they have no developed technical skills or they just seem unable to conform to company rules such as reporting for work at 8 A.M. After canvassing the country and mobilizing the business community, the NAB was able to report dramatic success. Today its programs continue and firms that are participating are keeping the emphasis on minority hiring.

Minority capitalism

Another important business-sponsored program has been that of helping minority entrepreneurs start and maintain their own businesses. At the present time only about 3 percent of all firms in America are minority owned. To increase this number, businesses are providing direct financial assistance, giving contracts, and offering advice. General Motors, for example, uses minority businesses as suppliers for some of the auto-related equipment it needs. Meanwhile, a number of corporations (such as Sears, Roebuck; Glen Alden; and Montgomery Ward) have placed substantial deposits with minority banks to help ensure their success.

Women in business

Business is also beginning to take a more active interest in hiring, training, and promoting female employees. In many cases companies are changing their traditional recruiting practices in an effort to hire more women. Some are also setting up training programs for those women with supervisory potential but no previous business background. Another current trend is toward evaluating and promoting both sexes on the same basis. This is quite a change from the past, when women were promoted on the basis of technical ability while men were advanced on the basis of their long-run potential to the firm. If these present trends continue, women will find their chances for better pay and advancement coming closer and closer to those of men.

13. What are some steps business can take to help minority businesspeople start their own companies?

14. What can a business do to prevent women in the company from being discriminated against?

In recent years business has responded to social issues through active minority hiring programs by providing financial assistance and consultation to minority entrepreneurs and by hiring, training, and promoting female employees.

A getting-acquainted session at Western Electric's Industrial Skill Center in Chicago.

Protecting the Environment

Business has taken a number of important steps to protect the environment. In particular, it has developed programs to fight air, water, and noise pollution.

Fighting air pollution

As one drives into a major metropolis on a cold day, great amounts of air pollution can be seen hanging over the city. Much of this pollution is a result of smokestacks and automobiles. In recent years business has begun cleaning up this pollution.

For example, antipollution equipment is being installed on smokestacks. One of the most popular approaches is to send the fumes and other material through a "scrubber" before letting them go up the smokestack. The scrubber eliminates much of the sludge and particulates that would otherwise be thrown out into the air.

Meanwhile, in the case of automobiles, the Big Three (General Motors, Ford, and Chrysler) are putting millions of dollars into research and development in the field of engine modification. In addition, in recent years all new autos have come equipped with their own antipollution devices. The result has been a drastic reduction in the pollution caused by new autos. This has led a Chrysler spokesperson to predict that by the early 1980s air quality from an automotive standpoint will be comparable to that of the 1940s.

Fighting water pollution

Water pollution takes two forms. The first occurs when garbage and chemicals are thrown into the water. These waste materials upset the natural environment and often prove dangerous to the fish and other life in the water. To prevent further deterioration of our waters, business is now treating its wastes before putting them in the water or are looking for other, safer ways to dispose of them.

A second common problem is thermal, or warm-water, pollution. Hydroelectric power plants, in particular, tend to cause this type of pollution. In creating electricity, utilities take water from a nearby lake or river, convert it to steam for turning the plant's turbine engines, change the steam back to water, and then return it to the original lake or river. The problem is that the water is often returned at 5 to 10 degrees above the original temperature. This causes a change in the environment of the lake or river and can be harmful to the aquatic life there. Utilities are now studying this matter to determine exactly what effect the warmer water is having and what steps need to be taken to correct any problems.

Reducing noise pollution

Business firms all over America are trying to reduce noise pollution. One of the most common approaches by manufacturing firms is to either modify their machines or put casings around the parts that make the most noise, thereby muffling the sound. Another method is to give employees headsets similar to those used for listening to music. These headsets reduce the amount of noise people can hear while still allowing them to communicate verbally with their fellow workers. In some newspaper-printing plants, those individuals running the presses wear plastic earmuffs that are wired for sound. Since these individuals do not have to do much communicating with others, the company pipes in soft music to them as they go about their work. This is a welcome relief from the deafening roar of the presses.

Engineers are also working to reduce the noise caused by aircraft flying overhead, especially as they slow up for their approach to an airport, since this is when the noise is most noticeable. Engineers are also studying ways to make our daily lives more quiet. In the future, autos will make less noise as quieter cars are designed and built. Auto horns, for example, can now be heard for blocks; this is going to change as the noise level permitted for such horns continues to be lowered. Even construction equipment will improve. The latest types of pneumatic drills are much quieter, lacking their previous rat-a-tat-tat, ear-splitting sound.

Providing Consumer Protection

In providing consumer protection, business programs fall into two general categories: consumer information and product safety.

Consumer information

Today business realizes that it must do more than merely sell a product or a service. Modern consumers want to know what they are buying, how it works, and what to do in case of a problem. Business has responded in a number of ways.

Some firms have established twenty-four-hour, toll-free telephone service. Anyone, anywhere in the country, can place a call, register a complaint, or obtain information on a product purchased from the company. Other firms have set up "consumer clinics," in which they hold short sessions showing the customers the various ways in which their products can be used. Companies selling food products, in particular, tend to do this by giving out different recipes and providing information on how to cook the food. Still other firms go out of their way to help the customer understand *exactly* what is being purchased and what the special features of the product are. Recent research shows that consumers appreciate these efforts because it makes them more knowledgeable about the products they are buying.

Equal Credit for Women

One of the major consumer laws is the Equal Credit Opportunity Act of 1975. This legislation prohibits creditors from discriminating on the basis of sex and makes it easier for married women to establish their own credit ratings.

Recently the Federal Trade Commission (FTC) announced an agreement on the first test of the law. The FTC has alleged that Bloomingdale's violated the law by not considering child support, alimony payments, or income from part-time jobs when considering credit applications from women. The governmental agency also charged that the giant retailer failed to comply with rules requiring stores to tell rejected credit applicants why they were denied credit.

Bloomingdale's did not admit any violation of the law. However, in the settlement it struck with the FTC, the retailer agreed to pay a $50,000 civil penalty. The company also agreed to contact all women who had been denied credit and invite them to reapply.

Product safety

The last ten years have seen a tremendous increase in the number of lawsuits filed against firms for manufacturing and selling defective products. Perhaps even more upsetting to business is the fact that injured parties have been winning more of these suits and getting larger awards from the courts. To meet this challenge business has been taking a number of important steps to improve product safety.

In automobiles, for example, the Big Three have been spending millions of dollars on safety research. As a result, the latest cars all have more safety equipment, including shock-absorbing steering columns, padded dashboards, and stronger fuel tanks capable of withstanding severe accidents without bursting and causing a fire or an explosion. The automakers are also working on improved seat belts that are safer and easier to use. Recent statistics show auto deaths running at a lower rate than previously predicted, and it would seem that improved auto safety, as well as lower speed limits, is helping account for this.

Other manufacturers are also taking steps to improve the safety of their products. For example, it is common to find firms establishing product safety committees to review and make safety proposal recommendations for all products. Many of these committees are chaired by an engineer who has a direct line to the president. In this way, safety recommendations can be conveyed right to the top man. A second approach is to place an identification number on every product or group of products. Then, if there is any need to have a product recalled because of a production defect, the company can trace the item more easily. Some firms even enclose a card with the product, asking the purchasers to identify themselves. This helps the company contact the owner in case of a product recall. In all of these cases the goal is the same—improve product safety and, if a problem arises, straighten it out as soon as possible.

15. In addition to those things mentioned above, what else do you think business will be doing over the next ten years to meet its obligations in the area of ecology?

16. Product safety can not only give a company a good reputation, it can also save it millions of dollars in lawsuits. Explain this statement.

Q. Checking tire pressure is a pain. Why bother?

A. Here's why. A tire that's only 25 percent low — hardly enough to see — can lose *one-fifth* of its useful life. On top of that, underinflated tires waste gasoline.

Checking pressure is *free*. I do it about once a month.

Radial tire owners: The "radial bulge" can sometimes disguise a tire that really is underinflated. Don't rely on looks. Use a gauge.

Q. When does a worn tire become a dangerous tire?

A. Look for the tread wear indicators that show up when your tread gets down to the last 1/16 inch. When they show across two or more grooves (as in photo), that can be dangerous. When a tire of mine gets that worn, I get rid of it.

Q. Are my shock absorbers doing their job?

A. If your shocks are more than 15,000 miles old, do this check.

Bounce the car up and down hard at each wheel. Once it's going good, let go and see how many times it bounces. Good healthy shocks will stop it after one. Weak shocks that bounce twice or more will give you unnecessary tire wear and maybe even handling problems.

Q. Won't most problems be obvious?

A. No. You can overlook things that are practically under your nose. There are several things to check right from the driver's seat.

1. Do your dashboard warning lights work? They should all light up when the engine is cranking and the parking brake is on. Common warning lights: alternator, brakes, temperature, oil pressure. Check your owner's manual if you're not sure which ones your car should have.

2. Does your horn honk? Easy to check. Bad to wait til you need it to make sure it works.

3. Windshield washers and wipers. Do they spray right? Do they wipe clean?

4. What about outside lights? Get a helper to check headlights (high and low), emergency flashers, side markers, parking lights, license plate lights, taillights, brake lights, backup lights (shift to reverse), and turn signals. (Most cars need the key on for the last two.)

FIG. 3.3 *Tips from Shell Oil*
(*Source:* Shell Answer Book #1, The Early Warning Book *by A. J. Russo.*
Copyright 1976 by Shell Oil Co. Reprinted by permission.)

Keeping the consumer informed is a top priority for business watchdog agencies such as the Better Business Bureau.

The New Loan Program

The First National Bank has established a new minority loan program. Convinced that minority business people, including women, have not been getting the attention they deserve, the bank president, Rodger McHarris, decided to go out and actively solicit business from both new and established minority entrepreneurs.

During the first six months of this year the bank has helped seven new minority businesses get started and has encouraged twenty-three others to move their accounts to First National. Additionally, the bank is offering an in-house-sponsored course dealing with the fundamentals of setting up and running a business. The course is taught by a professor from a local business college, and the class meets once a week in the First National board room.

The program is proving so successful that the bank has had calls from some current owners of small businesses asking if they could come to the course. Rodger believes that if this trend continues it will be necessary to expand the size of the group handling minority loans from two to four people. This will also open up opportunities for minorities in the bank because Rodger is determined to staff the loan program with minorities. "After all," he told a friend, "who best understands minority business people and their needs if not minority banking personnel?"

1. Which social responsibility is the bank meeting with this program? Explain.

2. Is this a socially oriented program or a profit-making strategy for the bank? Defend your answer.

3. What else could the bank do to meet its social responsibilities? List three examples.

SUMMARY

Social responsibility is the obligation business has to assume concern for the welfare of the society in which it operates. This responsibility extends to a number of important groups, including owners, customers, creditors, employees, the government, and the community. At the present time the social responsibility of business can be categorized into three main areas: equal opportunity, ecology, and consumerism.

Why is business involved in this social responsibility arena? There are several reasons, which relate to changing personal values, enlightened self-interest, managerial "know-how," and government legislation. Each of these is a sufficient reason alone, but together they create a great willingness on the part of business to do its part in helping society. As a result, there are many business programs today for providing equal opportunity, including minority hiring programs, support for minority capitalism, and the hiring, training, and promoting of female employees. There are also programs for protecting the environment by fighting air, water, and noise pollution. Finally, there are programs to ensure consumer protection by providing information and product safety. The development of these programs illustrates that business not only is aware of its social responsibility but is also meeting the challenge with positive action.

KEY TERMS FOUND IN THIS CHAPTER

social responsibility, 44
equal opportunity, 46
ecology, 46
consumerism, 46
air pollution, 48
water pollution, 49
noise pollution, 49
caveat emptor, 50
enlightened self-interest, 50
Equal Pay Act of 1963, 52

Civil Rights Act of 1964, 52
Truth in Packaging Act, 52
Truth in Lending Act, 52
product safety, 52
National Alliance of Businessmen, 54
minority hiring programs, 54
minority capitalism, 54
thermal pollution, 55
consumer protection, 56

1. Exactly what is social responsibility and in what way does it involve business?

2. What types of social responsibility does a company have to the employees? The creditors? The government?

3. Women will never really receive equal opportunities in business, no matter what laws are passed or actions taken. Do you think this statement is true or false? Explain.

4. How useful is legislation in helping clean up the environment? Would business take voluntary action or are these laws necessary?

5. In what way is the Truth in Lending Act helpful to the consumer?

6. If the economy turns down, how much of a negative effect would this have on minority training programs? Would companies have to cut back their efforts in this area?

7. How likely is it that our environment will be in poorer shape in 1985 than it is today?

8. What are some steps a company could follow in helping to ensure that its products are safe for the consumer? List and explain them.

II

Business and Its Operations

Our major goal in this part of the book is to answer the question: what is business all about? You will learn that this is a difficult question to answer because there are so many things going on simultaneously. In order to describe all of these business operations, therefore, we are going to have to look at them in segments. The model shown at the beginning of each section will serve as a basis for our discussion.

We have already examined the external environment in which business functions. Now we are going to analyze the internal environment by studying six specific areas of business operations. This part of the book is divided into six sections for this purpose.

In Section A, we will review the three major forms of business enterprise: the sole proprietorship, the partnership, and the corporation. In this section you will learn the advantages and disadvantages of each of these forms, as well as other information useful to the internal organization of a business.

Section B is concerned with the way a business produces the goods and services it sells, and will emphasize such important areas as production processes, purchasing, and inventory control.

Section C will examine how a company manages its human assets, and will emphasize how to motivate company personnel and lead them effectively.

Section D is devoted to the marketing of the company's goods and services. We will be looking at how a business moves its goods and services from where they are produced to where they are desired. Particular attention will be given to topics such as pricing, personal selling, and advertising.

In Section E we will be studying the ways in which a business finances its operations. Some of the areas we will be covering are short-term financing, long-term financing, and the use of insurance for handling risks.

Finally, in Section F, we will examine the ways in which a business controls operations. Particular consideration will be given to the use of accounting, statistics, and computers in performing this function.

As you can see in the model shown at the beginning of each section, business operates within the constraints of an external environment. At the same time, the firm itself is organized as either a sole proprietorship, partnership, or corporation. And within this particular organizational form, the company will undertake five basic functions: production, management, marketing, finance, and control of operations. As is also seen in our model, these operations are all *interrelated*. For example, production of goods and services depends upon how well the company manages its people, markets its goods and services, finances operations, and controls the overall organization. This same interactive relationship holds for all of the other operations as well. We put control in the center because the control process is the one that tells us how well we are doing and what changes, if any, should be made.

As you read these six sections, remember that each contains information important to a solid understanding of how the modern business firm functions. Keep in mind also that these operations are all being performed by individuals and departments that are working both *independently* and *in conjunction* with others. Thus, while we are studying business operations in segments, you should continually refer to the model so that you remain aware of how each segment fits into the overall scheme.

BUSINESS AND ITS OPERATIONS

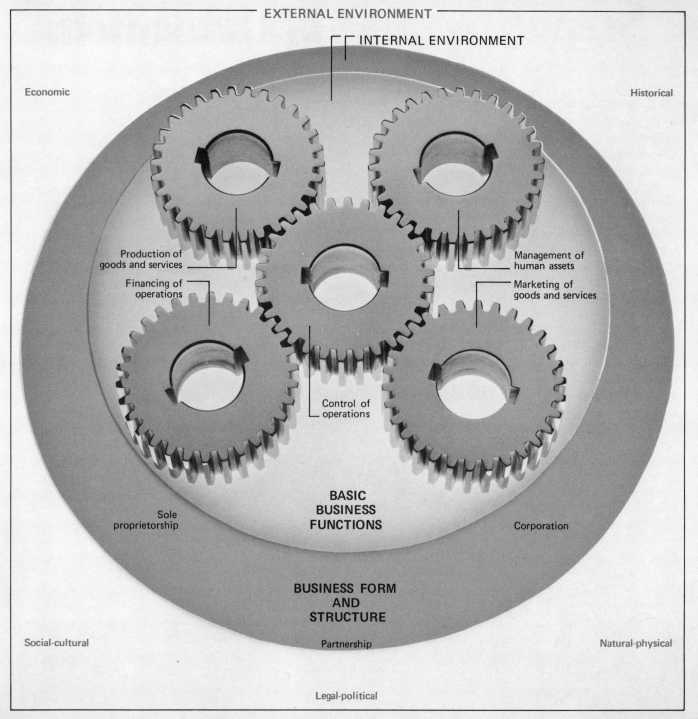

EXTERNAL ENVIRONMENT

INTERNAL ENVIRONMENT

Economic

Historical

Production of goods and services

Management of human assets

Financing of operations

Marketing of goods and services

Control of operations

BASIC BUSINESS FUNCTIONS

Sole proprietorship

Corporation

BUSINESS FORM AND STRUCTURE

Social-cultural

Partnership

Natural-physical

Legal-political

Determining the Firm's Structure and Management

In the first part of the book we studied the external environment in which business operates. Now we will turn our attention to the firm itself. The goal of this section of the book is to analyze the *internal* workings of the firm. Remember that although the company's structure and management may be influenced by the outside environment, the final decision on the *specific* type of structure or management used by the firm is made by the company itself.

In Chapter 4 we will first examine the sole proprietorship and the partnership. These are two of the more popular forms of business ownership today. Then the corporate form of ownership will be studied. Here you will learn about how a corporation is formed, what the rights and duties of the stockholders are, and what the basic advantages and disadvantages of incorporation are.

The basic objective of Chapter 5 is to acquaint you with how business firms are organized. Remember that no matter what form of ownership the firm takes, its resources must be efficiently organized. In this chapter major attention will be given to explaining the basic types of organization structures. Consideration will also be given to identifying and explaining some of the major principles for sound organizing.

Finally, in Chapter 6, the manager's job will be examined. Particular emphasis will be placed on identifying and describing the functions that managers perform. The importance of effective communication will also be highlighted, for this is the key to management effectiveness.

When you have finished reading this section you should have a solid understanding of the three basic forms of business ownership. You should also be familiar with a number of key business terms, including *sole proprietorship, limited liability, partnership, corporation, organization structure, principles of sound organizing, management functions,* and *two-way communication.* Finally, you should have gained an appreciation for the process involved in organizing a firm internally.

4

OBJECTIVES OF THIS CHAPTER

One of the major questions facing a business is, What legal form of ownership will be best? There are three choices: the sole proprietorship, the partnership, and the corporation. In this chapter you will learn about these three forms. When you have finished reading the chapter, you should be able to do the following:

a. define what is meant by a sole proprietorship;

b. identify some of the major advantages and disadvantages of this form of ownership;

c. explain what a partnership is;

d. describe the more common types of partners;

e. outline some of the major advantages and disadvantages associated with a partnership;

f. explain how a corporation is formed and identify/discuss articles of incorporation and corporate charter;

g. describe the rights and duties of stockholders, boards of directors, and officers of the corporation; and

h. outline the basic advantages and disadvantages of a corporation.

Choosing A Legal Form

THE SOLE PROPRIETORSHIP

A **sole proprietorship** is a business that is owned and controlled by one individual. At the present time this is the *most common* form of ownership in America. Over 75 percent of all businesses in this country are sole proprietorships (see Fig. 4.1).

FIG. 4.1 *Number of proprietorships, partnerships, and corporations in the U.S. (in thousands)*
(*Source:* Statistical Abstract of the United States, *1978, p. 561.)*

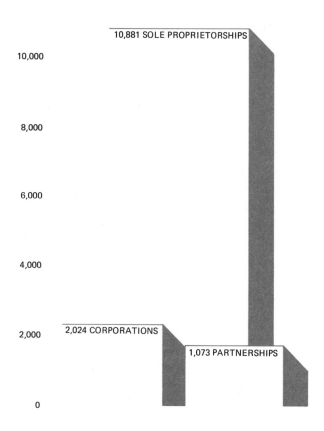

Advantages of the Sole Proprietorship

What makes this form of ownership so popular? The answer is found in the many advantages it offers, including (a) financial advantages, (b) lack of restrictions, (c) secrecy, and (d) personal satisfaction.

Financial advantages

Because the proprietor owns the entire business, all of the profits belong to him or her. They do not have to be shared with anyone else. Of course taxes must be paid on these earnings, but these are just regular plus business taxes (unlike for corporations, which, as we will see in the next chapter, are subject to double taxation). In addition, proprietorships can often obtain a higher credit standing than a similar-sized business owned some other way because the personal as well as business assets of the owner stand behind the firm.

Lack of restrictions

A sole proprietor has a great deal of freedom in deciding how the firm will be managed. There are no partners or stockholders to be consulted. In addition, because its operation is usually much smaller than that of other business forms, a sole proprietorship is easier to manage. There are fewer people to worry about and fewer complicated business affairs with which to be concerned. Furthermore, except in those cases where a license is required, such as for establishing a barbershop or opening a bar, there are no restrictions on either starting or terminating operations.

Secrecy

Success is sometimes based on secrecy. The less the competition knows about one's sales, profit margins, secret processes, and overall financial strength, the better off one may be. Most sole proprietorships are required to release no business information other than that contained in the income tax forms filed with the government. Thus this form of ownership offers the best possibility for maintaining secrecy of operations.

Personal satisfaction

The right to run the operation *their* way provides most proprietors with a great sense of personal satisfaction. The individual can work as many hours a week as he or she wants and the goals being pursued are the proprietor's own. If successful, the owner can then look back with a sense of personal satisfaction, realizing that he or she contributed in great measure to the firm's success. In fact, many proprietors admit that they are in business primarily for the personal satisfaction that they receive from operating their own firm rather than for the profits they make.

1. In contrast to any other type of business form you can imagine, why is the sole proprietorship so popular?

2. How important is secrecy to the success of a sole proprietorship?

3. Most sole proprietors are in business to become wealthy. Do you agree or disagree with this statement? Explain.

Disadvantages of the Sole Proprietorship

In deciding whether or not to form a sole proprietorship, it is necessary to examine the disadvantages of this legal form and then compare the pros and cons. Some of the major disadvantages of a sole proprietorship are (a) unlimited liability, (b) limited size, and (c) limited life.

Unlimited liability

A sole proprietor is *personally* responsible for all the debts he or she incurs. This means that creditors have a claim against the business and the proprietor *simultaneously.* If the firm does not have the money to pay its bills as they come due, the creditors can force the owner to sell his or her personal possessions in order to meet these obligations. Thus sole proprietors risk everything they own.

Limited size

Since there is only one owner there is a limit to the amount of capital that can be raised for operations. If the proprietor puts all the money from his or her personal estate, as well as whatever can be borrowed, into the business, this is as far as he or she can go. Further growth of the business will depend entirely upon reinvested profits. Therefore, from a financial standpoint growth is limited. This in turn means that sole proprietorships are virtually unable to enter any areas where large capital expenditures are required. Mass-production operations are an illustration of such an area.

In addition, because there is only one owner, all the responsibility for buying, selling, extending credit, advertising, hiring, firing, and other business-related matters falls on his or her shoulders. This is quite a burden, and if the business gets very large these duties will soon weigh down the proprietor. Of course one way of coping with the problem is to delegate authority to subordinates. The major decisions, however, must still be made by the owner. As a result, there is a limit beyond which the proprietorship cannot expand. To grow beyond this limit results in uncontrollable operations.

Limited life

The firm's existence depends exclusively upon the proprietor. If he or she dies, goes bankrupt, is imprisoned, or simply chooses to cease operations, the business dies. This presents a risk not only to the employees who depend upon the firm for their livelihood but also to any creditors who lend the firm money. To offset some of the financial problems that might arise should the owner die suddenly, creditors will often require the owner to have a sufficiently large life insurance policy to cover all financial obligations. In this way the face value of the policy can be used to pay all of the firm's debts. It is important to note that, should this be necessary, most proprietorships are unable to continue operating under new management. The owner's widow or heirs often lack the ability to carry on the operations, so the company goes out of existence. As a result, sole proprietorships have a limited life.

4. What is meant by unlimited liability?

5. Why might a sole proprietorship have difficulty in increasing its sales revenue from $30,000 a year to $3 million a year?

6. If the sole proprietor dies, what problems might this create for the business?

THE PARTNERSHIP

A **partnership,** as defined by the **Uniform Partnership Act,** is "an association of two or more persons to carry on as co-owners of a business for profit." In recent years this form of ownership has not proved as popular as the sole proprietorship or the corporation. At present only about 7 percent of all business firms in America are partnerships. Nevertheless, there are currently over 1 million of them with total business receipts of over $140 billion. Most partnerships consist of two owners, although there can be more. Common illustrations of this ownership form include advertising agencies, public accounting firms, stock brokerages, and retail stores.

Partnership Contract

A partnership can be formed by two people simply getting together and agreeing to operate a business. However, it is unlikely that either side will be willing to be bound by such an informal, verbal arrangement. It is more common for both parties to draw up a formal, written agreement. This is known as the **partnership contract.** Figure 4.2 shows a standard form for the beginning of the contract. After item 5

FIG. 4.2 *Simple partnership contract (partial form)*

Agreement executed this_____ day of_____ , 19_____ ,

between_____ , _____ and_____ , all of

_____ .

1. The name of the partnership shall be_____.

2. The principal place of business of the partnership shall be at_____.

3. The partnership will engage in the business of_____ and in such other related business as agreed upon by the partners.

4. The partnership shall commence on_____ , 19_____ , and continue until terminated as herein provided.

5. The initial capital of the partnership shall be $ _____ . Each partner agrees to contribute cash or property at agreed valuation as follows:

Partner	Amount	Percent
_____	$_____	_____%
_____	_____	_____
_____	_____	_____

in Fig. 4.2, more specific terms will be spelled out. These often cover areas such as

1. how the profits and losses will be distributed;
2. the method to be followed if old partners withdraw or die or new ones enter the business;
3. how the assets will be divided in case of dissolution;
4. the duties of the partners; and
5. the manner in which any controversies arising out of this contract will be settled (such as through arbitration).

At the bottom of the agreement, after all these provisions are listed, there is a place for the partners to sign their names. This document then serves as a binding contract on all parties involved.

Types of Partners
The people who own the business are called partners or copartners. However, there are various *types* of partners. Some may run the business while others play no active role. Some have unlimited liability, others do not.

General partners
General partners have **unlimited liability** and are usually very active in the firm's operations. Every partnership must have at least one general partner, who assumes ultimate responsibility for all the firm's obligations and is empowered to enter into contracts in the name of the business. If all the partners fall into this category, the organization is known as a *general partnership.*

Limited partners
Under the Uniform Limited Partnership Act, currently adopted by most states,[1] individuals who want to invest in a partnership but do not want to risk all of their assets can do so as **limited partners.** These individuals have their liability *limited* to the amount

"Do you promise to love, honor, and stimulate the economy?"

Al Kaufman, The Wall Street Journal

of money they have invested in the company. Such partners do not play an active role in the operation of the firm. It should be noted, however, that if these limited partners do enter into contracts for the partnership by passing themselves off as general partners, they can become liable for any losses resulting from their action.

Other partners
While the general and limited partners are the most common types, there are other categories of partners, including silent, secret, dormant, and nominal. **Silent partners** are those who are known as owners in the business but who take no active role in managing the operations. They have no voice in the matter, hence the term silent. **Secret partners** do take an active role in running the business, but they are not known as partners by the public. **Dormant partners** take no active role in running the firm nor are they known as partners by the general public. **Nomi-**

From Humble Beginnings

One day in 1886 a local jeweler refused to accept a consignment of watches that had been shipped by a Chicago jewelry firm. The railroad agent, Richard Sears, decided to purchase them himself. Setting his price low enough to make the watches an attractive buy, he soon sold all of them to other agents on the line. Soon Sears left his job and began to devote all his energies to selling watches.

He set up the R. W. Sears Watch Company, first in Minneapolis and then in Chicago, and sold his watches through express agents, by mail, on the club plan, and by installment. The business grew. Inevitably, however, some of the watches needed repairs and Sears advertised for a watch repairman. Alvah C. Roebuck answered the ad and Sears hired him for $3.50 a week plus room and board. Over the years the two men built one of the greatest retail empires the world has ever known--Sears, Roebuck. Today the company accounts for over 1 percent of America's gross national product, selling everything from suits and sporting goods to television sets and microwave ovens.

nal partners are individuals who lend their names to the enterprise but invest no money in the firm and play no role in its management.

As with limited partners, nominal partners can end up with unlimited liability for partnership debts if they are not careful. For example, if a nominal partner passes himself or herself off as a general partner and commits the firm to a contract, he or she may be liable for any losses incurred by the action. In this case the nominal partner should have remained inactive. On the other hand, there are times when nominal partners must take an active stand by speaking up and letting everyone know that they are partners in name only. For example, Ms. Jones believes that Mr. Smith, a local millionaire, is a general partner. On the basis of this assumption, she agrees to lend the partnership $25,000. If Mr. Smith is actually a nominal partner and knows the loan is based on an erroneous assumption, he must come forward and tell Ms. Jones this fact. Otherwise, he is misleading the lender with his silence and can be adjudged a general partner. If this happens, Mr. Smith can be liable for debts of the partnership.

7. Do nominal partners have limited or unlimited liability? Explain.

Advantages of the Partnership

The partnership offers a number of important advantages. Some of these are (a) increased sources of capital and credit, (b) improved decision-making potential, (c) possibilities for expansion and growth, and (d) definite legal status.

Increased sources of capital and credit

While the sole proprietorship relies upon the personal fortune and borrowing power of one individual to raise money, the partnership offers numerous sources of capital. First, there are the direct contributions from the partners themselves. Second, there are the loans that friends, investors, and lending institutions are willing to make. Third, there is the credit that suppliers will extend. As the partners increase in number, especially if they are general partners, it is likely that the business will be able to raise more capital and have its credit line extended. After all, if there is a financial setback the creditors will have a number of partners who are personally responsible for the debts. Thus a partnership can offer creditors less risk than a sole proprietorship, thereby making it an attractive investment to creditors.

Improved decision-making potential

Because it has more than one owner, there is a good chance that a partnership will make better decisions than a sole proprietorship. After all, with two or more people contributing their ideas to the solving of problems, superior solutions should be forthcoming. This is particularly true if the partners are specialists in different areas. For example, one might be the individual who thinks up new ideas and services to provide to customers, a second might know a lot about personal selling, and a third might be an accountant. Furthermore, in many partnerships skilled personnel are taken in as partners, a useful technique in maintaining the services of key employees. As a result, there can be a host of partners who each contribute to a particular specialized area. Thus overall decisions are improved.

Possibilities for expansion and growth

With the increased sources of capital and the improved decision-making ability of the owners, partnerships are in a much better position to expand and grow than are sole proprietorships. In particular, partnerships have the money and/or manpower to supervise more employees and greater facilities. Thus, as operations increase the owners are able to control the specific types of products and services being sold. In contrast to a sole proprietorship, there is minimal chance of operations getting out of control.

Definite legal status

Partnerships have been in existence for centuries. During this time many court decisions have been rendered in answer to all sorts of legal problems. As a result, today's partner can be assured that a competent lawyer can answer virtually any question he or she might have about this form of ownership, from defining the rights and duties of partners to identifying the liability of each partner in case of financial failure.

8. Why are partnerships usually able to obtain more capital and credit than are sole proprietorships?

9. Many accounting firms make their most promising employees partners in the company. How is this useful in terms of both maintaining and motivating key personnel?

10. Three men have decided to form a partnership and share all profits equally. However, they want to share losses in a different way. One of the partners is to be responsible for 50 percent of all losses, a second will take responsibility for 30 percent of any losses, and the third partner will assume liability for the other 20 percent. What is the likelihood that other partnerships have used a similar, if not identical, arrangement? How much difficulty will this raise for their lawyer in drawing up the partnership agreement?

Disadvantages of the Partnership

The partnership has a number of disadvantages. Some of these are similar to those of the sole proprietorship; others are unique to the partnership. In deciding whether or not to adopt this form of business ownership, it is important that you examine the situation in perspective. The advantages of a partnership have just been examined. The disadvantages that may counterbalance them include (a) unlimited

liability, (b) the problem of continuity, (c) managerial problems, and (d) size limitations.

Unlimited liability

As with the sole proprietorship, there is the matter of unlimited liability. Some partners, as we have seen, are limited partners and in case of financial difficulties will lose only their investment in the partnership. The others are general partners, and must assume unlimited liability for all obligations. Of course the partnership contract stipulates the manner in which profits and losses are to be shared. In general partnerships, it is common to find everything being divided according to one's percentage of contribution. For example, the partner who puts up 50 percent of the money gets half the profits or pays half the losses, and the same type of approach applies to all of the other partners. However, it must be remembered that because these general partners can make commitments for the company, an unwise decision by one of them can spell trouble for all. For example, if there are four general partners and a year-end loss of $20,000, the owners are *individually and collectively liable* for the entire amount of this loss. This means that each is responsible for his or her share of the loss, but that if someone is unable to pay the others must take up that loss themselves. If one of the partners is very wealthy, he or she may end up paying the bulk of the debt. Thus there is not always a division of losses along the lines called for in the partnership agreement. The very rich partners may end up carrying the very poor ones.

Problem of continuity

The partnership is a temporary form. If one of the partners dies, is adjudged insane, goes to jail, or simply wishes to withdraw from the business, the partnership is terminated. As the number of partners increases, the likelihood of one of these events occurring becomes greater. When one does occur, it is necessary for the remaining partners to buy out the interest of the individual who has died or withdrawn and reorganize the operation. Yet this can be difficult because no one may be able to determine the

Kemmons Wilson

Kemmons Wilson was always something of an entrepreneur. As a boy growing up in Memphis, he bought a popcorn machine for $50 and set up shop inside a local movie theater. Within a short period of time he was making more than the theater manager, who fired him and took over the operation himself. No matter— Wilson sold the popcorn machine for $50 and bought five pinball machines. In the years that followed he moved on to home building, and apartment and theater acquisitions.

During World War II he sold everything for $250,000 and joined the service. But after the war he got back into construction.

It was not until 1951, however, that he got his idea for Holiday Inns. During a vacation he had found hotels costly, cramped, and uncomfortable. As a result, he borrowed money that year and set up his first Holiday Inn in Memphis in 1952. Business was so good that he built three more units. And before you knew it, he had constructed and franchised his operations to where today there are Holiday Inns worldwide from Greece to Swaziland and from Hong Kong to Morocco. Along the way Wilson pioneered a number of new services, including putting up children at no extra cost when they share a room with their parents, free cribs for babies, free TV sets and telephones in every room, a swimming pool in every motel, and a kennel for traveling dogs.

Today Holiday Inns have more hotel and motel rooms than any other company in the world including Ramada Inn, Sheraton, or Hilton, and the company's gross annual revenues are in excess of $1 billion. And Wilson, whose personal wealth is estimated at over $200 million, has been cited by the *Sunday Times* of London as one of the 1,000 most important men of the twentieth century.

All of this, of course, makes Kemmons Wilson a happy man. However, he sees these Holiday Inns as more than just a money-making machine, as is illustrated by his personal philosophy. "I think," he says, "that I can do more for world peace through tourism and building Holiday Inns around the world than anything else. We get to know other people and they get to know us and that's good."

value of the partner's share. Furthermore, if a figure can be set, the remaining partners must raise that amount. If everyone has their assets tied up in the business, however, this is impossible. The only alternative is to bring in a new partner with the money to buy out the old one. Yet it is often difficult to find a person who is acceptable to all of the partners, a mandatory requirement for bringing in any new partner. As a result there is the problem of continuity in partnership.

Managerial problems

Because all of the general partners have the right to make decisions for the firm, the business can become a good illustration of the adage that "too many cooks spoil the broth." One way of overcoming these managerial problems is to have each person agree to restrict his or her activity to one area of the operations. For example, one partner works exclusively in the financial area, with responsibility for determining the financing needs of the

The Pizza Parlor Problem

Frank Jones teamed up with two friends, Bob Adams and Jim Burke, and together the three men formed a general partnership for the purpose of operating and managing a pizza parlor. The total estimated start-up cost was $15,000. Each of the men put up $1,000 in cash, signed a personal note at the local bank for $4,000, and agreed to share profits and losses equally.

After two years of operations things were going so well that the group opened a second parlor. At about this same time they were approached by a local businessman who offered to finance a third pizzeria for them. He would put up all the money in return for 40 percent of the profits from this parlor. However, he wanted no active interests in the management and refused to be responsible for any losses suffered by the new pizzeria. The three founders agreed that the businessman would be taken in as a limited partner. The legal work was taken care of by the firm's attorney and the parlor opened two months later.

With the increase in operations, each of the three general partners began managing one of the parlors on a full-time basis. It was not long, however, before a problem arose that threatened the firm's existence. It seems that one of the local furniture dealers had purchased seventy-five very expensive, made-to-order tables and delivered twenty-five to each store. The owners were aghast. They had ordered no new furniture. Upon investigating they learned that the limited partner had ordered them in the partnership's name. He believed that the current furniture

firm, while another is responsible for manufacturing the company's product line. Yet even when these assignments are spelled out in writing it is possible for petty jealousies to arise and for partners to start interfering in each other's areas.

Size limitations

While a partnership can usually raise more money than a proprietorship, there is a limit to the capital and credit that bankers and suppliers are willing to provide. Therefore, sooner or later the firm will find its growth limited. This can be particularly disconcerting when more money is needed to take advantage of lucrative market opportunities or to develop a patent for a new product. It is also a serious setback when the competition consists of corporations that are able to raise far more capital merely by selling additional shares of ownership.

11. Why might it be a poor idea for a millionaire to become a general partner in a high-risk business?

was unbecoming and that this would give the parlors the type of distinctive atmosphere they needed. The partners ordered the furniture store to take back the tables, but the store said that special orders of this nature could not be returned to the factory. Furthermore, the businessman had signed the sales order after telling the clerk that he was a general partner and was authorized to enter into contracts for the business. With all of their funds already invested in their second parlor, the owners had no money left to meet this furniture bill.

1. How does this case illustrate a partnership's ability to raise money to start up operations? Why might a sole proprietorship not have been able to raise the $12,000 from the bank?

2. If this case went to court, could the businessman be found responsible for any obligations arising from his action? After all, is he not a limited partner?

3. If the partnership survives this crisis and decides to take on other limited partners who agree to finance individual parlors, could they not use this idea to set up 1,000 pizzerias across the country? What major disadvantages of a partnership might prevent such action? Explain.

12. What are some of the reasons that might account for partners being unable to agree on whether or not to bring in a particular person as a new partner?

13. What guidelines can be used in preventing partners from interfering with each other in the operation of the business?

THE NATURE OF THE CORPORATION

While sole proprietorships and partnerships played a significant role in the early development of American business, the **corporation** is the most important form of ownership today. Why? Perhaps the major reason is the size of most corporations and their financial impact on our modern economy. Although they constitute only around 15 percent of all business firms, corporations account for over 85 percent of all business receipts and 70 percent of all net profits. In addition, they hire so many people that over 70 percent of all wages paid to workers in America go to corporate employees. Figure 4.3 presents statistics on business receipts and net profits of corporations in the United States.

Who are these companies? Some of them are firms you probably do business with on a regular basis. Examples include American Telephone & Telegraph; Ford Motor; General Motors; Sears, Roebuck; General Electric; Goodyear Tire; Montgomery Ward; and J.C. Penney, to name but a small group.

What makes the corporate form of ownership so important to business? The answer is that the corporation is regarded, at least from a legal standpoint, as an artificial being that has the right to conduct business affairs in its own name. In addition, the corporation can exist for an indefinite period of time, in contrast to sole proprietorships and partnerships. It is also able to enter into contracts, file suits, be sued, and do anything else a regular person might do in conducting a business.

14. Are the twenty largest business firms in America more likely to be sole proprietorships, partnerships, or corporations? Explain.

ORGANIZING A CORPORATION

In order to organize a corporation, *it is necessary to obtain permission from the state in which the company intends to do business.* The first step is that of filing the required application form with the appropriate state official. Figure 4.4 contains a basic form often used in this process. As long as there are at least three incorporators, each of whom is an adult, who want to form the corporation, and the necessary fees are paid by filing time, there is usually little other paper work with which to be concerned.

Of course, many incorporators want to write their application in such a way that the activities and objectives of the firm are not very limited. In addition, they want to pay the smallest incorporation fees and the lowest taxes. Some states such as Delaware, Maryland, and New Jersey offer these benefits and have proven to be very popular ones in which to incorporate.

Once the filing is complete and approval to incorporate is given, the secretary of that state issues

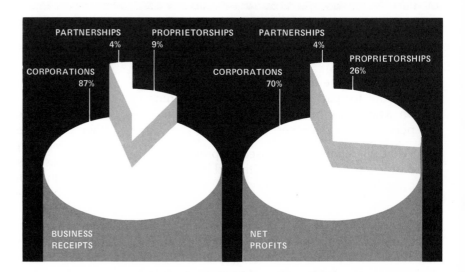

FIG. 4.3 *Receipts and net profits of business firms*
(*Source:* Statistical Abstract of the United States, *1978, p. 561.)*

ARTICLES OF INCORPORATION
OF

_____

We, the undersigned natural persons of the age of twenty-one years or more, acting as incorporators of a corporation under the _____ Business Corporation Act, adopt the following Articles of Incorporation for such corporation:

FIRST: The name of the corporation is _____

_____

_____

SECOND: The period of its duration is _____

THIRD: The purpose or purposes for which the corporation is organized are: _____

_____

_____

FOURTH: The aggregate number of shares which the corporation shall have authority to issue is: _____

_____

_____

FIFTH: The corporation will not commence business until at least one thousand dollars has been received by it as consideration for the issuance of shares.

SIXTH: Provisions limiting or denying to shareholders the preemptive right to acquire additional or treasury shares of the corporation are: _____

_____

SEVENTH: Provisions for the regulation of the internal affairs of the corporation are:

_____

EIGHTH: The address of the initial registered office of the corporation is: _____

_____

_____

and the name of its initial registered agent at such address is: _____

_____

_____

NINTH: The number of directors constituting the initial board of directors of the corporation is _____, and the names and addresses of the persons who are to serve as directors until the first annual meeting of shareholders or until their successors are elected and shall qualify are:

Name   Address

_____   _____

_____   _____

_____   _____

_____   _____

TENTH: The name and address of each incorporator is:

Name   Address

_____   _____

_____   _____

_____   _____

_____   _____

                                   _____

                                   _____

                                   _____

Dated _____ , 19_____.   Incorporators

FIG. 4.4. _Basic form for applying for incorporation_

the company a **corporate charter.** The charter relates such things as the type of business the firm is in and the number of shares of stock it intends to issue. The corporation must operate within the confines of this charter. Any changes must come from either the stockholders or new government legislation that affects the old specifications in the charter.

15. Must all corporations have permission from the state in order to come into existence? Explain.
16. What are articles of incorporation? (Review Fig. 4.4 in answering this question.) Put it in your own words.

THE CORPORATE STRUCTURE
The corporate charter provides the basis for the corporate structure. According to the charter, the **stockholders** or **shareholders** own the firm and have the right to elect a **board of directors.** In turn, the members of the board decide who the president will be. This person then appoints other top-ranking officials of the company. These top managers, including the president, are all responsible to the board for seeing that the organization runs smoothly. Figure 4.5 illustrates the corporate structure.

Stockholders
The *stockholders* are individuals who have purchased **shares of stock** in the corporation (see Fig. 4.6). These shares represent **ownership.** For example, a newly founded corporation might issue and sell 50,000 shares of common stock. Each person buying one share would then own 1/50,000 of the firm. Small corporations will often issue only a few thousand shares of stock, and these are often held by a

FIG. 4.5 *Corporate structure*

STOCKHOLDERS

WHO ELECT

THE BOARD OF DIRECTORS

WHO CHOOSE

A PRESIDENT

WHO APPOINTS

TOP CORPORATE OFFICERS

WHO IN TURN CHOOSE

SUBORDINATE MANAGERS

AND THIS PROCESS CONTINUES ON DOWN TO THE

WORKERS' LEVEL

small group of stockholders who control the firm. Large corporations, however, have millions of shares of stock outstanding and few stockholders will own even 1 percent of the firm. Yet regardless of their holdings, all stockholders have a right to vote for the board of directors. This voting usually occurs on an annual basis, with each person permitted one vote for every share owned. In this way, large stockholders have more power in deciding who will be on the board than do small stockholders.

Large corporations will often rent a hall or auditorium for their annual meeting. All stockholders who wish to attend are free to do so. Most stockholders, however, will be unable to come to the meeting because of the great distance involved. Yet in many cases a corporation must have at least half of the voting stock represented if there is to be a quorum. Therefore, it is common to find most stockholders of large corporations voting by proxy. A **proxy** is a written authorization that allows someone to cast the stockholder's vote for him or her. Usually it permits the board members to cast a vote for their own proposed slate. In major corporations this means that the board perpetuates itself or chooses its own successors. This does not have to be the case, of course. Angry stockholders can put up their own slate of board members and solicit support for them via a proxy fight. The larger the number of stockholders, however, the less the likelihood of such an action succeeding.

In addition to voting for the board of directors, stockholders vote on such things as amendments to the corporate charter, the certified public accounting firm that will audit the firm's financial records, and

FIG. 4.6. *A stock certificate issued by General Motors*

the retirement or pension plans that will be made available to the firm's employees. Stockholders also have the right to (a) sell their stock whenever they wish, (b) buy additional stock from a new issue before it is made available to the general public, and (c) inspect the firm's records if good cause can be shown for requesting such action.

Board of Directors

The **board of directors** is responsible for seeing that the business is managed properly. In this capacity it helps formulate long-range strategy, approves plans from top management, and sets the major policies within which all operations will be carried out. The board is also empowered to declare stock dividends.

These are all very important decisions. In large corporations they can involve billions of dollars. For this reason, it is common to find the boards of widely held companies recommending to the stockholders the election of highly talented people. Often these directors come from outside the firm and offer a fresh, unbiased view of things. In small corporations, of course, one is more likely to find company officials or large stockholders serving on the board. Regardless of a company's size, the directors' job is to assist the operating management team by offering general direction and advice. If the directors are successful, the stockholders may reelect them at the end of their term, which is usually one year. If they are not successful, there may be a whole new board voted in. In either case the board members are not personally liable for any corporate acts except those resulting from fraud, neglect, or the exceeding of the authority given to them in the charter.

Officers

The **officers** of the corporation are determined by the board of directors through either election or appointment. They generally include the president and the vice-presidents, the secretary, and the treasurer. All of these individuals can act as agents of the corporation by binding it to contracts. Other individuals in the firm may also have this right, of course, depending upon the corporate charter, but the above individuals are the most likely to.

17. What rights do stockholders in a corporation have?
18. What is meant by "voting by proxy"?
19. What is the job of a board of directors?
20. Who are the officers of a corporation? Explain.

ADVANTAGES OF A CORPORATION

The corporate form of ownership offers some very important advantages. These include (a) limited liability, (b) indefinite life, (c) growth potential, (d) managerial efficiency, and (e) transfer of ownership.

Limited Liability

Stockholders are like limited partners in that they have their liability restricted to the amount of money they have invested in the corporation. An individual buying ten shares of stock at $20 per share in the XYZ Company loses only $200 if the firm declares bankruptcy. Because the corporation is a legal entity, it is responsible for its own debts; the stockholders are not.

Indefinite Life

A corporation can continue in existence for an indefinite period of time. The deaths of stockholders or employees seldom threaten its existence. As long as the company keeps making money, it can remain in operation. This, of course, is in direct contrast to the sole proprietorship, which ends with the death of the owner. It is also quite different from the partnership which may dissolve if one of the partners dies. Most of the large corporations in this country today have been in existence for decades. Examples include such well-known firms as Standard Oil of Indiana (1889), General Electric (1892), IBM (1911), General Motors (1916), and Ford Motor (1919).

Growth is the Name of the Game

For the past thirty years, growth has been a primary objective for most corporations. Right after World War II, a corporation called the Haloid Company was in the process of looking for new products that were related to its own field of photocopying but that would not put it into direct competition with Eastman Kodak.

It was then the firm learned of an inventor, Chester Carlson, who had developed and patented a method of photoelectrical copying. However, none of the large corporations, such as DuPont, wanted the process; they did not feel it would be a big profit item. But Haloid did, and by 1947 it had a contract with Carlson and his associates.

It was 1950 before the company brought out its first copying machine. Cumbersome and difficult to use, it still managed to pay its own way. Meanwhile the firm had undertaken further development to improve the process and the method of operation. By 1955 the company's sales had risen to $21 million, up from $7 million in 1947. By 1962 revenues had reached $100 million and by 1978 they were over $5.9 billion.

During all of these years the company continued to bring out many new types of office copying machines that today can be found in virtually every business and government office in the country. The firm also changed its name --you guessed it--Xerox Corporation.

"My, what a glorious day for a proxy fight!"

From The Wall Street Journal; permission Cartoon Features Syndicate

Growth Potential

Corporations have greater growth potential than sole proprietorships or partnerships because they can raise more capital. By selling shares of stock the company can obtain millions of dollars from thousands of different stockholders, each of whom may be buying only ten or twenty shares. While this might appear to be a rather awkward process, it has been very successful in helping major corporations. By the early 1980s the number of stockholders in some of our largest firms was very, very large. And with their stock purchases, the corporations were able to generate billions of dollars in sales. Some examples are given in Table 4.1.

TABLE 4.1 TEN COMPANIES WITH THE LARGEST NUMBER OF STOCKHOLDERS

COMPANY	NUMBER OF STOCK-HOLDERS	SALES (IN THOU-SANDS)†
American Telephone & Telegraph	2,879,000	$40,993,356
General Motors	1,225,000	63,221,100
Exxon Corporation	684,000	60,334,527
International Business Machines	582,000	21,076,089
General Electric	545,000	10,653,800
General Telephone & Electronics	443,000	8,723,483
Texaco, Inc.	414,000	28,607,521
Gulf Oil	357,000	18,069,000
Ford Motor	335,000	42,784,100
Southern Company	293,000	17,946,336

* As of early 1978. Source: New York Stock Exchange
† For 1978. Source: *Fortune*, 1979.

Managerial Efficiency

Sole proprietorships, partnerships, and small corporations are often managed by their owners. However, as corporations increase in size a division develops between owners and managers. The stockholders do not directly manage the operations of most medium-size and large corporations. These duties are delegated to the officers of the firm and their subordinates. Such a **division of responsibility** allows the company to hire specialists and professionals, such as sales managers, accountants, advertising executives, and lawyers, to run the operations for the

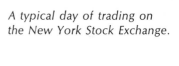
A typical day of trading on the New York Stock Exchange.

stockholders. These individuals are all skilled in their particular areas and can bring about a level of managerial efficiency that would not be possible if one or two owners attempted to carry out all these duties by themselves. In addition, the use of **professional managers** allows the corporation to maintain a high degree of managerial efficiency even in the face of dynamic growth.

Transfer of Ownership

When an individual buys stock in a firm, a stock certificate is issued to him or her (see Fig. 4.6). In

TABLE 4.2 ADVANTAGES AND DISADVANTAGES OF THE THREE ORGANIZATIONAL FORMS

	SOLE PROPRIETORSHIP	*PARTNERSHIP*	*CORPORATION*
Advantages	1. Financial advantages 2. Lack of restrictions 3. Secrecy 4. Personal satisfaction	1. Increased sources of capital and credit 2. Improved decision-making potential 3. Possibilities for expansion and growth 4. Definite legal status	1. Limited liability 2. Indefinite life 3. Growth potential 4. Managerial efficiency 5. Transfer of ownership
Disadvantages	1. Unlimited liability 2. Limited size 3. Limited life	1. Unlimited liability 2. The problem of continuity 3. Managerial problems 4. Size limitations	1. Heavy taxation 2. High organizing expense 3. Government restrictions 4. Lack of secrecy

Mama Mia's Pizzeria, Inc.

Things became hectic for Frank, Bob, and Jim when their limited partner went out and ordered seventy-five special tables for their pizzerias. However, thanks to their banker, Barbara Williams, they were able to borrow enough money to meet their bills and buy out the limited partner. Within twenty-four months it was evident that their banker's trust had not been misplaced. In fact, the firm was making so much money that it had paid off all its debts, and its accountant and lawyer both suggested that the partners incorporate.

The three men agreed and the lawyer, in turn, drew up the articles of incorporation. These were then filed with the secretary of the state and a charter was issued to the company. The firm was to be called Mama Mia's Pizzeria, Inc. The owners decided to have seven people on the board of directors: the three original partners, their wives, and the lawyer. They also decided to issue a total of 1,000 shares of stock. Each of the owners was given 332 shares while the wives and the lawyer each received 1 share. In addition, it was agreed that Frank would be

most cases this certificate can be sold at the individual's option. If the corporation is very small, the owner may have to find a buyer on his or her own. If the stock is that of a major corporation, however, it is traded at one of the **stock exchanges,** such as the New York Stock Exchange or the American Stock Exchange. In this case all the individual has to do is take the certificate to a stock brokerage firm and they will see that the stock is sold and the money (minus the brokerage fee) is turned over to the seller. More will be said about this topic in Section E, where the finance function will be studied.

21. If the president of a corporation dies, can the company continue in existence?

22. Why are most of our large companies incorporated?

23. Can an owner of ten shares of General Motors sell these shares if he or she wants?

DISADVANTAGES OF THE CORPORATION

While the corporate form of ownership offers some important advantages, there are also drawbacks associated with its use. Some of the more common ones include (a) heavy taxation, (b) high organizing expenses, (c) government restrictions, and (d) lack of secrecy.

Heavy Taxation

Corporations are subject to heavier taxes than are proprietorships or partnerships. First, they are required to pay federal income tax. In recent years this rate has been 17 percent on the first $25,000, 22 percent on the next $25,000 and 48 percent of everything above this amount. Then they are taxed annually by the state in which they are incorporated. Finally, if the company gives a dividend to its stockholders, these individuals must pay personal income taxes on all dividends in excess of $100. In this case the corporate earnings are subject to **double taxation.**

named chairman of the board, Bob would be the president, and Jim the executive vice-president.

Frank and Bob liked the new arrangement. Jim, however, was confused. "I don't see why we went through this whole procedure of incorporating," he said. "What specific advantages were supposed to be gained from all of this?"

1. How would you answer Jim's question? What are some of the advantages the new corporation will have over the partnership form of ownership?

2. In this case, the owners are also the managers. Has incorporation improved their managerial efficiency?

3. How can the owners raise money, besides borrowing funds from the bank, if they decide to expand their operations?

High Organizing Expenses

When a business decides to incorporate, there are a number of fees that must be paid. First, the company must pay for its charter. Then, if it wishes to operate in another state it must either incorporate there as well or pay a tax for the right to do business there. Finally, in order to determine all the legal procedures and red tape that must be dealt with, the company usually has to hire an attorney. All of these expenses can add up to quite an incorporation bill.

Government Restrictions

While the proprietorship and partnership are virtually free from government restrictions, the corporation is not. The firm is regulated by both federal and state governments in its sale of stock. It is also required to comply with certain laws if it merges or consolidates with another organization or if it reorganizes. Corporations are also required to maintain records and reports, which governmental agencies have the right to examine. In the case of regulated industries, such as utilities, some of these reports must be filed on a periodic basis with a particular government bureau.

Lack of Secrecy

In that the corporation is required to make certain records available to the government, its operations are not as secretive as those of other organizational forms. In addition, the corporation must provide an annual report to each stockholder. When there are only a few, some secrecy is possible. When there are many stockholders, however, the annual report becomes public record. Everyone, including the competition, can find out the firm's sales revenue, gross profit, total assets, net profit, and other financial data.

24. In what way are corporate earnings subject to double taxation?

25. To what types of government restrictions are corporations subject?

SUMMARY

When an individual decides to go into business for himself or herself, an evaluation must be made of the various possible forms of ownership. In this chapter three of these forms were examined: the sole proprietorship, the partnership, and the corporation.

The sole proprietorship is the easiest form of ownership to start or to dissolve. Some of its common advantages include the fact that the owner gets to keep all the profits, has freedom of action in deciding what he or she wants to do, can keep the operations very secretive, and often derives a good deal of personal satisfaction from all business successes. On the other hand, sole proprietors must assume unlimited liability for all obligations. Other disadvantages are that the size to which proprietorships can grow, as well as the life of the business, are both limited.

A partnership consists of two or more people who get together to operate a business. The most common type of partner is the general partner, who has unlimited liability. However there are other types as well, including limited, silent, secret, dormant, and nominal partners. In contrast to the sole proprietorship, the partnership form of ownership offers the partners a better chance to raise capital and credit and to improve their decision making by having two or more people thinking through business problems. In addition, there is the possibility for expansion and growth with few problems about the legal status of the partners, because these issues have now virtually all been resolved by the courts. On the other hand, all the partners except those with limited liability must assume responsibility for all obligations of the firm. Also, there are problems with continuity, management of the partnership, and size of the organization.

Major business firms today are not sole proprietorships or partnerships; they are corporations. Perhaps the reason why so many large firms choose to incorporate is the advantages offered by this form of ownership. One plus factor is that all stockholders have limited liability. Second, a corporation can exist indefinitely. Third, it has greater growth potential and managerial efficiency than do most proprietorships or partnerships. Finally, if any stockholders are dissatisfied with the way the company is performing, they can usually sell their stock and withdraw from ownership.

Of course, these advantages must be compared with the disadvantages. Not only is the corporation subject to heavy taxation, it also has high organizing expenses. In addition, there are government restrictions on operations, and also a lack of secrecy that permits competitors at least some information about what the company is doing.

KEY TERMS FOUND IN THIS CHAPTER

QUESTIONS FOR DISCUSSION AND ANALYSIS

1. Most sole proprietorships do not make much profit. Why then do so many business people initially choose this form of ownership?

2. Why is a partnership usually able to raise more capital than a sole proprietorship?

3. How does the adage "too many cooks spoil the broth" apply to the management of a partnership?

4. Is it not unfair for both sole proprietors and general partners to have to assume unlimited liability? Should not liabilities be restricted solely to the assets of the business, with personal assets protected from creditors?

5. Why is a corporation regarded, at least in legal terms, as an "artificial being"?

6. How difficult is it for a group of angry stockholders in a major corporation to oust the board of directors and replace them with a new board?

7. Why is it likely that a corporation will have greater managerial efficiency than a sole proprietorship or partnership?

8. Corporations have to pay taxes on their earnings and then stockholders pay taxes on any dividends they receive from these earnings. Is this double taxation unfair?

9. If an individual wants to maintain strict secrecy of operations, the corporate form is a poor choice. Explain this statement.

5

OBJECTIVES OF THIS CHAPTER

Every organization, whether it be a sole proprietorship, partnership, or corporation, needs to be effectively organized. In this chapter you will learn about how business firms are organized. The objectives of this chapter are to review the organizing process and present some of the basic information every manager must know about this process. When you are finished reading this chapter you should be able to do the following:

a. describe the organizing process;

b. explain the three essentials of an efficient organization;

c. relate what is meant by the term formal organization;

d. outline the four basic types of organization structures with their accompanying advantages and disadvantages;

e. identify seven of the major principles for sound organizing; and

f. understand the importance and value of the informal organization.

Organizing the Firm's Resources

WHAT IS ORGANIZING?

Organizing is a process in which the individuals and the resources of a company are brought together for the purpose of attaining the enterprise's objectives. In carrying out this process, the firm needs to (a) determine the activities that will have to be performed, (b) group these activities into some logical framework, and (c) assign the activities to the people in the organization. Because the firm itself decides how these steps are to be implemented, the organizing process is an *internal* one. All the company has to do is work out the best arrangement for carrying out its goal-related activities.

Some firms employ a very loose process in which jobs are informally assigned and people have a lot of leeway in deciding what they are going to do and when it will be accomplished. It is common to find this relatively simple, unsophisticated approach used by many sole proprietorships. On the other hand, in large companies it is likely that the individuals will all have job titles, written job descriptions, and specific objectives that they are to be pursuing. The organization will also have a formalized organization chart depicting the formal relationships between all the different jobs. Of course, the final decision about what kind of structure to use must rest upon the answer to the following question: with what type of organization will the company be most *efficient*?

1. What is meant by the term organizing?

THE ESSENTIALS OF AN EFFICIENT ORGANIZATION

In order to be efficient, there are three essentials that must be present in an organization. These are (a) objectives, (b) coordination, and (c) the proper delegation of authority.

Objectives

The first essential ingredient of an efficient organization is the presence of **objectives.** These are simply goals that the organization wants to attain. Some of the more common objectives among business firms are survival, profit, and growth. Naturally the identification of objectives is not, in and of itself, sufficient to ensure a successful organization. However, without objectives a company will lack direction and be unsure of the activities it should be carrying out. Objectives provide the basis for job assignments.

Coordination

The second essential ingredient of an effective organization is coordination. **Coordination** requires individuals to synchronize their efforts cooperatively in pursuing the objectives of the enterprise. At the heart of coordination is *teamwork,* which depends on two things. First, there must be a willingness to cooperate with others. This often means that individuals must put aside doing what they want to do and help out where they are needed. Second, everyone has to be given a specific job. This means breaking down overall objectives into departmental goals and then into individual work assignments. After all, no matter how willing people are to help out, if they are not assigned specific jobs, there is no basis for coordinating their efforts.

Proper Delegation of Authority

The third essential ingredient for an effective organization is the proper **delegation of authority. Authority** is the right to command. In an effective organization everyone has *some* authority. The managers have authority over their subordinates on down the hierarchy to the workers, who have authority over their equipment and their work. The flow of authority in the formal organization is downward.

The challenge for the manager is knowing *how much* authority to delegate and how much to hold on to. In many businesses it is common to find people far down in the organization making rather important decisions. These companies are known as **highly decentralized.** In other businesses, however, most such decisions are made at the top. These firms are known as **highly centralized.** Either of the two approaches can be successful depending upon the situation. However, in recent years many businesses have moved toward decentralization because they feel it is more efficient. Managers in these firms are encouraged to delegate authority, thereby freeing themselves for more important duties. Subordinates, meanwhile, feel a sense of participation when they are delegated this authority, the result being higher company morale.

The manager does not delegate *all* of his or her authority, of course. The subordinate is given only the authority needed to get the job done. In addition, no matter how much authority is delegated, *both the manager and the subordinate are responsible for the final outcome.* This has led to the well-

---

Katharine Graham, chief executive officer of the Washington Post Company, is one of the most influential people in America. She is best known to the general public as the owner of the *Washington Post* newspaper, which played a major role in breaking the Watergate scandal. What is unknown to many, however, is that she is also a very prominent business executive, whose holdings include not only the *Post,* but *Newsweek,* television stations, and one radio station.

Ever since she took the helm of this business empire in 1969 she has been concerned with the organization and management of operations. Her basic strategy has been to keep a tight rein on the operations of the *Post* while delegating authority over the other divisions to a team of managers.

Some people regard the management structure of the firm as slightly irregular. Much of this irregularity, however, has been brought about by the painful process of substituting formal planning and control for, heretofore, family management. Graham's current efforts are geared toward assessing changes in the mar-

ket and making the moves necessary to take advantage of these changes.

At the same time she has been pushing hard to maintain editorial budgets at the *Post* and *Newsweek* while cutting away at production and distribution costs. By 1978 the pretax margin on operations for the *Post* stood at 15.6¢ per $1 of sales, reaching a goal Graham set for the firm in 1975. Today overall sales are in excess of $500 million and net income is in the $50 million range.

Meanwhile, a good many publishers would like her to sit down and write an autobiography. She is not yet ready for that, however, noting that "If there's any book I want to write now, it would be about management—how I've learned to handle it and how it has changed this company." If she ever gets around to doing so, the book should prove worthwhile reading for all who are interested in learning how she used her managerial power to convert a loosely structured, family-owned enterprise that she took over in the early sixties into a professional, publicly held major corporation of the seventies.

Katharine Graham

known cliché that "you can delegate authority but you can never delegate responsibility." If the manager feels the subordinate is doing a poor job, the authority should be recalled and the manager should either do the job personally or redelegate it to a different subordinate.

No organization can function effectively if the manager does not delegate authority to the subordinates. However, delegating the *proper* amount to the *right* people is no easy task. In order to prevent making a serious mistake, the intelligent manager notes the type of authority needed to effectively carry out each job. The astute manager also identifies the capabilities of each subordinate, so that every one of them is given, to the highest degree possible, the type of work he or she finds both challenging and interesting. If the manager can do these things, there is an excellent chance that high efficiency can be attained.

2. How important is coordination to an organization's efficiency?

3. What is the difference between a centralized and a decentralized organization?

THE FORMAL ORGANIZATION

The essentials of an efficient organization give order and direction to the firm. Objectives are set, jobs are assigned, work quotas are established, an organization chart is drawn up. As these things happen, the **formal organization** begins to take shape. Some people like to refer to the formal organization as "the way the company operates on paper." By this they mean that the adoption of objectives and the establishment of work standards help to let people know what management expects. In practice, however, things never seem to work exactly the way the company wants. Nevertheless, the formal organization is very important because it serves as a starting point in bringing together the people and the work. One way in which this is done is through the formation of an organization structure.

4. What is meant by the term formal organization? Put it in your own words.

Types of Organization Structures

There are four basic types of organization structure found in modern businesses: (a) line, (b) line and staff, (c) functional, and (d) committee. Each of these offers a framework within which the manager can coordinate the activities of his or her people, although most companies prefer to use a combination of these structures rather than any one "pure" type.

Line organization

A **line organization** is one in which there is a direct flow of authority from the top of the organization to the bottom. Line organizations have a number of common characteristics. First, each manager has direct authority over his or her subordinates, who in turn have direct authority over their subordinates, on down the organization. Second, everyone in the organization reports to only one immediate superior. This concept, known as the **unity of command principle,** means "one man, one boss." Third, managers have complete authority over their own areas. For example, the head of advertising has authority over his or her department while the credit manager controls credit operations. This type of organization structure, diagramed in Fig. 5.1, is a very simple one and has both advantages and disadvantages.

Advantages

a. The structure is easy to understand.

b. All people know to whom they report and who reports to them.

c. Authority and responsibility are clearly defined.

d. Everyone has one and only one boss.

e. Decisions can often be made quickly.

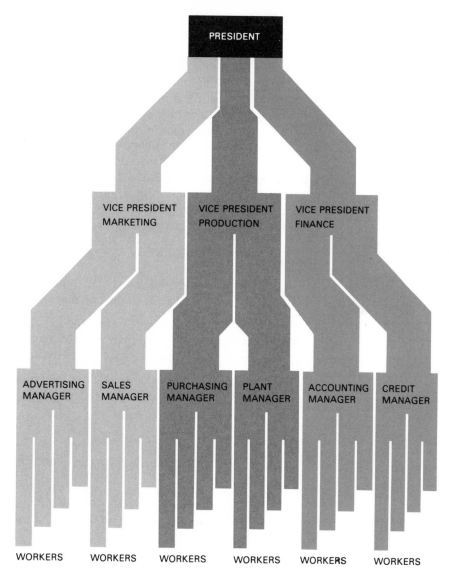

FIG. 5.1 *Line type of organization structure*

Disadvantages

a. Managers have to handle a lot of detail work because they are directly responsible for approving the work of their subordinates.

b. Managers have to be able to do a lot of things well; as a result there are few specialists in the organization.

c. Each department is concerned basically with its own work; little attention is given to coordination with other departments.

d. If a manager resigns or retires it is often difficult to find someone with the necessary broad knowledge and skills to replace him or her.

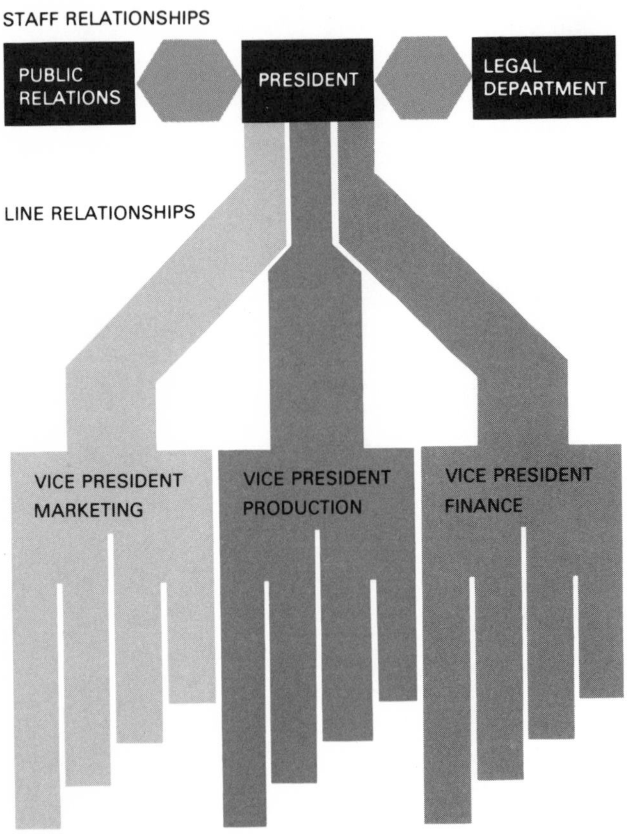

STAFF RELATIONSHIPS

LINE RELATIONSHIPS

PUBLIC RELATIONS — PRESIDENT — LEGAL DEPARTMENT

VICE PRESIDENT MARKETING   VICE PRESIDENT PRODUCTION   VICE PRESIDENT FINANCE

FIG. 5.2 *Line and staff type of organization structure*

Line and staff organization

As a company grows larger the manager's job becomes more and more complex. As a consequence, it is often necessary to use staff specialists with knowledge and skills in areas such as law or public relations to help out the manager. The line departments, which are doing the work necessary to attain the company's objectives, are supplemented by staff departments that provide advice and other special services to them. When this occurs, a **line and staff organization** emerges (see Fig. 5.2). Today this type of structure is very common in large business firms. Again, however, there are advantages and disadvantages in using such a structure.

Advantages

a. Highly trained professionals are available to give advice in specialized areas to the line manager.

b. The line manager can devote more time to regular responsibilities and does not have to worry about handling highly specialized matters.

c. Despite the addition of staff specialists, everyone still reports to only one superior.

Disadvantages

a. Line managers may resent receiving advice from staff specialists.

b. Staff specialists may go overboard in trying to persuade line managers to use their recommendations.

c. The use of staff specialists may dramatically increase the company's salary expenses.

Functional organization

A **functional organization** is one in which specialists are placed in line positions. As such they are able to give orders in their areas of expertise. Figure 5.3 provides an illustration of such an organization. In this structure employees have more than one su-

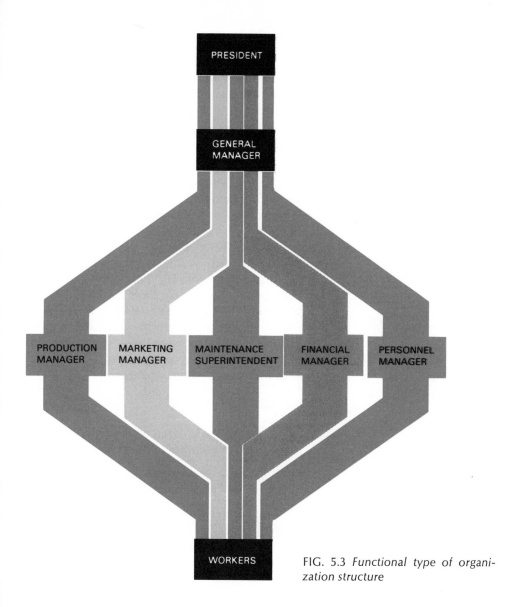

FIG. 5.3 *Functional type of organization structure*

perior. This may result in some confusion. However, many firms feel that the efficiency obtained with this structure more than offsets any losses brought about by the use of multiple bosses. Other commonly cited advantages and disadvantages associated with this organizational form are as follows.

Advantages

a. Experts are available to help the workers on any job-related problem.

b. Each specialist is working in only one area, the one he or she knows best.

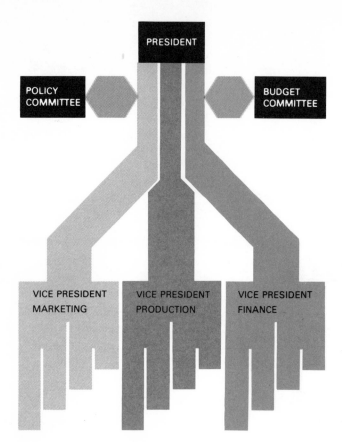

FIG. 5.4 *Committee organization used with line type of structure*

"We've made a decision, five to one. You look stupid in that mustache!"

From The Wall Street Journal; permission Cartoon Features Syndicate

Disadvantages

a. The fact that the workers have more than one boss can result in confusion regarding which superior to obey. Discipline can also break down.

b. With such great emphasis on specialization, managers never get a chance to learn anything outside their own areas of expertise.

Committee organization

In the **committee organization,** individuals from different areas are brought together to study organization problems. This type of organization is usually combined with one of the others, such as the line type of organization (see Fig. 5.4). Some committees are formed on a permanent basis and are known as **standing committees.** Others are formed to achieve a particular purpose and are then disbanded; these are known as **ad hoc committees.** There are some very commonly cited advantages and disadvantages to this committee type of organization.

Advantages

a. Decisions are made based on the combined judgment of a group of individuals.

b. Committees can often examine an issue with less personal involvement than can an individual.

c. Committees can draw upon the expertise of their individual members in analyzing many important problems in far greater depth than can the average individual manager.

Disadvantages

a. Committees often take a long time to make a decision, which makes them an expensive form of organization.

b. Some committee decisions are a result of compromise and modification, and often achieve rather poor results.

c. Some issues may split the committee so badly that they result in disputes and hurt feelings among the members.

5. The line organization is referred to as the simplest type of structure. Why?

6. Why is it common to find organizations changing from a line to a line and staff structure as they increase in size?

7. After evaluating the advantages and disadvantages of each of the four basic types of organization structure, which do you think is most widely used? Explain.

Major Principles for Sound Organizing

For years managers have been looking for guidelines to use in coordinating the efforts of their people. Fortunately there are some general rules of the road that are now available to the modern manager. One which we have already noted is the principle of unity of command. We call them **principles for sound**

The Hughes Organizational Empire

When Howard Hughes died in 1976 he left behind an empire with two major divisions. One was the Howard Hughes Medical Institute; the other was the Summa Corporation. The latter is seemingly directionless and complex, consisting of hotel, gambling, real estate, transportation, mining, television, engineering, and manufacturing interests. When Hughes died, the empire was so entangled that experts wondered if the organization's holdings would ever get sorted out. Now it seems that they might.

The Landmark Hotel and Casino in Las Vegas are being sold; the organization had never made a profit from them. KLAS-TV, Las Vegas, the Hughes TV network; some Nevada mining claims; and a 2,000-acre ranch in Nevada have also been sold, and Hughes Helicopter and the North Las Vegas Airport are said to be on the selling block.

However, the other four Las Vegas hotels and five casinos, as well as Harold's Club in Reno, are all profit-able. So, Summa is hanging onto them. It is also holding Hughes Airwest, Paradise Valley Country Club, the Hughes Executive Terminal at the Las Vegas airport, and the Xanadu Hotel in the Bahamas. The court-appointed trustee, William E. Lummis, has invested $55.5 million of land and cash in a new high-rise fashion shopping center adjacent to the Summa-owned Frontier Hotel in Las Vegas and is renovating and expanding the Desert Inn. Nevertheless, the Hughes empire is still a tangled organizational mess. Even its dollar value is currently unknown. Merrill Lynch, the stock brokerage house, estimates it at $167 million while Las Vegas observers say that the hotels and casinos alone are worth $300 million.

It took a tremendous amount of time and effort to organize the Hughes empire. But it looks like it's going to take even more time and effort to determine what will now be done with it.

organizing. Before we examine seven of the other most significant, you should be aware that a principle is a *general guideline* and must be adapted to the situation. Sometimes these principles must be modified; other times they can be ignored. In general, however, the manager will find that they are beneficial in achieving a more effective organization. The principles we will examine are the (a) unity of objective principle, (b) span of control principle, (c) principle of work similarity, (d) principle of delegation of authority, (e) principle of equality between authority and responsibility, (f) principle of minimum levels, and (g) principle of flexibility.

Unity of objective principle

As applied to a business, the **unity of objective principle** states that each department in a company must assist in attaining the overall objectives of the firm. This means that everything the production people do must help not just the production department but the entire company. There must be cooperation between all the units in the firm. For example, the production people must coordinate their activities with the sales department so that the goods being manufactured are also sold. If demand is declining and sales are dropping, production must slow up its efforts. On the other hand, if demand is high the production people must turn out more goods to help meet this demand. If all the departments are working together, they will attain not only their own individual objectives but those of the overall company as well.

Span of control principle

The **span of control principle** states that managers can effectively handle only a limited number of subordinates. Naturally the right number for one manager will be different from that for another. It will depend to some degree on the *type of work*. Subordinates doing new or complex jobs will have to ask their superiors more questions (or ask for more help) than someone doing a simple job. As a result, managers may find their span of control lim-

ited to three or four subordinates. Another factor influencing the span of control is the manager's *own ability*. Some superiors are able to manage ten subordinates regardless of the situation; others are more effective if they have only three. Each manager must analyze the situation and decide what is ideal for him or her.

Principle of work similarity

According to the **principle of work similarity,** it is more efficient in organizing a work force to group together people who are doing the same things. For example, in a manufacturing firm it is common to find marketing, production, and finance departments. People in each of these departments are further organized by work similarity (see Fig. 5.5). This basic idea is used by many companies. Another illustration would be a large auto firm such as General Motors, which is organized by product lines. There are Chevrolet, Pontiac, Oldsmobile, Buick, and Cadillac divisions. People in each division work on one particular type of car only.

Principle of delegation of authority

In order to ensure an effective organization, managers must *delegate authority to competent individuals at the lowest level of the hierarchy.* By getting everyone to participate, they create a climate of teamwork, high morale, and effective coordination. Many managers want this climate, but they confine all decision making to the upper levels. Effective managers delegate minor work down the line and spend their own time making important decisions. Since most of the work in an organization is not of major importance, it is easy to see that delegation of authority can get everyone involved with no loss of efficiency.

Principle of equality between authority and responsibility

The manager who delegates work to be done must give the subordinate the authority to carry out the task. This principle holds that, for an organization to be most effective, *authority must be equal to responsibility*. Unfortunately, many managers hold their subordinates responsible for doing a job right, but they never give the person the adequate authority for getting the job done.

Principle of minimum levels

Every firm should operate as efficiently as possible. Within this guideline, the **principle of minimum levels** states that a firm should have as few levels in the hierarchy as possible. The basic reasoning behind this principle is that as the number of organization levels increases communication problems arise. This happens because there are too many people through whom a message must pass as it moves from the top to the bottom of the hierarchy.

This principle ties in very closely with the span of control principle. After all, if every manager has three subordinates there will be more levels in an organization consisting of 500 employees than if each manager has six subordinates. As one increases

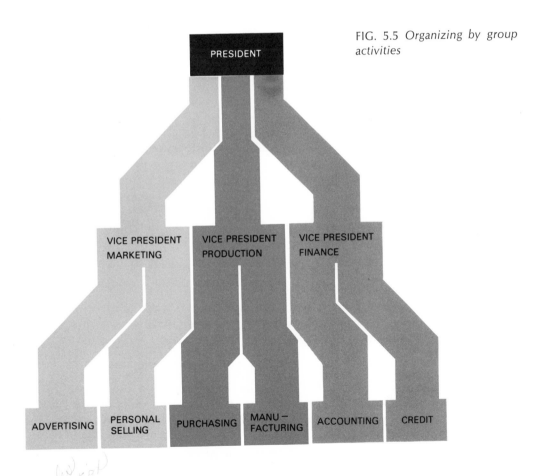

FIG. 5.5 *Organizing by group activities*

More than Just a Pizzeria

After incorporating their business, the owners of Mama Mia's Pizzeria, Inc., decided to expand their operations by doubling the size of each of the three pizza parlors. Instead of restricting their business to pizza, however, they decided to turn their establishments into Italian restaurants and change their name to "Mama Mia's Restaurant." The money to finance the operation was secured by plowing the profits of the last two years back into the business. The problem facing the owners was how to organize the three restaurants so as to operate them as efficiently as possible.

After examining the situation, they decided to organize them identically. Each of the owners—Frank, Bob, and Jim—agreed to manage one restaurant. Reporting directly to each would be the individuals in charge of (a) the bar operations, (b) the kitchen, and (c) the table service. The bookkeeper, who would be responsible for keeping the financial records of the restaurant, would also report directly to the manager. Each of these four people, in turn, had from one to eight subordinates directly under his or her command, depending upon the area. For example, the bookkeeper had only one subordinate, while the maitre d' was in charge of the eight waiters and waitresses who took care of the table service.

The owners felt that this organizational arrangement would be efficient because it adhered to certain principles of effective organization. In particular, they believed it was in line with the unity of command principle, the principle of work similarity, and the principle of unity of objective. Six months after the owners opened their three new restaurants, their local banker admitted that she was unsure of exactly what these organizing principles were but she did know that the new restaurants were making a great deal of money.

1. What type of organization structure is each of the restaurants using? What are the advantages and disadvantages of this type of structure?

2. Draw the organization chart for one of the restaurants.

3. Describe the three principles of organization mentioned in the case: unity of command, work similarity, and unity of objective. In what way might these account for the financial success of the restaurants? Explain.

the span of control, the organization moves from a "tall" structure to a "flat" one (see Figs. 5.6 and 5.7). Remember, however, that the *situation* determines whether or not to have a flat or tall structure. The guideline must be *efficiency*. If the company feels it can be just as profitable with four levels in the hierarchy as it can with six, it should choose the former.

Principle of flexibility

If an organization is to be successful, it must be flexible. This means that it must be *capable of adapting to changing conditions*. Upturns or downturns in the external environment are certain to have an effect on the firm. So, too, are changes in personnel attitude and morale. The firm must be able to adjust to these conditions if it is to survive.

8. Why are the principles of organizing known as general guidelines? Why are they not considered fixed rules that should always be followed?

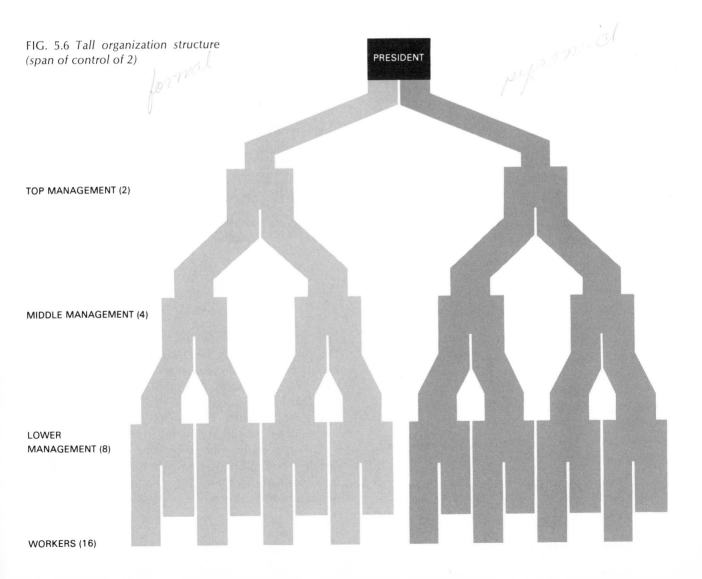

FIG. 5.6 *Tall organization structure (span of control of 2)*

PRESIDENT

TOP MANAGEMENT (2)

MIDDLE MANAGEMENT (4)

LOWER MANAGEMENT (8)

WORKERS (16)

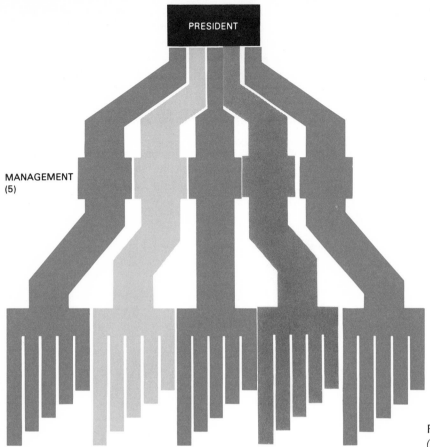

MANAGEMENT (5)

WORKERS (25)

FIG. 5.7 *Flat organization structure (span of control of 5)*

9. What is meant by the unity of objective principle? Put it in your own words.

10. How useful is the span of control principle to the practicing manager? Explain.

11. What is meant by the principle of minimum levels?

12. What is the difference between a flat and a tall structure?

13. Of the principles presented in this section, which is of the most value to the manager? Explain.

THE INFORMAL ORGANIZATION

The organization we have been examining thus far is called the *formal organization.* However, we know that no business operates completely "by the book." In a real business setting the relationships that actually exist between the personnel do not follow formal lines. People in one department know people in other departments. They may have met them during a coffee break; they may be on the company bowling team together; or they may live in the same neighborhood. When these people need information or help, they will often cross departmental lines and ask their friends for it. This type of friendly interaction among the people in an organizational setting helps create the **informal organization.**

As you can imagine, it is impossible to draw the informal organization on a chart because it is con-

tinually changing. People who helped each other out yesterday may be associating with other people today. Furthermore, these associations may be between people on the same level of the hierarchy or on different levels. They may even cross unit or plant lines. For example, a new plant supervisor may con-

CASE

A Hodgepodge of Efficiency

Barbara Williams, the banker for the Mama Mia's Restaurant Corporation, was so impressed with its financial success that she decided to drop by and visit one of the restaurants. After saying hello to the owner/manager and taking a table at the side of the room, she sat back and watched the restaurant in operation. At the end of the evening, she and the manager had a talk.

Well, what did you think of our operation? Pretty efficient, huh?

Yes, it was. But what confused me was all these principles of effective organizing that you said you follow in your operation. I couldn't see any of them.

What do you mean?

Well, early in the evening I noticed some of the waiters getting a little behind in serving their tables, and some of the other waiters came over to help out. I thought good organizing required everyone to do his or her own job and leave others alone. Also, I saw a doctor come in and ask for a quick order because he was due at the hospital. He was served before some of the other people who came in before him. I thought good organization principles required everyone to be treated equally with no favoritism. The big thing that confuses me about your restaurant is its lack of formal organization. It seems to me that the waiters, the cooks, and everyone else are teaming up together in some hodge-podge type of organization to get things done. I admit it is efficient, but is it really organization?

1. What is Barbara telling us about the informal organization that exists in the restaurant?

2. What do you think of Barbara's statement about the restaurant having a lot of efficiency but no real organization?

3. How well would a restaurant run if it relied exclusively on the formal structure in getting things done? Explain.

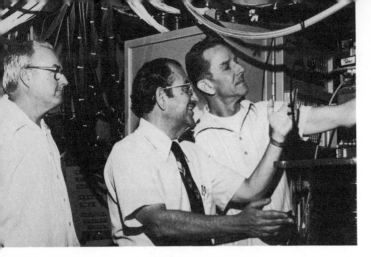

Organizations operate both formally and informally. Can you tell whether these employees are talking about a job-related problem or about how the local sports team fared?

tact an experienced supervisor to ask him or her a question about effective discipline. The new employer feels the experienced one will give good advice (see Fig. 5.8). In another instance a plant manager may contact a foreman to ask if he or she will read a report scheduled for top management. The report deals with worker attitudes and the plant manager may want the foreman's opinion of the report's accuracy. In a third case, a supervisor may contact the manager in another plant, describe a good article he or she just read on management, and recommend that the manager also read it. In a fourth instance, a worker may contact his or her plant manager, a fellow member of the company bowling team, and remind the manager that they are bowling for the league championship that night.

Each of the above illustrations showed an informal relationship. Three of these were job related, one was not. Yet all represent typical day-to-day relationships in the work environment. When one realizes that the average employee may have a dozen informal contacts with other employees on the job, it becomes evident that the informal organization is relied upon heavily in accomplishing company goals.

There is, of course, a negative side to the informal organization. If everyone spent their entire day crossing formal lines and talking about activities that were not job related, very little would get done. Efficient managers try to be aware of the informal organization that exists within their unit and between the unit and the rest of the company. They then discourage communications for solely personal pleasure and try to get the workers to use their informal contacts to help solve job-related problems. Naturally it is impossible to ever accomplish this objective fully. However, the effective manager knows that the informal organization cannot be eliminated. He or she should therefore seek to use it for the good of the company. For example, informal relationships often develop when formal channels foul up. If an order from the plant to the warehouse is lost, formal procedure may require a duplicate order. Using informal channels, however, a plant supervisor may call the warehouse foreman and ask him or her to ship the material immediately without waiting for a new order. In this case, people got things done by going outside of formal channels. Another use of the informal organization is to facilitate communication. When there is a breakdown in the formal lines of communication, an informal channel will spring up. This is called the **grapevine.** Often the grapevine carries rumor and gossip; sometimes it conveys accurate information. In either event, managers who are aware of the grapevine can not only find out the latest rumors, they can use the informal network for passing on accurate information of their own. Thus the grapevine supplements and strengthens formal communication channels. The effective manager uses the informal organization in getting things done.

14. Do all business firms have informal organizations?

15. What are some of the reasons why people in a business firm communicate informally?

16. Why is it impossible to draw a chart of the informal organization?

FIG. 5.8 *The informal organization*

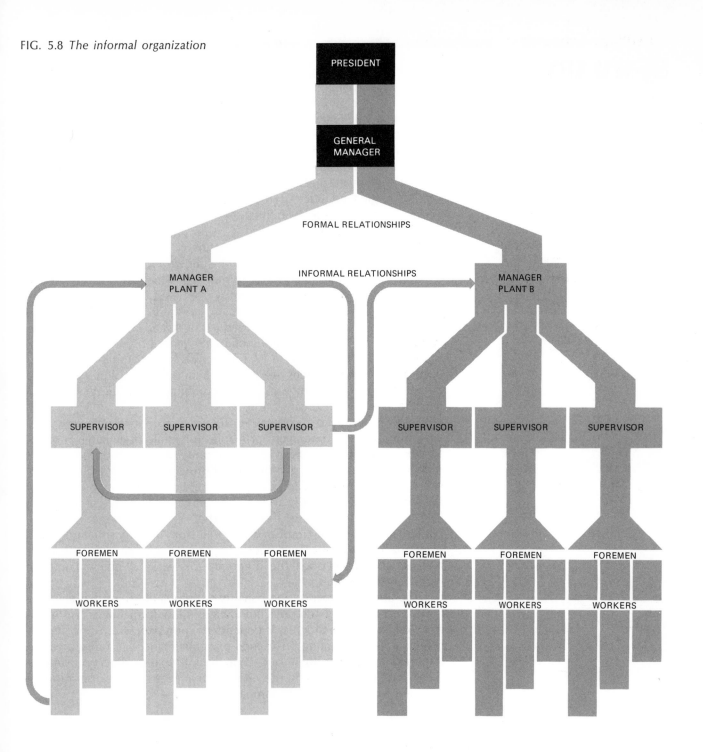

SUMMARY

In this chapter the organizing process was examined. This is a process in which the people and the other resources of the company are brought together for the purpose of attaining the enterprise's objectives. In order to organize efficiently there are three essentials one must take into consideration. First, the company must have objectives. Second, there must be coordination via teamwork and individual job assignments. Third, there must be a proper delegation of authority. If these three things are present, the organization's effectiveness will be improved.

In bringing together the people and the work, the business must define duties and responsibilities. As these things are done, the organization begins to take shape—at least on paper. This is known as the formal organization. The eventual structure of one firm may differ from that of any other firm. In general terms, however, there are four basic types of organization structure. The simplest is the line organization, in which there is a direct flow of authority from the top of the organization to the bottom. A second type of structure is the line and staff organization, in which staff specialists are used to advise and assist line managers. A third type of structure is the functional organization, in which specialists are placed in line positions. A fourth type is the committee organization, in which committees are used to help make decisions. The committee type of organization is usually combined with one of the other types such as the line organization.

In trying to make an organization structure operate efficiently, it is useful to consider some major principles for sound organizing. Some of the more common are the principle of unity of command, the unity of objective principle, the span of control principle, the principle of work similarity, the principle of delegation of authority, the principle of equality between authority and responsibility, the principle of minimum levels, and the principle of flexibility. These principles are only general guidelines. There is no proof that they will work in every situation. However, the effective manager checks to see if he or she can use them because they often spell the difference between an efficient and an inefficient organization.

The informal organization consists of the relationships that exist between the personnel and does not always follow formal lines. Yet much of an organization's progress is dependent upon people crossing departmental lines and calling on friends or acquaintances in other areas of the company to help them out. Thus the informal organization supplements the formal one, and the effective manager seeks to use informal channels for the good of the company.

KEY TERMS FOUND IN THIS CHAPTER

QUESTIONS FOR DISCUSSION AND ANALYSIS

1. What are the steps involved in the organizing process? Explain.

2. What are the three essentials of an efficient organization? How are they of value to modern business?

3. What is a line organization? What are its major advantages or disadvantages?

4. Describe a line and staff organization. What are its major advantages and disadvantages? Why do so many firms use this type of structure?

5. A functional organization is a poor one because it violates the unity of command principle. Support or oppose this statement.

6. Why do businesses employing the committee type of organization often combine it with one of the other types rather than using it by itself?

7. How beneficial are principles of organization to the practicing manager?

8. In getting things done, how important is the informal organization to a business? Should the manager encourage or discourage it? Explain.

6

Never tell people how to do things. Tell them what to do and they will surprise you with their ingenuity.

General George Patton

OBJECTIVES OF THIS CHAPTER

The group of individuals in the business firm who are responsible for seeing that things get done is known as the managers. In this chapter you will be learning about what these people do. The objectives of this chapter are to examine the management process and study the functions and skills needed to carry out this process effectively. By the end of the chapter you should be able to do the following:

a. define what is meant by the term management;

b. tell why management is both a science and an art;

c. identify the three levels of management;

d. describe the four functions every manager performs;

e. relate the three skills all effective managers must have; and

f. explain why communication is the key to management effectiveness.

The Manager's Job

WHAT IS MANAGEMENT?

Management is the process of getting things done through people. In the previous chapter we saw that part of this process is carried out with the development of an organization structure. However, there is more to management than just organizing the people and the work. Objectives must be set, plans formulated, people directed, and operations controlled. In making the necessary decisions, management must rely on all the skills at its command. As a result, **management is both a science and an art.**

As a **science,** management entails the use of organized knowledge. Many of the things managers do are a result of information obtained through formal research and study. One area in which a great deal has been done is that of quantitative decision making or, as it is known today, **management science.** We know that by using certain mathematical formulas we can often control inventory and project demand more accurately than by merely using trial and error.

Yet management is also an **art.** Through experience the manager develops judgment and intuition. These subjective factors are useful in evaluating situations. For example, the manager may have to choose between two strategies: A and B. All research and study may indicate that neither of the two is any better than the other. However, what if the manager chooses strategy A on the basis of intuition and proves to be right? In this case it is difficult to say precisely *why* the manager was able to choose so well, but there must be some special ability he or she has. This same type of ability is useful in managing people. Effective managers know when to flatter their subordinates and when to be stern. Such human behavior skills cannot be quantified; they can only be learned through experience and training.

Effective management is a combination of art and science. Neither should be ignored; neither ought to be relied on exclusively. In getting things done through people, management must seek the right blend of art and science. At the upper levels of the hierarchy there will be more emphasis on the

"I'm back! Did everyone enjoy my vacation?"

From The Wall Street Journal; permission Cartoon Features Syndicate

former; at the lower levels there will be more emphasis on the latter.

1. In what way is management a science? In what way is it an art?

LEVELS OF MANAGEMENT

In a small business firm the owner is often the manager. Major corporations, however, rely upon large numbers of professional managers to conduct the affairs of the company. This management team consists of three levels: top management, middle management, and operating management (see Fig. 6.1).

The **top management** group includes the board of directors, the president, and other officers of the corporation such as the secretary, the treasurer, the

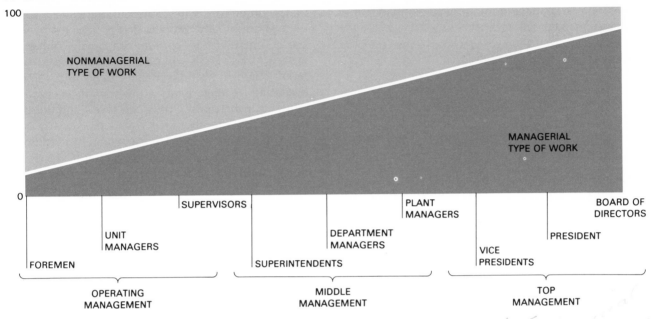

FIG. 6.1 *The manager's job*

vice-presidents, and the general managers. The duties of this group are to set long-range objectives for the firm and to evaluate overall progress.

The **middle management** group reports directly to the top managers. This group includes persons such as plant managers, department managers, chief engineers, controllers, and superintendents. The duties of this group are to carry out the long-range objectives set by top management. Therefore the middle managers are more interested in day-to-day activities than are their superiors.

The **operating management** group reports directly to the middle managers. These operating managers include foremen, supervisors, and unit heads. They are responsible for seeing that performance goals are met by all the workers. As a result, a good part of their day consists of assigning people to specific jobs and tasks and then watching their performance very closely. If problem areas arise, these managers will often take corrective action right on the spot.

As one moves up the hierarchy from operating management to top management, one finds a change in the type of work being done. Operating managers are very concerned with specific jobs and performance, while top managers are more interested in the overall objectives and long-range planning. The operating managers tend to handle problems that can be solved with physical labor, while top managers tend to deal with issues that can only be solved with careful thought. Thus the operating manager may be concerned with how to repair a machine, while the top manager is trying to formulate a plan for capturing a large share of the competition's market. Because of the differences in the type of work they do, we say that operating managers are most concerned with nonmanagerial types of work while top managers are most concerned with managerial types of work. As one moves up the hierarchy the emphasis changes from heavily nonmanagerial to heavily managerial.

2. Why are top managers often referred to as "thinkers," while operating managers are called "doers"?

MANAGEMENT FUNCTIONS

How do managers succeed in getting things done through people? In order to answer this question it is necessary to break down the manager's job into its basic duties or *functions*. **Management entails planning, organizing, directing, and controlling.** By performing well in each of these areas the manager can get things done through people. However, it must be remembered that the manager does not do these things in any specific order. Planning and controlling, for example, may be going on simultaneously. Also, the functions are all interdependent in that effective planning depends on competent control, and proper directing relies on good organizing (see Fig. 6.2).

Planning

Planning consists of two basic activities: (a) setting objectives, and (b) deciding how to attain these objectives. By its very nature, planning is concerned with the future. The firm needs to have some direction to take it through the next couple of years. The plan provides this direction.

The first major step in planning is *setting the objective.* Many people believe that this means deciding how much profit the firm wants to attain. Actually, businesses are more realistic in their thinking. They know that their major purpose for existence is to provide some good or service to the customer. Therefore, they will set not only a profit objective but also some goals related to the goods or services they intend to make available. The result

is a group of multiple *major objectives.* From these major objectives will come subobjectives; so the plan is eventually broken down into many small pieces, each with its own accompanying objectives. Some of these goals will be pursued by top management, some by middle management, and some by operating management. However, if everyone is working in harmony, the three levels should all be supporting each other.

The second major step in planning is *deciding how to reach the chosen objectives.* Often there are two or three possible approaches to the same objective. Management's task must be to determine which one will give the best results for the least investment. We call this a **cost-benefit ratio.**

In order to find the best cost-benefit ratio, one must first identify the various plans that can be used to reach each objective. Then the premises or assumptions on which the plans are based must be evaluated. Some plans will be most successful if the economy is good, others are based on the assumption that there will be an economic slump, while

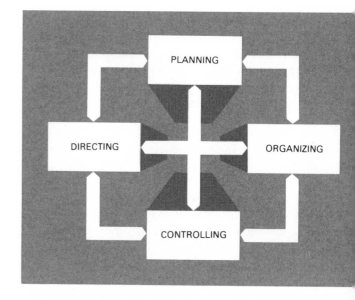

FIG. 6.2 *Interdependent management functions*

still others assume a generally stable economy. Which of these is most likely to occur? By evaluating the conditions under which each plan will be successful, management can decide which offers the best results. To some degree, of course, the company will be guessing because there is no assurance that its projection of future conditions will be correct. Nevertheless, there is little more that can be done except to analyze the situation and play the odds.

Consider, for example, a company that has $50,000 to invest and has narrowed its decision down to four plans of action. The expected profit from and the probability of success of each plan is as follows:

Strategy	Profit to the firm	Probability of success
1	$200,000	.40
2	250,000	.30
3	350,000	.20
4	500,000	.10

Which of the four strategies should the firm choose? The answer will depend upon the profit involved *and* the probability of success. Therefore, the two must be multiplied. When they are, you will see that the totals are $80,000, $75,000, $70,000, and $50,000 respectively. In this case, then, given the possible profit and the likelihood of the plan succeeding, strategy 1 is best.

This is the exact process a manager will use when planning. Each alternative plan will be analyzed for the purpose of determining which will give the best results for the investment. In the above illustration, strategy 1 has an expectation of $80,000 for a $50,000 investment. This is the best cost-benefit ratio available to the firm. It should therefore choose this strategy.

Organizing

As we saw in the previous chapter, **organizing** is the function or process of dividing the work to be done into small units and assigning the units to people. Plans are put into effect by the organizing process.

Management entails planning, organizing, directing, and controlling. A manager's job is to get things done through people.

Don Shula

The manager's job is to get things done through people. And this is exactly what Coach Don Shula of the Miami Dolphins does.

Born in 1930 and raised in Painesville, Ohio, he was a running back at John Carroll University in Cleveland. He then went on to the pros, playing for the Cleveland Browns, Baltimore Colts, and Washington Redskins. From here he entered the coaching ranks, first as an assistant coach at Virginia and Kentucky and then as a defensive coordinator for the Detroit Lions.

In 1963 he became head coach at Baltimore and his capabilities as a manager were immediately apparent. The youngest head coach in NFL history, he guided the team to a conference championship within two years. And during his seven years at Baltimore, the Colts finished first in their conference four times.

In 1970 he took over as head coach of the Miami Dolphins. Turning around a team that was 3–10–1, he won two Super Bowls within the first four years. During this time period the Dolphins won 17 straight games, an NFL record. And he had the best winning percentage in pro football during the 1970s, emerging victorious in over 73 percent of all games.

How does Coach Shula do it? There are several answers, all tied directly to effective management. First, as one of his players put it, he has total commitment to goals and objectives and he can transfer his commitment to his players. Second, he works hard to get that extra edge needed for success. Third, he explains things simply and completely so that those working with him understand what is to be done. Fourth, he drills his people through practice so that they can execute their assignments with precision. Finally, he has a philosophy that keeps success and failure in perspective. He puts it this way: "Success is never final; defeat is never fatal." And his record as a coach shows that both his philosophy and his ability to get things done through others reveals him to be a superb manager.

When plans or objectives are changed, it is common to find changes also being made in the organization structure.

In addition to job assignment and the formation of an organization structure, organizing involves the delegation of authority to managers and workers for the purpose of getting the job done. Yet even with all this formal design, effective organizations depend on teamwork. There must be cooperation and understanding between and within all units of the company. The manager's job is that of both creating and maintaining this *psychological* climate within the organization. Remember that people who want to work together will use the informal organization if the formal structure fails them. Thus the key goal in organizing is to create a desire on the part of personnel to be members of the team. If the manager can achieve this goal, the rest will follow.

Directing

Directing is the management function of supervising and guiding subordinates. Much of this is done on a face-to-face basis with the employees as they perform their tasks. One of the major challenges facing management in carrying out this function is seeing that orders are understood. This requires effective *communication.* Orders must be clear and precise. Also, there must be an opportunity for the employees to ask questions and receive feedback on how well they are doing.

A second major challenge for management is that of **motivating** the personnel. Management needs to understand the types of rewards the employees want. These commonly include money, good working conditions, job security, meaningful work, and a feeling of accomplishment. Every individual will be different, of course, so management will have to put together just the right combination of these rewards for each.

The third major challenge is that of providing effective **leadership.** Some people want to be directed very closely, others want to be left alone. Some want a little responsibility, others want a lot. Management must have a flexible leadership style that permits it to adapt to the particular needs of each employee. Only in this way can it hope to achieve effective direction of the employees.

Controlling

Controlling is the function or process in which management compares expected results with actual performance and then takes steps to correct any significant deviations that have occurred. Figure 6.3 illustrates the control process in action.

The purpose of this control process is to provide management with a basis for keeping its operations in line with the plan. If something goes wrong, management needs to know. One of the most common methods for controlling operations is the *budget.* A second is a *quality control program.* A third is simply *personal observation* on the part of management. These and other similar techniques are widely used to provide **feedback** to management for control purposes.

One of the major requirements of a control system is *timeliness.* Unless management receives control information in time to take the necessary action, the control system is useless. A second characteristic is *economy.* The system must be worth the cost. For example, a quality control program that costs $10,000 to set up but saves the company only $1,000 a year is not worth the investment. How, then, can a firm control all problem areas if the costs of some control systems are too high? The answer is that the management does not have to control *every* deviation. In fact, no firm tries to do so. Instead, management relies on the **exception principle.** This principle states that management should concern itself only with significant deviations or exceptions. For example, a business may set a goal of $250,000 in sales for the first quarter of its fiscal year. At the end of three months the company will compare its actual sales to its expected goal of $250,000. Whether or not corrective action is needed will depend upon what the firm has predetermined to be a *significant* deviation. If the acceptable deviation is 10 percent,

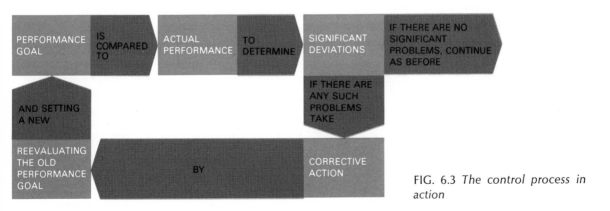

PERFORMANCE GOAL IS COMPARED TO ACTUAL PERFORMANCE TO DETERMINE SIGNIFICANT DEVIATIONS IF THERE ARE NO SIGNIFICANT PROBLEMS, CONTINUE AS BEFORE

IF THERE ARE ANY SUCH PROBLEMS TAKE

AND SETTING A NEW

REEVALUATING THE OLD PERFORMANCE GOAL BY CORRECTIVE ACTION

FIG. 6.3 *The control process in action*

then the management will accept any sales figure between $225,000 and $275,000 because this is within the acceptable range. If sales are less than $225,000 the management must decide what type of corrective action is needed. It may be necessary to reduce the next quarter's sales projection because there is simply insufficient demand for the goods or services being provided. Or it may be necessary to increase advertising or personal selling to bolster sales. Similarly, if sales are greater than $275,000 the management can increase its goals for the next quarter. By establishing a control system that is timely, economical, and administered with the help of the exception principle, management can develop an *effective* overall control system.

3. What do we mean when we say that the management functions are interdependent?

4. What are the two basic activities involved in planning?

5. Which one of the management functions is most concerned with motivating employees?

6. What are some of the major requirements of an effective control system?

MANAGEMENT FUNCTIONS AND MANAGEMENT LEVELS

One of the most commonly accepted principles of management is **universality of management functions.** By this we mean that all managers perform the same basic functions. Whether we are talking about business managers, hospital administrators, military officers, or directors of government agencies, they all plan, organize, direct, and control their subordinates.

However, managers do not all devote the same amount of time to each of the four functions. We know from research that as an individual progresses up the management hierarchy he or she will spend

Directing is the management function of supervising and guiding subordinates. Much of this is done on a face-to-face basis with the employees as they perform their tasks.

DISTRIBUTION OF EFFORT

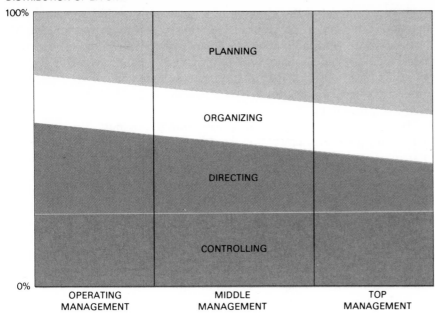

FIG. 6.4 *Management functions and management levels*

less time directing and controlling and more time planning (see Fig. 6.4). Thus the importance of each function to the individual manager will depend on his or her level in the hierarchy.

7. While all managers perform the same basic functions, how does the amount of time devoted to each change as one moves up the management hierarchy?

MANAGEMENT SKILLS

In order to be effective, managers must be able to carry out the functions of planning, organizing, directing, and controlling. However, their success in doing this depends upon certain *managerial skills* or abilities. These skills help the individual manager in sizing up situations, making decisions, and seeing that they are properly implemented. We call these skills (a) technical, (b) human, and (c) conceptual.

Technical Skills

Technical skills are those that allow the manager to use techniques, methods, and equipment in performing specific tasks. To a large degree, these skills are developed through experience and education. As shown in Fig. 6.5, technical skills are most important to operating managers. This is because many of the things they are called upon to do require them to have some knowledge of "how things work." In a manufacturing firm this may mean the ability to operate complex machinery. After all, how can supervisors or foremen tell the workers how to do something if they cannot do it themselves? Another type of technical skill is the ability to draw up and

Thinking versus Having Fun

Eighteen months after the opening of their three Mama Mia restaurants, the owners decided to expand their operations. They felt that they could be even more profitable if they set up other restaurants around the state. Their banker, Barbara Williams, agreed that they were in such a strong financial position that as long as they limited their expansion to three more restaurants, they could survive even if these last three proved unprofitable.

However, there was one thing bothering the owners. They realized that as they grew ever larger they could no longer restrict their activities to being simply restaurant managers. With six restaurants they would have to start looking around for competent help to manage some of their operations. More importantly, they knew that if they continued to grow as quickly as they were, they would have to start taking themselves out of the day-to-day operations of the business and begin doing long-range planning and other top management activities. This worried them because they felt it would take the fun out of owning their own corporation. One of them put it this way: "Top managers have to do all the thinking. Operating managers have all the fun."

Barbara assured them that this was not true. "All managers have enjoyable jobs. There are many challenges and interesting decisions you will make as members of the board of this corporation. Give yourself some time to be a top manager. You have all been acting as operating and middle managers too long. You'll find the role of top manager just as enjoyable."

1. In what way will the job of the owners change if they decide to get out of the operating side and start taking on more top management responsibility?

2. What did the owner mean when he said that top managers do all the thinking while operating managers have all the fun?

3. If you were in agreement with the banker, what other things would you tell the owners about the interesting work of top managers?

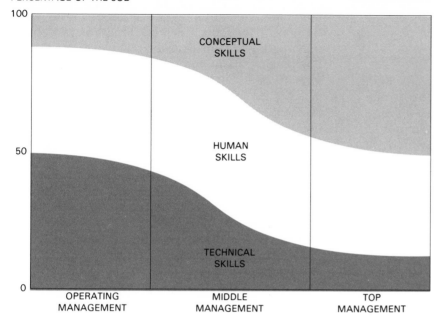

FIG. 6.5 *Management skills in the management hierarchy*

interpret meaningful financial data. This would be very important to a supervisor in an accounting department. The individual's training would have provided him or her with the technical skills necessary to manage employees who are collecting production or cost data from around the firm and compiling it for control purposes. In every type of organization the managers at the lower levels need to understand the mechanics of the job if they are to supervise effectively. However, as they begin moving up the hierarchy, technical skills become less important in relation to other skills.

Human Skills

Human skills are those that help the manager work effectively with others on a person-to-person basis. All effective managers have these skills, and of all three—technical, human, and conceptual—they are the most important. When we examined the directing function earlier in this chapter, we touched on

some of the human skills managers must have. In particular, these include the ability to communicate, motivate, and lead.

Communication ability will be discussed in greater detail later in this chapter, and motivation and leadership will be the focus of attention in Chapter 9. For the moment, however, there is one thing you should note about human skills. Some people like to refer to them as "human relations" abilities. Today that term is no longer used by knowledgeable managers because its meaning is too restricted. Over the years the term human relations has come to mean that by making employees happy we also make them productive. We now know that happy workers are *not* necessarily productive workers. We also know that employees want managers to do more than merely keep them happy. Employees are *human assets*. Without them the firm cannot operate. How do managers tap the full potential of their people? The answer is by giving them chal-

A Profile of Today's Black Executive

What does the current profile of today's black executive look like? Recent findings report that this individual is a 43-year-old vice-president or manager earning $40,000 or more annually and working for a billion-dollar industrial corporation in the east or midwest. Born in the south or southwest, the person is a college graduate with at least some study toward an advanced degree. He is committed to his job and works 50–60 hours a week. He wants to succeed and is not easily deterred in these efforts.

Among those black executives who have had the greatest success in moving up the hierarchy, the largest percentage have come from sales, marketing, manufacturing, and finance. And what does the future of the typical black executive look like? One expert in the field has concluded that they "will make a long-term impact upon corporate America." The statistics certainly seem to support this.

Source: Boston Globe, January 15, 1980.

lenging work, treating them like adults, and assuming that they want the business to succeed just as much as the managers do. Research shows that when employees are handled in this manner, they tend to respond favorably. They like to be treated as important contributors to the firm; and, generally speaking, they want to do their share of the work. In a positive sense, the employees "want to be used well." This type of thinking is known as a *human resources philosophy*. Effective managers see their people as important human resources that must be used well. As a result, they spend as much time worrying about the proper way to manage their human assets as they do thinking about the right way to care for their physical assets.

Conceptual Skills

Conceptual skills are those that help the manager see the whole enterprise as well as the relationships that exist between the various parts. Top managers in particular need these skills because they are of maximum importance in long-range planning. After all, unless one is aware of how the total organization operates it is difficult to determine the direction that should be taken for the next one to five years.

The further up the management hierarchy one goes, the greater the need for conceptual skills. Members of the board, for example, must rely heavily on their conceptual abilities in making decisions. On the other hand, supervisors and foremen have little need for conceptual abilities; their prime interest is in using technical and human skills (see Fig. 6.5).

8. Why are technical skills more important to an operating manager than are conceptual skills?

9. If a manager has no human skills or abilities, can he or she be an effective manager? Explain.

10. In what way are employees assets of the firm?

11. What types of skills would a company president need in order to be effective? Which would be most important? Which would be least important?

COMMUNICATION: THE KEY TO MANAGEMENT EFFECTIVENESS

Whether the manager is planning, organizing, directing, controlling, or using one of the three types of managerial skills, communication is the key to effectiveness. Unless subordinates know what managers want them to do, no amount of planning will help an organization. Nor can managers hope to use technical, human, or conceptual skills effectively if they are unable to communicate well with their people.

The Communication Process in Action

Communication is the process of conveying meanings from sender to receiver. Sometimes this process is **interpersonal** and involves, for example, a manager and a subordinate. Other times it is **organizational** and involves three or four levels in the hierarchy. In either case, the communication process is the same. First there is a sender, who puts the message in some form (written, verbal), chooses a method for conveying it (memo, telephone), and sends it off. Then there is the receiver, who gets the message, interprets it, and takes appropriate action. Unfortunately, the message the sender intended to convey and the one the receiver actually got are frequently completely different. Something prevented the message from getting through. We call such obstacles *barriers to effective communication*.

Barriers to Effective Communication

There are many barriers to effective communication (see Fig. 6.6). Some of these are more common in written communications; others tend to occur more frequently in verbal communications. Three of the most common, found in all forms of communication, are perception, inference, and semantics.

Perception

Perception is a person's view of reality. It is based on an individual's experience and training. Since no two of us ever lead identical lives, we often have different views of or attach different meanings to the same situation. For example, a plant manager tells a supervisor to increase the efficiency of her subordi-

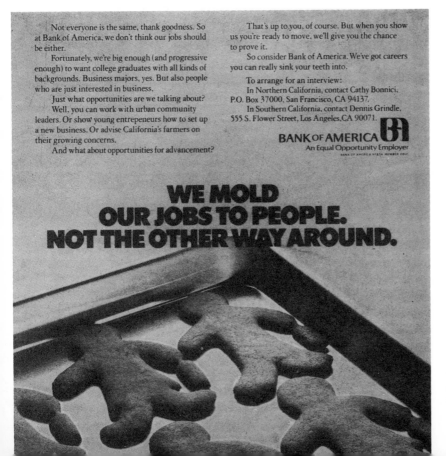

© Bank of America NT&SA 1980
Agency D'Arcy-MacManus &
Masius, San Francisco

123

FIG. 6.6 *Barriers to effective communication*

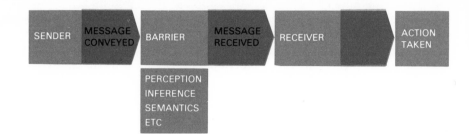

nates. The supervisor, in turn, announces that from now on anyone arriving late in the morning will be fired. This results in a complaint from the union that the workers are being threatened with the loss of their jobs for a minor reason. Upon investigation it turns out that the plant manager merely meant that the supervisor should encourage the workers to try harder. The supervisor, however, thought the plant manager wanted her to get tough and start cracking down on them. This type of perception problem is very common in business firms.

Inference

An **inference** is an assumption made by a receiver of a message. Sometimes the assumption is correct; other times the receiver "reads in" something that was not intended by the sender. For example, a subordinate calls the sales manager long distance to get some information on how to close a sale. The secretary tells the caller that the manager cannot come to the phone because he or she is "in conference and probably will be most of the day." The secretary may feel that this message was accurate and honest. He or she has communicated effectively. The subordinate, however, may feel that the reason being given is false and the manager just does not feel that the salesperson is important enough to talk with. Or consider the case of the top manager who calls and is given the same answer. The secretary may feel that the top executive should know that his or her boss is working hard. The executive, however, may feel that the sales manager is really out on the golf course and is being covered for by the secretary.

"What do you mean, I don't communicate? Didn't you read the memo I left you at breakfast?"

From The Wall Street Journal; permission Cartoon Features Syndicate

Any time messages are unclear or their believability is open to question, the receiver may start to make assumptions or inferences about their true meaning.

Semantics

By **semantics** we mean that the same words may have different meanings for different people. For example, a manager may call in a new secretary and ask him or her to "burn" a copy of a particular blueprint. Since there is only one copy with all the corrections on it, the manager may want more copies made. But the secretary, being unfamiliar with this "technical jargon," may literally put a match to the blueprint. Whenever managers are dealing with new employees it is important to acquaint them with technical terms.

Developing Two-Way Communication Techniques

One of the best ways to overcome these barriers is to develop **two-way communication techniques.** By this we mean that managers should allow and encourage subordinates to ask questions and seek advice. If a receiver is unclear as to exactly what was meant, he or she should feel free to ask the manager to repeat and further explain the message.

In turn, the manager must try to develop good listening habits. Many superiors prefer to give orders and not be bothered with questions. We call these individuals *one-way communicators.* From research we know that they are less effective than are two-way communicators.

What are some of the things two-way communicators do? One is that they **listen** to their people. When a subordinate comes in to talk to them, they put the individual at ease. They also both *look and act interested.* Second, they try to put themselves in their subordinates' shoes by **empathizing** with them. Third, they try *never to get angry* at their subordinates because this only discourages people from giving feedback in the future. Fourth, they **ask questions** to both encourage further feedback and show the person that they are listening. Fifth, they maintain an **open-door policy,** so that subordinates can

Inference and Meaning

A corporate president recently made a visit to a nearby Indian reservation as part of his firm's public relations program. "We realize that we have not hired any Indians in the five years our company has been located in this area," he told the assembled tribesmen, "but we are looking into the matter very carefully." "Hora, hora," said some of the Indians. "We would like to eventually hire 5 percent of our total work force from this reservation," he said. "Hora, hora," shouted more of the Indians. Encouraged by their enthusiasm, the president closed his short address by telling them that he hoped his firm would be able to take some hiring action within the next couple of years. "Hora, hora, hora," cried the total group. With a feeling of satisfaction the president left the hall and was taken on a tour of the reservation. Stopping in a field to admire some of the horses grazing there, the president asked if he could walk up closer to the animals. "Certainly," said his Indian driver, "but be careful not to step in the hora."

drop by whenever they have questions. At the same time they try to follow the principles of effective communication.

Principles of Effective Communication

Over the years a number of principles of effective communication have been developed to improve the manager's ability to convey meaning to subordinates. The following presents four of the most widely accepted ones.

Principle of open communication

This principle states that employees will be motivated to achieve results if they are informed about what they are doing. We know from research that managers who tell their people what they want done and why they want it done are more likely to get good results than are those who keep their people in the dark. Open communication leads to positive motivation.

Principle of clarity

Messages should be clear! This means that they should be framed in such a way that when they are communicated they are easily understood by the receiver. In carrying out this principle, the manager should sometimes use written communication, sometimes employ verbal communication, and still other times rely upon a combination of the two. In all cases the message must be clear.

CASE

An Important Asset

The owners of Mama Mia's decided that over the next couple of years they would turn over the management of their restaurants to professional managers, while they concerned themselves more with setting long-range objectives, checking out sites for new restaurants, and controlling overall operations. Their banker was delighted with the decision for she felt it would result in more success for the corporation.

A few months after making their decision, the owners were confronted with a serious problem. The manager of their most successful restaurant, William Johnson, called them to say that he was thinking of leaving and taking a job with another restaurant. The three owners asked Bill to come by the home office for a chat later in the week. Part of the conversation between Bill and the chairman of the board went as follows:

Bill, we asked you to drop by because we would like to know why you are thinking of leaving.

Well, quite frankly I'm not sure of my future with your company. I don't know how many more restaurants you are going to open up, how many new owners you'll eventually have in the corporation, or how much opportunity I'll have to grow with the firm.

Quite honestly, Bill, we don't know how large we are going to grow either. However, you are our number-one manager and as we expand to other cities we are going to be relying heavily on your judgment to

Principle of conciseness

If at all possible, messages should be brief and to the point. Short messages tend to get more attention than do long ones. Consider the advertisements you read every day. They are seldom over one hunderd words in length and this is one reason why they have such high readership. People tend to listen to concise messages, and to ignore long ones.

Efficient use of the informal organization

In receiving and transmitting information, managers should use the informal organization to supplement formal communication channels. Whenever possible, of course, managers should rely on the formal organization and go through channels. But when it is more efficient to use the informal organization, the manager should do so.

12. How does the communication process work? Put it in your own words.

13. In what way is perception a communication barrier?

14. What are some of the ways of developing two-way communication?

15. What is meant by the principle of open communication?

---

tell us whether or not a particular locale would be profitable. We also have hopes of putting you on a profit sharing plan and, if we ever start selling stock to the public, giving you a stock option and perhaps even making you a member of the board of directors. You are an important asset to our corporation and we want to keep you.

Gee, I never realized you were thinking in those terms. What do you think the chances are that these things will ever come about?

Naturally, Bill, we can't make any promises, but I believe we'll know quite a bit in the next twenty-four months.

Well, in that case you've sold me. I'd be willing to stay until then to see how things develop.

1. What types of management skills was the chairman of the board using when he talked to Bill?

2. How was the chairman of the board able to persuade Bill to stay? What things did he say that influenced Bill?

3. Which principles of effective communication did the chairman of the board use? Explain.

SUMMARY

In this chapter we saw that management is the process of getting things done through people. As such it is both an art and a science. The manager must use organized knowledge and information that have been obtained through research and study (science) as well as intuition, judgment, and experience (art) in achieving objectives.

Management has three levels: top, middle, and operating. The top managers, such as the board of directors and the president, are concerned with setting long-range objectives and evaluating overall progress. The middle managers, such as the plant managers and superintendents, are responsible for translating long-range objectives into action plans. The operating managers, such as foremen and supervisors, are responsible for seeing that the day-to-day operations are carried out by the workers.

In getting things done through people, managers perform four basic functions: planning, organizing, directing, and controlling. Planning involves setting objectives and deciding how to reach them. Organizing consists of dividing up the work to be done and assigning it to people. Directing entails the supervision and guidance of subordinates. Controlling is the process in which management compares actual performance against expected results and takes any steps necessary to correct problem areas. All managers perform these functions, although the amount of time they devote to each will depend on their level in the hierarchy. For example, top managers will spend more time planning than anything else, while operating managers will spend more of their time controlling.

In carrying out these functions managers need to use three basic skills: technical, human, and conceptual. Technical skills require a knowledge of how things work. Human skills are those that help the manager work with employees on a person-to-person basis. Conceptual skills help the manager see the whole enterprise as well as the relationships that exist between the various parts. The further up the hierarchy one goes the less important technical skills become and the more important conceptual skills become.

The overall key to management effectiveness is communication. Without communication managers can neither carry out their functions nor use their managerial skills. In its essence, communication is the transmission of meaning between sender and receiver. Some of the common barriers to effective communication are perception, inference, and semantics. These can be overcome through two-way communication and the use of the principles of effective communication.

KEY TERMS FOUND IN THIS CHAPTER

QUESTIONS FOR DISCUSSION AND ANALYSIS

1. What is management? Put it in your own words.

2. Many operating managers make poor middle managers because they are too interested in the mechanical side of the job. Explain this statement.

3. What are the four basic functions every manager performs?

4. How is the exception principle used by modern managers?

5. What are technical skills? Human skills? Conceptual skills? Put it in your own words.

6. Why are conceptual skills so important to top management?

7. What are some of the most common barriers to effective communication? Explain.

8. Identify and describe the following principles of effective communication: principle of clarity, principle of conciseness, and efficient use of the informal organization.

CAREERS
IN MANAGEMENT

There are many career opportunities available in the field of management. This is a very broad area of interest with opportunities extending to many different fields. Production, human resource management, marketing, finance, accounting, statistics, computers, government, law, and small business, are but some. We will be discussing management career opportunities *throughout* this book, but at this point we merely want to provide some examples of careers in management without getting too much into these other functional areas. At the same time, we are going to provide some information related to salaries and career outlook through the 1980s. These salary statistics are a result of government studies and may now be a little low given the high rate of inflation in recent years.

Also, keep in mind that the beginning salaries for many of the occupations in the career sections of this book will vary. However, some jobs require only a high school education or a few years of college, while others call for a college degree or even an advanced degree. Because the entry requirements are higher for some jobs than for others, the starting salaries will fluctuate. Finally, as you will see in the discussion of careers in finance, some occupations such as security sales worker pay a great deal of money. However, there are limited openings, so the chances of securing employment there are small. Also, the average security sales worker has a large number of clients who are actively trading securities. The individual who does not have active clientele will make far less money, as shown in the matrix following the occupational description.

The following are some management occupations that promise a challenging career in the field.

Remember, however, that in most cases these are not the top positions in the field. They represent entry or middle-level jobs and as one works his or her way up the hierarchy, both the salary and the challenge will increase.

SUPERVISOR, BLUE-COLLAR WORK
Most blue-collar managers are known as supervisors or foremen, although in some industries such as textiles they are called "second hands" and on ships they are known as "boatswains." Regardless of job title, however, their work is very similar. They tell other employees what jobs are to be done and make sure that the work is performed correctly. For example, loading supervisors at truck terminals assign workers to load trucks and then check to see that the material was loaded correctly. In some industries, such as brick laying, the supervisor also does the same job as the workers being supervised. Overall, however, supervisors are responsible for preparing work schedules, keeping production and employee records, using judgment in dealing with unforeseen problems such as absenteeism and work-machine breakdowns, teaching workers safety habits, and enforcing rules and regulations. They also hire people and, in some cases, are called on to fire people. And in those companies where there is a union they are also responsible for meeting with union representatives to discuss union work problems and grievances. For this reason, they must know the provisions of the labor-management contract and act within the parameters of this agreement.

SOURCE: *Occupational Outlook Handbook*, 1978–79 Edition, U.S. Department of Labor, Bureau of Labor Statistics

CITY MANAGER

A city manager is responsible directly to the municipality's elected officials (usually the mayor). While duties vary by city size, the city manager generally administers and coordinates day-to-day operations of the city and is responsible for such functions as tax collection and disbursement, law enforcement, and public works. This individual also hires department heads and their staff, prepares the annual budget, studies problems such as urban renewal, traffic congestion and crime in the city, and reports the findings to the elected council. In addition, the manager is responsible for planning for future growth and development, providing for the expansion of future public services, appearing at civic functions, and informing the citizens of current government operations. While it can take years to reach the position of city manager, many cities offer a road to this position in the form of management assistants, assistant city managers, department head assistants, and administrative assistants.

HOTEL MANAGER AND ASSISTANT HOTEL MANAGER

The hotel manager is responsible for operating the establishment profitably. The individual determines room rates and credit policies, directs the operation of the kitchen and dining rooms, manages the housekeeping, accounting and maintenance departments of the hotel, and handles unexpected problems. In small hotels the manager may also work the front desk, taking care of reservations and assigning rooms. In these cases the individual is often the owner. In large hotels there are assistants who help perform these functions. The assistants handle areas such as advertising, accounting, personnel, and rental of banquet and meeting facilities. Meanwhile, in the very large hotel chains certain functions, such as purchasing and advertising, are often centralized and handled by the main headquarters.

STATION AGENT

A station agent is the customers' contact with the railroad. Most agents work in small freight stations where they take orders from companies that need cargo shipped and arrange for railroad cars to transport their product. When loaded cars are delivered to the station, the agent's job is to inspect the merchandise for damage and inform the person receiving the goods that they are ready for unloading. The agent also prepares customer bills and must be knowledgeable about the complex railroad billing procedure. At passenger stations, agents coordinate and supervise the activities of workers who sell tickets and check baggage. At major freight stations and passenger stations, the agent's duties are primarily administrative and supervisory in nature.

HEALTH SERVICE ADMINISTRATOR

The health service administrator coordinates the various functions and activities that make a health organization function properly. If the organization is small, they do the work personally; if the organization is large, they work through a staff of assistant administrators. The responsibilities of the health service administrator varies depending on the organization, but some of the common functions include overseeing nursing, food services, and in-service

CAREERS
IN MANAGEMENT (continued)

training programs, directing the daily operations of departments, holding meetings with organizational personnel, and carrying out fund raising and public relations activities.

MEDICAL RECORDS ADMINISTRATOR
All health care institutions keep records that contain medical information on each patient. These records are vital to correct, prompt diagnosis and treatment of illnesses and injuries. The medical records administrator directs the activities of the medical records department and develops systems for documenting, storing, and retrieving medical information. The individual also supervises the medical records staff, trains members for specialized jobs, compiles medical statistics required by state and national health agencies, and assists the staff in evaluation of patient care.

COLLEGE STUDENT PERSONNEL WORKER
A college student personnel worker, depending on the specific job, is one who provides for the housing, social, cultural, and/or recreational needs of the students. Individuals who fall into this category include the dean of students, the registrar, and the career planning and placement counselor. The dean of students, or vice president for student affairs, heads the student personnel program at the school. This individual's duties include evaluating the changing needs of the students and helping the president of the institution to develop policies. The registrar maintains the academic records of students and provides current enrollment statistics to those who require them, both within the college and in the local community. The career planning and placement counselor, sometimes call the college placement officer, assists students in career selection and sometimes help them get summer jobs. The individual also arranges for prospective employers to visit the campus to discuss their personnel needs and to interview applicants.

URBAN PLANNER
Sometimes called a community or regional planner, this individual develops programs to provide for the future growth and revitalization of urban, suburban, and rural communities. The individual also helps local officials make decisions for solving economic, environmental, and social problems. The urban planner keeps abreast of current community facilities and the growing needs of the area and makes plans for dealing with new transportation, housing, and business needs. In carrying out this job, the individual often confers with private land developers, civic leaders, and officials of public agencies that do specialized planning. In large urban planning offices, the individual often supervises the work of 5 to 10 people; while in smaller offices, the person will often work alongside the other planners.

CAREERS	LATEST EMPLOYMENT FIGURES	EARNINGS	EMPLOYMENT OUTLOOK
Supervisor, Blue-Collar Work	1,445,000	$15,000–$20,000	Increase at about the same rate as for occupations in general
City manager[a]	3,000	$25,000 +	Better than for occupations in general
Hotel manager[b] and assistant hotel manager	137,000	$16,000–$50,000	Expected to grow more slowly than for occupations in general
Station agent	7,000	$15,000–$20,000	Expected to grow more slowly than for occupations in general
Health service administrator	160,000	$20,000–$50,000	Expected to increase more rapidly than for all occupations in general
Medical records administrator	12,300	$15,000–$18,000	Expected to grow more rapidly than for all occupations in general
College student personnel worker	5,700	$15,000–$25,000	Expected to grow more slowly than for occupations in general
Urban planner	16,000	$14,000–$17,000	Expected to grow more rapidly than for occupations in general

[a] College degrees and experience are required.
[b] Very often owner-manager.

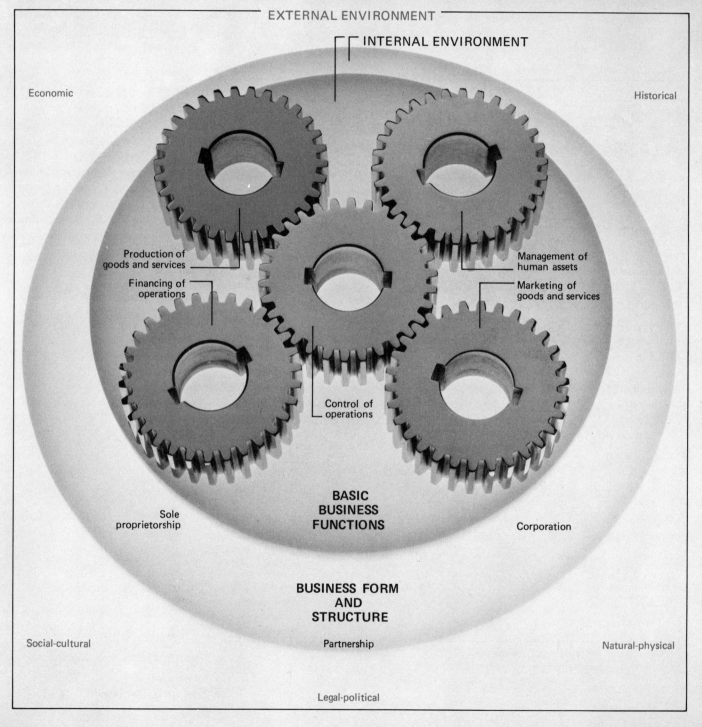

EXTERNAL ENVIRONMENT

INTERNAL ENVIRONMENT

Economic

Historical

Production of goods and services

Management of human assets

Financing of operations

Marketing of goods and services

Control of operations

BASIC BUSINESS FUNCTIONS

Sole proprietorship

Corporation

BUSINESS FORM AND STRUCTURE

Social-cultural

Partnership

Natural-physical

Legal-political

Producing the Company's Products

Every profit organization has to produce a good or service if it wishes to remain in existence. The goal of this section of the book is to examine the production process used in making goods and services for sale.

In Chapter 7, product planning and production will be examined. You will learn about how inputs such as raw materials are transformed into outputs such as goods and services. Attention will also be devoted to product planning, the process of deciding how to actually turn out the good. Finally, you will learn about the various methods of plant layout used in producing various types of goods.

In Chapter 8, purchasing and production control will be studied. Particular emphasis will be given to inventory control, purchasing, maintenance, production scheduling, and quality control. These are all areas of major importance in maintaining production operations.

When you are finished reading this section, you should have a good understanding of the production process. You should also be familiar with a number of key production terms, including *break-even point, fixed costs, variable costs, continuous production, perpetual inventory system, sampling, and preventive maintenance*. Finally, you should have gained an appreciation for the importance of the production function in business.

Product planning is an increasingly vital activity in a modern economy because it is no longer very profitable to sell just "commodities." And product planning must be continuous to meet the dynamic and innovating competition which is causing product life to shorten.

E. Jerome McCarthy

OBJECTIVES OF THIS CHAPTER

In this chapter we will be studying the ways in which a company plans for and then manufactures goods. The first objective of the chapter is to look at what production management is all about. The second is to examine how a company decides specifically what goods to produce. The third goal is to point out the way a plant location is chosen. The fourth objective is to examine how a business decides on the size of its factory and its plant layout. By the end of this chapter you should be able to do the following:

a. describe the production process;

b. identify some of the key areas of consideration used by firms in deciding which goods to produce;

c. explain how a plant location is chosen;

d. relate some of the important factors involved in deciding the size of the plant; and

e. outline the analysis a company will undertake in determining the layout of its factory.

Product Planning
and Production

THE NATURE OF THE PRODUCTION PROCESS

Production is the process of transforming inputs such as raw materials into outputs such as goods and services. This process involves three phases: (a) input, (b) transformation, and (c) output. When applied to the manufacture of an automobile, for example, it would work in the manner illustrated in Fig. 7.1. In its very essence, this is what production management is all about: converting inputs into finished outputs.

Inputs

The **inputs** to the production process are those resources that will be needed to produce the desired good or service. These can be divided into three major categories: material inputs, human inputs, and other input considerations. The *material inputs* include things such as machines, raw materials, and parts. The *human inputs* consist of labor, both skilled and unskilled, and management. *Other input considerations* involve plant location, electric power and other energy sources, storage facilities, and anything else that does not fit directly into the categories of material and human inputs.

Transformation

Transformation consists of those production activities that take the inputs and combine them in some special way to produce the output. In the building of an automobile, transformation involves both manufacturing and assembly. In the manufacturing stage the desired parts are produced. In the assembly phase they are all brought together in just the right way. This is particularly evident as one watches an auto frame make its way down the assembly line. As the car moves along one can see the actual transformation of individual parts into a finished product.

Output

The **output** is the final result of the production process. In the case of a car, it is the final assembled automobile. However, this same approach can be used in manufacturing almost anything. The inputs may be different, the transformation may be slightly changed, the outputs may be of a different type; but the overall production process is the same: input, transformation, and output.

1. In what way might the production process for manufacturing automobiles be similar to that for making television sets?

2. Do all production processes have the same three phases of input, transformation, and output?

PRODUCT PLANNING

The first major question in production is: what goods should be manufactured? Assuming that the firm has already done marketing research, it knows the types of products being demanded by consumers. However, before designing and manufacturing these goods, it is first necessary to look at the products' profitability. After all, there is no sense producing a losing line.

FIG. 7.1 *The production process and the automobile*

INPUT
MACHINES
RAW MATERIALS
PARTS
LABOR
MANAGEMENT

TRANSFORMATION
MANUFACTURING
ASSEMBLING

OUTPUT
FINISHED
AUTOMOBILE

Can you identify the three phases—input, transformation, and output—of the production process of the automobile?

Product Profitability

In deciding whether or not to manufacture a particular product, two analyses must be undertaken. The first, by the marketing department, identifies the number of units that can be sold. The second, by the production department, examines the costs associated with this production for the purpose of determining how many units will have to be sold for the firm to break even. This latter analysis takes into account the two basic types of costs associated with producing anything: fixed costs and variable costs.

Fixed costs are those expenses that remain the same in the short run regardless of how many units the firm manufactures. Property taxes are an illustration. Whether the company produces 10,000 units or shuts down completely, it must still pay these taxes.

Variable costs are those expenses that change in relation to output. If production goes up, so do these costs. If output declines, these expenses go down. Illustrations include the cost of raw materials and labor to manufacture the product. It can thus be seen that variable costs are directly related to production activity.

In order to make *any* profit, the company must cover *all* fixed costs *and* variable costs associated with producing the good. Therefore, if the marketing department estimates total sales for a new product at 17,500 units per year, should the company consider manufacturing it? The answer will depend on the fixed and variable costs associated with the good as well as on the selling price. In this regard, assume the following to be true:

Selling price = $10,
Fixed cost = $50,000,
Variable cost = $6.

Should the firm undertake production? One way to answer this question is to determine both the break-even point and the total profit associated with the venture. The **break-even point** in terms of units can be computed as follows:

$$\text{Break-even point} = \frac{\text{Total fixed cost}}{\text{Selling price} - \text{variable cost}},$$

$$\text{Break-even point} = \frac{\$50,000}{\$10 - \$6},$$

$$\text{Break-even point} = \frac{\$50,000}{\$4},$$

$$\text{Break-even point} = 12,500 \text{ units.}$$

The company will cover all costs if it can sell 12,500 units. (See Fig. 7.2 for a graphic illustration of this

FIG. 7.2 *Break-even point computation*

COST OR REVENUE (IN THOUSANDS OF DOLLARS)

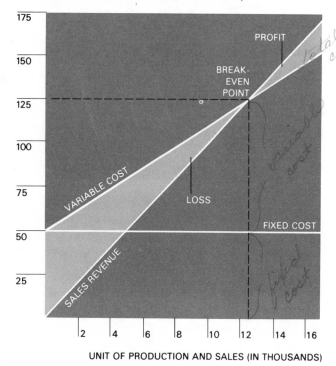

UNIT OF PRODUCTION AND SALES (IN THOUSANDS)

break-even point.) For every unit over this amount it will make $4, a figure that is reached by subtracting the variable cost ($6) from the selling price ($10). Therefore, if the firm can sell 17,500 units every year, it will make an annual profit of $20,000 ($4 × 5,000). If this profit is not satisfactory to the company, it will abandon all manufacturing plans at this point. If this profit is satisfactory, the firm will push on and begin designing the product.

3. If a firm's fixed costs are $35,000, the variable costs are $10, and the selling price is $17, what is the break-even point in units?

4. If the fixed costs are $75,000, the variable costs are $17.50, and the selling price is $25, what is the break-even point in units?

Product Development

In the **product development** stage the good is put in final form—at least on paper. All of the ideas people have for the product are reviewed and are either discarded or incorporated into the design. During this stage it is sometimes necessary to build a "pilot model," or a mockup, of the good in order to examine it in greater detail. The firm may even manufacture a small number of the items to get an idea of the production problems associated with mass producing the good. At the end of this stage the company will agree on the final design for the product.

Product Specifications

The last step in product planning is that of determining the **specifications for production.** What kinds of raw materials or parts will be needed? What types of operations, such as boring or threading, will have to be performed? What kind of machinery will be needed? As these questions are answered, the production process becomes clearer. Another of the key

In the product development stage, the good is put in final form—at least on paper.

"Actually, we haven't quite decided whether your proposal will fly."

From The Wall Street Journal; permission Cartoon Features Syndicate

A New Product Proposal

Rolfson, Inc., a large midwestern manufacturing firm, recently decided to look into the possibility of producing a new consumer product. After conducting marketing research in a six-state area, the company found that demand existed for a small, portable radio. Based on research findings, Rolfson estimates total demand to be 100,000 units per year in this six-state area. After computing all of the expenses that would be involved in manufacturing the radios, the firm put the total fixed costs at $360,000 and the variable cost per unit at $9.

The firm has contacted a large regional retail chain that has agreed to market the product. The retailer estimates that these radios should be priced at $22.50.

Under the proposed arrangement, Rolfson will receive 60 percent of this selling price for each radio that is manufactured, delivered, and sold by the retail chain. Before deciding whether or not to proceed with the venture, however, Rolfson's management has set down a minimal profit figure. It is $100,000 per year. If this profit can be obtained, the company will proceed with the new product. Otherwise, it intends to drop the idea.

1. How many units will have to be sold before Rolfson, Inc. will break even on the venture?

2. How much profit will Rolfson make if it manufactures 100,000 units and they are all sold?

3. Based on its criterion of $100,000 profit, should the firm proceed with the venture or drop the idea? Explain.

areas of consideration in this process is the location of the physical facilities.

5. In manufacturing an automobile, what kinds of decisions would be made in the product development stage?

6. What kinds of decisions would be made in the product specifications stage?

PLANT LOCATION

Plant location can mean the difference between profit and loss for the firm. Most companies will choose a site based on such important factors as (a) location of their customers, (b) source of raw materials, (c) the adequacy of a labor supply, (d) the availability of power or water, and (e) community considerations.

Customer Location

Many firms find they must locate close to their customers. This is particularly true for companies producing perishable items such as bread and cake. It is also the case for firms in industries where competitive advantage depends on rapid delivery, or for those companies that sell heavy or bulky products such as bricks or automobiles. Most brick factories are located close to their construction-firm customers because of the high expense of transporting the product any great distance. Likewise, many auto assembly plants today are placed near population centers so that the finished car needs to be shipped only a short distance to the dealer.

Source of Raw Materials

Many companies find it most profitable to place the plant near their source of raw materials. Steel mills, for example, have tended to locate near Pittsburgh because the coal supplies they need to process iron ore are located there. Furthermore, this ore is very heavy and the transportation costs associated with shipping it any great distance would be very high.

Other businesses locate near their raw materials because of the perishability factor. For example, firms in the food-canning business set up their plants close to the fields where the crops are being grown. By so doing the company can process the food before it spoils. These crops could be frozen and then shipped to a plant hundreds of miles away, of course, but it is often cheaper to locate nearby.

Labor Supply

All production operations require some manpower. Therefore the firm must identify the type of labor it needs and then try to locate its facilities at least within commuting distance of these people. This is especially important in the case of those companies that need highly skilled people, for these people cannot be found everywhere. As a result, firms have to identify those areas of the country where these people live, evaluate the benefits of each locale, and then choose one.

Power and Water

Some firms need a great deal of electric power to produce their goods. Aluminum, chemical, and fertilizer companies are illustrations. As a result, businesses in these industries must locate in areas having sufficient power to meet their needs.

Other firms require a location near water. Companies that make paper, for example, need water for washing the logs, transporting the wood pulp, accomplishing the matting process, and eliminating impurities. And in the case of high-quality paper, clean water must be used. When one realizes that around 50,000 gallons of water are needed to make one ton of paper, it is easy to see why paper mills locate in areas where clean water is available in large quantities and at low cost.

Community Considerations

In plant location the company also needs to look at the services available in the community. Some cities and towns will offer low taxes. In fact, some will sell land to new businesses at a very low cost and levy no local taxes for up to five years if the firm will locate there. Others offer fine educational systems and have many of the good things in life such as clean air, clean water, and a low cost of living. Still others will provide special services to businesses that locate there, such as extending the city water and sewerage lines out to the plant at no expense to the firm.

Some states try to help out by working with businesses that are looking for a location. Today almost every state has a Department of Economic Development or a Department of Commerce that provides information and assistance in location planning. Notice that many of the important factors we

discussed above are incorporated into the advertisement run by Michigan's Department of Commerce.

7. When would you expect a firm to set up its plant close to its customers?

8. Do all companies locate near their source of raw materials? Explain.

9. Of the five factors listed in this section, which is most important in plant location?

PLANT CAPACITY

Once a decision has been reached regarding plant location, attention can be focused on **plant capacity.** How large will the factory have to be to produce the desired goods? In addition, what provisions, if any, should be made for increasing the size of the plant at some future date? Other considerations relating to plant capacity are the sales pattern and the types of machines that will be used.

Size and Cost

If the firm's plant is too small, the firm will end up losing sales. If the plant is too large, the extra capacity will go unused and the company will have wasted part of its investment. Therefore, the firm must seek to balance product demand with plant capacity.

It is important to note that as the size of a plant increases, the cost of production usually declines—at least for a while. This is illustrated in Fig. 7.3, where a cost-per-unit curve is shown. Note that as the firm produces 5,000, 10,000, 15,000, and then 20,000 units, the cost per unit drops from $4 to $2. What is the cause of this? The answer is simple. As we begin to use the factory to turn out more and more goods, we are able to spread the fixed costs over more units. For example, if we have a property tax of $1,000 and produce 1,000 units, $1.00 must be

added to the costs of each unit to cover the tax. However, if 20,000 units are manufactured, only 5¢ needs to be added to each. In addition, machines can be made to go faster with little real increase in overall cost. Because of these factors, as production increases, cost per unit declines. However, these increases in efficiency do not continue indefinitely. If the factory tries to produce too much, inefficiencies will occur and cost per unit will begin to increase.

As a result, there is a relationship between size and cost. Using Fig. 7.3 as an illustration, we can see that the firm would attempt to manufacture up to 20,000 units if it wants to maximize its profit. If more units are demanded, consideration must then be given to increasing the size of the plant.

FIGURE 7.3

COST PER UNIT (IN DOLLARS)

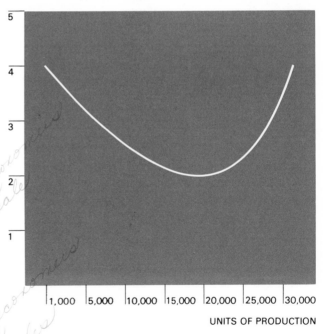

UNITS OF PRODUCTION

Sales Pattern

Another consideration in determining plant capacity must be the sales pattern. At what period during the year will the goods be demanded? If the product is purchased year round, the company can plan for continuous production. If the product is seasonal, however, the company must decide whether to store the goods or simply stop manufacturing them for a while and go to something else. These issues will all affect the firm's cost per unit, so the product's sales pattern and the plant's capacity must be blended carefully.

Types of Machines

A final consideration in planning for capacity must be the types of machines that will be required. These

Henry Ford

As a boy of thirteen, Henry Ford took a watch apart and then reassembled it. It was obvious that he had mechanical ability. However, his main chores were on the family farm. He was the oldest of six children, and his father relied on him to help with the work after school.

At sixteen young Henry left the Dearborn farm and ran away to Detroit, taking a job during the day as a machine-shop apprentice and working four hours a night for a jeweler. He returned to Dearborn once to try farming, but his interest in mechanical problems continued and he again left for the city.

In 1890 he secured a job as an engineer and machinist with the Detroit Edison Company. He continued experimenting in the workshop in his back yard, however, and in 1892 he developed the first "gasoline buggy." Meanwhile he continued to do very well with Detroit Edison. So well, in fact, that in 1899 they offered to make him general superintendent of the company—if he would drop his ideas about gasoline buggies and devote himself to electricity full time. He refused and quit.

He then organized the Detroit Automobile Company to manufacture his car, but the arrangement with his partners did not work out so he broke the association.

Ford wanted to mass produce autos for a national market. In order to do so, he built two racing cars for the purpose of creating consumer demand. One of them, the "999," driven by the legendary Barney Oldfield, won all of its races. The public was interested and in 1903 Ford sold 1,708 two-cylinder, eight-horsepower cars. He formed the Ford Motor Company in 1903, and in 1908, thanks to the use of mass-production techniques, he started to produce the Model T, which sold for $850. In 1909 he sold 10,600 Model Ts and within seven years over 1,000,000. By 1925 Ford was turning out 2,000,000 cars a year. And as the number of autos increased, assembly-line techniques were developed to make the job easier and thereby speed production. While Henry Ford certainly did not invent the concept of the assembly line, he developed it to a greater degree than anyone before him and introduced a whole new way of life to America and the world. As Marshall McLuhan was to remark, "The car has become an article of dress, without which we feel uncertain, unclad and incomplete."

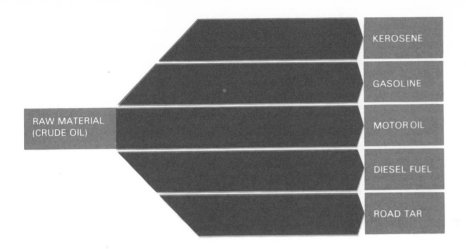

FIG. 7.4 *Analytic process for "cracking" crude oil*

will, of course, be determined by the kinds of products the firm makes. However, the company will have to calculate how much work each machine can do, how long this will take, and how much it will all cost. On the basis of these calculations, the company can decide the most efficient type of machinery for its purposes.

10. In choosing a plant size, why does a company not simply choose the capacity that gives it the lowest cost per unit?

11. As production increases, why does cost per unit tend to fall and then rise?

PLANT LAYOUT

Once a plant site has been chosen and the plant capacity determined, the firm can turn its attention to plant layout. This is simply the arrangement of the machinery and other facilities in such a way as to facilitate production. Deciding on plant layout entails a careful analysis of (a) the production processes, (b) the production sequences, (c) the flow of materials, (d) the possible types of layout, and (e) worker safety considerations.

Production Processes

Most goods are manufactured through the use of some production process. These processes can be narrowed down to two types: (a) analytic, and (b) synthetic.

Analytic process

An **analytic process** is one in which a raw material is reduced to its component parts for the purpose of extracting one or more products. In an oil refinery, for example, crude oil is broken down and gasoline, motor oil, and other products are obtained. In a meat-packing plant, cattle are slaughtered for the purpose of obtaining various cuts of meat for consumption, animal hides for wearing apparel, and hooves and horns for glue. In a mining firm, ore is processed by separating the metal from the dirt and other useless material. In many cases the raw material produces a number of useful products. The process in the case of crude oil can be diagramed as in Fig. 7.4.

FIG. 7.5 *Synthetic process using fabrication to build an auto*

Synthetic process

A **synthetic production process** is somewhat the reverse of the analytic process. Quite often the synthetic process involves either converting a number of different raw materials or parts into a finished product or changing a raw material into a completely different product. The two most common ways in which this is done is through either fabrication or modification.

Fabrication involves combining a host of materials or parts in such a way as to form a finished product. The auto assembly line is an example of this process, and is illustrated in a simplified fashion in Fig. 7.5. Other examples would include the making of nylon, glass, and chemical compounds, which are all produced by synthetic processing.

Modification is a synthetic process in which raw materials are changed into a product by being altered in some way. In this treatment process, the materials are converted into the desired form. A common illustration would be the production of steel, in which the ore is converted into steel ingots or blocks. Another example would be the modification of these ingots into steel pipe.

12. What type of production process is used in mining gold?

13. Which type of production process is used in building a commercial airplane for carrying people on transcontinental flights? Would fabrication or modification be used in this process?

FIG. 7.6 *A continuous production sequence*

Production Sequences

In choosing the most efficient type of plant layout, one must also examine the production sequence. Some products will use one type of sequence while others will employ another. In essence, however, all production sequences fall into one of two categories: (a) continuous, or (b) intermittent.

Continuous production

Continuous production is characterized by a *constant* flow of materials. In this production sequence goods are produced at a steady, constant rate. This approach is widely used by firms manufacturing standardized, high-volume goods. Perhaps the most familiar illustration is, again, the auto assembly line. In continuous production goods are manufactured in very large quantities and are then stocked in the warehouse until demanded by the consumer. Many times we hear the term "mass production" used to describe this approach. The continuous production sequence can be diagramed as in Fig. 7.6.

Intermittent production

Some goods are produced **intermittently** or **noncontinuously,** such as those produced in batches or as "one-of-a-kind." Illustrations include airplanes, locomotives, and weather satellites. Quite often these products are manufactured in response to a specific customer order. Thus only a limited number are produced and, instead of being stocked in the warehouse, they are shipped out when completed. Since this process involves manufacturing "to order," it is often referred to as **job-order** or **job-lot production.** The production flow can be diagramed as in Fig. 7.7.

Whitney's Revolution

What was Eli Whitney's greatest contribution to the business world? If you said interchangeable parts, you're right. Whitney never made much money from the cotton gin. In fact, people began stealing his patent and making their own cotton gins. While fighting them in the courts, however, Whitney turned his mind to other things.

Approaching the federal government, he managed to secure a contract to produce 10,000 muskets at $13.40 each. He proposed to build the guns by making a metal mold or "jig" for each part of the firearm. This would enable ordinary metalworkers rather than skilled gunsmiths to make the parts, which would be identical from gun to gun. When completed, the muskets proved satisfactory and a whole new era in factory mass-production work began. Thanks to Whitney it was now possible to manufacture a very large number of products by having each worker concentrate on one part of the good. This approach is still used in the production and assembly of products, the most notable example being the automobile. Whitney's contribution of interchangeable parts has played an important role in helping to raise the standard of living everywhere in the world.

FIG. 7.7 *An intermittent production sequence*

Mixed production sequences

Sometimes manufacturers will use a combination of continuous and intermittent sequences. For example, some models of television sets are very similar. The basic differences may consist of a few extras on one model or a different type of channel tuner on another. The manufacturer can use a continuous production sequence for each model. When the demand for one model is satisfied, however, the company then switches production to the next.

14. Which production sequence would you expect to be used in the manufacture of tires: continuous or intermittent? Explain.

15. Which production sequence would you expect to be used in making telecommunication satellites? Explain.

Materials Flow

Once the company has analyzed its production processes and sequences, it is in a position to determine the most efficient flow of materials. For ex-ample, in multistoried factories some firms use a **vertical flow,** in which products move from one floor to the next. In **downward processing** the raw materials are placed on the top floor and the finished goods come out on the bottom. In **upward processing** the completed products come out on the top and are then shipped to the bottom floor on the service elevator. For those firms manufacturing heavy products, however, this approach is often not feasible. The building's structure will simply not support heavy equipment or material on the upper floors. As a result, these companies often have only one floor in the factory and must use horizontal flow.

In **horizontal flow** all the materials move on the same floor. The simplest flow is called the "I" flow, in which materials come in from one end of the building and leave the line at the other. A second type, which is used when the "I" flow cannot be accommodated, is the "L" flow. As can be seen in Fig. 7.8, it is very similar to the "I" flow. A third is the "U" flow, in which materials can be received and goods shipped from the same end of the building. A fourth is the "S" flow, which is used when space is at a premium. These four arrangements are

A tire-sorter at Uniroyal puts different sizes and types of tires on separate lines to facilitate shipping.

illustrated in Fig. 7.8. Any one or a combination can be used, depending upon the needs of the firm.

Types of Layout

The flow of material is usually worked into one of three general types of layout. The first is the **process layout,** in which machines and equipment are grouped by function. Those that perform welding functions are placed in one location, those that do sanding are put in another. The products are then moved from one locale to another, and at each place a specific function is performed on them. This layout is very efficient when producing smaller quantities of goods, for which an assembly-line approach would be far too costly. And one of the major benefits of the process layout is that if one machine breaks down the others may be able to take up the slack, in contrast to a production line where one machine breakdown will halt the line.

A second type is the **product layout.** Here all the machines and services are set up along a product-flow line. The goods come down the line and at each step something is done to them. This approach is often used for continuous production as in the

In multistoried factories some firms use a vertical flow, in which products move from one floor to the next.

FIG. 7.8 *Some basic forms of horizontal materials flow*

"I" FLOW

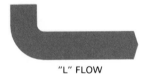

"L" FLOW

"U" FLOW

"S" FLOW

case of the auto assembly line. It is very efficient when it comes to producing large quantities of a product.

A third common type is the **static product layout.** In this case the good is usually too bulky or heavy to be moved around the factory. Therefore the workers come to the product. In building spacecraft vehicles, for example, the assemblers and electricians all bring the parts to the craft for installation. The same is true in the construction of large aircraft, where it is more efficient to move the people rather than the plane.

CASE

Here Come the TVs

Rolfson, Inc. was recently approached by one of the nation's giant mass merchandisers. The merchandiser was looking for a firm to mass produce television sets, which would then be sold under its own brand name. The Rolfson management examined its current manufacturing facilities and decided that it had both the plant space and the work force to build the televisions. All that had to be done was to purchase the proper machinery and lay out the facilities. This promised to be no real problem, and so Rolfson entered into a contract with the giant retailer. According to the terms of the contract, Rolfson will manufacture these televisions on a year-round basis. After they are assembled they will be shipped to the retailer, who will assume all responsibility for storage.

A few weeks ago a group of production management students from a nearby business college toured the company's plant. During the tour they were told that the televisions are built via a synthetic production process, specifically fabrication. In addition, they learned that the firm uses a continuous production sequence and that the materials move along an "I" flow. Finally, they heard the tour guide refer to the fact that the firm uses a type of layout known as a product layout.

1. How does Rolfson use a synthetic production process in manufacturing the TV sets? Explain.

2. Why does Rolfson use a continuous production sequence rather than an intermittent production sequence in manufacturing the televisions?

3. What is a product layout? Why does Rolfson use this type of layout rather than a static product layout?

Worker Safety

Another consideration in plant layout is **worker safety.** Once the company has decided on the ideal layout it must bring the workers and the work place together. This often means changing part of the layout. Such things as exposed gear boxes, moving machine parts, and toxic chemicals can all constitute dangers for the employees. The firm must work around these hazards by either removing them or providing safety equipment. Sometimes this equipment takes the form of covers or shields placed on machinery; other times it involves issuing safety glasses or special clothing to the workers. In all cases, worker safety must be at the very top of management's list as it decides on the most efficient type of plant layout.

For example, at its Saginaw, Michigan plant, General Motors has spent over $1 million reducing factory and machine noise. All around the plant, ceilings and walls are covered with sound-absorbing materials, and machines are either slowed down or provided with sound-absorbing hoods. In another case, a textile plant has developed special replacement parts for its looms so that those parts of the machine involved in throwing and catching the shuttle make far less noise. As a result, "weaver's deafness" is being eliminated. Developments such as these are helping businesses meet the new federal safety regulations while at the same time making the work more enjoyable.

16. Which type of material flow is most widely used: vertical or horizontal? Give your reasoning.

17. How does process layout differ from product layout?

18. Worker safety is the most important factor in plant layout. Comment on this statement.

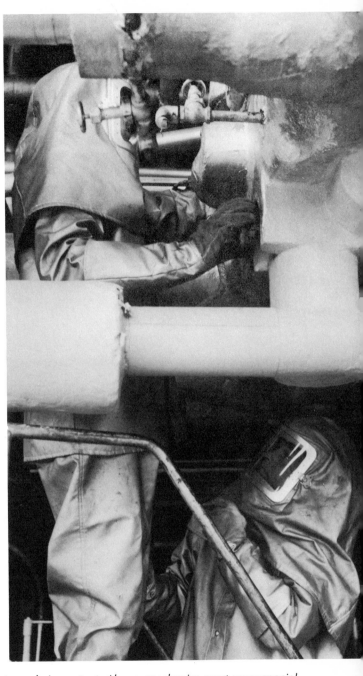

Worker safety is extremely important. Above, mechanics must wear special protective suits while changing filters in a chemical supply line.

SUMMARY

Production management involves three phases: input, transformation, and output. However, before deciding to produce a good, the firm must examine the profitability of the product. At what point will break-even occur? How much profit does it stand to make if market projections hold up? If the profit is assessed as sufficient, the company will move to product development, and then on to determining product specifications.

From here, other areas of consideration include plant location, plant capacity, and plant layout. Plant location should be based on such factors as customer location, the source of raw materials, the adequacy of a labor supply, the availability of power or water, and community considerations. In plant location the firm must examine the relationship between plant size and cost per unit, the sales pattern of the goods, and the type of machinery that will be required. Plant layout involves an analysis of the production processes and sequences, the flow of materials, types of layout, and worker safety considerations. When all of this is done the firm is ready to begin its production operations.

KEY TERMS FOUND IN THIS CHAPTER

production, 138
input, 138
transformation, 138
output, 138
fixed costs, 140
variable costs, 140
break-even point, 140
product development, 141
product specifications, 141
plant location, 142
plant capacity, 145
analytic process, 147
synthetic process, 148
fabrication, 148

modification, 148
continuous production, 149
intermittent production, 149
job-order or job-lot production, 149
mixed production sequences, 150
vertical flow, 150
downward processing, 150
upward processing, 150
horizontal flow, 150
process layout, 151
product layout, 151
static product layout, 152
worker safety, 153

1. What are the three phases in the production process?

2. How is the break-even point for a good computed? Put it in your own words.

3. What goes on in the product development stage?

4. What kinds of businesses need to be situated near a source of skilled labor? Identify some.

5. In choosing a plant location, in what types of community considerations would a business be interested?

6. How does a firm go about deciding on its plant capacity?

7. How does an analytic production process differ from a synthetic production process?

8. Which production process is used in manufacturing television sets: continuous or intermittent? Explain.

8

The first thing to know is that controlling the work process means control of the work, and not control of the worker. Control is a tool of the workers and must never be his master. It must also never become an impediment to working.
Peter Drucker

OBJECTIVES OF THIS CHAPTER

In the production process the firm manufactures various types of goods. However, it also needs to replenish raw materials and ensure that the product is being made according to specifications. This requires attention to the areas of purchasing and production control. The objectives of this chapter are to examine these two activities. We shall begin by looking at the area of inventory control, because purchasing is tied directly to inventory. Then we shall proceed to study purchasing, maintenance, scheduling, and quality control. By the end of this chapter you should be able to do the following:

a. describe the ways in which a firm decides when and how much inventory to reorder;

b. define some of the major duties of a purchasing department;

c. relate the importance of maintenance to production scheduling;

d. identify some of the most popular scheduling techniques used in industry today;

e. explain how a firm employs quality control in its operation; and

f. describe some of the latest techniques for overcoming job boredom in production-line work.

Purchasing and Production Control

INVENTORY CONTROL

One of the most important activities in the production management area is **inventory control.** No firm wants to have either too much or too little inventory on hand at any time. One reason is the cost associated with carrying this inventory.

Inventory Costs

Every time the firm purchases some raw materials, parts, or other kinds of inventory, it must pay for these items and store them until they are ready to be used. The more inventory a firm buys, the greater its **carrying costs** will be. These costs include warehouse expenses, depreciation of the inventory, insurance against such dangers as fire and theft, and, in some cases, the expenses associated with replacing obsolescent material.

On the other hand, if the firm has too little inventory, it also faces problems. One of the most common problems is that of running out of inventory and thereby losing sales. Other problems include production slowdowns, wasted time, and the firm's inability to use the full potential of its equipment.

Some firms try to solve their inventory problems by placing frequent orders for small amounts of goods. Then if production is moving more slowly than anticipated, or sales orders are not coming in as expected, the company will cancel some of these inventory orders. Unfortunately, inventory control is

Every time the firm purchases some raw materials, parts, or other kinds of inventory, it must pay for these items and store them until they are ready to be used.

usually too complex a matter to be solved by such simplistic procedures.

The first problem with the above solution is that it does not help the firm deal with a flurry of large orders. If such sales were to materialize the company would quickly run out of inventory.

A second problem is that every time the firm places an order there is an **order cost** involved. It costs money to type up an invoice, send it to the supplier, follow up to ensure delivery, and then see that payment is made. In fact, it costs virtually no more in paperwork time to order 1,000 units than it does to order 10 units. Therefore, those firms that order 10 items each time will have order costs 100 times higher than those that order 1,000 units each time.

Third, some suppliers grant quantity discounts. The following is an illustration:

Units	Cost per unit
1–10	$10.00
11–99	9.50
100–999	9.00
1,000 or more	8.00

The company that orders in quantities of 10 will pay $10,000 for 1,000 units. The firm that orders in quantities of 1,000 will pay $8,000 for these units. This can be quite a saving for those businesses willing to buy in large lots.

Although this does not solve the problem of how much inventory to carry and when and how much to reorder, it does point out the magnitude of the situation. An error either way, resulting in too much or too little inventory, can be costly.

1. What are carrying costs?

2. What problems are associated with having too little inventory? Too much inventory?

Lead Time and Safety Stock

In constructing a reordering system, two important points must be kept in mind. First, the amount of raw materials that are used will vary from day to day depending upon sales and production. Second, the time required to obtain new stock from a supplier is also going to vary. We use the term **lead time** to refer to the time difference between when an order is placed and when it is received. Both the rate of depletion of raw materials and the lead time for reordering can be difficult to predict. As a result, most firms make use of what is called safety stock.

Safety stock is basically a protective cushion that prevents a business from running out of inventory. When the number of units on hand reaches the safety stock level, a reorder is placed with the supplier. Thus a television manufacturer who purchases his TV cabinets from a supplier, and who wishes to maintain a safety stock of 300 cabinets, will reorder when the number of cabinets reaches this point. If the level has been properly chosen, the new cabinets will arrive before, or just as, the last one is being used. In this way the firm will not lose any sales due to lack of inventory.

Figure 8.1 provides an illustration of safety stock over three reorder cycles. Note that this manufacturer begins by ordering 1,200 TV cabinets. These are used at the rate of 60 per day. Therefore, in twenty days the supply will be exhausted. In fifteen days, however, the manufacturer reorders another 1,200, which arrive five days later, bringing the inventory level back to 1,200.

A close analysis of Fig. 8.1 reveals that the manufacturer assumes 60 TVs will be assembled every day and that a lead time of five days will be sufficient. These, of course, can be erroneous assumptions. For example, the manufacturer may produce an average of 60 TVs a day, but the actual number may vary from a high of 80 to a low of 40 depending upon machine breakdown, worker morale, and a host of other factors. Furthermore, lead time may have to vary depending upon the season of the year. For example, around August and September the supplier's factories may be jammed with Christmas

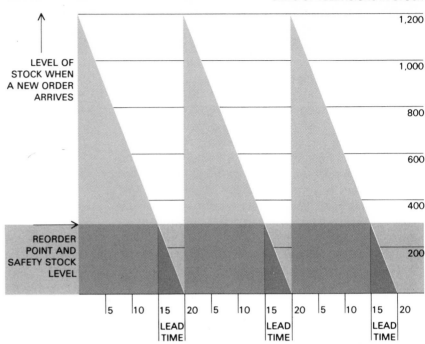

UNITS OF TELEVISIONS IN STOCK

LEVEL OF
STOCK WHEN
A NEW ORDER
ARRIVES

1,200

1,000

800

600

400

200

REORDER
POINT AND
SAFETY STOCK
LEVEL

FIG. 8.1 *Inventory depletion, safety stock, and lead time*

5   10   15   20   5   10   15   20   5   10   15   20
LEAD   LEAD   LEAD
TIME   TIME   TIME

TIME IN DAYS

orders and it may take as long as fifteen days to receive delivery. The system shown in Fig. 8.1, therefore, is simply one company's method of trying to solve its inventory problems.

3. Why would a firm want to have safety stock?

4. How does a company decide the level to which inventory must fall before reorders are placed?

5. If a company misjudges the reorder time needed to replenish its stock, how might this affect the firm's financial position?

Reordering Systems

In practice there are two types of reordering systems. The first, and simplest, is the **periodic reordering system.** This system is used for raw materials or goods that are inexpensive, used often, and easily obtainable. Examples are nuts, bolts, and nails, which are reordered on a periodic basis such as every sixty days.

The other approach is known as a **perpetual inventory system.** This is the system that uses reorder points and safety stock levels. Under this system, constant track is kept of stock inventories and reorders are placed when they reach a predetermined level. These levels are set to cover such things as lead time, stock spoilage, and obsolescence. Whenever such factors are involved in inventory control, it is common to find a perpetual inventory system being employed.

Maintaining Physical Inventory

In order to determine when the reorder point has been reached, some method for inventory management must be established. Many firms take a **physical inventory,** counting how much raw material or how many parts are actually on hand. This method is useful for comparing the actual amount of each material on hand with what the company books indicate should be there. The firm can note how much has been lost due to either spoilage or pilferage, and can adjust its books to reflect the correct amount.

In recent years many companies have turned to the computer for inventory bookkeeping. Factories with large amounts of raw materials and parts could end up spending thousands of staff hours entering inventory that is received and then deducting it from the books after it is used. The computer can handle all of this in far less time, and with an accompanying cost saving. In fact, computers have become so widely used for inventory control that we are now finding them in many retail stores. Every time we buy merchandise at these stores the clerk enters the appropriate information in a special keyboard on the cash register. These data are used for sales purposes as well as for inventory control.

Determining the Right Reorder Quantity

When inventory does reach the reorder point the firm must decide how much more it wishes to purchase. If the materials or parts are standard items and demand for them is fairly stable, it is often possible to determine reorder quantities by using mathematical formulas. The best known of these is the **economic order quantity formula,** often abbreviated as EOQ. This formula helps the production manager balance carrying and order costs while keeping total inventory to a minimum. The basic equation states that the ideal reorder quantity is

$$\sqrt{\frac{2 \times (\text{Yearly demand}) \times (\text{Order cost})}{(\text{Annual carrying cost for one unit})}}.$$

This formula can be applied directly to our earlier illustration of the television cabinets. Assume the following facts to be accurate: (a) the production demand for these cabinets is 60 per day or, based on a 260-day year, 15,600 per year; (b) the order cost is $100; and (c) the annual carrying cost for one unit is $2.165. Applying these data to our formula results in the following:

$$EOQ = \sqrt{\frac{2(15,600)\ (\$100)}{\$2.165}},$$

$$EOQ = \sqrt{\frac{(31,200)\ (\$100)}{\$2.16}},$$

$$EOQ = \sqrt{\frac{\$3,120,000}{\$2.16}},$$

$$EOQ = \sqrt{1,441,108},$$

$$EOQ = 1,200.$$

The company should reorder in lots of 1,200. Given our demand and cost data, this is the least expensive lot size. However, because these inventory control techniques are highly mathematical in nature, we will not concern ourselves with any further analysis of them. Suffice it to say that modern managers can draw on mathematical formulas to help them make reorder decisions.

6. Most firms use both a periodic and a perpetual inventory system, depending upon the raw material. Explain this statement.

7. In what way can a physical inventory be of value to a company?

8. How important is it for a firm to know how much inventory to reorder?

The Systematic Approach

Rolfson, Inc. recently examined its production operations and discovered that Plant 3 was continually having inventory control problems. Sometimes the plant had so much inventory on hand that it had to ask other plants to stock some of it for them. Other times the plant was producing hardly anything because there were no raw materials left. Someone in the plant had placed a reorder too late or the supplier had been delayed in delivering the order.

After looking into the matter, the top management of the firm fired the plant manager and brought in a new man, Hank Wilson. The first thing Hank announced was that he intended to systematize the inventory control situation. He brought in two inventory control experts who studied the situation very carefully. The workers noticed these individuals looking into such things as the cost of ordering new inventory, warehouse expenses, inventory depreciation, and the cost of inventory insurance. When the experts were finished, they presented Hank with a list of all the raw materials and parts that the firm had to have on hand. After each item the inventory control people had indicated when the good should be reordered. In some cases this was to be done periodically; in other cases it was to occur when inventory reached a particular level. Hank promised to follow their instructions to the letter.

A few months later the plant had had only one problem with inventory reordering. A vendor had been late in delivering the order. Aside from this everything was going smoothly. When Hank talked to the president of the firm a week later, he told the president that the inventory control people had worked out a plan that would prevent inventory problems in the future. "You know," he said, "it's amazing how the careful analysis of a production problem can result in its solution. It's really too bad that the last plant manager didn't use a more systematic approach to reordering inventory. If he had, things never would have gotten out of hand."

1. Why would inventory control people be interested in such things as the cost of ordering new inventory, warehouse expenses, inventory depreciation, and the cost of inventory insurance? Explain, bringing into your discussion carrying and order costs.

2. If a new system is so good, how come the plant still had an inventory reorder problem?

3. If this new system is as good as it appears, why did the old plant manager not use it?

PURCHASING

In addition to controlling inventory, the firm must decide what raw materials and capital equipment, such as heavy-duty machinery, need to be purchased. If the company is small and decentralized, these decisions will often be made by the production manager. If the organization is large and centralized, the decisions will probably be made by a purchasing manager.

Centralized and Decentralized Purchasing

Many managers favor a **decentralized purchasing** policy in which each department buys the things it needs. The rationale for this approach is simply that each department knows its own requirements best. However, there are many reasons favoring a **centralized purchasing** plan. First, the individuals placing the orders become highly proficient at this task and soon learn how to cut through red tape. Second, by coordinating the purchases of similar goods from many different departments, the purchasing manager can often place one large order and obtain a quantity discount from the supplier. Third, by centralizing purchasing the company frees the production people for more important duties.

How Purchasing Is Done

The purchasing department is the firm's representative with external vendors. Its job is to purchase the necessary goods and services as efficiently as possible. In addition, the department is responsible for maintaining records on the performance of suppliers (Were the goods received on time and in satisfactory condition?) and for paying the agreed-upon price.

Once goods are received they are often stocked in a storeroom and drawn out as needed. If more than one unit or department will be using them, it is common to find the purchasing department also supervising the disbursement of the materials. In this case, each production unit will present a requisition for the goods it needs, specifying the desired quantities. The material is then given to the department, charged to its account, and subtracted from the currently recorded inventory level. When this level falls to the reorder point, a purchase order is prepared and placed with a vendor. Then, when the goods are received, the storeroom is restocked and the merchandise is paid for by the purchasing department.

Purchasing Capital Equipment

The above discussion illustrated the role of the purchasing department in buying raw materials and other necessary goods. However, the firm will occasionally need to buy **capital equipment,** such as a new machine. An example would be a forklift truck that will transport materials around the plant. Another

example would be a lathe that will assist in converting raw materials into finished goods. A third would be specially designed hand drills used in the production process.

In each case the purchasing department will determine what companies make these goods. Then the price, service, and reputation of each company will be evaluated in reaching a final decision on the vendor. The next important decision will be that of financing the equipment. This, however, is not a matter for the purchasing department alone. Many others, including the finance department, will often become involved at this point.

The most obvious method of financing new equipment is to buy it outright. However, the company may be unable to afford such an outlay of cash. As a result, many firms lease or rent equipment. In this way they not only save the large initial capital outlay needed to pay for the machine but also the costs of maintaining the equipment, which fall on the lessor who is providing the machine. An added advantage is that the cost of leasing the machines can be deducted from the firm's income tax.

In the final analysis, however, the question of purchasing capital equipment comes down to dollars and cents. How much money will the firm have to pay for the machinery and how much of an increase in efficiency can it expect from the new machines? In determining the expenses associated with the machines the company has to examine not only the selling price but also such costs as maintenance of the equipment, power to run the machines, and insurance on the equipment. These are often referred to as **operating costs.** The company will also examine the **opportunity cost of capital.** The opportunity cost is the return that could be expected if, instead of buying a new machine, the firm put the money into a different investment, such as a savings account at the local bank. Here it might have been able to obtain 6 percent a year on the investment. Of course, if the machine will return more than this to the company, it is wiser to invest in the capital equipment. And, of course, there is always the

possibility that the machine will have some scrap value at the end of its useful life, so that some of the purchase price can be recovered upon resale.

Drawing upon the information in the above paragraph, it is possible to illustrate how a company that has decided to purchase a new machine will evaluate the alternatives. Let us assume that a firm has two machines under consideration: one costs $250,000, the other 300,000. Each is just as efficient as the other and both will last for five years. In addition, the current rate on investments is 6 percent simple interest. Given this data, and subtracting the salvage value, we can compare the two as follows:

	Machine 1	Machine 2
Purchase price (+)	$250,000	$300,000
Operating costs for 5 years (+)	110,000	65,000
Opportunity costs at 6% for 5 years (+)	75,000	90,000
Net cost	$435,000	$455,000
Salvage value (−)	20,000	60,000
Net cost	$415,000	$395,000

If just the purchase price is considered, Machine 1 is the best choice. In this case, however, the more expensive piece of equipment, Machine 2, has such low operating costs and high scrap value that it makes the better investment. Calculations such as the above are widely used in making capital equipment investments.

9. Why do many companies centralize the purchasing function?

10. What functions does a purchasing department perform for the firm?

11. What are some of the things a firm will evaluate in deciding which of two machines to purchase?

MAINTENANCE

Another key production activity is **maintenance.** Sooner or later every machine will break down. This in turn can mean lost sales, as idle equipment and operators wait for someone to fix the machine. And in the case of a production line, one machine going down may halt the entire line.

Companies use various methods for dealing with these problems. One is to set up the production process in such a way that when a machine goes down they can continue to operate with the other machines. A second method is to build up inventories at each stage of the production process. Then if one stage breaks down, the others can at least continue on until the inventories run out. A third is to use preventive maintenance.

Preventive maintenance is a term that means fixing a machine before it breaks down. The benefit of preventive maintenance is that the company can choose when it wants to perform these repairs,

---

Whenever someone on radio or TV says, "With a name like Smucker's, it has to be good," the listener is liable to chuckle out loud. But there's nothing funny about Smucker products—especially their quality, as can be attested by the millions of consumers who buy them.

The Smucker story all began back in 1897 with J. M. Smucker, who founded the concern to make and sell apple butter. On the jar labels was the statement that the apple butter was "manufactured and personally guaranteed by J. M. Smucker." There is no evidence that he ever had a dissatisfied customer. The company's current president, Paul Smucker, is as dedicated to quality as was his grandfather.

Paul took over as president of the firm in 1961 and sales began to spurt shortly thereafter. The product line was by this time quite large, and it was further expanded by the addition of other food products such as pickles and a jelly and peanut-butter combination. At the same time the company began to expand by buying up additional plants and reducing its dependence on independent fruit farmers and processors.

In 1961 the company's sales were $14.6 million. Today they are well in excess of $145 million. And the firm's success story can be related in two words—product quality. While building a bigger and better company is always on Paul Smucker's mind, he resolutely refuses to do anything that will hurt product quality in any way. As one top manager in the firm has noted, "Everybody here knows it. Unless whatever you've got in mind will improve the quality, you can forget it. Paul just won't stand for it."

Speaking for himself, Paul has set forth his philosophy of management in this way: "I just can't imagine a nicer business to be in. To me, it all starts with what you put in the jar. If it's honest and of good quality —and if you deal that way with your people—then all the rest will come. That was the way my grandfather felt when he started out making apple butter with an old Dutch recipe that his grandmother had. All I've inherited is the base, and I'm trying to carry that base further." Consumers who buy Smucker products agree that he is doing well in this effort.

Paul H. Smucker

ORDER NUMBER	QUANTITY DESIRED	JANUARY					FEBRUARY				MARCH				APRIL			
		3	10	17	24	31	7	14	21	28	7	14	21	28	4	11	18	25
125	5,000																	
211	2,750																	
342	3,100																	
401	700																	
475	1,500																	

FIG. 8.2 *A Gantt chart*

rather than waiting for the machine to actually go down. For example, if a machine has a record of breaking down every one hundred hours and it had maintenance fifty hours ago, the firm knows that it can operate for approximately fifty more hours before going down again. If the machine is scheduled for a job requiring sixty-five hours, the company can do maintenance on it now and virtually assure itself that no further repairs will be needed until the job is complete. Of course, in some cases it is cheaper to let the machine break down and then simply repair it. So the firm has to determine the costs associated with both of these maintenance policies to decide which is the most efficient.

12. When might it be profitable for a firm to use preventive maintenance? When might it not?

PRODUCTION SCHEDULING

As we noted in the last chapter, most products follow some production sequence. For example, the goods are first manufactured, then treated with a special coating, and then assembled. In order to do this, the company must have planned out a **production schedule.** In essence, scheduling involves determining when work should begin on a particular order and when it should finish. And the company would also like to be able to determine the amount of progress that has been made to date. These things are often accomplished through the use of scheduling techniques.

Scheduling Techniques
Most firms rely on one or more scheduling techniques to help them solve their production coordination problems. These techniques can be grouped into two basic categories: (a) charts and graphs, and (b) operations research methods.

Charts and graphs
There are all sorts of charts and graphs used for scheduling. Perhaps the best known is the **Gantt chart,** which is illustrated in Fig. 8.2. This chart gives the numbers of the orders currently being worked on and the quantities of each that are being manufactured. For example, order 125 calls for 5,000 units of a particular good. The chart also indicates when work on the particular job was started and when it is scheduled to finish. For example, order 211 is scheduled to start on January 10 and be finished by the end of the week of February 28, namely March 4. Progress on each order is designated by the dark purple bar that extends from the open angle on the left toward the open angle on the right. Finally, the "V" on the top of the chart after the week of February 28 indicates the current date, which is March 4.

A visual examination of the chart reveals the following progress on each job:

Order 125   finished on time
Order 211   currently one week late
Order 342   currently one week ahead of schedule
Order 401   on time
Order 475   currently one week late

One of the reasons why many firms like the Gantt chart is that it allows the manager to determine the progress of each order simply by examining the chart. Those jobs that are running late, therefore, can be easily identified and the manager can take quick corrective action. The manager can also schedule more work for those individuals finishing early.

Operations research methods

Operations research is a term used to describe mathematical decision-making techniques. Most of these are far too technical for discussion here. There is one, however, that is fairly easy to understand. It is called **PERT,** which is an acronym for Program Evaluation and Review Technique (see Fig. 8.3).

PERT is widely used in scheduling complex jobs that are "one-time" operations for the firm. In essence, PERT requires the company to determine both

FIG. 8.3 *A PERT diagram showing the critical path*

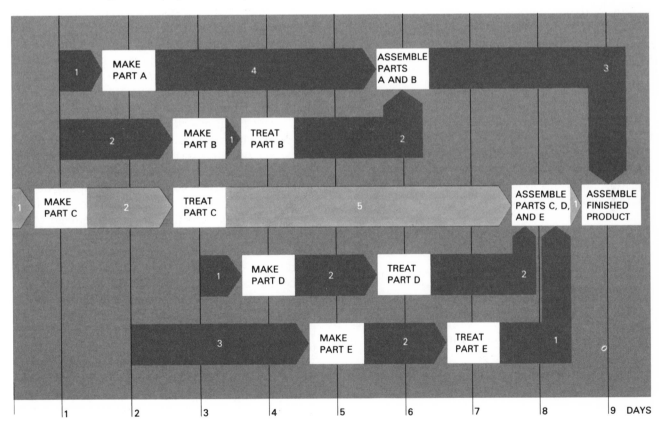

the activities that must be performed on a project and how long each will take. Figure 8.3 is an illustration of a simple PERT diagram. As can be seen in the figure, Part A will take one day to make. Part B, meanwhile, will take two days to make and one day to treat. The two parts, A and B, will then be assembled into a subunit and, finally, assembled once more as part of the finished product. This same method of explanation applies to the other parts of Fig. 8.3.

The reason companies like to use PERT on complex projects is that it helps them to (a) identify all the things that have to be done, (b) determine how long each will take, and (c) work out the sequence in which everything must be accomplished. In addition, a PERT network allows the manager to identify the longest possible time the project will take. This is done by determining the sequence or path requiring the greatest amount of time. In Fig. 8.3 it is the gray path, for Part C. This path, often called the **critical path,** will take nine days. Therefore the entire project should take no more than nine days to complete.

By identifying the critical path the company can schedule its operations accordingly. Primary attention must be given to those activities on the critical path. The others are important, of course, but they are secondary. By concentrating its efforts on finishing those activities along the critical path on time, the firm ensures that the project will not run late.

13. What are the two basic types of scheduling techniques?

14. How does a Gantt chart work?

15. Why do so many production managers like the Gantt chart?

16. How does PERT help a production manager in scheduling work?

QUALITY CONTROL

While production scheduling helps ensure that the goods will be completed on time, quality control ensures that the products will meet minimum standards. These standards are often related to the size, shape, weight, or performance of the good. To ensure this quality, it is common to find some form of inspection taking place.

Inspection

Some goods are **inspected** after they are manufactured. Others are examined at various stages in the production process to ensure that a mistake is not allowed to go undetected for too long a period. In addition, some are inspected before being finally shipped and some are not. Which of these latter methods is best? The answer will depend upon the cost of inspecting. For example, the cost of inspecting a new auto before shipping is very low when compared to both the selling price of the car and the legal fees involved if the auto has a defect that is not discovered in time. On the other hand, the cost of inspecting inexpensive items such as light bulbs would be very great if every bulb were tested. As a result the firm will examine only a representative sample of the bulbs.

Some firms do not like to use a **sampling** approach because of the possible error associated with a poor sample. For example, if the company decides to test every tenth light bulb and one out of one hundred proves defective, what percentage of the total production run are *really* defective? The answer depends on how well the sample represents the total production run. If it is truly representative, then 1 percent of all the bulbs are defective and the company saved a lot of money by inspecting only 10 percent of them. However, if 5 percent of all the bulbs are defective, the sample is inaccurate and the firm could be in trouble.

One way of obtaining a representative sample is to consult quality control people who are familiar with sampling theory. These individuals have a good

THE BMW 528i.
A CAR THAT MEETS THE DEMANDS OF THE 80's WITHOUT VIOLATING THE CONCEPT OF A BMW.

Conventional automotive wisdom has it that any increase in a car's environmental control paraphernalia must inevitably result in a corresponding decrease in performance.

Indeed, many serious automotive writers have warned that pollution systems and fuel efficiency regulations have all but sounded the death knell for high-performance automobiles.

These gloomy predictions, however, do not take into consideration the determination of the engineers at the Bavarian Motor Works to build extraordinary automobiles.

Against all odds, the BMW 528i not only meets the demands of society, it also provides the kind of exhilarating driving experience that most people have all but given up for lost in today's luxury automobiles. AMIDST INCREASING MEDIOCRITY, BMW GETS EVEN BETTER.

Press the accelerator and the 528i's fuel-injected, six-cylinder, overhead cam engine responds in a manner that can only be described as exhilarating.

And yet, the 528i (with standard transmission) delivers an impressive 17 EPA estimated mpg, 26 estimated highway mileage and, based on these figures, an estimated mpg range of 279 miles and a highway range of 426 miles.

(Naturally our fuel efficiency figures are for comparison purposes only. Your actual mileage and range may vary, depending on speed, weather and trip length. Your actual highway mileage and highway range will most likely be lower.)

Its four-speed manual transmission (automatic is available) runs smoothly and precisely up through the gears.

Its suspension system—independent on all four wheels—provides the driver with an uncanny feel of the road.

And, while the 528i provides as long a list of luxury items as one could sanely require—AM/FM stereo cassette, full-power accessories, air conditioning, etc.—its luxury is purposefully engineered to help prevent driver fatigue.

Vital controls are within easy reach; the tachometer, speedometer and ancillary instruments are well-marked and easy to read.

Its front seats are designed to hold their occupants firmly in place, and are so thoroughly adjustable that it is all but impossible not to find a comfortable seating position.

If you'd care to judge the extraordinary performance of the 528i for yourself, phone your nearest BMW dealer and he will arrange a thorough test drive at your convenience.

THE ULTIMATE DRIVING MACHINE.
Bavarian Motor Works, Munich, Germany.

Where Quality Counts

Quality control is just as important in the production of food items as it is in the manufacture of hardware goods. The J. M. Smucker Company provides an illustration of how quality control in food products can be attained. For example, when Smucker's buyers purchase fruits and berries, they always buy a full year's supply of each variety at harvest time to ensure uniform quality throughout the year. The produce is then shipped by rapid transportation to processing plants, where it is washed, sorted, quick-frozen, and then shipped on to one of three preserving plants. There the produce is quick-cooked in special vacuum kettles at low temperatures so that it retains the original flavor and color. Using a process called "essence recovery," Smucker's condenses the cooking vapors and returns them to the kettle. This makes it possible to retain maximum fresh-fruit flavor--a great deal more flavor than homemakers can retain in their own kitchens. Finally, the product is placed in airtight glass jars, pioneered by Smucker's, so that top-quality products will reach every family table. Similar high-quality procedures are used in making all of the goods, from jellies and fruit syrups to peanut butter and Goober spreads. Is it any wonder that Smucker's has gained a national reputation for high-quality food products?

working knowledge of how to choose samples, how many of them to conduct, and how to judge the accuracy of the results. Although these methods are too complex to warrant further discussion here, they are vital to production operations. When the firm can obtain accurate results from sampling, it can decide whether machine repairs are needed or whether the workers are becoming careless and closer control by supervisors is in order. Good sampling techniques can help a company spot the error early and take effective action.

17. What are the benefits of sampling as opposed to testing every unit?

NEW CHALLENGES

Thus far in this chapter we have presented the operational side of production management in a technical manner. And to a large degree, this is precisely what the subject entails—routine, mechanical work. However, in recent years the production area has been undergoing many changes. Many of them are directly related to the area of social responsibility; specifically, product quality and the demand by employees for meaningful work.

The Consumer and Quality

As seen earlier in this book, consumerism is a current social issue. One of the major demands of modern consumers is for a quality product. Unfortunately, many businesses operate in a highly competitive environment and quality can add a great deal of expense to the total cost of operation. As a result, quality is sometimes sacrificed for quantity at the production planning level. Other times it adds so much to the total cost of the product that few customers are willing to buy it. Prior to the current demand for automobile safety, for example, the Big Three were unable to get consumers interested in

You Gotta Believe

June Andersen, a new employee at Rolfson, Inc., works in the purchasing area. However, in order to get a better understanding of the needs of the production people, she likes to get out in the plant and learn a little bit about the operations. The other day she was over in the quality control area where one of the inspectors was sampling some components. After randomly choosing 100 components from a batch of 1,000, the inspector noted that 2 percent of them were defective. Since the firm has a standard acceptance rate of anything under 5 percent the man allowed the components to be shipped. This confused June, who decided to discuss the matter with Bob Raffel, a friend of hers in quality control. Part of the conversation went as follows:

Bob, I don't understand how the inspector knew that 2 percent of the components were defective and the rest were all right.

Well, June, he picked out some of them, tested them, and found that 2 percent were defective. It's that simple.

I don't get it. How does he know that 2 percent of the entire 1,000 were defective? He only examined 100 of them.

In sampling, June, you don't test each one, you generalize from the sample to the entire batch. If your sample is representative, and ours is because we are very careful in the way we choose a sample, then everything is going to be all right.

June, however, was still unconvinced. Therefore, Bob decided to let her find out for herself. They went over to the line where the inspector had just finished testing another batch. The man said that 2 percent of this 1,000 were also defective. Bob then suggested that June test each of the 1,000 components herself to see how accurate the 2-percent figure was. Since it only took five seconds to test each one, June agreed. Two hours later she had found nineteen defective components. "Bob," June said, "I still don't get it, but I'll admit your inspector was right." "Well," said Bob, "for those of you who are unfamiliar with sampling techniques, it's just a matter of faith. You gotta believe in us if you don't understand."

1. What does Bob mean by a "representative sample"?

2. Do you think the company's sampling procedures are good or was Bob just lucky in that June drew a batch of components that had 2 percent defects?

3. What are the advantages of sampling over 100-percent inspection?

Today packing bread, tomorrow baking bread! Job enrichment involves rotating employees through jobs as a means of relieving job boredom.

consideration will be given to building things *well* and less to just building them for production's sake.

Overcoming Job Boredom

A second major area of production consideration today is that of job boredom. We know from research in industry that many people are bored with their jobs. For example, assembly line workers who spend their entire day doing the same operation over and over complain that the work is painfully dull and unrewarding. Many of them have no pride in their jobs. On the other side of the coin, however, is the fact that without this division of labor, in which everyone performs a simple task, industry could never achieve high production.

How can the workers and the work be brought together in a meaningful way? Today a number of methods are being tried, including job enlargement and job enrichment. **Job enlargement** involves giving the workers added duties, such as having them perform more operations or move from job to job on an assembly line. By making the work less routine, the company tries to break down the boredom factor. **Job enrichment** involves changing the jobs, so as to build into them things that motivate the workers. These include increased responsibility, challenging work, opportunity for advancement and growth, and a greater feeling of personal achievement.

Both of these methods, job enlargement and job enrichment, are being used to break down the monotony of many production-type jobs. Some work, of course, does not lend itself to these methods, and some companies still see production as a mechanical process. However, most firms realize that the worker is as important to the creation of a product as is the machinery and equipment. As a result, we should see a great deal more of job enlargement and job enrichment in years to come.

18. How does job enrichment differ from job enlargement?

purchasing safety-related auto equipment. Today, of course, all of this has changed and there is great emphasis being placed on **quality of life.** As the emphasis continues, we can expect to see accompanying changes in the production area. More

They Do It in Scandinavia

Autos in the United States roll down the assembly line, with each worker performing some operation on each of them. However, not every auto maker uses this assembly-line approach. For example, at Volvo's Kalmar assembly plant in Sweden, car bodies are carried on a big dolly-type vehicle rather than a conveyor. Working in teams, the employees perform a series of operations, rather than just one as is common in many American auto plants. This method of job enlargement has helped the Swedish auto maker reduce absenteeism and improve efficiency.

The same basic concept is being used in a Norwegian paper plant. In one department there the workers all learned how to do every job in the department. This allowed them to switch jobs and thereby reduce the boredom and monotony associated with doing the same thing day after day. The workers also set their own schedules, decided when to take vacations, and eventually voted to eliminate the foreman's job.

This idea of enlarging the work and making it more interesting and challenging is also being used in the United States. However, it will probably not be introduced into auto assembly. Some American workers who studied its use overseas said that they preferred doing just one operation because it is less tiring! In other operations, however, it does seem to be receiving more interest.

SUMMARY

Production consists of more than just the manufacture of goods. It is also necessary to decide when inventory should be reordered and in what quantities. Many firms use periodic and/or perpetual inventory systems to determine when they should reorder, and rely upon mathematic techniques such as the EOQ to determine how much to reorder. These orders are then placed with suppliers or vendors. Sometimes a department will do this itself. However, it is more common to find a purchasing department coordinating orders for the entire firm.

Another important production-related activity is maintenance. Because all machinery will eventually break down, the company must decide whether it wants to fix things after they go down or employ a preventive maintenance policy. Preventive maintenance calls for fixing machinery at scheduled intervals, regardless of the equipment's condition. In choosing a maintenance policy, of course, the firm will evaluate the costs associated with each approach and choose the one offering the greatest saving.

A third production-related technique is scheduling, a planning tool used to coordinate the work. Scheduling involves deciding when jobs should begin and when they should be finished. It also allows the production manager to determine how much progress has been made on each job. Two of the best-known scheduling methods are the Gantt chart and PERT.

If everything is on schedule, the company can then turn its attention to quality control. Are the goods being made according to specifications? This can be determined through inspection, either when the item is finished or at various intervals in the production process. To examine every unit, of course, can be expensive. However, quality control can be maintained through carefully conducted sampling techniques.

Before finishing our discussion of the production side of business, it should be noted that not all of this work is routine, technical, and mechanical. There is also the human side of operations. For example, business realizes that production work can be boring. For this reason attempts are now being made to introduce interest-creating techniques into the production area. Illustrations include both job enlargement and job enrichment, and the future should see even more attention devoted to this area.

KEY TERMS FOUND IN THIS CHAPTER

QUESTIONS FOR DISCUSSION AND ANALYSIS

1. What types of costs are associated with buying inventory? Identify and describe them.

2. In what way is lead time related to the reordering of inventory?

3. How does a perpetual inventory system work?

4. What are some of the advantages of centralized purchasing?

5. What is meant by the opportunity cost of capital?

6. Why do all firms not use preventive maintenance?

7. What is the purpose of a production schedule?

8. Why do many firms sample the quality of their products rather than test each one?

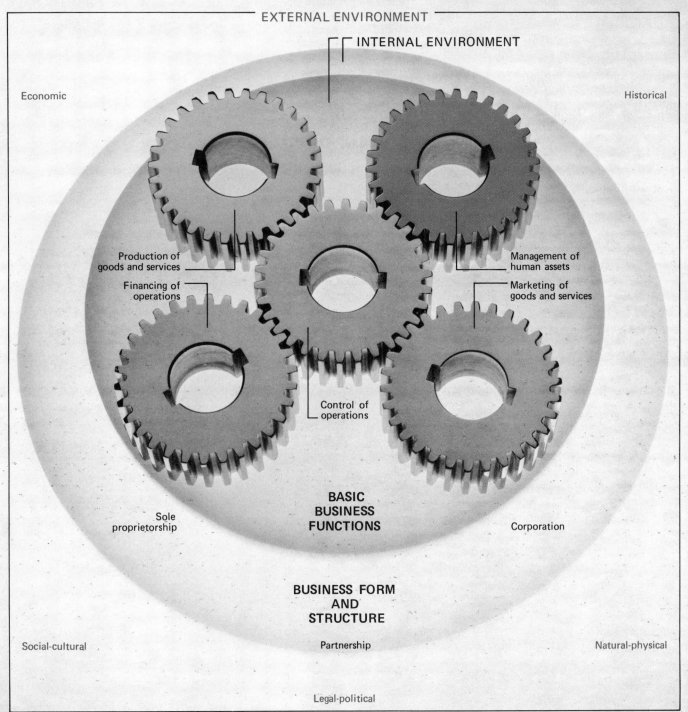

EXTERNAL ENVIRONMENT

INTERNAL ENVIRONMENT

Economic

Historical

Production of goods and services

Management of human assets

Financing of operations

Marketing of goods and services

Control of operations

BASIC BUSINESS FUNCTIONS

Sole proprietorship

Corporation

BUSINESS FORM AND STRUCTURE

Social-cultural

Partnership

Natural-physical

Legal-political

Managing the Human Resources of Business

An organization's most important asset is its people. Unless these individuals are managed and motivated properly, the business is in trouble. In this section of the book we will study the ways in which the modern business goes about managing its human assets.

In Chapter 9, the area of "human resource management" will be studied. Particular emphasis will be given to the topics of motivation and leadership. What is it that people want from their jobs? What "turns them on"? Furthermore, what kinds of leadership styles are most effective in directing people toward the attainment of company objectives? In Chapter 9 some answers to these questions will be given.

Then, in Chapter 10, the focus of attention will be placed on the personnel department. This is the in-house department that helps a firm manage its human assets by helping to provide much of the formal training to the people. This department also plays an active role in developing competitive wage and salary programs and benefit programs.

In the final chapter of this section, Chapter 11, the area of management-labor relations is examined. Whenever one discusses human assets, it is important to ask why there are unions. Chapter 11 attempts to answer this question by explaining the role and objectives of unions. It also explains how labor contracts are negotiated, and describes some of the techniques used by both management and labor in settling disputes.

When you are finished reading this section, you should have a solid understanding of how businesses attempt to motivate and lead their people. You should also be familiar with a number of key terms in this area, including *Theory X, Theory Y, situational leadership, vestibule training, job rotation, union shop, collective bargaining, picketing,* and *arbitration.* Finally, you should have gained an appreciation for the importance of managing human assets well.

9

The real leader has no need to lead—he is content to point the way.

Henry Miller

OBJECTIVES OF THIS CHAPTER

The organization's personnel are its most important assets. Therefore, today's business firms must be very careful to treat their employees well. In this chapter we are going to be looking at some of the ways in which this is done, and our objectives are to examine two of the major areas of human resource management: motivation and leadership. In particular, we will look at some of the most important human behavior research that has been conducted in these areas. By the end of the chapter you should be able to do the following:

a. identify the five basic needs of every individual;

b. describe some of the most important motivators for getting workers to attain company objectives;

c. outline some of the common assumptions managers have about their subordinates;

d. define the four basic styles of leadership; and

e. explain what is meant by the saying, "there is no such thing as one best leadership style."

Human Resource Management

MOTIVATING PEOPLE

One of the key elements in human resource management is motivation. Simply defined, **motivation** is the process of creating organizational conditions that will result in employees striving to attain company goals.

Perhaps the most difficult question for the manager, however, is *what motivates people?* All sorts of factors can be listed, including money, good working conditions, interesting work, a chance to do something one likes, and an opportunity for growth and development. Depending on the individual, of course, our list could contain hundreds of factors. Yet if we were to look for one overriding theme in motivation, it might well be **need satisfaction.** By this we mean that people have desires or needs that require satisfaction. If the company provides the means for meeting these needs, it can motivate its employees. For example, if a firm has a job that pays $500 a day, some workers may be willing to take it. The fact that the job involves driving a truck carrying dynamite is of no importance to these people. For them, the high daily wage justifies the risk. In this case we would say that the worker's need for money is greater than his or her need for safety.

1. What is motivation? Put it in your own words.

"The motivational research firm wants to know why you're hiring them."

From The Wall Street Journal; permission Cartoon Features Syndicate

Motivation and Needs

In analyzing motivation, it is possible to use a "needs" approach. Needs can be classified broadly into two categories: primary and secondary. **Primary needs** are physiological in nature, such as the need for food, clothing, and shelter. **Secondary needs** are psychological, such as love, the need to feel wanted,

It can be the job, the employee, or the organization that provides the motivation to get the job done properly.

180

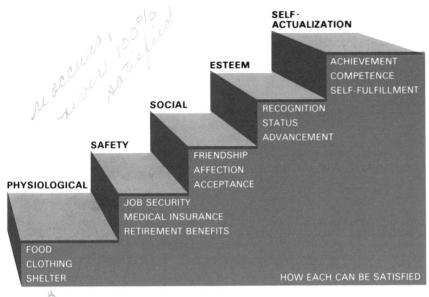

FIG. 9.1 *Maslow's hierarchy of human needs*

and the desire to associate and interact with other people. Both of these need categories, of course, are important to an understanding of motivation.

In taking a closer look at needs, we are going to examine the best-known list, which was put forth by the noted psychologist Abraham Maslow. According to Maslow, there are five levels of needs that every human seeks to satisfy: (a) physiological, (b) safety, (c) social, (d) esteem, and (e) self-actualization. Each of these is considered important, but the lower ones must be fulfilled before the upper ones merit attention. For example, the first (physiological) must be basically satisfied before one goes on to the second (safety). A diagram of these needs and how they can be satisfied is given in Fig. 9.1.

Physiological needs

The most basic needs are **physiological.** People require food, clothing, and shelter, and acquiring these is their first concern. These needs cannot, of course, be directly satisfied on the job. But they can be taken care of with the money earned on the job. Once these physiological needs are satisfied, attention can be focused on the next level.

Safety needs

Every individual has a desire for **safety** not only from physical dangers but also from illness, unemployment, and a host of other factors. These needs are met by many firms in the form of safety equipment, medical insurance, retirement benefits, and so forth.

Social needs

People like to interact and **socialize** with others. On the job this is often done through conversation and friendship. Employees talk among themselves, form groups, and, in general, enjoy each other's company. Thus the workplace is more than just a locale where people go to work; it is a place where they have an opportunity to socialize.

Esteem needs

Every person needs **esteem** or **self-respect.** People have to feel that they are important. When they do, their self-confidence increases. Some of the ways that esteem needs are fulfilled on the job include recognition for work well done, an increase in status among fellow workers, and advancement up the hierarchy in the form of promotion.

Self-actualization needs

When all the other needs have been basically satisfied, the **self-actualization** need becomes prominent. This is the desire to be the "best possible person one can be." Sometimes the terms *self-fulfillment, self-development,* and *creativity* are used instead of self-actualization. When people are operating at this level, they are attempting to realize their full potential. Unfortunately, less is known about this need than any other because people satisfy it in so many different ways. However, we do know that on the job people try to fulfill their self-actualization need through competence and achievement.

2. How can one distinguish between primary and secondary needs?

3. What are social needs? Does everyone have them?

4. How do esteem needs differ from self-actualization needs?

People and Individual Needs

Of course, Fig. 9.1 presents only a general picture of people and their needs. It is important for the manager to realize that not everyone follows this five-step hierarchy in precisely the order shown in the figure. For example, for some people social needs are more important than esteem needs. In addition, not everyone moves from one level of the hierarchy to the next. For some the physiological level may be as far as they want to go; money is the only thing that motivates them. Some researchers claim that 20 percent of the population operate basically in the first two levels of the hierarchy (physiological and safety needs), less than 1 percent in the top two levels (esteem and self-actualization), and the remainder (about 80 percent) at the third level, namely social.

Maslow's research is important for the manager because it shows that when a need is basically satis-

fied, it is no longer a motivator. To motivate the individual, then, one must move to the next level of the hierarchy. However, the difficult question for the manager is: what *specific* need does the worker want satisfied? If it is physiological, the company might be wise to offer more money. If it is esteem, the firm could consider giving recognition to those doing a good job. In answering this question the manager must make some assumptions about the workers. Unfortunately, these assumptions are sometimes incorrect. For example, one survey conducted in American industry asked supervisors what their workers wanted from their jobs. Table 9.1, which presents the results, shows that the supervisors tended to underrate what we might call **psychological rewards**—those that help meet upper-level needs. In fact, a close review of Table 9.1 shows that what the workers ranked 1, 2, and 3, the supervisors ranked 8, 10, and 9 respectively.

TABLE 9.1 WHAT DO WORKERS WANT FROM THEIR JOBS?

	RESPONSES	
	SUPERVISORS	WORKERS
Good wages	1	5
Job security	2	4
Promotion and growth with the company	3	7
Good working conditions	4	9
Interesting work	5	6
Management loyalty to workers	6	8
Tactful disciplining	7	10
Full appreciation for work done	8	1
Sympathetic understanding of personal problems	9	3
Feeling "in" on things	10	2

Source: Paul Hersey and Kenneth H. Blanchard, *Management of Organizational Behavior,* 3rd ed. (Englewood Cliffs, N.J.: Prentice-Hall, 1977), p. 47.

In recent years Frederick Herzberg has tried to make this area of motivation more understandable and applicable in the work place by illustrating the importance of satisfying *both* upper- and lower-level needs.

5. Why do so many managers underrate the importance of psychological rewards?

Herzberg's Two-Factor Theory

Unlike Maslow's theory, Herzberg's ideas were obtained from research conducted in industry. Beginning their research with a group of accountants and engineers in Pittsburgh, Herzberg and his associates sought answers to two questions: (a) what is it about your job that you like? and (b) what is it about your

Peter F. Drucker

When one talks about human resource management, it is almost impossible to avoid discussing management theory and practice. Who knows more about this subject than Peter F. Drucker, currently the most influential management writer in the world. Born in Vienna in 1909, he received an LL.D. from the University of Frankfurt in 1931. Two years later he was teaching international law in Germany, writing for a newspaper, and publishing his first book. Moving on to London and then to the U.S. in 1937, he began publishing the first of a long list of major books, *The End of Economic Man.* However, the one for which he is best known is the *Concept of the Corporation,* the result of work he had done at General Motors. The book proved so popular that it established him as a management philosopher and a leading authority in the field.

Over the last thirty years Drucker has turned out scores of articles for such prestigious publications as the *Wall Street Journal, Harvard Business Review, Harper's,* and *Fortune,* to name but four. He has also penned over a thousand articles and written twenty books. Some of his most popular have been *Managing for Results, The Effective Executive, The Unseen Revolution,* and *Management: Tasks, Responsibilities, Practices.*

He is also one of the most sought-after consultants in the country, providing advice to giant corporations such as General Motors and General Electric, as well as to government leaders and the heads of nonprofit organizations. He is widely hailed as one of the greatest living authorities on management. Many of his books end up on the best seller list, illustrating that he has a broad following both inside and outside of the business arena. Although Drucker is not writing as prolifically as he did during his younger days, his image and reputation seem only to have grown with time. A recent survey found him to be one of the most important contributors to twentieth century management thought.

Who Gets the Money?

Money is one of the biggest motivators for most people. Among top managers in U.S. industry, total compensation can run into the millions of dollars. In many cases this compensation is a combination of many different things including salaries, bonuses, deferred payments, personal benefits, and payment on stock appreciation. The following are the highest paid 25 executives according to a recent report.

Company	Chief Executive Officer	Total Compensation
1. Metro-Goldwyn-Mayer	Frank E. Rosenfelt	$5,063
2. Mobil	Rawleigh Warner, Jr.	4,313
3. McGraw-Edison	Richard W. Vieser	2,635
4. Metro-Goldwyn-Mayer	Barrie K. Brunet	2,451
5. Revlon	Paul P. Wollard	2,368
7. Mobil	Michel C. Bergerac	2,339
6. Revlon	William P. Taboulareas	2,313
8. Hughes Tool	R. M. Holliday	2,124
9. MCA	Sidney J. Sheinberg	1,984
10. General Dynamics	James M. Beggs	1,975
11. Metro-Goldwyn-Mayer	James D. Aijian	1,840
12. Fluor	Robert Fluor	1,784
13. Walt Disney Productions	E. Cardon Walker	1,521
14. Atlantic Richfield	T. F. Bradshaw	1,516
15. Gulf Oil	Edward B. Walker III	1,492
16. Boeing	O. C. Boileau	1,338
17. Kennecott Copper	Thomas D. Barrow	1,309
18. Storage Technology	Jesse I. Aweida	1,296
19. Rockwell International	Willard F. Rockwell Jr.	1,270
20. Chrysler	Lee A. Iacocca	1,266
21. SmithKline	Henry Wendt	1,256
22. Boeing	M. T. Stamper	1,159
23. SmithKline	Robert F. Dee	1,142
24. ITT	H. S. Geneen	1,116
25. Exxon	C. C. Garvin, Jr.	1,078

job that you dislike? The responses appeared to fall into two general categories.

The things that people seemed to like about their work were directly related to the job itself. For example, one supervisor indicated that he enjoyed being put in charge of installing some new equipment. He liked the challenge, the responsibility, and the recognition. Herzberg called these factors **motivators.**

The things people seemed to dislike about their work were related to the environment in which they performed their jobs. Illustrations included working conditions, supervision, company policies, and money. These factors, Herzberg concluded, do not motivate people; if they are adequate, they merely prevent dissatisfaction. He called these factors **hygiene,** because like physical hygiene they simply maintain a current status. For example, if you take proper care of your teeth by brushing and making regular trips to the dentist, your teeth should remain healthy; they should get no better or worse. If you do not take these hygiene steps, your teeth could deteriorate. In other words, Herzberg found that his hygiene factors helped maintain what can be termed a "zero level of motivation" if they were given to the workers, and dissatisfaction if they were not given. See Table 9.2 for a list of Herzberg's motivators and hygiene factors.

TABLE 9.2 HERZBERG'S MOTIVATORS AND HYGIENE FACTORS

MOTIVATORS	HYGIENE FACTORS
Work itself	Money
Recognition	Security
Responsibility	Working conditions
Advancement	Supervision
Achievement	Company policies

If we take Herzberg's theory and apply it to business, two important motivational ideas for managing human resources can be extracted. First, there are some things that simply do not motivate people. Of course, Table 9.2 is only a *general* scheme. For

Full appreciation for work done is an important psychological motivator.

The Man Who Didn't Understand

Clark Dolson, one of the press operators at Harrow Printing, a large eastern printing firm, quit the company last week. When asked why he was leaving Clark explained that he had been offered a more challenging job with a printing firm in the nearby vicinity. This was the third person in Fred Baker's department who had quit in the last two months. When asked about this increase in the turnover rate, Fred indicated that he was unable to explain it. An investigation by Fred's boss, however, revealed that the men were dissatisfied with Fred's treatment of them. One of the operators said that Fred treated his people as if they were incompetent. The remark was in reference to a list of rules and regulations that Fred had formulated and sent around to them the week before. Another operator said that Fred not only spent a lot of time looking over their shoulder but that he never stopped telling them how lucky they were to be working for Harrow Printing. "You know," said the operator, "you get a little tired of hearing how well the firm pays you and how good our working conditions are here. I'll bet there are plenty of other printing firms that have just as good a pay scale and probably even better working conditions. Besides, if Fred thinks all we are doing here is working for a paycheck he's sadly mistaken. I like this job but it's the people as well as the work. If the rest of the operators quit, I'd leave too."

Fred's boss decided to talk to him about these comments. However, Fred just did not seem to believe that there was any problem. "Oh, you know as well as I do," he told his boss, "that the men are always complaining. The only thing they work for is money and that's never enough. They always want another big raise. And you know that the workers are basically lazy. You've got to keep the screws on if you want any efficiency." Fred's boss asked him how this could be true in light of the fact that while Fred was keeping the men under pressure he was not achieving any increases in efficiency. In fact, noted his boss, Fred's men did less work than any other group in the entire plant. Fred again admitted that he had no answer to this problem, but he believed that if he cracked down hard for the next six months the workers would begin increasing their output.

1. In Herzberg's terms, is Fred more interested in motivators or hygiene factors?

2. What is Fred's problem in terms of motivating his workers?

3. What recommendations would you make to Fred? Explain.

Theory X management in action

© 1963 United Feature Syndicate, Inc.

some individuals, the factors Herzberg lists as hygiene are actually motivators. But the important thing is that for each of us there are some items that fall under the heading of hygiene. As a result not everything the company does will motivate workers. Some will just stop them from becoming unmotivated. For example, do good working conditions really motivate people? Probably not. But without good working conditions people might do less work.

Second, Herzberg's theory points out the importance of satisfying upper-level needs. Workers want recognition, increased responsibility, and a chance for advancement. In fact, when comparing the same job in different companies, it is common to find people receiving identical pay and having similar working conditions. The differences occur at the psychological level (Herzberg's motivators), and they account for the differences in worker performance.

6. In Herzberg's view, how do motivators differ from hygiene factors?

7. What do we mean when we say that hygiene factors create a "zero level of motivation"?

8. Does Herzberg's two-factor scheme as shown in Table 9.2 hold for everyone? Explain.

9. Of what value is Herzberg's theory to an understanding of employee motivation?

Theory X and Theory Y

Given the above findings, it is easy to see that managers who want to properly motivate and lead their subordinates will stress the psychological rewards of the job. Unfortunately, in American industry today we find many managers holding erroneous beliefs about the way to manage people. In his book *The Human Side of Enterprise,* Douglas McGregor called these individuals "Theory X managers." A **Theory X** manager is someone whose assumptions about people can be summarized as follows:

1. The average person dislikes work and, whenever possible, will avoid it.

2. To get people to really work it is necessary to use close control, threats, and constant pressure.

3. People actually like to be directed and supervised very closely.

Needless to say, the above description does apply to some people. However, it does not really represent an accurate picture of *all* employees. In fact, managers who are Theory X advocates actually underrate the abilities of many of their people.

Another set of assumptions set forth by McGregor are called **Theory Y** assumptions. These are more optimistic and are probably much more representative of the average worker. They are:

1. Work is a natural activity, just as are playing and resting.

NUMBER OF PEOPLE

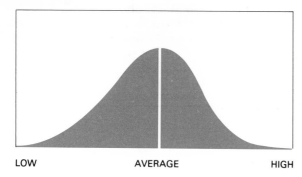

LOW   AVERAGE   HIGH

FIG. 9.2 *Ability of the work force*

NUMBER OF JOBS

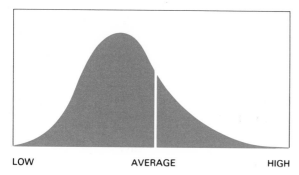

LOW   AVERAGE   HIGH

FIG. 9.3 *Job demands*

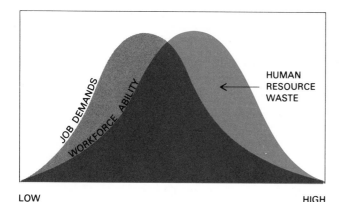

FIG. 9.4 *Workforce ability versus job demands*

2. Close control and threats of punishment are not the only ways to get people to do things. If individuals are committed to certain objectives, they will willingly work toward them.

3. Commitment to objectives is determined by the rewards associated with their achievement.

4. Under the right conditions, people not only accept responsibility, they seek it.

5. A large percentage of the population have high degrees of imagination, ingenuity, and creativity, which can be used in solving organizational problems.

6. In the world of business, the intellectual potential of the average person is only partially used.

Human Resource Utilization

In supervising human resources, the modern manager realizes that Theory Y offers a better description of people than does Theory X. Of course, there are some individuals who are lazy and need to be threatened or controlled very closely. However, far more people respond better to a manager who employs a leadership style that is Theory Y in orientation.

In fact, we know from research that many jobs in industry can be handled with less ability than the average person possesses. For example, if we were to draw a diagram of the ability of all the people in American industry, it would take the form of a bell-shaped curve, showing a small number having low ability, a large number possessing average ability, and a small number having high ability (see Fig. 9.2). If we were to diagram job demands, however, the curve would reveal that the difficulty of most work in business organizations is not that great (see Fig. 9.3). As a result, when the abilities of personnel are compared to job demands, we find that the people have greater talents than are needed for the jobs. We call this gap **human resource waste** (see Fig. 9.4). Theory Y managers are aware of this waste and attempt to eliminate it by building motivators such as those identified by Herzberg into the work. They also use leadership styles that allow their people to get the work done with a minimum of interference and control.

10. How accurate is the Theory X manager's view of subordinates?

11. How accurate is the Theory Y manager's view of subordinates?

12. Which of the above descriptions is more accurate? Explain.

LEADERSHIP

Leadership is the process of directing people toward the attainment of predetermined objectives. This, of course, can be a tall order. Nevertheless, leadership is crucially important to the success of an organization and has long been the object of serious study.

For a long time many people believed that effective leaders were born with certain personal characteristics or traits that other individuals did not possess. After years of research, however, this area of **trait theory** has declined in popularity because it has proved impossible to come up with a complete and specific list of leadership characteristics. Yet this is not to say that leaders have nothing in common. There are some traits that do seem to be present in most successful leaders.

One of these is *intelligence*. Leaders are usually more intelligent than their average follower. Another trait is *social maturity*. Leaders are emotionally mature, able to socialize well with other people, and capable of handling critical situations. They also have *high motivation and achievement drive*. They want to accomplish things. A fourth trait is a *human relations attitude*. Leaders are as interested in the well-being of their workers as they are in getting the work done.

Despite these common traits, however, effective leadership **is situational** in nature. By this we mean

"And just how long have people accused you of being a 'take charge' type?"

From The Wall Street Journal; permission Cartoon Features Syndicate

189

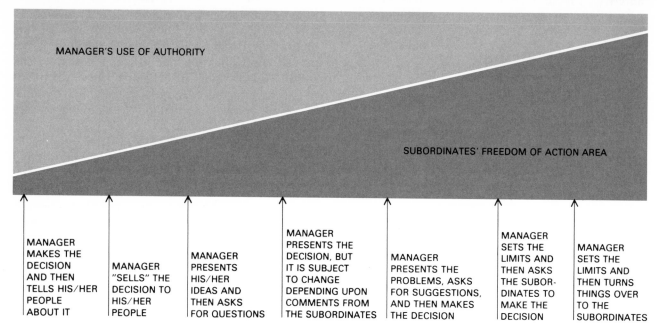

THE BOSS-CENTERED
LEADER

THE SUBORDINATE-CENTERED
LEADER

MANAGER'S USE OF AUTHORITY

SUBORDINATES' FREEDOM OF ACTION AREA

| MANAGER MAKES THE DECISION AND THEN TELLS HIS/HER PEOPLE ABOUT IT | MANAGER "SELLS" THE DECISION TO HIS/HER PEOPLE | MANAGER PRESENTS HIS/HER IDEAS AND THEN ASKS FOR QUESTIONS | MANAGER PRESENTS THE DECISION, BUT IT IS SUBJECT TO CHANGE DEPENDING UPON COMMENTS FROM THE SUBORDINATES | MANAGER PRESENTS THE PROBLEMS, ASKS FOR SUGGESTIONS, AND THEN MAKES THE DECISION | MANAGER SETS THE LIMITS AND THEN ASKS THE SUBOR-DINATES TO MAKE THE DECISION | MANAGER SETS THE LIMITS AND THEN TURNS THINGS OVER TO THE SUBORDINATES |

FIG. 9.5 *Leadership continuum (Adapted from Robert Tannenbaum and Warren H. Schmidt, "How to Choose a Leadership Pattern," Harvard Business Review, May– June 1973, p. 164.)*

that the manager's leadership style must be determined by the situation. Sometimes it is important to be lenient and easy-going; other times it is necessary to be firm and decisive. A closer look at leadership behavior should make this clearer.

Leadership Behavior

Perhaps the easiest way to examine leadership behavior is on a leadership continuum. One of the most popular continua is presented in Fig. 9.5. On the left side of the continuum is the **boss-centered leader.** This is the individual who makes the decisions and then communicates them to the subordinates. As one moves across the continuum, the

amount of authority delegated to subordinates increases. We call the manager at the right-hand side of this continuum a **subordinate-centered** leader.

13. What is meant by the term leadership?

14. Are there any traits most leaders seem to possess? What are they?

15. How does a boss-centered leader differ from a subordinate-centered leader?

Management Systems

In taking a closer look at the leadership continuum, it is helpful to use a **management systems** approach. This idea has been well developed by researchers such as Rensis Likert at the University of Michigan. In essence, it involves breaking leadership behavior into four basic styles or systems, from heavily autocratic to heavily democratic (see Table 9.3). Each of these four systems differs from the others. An illustration of the four is as follows:

System 1
Exploitive
Authoritative

System 2
Benevolent
Authoritative

System 3
Consultative
Democratic

System 4
Participative
Democratic

A **System 1** manager is an individual who has very little confidence in the subordinates. For the most part, decisions are made and then passed down the line for action. If necessary, pressure and threats of punishment are used to get things done. Basically, the manager distrusts the subordinates and vice versa. Any informal organization that develops generally opposes the goals of the formal organization.

A **System 2** manager is heavily benevolent. By this we mean that the manager acts toward the sub-

TABLE 9.3 LIKERT'S MANAGEMENT SYSTEMS

LEADERSHIP VARIABLE	SYSTEM 1 (EXPLOITIVE/ AUTOCRATIC)	SYSTEM 2 (BENEVOLENT/ AUTOCRATIC)	SYSTEM 3 (CONSULTATIVE/ DEMOCRATIC)	SYSTEM 4 (PARTICIPATIVE/ DEMOCRATIC)
Degree to which superior has confidence and trust in the subordinates	No confidence and trust	Very little confidence and trust	Substantial confidence and trust	Complete confidence and trust
Degree to which subordinates feel free to discuss important job matters with their superior	None at all	Very little	A good deal	Feels completely free
Degree to which superior seeks and uses subordinates' ideas and opinions in the solution of job problems	Seldom uses subordinates' ideas and opinions	Sometimes uses subordinates' ideas and opinions	Usually gets subordinates' ideas and opinions and tries to use them constructively	Always gets subordinates' ideas and opinions and always tries to use them constructively

Adapted from: Rensis Likert, *The Human Organization* (New York: McGraw-Hill, 1967), p. 4.

Which of Likert's Management Systems do we see in operation—System 1, 2, 3, or 4?

ordinates the way a parent would toward children. Most decisions are made by the manager and the subordinates are asked to "trust" in these decisions. The leader gives the followers little opportunity to get involved in decision making. As a result, subordinates are very wary and fearful of the System 2 manager.

A **System 3** manager consults with subordinates about decisions. This manager has quite a bit of confidence and trust in subordinates. Of course, major policy decisions are still made at the top of the organization, but subordinates are active in all other types of decision making. As a result, there is confidence and trust between the manager and the subordinates.

A **System 4** manager has complete confidence and trust in subordinates. Decision making is highly decentralized and there is a great deal of communication and cooperation between the leader and the followers. If there is an informal organization, it supports the formal organization.

Table 9.3 shows a classification of these four management systems in terms of certain leadership variables. Notice that as one moves from System 1 to System 4 in each variable, the amount of interaction between the leader and the subordinates increases dramatically.

Choosing the Right Style

We know from leadership research that more people seem to prefer a manager who uses a System 3 or System 4 style than one who employs a System 1 or System 2. In addition, people seem to do better work under System 3 and 4 conditions. For example, employees working under general supervision (Systems 3 and 4) are usually more productive than those operating under close supervision (Systems 1 and 2). People are also more productive under managers who are helpful or tolerant of mistakes than under those who are critical and believe in punishing the workers for every error they commit. Likewise, people seem to do a better job when they are allowed to set their own pace, as opposed to being told how fast to work.

When we take these findings into consideration it is easy to see why participative leaders, who treat their workers well and delegate authority to them, are more effective than their nonparticipative counterparts. Some people feel that it all comes back to Theory X and Theory Y leaders, with the latter being far more effective than the former. However, before concluding our discussion of leadership it is important for us to remember that *effective leadership depends on the situation*.

"Ms. Ryan, send me in a scapegoat."

From The Wall Street Journal; permission Cartoon Features Syndicate

The Productive Manager

Harrow Printing made a big profit last year. To a large degree, this profitability was accounted for by the increased productivity of the workers. In particular, Lara Day, one of Harrow's top managers, was able to achieve a 15-percent increase in the efficiency of her people. When asked about her success, Lara explained that she felt she really tried to understand and to empathize with her subordinates. She also treated them well and went out of her way to let them set their own work pace. Lara believes that if you leave people alone they will perform much better than if you look over their shoulder all day long.

The workers apparently believe this also. When interviewed, they said that they felt little pressure or fear over getting things done on time. If they were a little late on one job they would make it up on the next. "The important thing," one of them noted, "is that Lara never jumps on your back or asks her supervisors to start cracking the whip. This is really a great place to work. I don't think there is another printing firm like it anywhere else in the country." The workers who were standing around listening all agreed that the individual had summarized their feelings on the matter as well.

The company president apparently likes Lara's approach, too. He called Lara last week and told her that he'd like to start having weekly meetings with all the top managers. During these meetings the president said he would like to discuss what some of the managers were doing to improve efficiency. In particular, he said that he would like Lara to give her opinions on effective leadership. "You've got a successful leadership style, Lara," the president said, "and I'd like you to share your ideas with some of our other people to see if you can't help them in some way."

1. Based on the data in this case, would you say Lara is a Theory X or a Theory Y manager?

2. Under which management system would you classify Lara: 1, 2, 3, or 4? Explain.

3. What might Lara be doing that makes her more effective than some of the other managers? Give your reasoning.

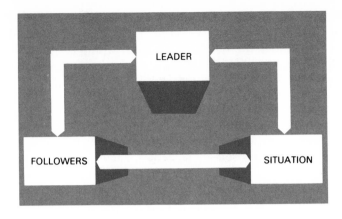

FIG. 9.6 *Effective leadership variables*

In many cases Theory Y and Systems 3 and 4 work well. There are situations, however, when a System 1 or 2 manager is needed. Consider, for example, the case of a sinking ship. How can all the passengers be moved into the lifeboats quickly and efficiently? The solution will call for a no-nonsense leader who can make fast decisions. There is no time to get everyone involved in a discussion of the problem. A "get-tough" manager is required. This person may have a gun, and will in all likelihood not stand for any challenge to his or her authority. This may seem like a cruel way to solve the problem, but in a crisis a Theory X manager is often superior to a Theory Y manager.

This same analogy is true in handling business problems. When a crisis situation arises, such as the firm being on the verge of bankruptcy, a System 1 or 2 manager may prove superior. In fact, many management consultants believe that the first question to be answered in determining leadership effectiveness is: what is the financial situation of the company? If things are critical, use a System 1 or 2 manager. If things are going along fine, use a System 3 or 4 manager.

It is also important to remember that different subordinates react differently to the same leadership style. Some like a highly decentralized approach in which they play an important part in decision making. Others want a less decentralized approach with close control. The former will not do well under a System 1 manager; the latter will perform poorly under a System 4 manager. Thus the leader must gear his or her style to the needs of the subordinates. It is erroneous to believe that any one style always works best. Effective leadership style is determined by the leader, the followers, and the situation itself, and each affects the others (see Fig. 9.6). In short, the effective manager examines the situation and analyzes the type of leadership the subordinates seem to like best. Then, given these conditions, the leader tries to adapt his or her style to fit the challenge.

16. How does a System 1 leader differ from a System 2 leader?

17. How does a System 3 leader differ from a System 4 leader?

18. In what way do the leader, the followers, and the situation all influence the type of leadership style needed in a given situation?

SUMMARY

Every organization needs to treat its people well. This calls for an understanding of both motivation and leadership.

Motivation is the process of stimulating employees to attain company goals. Yet what is it that motivates people? The answer, of course, will differ from person to person. One way of analyzing motivation is to use a "needs" approach. According to Maslow, everyone has needs that require satisfaction. These can be divided into five levels: physiological, safety, social, esteem, and self-actualization. Each level must be basically satisfied before one goes on to the next. On the job there are numerous ways in which business firms try to satisfy each of these needs.

The problem with Maslow's hierarchy, however, is that it is too theoretical and does not directly address the problem of motivation on the job. Herzberg has attempted to remedy this with his two-factor theory. His research findings indicated that there are factors that motivate people and factors that merely stop people from becoming dissatisfied. The former consist of things such as recognition, responsibility, and advancement. He labeled these motivators. The latter consist of things such as money, security, and working conditions. He labeled these hygiene factors. This model does not hold for every worker, of course, but it does point out the importance of psychological rewards, something often overlooked by managers in their attempts to motivate workers.

Why do many managers fail to give proper attention to psychological rewards? A good part of the answer rests in their assumptions about the workers. Many see the employees as lazy and in need of constant direction. We call these individuals Theory X managers. Their counterparts, who believe that people are actually willing to accept responsibility and work hard, are called Theory Y managers. These individuals are more likely to be effective because they treat their people better, delegate authority to them, and tend to be more System 3 and System 4 in orientation. Of course, there is no guarantee that a participative manager will always be more effective than an autocratic manager. It depends on the situation, the subordinates, and the leader. However, more people do prefer a System 3 or 4 manager to a System 1 or 2. Companies that use this approach tend to achieve better results.

KEY TERMS FOUND IN THIS CHAPTER

QUESTIONS FOR DISCUSSION AND ANALYSIS

1. What are the five needs in Maslow's hierarchy? How do business firms attempt to satisfy each?

2. Why is there less known about the self-actualization need than about any other need in Maslow's hierarchy?

3. In his two-factor theory, what did Herzberg mean by motivators? Identify some of them.

4. In his two-factor theory, what did Herzberg mean by hygiene factors? Identify some of them.

5. How do Theory X managers view their subordinates?

6. How do Theory Y managers view their subordinates?

7. How does a System 1 manager differ from a System 4 manager?

8. What is meant by the statement that "there is no such thing as one best leadership style"?

10

The training which makes men happiest in themselves also makes them most serviceable to others.
John Ruskin

OBJECTIVES OF THIS CHAPTER

In the previous chapter we examined some important ideas for motivating and leading personnel. Yet the firm must do more than just this if it is to manage its human assets well. The modern firm must also select its personnel carefully, train them well, pay them competitively, and provide them with health, safety, and benefit programs. The department most responsible for assisting the company in doing these things is the personnel department. The objectives of this chapter are to examine the role and functions of this department. By the end of the chapter you should be able to do the following:

a. describe the steps in the employee selection process;

b. explain some of the most common on-the-job and off-the-job training methods;

c. relate the role played by personnel in developing wage and salary levels; and

d. describe some of the health, safety, and benefit programs provided to employees.

Personnel: Its Role and Functions

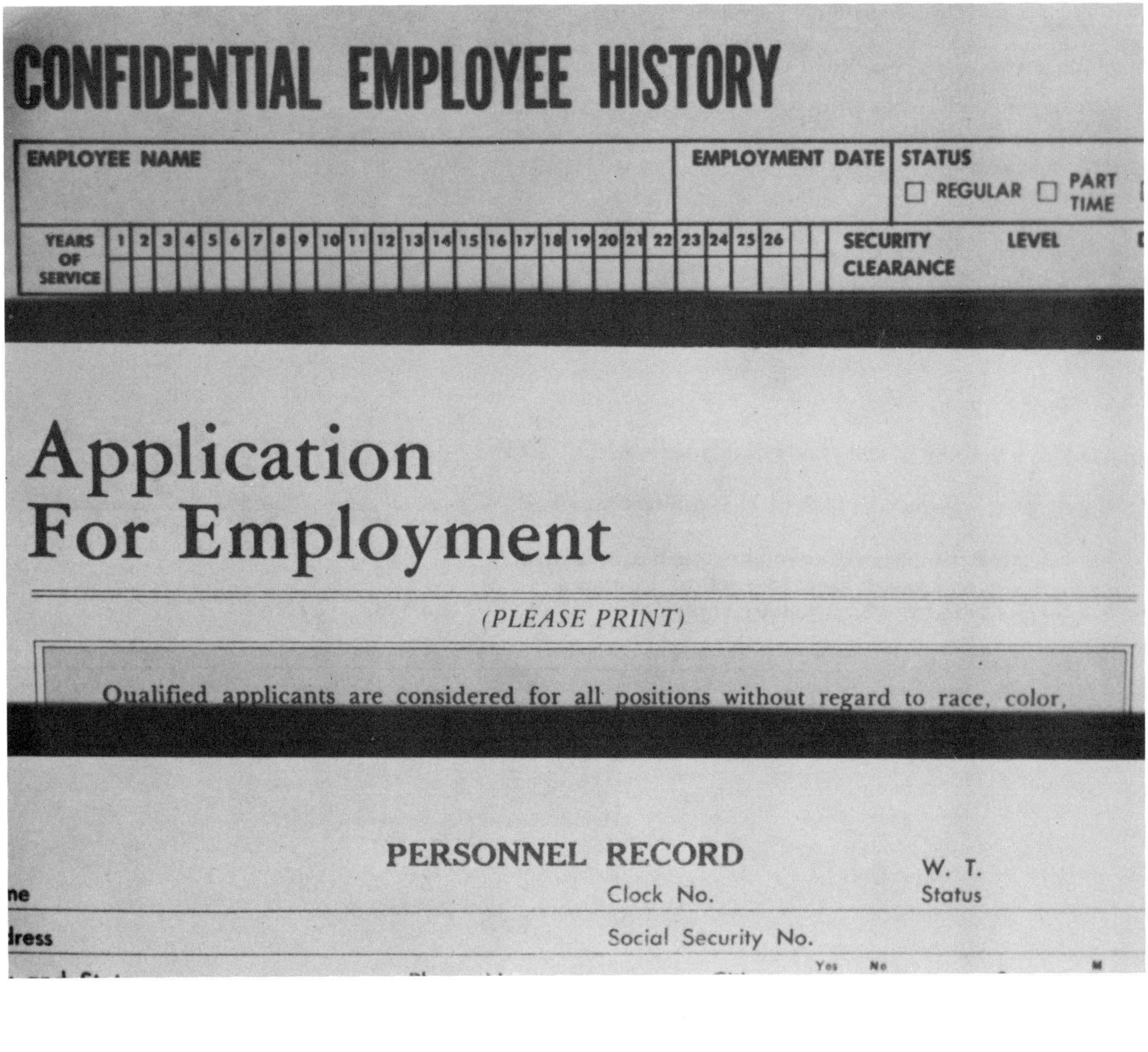

CONFIDENTIAL EMPLOYEE HISTORY

EMPLOYEE NAME																								EMPLOYMENT DATE	STATUS	
																									☐ REGULAR ☐	PART TIME

YEARS OF SERVICE	1	2	3	4	5	6	7	8	9	10	11	12	13	14	15	16	17	18	19	20	21	22	23	24	25	26		SECURITY CLEARANCE	LEVEL

Application For Employment

(PLEASE PRINT)

Qualified applicants are considered for all positions without regard to race, color,

PERSONNEL RECORD

W. T. Status

Clock No.

ne

Social Security No.

dress

Yes   No   M

THE NATURE OF THE PERSONNEL DEPARTMENT

Over the last twenty years business has begun paying more and more attention to the well-being of its **human assets.** Successful firms have finally come to realize that their people are far more important than their machines or equipment. As a result, most businesses today have a **personnel department** that helps select, train, and develop company employees. It is also common to find this department playing an active role in developing wage and salary programs as well as other programs related to health, safety, and benefits.

This department has become so important to many firms that it often occupies a status equal to that of other primary business departments such as marketing, production, and finance. Figure 10.1 shows the organization of the personnel department in a typical medium-size or large business. In a smaller company, of course, there would be fewer people in the personnel department; so some of these duties would be combined.

FIG. 10.1 *Organization chart of the personnel department*

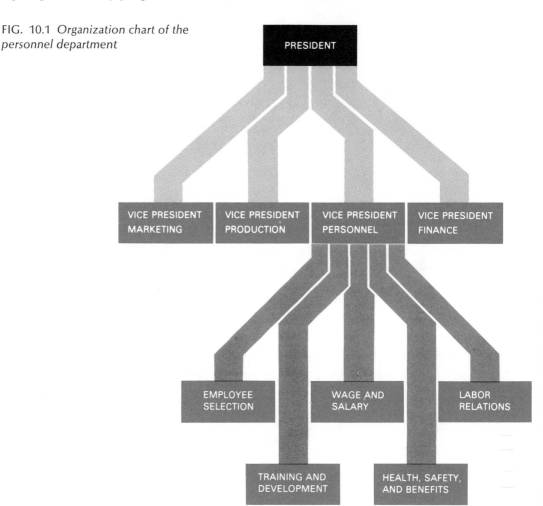

In general, the personnel department's job is to provide advice and assistance to other departments. For example, the department may place employment ads in the local newspapers. It may even interview the job applicants. However, it does *not* make the final decision regarding whether or not to hire the person. This is the responsibility of the manager in whose department the applicant will be working.

Another important personnel function is the training and development of the company staff. Some people need *pre-job training* before they can take on a particular job. Others need *on-the-job training* to ensure that they master the work as quickly and completely as possible. Some of this training will be required at the foreman or supervisory level; some of it will be needed at the upper management levels. The personnel department is often called upon to provide this training. Once again, its job is to *assist* the other departments with these services; it does not play any part in deciding who is to receive this training and plays only a limited role in determining the type of training that will be given.

Likewise, when it comes to wage and salary administration, the personnel department will perform many important functions. Some of these include analyzing jobs, writing job descriptions, and determining how much money other firms are paying for comparable work. However, the final decision on wages and salaries is made not by the personnel department but by the top management of the company.

This same advisory role is assumed when it comes to health, safety, and retirement. Personnel will examine the current programs and evaluate the needs of the employees. It will also determine the type of benefits being offered by other companies in the industry. Then, based on this information, it may make suggestions to management regarding any needed changes in the firm's current programs.

The personnel department's role in the area of labor relations is basically the same. Personnel tries to work out many of the problems that arise between the company and the employees. These can cover a very large area, from union grievances to someone who was shorted $10 on the weekly paycheck. In some cases the personnel department can take steps to straighten out the situation. In most instances, however, its job is that of assisting in the solution of the problem.

In the rest of this chapter we will be examining some of the functions performed by the personnel department. First, we will study the employee selection process. Then training and development, wage

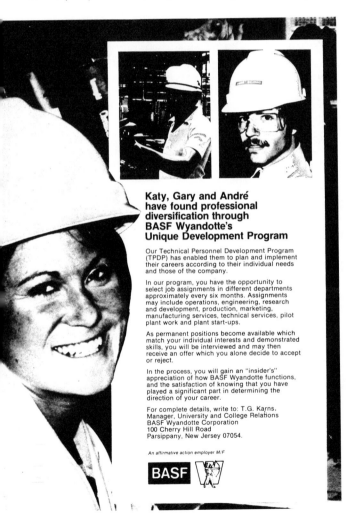

Lewis W. Lash

One of the most important personnel functions is that of training and development. In the major corporations, this is often handled, at least partially, through a central training and development department. At Eastern Airlines, Lewis Lash is the individual in charge of this function.

Starting his academic career in the field of accounting and economics, and then getting a master's degree from the University of Michigan in business education, Lew's career gradually took him out of the accounting area and into personnel and training. What kinds of training does a corporation like Eastern provide to its people? The answer is all kinds. As Lew puts it, "We have three major areas of emphasis in management development and training today: management training, assessment centers, and performance improvement. Management training is directed toward providing a broad range of courses and experiences that will help the manager better perform his or her job. Some of these types of training include supervisory training, problem-solving and decision making, counseling, and labor relations. Assessment centers are designed to help us perform a job analysis for determining the key tasks involved in positions; select and structure simulation exercises which will measure the dimensions we have identified during the job

analysis; provide feedback to individuals on how well they are doing; and assist them in their development as managers. Then there is performance improvement, an area that is not conveniently handled in a classroom setting. We have corporate responsibility for designing various performance appraisal systems and conducting team building sessions. We also serve as a liaison group between our departments and outside consultants. In all of these three activities, however, the objective is the same—increase productivity. At Eastern we believe that people are our most important asset. From the people who service our aircraft to our top corporate officers, everyone can profit if they are given proper training and development."

At the present time Lew is completing his doctorate in business administration, a step he feels has helped him professionally as well as personally. "This blend of real world experience and academic theory and practice has helped me better understand the value of training and development in the business arena," he notes. "So, to extend my earlier comment, even those in training and development can profit from further education."

At Eastern they like to say "we have to earn our wings every day." Those who know Lew feel he is helping Eastern in this effort.

and salary administration, and health, safety, and benefit programs will be reviewed. The area of labor relations, meanwhile, will be delayed until the next chapter.

1. What are some of the functions performed by the personnel department?

2. Is personnel a line or a staff department? Give your reasoning.

EMPLOYEE SELECTION

One of the most important jobs of the personnel department is to help the firm fill its manpower needs. Some workers will be quitting, others will be retiring. These positions will need to be filled. In addition, if the company is expanding operations, more workers will be needed for the new jobs that will be opening up. Yet the firm does not want to hire just anyone. Therefore, a careful **employee selection** process must be established. This process usually includes seven steps, which are illustrated in Fig. 10.2. If the employee completes all of the seven steps successfully, the company will often hire the individual.

Preliminary Screening Interview

Many times a firm will have far more applicants than job openings. In order to reduce the number, the company will begin with a **preliminary screening interview.** During this interview the personnel department will compare the applicant's abilities and skills with those required by the job. This latter information is usually available in the form of a job description (see Fig. 10.3). If the applicant lacks some of the job requirements, such as the minimal edu-

1. PRELIMINARY SCREENING INTERVIEW
2. APPLICATION FORM
3. EMPLOYMENT TESTS

4. BACKGROUND AND REFERENCE CHECKS
5. EMPLOYMENT INTERVIEW

FIG. 10.2 *Steps in the employee selection process*

6. PHYSICAL EXAMINATION
7. EMPLOYMENT DECISION

PLACEMENT ON THE JOB

FIG. 10.3 *Job description for a stenographer-clerk*

JOB TITLE:

Stenographer-Clerk

Description of Duties

Under direct supervision, takes and transcribes moderately difficult dictation from one or more individuals, performs a variety of clerical duties, and usually carries out a regularly assigned specific clerical task related to the functions of the unit. Performs miscellaneous typing and related duties as assigned.

Typical Examples of Work

Takes dictation of moderate difficulty using shorthand or stenotype machine. Transcribes notes by typing.

Performs rough draft or copy typing.

Performs a variety of clerical duties, which may involve the following related duties:

maintaining office files, including making additions, deletions, and revisions; looking up materials from the files such as correspondence, reports, and requisitions;

composing and typing simple memoranda and correspondence;

maintaining reports and letters, recording data on predesigned forms, and, as requested, summarizing data in weekly and monthly reports;

maintaining follow-up records on reports and correspondence;

distributing mail;

answering the telephone;

requisitioning office supplies.

Minimum Qualifications

Education

Graduation from high school or its equivalent, with sufficient mental development to perform clerical and stenographic duties. Requires training in stenography, typing, and routine business procedures.

Experience

At least three months' experience in the company to become familiar with company and departmental organization, policies, procedures, terminology, and general office procedures. Requires 120 hours of on-the-job training to learn the details of departmental assignments.

Knowledge

Knowledge of clerical methods and office procedures.

Ability and Skill

Ability to take general dictation using shorthand or stenotype machine, to record statistics and arithmetical data on standard records and reports, and to compose and type routine correspondence. Must be skilled in the use of the typewriter.

Personal Characteristics

Accuracy; dependability; mental alertness; thorough, pleasing personality; and good memory for details.

Physical Requirements

Must pass company physical examination.

cational level necessary for this job, the selection process need go no further.

Application Form
Almost every company requires applicants to fill out an **application form.** In this form the individual will provide personal information (name, address, marital status, and so forth), educational information (high school and colleges attended, diplomas or degrees awarded), military service information (dates of service, rank, type of discharge, current military status), work experience (types of work, dates of employment, reasons for leaving), personal health information (physical defects, current health problems), and personal references (names and addresses of individuals who know the applicant and can vouch for him or her).

The application form is often used in conjunction with the preliminary screening interview. It is also a helpful device for gathering personal information on the individual, and serves as a guide for the employment interview to follow.

3. What is the purpose of a preliminary screening interview?

4. How does the application form help a company in the employee selection process?

Employment Tests
Employment tests are designed to help the firm pinpoint the best candidates for each job. The most common type of test is that used to measure *intelligence and mental ability.* Others are designed to determine the individual's *interests, personality, attitudes,* and so forth. The specific type of test that is administered will, of course, depend on the job.

In recent years a great deal of attention has been given to testing, because many times employment tests have been misused. For example, a machinist's general intelligence may have no relation to his or her job ability. Therefore, to screen out such an

individual for not having a high IQ is questionable. Today business firms are trying to use tests that have proved to be both valid and reliable. By **valid** we mean that the test measures what it is supposed to measure. If a machinist is given a test to determine his or her manual dexterity and receives a high rating, this should mean that that person has good hand coordination and speed. If that person is in fact slow and clumsy, the test is not valid because it has not really measured manual dexterity. **Reliability** means that the test accurately and consistently measures the person's skill. Thus the machinist should do well on the test each time. As long as the firm uses tests that are valid and reliable, it should be able to successfully screen out those applicants who lack the required job abilities.

Background and Reference Checks
Many firms also run **background and reference checks** on the applicant. Most of these are in regard to previous work employment. The company wants to know how well the individual has performed in the past and why he or she left the job. Another common check is on personal references, although many firms tend to discount these because no one knowingly puts down a reference who will give them a bad recommendation. A third type of check is on school references, in which former teachers are asked about the applicant. A fourth is the credit check, which is used to obtain information such as whether the person pays bills on time. Of all of these, business relies most often on employment references because they provide the best insight into how well the person may perform in the future.

5. What are some of the common types of employment tests given by business firms?

6. Why is it so important that employment tests be both valid and reliable?

7. Are background and reference checks really of any value in the employment screening process?

Employment Interview

The most widely used screening technique is the **employment interview.** Recent statistics show that 98 percent of all firms use it. During this meeting the interviewer gets an opportunity to size up the applicant on a face-to-face basis. How well does the person communicate? Does the individual have a pleasing personal appearance? Does the person seem to be interested in the job? What is the applicant expecting from the firm in the way of salary and job opportunities? How well does this individual seem to fit the organization's needs? These are the types of questions the interviewer will often have in mind.

In terms of actually asking these questions, most firms use either a **structured interview** or a combination **structured-unstructured interview.** In a structured interview the interviewer follows a prepared format, asking one question after another. The purpose of this approach is to help gather specific data. In the structured-unstructured interview the interviewer often begins with a very unstructured approach, using questions designed to put the applicant at ease. As the interview moves along, the

---

CASE

Three Out of Ten

Harrow Printing had sales of $37 million last year. However, the company has been concerned over the fact that its labor turnover is high. Already this year 12 percent of the work force has quit. In an effort to fill these positions, the company has advertised in the local papers and has had a good response. This week it had openings for three press operators and received ten applications.

The personnel department performed the screening process and eliminated seven of the individuals almost immediately. Two of them had no prior experience in the printing industry. One had a heart condition and was screened out with the physical exam. Two others were turned down because a background check revealed that they had been fired from their previous jobs for drinking on the premises. The last two were eliminated because during the employment interview they indicated a minimum salary much higher than the job called for. The final three were sent to the plant floor, where they were hired by the supervisor.

1. What are the steps in the employee selection process?

2. If this company gave an employment test to these applicants, what might this test be like? Describe it.

3. In what way can the employee selection process help a company choose the best applicants? Explain.

interviewer then begins using structured questions to help gather data about the person and to direct the interview toward its objective. Many people prefer this approach to the structured interview.

Physical Examination

Many organizations require job applicants to take a *physical exam*. There are several important reasons for this. First, it can help determine whether the person is capable of performing the job in question. Second, if the individual has any serious or communicable diseases, they can be identified and treated. Third, if the person is injured on the job and files for workmen's compensation, his or her physical condition at the time of employment is known and the validity of the claim can be readily evaluated.

The physical exam is widely relied upon by firms hiring manual workers for hard labor. It is also helpful in identifying executive personnel who have not had the opportunity to do much physical labor and are now prone to heart attacks or other physical ailments. Screening these people out at this stage can be very important to the future of the firm.

8. Why do most people like the structured-unstructured interview better than the structured interview?

9. The physical exam is more important for incoming executives than for incoming workers. Explain this statement.

Employment Decision

If the applicant gets this far, the question now is: should he or she be hired? This decision will, of course, be made by the *manager in the department where this person will work*. With all of the background, testing, and interview information available for analysis, this manager should be in a good position to make the decision. Naturally, sometimes a competent person will be passed over and rejected; other times an individual will be hired and will not work out. With a carefully designed selection process, however, the chances of this occurring are greatly diminished.

TRAINING AND DEVELOPING THE PERSONNEL

Once employees are selected, it is necessary to train and develop them and keep them up to date. This last point is very important because much of the knowledge and skills obtained ten years ago are no longer very useful to the modern employee. Thus, training is a continuing challenge to the firm.

This training will vary, of course, depending upon the individual and his or her place in the organization. For example, workers often need one type of training while managers require another. In deciding who needs what, the firm will first review its training needs. This often entails interviewing department heads and managers to see what their people should have. From here a program is put together to meet these needs. This training can be done with either on-the-job methods or off-the-job methods.

On-the-Job Methods

The most widely employed methods of training and development take place **on the job.** The three most commonly used techniques are coaching, job rotation, and special assignments. For the most part the personnel department plays little role in this training.

Coaching

On-the-job **coaching** is very similar to that used by sports coaches. The manager responsible for coaching is charged with teaching, motivating, and counseling the trainees. Many people tend to regard coaching as simply encouraging and helping one's people, rather than a formal training and development technique. However, it is a very important method of teaching people the right way to do their jobs.

Training: the way it was.

Training: the way it is.

Job rotation

Another training and development technique is **job rotation.** This consists of moving an individual from one job to another, often for a month or two in each position, for the purpose of providing the trainee with different types of experience. If this rotation is carefully planned, it can serve not only to overcome job boredom but also to give the employee first-hand knowledge of the jobs he or she will be doing in the future.

Special assignments

Many firms give temporary **special assignments** to employees to provide them with the type of training they will need later in their careers. An illustration is that of assigning up-and-coming managers to top decision-making committees in the firm for the purpose of obtaining important experience.

Off-the-Job Methods

Off-the-job training is done away from the actual work place, with the personnel department often coordinating the activities. For example, many companies have their own classroom facilities. Those who do not will often hold their training sessions at a conference room in a nearby hotel. The actual training is often done by company personnel. However, in some cases the firm will rely upon professional training organizations such as the American Management Association, the American Society for Training and Development, or local university professors who are skilled in a particular area. Some of the most widely used off-the-job techniques include vestibule training; lecture, conference, or group discussion; and cases and role playing.

Vestibule training

In **vestibule training** the trainee is taught how to do the work in an environment that duplicates the on-the-job situation. For example, the individual may run a machine under the careful supervision of a foreman. When the person knows how to operate the machine properly, he or she is then sent to the shop floor. Once the necessary equipment and machinery is set up, the firm can use these facilities over and over again, making it an economical training method.

Lecture, conference, and group discussion

Some training consists of more than simply "how to do it." Managers, for example, need training and development in areas such as communication, motivation, and leadership. One way to carry out this training is through formal **lecture** presentation. However, many firms find that there is a need for discussion and interaction among the participants for the purpose of answering questions and stirring discussion. Did everyone understand the material? Are there any questions or comments anyone would like to make? Does anyone have a problem similar to the ones discussed here this morning, and did they use a solution like the one recommended in the lecture? To obtain this two-way communication, many companies supplement the lecture approach with **conference or group discussion** techniques. In this way more interaction among group members themselves, as well as between the members and the trainer, are obtained.

Cases and role playing

Cases and role playing are used to develop trainee sensitivities and analytical ability. In **case analysis,** the trainees are often given a written case that presents a situation or incident that might confront them on the job. For example, the case might relate the story of a subordinate who is continually late for work. The question then is what should the manager do? In case analysis, there is often no right answer. But by making individuals aware of various issues and problems, the cases prepare them for situations that will confront them on the job.

Role playing involves having the trainees act out a part as if they were in a stage play. In handling the problem of the late employee, for example, one trainee would play the role of the manager, another would assume the part of the subordinate. Each

The personnel department often coordinates the firm's training and development activities.

would then act out his or her part. The person playing the employee would get a much better idea of that individual's feelings and emotions, and the person playing the manager would gain experience in handling the problem. At the same time, the audience would obtain important insights into the problem and some potential solutions. One of the major reasons why companies use role playing in training and developing their people is that it helps create a better understanding of the problems and issues that will confront them on the job.

10. What are the most common methods of on-the-job training? Explain each.

11. How is vestibule training useful in teaching people "how-to-do-it" skills?

12. When might role playing be a useful training technique?

FIG. 10.4 *The proper way to train someone*

Keeping Up to Date

The big challenge in training and developing personnel is to identify the needs of the people and then to develop the right techniques for meeting these needs. New training methods in such behavioral areas as communication, motivation, and leadership will be needed. Greater application of cases and role playing, especially in management training and development, will also be required. The personnel department's job is that of keeping up to date in these areas so as to provide the best training in the most efficient manner. One way in which this can be done is simply by following the steps suggested in Fig. 10.4.

WAGE AND SALARY ADMINISTRATION

Another important personnel function is that of helping to develop an effective wage and salary program. The company needs to decide how much it will pay for each job in the firm, and what kinds of financial raises will be given in the near future. Because money is an important job factor, a firm's wage and salary program can spell the difference between maintaining skilled, productive employees and losing them to the competition.

Determining Wage and Salary Levels

There are many ways to determine the level of wages and salaries for employees. Some of the most common factors affecting these levels are discussed below.

Competitive wage rates

One factor that plays a key role in determining salary levels is **competitive wage rates.** How much are other firms paying for similar work in their company? The personnel department will often make use of community and industry surveys to determine competitive salary levels. Then the firm can compare its salaries to those of others to determine if it is paying too little, too much, or just the right amount. Many times the company will find that it has jobs that fit into each of these three categories. In such cases the company must be most concerned with those being paid too little, for it is these individuals who are most prone to being hired away by the competition.

Cost of living

A second key factor in salary level determination is **cost of living.** Especially during periods of inflation, there is pressure on management to raise salaries and keep wages up with prices. In many companies, employees are given cost-of-living raises on a semiannual or annual basis. At the end of whatever period has been chosen, the rise in the cost of living in the area is computed and the personnel are given salary increases based on some predetermined formula. These "built-in" raises help protect the personnel against spiraling inflation. In firms that have no cost-of-living raises there is, of course, constant pressure on the company to meet the competitive salaries offered by firms that do have such benefits.

Productivity

Productivity is another name for efficiency. As a firm becomes more and more efficient, it can afford to pay higher salaries. Conversely, if worker productivity declines, the company may have to hold the line on wages because its costs are going up and its profits are declining. Productivity is a key factor in wage and salary determination.

Ability to pay

Perhaps the most important factor in salary determination is **ability to pay.** Regardless of what the competition is offering, the firm must examine its own financial situation. Some companies are simply unable to meet the salaries paid by a firm across the street. They are always on the low end of the pay scale. Other companies are very profitable and tend to always pay above the industry average.

A Cost-of-Living Issue

Last year Harrow Printing agreed to give its employees an annual cost-of-living adjustment. The rise in the cost of living is computed at the end of each fiscal year, and all employees are given this percentage in addition to any merit increases they may have earned.

Some of the stockholders at the annual meeting objected to this development. They believed that this salary adjustment could be detrimental to the firm because it was in no way tied to productivity. If the inflation level rose all personnel would receive an increase in pay, regardless of their efficiency. These vocal opponents wanted the company to tie all salary raises directly to productivity.

When called upon to speak by the chairman of the board, the vice-president of personnel said that both cost of living and productivity were important factors in determining salaries. However, he pointed out that competitive wage rates also had to be considered. All the competitors in the nearby area offered their people cost-of-living adjustments and, to keep up, Harrow would have to also. After discussion between the vice-president and some of the stockholders, a motion was put forth giving support for management's decision to provide cost-of-living adjustments. The motion carried overwhelmingly.

1. In addition to the four factors mentioned in the case, what else helps determine wage and salary levels?

2. How important is it for a firm to offer competitive wages and salaries?

3. Do you agree with the cost of living adjustment? Explain.

Establishing a Wage and Salary Structure

After examining the above four factors, a company will establish a **wage and salary structure.** This is simply a process for determining how much money to pay each job. Quite often jobs will be divided according to type, such as clerical, machinist, and administrative. From here a salary range will be established for all jobs in each category. The minimum, average, and maximum for each will be determined. Then periodical appraisals of each job will be made to see if the salary is equitable. On occasion some employees will find their wages raised because the salary structure set them too low. If a salary is too high, on the other hand, further increases might be halted until the salary is brought into line with those of the other employees in that category.

In the case of top managers, salary is not as regulated. Usually the president sets the pace for all the rest, but there is no universal rule on how much everyone should receive. Quite often salaries are established based on what the competition is paying its managers. Recent research shows that in companies today the highest-paid executives tend to be in marketing. After this, in order, come manufacturing, product engineering, control, personnel, industrial engineering, and purchasing. Naturally, this order may differ by firm. If the personnel department is doing its job, however, it will be providing the company with the information needed to establish wage and salary structures at the low and medium levels of the organization as well as data related to competitive executive salaries for use at the upper levels of the hierarchy.

13. What are some of the factors that help determine the level of wages and salaries in a firm?

14. What is the most important factor in determining a firm's wage and salary levels?

15. How does a firm decide how much to pay its executives?

HEALTH, SAFETY, AND BENEFITS

The personnel department is often charged with putting together health, safety, and benefit programs for the firm. Many times this department is also responsible for seeing that these programs are implemented.

Health and Safety Programs

Employees who are sick or injured on the job are of little use to the company. For this reason, business has long been interested in the health and safety of its people. Since 1970, when the **Occupational Safety and Health Act (OSHA)** was enacted, particularly strong attention has been given to job safety. In fact, American business today is spending around three times as much for industrial safety as it did prior to the passage of OSHA. Measures to improve work safety include providing safety equipment to the employees, putting safety devices on machinery, and developing safety procedures to be used at all times.

In regard to the health needs of employees, just about every firm has some type of medical insurance. Many are also developing programs to help workers who have alcohol or emotional problems.

Since 1970, when the Occupational Safety and Health Act (OSHA) was enacted, particularly strong attention has been given to job safety.

Meanwhile, again in the safety area, there are accident and disability insurance programs in addition to those required by OSHA. The personnel department plays an important role in designing and implementing many of these programs.

Benefit Programs

Today most firms offer their employees a number of **benefit programs.** Typical examples are life insurance, pensions, severance pay, vacations, paid holidays, parties, and picnics. These programs used to be referred to as fringe benefits, but today the term "fringe" has been dropped because it implies extra frills. The cost of these benefits often runs between 25 percent and 33 percent of the company's total labor costs. In order to ensure the best coverage at the lowest price, many firms use their personnel department to coordinate and implement these programs for the entire organization.

16. Why has greater attention been given to worker safety in recent years?

17. What kinds of benefit programs do most firms make available to their personnel?

18. If the health, safety, and benefit programs cost so much, why does business not eliminate them?

Emotional Help

One of the most recent benefits being provided to employees is the Employee Assistance Program (EAP) that offers assistance in dealing with emotional problems. Large companies are now creating EAP departments staffed by psychologists and others skilled in dealing with employee problems such as alcoholism, drug abuse, and other emotional dilemmas. Small firms, meanwhile, are finding that they cannot justify such a department since the general rule is one in-house mental health professional for every 2,500 employees. However, small firms are able to contract EAP services from the large firms, which charge as little as $10 per covered employee. For this fee the EAP will train a client company's supervisors to spot a falloff in performance that can indicate emotional problems or alcoholism. They also provide literature for the employee, do diagnostic interviews with troubled workers, and either offer basic treatment or make referrals to more extensive treatment organizations.

Do workers like this new benefit? Many of them do, although some are afraid that if they are diagnosed as needing such counseling, or tell the specialist that they have a drinking problem, they are likely to suffer a career setback. After all, who wants to promote a confessed alcoholic? An astute business firm, however, does not attempt to pry into the activities of the EAP. Nevertheless, because of a desire for anonymity or secrecy, many employees admit that they prefer independent EAPs as opposed to in-house departments where confidentiality might be more difficult to maintain. In any event, it does seem that these programs are here to stay and according to social scientists, EAP is one of the best benefits a firm can offer its people.

SUMMARY

The personnel department plays an important role in helping the firm care for its human assets. Some of the areas where personnel is especially active include employee selection, training and development, wage and salary administration, and the implementation of health, safety, and benefit programs.

In employee selection, the personnel department helps by screening out those applicants who are not qualified for the job. This may occur at any of the seven stages of the employee selection process: the preliminary screening interview, review of the application form, employment testing, background and reference checks, the employment interview, the physical exam, or the employment decision. If the individual is hired, however, contact with the personnel department is far from over.

Personnel is often very active in helping to train and develop employees. Some of this is done on the job. A good deal of it, however, takes place off the job in the form of vestibule training, lectures, and case analysis and role playing.

A third important personnel activity is that of helping to develop a wage and salary structure for the firm. A fourth is the development and implementation of health, safety, and benefit programs. In both of these cases the personnel department assists the firm in providing some of the rewards necessary for maintaining competent personnel. It does this by conducting research and keeping the company aware of the most recent economic and competitive changes related to these areas.

KEY TERMS FOUND IN THIS CHAPTER

QUESTIONS FOR DISCUSSION AND ANALYSIS

1. In what way does the personnel department help a firm take care of its human assets?

2. What is a job description? Of what value is it to the company?

3. What types of information are usually contained on an application form? What is the purpose of collecting these data?

4. What does it mean to say that a test is valid? Reliable?

5. In terms of on-the-job training, what is meant by coaching? Job rotation?

6. How does vestibule training differ from role playing?

7. In what way do competitive wage rates influence a firm's wage and salary structure?

8. What are some of the common health, safety, and benefit programs provided by business to its personnel?

11

With all their faults, trade unions have done more for humanity than any other organization of men that ever existed.
Clarence Darrow

OBJECTIVES OF THIS CHAPTER

As noted in the last chapter, the personnel department plays an important role in seeing that employees are trained properly and paid equitably. In some companies, however, the workers are unwilling to rely exclusively on the firm to look after their interests. As a result, the workers unionize and directly negotiate salary, working conditions, and benefit packages with the company. In this chapter we will be examining management-union relations. The first objective is to present a brief history of the labor union movement in the United States. The second is to examine the organization structure and objectives of unions. The third is to review some of the important labor legislation that has been enacted over the last sixty years. And the final objective is to take a look at some of the tactics employed by labor and management during disputes and some of the methods used for resolving these disagreements. By the end of this chapter you should be able to do the following:

a. trace the rise of labor unions in this country;

b. describe the three levels of union organization;

c. explain how collective bargaining works and why it is so important to management-union relations;

d. identify the major goals of unions;

e. present a brief description of some of the major labor legislation enacted in the last sixty years; and

f. relate some of the common union and management tactics employed in labor disputes and some of the methods used in resolving these disagreements.

Management–Labor Relations

HISTORY OF LABOR UNIONS

Labor unions in the United States can be traced back hundreds of years. For example, in 1778 journeyman printers in New York City banded together to demand an increase in wages. Their attempts were successful and the organization soon disbanded. Eight years later, in 1786, Philadelphia printers struck for a $6-a-week minimum wage. They too were successful. The problem with these early unions, however, was that once they attained their objective, they often broke up.

By 1869 this was no longer true. In this year the first important national union, The Noble Order of the Knights of Labor, was founded. One of its early successes came against the railroads. After this, its membership began to grow. By 1886 it had over 700,000 members, but internal difficulties led to its eventual demise. However, a new union known as the **American Federation of Labor (AFL)** arose in its place. Led by Samuel Gompers, this union grew at a spectacular rate. By 1920, three-fourths of all organized workers were members of the AFL.

The AFL was a **craft union,** consisting of skilled workers such as carpenters, electricians, and plumbers. In 1935 a union was formed within the AFL for **industrial** workers, who were ineligible for membership in a craft union. This union was called the Committee for Industrial Organization. Membership in this new union grew as it quickly sought to bring in groups such as the auto workers and garment workers. In 1938, however, the union (which had now changed its name to the **Congress of Industrial Organizations (CIO)**) was expelled from the AFL because the latter feared it would lose status and security due to its affiliation with an industrial union. From 1938 to 1955 there were frequent confrontations between the AFL and the CIO. In 1955, however, these ended with their merger into the AFL-CIO, which we still have today.

1. What is the difference between a craft union and an industrial union? Put it in your own words.

WHY ARE THERE LABOR UNIONS?

The basic reason for labor unions is found in the adage that "in union there is strength." With the rise of the factory system in America, it did not take the workers long to realize that as individuals they were at a distinct disadvantage when dealing with a well-organized management. They too needed to attain a united front, and the best way was through a union.

Thus one of the major reasons for labor unions is that they provide a system of checks and balances against the arbitrary use of power by the company. A second, and complementary, reason is that they

Labor unions provide a system of checks and balances against the arbitrary use of power by the company.

serve as a spokesman for the workers in ensuring fair wages, job security, good working conditions, and equitable retirement benefits. A third reason is that they provide a means of satisfying some of the workers' psychological needs for such things as security, belongingness, and esteem.

The above three reasons are all intertwined. Yet each is important to the workers. As a result, it is highly likely that workers will *always* have a need for unions. In their efforts to meet this need, unions have become very well organized today.

2. What are some of the reasons for labor unions?

THE ORGANIZATION OF UNIONS

There are three major levels of organization in unions. Starting with the lowest, these are (a) the local, (b) the national or international, and (c) the federation.

The Local

The basic organizational unit for all labor groups is the **local union.** A local craft union, for example, would consist of all electricians in a particular city. A local industrial union will often be made up of all the workers in an assembly plant. Each of these locals will elect officers, admit new members, recruit others, and generally try to fashion the group into a cohesive organization. Locals tend to be very democratically run, with each member of the rank and file eligible to vote for local officers. At the present time there are around 70,000 locals in the United States.

The elected officials usually consist of a president, a secretary-treasurer, and an executive board. Some unions also have a business agent, a negotiating committee, and a grievance committee.

The president of a local is usually a worker who has been elected by the membership but who devotes only a part of his or her time to union duties. (Only large locals can afford a salaried, full-time president.) The president usually has a regular job with the firm and is paid a wage by the company. However, he or she is given time off by the firm to devote to union affairs, and works evenings and weekends as well at this union job. The local president is the chief union spokesman in contract negotiations with the company and, if unable to deliver what the membership consider a "suitable wage and salary package," will often be defeated in a bid for re-election.

Another important person in the local union organization is the **shop steward.** This individual is usually elected for a one-year term and it is his

A major goal of unions is to provide adequate compensation and insurance coverage for members whose work involves a high degree of risk.

How large is the membership in these nationals and internationals? The total was over 19 million by the early 1970s. Today, with such situations as unemployment and inflation confronting workers, this figure is estimated to be around 21 million as employees have sought the assistance of unions. Some of the largest unions are listed in Table 11.1. Overall, approximately 33 percent of the eligible nonagricultural civilian labor work force are organized.

TABLE 11.1 TEN LARGEST LABOR UNIONS IN THE U.S.

UNION	MEMBERSHIP
Teamsters	1,888,895
Automobile workers	1,358,354
Steelworkers	1,300,000
Electrical	923,560
Machinists and aerospace	917,226
Carpenters	820,000
Retail clerks	699,200
Laborers	627,406
Meat cutters	509,903
Clothing and textile	502,000

Source: Bureau of Labor Statistics.

or her duty to see that management lives up to its contract. This individual is to the union what the supervisor is to management. If a supervisor wants to take action against a worker, the shop steward will always be called in to represent the worker. This person is the backbone of the union local.

The National
Most local unions are "affiliated," or associated, with a **national** or **international union.** (The only difference between a national and an international is that the latter takes in locals from other countries, such as Canada or Mexico.) The **national union** provides strength and support to the affiliated locals. For example, if the local electricians union in one city affiliates with the national electricians union, it is combining its forces with those of many other local electricians unions. In turn, the national can help each of them negotiate contracts and work for better conditions. Well-known national unions include the Teamsters, the Steelworkers, and the United Auto Workers. Each plays an important role in helping its affiliated locals.

The Federation
Just as the locals join together into a national union, so also many of the nationals have joined the AFL-CIO **federation.** The theory behind such a federation is the same as that for locals affiliating with a national—"in union there is strength." Most of the large nationals are members of this federation—although some, such as the Teamsters, United Auto Workers, and United Mine Workers, are not. These three nationals withdrew from the federation some years ago.

The AFL-CIO provides a number of important services to the affiliated national unions. Perhaps the most important of these is its efforts to secure passage of legislation at the local, state, and federal levels that is favorable to organized labor. An organization chart of the AFL-CIO is presented in Fig. 11.1.

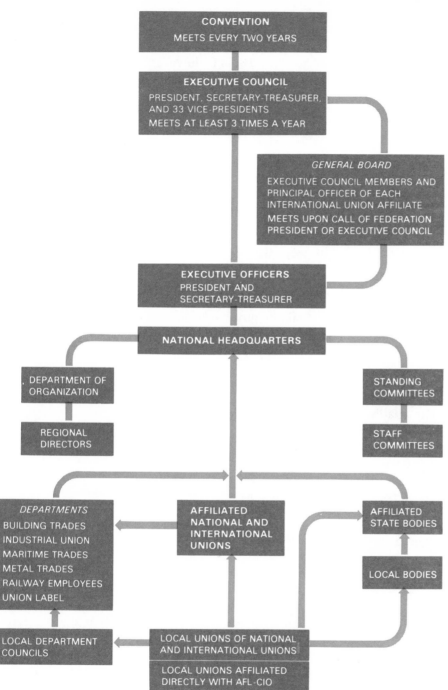

FIG. 11.1 *Organization structure of the AFL-CIO*
(*Source:* Bureau of Labor Statistics, Directory of National Unions and Employee Associations, *1971*).

Every two years delegates from the national and international unions hold a policy-making convention. Between these convention meetings, the AFL-CIO is run by the Executive Council. The General Board considers policy questions referred to it by the officers or the Executive Council.

The federation is the most powerful labor organization in the country. Over 75 percent of all organized labor hold membership in unions affiliated with the AFL-CIO. As a result, the federation can be very helpful in providing both assistance and advice to its member unions.

3. What benefits can a national union provide to the affiliated local unions?

4. What benefits can the AFL-CIO federation provide to the national unions affiliated with it?

COLLECTIVE BARGAINING

Workers form a union so that they can bargain as a united group. The process of the union and management coming together to negotiate a labor contract is known as **collective bargaining.** It is at this time that management puts forth an offer and the union relates what it is looking for from the company. For example, management may offer an 8-percent across-the-board salary increase and a 6-percent increase in the benefit program, while the union seeks 10 and 7 percent respectively. In addition, both sides will discuss other contract matters such as overtime pay, seniority rights, working hours, paid vacations, and holidays.

In these discussions, both sides will explain the reasons for their demands. From here it is a matter of negotiation. Management will often give on one point if the union will give on another. Keep in mind, however, that this process is not a simple one. Each side may bring up a number of unimportant issues simply so it can drop them if the other side

gives in on another particular issue. For example, the union may not believe that a four-week vacation for workers with over twenty years on the job is really worth pursuing. However, it may bring it up in the hopes that management will counter by saying, "We can't give you that but we will give you an increase in the benefit package." Both sides will load up on issues, real and imaginary, before going into the bargaining session.

Of course, each knows that the other has some minor issues that it will raise. As a result, both sides will spar with each other very carefully. Neither wants to give up on an issue the other side will give in to; by the same token there is no sense in fighting over a minor matter that has little relevance to the overall contract.

When all is said and done, a labor agreement will have been hammered out. Some students of labor relations believe that this contract is always a middle-ground position. That is, if management offers a 6-percent salary raise and the union wants 12 percent, they will settle on 9 percent. This is totally wrong. The final contract will be determined by which side is strong enough to work its will on the other. During good economic times, the contract may call for a 10 or 11 percent salary increase. During poor times, the agreement may be for 6 or 7 percent.

A relatively new technique employed by unions to improve their strength at the bargaining table is known as **coalition bargaining.** Some companies have a number of different unions with which they must bargain. For example, there may be electricians, plumbers, steelworkers, and carpenters unions all representing various groups within one company. General Electric deals with more than eighty unions, Union Carbide with over twenty-five, and American Standard, Inc., with five. In order to strengthen their hand, some unions have begun aligning themselves into a coalition or united front and started pushing for standard fringe benefits for *all* personnel, standard wage increases, and a common expiration date for *all* contracts. In short, coalition bargaining allows

A New Arrangement

Chrysler Chairman Lee Iacocca and UAW President Douglas Fraser after Fraser was elected to Chrysler's board of directors. It marked the first time a national union leader has penetrated the directorship of a major corporation.

People talk a lot about the conflict that often exists between unions and management. However, conflict does not always present the same face. For example, recently the Chrysler Corporation has found itself in dire financial straits. Its share of the auto market has been falling and in 1979 the firm reported record losses. This bodes badly not only for stockholders but also for the union. After all, if the firm is not doing well, the union can hardly hope to get large increases in its wage or benefit package.

However, while it appears that the union will have to yield on pay demands, it is apparently going to insist on a new relationship with the firm. In particular, union leaders feel that Chrysler has been badly managed, and they now want to have a voice in such management decisions as production scheduling. While this idea of union involvement in decision making has been popular in western Europe, it is foreign in this country. In fact, many union leaders have long felt that obtaining representation on the board of directors would mean giving up their adversary bargaining position and thereby weaken their ability to speak for the workers. However, the idea does appear particularly feasible at Chrysler. Over 16,000 of their salaried workers are involved in a thrift stock purchase plan, through which they have secured more than 15 percent of the company's common shares outstanding. Thus the workers already hold a substantial share of the ownership, so why not give them more of a voice in the management? Will this come to pass? While it is still too early to tell, one union official has put it this way, "I'm no socialist, but if a guy works for the company, he just works for it. If he owns it, he has a right to call the shots." Thus the future may see greater involvement of unions in the decision-making process of American businesses.

unions to present a united front and prevent the management from negotiating separate contracts with each of them. Management, of course, has viewed this development of coalition bargaining with great alarm, feeling that it gives the unions too much power. Despite management protests, however, the courts have upheld the use of this form of bargaining.

5. Define the term collective bargaining.

OBJECTIVES OF THE UNION

Unions have two basic objectives. First, they want to secure better economic conditions from the management for their members. Second, they want to obtain favorable legislation at the national and state levels. This latter objective becomes particularly evident on election day, when the unions try to bring about the election of candidates who support pro-labor legislation. Meanwhile, in the economic arena, the union has tried to help the workers by securing (a) higher wages and shorter hours, (b) guaranteed seniority rights, (c) union security, and (d) job retention.

Higher Wages and Shorter Hours

One of the primary aims of every union is to obtain *higher wages* and *shorter hours* for its people. These two factors are actually interrelated, in that shorter hours can often result in higher wages. For example, if workers secure a thirty-five-hour week but management still requires their services for forty hours, they are paid overtime (often 1½ times the normal rate). In addition, every wage increase means more money, whether or not they get overtime.

Guaranteed Seniority Rights

Another major goal of unions is to secure contracts that guarantee **seniority rights.** This means that those who have held their jobs for the longest period of time are given certain privileges. For example, in the case of layoffs those with seniority are often laid off last and rehired first. Some contracts allow a worker who is laid off from one job to **"bump"** an individual on another job. For example, lathe operator #4, if laid off, can replace or bump lathe operator #3. Other contracts permit bumping on a less restricted basis. In many cases, for example, bumping is not confined to specific jobs but is done on a departmental or overall company basis. In this case, a lathe operator may end up bumping a painter. Regardless of the particular method of bumping, individuals with seniority manage to keep a job.

Union Security

Union security is obtained when the company agrees to recognize and negotiate with the union chosen by the workers. Unions have sought to attain this security in numerous ways.

Closed shop

The **closed shop** is one in which the company agrees to hire only union members in good standing. This type of shop was outlawed in interstate commerce by the National Management Relations Act of 1947. However, it still continues to exist in some industries such as construction and printing.

Union shop

A **union shop** is one in which the company can hire nonunion people, but they have to join the union after a prescribed period of time and remain in good standing as members. If they do not, they can be fired.

Agency shop

In an **agency shop** employees who are not members of the union are still required to pay union dues. However, they do not have to join the union. Union members feel that this is only fair, since it is the labor union that fights for higher wages and better conditions for them. Nonunion members, of course, might disagree. However, the agency shop has been held by the courts to be a lawful form of union security.

At the age of seventeen, Addie Wyatt started her career in business by putting lids on cans of stew at Armour and Company. It was not long, however, before she became involved in union activities. A member of the United Packinghouse, Food and Allied Workers Union (now merged with Amalgamated Meat Cutters), she eventually served as an organizer, negotiator, and program coordinator. In 1954 she became the first woman president of a packinghouse local and later was appointed one of the five women international representatives of the United Packinghouse. In 1974 she was made director of the Women's Affairs department of the Amalgamated Meat Cutters and Butcher Workmen of North America, AFL-CIO.

In her active union roles, Addie Wyatt has continually fought to eradicate all vestiges of discriminatory employer practices, particularly those leveled against women. Expressing her feelings on this matter, she has said, "Amalgamated women know that they have made

progress because of the union. They know too that banding together in true trade union solidarity will attain for them improved benefits. They know that the men in the union cannot and should not be asked to do the job of achieving progress for all alone. Women are ready to become full partners in the struggle for a decent way of life. Their skills and talent are needed and they are willing to contribute to the union cause."

Currently she is the International Vice–President, Director, Civil Rights and Women's Affairs Department of the United Food & Commercial Workers International Union, AFL–CIO & CLC. This union is a new one based on the merger of the Amalgamated Meat Cutters Union and the Retail Clerks Union. The recipient of many awards, Addie Wyatt recently was selected as an Outstanding Illinois Woman. She also received the 1979 Outstanding Achiever in Community Leadership award, presented by the YWCA of Metropolitan Chicago.

Addie Wyatt

Open shop
The **open shop** is one in which the workers decide whether or not they wish to join a union. As a result, both union and nonunion employees may be working in the organization. A major distinction between the open shop and the agency shop is that those open-shop employees who choose *not* to join the union *do not* have to pay dues as they do in the agency shop. While labor unions are opposed to the open shop, it continues to exist, particularly in those states that have "right-to-work" laws, which prohibit union

shops and other security agreements. For the most part, these are states that are not heavily industrialized.

Maintenance of membership
Under a **maintenance of membership** arrangement, employees do not have to belong to a union to obtain or keep their jobs. However, union members who are employed by the firm at the time such an arrangement becomes effective, or who join at a later date, must maintain such membership in good

standing for the rest of the contract period. Otherwise they can be fired. This arrangement could exist in all situations described above except the open shop.

Job Retention

Another major union goal is *job retention*. The union wants to preserve jobs so that it loses none of its members. One common method of accomplishing this is to urge a **"spread-the-work" policy.** This means that instead of laying people off, the company merely cuts the number of hours everyone is working. Another method, which is currently being eliminated, is *featherbedding,* in which jobs have continued in existence long after the need for them has disappeared.

6. In the case of job layoffs, what is meant by bumping?

7. How does a union shop differ from an agency shop?

8. What is a maintenance of membership arrangement? Explain.

CASE
Contract Time

Every three years, the union at Harrow Printing negotiates a new labor contract with the management. A number of years ago it got management to agree to a union shop. This time around the union's big push is going to be for higher wages and more guaranteed seniority rights.

Due to poor economic conditions in the area, the union believes management will fight hard to keep wage increases under 8 percent. The union, however, feels that because inflation in the immediate area has averaged 10.6 percent over each of the last three years, a minimum salary raise of 11 percent across the board is in order. In fact, it would really like to see the company agree to cost-of-living adjustments every six months instead of annually. However, this is probably too much to hope for. In addition to better wages and seniority rights, of course, the union intends to push for an increase in the benefit package. At the present time it is unsure of how many of its demands will be met, but it is optimistic.

1. What else besides that mentioned in the case do you think the union will be seeking in a new contract?

2. How does this labor negotiating process work? What goes on during contract negotiations?

3. If this local is affiliated with a national, how might the latter help them in securing the best possible contract?

LABOR LEGISLATION

Over the past sixty years a number of important pieces of labor legislation have been enacted. Some of the most important of these are presented below. Each has been useful in helping to shape the current status of unions.

Railway Labor Act of 1926

This act applied only to the railroad industry. However, portions of it were used to help frame other labor legislation in the years that followed.

The main provision of the **Railway Labor Act** was the requirement that employers bargain collectively with their employees. The act also outlawed the **yellow-dog contract,** which was a written pledge not to join a union or attempt to form one. Prior to this legislation, many railroads refused to hire individuals who would not sign such an agreement. A third provision of this act was the establishment of procedures for settling management-labor disputes.

Norris-LaGuardia Act of 1932

Enacted in 1932, this legislation took some of the provisions of the Railway Labor Act and expanded them to include all workers. For example, it outlawed the use of yellow-dog contracts in all industries. The act also prohibited employers, except in specific instances, from using injunctions to prevent work stoppages by employees. Many people feel that this law guaranteed the survival of unions.

National Labor Relations Act of 1935

This act, often known as the *Wagner Act,* was designed to help workers organize into unions that were free from employer domination. The law was also intended to secure recognition for these unions from their own companies. In achieving these objectives, the act listed five unfair labor practices in which employers were *forbidden* to engage. These included

1. interfering with or restraining employees involved in either self-organizing activities or collective bargaining with the firm;

2. dominating or interfering in the formation or administration of any labor organization or contributing financially to its support;

3. taking any action against employees as a means of either encouraging or discouraging union membership;

4. firing or taking action against employees because they had filed or given testimony under the act; and

5. refusing to bargain collectively with those representatives chosen by the employees.

The act also set up a **National Labor Relations Board.** The board consisted of three members (later expanded to five) who were affiliated with neither industry nor labor. The job of this board is to prevent employers from engaging in the unfair labor practices listed above and to conduct elections among employees to determine who will bargain collectively for them. These elections are held when employees decide they would like to consider unionizing. In the election they can then vote whether or not to do so and with which union they would like to affiliate. If the vote is for unionizing, this union will represent the employees in all matters of wages, hours, and other conditions of employment. From 1935 to 1947 the **National Labor Relations Act** provided a fertile ground for unionization and organized labor increased its membership dramatically.

Labor-Management Relations Act of 1947

Many people felt that the Wagner Act went too far in that it was overly favorable to labor. As a result, in 1947 the **Labor-Management Relations Act** was passed. Often known as the *Taft-Hartley Act,* its purpose was to swing the pendulum back toward management so that there was a more equal balance of power between management and labor. Taft-Hartley is actually an amendment to the Wagner Act. Thus the Wagner Act, except as amended or repealed by Taft-Hartley, still remains in effect today.

A striking firefighter stands before a blazing vacant house a few hours after the city's 900 firefighters walked off the job. They were protesting the dismissal of 42 co-workers who took part in a previous strike.

In particular, Taft-Hartley enumerated specific unfair *labor* practices. Some of these are

1. pressuring employees into joining the union (except in the case of a union shop) or attempting to coerce employers in selecting their representatives for collective bargaining;

2. refusing to bargain collectively with the employer;

3. charging excessive or discriminatory initiation fees to its members; or

4. charging the employer for services that were not performed.

Labor-Management Reporting and Disclosure Act of 1959

Also known as the *Landrum-Griffith Act,* this law was passed as a result of the McClellan Committee investigations, which found racketeering and financial irresponsibility in some unions. The act's provisions require that all unions file a complete and detailed annual report with the secretary of labor, and that this same information also be made available to the union members. They make embezzlement of union funds a crime and require that union officers be bonded by American firms in order to protect these funds. Another major provision of the act provides for the protection of union members' rights. All members can nominate candidates for union office, vote in union elections, attend union meetings, and have a voice in union matters. The Landrum-Griffith Act has resulted in the government playing a much more active role in management-labor relations. Some individuals feel it is an attempt to regulate union morality. Most, however, believe it is a positive step toward protecting the average union member and seeing that all of them get a fair deal.

9. How did the Norris-LaGuardia Act help the unions?

10. What are the major provisions of the National Labor Relations Act?

11. How did the Labor-Management Relations Act modify the Wagner Act?

UNION TACTICS

Working within the framework provided by the above legislation, unions have been able to attain many of their objectives. Sometimes, however, labor and management have been unable to reach agreement. When this occurs unions tend to employ a number of bargaining tactics designed to win them their way.

Strike

A **strike** is a temporary refusal by workers to continue doing their jobs until their demands are met by management. The most common form of strike occurs when the employees stay away from the plant. There is also the *sitdown strike,* in which the workers go to their jobs but refuse to do anything. This form of strike has been declared illegal. Another version is the *slowdown strike,* in which the employees simply reduce their work tempo so that very little gets done.

Boycott

A **boycott** is a technique by which union members try to bring economic pressure against a company by encouraging people not to buy the firm's goods. If the union refuses to buy the goods, it is called a *primary boycott.* If the union uses these boycott tactics against other firms doing business with their company, it is called a *secondary boycott.* Most secondary boycotts are illegal.

Picketing

In an effort to bring pressure on management, unions will sometimes use **picketing.** This is a practice in which workers march at the entrance of a company's building or plant, usually carrying or wearing signs that identify their complaints against the firm. This procedure can not only be embarrassing to the company but it can keep other employees away from the job, because they do not wish, or are afraid, to cross the picket line. This is

A **lockout** consists of refusing to allow the workers to enter the company's facilities.

especially true when there is more than one union in the firm. For example, the telephone operators are members of the Communication Workers of America while some of the other employees are members of the Electricians Union. If one pickets, the other will often "honor" the picket line.

12. Why do unions go on strike?

13. What is a boycott?

MANAGEMENT TACTICS

Management also has tactics it employs when bargaining with the union. These are designed to apply pressure and/or counter some of the union tactics described above.

Lockout

The **lockout** is management's strongest weapon. It consists of simply refusing to allow the workers to enter the company's facilities. In a manner of speaking, the lockout is a management strike. Quite often it entails a shutting down of all the operating facilities. Sometimes, however, if the work is not too technical, the managers will try to keep the company going by performing these operations themselves.

Injunction

An **injunction** is a court order, obtained by the employer, that forbids the union from interfering

Twin lines of cars and pedestrians cross the Brooklyn Bridge to Manhattan during New York City's transit strike. About 30,000 walked, 25,000 rode bikes, and 10,000 boated to work.

229

with the company's operations. Often an injunction is issued to restrict mass picketing or to prevent damage to company property. If the union refuses to obey the injunction, it can be held in contempt of court and its leaders are subject to fine and/or imprisonment.

Employer's Associations

In recent years unions have been demanding industry-wide bargaining in which all unions and companies in a particular industry negotiate contracts at the same time. To meet this united union front, business firms have begun forming **employer's associations.** These associations, acting as representatives of the individual employers, bargain with the unions. This approach is useful in strengthening management's hand at the contract table, especially among those unions using coalition bargaining.

14. What is an injunction? What is its purpose?

SETTLING LABOR DISPUTES

Sometimes management and labor simply cannot reach an agreement on a particular dispute. When this occurs it is necessary to bring in an outside party to solve the problem. The most common roles for this third party are (a) conciliation, (b) mediation, and (c) arbitration.

CASE

Here Comes the Judge

The union at Harrow Printing recently had a labor dispute with the company. It seems that one of the men had gotten into an argument with a supervisor. After a heated exchange, the man was laid off for ten days. The union objected to this, saying that the penalty was too stiff. The management, however, refused to back down. Since an impasse had been reached, both sides insisted that the labor contract clause calling for automatic arbitration be initiated.

As a result, an arbitrator was brought in and both sides presented their arguments to him. After evaluating them, the arbitrator agreed with the union that the penalty was too stiff. Five days suspension would have been enough. Since the man had already been laid off for ten days, the firm was directed to reimburse the individual for one week's back wages. Although the contract called for voluntary arbitration, the company did not hesitate to pay the man. The payroll department was directed to draw up a check immediately.

1. When is it common to find both sides willing to submit an issue to arbitration?

2. What are the benefits of arbitration?

3. Since this was voluntary arbitration, did the company have to comply with the ruling? Explain.

Conciliation

Conciliation occurs when the parties to the dispute invite in a third person to help them out. This individual's role is to encourage both labor and management to rethink their positions and work toward a solution of the problem. The conciliator serves as a catalyst in resolving the dispute.

Mediation

In **mediation** this third party takes a more active role. For example, unlike the conciliator, the mediator will often make suggestions for resolving the problem. Of course, neither side is required to accept these recommendations, but this person's participation can help the parties reach a solution.

Arbitration

In **arbitration** both sides actually turn the case over to a third party. Sometimes this individual acts as the sole umpire in resolving the dispute; other times the person serves on a board with one representative from management and one representative from the union.

After hearing the facts, the third party makes a decision. If management and labor are operating under *voluntary arbitration,* they are *morally* bound to accept the decision. If they are operating under *compulsory arbitration,* they are *legally* bound to accept the decision. In most cases, the parties prefer voluntary arbitration, because compulsory arbitration has never really proved to be a satisfactory method of achieving good management-labor relations.

15. How can conciliation help settle a labor dispute?

16. How does a mediator differ from an arbitrator?

17. What is the difference between voluntary and compulsory arbitration?

A New Ballgame

The economic recession of the late 1970s may have tamed some of the restiveness of the work force, but it has not altered the values of many of these workers, especially the young ones. With the current upsurge in the economy, these workers will again be making themselves heard. And researchers report that today's young workers are very different from their older counterparts. For example, they are less likely to just obey orders and much more likely to ask "why." In addition, they tend to have much higher expectations. For example, younger workers want better working conditions, greater health-care coverage, more meaningful work, and more secure retirement programs than do the older workers. More importantly, perhaps, is the fact that in a few years the post-World War II generation that holds these values will make up a majority of the nation's work force. What does this mean for corporations and unions? It means that unless these two groups can get together and find ways for meeting these new demands, there is going to be growing worker dissatisfaction. What made workers happy thirty years ago will not do today. It is a whole new ballgame.

THE NEED FOR COOPERATION

In this chapter we have examined management-labor relations. Before concluding, however, it is important to remember that the success of these relations depends upon mutual cooperation. Management must do its best for its workers by offering a contract that provides a fair salary, good working conditions, and reasonable benefits. Unions must make management live up to these obligations. At the same time, however, unions must refrain from demanding too much from the company.

In the final analysis, cooperation is based on fair play by both sides. Any attempt by one to exploit the other will result in a backlash. Each side has tactics it can use. The history of management-labor relations in this country has made this all too clear. As we move through the 1980s it is likely that the economic growth of the United States will begin to stabilize. Operating in such an environment will require a great deal of cooperation by both labor and management. Remember, each needs the other.

SUMMARY

Over the last one hundred years we have witnessed the rise of labor unions in America. The primary reason for them is that "in union there is strength."

The basic organizational unit for all unions is the local. Whether it be a craft or industrial union, the local's members vote for officers and participate in the running of the organization. In order to gain strength, most locals are affiliated with a national or international union. Likewise, most of these nationals are members of the AFL-CIO federation.

One of the main functions of a union is to bargain collectively for its members. This involves negotiating the labor contract. In this contract the union attempts to attain its basic goals, including higher wages, shorter working hours, guaranteed seniority rights, union security, and the retention of workers' jobs.

Over the last sixty years a number of important pieces of labor-related legislation have been enacted. Some of these have been pro-labor, such as the Railway Labor Act, the Norris-LaGuardia Act, and the National Labor Relations Act. One, however, the Labor-Management Relations Act, strengthened management's hand by identifying unfair labor practices. Meanwhile the latest major legislation, the Labor-Management Reporting and Disclosure Act, has attempted to protect union members from exploitation by those running the union.

Within the above legal framework, management and labor conduct their activities. When one side feels it is not getting a fair deal, however, it is likely to rely upon some special bargaining tactics. Unions tend to use the strike, boycott, and picket. Management employs the lockout, injunction, and employer's associations. If the two find they simply cannot reach agreement in a dispute, however, it is then common to find them turning to conciliation, mediation, or even arbitration. In the final analysis, of course, it is beneficial to both sides if they can cooperate and work in harmony.

KEY TERMS FOUND IN THIS CHAPTER

QUESTIONS FOR DISCUSSION AND ANALYSIS

1. Will there always be a need for labor unions? Explain.

2. How does a shop steward help out union members?

3. How does an open shop differ from a closed shop?

4. What is meant by a spread-the-work policy?

5. In what way did the Railway Labor Act affect unionization?

6. What is an employer's association?

7. How does conciliation differ from mediation?

8. Why do many companies and unions dislike compulsory arbitration?

CAREERS
IN PRODUCTION AND HUMAN
RESOURCE MANAGEMENT

In one way or another, all businesses produce some kind of a good or service. As a result, production management and its key subareas such as purchasing and production control offer business career opportunities. So does human resource management, which has openings in areas such as personnel management and labor relations. In more specific terms, the following paragraphs provide descriptions of a handful of the careers that are available in these fields. The accompanying matrix shows the employment outlook through 1985. While reading the salary ranges and employment information, remember that these are entry-level averages for these careers, and many of those employed have college degrees.

SUPERVISOR

A supervisor manages workers directly, telling them what is to be done and ensuring that the work is carried out properly. The supervisor maintains work schedules, keeps production and employee records, and uses judgment in planning and dealing with control problems. The manager is also charged with telling the subordinates about company plans and policies, rewarding high performance by recommending wage increases and promotions (as well as laying off or firing poor workers), and in those firms where there is a union, knowing the provisions of the labor-management contract and running the operation in accord with this agreement.

PURCHASING AGENT

This person is responsible for obtaining goods and services of the required quality and at the lowest possible cost. In a manufacturing firm this individual buys machinery, raw materials, product components, and services; in a nonmanufacturing setting the person is responsible for buying office supplies, furniture, and business machines. Additionally, when stocks on hand reach a predetermined reorder point, the purchasing agent buys more of them. Finally, when the goods are received this individual checks to see that the quality and quantity are in conformance with the company's order and then authorizes payment to the shipper.

INDUSTRIAL TRAFFIC MANAGER

Industrial firms want to receive raw materials and deliver the customer's goods promptly, safely, and with minimum cost. Arranging for the transportation of materials and finished products is another task for the industrial traffic manager. This individual also analyzes various transportation possibilities and chooses the most efficent one for the firm— air, rail, road, water, pipeline. These activities range from checking freight bills to deciding whether the company should buy its own fleet of rail cars or trucks or should contract for these services. The individual is also responsible for keeping records of shipments, freight rates, commodity classifications, and applicable government regulations.

INDUSTRIAL ENGINEER

This individual is responsible for determining the most effective ways for the organization to use the basic factors of production: people, machines, and materials. In solving organizational, production, and related problems most efficiently, this person

SOURCE: *Occupational Outlook Handbook*, 1978–79 Edition, U.S. Department of Labor, Bureau of Labor Statistics

designs data processing systems and applies mathematical concepts. The individual also develops management control systems to help in financing planning and cost analysis, designs production planning and control systems to coordinate activities and to control product quality, and designs and improves systems for the physical distribution of goods and services.

PERSONNEL AND LABOR RELATIONS WORKERS

There are many people who fall into this career category, from personnel and employment recruiters to job analysts, wage administrators, and labor relations specialists. Speaking in overall terms, these people are responsible for interviewing, selecting, and recommending applicants to fill job openings. They also handle wage and salary administration, training and career development, and employee benefits. Another important assignment is helping officials of the firm prepare for collective bargaining sessions with the union. In a small firm, one or two workers may perform many of these functions, while in a large organization there will be numerous people in the personnel and labor relations department(s).

PSYCHOLOGIST

The psychologist studies the behavior of individuals and groups in order to understand and explain their actions. In so doing, the person gathers information about the capabilities, interests, and behaviors of people. In a business setting the most common type of psychologist is the industrial or organizational

psychologist. The person engages in personnel research, policy and planning, training and development, counseling, and organizational development.

SOCIOLOGIST

The sociologist studies human society and social behavior by examining the groups that people form. In a business setting the individual is interested in organizational groups and works closely with other behavioral scientists in the firm to provide counseling, guidance, training and development for the personnel.

MANUFACTURING INSPECTOR

Most products need to be checked by inspectors at some point during the manufacturing process to ensure that they are of desired quality. The manufacturing inspector may use a variety of methods in doing this. Some of the most common responsibilities include physically examining the goods produced, using tools or calculations to measure parts, and examining blueprint to verify that the product conforms to standards. While the semiskilled inspector usually works under close inspection, the skilled inspector typically has authority to accept or reject most products, analyzes the reasons for faulty construction, and recommends corrective action.

OCCUPATIONAL SAFETY AND HEALTH WORKER

Workers in this field are responsible for ensuring a safe and healthful environment for workers and safe products for consumers. These individuals strive to

CAREERS IN PRODUCTION AND HUMAN RESOURCE MANAGEMENT (continued)

control occupational accidents and diseases, property losses, and injuries from unsafe products. The largest group of these workers are safety engineers. In large manufacturing plants, these people are responsible for developing a comprehensive safety program. This usually involves a detailed analysis of each job in the plant, to identify potential hazards so that preventive measures can be taken. When accidents do occur, the safety engineer's job is to investigate the cause of the problem and to use technical skills to correct the situation and prevent recurrence.

EMPLOYMENT COUNSELOR

The employment counselor provides advice and assistance to those seeking jobs. Many of the latter are handicapped, have been displaced by automation, or are unhappy with their present occupational choices and are seeking to change jobs. Others have little education and marketable skills and need intensive training to prepare for jobs. The counselor interviews job-seekers, learns about their employment-related background, interests, training, work experience, attitudes, physical capacities, and personal traits. In some cases the counselor may also arrange for aptitude and achievement tests and interest inventories so that more objective advice can be given.

Then the individual provides assistance such as suggesting employment sources and appropriate ways of applying for work. After job placement, the counselor may follow up to determine if additional assistance is required.

MAINTENANCE ELECTRICIAN

The maintenance electrician keeps lighting systems, transformers, generators, and other electrical equipment in good working order. The individual is also able to install new electrical equipment. Depending on where the person is employed, duties will vary greatly. The person who works in a large factory may repair particular items such as motors and welding machines; while the individual who works in an office building or small plant usually fixes all kinds of electrical equipment. Regardless of the organization's size, the individual makes periodic inspection of equipment to locate and correct defects before breakdowns occur and, if they do, finds the cause and eliminates it as efficiently as possible. Sometimes the individual must also be able to work from blueprints or wire diagrams, and to use meters and other testing devices to locate faulty equipment, and make repairs using such common tools as pliers, screwdrivers, drills, and wire cutters.

CAREER	LATEST EMPLOYMENT FIGURES	EARNINGS	EMPLOYMENT OUTLOOK
Supervisor	1,445,000	$15,000–$18,000	About the same as the average for all occupations
Purchasing agent	190,000	$16,000–$25,000 [a]	Faster than the average for all occupations
Industrial traffic manager	21,000	$12,000–$15,000 [b]	Faster than the average for all occupations
Industrial engineer	200,000	$16,000–$18,000	Faster than the average for all occupations
Personnel and labor relations	335,000	$13,500–$15,000	About as fast as the average for all occupations
Psychologist	90,000	$13,000–$15,000+[e]	Faster than the average for all occupations
Sociologist	19,000	$13,000–$15,000+[e]	Slower than the average for all occupations
Manufacturing inspector	692,000	$14,000–$17,000	Faster than the average for all occupations
Occupational safety and health worker	28,000	$15,000–$18,000	Faster than the average for all occupations
Employment counselor	7,500	$12,000–$15,000	About the same as the average for all occupations
Maintenance electrician	300,000	$13,000–$15,000	About the same as the average for all occupations

[a] Although senior purchasing agents can earn over $50,000
[b] Although some senior executives earn over $50,000
[e] Salary depends heavily on whether the individual has a master's or doctor's degree

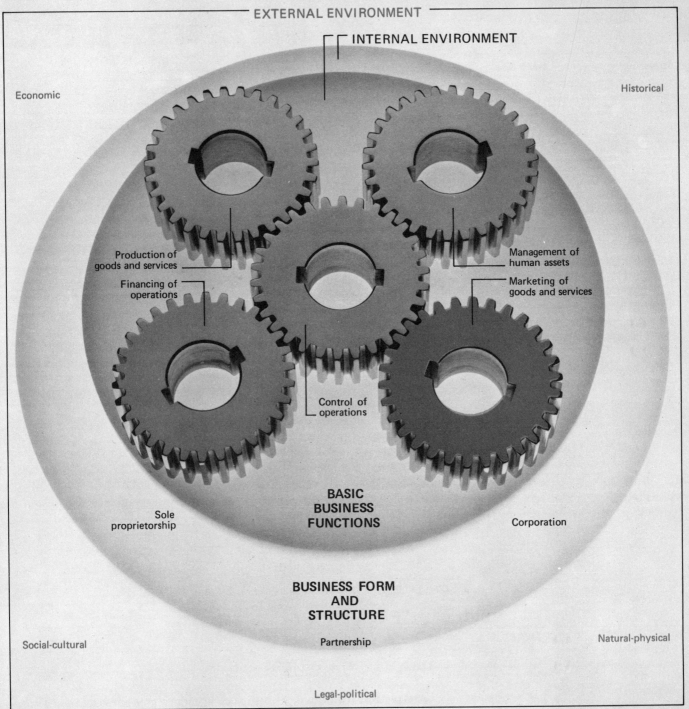

EXTERNAL ENVIRONMENT

INTERNAL ENVIRONMENT

Economic

Historical

Production of
goods and services

Management of
human assets

Financing of
operations

Marketing of
goods and services

Control of
operations

**BASIC
BUSINESS
FUNCTIONS**

Sole
proprietorship

Corporation

**BUSINESS FORM
AND
STRUCTURE**

Social-cultural

Partnership

Natural-physical

Legal-political

Marketing the Company's Goods and Services

The success of every company depends upon its ability to market its goods and services. As a result, marketing is one of the most important functions of a business enterprise. In this section of the text we will be examining what goes on in this marketing process.

In Chapter 12 the fundamentals of marketing will be discussed. Particular attention will be given to the types of goods sold by marketers and the pricing strategy used in selling them.

Chapter 13 is devoted to an analysis of distribution channels. How does a firm move its goods from the plant to the customer? In this chapter you will study the various types of wholesale and retail activities performed in transporting these goods from those who are producing them to those who wish to use them. You will also learn about the major kinds of transportation facilities available for carrying these products.

In Chapter 14 promotion, personal selling, and advertising are examined. Some products seem to sell themselves. Most, however, need to be promoted in some way. In this chapter you will learn how promotion is carried out. In addition, considerable attention will be given to the steps involved in personal selling. Finally, the area of advertising will be studied. The focus of interest here will be on developing effective advertising copy by getting the right mix of ingredients such as layout, typeface, and color.

The last chapter in this section deals with international trade. When we speak of marketing goods, it is important to remember that this business activity can be carried on overseas as well as within the United States. Therefore, international trade is an important marketing area. In this chapter you will learn why countries trade with each other and what role the United States plays in this international trade arena.

The goal of this section is to acquaint you with the area of marketing. When you are finished reading Chapter 15 you should have a solid understanding of how businesses go about marketing their goods and services. You should also be familiar with a number of key marketing terms, including *the 4 P's of marketing, brand name, convenience good, trade discount, channel of distribution, merchant wholesaler, order taking, advertising agency, network ad, readership report, absolute advantage,* and *protective tariff.* You should also have gained a basic appreciation of the importance of marketing to the business world.

12

It is our intention always to give value for value in every sale we make, and those who are not pleased with what they buy do us a positive favor to return the goods and get their money back.
John Wanamaker

OBJECTIVES OF THIS CHAPTER

As we noted in Chapter 1, the purpose of business is to provide goods and services to mankind. The marketing process involves moving these goods and services from the point of production to the point of consumption. The first objective of this chapter is to examine what marketing is all about. The second is to review the types of goods sold by marketers. The third is to present some of the pricing strategies often used in selling goods. By the end of the chapter you should be able to do the following:

a. explain what is meant by the term marketing;

b. describe the eight basic marketing functions;

c. relate the four major elements contained in the marketing mix;

d. identify the three basic types of goods sold by marketers;

e. understand the method employed by sellers in identifying their products; and

f. describe some of the most commonly used pricing strategies.

Fundamentals of Marketing

THE NATURE OF MARKETING

Marketing involves two important activities: (a) identifying the goods and services the consumer wants, and (b) providing them where they are needed, when they are desired, and at a price the purchaser is willing to pay. This idea is the same one we described in Chapter 1 when we noted that in this country business should be *consumer oriented.* For many of us, this is not a new idea. However, it is important to note that this consumer orientation is the result of an evolution in marketing that began fifty years ago and encompassed four stages or "eras."

The first of these was the **production era.** During this period products were relatively scarce and the primary function of business was to produce goods. Then during the 1930s we saw the rise of the **sales era.** It was now evident to many firms that they had to go out and get customers. People were no longer going to beat a path to their door. Product promotion became very important during this era. The third period, called the **marketing department era,** emerged in the early 1950s. During this period business began to realize that, with all of their product lines, it was necessary to coordinate and organize their total effort in the areas of production and sales. Heavy emphasis was placed on short-run planning in the marketing area. Finally, in the late 1950s, we entered the **marketing company era.** This period is characterized by short- and long-run marketing planning, with the emphasis on gearing all company effort toward satisfying consumer needs.

Since the 1950s we have been in our present consumer-oriented economy. As our gross national product has risen and people have taken more and more money home every week, marketing has increased in importance. The consumer now has the final say regarding what goods and services will be provided. Today, a large percent of our labor force works in the marketing area. Their job is to help identify what consumers want and then get it to them. Wherever we go in this country we can find people engaged in this activity. The local gasoline-station owner is a marketer. So too is the big petroleum company that discovers new fields, pumps out the oil, and converts it to the gasoline sold by the station owner. And there are millions more, from the person who sells us a Big Mac and a Coke to the car dealer who lets us take a test drive in the latest-model Chevy.

In evaluating what these people are doing, it is important to remember that there are two aspects to marketing. First, there are the marketing activities or functions, such as buying and selling. Second, there is marketing philosophy—the belief that the primary reason for a company's existence is the satisfaction of customer wants. Both of these aspects are important in modern marketing, although in this chapter we will be concerned more with marketing functions than with marketing philosophy.

1. Today, "the consumer is king." How is this idea related to modern marketing?

MARKETING FUNCTIONS

Marketing consists of certain specific tasks or *functions* that must be performed. These functions, which are of major importance in moving goods and services from producer to consumer, are (a) buying, (b) selling, (c) transportation, (d) storage, (e) standardization and grading, (f) financing, (g) risk taking, and (h) marketing information.

Buying

Buying involves the selection of both the type and amount of goods to be purchased. This quality and quantity are determined, of course, by the firm's estimate of what the consumer wants. A store that hopes to appeal to a large number of customers, for example, will purchase a wide range of goods. One that intends to cater to only a small, select group, however, will buy a much narrower line of merchandise. In each case, the purchased goods will be those the firm believes will be demanded by the consumer.

Selling

Selling involves more than just a transaction in which a buyer pays money for a good and the seller hands over the item; it also entails the identification of buyers and the use of advertising and sales promotion. Most businesses purchase merchandise before they have a customer for it. However, a carefully constructed sales campaign can help them move the goods to the consumer. More will be said about this later.

Transportation

Quite often goods are produced in one location but are sold to consumers in another. **Transportation** moves the goods from where they are manufactured to where they are needed. This function can be carried out by the use of one or more forms of transportation, including railroad, motor vehicle, waterway, pipeline, and airplane. The company will evaluate the time and costs associated with moving goods by each of these methods, and then decide which best meets their needs.

Transportation moves the goods from where they are manufactured to where they are needed.

Storage

To ensure that they have enough goods on hand, business firms will often order a two- or three-month supply. This, however, requires the company to **store** the merchandise until it is demanded. Some businesses have their own storage facilities; others rent space from public storage warehouse companies. In either event, firms realize that if goods are to be available when they are demanded, someone has to perform the storage function.

Standardization and Grading

With so many types and varieties of products to choose from, today's consumer could be completely confused if it were not for standardization and grading. **Standardization** is the establishment of specifications or categories for products. For example, when we buy a shirt with a 15½-inch collar, we know how large that is because there is a standard measurement for shirt collars. Likewise, when we order a 100-watt bulb, we know how much light we should get from it because lightbulbs are all manu-

Standardization is the establishment of specifications or categories for products. White sidewall tires must meet specifications in order to pass inspection.

Stanley Marcus

What Christmas present do you give to an individual who claims to have everything? Well, obviously, you look for something you just know the person doesn't have. And where do you look? Why in the Neiman-Marcus Christmas catalogue, of course. Over the years Neiman's has offered some unique ideas for Christmas presents, especially of the "his and hers" variety. For example, one year the store offered "his and her" airplanes. Other Yuletide selections included miniature submarines, robes made of shahtoosh (the rarest and most costly fabric in the world, the fiber of which comes from the neck of the ibex goat that lives on the upper slopes of the Himalayas), jaguars ("his" was a roadster, "hers" a coat), saunas, Chinese junks, and (no kidding) "his and her" mummy cases.

The guiding light behind this sales strategy has been H. Stanley Marcus. Born in 1905, he was educated in Amherst and Harvard and joined his father in the family store of Neiman-Marcus in 1926. Learning the business from the ground up, at one time or another he purchased products for almost every department in the store.

In 1950 he succeeded his father as president, and became chairman in 1973. Drawing on his taste in music, art, books, and fine clothes, Marcus has developed the store into one of the leading high-quality retailers in the nation, with outlets on both coasts as well as in the central United States. Known by its customers for adherence to high quality, the store is run on the general philosophy that "There is never a good *sale* for Neiman-Marcus unless it's a good *buy* for the customer."

In the late 1960s Neiman-Marcus sold out to Broadway-Hale. However, Marcus continues to be active in the management of the store. And Neiman's continues to be regarded as one of the finest retail stores in America. Perhaps the reason is found in Stanley Marcus's own personal philosophy about quality. As he put it, "I firmly believe that quality is remembered long after the price is forgotten." The store's customers would tend to agree.

factured to predetermined specifications. There are many types of standards we use in differentiating items, including weight, height, and size.

Grading involves the sorting of goods into classes, or grades, on the basis of quality. We see this done quite often with agricultural products such as meat, fruit, and other farm produce. The federal government has established specifications for each grade of a commodity, such as grade A and grade B eggs. When goods are already graded, the consumer has an easier time deciding what to buy.

Financing

Whenever goods are bought or sold, **financing** is necessary. Some consumers may handle this function by paying cash. Others will use credit and pay the bill at the end of the month or a little each month until all is paid off. The seller, meanwhile, has probably ordered quite a lot of merchandise and is paying for it over a given time period, relying upon the supplier for credit. Sometimes these financial transactions involve banks or lending agencies. Many of them, however, are handled by the parties themselves. For example, local retailers extend credit to their own customers and, in turn, are given credit by their suppliers.

Risk Taking

Whenever someone takes possession of merchandise, there is a risk involved. The goods may be stolen. A fire may destroy them. The selling price may suddenly drop, forcing the owner to sell at a loss. New, competitive products may reduce demand for the goods. All of these conditions are possible. So too is the likelihood that when merchandise is sold on credit the buyer will not pay the bill. Therefore, **risk taking** is an inherent part of marketing.

Marketing Information

From the very beginning of this chapter we have been emphasizing the importance of **marketing information.** By this term we mean *data upon which marketing decisions can be made.* Marketing information can be obtained through the use of marketing research.

Marketing research helps business answer all kinds of questions related to topics such as consumer buying habits, advertising, the proper way to promote sales, and the location of markets. The primary goal of marketing research is to identify the market for particular goods. For example, before one of the Big Three comes out with a new automobile it will do marketing research to determine what types of features potential buyers want in new cars. It will also be interested in who these buyers are, how much money they make, how well educated they are, and what their average age is. By finding these things out, business pinpoints a market for the auto. The next step is to decide whether the demand for the car is large enough to warrant producing it. After all, Detroit does not want to lose money on the venture. If the marketing research indicates that the car is desired by enough people, plans will be made for manufacturing it. Marketing

research helps business analyze and evaluate its consumer market in a scientific manner.

2. How are the buying and selling functions related?

3. In what way are standardization and grading of importance to marketers in selling their goods?

4. Marketing research must be carried out before the firm really knows who its customers are. Comment on this statement.

THE MARKETING MIX

In carrying out the marketing functions, the firm needs to have a marketing program or strategy. This is known as the *marketing mix.* It contains the following major elements: (a) product, (b) price, (c) place, and (d) promotion. These are sometimes referred to as "the 4 P's" of marketing.

Product

The **product** consists of the item and accessories that the company offers to the consumer. This decision is made during product planning. *Product planning* involves identifying the buyer's needs, working up a preliminary design of the merchandise, checking to see that the product design meets the expectations of buyers, settling on the product's final specifications, selecting the brand name for the product, determining the type of packaging to be used, and deciding what services to offer with the product. Keep in mind that consumers view a good as something more than just a physical item. They see it as a *total product,* consisting of a physical unit *and* the satisfaction it will give them.

Choosing satisfactory products is important because it helps a firm replace old ones that have lost their market appeal. Remember, today's successful products were undoubtedly never heard of ten years

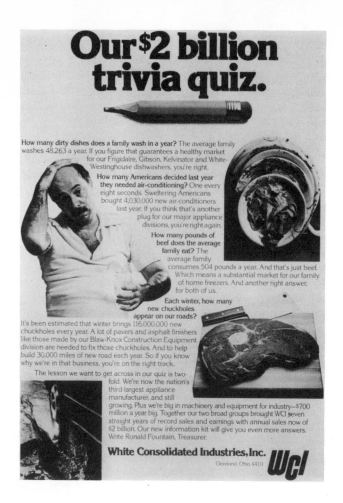

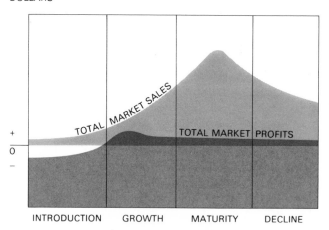

ago. Furthermore, they will probably be highly profitable for only a few years before they too start to fade. A typical life cycle for a product is shown in Fig. 12.1. Notice that total market profits are greatest when the market is growing. In the maturity stage, however, competition enters and the marketing expenses increase. So while total market sales continue to rise, total market profits decline. As a result, the company needs to find replacement products to bolster the profit picture.

Figure 12.2 provides an even more explicit illustration of the life cycle applied to products with which each of us is very familiar. Looking at the figure, we can see, for example, that trash compactors have a very small market demand because they are just catching on with the general public. Dishwashers are currently in the growth stage, refrigerators are in the maturity stage, and black-and-white televisions are in the decline stage. Meanwhile, wringers have virtually no market today, having been replaced by more modern conveniences.

DOLLARS

FIG. 12.1 *Typical life cycle for a product*

In some cases a firm will be able to keep a current product by increasing its life cycle. One way of doing this is to find other uses for the product. Nylon is an illustration. When nylon first came out it was used primarily by the military for things such as parachutes, thread, and rope. This was followed by nylon's entry into the women's hosiery industry. Since this time we have seen nylon used in the production of tires, sweaters, men's hose, and carpets, to name but a few. If a firm can find new uses for a good, it may be possible to extend the product's life cycle. If not, the good must be replaced.

Yet replacement can be difficult because for every one hundred ideas a company has for new products, only 2 percent will ever prove profitable. Most of the others (95 percent) are screened out after market testing, while a few (3 percent) will flop despite all initial signs to the contrary. The successful firm will want to replace those products whose profit levels make them marginal ventures with new lines of merchandise that have better profit potential.

Price

The **price** charged for the product must be high enough to give the company a profit, but low enough to entice the consumer to buy. In settling on a fair price, firms will evaluate their own costs, current pricing laws, what the competition is doing, and the types of discounts and terms of sales that are customary in the industry. On the basis of all of this information, a price will be agreed upon. This subject of pricing will be discussed in greater detail later in the chapter.

Place — DISTRIBUTION

Consumers are accustomed to looking for goods in a particular **place.** They go to drugstores to buy cold remedies, and to bookstores to purchase the latest best-selling novels. Business needs to have its goods available in the places consumers tend to frequent. This requires moving the merchandise from where it is produced to where it is desired. Such movement entails transportation, channels of distribution, and

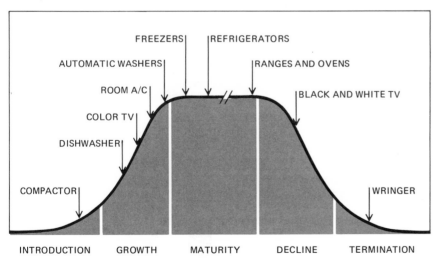

FIG. 12.2 *Life-cycle stages of various products (Adapted from John E. Smallwood, "The Product Life Cycle: A Key to Strategic Marketing Planning," p. 30,* MSU Business Topics, *Winter 1973. Reprinted by permission of the publisher, Division of Research, Graduate School of Business Administration, Michigan State University.)*

storage. The manufacturer needs to have a strategy for taking care of all these matters. Some use middlemen such as wholesalers to move their merchandise to the consumer. Others go directly to the final buyers themselves. In any case, the goods must eventually be moved to the right place for purchase. More will be said about these channels of distribution in the next chapter.

Promotion

The fourth element in the marketing mix is **promotion.** The purpose of promotion is to stimulate demand for the company's products. Common promotional techniques include advertising, packaging, branding, personal selling, sales manuals, enlisting of dealer cooperation in displaying goods at the point of purchase, and coupons and premiums. A firm may not use all of these promotional techniques to move a product, but many will rely on two or three of them because one alone cannot usually do the job. We will be discussing this area of promotion in more detail in Chapter 14.

Figure 12.3 illustrates how marketing research, the 4 P's, and the consumer are all related. In designing an effective marketing strategy, it is important for the firm to bring these three elements together in an interactive setting, as shown in the figure.

5. Why are the 4 P's known as the marketing mix?

6. In what way are product planning and marketing research related?

7. Of the 4 P's, which do you think is the most important? Why?

TYPES OF GOODS

The basic purpose of marketing is to get goods and services to the consumer. In order to understand this process, it is important to have some knowledge of the basic types of goods that are marketed. In all,

FIG. 12.3 *Marketing research, the four P's, and the consumer*

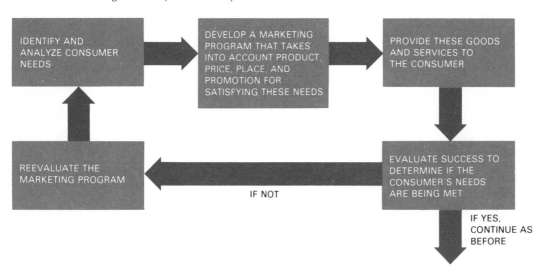

A "Mod" Proposal

Ted Billings is the manager of a men's clothing store in a large eastern city. The store is part of a retail chain, and Ted's job is to operate the store within the general guidelines established by the board of directors. For the most part, however, Ted is permitted to run operations as he sees fit.

In the past the store has offered a line of men's business suits ranging in price from $100 to $300. This selection is conservative in nature and tends to appeal to older professionals and business executives. Few young people shop here. The average age of the customers is fifty-three.

Recently some of the sales personnel have been suggesting that the product line be expanded to include more "mod" clothing. The argument in favor of this move is that it would bring more young people into the store and increase sales. Ted, however, has been reluctant to do this because he is afraid that the store will lose both its image and its current clientele. He believes the store is currently doing very well. Nevertheless, he has promised to look into the matter.

1. If Ted goes ahead with the proposed change, how will this affect the marketing functions of buying, storage, and risk taking?

2. How can marketing research be useful to Ted in arriving at a decision on whether or not to sell "mod" clothes?

3. If the store expands its offerings to include "mod" clothing, will there be any change in the marketing mix? Explain.

---

there are three: (a) industrial goods, (b) commercial goods, and (c) consumer goods.

Industrial Goods
Industrial goods are those used by industry or business to produce commercial, consumer, or other industrial goods. Illustrations include machinery, tools, raw materials, and supplies. Some of these goods, such as machinery, will remain in the company as industrial goods. Others, such as raw materials, are often converted into products that are eventually sold as consumer goods. Iron ore that will be used to make automobiles, or rubber that will become tires, are examples.

Commercial Goods
Commercial goods are those that are used by business in the form in which they are purchased but that are not intended for use in making other goods. Illustrations include typewriters, filing cabinets, office furniture, and cash registers. In recent years many firms have begun buying or renting computer hardware. This too would be included as a commercial good.

Consumer Goods

Consumer goods are those destined to be used by the consumer. There is no need for any further processing of these goods; they are complete in their final form. These goods can be classified into three subgroups: (a) convenience goods, (b) shopping goods, and (c) specialty goods.

Convenience goods

These goods are those that consumers like to purchase quickly and with a minimum of effort. Cigarettes, newspapers, candy, chewing gum, and toothpaste are all illustrations. **Convenience goods** can be found in many locations and, because they are quickly used up, tend to be purchased frequently. The cost per item is usually low and the quality contained in the product is standardized. In the case of toothpaste, for example, if we have a favorite brand, we ask for it with no hesitation. The only considerations might be the size of the tube and the flavor; for example, regular or spearmint. It should also be noted that convenience goods that are marketed nationally, such as toothpaste, gum, and cigarettes, usually receive national advertising coverage.

The Stanley Steamer

The Stanley Steamer was quite an automobile. Built by Francis and Freeland Stanley, these cars were manufactured from 1890 to 1925. Late models were very efficient, getting 200 miles on a fresh supply of water. And the average steamer could easily attain 70–80 miles per hour. In fact, in 1907 a Stanley racing car reached 197 mph!

Some people believed these Stanley steamers could blow up, but the car's construction design actually made this impossible. Early models did, however, have a tendency to let off steam in a noisy manner. One day, for example, a man in Boston entered a tavern after forgetting to turn off a valve on his Stanley Steamer. In protest the car gave off a thunderous blast of steam. The tavern shook, glasses fell off the shelves, and several patrons slipped to the floor. The car owner looked at the bartender and said, "Mighty powerful stuff you're serving here these days."

Yet, despite its speed and efficiency, the Stanley Steamer failed for a number of reasons, most of them related to marketing. First, the car was very highly priced--$2,500 in 1917. Second, the Stanleys "screened" all of their customers and refused to sell to those not having the "right personality." Third, after an order was accepted, if the customer did anything to offend the Stanleys, delivery was refused. One man, for example, asked for a written guarantee. Figuring their word was guarantee enough, the Stanleys showed him to the door. Fourth, the brothers sold for cash only--no credit or installment buying. Fifth, and finally, the firm did no advertising, believing the car would "advertise itself." The Stanleys were out of step with the market and sales dwindled, and in 1925 the firm finally went out of business.

Shopping goods

These are goods that the consumer buys only after comparing what competing stores have to offer in terms of such considerations as price, style, and quality. If they do have brand names these have no effect on the buyer. The goods are usually in a medium price range and have a fairly long life expectancy. Common examples include furniture, automobiles, and curtains and draperies. A microwave oven would be another illustration. A number of firms currently manufacture these ovens. Their cost is rather substantial, product quality varies depending on the manufacturer, and the average family will buy one very infrequently. In purchasing such an oven, consumers tend to shop around, read advertising material distributed by the merchants regarding the advantages of their particular unit, and spend a considerable amount of thought before finally making a decision.

Specialty goods

Specialty goods are those that consumers are willing to spend extra effort to locate and buy. The consumer purchases them on the basis of brand name, believing that the name implies the quality or characteristics being sought in such a product. Quite often these goods are sold by only a small number of stores in town. An illustration would be a Zenith television. Many consumers believe that Zenith's sets are the finest available and will purchase no other. Since they buy on brand name alone, for them the Zenith television is a specialty good. The same illustration holds for many people when they buy new cars. A person who will purchase only a Ford, or a Chrysler, or a Chevrolet buys on name brand. However, a specialty good purchase need not be expensive. An individual who will drink only one particular type of wine, eat only a specific kind of specialty cheese, or buy only shirts manufactured by one particular company, will go out of his way to obtain these goods. As a result, they too are specialty goods.

Would you consider this brass bed a convenience good, a shopping good, or a specialty good?

In classifying consumer goods, we have divided them into three exclusive groups. However, it should be realized that not all consumers are alike; what is a shopping good to one may be a specialty good to another. This is especially true as one's standard of living increases. For example, if we become richer and richer we might buy a living-room set the way we would a package of gum—quickly and with little thought. In this case, a shopping good would become a convenience good. On the other hand, no matter what our wealth, if we chew gum regularly it may have become a specialty good for us. For example, let us say you will chew only Dentyne and, if the local drug store does not have it, you will go to other outlets looking for it. In this case, chewing gum is a specialty good for you. Thus goods can be classified in general terms, but on a person-to-person basis there may be great differences in the ways they are viewed.

8. In what way does an industrial good differ from a commercial good?

9. What is a convenience good? How does it differ from a shopping good?

10. How would a shopping good become a specialty good? What change would have to take place?

PRODUCT IDENTIFICATION

Most marketers attempt to differentiate their products from those of the competition. Sometimes this involves giving better service than anyone else; other times the difference is psychological, such as brand image. Other ways of helping buyers identify the product are through packaging, labels, and brand names.

The package or container is part of the product.

Packaging

The **package** or container is actually part of the product. One of its basic purposes is to protect the contents. This is important because the item may have to withstand a lot of handling between the factory and the consumer. A second purpose of the package is to make the item look appealing to the buyer, especially through the use of appealing colors. For example, detergents are packaged in blue and white containers because people associate these colors with cleanliness. And products that are packaged in such a way as to catch the consumer's eye may well be purchased. A third purpose is to help identify the item. Coca-Cola, for example, is easily identified by its familiar-shaped bottle. Other common purposes of a package are to provide information about the contents inside, make it easy to carry the item, and provide convenience in using and reusing the product by allowing the consumer to open and reclose the package.

The container should help identify the product inside.

Labels

Labels are identification devices that are sewn, printed, or stamped on products or packages. These labels often include manufacturer's name, brand name, grade, quantity, ingredients, and instructions on how to use the good. In clothing, the label usually tells the name of the manufacturer, something about the materials used in making the garment, and, if made in the United States, instructions for cleaning it. On breakfast cereal the quantity and ingredients are specified. These labels help both to identify the products and to persuade the consumer to buy them.

Brand Names

Brand names are very useful in helping to identify products. As we saw earlier, they carry important connotations for the buyer, and many people buy on the basis of them. For example, when the consumer sees a well-known brand name, he or she often believes that the item is of good quality, that the price

HOW TO BUILD A BOEING.

Boeing is now building an airplane that'll save millions of gallons of fuel: the new generation 757.

How much will it save?

A 757 flying 1.3 million miles a year will save 1.8 million gallons of fuel annually over the airplane it will replace.

Fuel economy has always been a concern to an airplane designer. Now it's more critical than ever.

Heading up one engineering group is Doug Miller. His specialty is preliminary design and development.

Doug and the design team were involved in the development of an airplane wing that has exceptionally efficient aerodynamics. It

would never have been possible if Boeing had not been testing and perfecting components of lightweight carbon-fiber and high-strength pure aluminum alloys.

Result: The 757 wing will get the airplane off the ground and flying with less fuel consumption than any airplane its size.

New aerodynamics, new materials, and engineering inventiveness along with a long-term commitment to constantly reach out and explore the unknown have made the 757 a reality.

Boeing believes almost anything is possible. Doug and the team are but one part of the immensely complex process that has helped create a future world of efficient commercial aviation — a step that can keep air travel one of the best values in the world of rising inflation.

THE BOEING FAMILY
Getting people together.

is fair, and that the seller will stand behind any guarantees made about service or durability of the product.

Some sellers use a **family brand name** for all their goods. General Electric is an example. All its products carry the same brand. As a result, each of its promotion efforts serves to bolster sales for the entire product line. In addition, the introduction of a new product is made easier because of the company's reputation. Other family brand names include Heinz "57" food products; A & P brands such as Ann Page and Sultana; Sears, Roebuck's Kenmore appliances; and Pittsburgh Plate's line of paints and home products.

Other firms prefer to use **individual brand names.** For example, General Motors sells the Chevrolet, Buick, Pontiac, Oldsmobile, and Cadillac. Each is promoted separately. In this market people tend to have a preference for a *specific* type of automobile rather than just any car made by GM. The same is true for proprietary medications. We tend to buy by individual brand name with little regard for the specific manufacturer. For example, Sterling Drug makes both Bayer aspirin and Phillips Milk of Magnesia. Few of us know the manufacturer, but many of us request the product by brand name.

11. Is packaging really of any value in helping to sell a good?

12. What kinds of products might people buy by brand name? With what kinds of products is brand name of little, if any, value?

PRODUCT PRICING

Price is of major importance in marketing. If the seller asks too much for the merchandise there will be few, if any, buyers. If the seller asks too little, demand will be high but profit will suffer. In arriving at a price, the firm must consider (a) price level, (b) the cost of selling, (c) supply and demand, and (d) the competition.

Price Level

A company can price *above* the market, *at* the market, or *below* the market. Firms with products having a very strong demand often price above the market. This is frequently done with specialty goods where the buyer is willing to pay extra for the item. It is also the case when people believe that price and high quality are related, such as with medicines or drugs. Many consumers always buy the highest-priced items because they feel these goods have greater quality or potency than cheaper brands. Firms that offer products that are seen by the consumer as being of higher quality can often price above the competition.

Most firms price at the market; their goods are usually no better than average, and they offer no extra service or other demand-creating features. As a result consumers have no overriding reason to prefer their good over that of the competition. Many convenience goods fall into this category.

Some companies price below the market. Manufacturers selling stripped-down or low-quality models are illustrations. So too are discount stores that are willing to take a smaller profit on each item but try to make up the difference by selling a greater quantity of merchandise. Mail-order houses also fall into this category.

Cost of Selling

Regardless of what price is established, the seller must cover all costs and allow for a profit margin. Only in the short run can a "below-cost" price be permitted. This often happens when a company is trying to get rid of goods that have not sold well to make room for new merchandise. Barring this event, costs set the floor for price; the seller's decision must then be how far above this base to establish the asking price.

Supply and Demand

There is a relationship between supply and demand. Usually this relationship is *inverse,* which means that when one is high the other is low. Figure 12.4 provides an illustration of this relationship. In this case,

PRICE (IN DOLLARS)

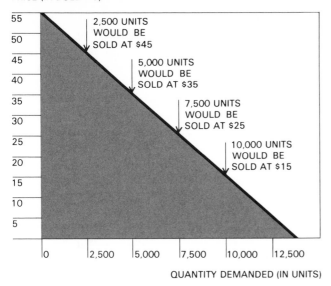

QUANTITY DEMANDED (IN UNITS)

FIG. 12.4 *The relationship between price and the quantity demanded*

the company can sell 2,500 units at $45. As this price declines, the number demanded rises. At $15 there will be 10,000 units demanded. If the four points on the demand curve in Fig. 12.4 are computed as to total revenue, the results are as follows:

2,500 units @ $45 each = $112,500
5,000 units @ $35 each = $175,000
7,500 units @ $25 each = $187,500
10,000 units @ $15 each = $150,000

In this case the firm would price at $25 because total revenue is highest at this price.

The problem with our illustration is that it assumes we will always be able to sell 7,500 units at $25. In fact, the needs of consumers are continually changing and the competition is always coming out with a new product or service. In addition, our costs will probably be going up so we will have to raise our prices. Given all these considerations, it is evident that our demand curve in Fig. 12.4 will not hold indefinitely, although it will help us in pricing the good in the short run.

The Competition

Unless a firm has a monopoly position, the competition will play a role in its pricing strategy. To a large degree, the effect of the competition will depend on its products, services, and price combinations. However, the thing to remember is that as one firm begins to increase its share of the market (company sales/industry sales), the competition will respond by making adjustments in its own strategy. Price is one of the major components that will be changed in an effort to win back market share. Therefore, the key question every firm must ask when deciding to change its price is: what will the competition do if we raise (or lower) our price, and what will the overall effect be for us?

13. When is selling below cost justified?

14. In what way does the competition have an effect on a company's price?

PRICING STRATEGIES

Most firms have a **list price,** which is their announced price for a good. On an automobile it is found on the window sticker. On a suit or blouse it is often located on a tag attached to the sleeve of the garment. On a book it is found stamped inside the cover or attached to the cover by a removable sticky label. Many times these prices are fixed and the seller refuses to negotiate on them. However, there are times when firms make discounts available.

Discounts

A **discount** is a reduction in the list price. Some of the most common forms of discounts are trade, quantity, cash, and seasonal.

Trade discounts

No one wants to sell for the same price they buy. As a result, as goods move through the distribution channel from producer to user, the middlemen are all given **trade discounts.** For example, a manufac-

Discounts are one way of stimulating sales.

turer may sell a watch with a list price of $200 to a jewelry store. The store gets a 50-percent discount and pays only $100. Or a publisher sells a $10 book to a bookstore for $8, thereby giving the buyer a 20-percent discount. These discounts, you will note, are based on selling or list price. Their purpose is to cover the merchant's cost of doing business while leaving a little room for profit.

Quantity discounts

Some sellers offer **quantity discounts.** The more a merchant orders the greater the discount. The following would be an illustration of a discount based on number of units purchased:

Units ordered	Discount
1–99	30%
100–1,000	40%
Over 1,000	50%

Cash discounts

Some businesses give buyers a discount if they pay their bills early. A common term of sale is 2/10; net 30, pronounced "two ten, net thirty." This means that if the buyer pays the bill within ten days, a 2-percent discount is given. Thus a $100 bill can be settled for $98 if paid early. Otherwise, the entire $100 is due in thirty days. In recent years it has been common to charge interest to those purchasers who fail to pay the bill within thirty days. Many buyers take advantage of the discount because it not only improves their credit rating but is a big saving to the firm. After all, failure to take the discount means that the firm pays 2 percent for the use of money for twenty days. This is a 36-percent annual rate of interest if computed on a 360-day year.

Seasonal discounts

Some manufacturers offer **seasonal discounts** to get buyers to order merchandise before peak periods. These discounts may be offered in August and September for Christmas-related items or February and March for summer merchandise. Other illustrations include hotels offering off-season rates, auto dealers giving big discounts just before the new models come out, and clothing retailers discounting merchandise that has not sold during the season, such as swimwear in late summer.

Other Pricing Methods

Discounts are one way of stimulating sales. Other ways include "loss leaders," flexible pricing, multiple-unit pricing, odd pricing, and new product pricing.

Loss leaders

A **loss leader** is a product that is priced either at or below cost. The objective of such pricing is to get people into the store where they may buy other goods as well. Loss leaders are often advertised on Thursdays and Fridays for the purpose of creating heavy weekend demand. It is common to find ads being run by supermarkets for loss leaders such as coffee, soft drinks, and toothpaste.

An airline's offer of large discounts resulted in congestion at the airport as an unexpectedly high number of people rushed to take advantage of the offer.

A recent phenomenon in supermarket selling is offering brand names at low prices by doing away with costly services.

"Doctor, that medication you prescribed for my husband did have a side effect. He fainted when I told him what it cost."

From The Wall Street Journal; permission Cartoon Features Syndicate

Flexible pricing

Flexible pricing can take a number of forms. Most commonly it involves selling merchandise to different buyers at different prices. For example, in most cases all wholesalers pay the same price to the manufacturer. So too do all retailers, but the price they pay is higher than what the wholesalers pay. In other words, the price is flexible between groups but consistent within them. Another example of flexible pricing is the auto dealer who allows different trade-in allowances on cars.

Multiple-unit pricing

Multiple-unit prices are similar to quantity discounts. The purpose of this pricing tactic is to encourage buyers to purchase in greater amounts. An illustration would be when a store sells shirts at $8 each or five for $35.

Odd pricing

Odd pricing occurs when a product is priced at an odd number, such as $9.95 rather than $10.00 or $499.95 rather than $500.00. It is difficult to evaluate the effectiveness of such a pricing technique. We do know, however, that some people feel they are getting a bargain with odd prices. Perhaps this is why they are also referred to as *psychological* prices.

New product pricing

In pricing new products there are two contrasting approaches. The first is called a **skimming** approach, where the marketer "skims the cream" off the top of the market by setting a high price on the product and capturing the market among those who are willing to pay this amount. Often this strategy is good only for a short period; then the price is lowered because either there is no demand left or competition enters the scene.

The other approach is called **penetration pricing** and is characterized by a low price that results in large quantities being purchased. This strategy may be more daring, but it also discourages competition. The major problem with it is that the seller may price too low and lose profit or be unable to supply the quantity demanded. In fact, many marketers believe that it is better to err on the high side; one can always lower one's price, but to raise it can often have disastrous results.

15. What is a cash discount? When would a company be willing to pass up such discounts? Why do most take advantage of them?

16. In pricing new products, what is meant by "skimming the cream"? How does this differ from penetration pricing?

After careful marketing research, Ted Billings decided to expand his store offerings to include "mod" clothes as well as conservative suits. The decision was not an easy one. However, the sales personnel had been right—there was a big demand for this type of clothing. Sales almost doubled within a year's time.

On the negative side, however, was the competitive factor. Ordering the right styles, in the right quantities, was difficult; and it had to be done very carefully if one was to remain competitive. In addition, if something did not sell, it was necessary to have a sale to move out the old merchandise to make room for new clothing. Ted found this to be a lot more hectic than just selling men's suits. For example, brand name seemed to have little effect. People tended to buy on the basis of style and color. And then there was the problem of what kinds of discounts and other pricing methods to use. For the most part the store tended to rely on seasonal discounts to move unsold merchandise. Meanwhile, on the regular merchandise it used odd pricing for suits and pants, and multiple-unit pricing for shirts and socks. On new goods that were judged to be fads the store employed a skimming strategy. These techniques seemed to work well, although Ted admitted he was considering the use of loss leaders in the future to generate sales.

1. Are the "mod" clothes convenience, shopping, or specialty goods? Give your reasoning.

2. Are seasonal discounts helpful in selling unmoved merchandise? Is odd pricing very effective in selling suits? How about multiple-unit pricing for selling shirts or socks?

3. How does a skimming strategy work?

4. Would loss leaders be of any value to Ted's store? Explain.

SUMMARY

Marketing involves identifying what consumers want and then getting the goods and services to them. In accomplishing these activities, there are eight basic functions that must be performed: buying, selling, transportation, storage, standardization and grading, financing, risk taking, and marketing information. These functions are carried out in the firm's marketing program or strategy. This strategy is called the marketing mix and contains four major elements: product, price, place, and promotion.

The goods a firm sells can be classified into three basic categories: industrial goods, commercial goods, and consumer goods. In turn, this last group is often subdivided into convenience, shopping, and specialty goods. In distinguishing their product from those of the competition, many companies use different forms of product identification, including packaging, labels, and brand names. Another important feature is price. Some companies offer various types of discounts such as trade, quantity, cash, and seasonal. Others use loss leaders, flexible pricing, multiple-unit pricing, odd pricing, and penetration pricing.

KEY TERMS FOUND IN THIS CHAPTER

1. What are the two basic activities involved in marketing? Describe them.

2. Can a marketer avoid risk taking? Why or why not?

3. Which of the marketing functions is the most important? Give your reasoning.

4. In a highly competitive market, how can promotion be of value to the marketer? In what way might it be harmful?

5. Is an automobile a convenience, shopping, or specialty good? Explain.

6. If price and quantity are inversely related, why do firms not always set the lowest possible prices?

7. What is a quantity discount? What is a seasonal discount? How might a company offer both at the same time?

8. Is odd pricing very effective? If you think it is, what is your reasoning? If you think it is not, why then do so many marketers use it?

13

Your product may be the best in the world, but it will be of little value to the customer if it is not where he wants it when he wants it.

E. Jerome McCarthy

OBJECTIVES OF THIS CHAPTER

Marketing involves not only finding out what goods consumers want but also getting these goods to the places where consumers will buy them. In this chapter we are going to examine the routes or channels that goods take in moving from where they are produced to where they are demanded. Our first objective is to review what some of these channels are. The second is to examine one of the major groups of middlemen who help move these goods, the wholesaler. The third objective is to explain the role and importance of the other major group of middlemen, the retailers; and the final objective is to review the major modes of transportation for moving goods. By the end of this chapter you should be able to do the following:

a. define what is meant by the term channels of distribution;

b. explain the role and importance of some of the major types of wholesalers;

c. identify some of the conventional mass-merchandising types of retail outlets used to sell goods to the final consumer; and

d. describe the five major kinds of transportation available to middlemen in moving their goods.

Channels of Distribution

TYPES OF DISTRIBUTION CHANNELS

Channels of distribution are those routes that goods take in moving from producer to consumer. These channels will vary depending upon the nature of the goods, the kind of demand that exists, and the type of competition that is present. Industrial and commercial goods, for example, have different channels of distribution from consumer goods.

Channels for Industrial and Commercial Goods

There are two types of distribution channels used for industrial and commercial goods. The most popular is as follows:

Manufacturer ⟶ Industrial or
                    commercial user.

In this case the goods are sold directly to the final buyer with no middlemen involved. The reason for this is that many of these goods are already in finished form, so there is no need for a company to use a middleman for functions such as grading, standardizing, or storing—its own sales force can handle the marketing directly. Illustrations can be found among manufacturers who build generators, computers, and heavy equipment.

The second common channel is one in which wholesalers are used. It is as follows:

Manufacturer ⟶ Wholesaler ⟶ Industrial or
                                commercial user.

In this case the manufacturer employs a wholesaler, such as a broker or an agent, to distribute the good. This is often the case when a producer needs to have the goods sold but does not want to hire a company sales force. We will see illustrations of this later in the chapter.

Channels for Consumer Goods

There are many different channels that can be used for marketing consumer goods. One of these is the *direct* channel, in which the manufacturer sells directly to the consumer:

Manufacturer ⟶ Consumer.

This approach is used by house-to-house sales firms such as Avon Products, and mail-order houses such as Sears, Roebuck.

A second channel involves retailers, who sell goods to consumers. For example,

Manufacturer ⟶ Retailer ⟶ Consumer.

These retail outlets take many different forms, including department stores, supermarkets, and discount houses. These are some of the retail outlets you and I generally use when buying merchandise.

A third channel involves wholesalers, who enter the distribution picture between the manufacturer and the retailer. The following is an illustration:

Manufacturer ⟶ Wholesaler ⟶ Retailer ⟶ Consumer.

In these cases, the manufacturer is often trying to sell a line of goods to retailers throughout the country. Contacting all of these retailers, however, can be quite a job. Wholesalers eliminate this problem by purchasing the manufacturer's output and taking over the job of selling to these retailers. This saves the manufacturer a great deal of time and effort.

The above are the three most common distribution channels for consumer goods. However, there are many, many different *combinations* in existence, which will vary depending on the good or service. For example, some manufacturers will use wholesalers to move some of their goods; other goods they will sell directly to retailers; and still others they will sell directly to the consumer. Regardless of the channel used, however, the marketing functions we mentioned in the previous chapter must *always* be performed.

1. Why are individuals such as wholesalers and retailers known as middlemen?

2. Why might a manufacturer who sells directly to the consumer be able to charge a lower price than one using wholesalers or retailers?

STEVENSON

Drawing by Stevenson; © 1976. The New Yorker Magazine, Inc.

FIG. 13.1 *Types and percentage of wholesalers* (*Source:* Statistical Abstract of the United States, *1978, p. 848.*)

WHOLESALERS

Wholesalers are middlemen who purchase goods and sell them to buyers for the purpose of resale. The Bureau of the Census lists five major types of wholesalers: (a) merchant wholesalers, (b) manufacturers' wholesale outlets, (c) merchandise agents and brokers, (d) petroleum bulk plants, and (e) assemblers of farm products. A chart showing the various types and the percentage of wholesale business they do in the United States is given in Fig. 13.1.

Merchant Wholesalers

Merchant wholesalers are wholesalers who take title to the goods. This means that they buy them for their own account. Over two-thirds of the wholesalers in the country fall into this category. Some of the more important ones in this group include (a) wholesale merchants, (b) wagon jobbers, (c) rack jobbers, (d) cash-and-carry wholesalers, and (e) drop shippers.

Wholesale merchants

Wholesale merchants are the most common form of merchant wholesalers. These individuals buy and sell merchandise for their own account, carry stocks of goods at their place of business, extend credit, make

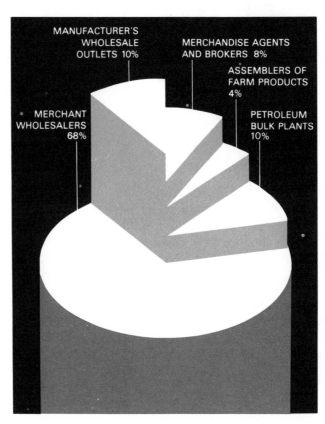

MANUFACTURER'S WHOLESALE OUTLETS 10%

MERCHANDISE AGENTS AND BROKERS 8%

ASSEMBLERS OF FARM PRODUCTS 4%

MERCHANT WHOLESALERS 68%

PETROLEUM BULK PLANTS 10%

Ray A. Kroc

Who is Ronald McDonald? The answer might be a mystery to some adults, but not to American schoolchildren. A 1973 survey revealed that 96 percent of them could identify Ronald McDonald—only Santa Claus had a higher rating. And who hasn't sung the jingle, "At McDonald's, we do it all for you"? Or tried to say, "Two all-beef patties, special sauce, lettuce er uh . . ."? Oh well, you know what we mean.

McDonald's is an American institution today. And we owe it all to Ray A. Kroc. In the 1940s Kroc became the exclusive salesman for a new invention, a milk-shake "multimixer" machine. A small hamburger restaurant in San Bernardino, California, owned by two brothers named McDonald, attracted his attention by purchasing eight of his machines. Realizing that a chain of similar restaurants would utilize many multimixers, Kroc began his own hamburger restaurants under a royalty arrangement with the two brothers.

As McDonald's restaurants began appearing across the country, Kroc soon realized that his future was in the restaurant and not the multi-mixer business. He eventually bought out the McDonald brothers. "I needed the McDonald name and those golden arches," he said. "What are you going to do with a name like Kroc?"

Since then McDonald's has established outlets all over the world, from New York to Paris to Tokyo. Operating under a strict set of rules (no cigarette machines, no selling of burgers that have been off the grill and under the infrared warming lights for more than ten minutes), the units provide high-quality service and good food for the whole family. In 1979, systemwide sales by all company-owned and licensed restaurants totaled over $5 billion. Ray Kroc has a personal fortune estimated in the hundreds of millions. And he achieved it by gearing his operations to consumer needs while at the same time making McDonald's a household word, as seen by the millions who have left his units humming, "Nobody can do it like McDonald's can."

deliveries, and provide a whole line of other services to their customers. Because of all the services they provide, they are often known as *regular full-service* wholesalers. They can often be found handling such items as drugs, groceries, hardware, and dry goods.

Wagon jobbers

Wagon jobbers, also known as *wagon distributors, truck jobbers,* or *truck distributors,* make sales and deliveries from the merchandise they carry in their trucks. These products are generally fast-moving, perishable items that have a rapid turnover, such as bakery and dairy products, snack foods, and tobacco goods. It is common to find these individuals selling their goods to retailers on a cash basis, although some wagon jobbers occasionally give credit. One of the biggest services they perform for their customers is that of risk taking. Because wagon jobbers visit their clientele frequently, it is unnecessary for the retailers to stock large quantities of perishable goods. Thus the wagon jobber assumes the risk associated with product spoilage.

Rack jobbers

Rack jobbers, also known as *rack merchandisers* or *service merchandisers,* are widely used by supermarkets that have added nonfood lines, such as hosiery, magazines, toiletries, and drug products, to their grocery stocks. The rack jobber is the person who supplies these nonfood items, sets up the display, stocks the shelves or racks with the product, prices the goods, and replenishes the merchandise as needed. Some rack jobbers sell their merchandise to the retailer. Others retain title to the goods and merely pay the store manager a certain percentage of the sales made to consumers. In this latter case, all risks associated with carrying the inventory are borne by the rack jobber.

Cash-and-carry wholesalers

These wholesalers usually sell to small groceries and other stores that buy in small quantities. Their products are typically grocery items or tobacco. These middlemen are called **cash-and-carry** because they provide neither credit nor delivery to their customers. The latter have to come and get the goods themselves.

Drop shippers

Drop shippers, also known as *desk jobbers,* buy and sell bulk items such as lumber and coal. Interestingly enough, these wholesalers do not take physical possession of the goods. The merchandise that drop shippers buy is usually expensive to ship, so it does not pay them to take direct delivery. Rather, it is common to find them buying the merchandise from a producer and then leaving the goods there until they can locate a buyer. They then notify the producer to ship the goods to the new owner.

3. When people hear the term wholesaler, they tend to think of a wholesale merchant as opposed to any other type of wholesaler. Why is this so?

4. How does a wagon jobber differ from a rack jobber?

Manufacturers' Wholesale Outlets

Some manufacturers are unable to find wholesalers who can handle their goods efficiently. As a result, they set up their own wholesale branches and offices. By using company-owned outlets, many firms have found that they are better able to market their products. Several reasons can be cited for this. One, a manufacturer's wholesale outlet will often sell its own goods more vigorously than will other wholesalers. Two, these company-owned outlets can often provide faster service to their customers than can other wholesalers. Three, if technical service or advice is needed the manufacturer's outlet is in a better position than anyone else to provide it.

Merchandise Agents and Brokers

Agents and brokers are those individuals who do *not* take title to the goods. Their job consists of negotiating purchases and sales for their customers, who in turn take ownership of the merchandise. For providing this service they are commonly paid a commission or a fee. The more important wholesalers in this group are (a) manufacturers' agents, (b) brokers, (c) selling agents, (d) commission merchants, and (e) auction companies.

Manufacturers' agents

A **manufacturers' agent** often works for several *noncompeting* manufacturers. This individual is very much like a company salesperson with an assigned territory. The agent's job is to sell the company's goods within the designated area, and she or he is paid a commission on all sales. These individuals are often used by small companies that cannot afford their own sales force. The agent's main job is to call on wholesalers and/or industrial customers and explain the company's product line to them. Orders are then sent to the firm, which sees that they are filled. Manufacturers' agents are frequently used in selling clothing, furniture, and dry goods.

Brokers

Brokers are individuals who bring buyers and sellers together. The broker's main product is *information;*

usually he or she does not physically handle the goods. By knowing what buyers need and where to get it, or what sellers want to dispose of and where potential customers are located, the broker can be a very important individual in bringing about sales. For their assistance in these transactions, brokers are paid fees by whichever party engages them. These individuals are used in many areas of business selling including real estate, used machinery, and seasonal products.

Selling agents

A **selling agent** is like a manufacturers' agent except that this person may handle competing lines. In addition, this agent often takes over the company's *entire* marketing job, not just the sales contacts in one area. As a result, it is common to find these individuals with almost complete control of pricing, advertising, and selling. In a manner of speaking, a selling agent is a producer's marketing manager. These wholesalers have often been used by producers who are in financial difficulty and need an individual with marketing know-how. They are especially found in

industries where marketing is more important to a firm's survival than is production. Illustrations include lumber, textiles, and coal.

Commission merchants

Commission merchants are widely used for selling agricultural products such as livestock and grain. Producers who want to sell their output in big-city central markets need to have someone there to handle the transaction if they do not want to accompany every shipment. Commission merchants do this by receiving the goods, finding a buyer, and then sending back to the seller the money remaining after commission.

Auction companies

Auction companies provide a common place where buyers and sellers can come together to negotiate transactions. These companies are very important in the sale of such lines as tobacco, fruit, livestock, and used cars. Supply and demand often change rapidly with these products, and the goods must be personally evaluated in order for a price to be decided

Auction companies provide a common place where buyers and sellers can come together to negotiate transactions.

No Middleman Involvement

The biggest challenge facing Ted Billings was that of offering his customers the type of clothing they wanted at a price they were willing to pay. The store's basic line of merchandise, and the one that Ted felt was his "bread and butter," consisted of conservative or business suits and accessories such as shirts, ties, and other articles of formal wear. The second line of goods was made up of "mod" clothes. These latter were lower priced and appealed more to younger people.

All of this clothing was purchased directly from the manufacturer. Usually the store sent two buyers to New York City to attend periodic fashion shows and to talk with the manufacturers. At these meetings the buyers were acquainted with the latest styles and fashions. To a large degree, the success of the store depended upon the buyers' ability to pick lines that would sell. It was known in the industry that a store's failure to carry a very popular line could result in a severe financial setback.

If a particular line was being sold faster than expected, reorders would be placed with the manufacturer. If a line did not move, a "special" was run and it was sold off as quickly as possible.

1. What distribution channel does Ted's store use in buying clothing? Draw it on a piece of paper.

2. Why do you think Ted's store buys directly from the manufacturer? Why does it not use wholesalers?

3. If, in the future, Ted does start using wholesalers, what kinds might these be? Explain.

---

upon. By bringing the buyers and sellers together, the auction company helps both sides reach an agreeable price. For its services and facilities, the company charges either a fixed fee or a commission.

5. Why do some manufacturers set up their own wholesale outlets?

6. In what way is a manufacturers' agent like a company salesperson?

7. How is a selling agent like a manufacturers' agent?

Petroleum Bulk Plants
Another major wholesale classification is **petroleum distribution.** These wholesalers work closely with major oil companies. Their major contribution to

marketing is the storage and handling facilities they provide.

Assemblers of Farm Products

The final category of wholesaler that we will be examining is the specialist who assembles agricultural products. This individual accumulates farm produce and sorts it into the most economical quantities for shipment to markets. It is also common to find these assemblers handling the transportation, storage, grading, financing, and risk taking associated with this activity.

RETAILERS

Retailers are those middlemen who sell goods and services to the final consumer. In recent years retailing has become a dynamic field, characterized by rapid change, new innovations, and vigorous competition. (Table 13.1 provides a list of the ten largest retailers in the United States.) The kinds of stores and types of services offered by today's retailers are quite different from those provided thirty years ago. Comparing the modern supermarket with the local grocery store of the 1940s, for example, would reveal many significant changes.

TABLE 13.1 THE TEN LARGEST RETAILERS IN THE UNITED STATES, 1979

RETAILER	SALES (IN THOUSANDS)
Sears Roebuck	$17,514,252
Safeway Stores	13,717,861
K–Mart	12,858,585
J. C. Penney	11,274,000
Kroger	9,029,315
Great Atlantic & Pacific Tea	7,469,659
F. W. Woolworth	6,785,000
Lucky Stores	5,815,927
Federated Department Stores	5,806,442
Montgomery Ward	5,251,085

Source: *Fortune,* July 1980.

There are a number of ways to examine what retailing is all about. We shall look at retailing from

Door-to-door retailing is an effective method for marketing new products or goods that require a demonstration.

two viewpoints. First, we will examine the types of operations often found in retailing, including both conventional and mass merchandising. Then we will look at the kinds of ownership that exist at the retail level.

There are all sorts of retail operations. Some of these are called *conventional retailing facilities* because they have been with us for a long time. Illustrations include (a) door-to-door retailers, (b) general stores, (c) single-line, limited-line stores, (d) specialty shops, (e) department stores, (f) mail-order houses, and (g) vending machines.

Door-to-door retailers

The **door-to-door retailer** can be traced back to the old Yankee peddler. While this is an expensive way to sell merchandise, it can be a very effective method for marketing new products or goods that

Most retail stores are both single-line and limited-line.

require a demonstration before they can be fully appreciated. Some vacuums, such as the Electrolux, are sold this way, and that firm still claims the number-one position in the vacuum-cleaning business. Other products sold door to door include encyclopedias, Avon products, and Tupperware.

General stores

The **general store** has been with us for over a century. Prior to the Civil War it was the main type of retail outlet in the country. Today general stores are still in existence in some small towns and rural areas. These stores are typified by the wide range of goods they carry, from food and clothing to hardware and appliances.

Single-line, limited-line stores

A **single-line store** specializes in a particular line of merchandise such as groceries, furniture, or clothing. Some of these stores are also **limited-line** in that

they carry only certain assortments of these goods. Most retail stores are *both* single-line and limited-line, tending to stock one type of merchandise and then restricting the offerings to those lines that are most profitable. In a men's clothing store, for example, the line of suits might be restricted to the $80–$150 range because these tend to sell more quickly than any others.

Specialty shops

Specialty shops are limited-line stores that offer a unique product to a particular group of customers. The sales personnel in the store are very knowledgeable about the product, and the service they provide is of high quality. Stores selling gourmet food products, high-fashion dresses, women's shoes, or men's exclusive ties are illustrations of specialty shops. One of the major advantages of such a shop is that it caters to the needs of a specific type of customer and comes to know its clientele very well. This helps the sales personnel continue to make available the types and quality of products and services that these customers want.

Department stores
Department stores offer a *wide* variety of goods. Some people like to think of them as a collection of specialty stores all located under one roof. In a way this is an accurate picture, for these stores have a large number of departments, each offering a limited line of merchandise. There are housewares, house furnishings, men's wear, boys' wear, women's apparel, televisions, records, and cosmetics departments in many of them. Today millions of Americans rely on these stores to provide them with many of the goods and services they need for everyday living.

Mail-order houses
Mail-order houses sell their merchandise by mail, using catalogs and newspaper ads to attract customers. The range of merchandise offered for sale is usually quite large, and often includes clothing, home appliances, and leisure goods. Some of the largest mail-order houses include Sears, Roebuck; Montgomery Ward; and Gamble-Skogmo. Many people like to purchase through these houses be-

cause the prices are lower. For example, Sears' mail-order prices are about 10 percent less than in their retail stores.

Vending machines
A wide variety of merchandise is sold through **vending machines.** Most of these products have a high demand and are repurchased frequently. Illustrations include cigarettes, soft drinks, coffee, candy, and sandwiches. The major problem with vending machines is the high cost of operation. Nevertheless, these machines are widely used and consumers seem willing to pay the added cost for the service.

8. Why is door-to-door retailing an expensive way to sell merchandise?

9. In what way is a department store like a specialty shop?

10. If mail-order houses sell for less than retail outlets, why do buyers not purchase all their merchandise by mail?

Mass Merchandise Retailing
The previous section examined some traditional retailing outlets. In recent years, however, some new approaches have emerged that do not fit into the previous classification. Supermarkets and discount stores are illustrations. We call these retailers **mass merchandisers.** Their basic marketing strategy is to offer low prices in order to achieve high sales volume and fast turnover.

Supermarkets
Supermarkets are large stores that sell primarily groceries, although they also carry nongrocery items. The stores emphasize self-service and tend to handle only fast-moving merchandise. The average supermarket is around 30,000 square feet and offers free parking to its customers. Other services that are beginning to be made available by some include

check cashing, film processing, extended hours of operation (including Sunday), and delivery service.

Discount houses

Since World War II **discount houses** have moved into the retail field. Initially these stores sold appliances, furniture, and cameras at greatly reduced prices to those who were willing to come to the store, pay cash, and assume all responsibility for repair and service. Since the 1950s, however, when war shortages ended, buyers have demanded more and better service. Today discount stores can be found in good locations and offer a wide assortment of products, services, and guarantees. Gone is the old emphasis on discounting only "hard goods" such as radios and television sets; now discount houses are mass merchandisers also selling soft goods, such as clothing and groceries. In fact, they sell more food per store than the chain supermarkets. To a great degree these mass merchandisers are simply giant, departmentalized stores offering a wide range of goods at low prices. Examples include K-Mart, Gibson's, and Woolco. These developments have resulted in a narrowing of the gap between discount stores and department stores to a point where it is now difficult to distinguish between them.

What will come next? What will the future see in terms of retail stores? Some people are predicting **superstores** even larger than the current mass-merchandising operations. Included among them would be huge supermarkets offering not just grocery-related items but also other goods and services the consumer routinely purchases, all at a low price. These would include magazines, books, cigarettes, laundry services, shoe repair, and bill paying. We have already seen some stores moving in this direction, and if the trend continues it could mean the end of the supermarket as we currently know it.

11. In what way is a supermarket a mass merchandiser?

Eugene Ferkauf Makes Good

In the era since World War II, consumers have begun to seek more for their money. This has resulted in the rise of discount stores. One of the most famous was that founded by Eugene Ferkauf. Starting with $4,000 and a retail store, Ferkauf brought discount pricing into eastern department stores. In particular, he was aware of the great migration of the middle class to the suburbs. He therefore chose high-traffic locations in the suburbs, minimized markup, and built his Korvette store chain into one of the largest in the country.

By the mid-fifties Ferkauf's firm was grossing $55 million. Ferkauf then launched a major expansion program and sold one million shares of stock to the public. The stock came out at $10 per share and reached, at one point, $110 during the stock-market heyday of the 1960s. Meanwhile, to keep pace with changing tastes the Korvette chain added furniture, grocery, and auto servicing lines. In 1961 its sales volume was $180 million. In 1966, when it merged and became part of Spartans Industries, this had risen to $800 million. Eugene Ferkauf had helped usher in a new era in mass merchandising.

12. How has the product offering in discount stores changed over the last thirty years?

13. How might superstores of the future spell the end for today's department store? General store? Supermarket?

Retail Ownership

There are two basic types of retail ownership: (a) independents and (b) chain stores. Each has particular advantages and disadvantages.

Independents

Independent retail stores are usually owned by local people, often the same individuals who operate the business. Common examples are shoe stores, drugstores, and liquor stores. Most of these stores are small and are usually run as sole proprietorships or partnerships. While many of them are criticized as not being aggressive enough with their advertising and pricing policies, they often cater to their customers very carefully and have a good deal of repeat business. In addition, while most of the owners may have little personal knowledge about bookkeeping or accounting, they frequently hire accountants to make out their bills every month and keep them advised of their financial position. As a result, these "Mom and Pop" stores can still be found all over the country, and many of them are doing quite well.

Chain stores

When two or more stores in the same general line of business are controlled and operated by the same

---

CASE

A Shuddering Thought

A group of marketing students recently visited Ted Billings to ask him his projection on the future of retailing. Ted indicated that he was very concerned with the trend toward mass merchandising. In particular, he felt that single-line, limited-line stores and specialty shops would both come under tremendous competitive pressure in the future from superstores.

> This is really going to hurt my retail outlet. These superstores can buy in much larger volume than we can, so they can offer lower prices and greater selection. If we're going to hang in there we have got to emphasize personal service and quality, fashionable merchandise. I think we've done well so far, but thinking about the future makes me shudder. I wonder if retailing as we know it today will still be with us in ten years.

1. Of the retail operations listed in this section of the book, which ones do you think will be most hurt by the development of superstores?

2. In what way might superstores change retailing?

3. What can Ted do to compete with these new developments?

firm, we call them **chain stores.** Some of the best-known chains have hundreds of stores all over the country. Illustrations in the grocery field include A & P, Safeway, Kroger, and Acme. While the costs of operating a chain are extremely large, there are a number of important advantages to them. First, chain stores can buy merchandise in large quantities, thereby securing significant discounts. In fact, many chains act as their own wholesalers, purchasing directly from the manufacturer. These savings can then be passed along to the customer. Second, chains invest money in marketing research and so they often know both what customers will want and when. Third, the opportunities for advancement in a chain store are often good because there is always a great need for those with sales and management potential.

14. Will independents ever be driven out by the chain stores?

15. What are the advantages of shopping at an independent? A chain store?

PHYSICAL DISTRIBUTION

In moving the goods from the producer to the middleman and then on to the consumer, there must be some physical distribution activities. In particular, these involve storage and transportation.

Storage

No one can say with certainty how many items will be sold on a particular day. Therefore, in order to have a sufficient supply on hand, both wholesalers and retailers are required to store merchandise. Some of these goods, such as auto supplies or home appliances, are demanded on a year-round basis. When the supply starts to run low, new orders must be placed. Other goods, such as bathing suits and snow skis, are seasonal, requiring the company to order them prior to the beginning of the period and sell them before the season ends.

If a large amount of merchandise is ordered, the company must either have a big warehouse of its own or rent space from a public warehouse. Businesses that continually store a great amount of goods often find it profitable to build their own warehouses. The others rent facilities, with the rental fee based on the space used and the length of time the goods are stored.

Transportation

Transportation decisions involve the choosing of a **transportation mode.** In all, there are five: railroads, motor vehicles, waterways, pipelines, and airplanes. Every company will want to weigh the costs and benefits of these particular modes in deciding which one to use.

Railroads

Of all transportation modes, railroads carry the greatest volume of goods (see Table 13.2). For years they have transported heavy and bulky freight such as steel and coal. However, they have run into vigorous competition from motor carriers in handling less bulky commodities. To meet this threat to profitability, in recent years the railroads have introduced a number of new services designed to attract shippers. One of these is the **piggyback service.** This involves placing a fully loaded truck trailer on a specially designed flatcar and shipping the goods "piggyback" style. Because the merchandise does not have to be taken out of the truck and put in a railroad car and then reloaded into a truck when the shipment reaches its final destination, costs to the shipper are greatly lowered.

A second service is called **fast freight,** which is employed when goods are perishable and must get to their destination quickly. The railroads using it can move goods sixty miles an hour, stopping only to change crews or load water and ice. Services such as these can be very useful to middlemen who are trying to ship their goods quickly.

Motor vehicles

Trucks are very useful for moving small amounts of goods for short distances. They can be both economical and fast. Some shippers also like motor vehicles because they can travel on almost any road and can cover areas located in any geographical locale, from a busy downtown city to an isolated prairie town. For short distances, trucks are cheaper than trains.

Waterways

Waterways are very important in moving bulky, non-perishable items such as sand, iron ore, and steel.

While water transportation is slow, it is also the cheapest way to ship goods. In recent years improvements in waterways have increased the potential of water transportation. In addition, with the redesign of some ships, there is now a **fishyback** *service* offered by some shipping lines. This is similar to railroad piggyback, and involves placing large standard-size containers and truck trailers on board ship.

Pipelines

Pipelines in the United States are used primarily to carry petroleum and natural gas. There are many pipelines in the Southwest, which carry oil from the

Trucks are very useful for moving small amounts of goods for short distances.

TABLE 13.2 DOMESTIC FREIGHT TRAFFIC BY MAJOR CARRIERS (MILLIONS OF TONS)

	1960		1970		1978	
	TON-MILES	PERCENTAGE OF TOTAL	TON-MILES	PERCENTAGE OF TOTAL	TON-MILES	PERCENTAGE OF TOTAL
Railroads	579,130	44.1%	771,168	39.8%	870,000	35.8%
Motor trucks	285,483	21.7	412,000	21.3	602,000	24.7
Inland waterways	220,253	16.8	318,560	16.4	389,000	16.0
Oil pipelines	228,626	17.4	431,000	22.3	568,000	23.3
Air carrier	778	—	3,925	0.2	4,632	0.2

Reported in *Information Please Almanac*, 1980, p. 68.

fields to the refineries. Other modes of transportation, such as trucks and ships, then carry the product through the rest of the distribution channel. Pipelines are cheaper than railroads but more expensive than water transportation.

Airplanes

Airplanes offer the fastest means of transportation possible. However, they are also the most expensive. For this reason, they are used primarily for shipping perishable goods. Flying tropical flowers from the South Pacific to the United States and fruit from Florida to New York during the winter season are illustrations. Air rates are usually twice those of trucks, but if speed is of the essence the added cost may be justified.

16. Why are motor vehicles often cheaper than railroads for hauling goods short distances?

17. In what way is piggyback service on the railroads similar to fishyback service on ships?

18. Which mode of transportation is cheapest? Which is most expensive?

Because of the comparative high cost, air transport is used primarily when speed is of the essence.

SUMMARY

Channels of distribution are those routes that goods take in moving from producer to consumer. Some manufacturers sell directly to the final customer. Most, however, use some form of middleman, such as a wholesaler or retailer.

Wholesalers purchase goods and then sell them to buyers for resale. There are many types of wholesalers, the most common being merchant wholesalers, manufacturers' wholesale outlets, merchandise agents and brokers, petroleum bulk plants, and assemblers of farm products. Some of these individuals take title to the merchandise, others do not. All, however, are helpful to producers because they offer specialized services useful in moving the goods through the distribution channel.

Retailers are those who sell merchandise directly to the final consumer. Common illustrations include door-to-door retailers; general stores; single-line, limited-line stores; specialty shops; department stores; mail-order houses; vending machines; supermarkets; and discount houses. Most of the goods purchased by the average consumer are bought in these retail outlets. However, there have been major changes in buying habits over the last twenty years, and some types of retail stores are losing business while others are gaining. One of the biggest trends has been toward mass merchandising. This consists of offering a large variety of goods at a low price. Illustrations of mass merchandisers include K-Mart and Gibson's. If the present trend continues, we may be making all our routine purchases in one store before the next decade is over.

In moving goods through the distribution channels, there are five modes of transportation available. Railroads carry the greatest amount of goods each year and are economical for long-haul shipments. Motor vehicles are economical and fast for short hauls. Waterways offer the cheapest means of transportation and are widely used for moving bulky, nonperishable items such as sand and iron ore. Pipelines are used primarily to carry petroleum and natural gas; they are cheaper than railroads but more expensive than water transportation. Airplanes offer the fastest means for shipping goods. However, they are also the most expensive.

KEY TERMS FOUND IN THIS CHAPTER

QUESTIONS FOR DISCUSSION AND ANALYSIS

1. What are the most common channels of distribution for industrial and commercial goods? For consumer goods?

2. Why are wholesale merchants known as full-service wholesalers?

3. How does a truck jobber differ from a cash-and-carry wholesaler?

4. In what way are merchandise agents and brokers different from merchant wholesalers?

5. What do we mean when we say that agents and brokers do not take title to the goods?

6. In what way are most retail stores both single-line and limited-line stores?

7. What is mass merchandise retailing?

8. When is it likely that goods will be shipped by railroad? By water? By air?

14

Doing business without advertising is like winking at a girl in the dark. You know what you are doing, but nobody else does.
Stuart Henderson Britt

OBJECTIVES OF THIS CHAPTER

Few companies manufacture products and then sit back and wait for customers to come calling. Intelligent business-people know that the firm has to go out and sell these goods. The first objective of this chapter is to examine what is involved in promoting products, as promotion is vital to the sale of goods. The second objective is to study the area of personal selling, with particular attention given to making a sale. The third objective is to acquaint you with the importance of advertising. By the end of this chapter you should be able to do the following:

a. explain the role of promotion in the marketing of goods;

b. discuss the important steps involved in making a personal sale; and

c. describe some of the major types of advertising and how they can help a firm in selling its products.

Personal Selling and Advertising

PROMOTION

Some products almost seem to sell themselves. Most, however, require some form of promotion. The most common methods of promotion are personal selling and advertising. Other forms include contests, premiums, and trading stamps. Of course, the *best* method of promoting a given product will vary depending on both the good itself and the behavior of the consumer.

The Importance of Communication

The basic objectives of promotion are to *inform* customers about the company's product, *persuade* them to buy it, and *remind* them to repurchase it. Why do some promotion efforts work well, while others do not? The major reason is *communication*.

The company must choose the *right* communication channel for getting the message to the consumer. Some people respond better to radio or television advertising. Others are better informed with newspaper ads. Still others respond best to personal selling.

Therefore, in promoting a product we must return again to the communication process (see Fig. 14.1). The marketer or company attempting to sell the product must send a message through a communication channel in such a way that the consumer receives and understands the information. The **encoding process** involves converting the marketer's ideas into some form, such as a written message and/or picture. The **message channel** is the means used to convey the information. It might be a newspaper, a magazine, or a television advertisement. The **decoding process** involves the interpretation of the message by the receiver. If the marketer encodes the message properly and uses the right channel to

convey it to the receiver, the consumer will interpret the information the way the sender intended. In this case, effective communication has resulted. Of course, we cannot say with certainty that the receiver will go out and buy the product. But at least the firm has gotten its promotion of the good across to the consumer.

Adoption Curve and Product Life Cycle

Few products are overnight successes. Most tend to go through an **adoption curve.** First, a small percentage (3–5) of the market, often called **innovators,** will use the new products. Then more people (10–15 percent), called **early adopters,** will buy. These are then followed by the **early majority** (34 percent) and **late majority** (34 percent). Finally there are the **laggards or nonadopters** (5–16 percent), who either purchase very late in the product's life cycle or never buy the good. (See Fig. 14.2 for a diagram of this product adoption curve.) In selling its product, the company must know which of these groups is buying at any given time, so it can use the proper promotional strategy.

This adoption curve can be tied right to the product's life cycle. As we noted in Chapter 12, all products go through four cycles or stages: introduction, growth, maturity, and decline. During the *introduction* stage, the basic objective is to *inform* the consumer about the product. The company must stimulate demand among the innovators. As the product begins to be accepted and moves into the *growth* stage, competitors will begin fighting with the company for market share. This will require the company to broaden its promotional emphasis to that of *both informing and persuading* customers to buy and stay with its products. During the *maturity*

FIG. 14.1 *The communication process*

PERCENTAGE OF PEOPLE ADOPTING THE PRODUCT

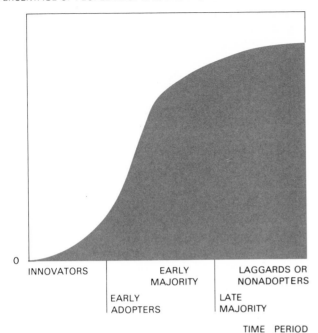

FIG. 14.2 *A product adoption curve*

stage, promotion programs tend to become less informative and *more persuasive*. People know the company's products, so it is now a matter of convincing them to repurchase them. During the sales *decline* stage, promotional expenses are reduced as the firm attempts to cut costs and remain profitable. Money spent on promotion will be directed toward the small group of people who still want the product.

1. What term is used to describe those individuals who are the first to adopt a new product? Why are they called this?

2. The adoption curve can be tied right to the product's life cycle. Explain this statement.

Promotion and the Purchaser

What type of promotion should be used in selling the company's products? This will all depend on who is the final consumer. In all, there are four different groups to whom business sells: industrial customers, wholesalers, retailers, and consumers.

Industrial customers purchase goods such as machinery or sophisticated equipment. These goods are often sold by personal salespeople who can answer technical questions about how the machinery works or what its specifications are. Because these sales often involve large sums of money and each customer has different needs and requirements, a personal approach is very helpful in promoting and closing the sale.

Personal salespeople are also very important in promoting goods to *wholesalers*. The latter tend to be very aware of cost and demand. If they are to buy a producer's goods, they need to be "sold" on the decision. In particular, they want to know what efforts the manufacturer will undertake to stimulate demand for the goods among retailers and consumers.

Promoting goods to *retailers* is also usually done with personal selling, although there is some emphasis given to advertising. Most retailers want to know how much the product will cost, what the markup will be, and what promotional assistance the manufacturer or wholesaler will provide in helping to sell the goods. As a result, much of the promotional effort is designed to *inform* the retailer of the terms of sale, although some of it is to *persuade* the individual to carry a particular line of merchandise. Personal selling is very important when dealing with retailers because they are the link with the customer. Unless the manufacturers or wholesalers can convince the retailer that he or she is an important link in their distribution channel, the retailer may never push their goods properly. Personal selling can create a warm relationship with the retailers and be invaluable in getting them to take on the company's products.

In most cases, promoting goods to millions of *final consumers* requires a nonpersonal approach.

This does not mean that personal selling is *never* used. However, if a producer wishes to reach a large audience at a low cost per person, advertising is often the most effective method. Every day in our local newspaper, as well as on television, we see and hear hundreds of advertisements designed to sell us all sorts of goods and services. This method of promotion has been highly successful in mass selling.

The key to choosing the most effective promotional approach is usually the product itself. If the goods are highly technical or questions about their use are likely to be raised, personal salespeople will be needed. If the goods are not very technical in nature or no explanation about their use is necessary, advertising or some other form of mass selling is often possible.

What you must remember is that in the final analysis effective promotion is possible only when the firm understands consumer behavior. The great difficulty in gaining a solid understanding of this behavior is in the complex nature of the consumer. This, in part, explains the complicated job promotion must perform, and points up why so much attention needs to be given to developing an effective promotional strategy. From here the firm can decide which promotional approach (or combination) will be best: personal selling or advertising.

3. Why is personal selling so important when dealing with industrial customers?

4. Why is a nonpersonal approach so widely used in promoting goods to final consumers?

PERSONAL SELLING

Personal selling is very important in moving certain types of goods. Regardless of the approach, however, the salesperson's job is a matter not so much of selling as of *helping the customer buy*. This is done by illustrating how the company's products can be of value to the purchaser. In discussing how this task is accomplished, we will consider four major aspects of personal selling: (a) order getting, (b) order taking, (c) making the sale, and (d) handling objections.

The salesperson's job is a matter not so much of selling as of helping the customer to buy.

Order Getting

Order getting, sometimes referred to as **creative selling,** involves seeking out potential buyers with a well-organized sales presentation. Often this presentation is designed to show the buyer how money can be saved or work made easier with the seller's product. Because effective sales personnel are highly knowledgeable about their product, they can often surprise their listener by pointing out short cuts or special jobs their product can perform. Another common approach is that of acting as an adviser or counselor to potential customers. The wholesaler, who works with the retailer in deciding what consumers want, frequently fills this role. So too does the encyclopedia salesperson who tries to get potential customers to see the encyclopedia as an investment that will last a lifetime and be of value to both them and their children.

Order Taking

Order taking is the completion of a sale to a customer who has expressed an interest in the product. Most sales transactions consist of order taking. A common illustration is the salesperson who helps a male customer choose a suit. The salesperson may show the man a number of different styles and colors, getting an idea of what the individual likes and is prepared to pay. Based on this information, the salesperson will then show the buyer a number of other suits, while commenting on the fabric, the cut, and the quality of the merchandise. After the buyer has chosen one, the salesperson will call for the tailor and see that the necessary alterations are made on the suit. He or she will also help the customer in choosing any shirts, ties, or other desired accessories. The last part of order getting consists of writing up the sales ticket, receiving payment or charging the purchase to the customer's account, and informing the individual about when the suit will be ready. Many people tend to downplay the job of order taking. This is unfortunate for it is at this point that the sale is actually made, and this is the major reason the company is in business.

Making the Sale

In actually making the sale, sales personnel must gear their presentation so that it takes the potential buyer through four phases: (a) attention, (b) interest, (c) desire, and (d) action.

Attention

Getting the buyer's attention can be difficult. If the salesperson knows the buyer, there is a basis for initial conversation. "Hi, how are you? It's nice to see you again. Can I help you with something today?" If the salesperson does not know the individual, a casual "Hello, can I help you?" is often a good opening. Another helpful feature in getting people's attention is a well-constructed sales display or a brochure that can be handed to the potential customer. Many times in selling equipment or machinery, the manufacturer provides a short written description of the product's features and advantages. Similarly, when promoting a washer, dryer, vacuum cleaner, or oven, it is common for the salesperson to provide some kind of short pamphlet, often printed on glossy paper and containing some pictures and a description of the product. These selling aids help to keep the buyer's attention.

Interest

An effective salesperson will try to get customers to tell a little about their interests. What are they looking for and what services do they want out of the product? As the individual talks, the seller has an opportunity to determine what is available and how it can satisfy the buyer's needs. The seller can also screen out those who are only "looking" from those who seem genuinely interested. After all, there is no point in going through an entire sales presentation for people who are obviously not interested. Among those who are, reference to sales brochures or comments on the high quality of the product can be helpful in maintaining interest.

Desire

If the customer does seem interested, the salesperson can then go on to illustrate exactly how the company's product can be of value. At this point it is often helpful to demonstrate the item. For example, the customer might like to know how the vacuum cleaner works, the way to use the accessories, or the proper method for changing the dust bags. In the case of sporting goods, some stores try to employ only salespeople who have actually used the products. After all, who can talk better about the advantages of a particular ski, for example, than someone who uses that brand all the time? When it comes to educational material such as encyclopedias, sales personnel often create desire by showing the individual how the books can be used as a reference source for gathering information on almost any topic in existence. Some have even gone so far as to provide purchasers with course outlines for home study. This technique is very appealing to adults who like to learn but do not have the time to attend formal classes. In the case of clothing such as suits or coats,

the seller may urge the individual to "try it on and see how it looks." Meanwhile, for individuals selling to middlemen, a common technique for arousing desire is to show statistics on how well the product is selling for other middlemen. In all cases, the seller's objective is to get the buyer to mentally examine the product and see how it meets his or her needs.

Action

The final step is to get the buyer to purchase the good. Many sellers fail to close the sale because they never ask for the order. Quite often they are afraid that the buyer will say no. One way of getting around having to ask directly is to review the strong points of the product and gear the discussion to the needs of the buyer. When this is done, the individual will often ask the salesperson for the merchandise. If this does not occur, there are many other indirect techniques that can help close the sale. One is to ask the

Displayed statistics represent a technique commonly used to prove how well a product is selling.

Nina Cohen

Many people believe that in the advertising and promotion area one rises to the top primarily on the basis of ability. A look at Nina Cohen's record would certainly support this statement. After graduating from the University of Florida, she soon made her way to Madison Avenue. It was six months before she was able to secure employment with an advertising agency. This did little to slow her progress. She eventually got a job at J. Walter Thompson and from here was "discovered" by the account executive, for the Ford Motor Company, who brought her onto his team. Within a year she was the Broadcast Buyer on the account, as well as handling other buying assignments on Scott Paper and Standard Brands. Eventually rising to the position of Senior Broadcasting Buyer, she was hired away by a Miami agency to be their buyer for a range of accounts including fast food, finance, and daily products. After working there for four years, she joined one of the individuals who had left that agency and started his own firm.

In seven years Nina rose to the position of Senior Vice-President/Media Director and is currently one of the most respected media people in the country. This statement is borne out in fact. One of the advertising industry publications has conducted an annual survey asking media salespeople during each of the last three years, throughout the Sun Belt, to name the Media Director they found to be the most competent and fair. Nina has ranked among the top three named people in these 11 states in all of the three surveys. Asked how she accounts for her success, she says, "It's all a matter of attitude and respect. We don't view the print/broadcast sales community as the enemy." For her and her agency, Caravetta Allen Kimbrough, her first principle of fairness still pays off.

person, "Shall we send that out to your house or would you like to take it with you?" Another is to start writing up the order. This may not only avoid embarrassment to the seller but serve as the little push the buyer needs in making the decision to purchase.

Once the sale is made, the salesperson should then be thinking about future business. How can the customer be persuaded to come back again? One of the most effective ways is to follow up by maintaining contact with the individual. If there is something wrong with the product, the salesperson handles the problem of getting it straightened out. If there is a special season sale a few months later, the salesperson sends the customer a postcard with a short note about the sale. In this way the seller maintains goodwill and rapport *after* the sale.

Handling Objections

At any point in the above process, especially during the last two steps, the seller is likely to encounter objections related to either the quality or performance of the product or its price. To handle these, many firms devote a great deal of time to helping their salespeople anticipate and overcome objections. In dealing with nonprice problems, the seller should usually handle them as they are raised. However, the further along one is in the presentation, the easier it is to respond to them. Price-related problems, meanwhile, should usually be handled only after the seller has demonstrated how the product can be of value to the buyer.

Many salespeople become nervous and edgy when confronted with objections. Actually, it is much easier to deal with buyers who communicate

CASE

The Ineffective Salesman

Ted Billings always had two or three college students working in his store on a part-time basis. When one graduated and moved on, he would fill the slot with another. Recently Ted hired a sophomore, George Hallar, who was majoring in business administration. George's primary interest was retail sales and Ted thought he would fit in well.

After a few weeks, however, it was evident that George was not very effective. In particular, he seemed to have trouble closing a sale. Sometimes things would seem to be going very well, and then suddenly the customer would leave the store without having purchased anything.

Ted decided to look into the matter. After working with and near George for a few days, three problems became evident. First, George was uneasy about starting a conversation with a customer. Second, he was embarrassed to ask the individual for the sale. He did not know how to close the transaction. Third, he sometimes disagreed with customers and drove them off. Ted decided that George needed some training in the basics of selling.

1. With which of the four phases of making a sale does George have the greatest difficulties? Explain.

2. How can Ted help George improve his performance in these areas?

3. What suggestions might Ted make regarding George's disagreeing with customers? How should objections from customers be handled?

their likes and dislikes than to sell to those who are noncommunicative. Most objections are a result of inadequate information. The buyer simply does not understand the benefits of the product or why it is necessary to set the price at its current level. Thus most objections are simply requests for more information. When they are not, a good salesperson listens attentively to them and tries to understand them. Sometimes the buyer has a valid point and the seller will be unable to sway the person. In all cases, however, effective salespeople never argue with customers and are very careful not to make them look foolish.

5. How does order getting differ from order taking?

6. Which of the four steps in making a sale is most important? Explain.

7. What are some general guidelines useful in helping a salesperson handle objections?

ADVERTISING

Every day of our lives we are exposed to hundreds of advertisements. From the morning paper that we read at breakfast to the late-night movie we see on television, we are subjected to advertising. Quite literally, advertising has become part of our way of life. Business relies heavily upon this *nonpersonal* or *mass communication* approach to help sell its products because, in contrast to personal selling, it is a far less expensive way of reaching mass markets. As a result, the advertising business is a multibillion-dollar industry today (see Table 14.1). In fact, it is predicted that by 1985 total annual advertising expenditures will be around $40 billion.

TABLE 14.1 THE TEN LEADING NATIONAL BUSINESS ADVERTISERS IN 1978

COMPANY	ADVERTISING EXPENDITURES*
Proctor & Gamble	$554,000,000
Sears Roebuck	417,900,000
General Foods	340,000,000
General Motors	266,300,000
K–Mart	250,000,000
Philip Morris	236,800,000
Warner-Lambert	211,000,000
Ford Motor	210,000,000
Bristol-Myers	192,800,000
Chrysler	188,900,000

Source: *Advertising Age*, September 6, 1979, p. 1.
* All totals are for the U.S. only and reflect expenditures by business firms.

Types of Advertising

There are two basic types of advertising: (a) product advertising and (b) institutional advertising. Each of these is used to attain particular objectives.

Product advertising

Product advertising, as is evident from its name, is concerned with selling a product. As we saw earlier, products have a particular life cycle. Advertising, therefore, must be geared to this cycle. Some advertising is used to introduce the product and build initial demand. This is called **pioneering advertising.** These ads inform people of the new product or service.

Once the product gets off the ground and starts to move, competition often enters the picture. The business must then switch to **competitive advertising,** which encourages the buyer to purchase the company's product over that of the competition. Emphasis is now given to the firm's brand name. For example, Chevrolet ads do not urge us to buy a car, they encourage us to "buy a Chevy." And the aspirin manufacturers tell us to buy *their* particular brand of aspirin. Meanwhile, airline ads, which are highly competitive, provide information on prices and timetables and the telephone number to call for reservations, encouraging us to fly *their* particular airline.

As a product reaches a mature stage, or starts to decline, firms then switch to **reminder advertising.** These ads are designed simply to keep the product's name before the public, because people tend to forget things such as brand names. As such, the ads often use a soft-sell approach. Illustrations include Coca-Cola, Kellogg's Corn Flakes, and Seven-Up advertisements, which remind us to repurchase particular products.

Institutional advertising

Institutional advertising is designed to remind people of the name or reputation of a company or industry. For example, General Motors is currently building an ad campaign around Mr. Goodwrench. The campaign is designed to support the corporation's dealer network by urging the customer to come to the dealer for auto service. Meanwhile, in the case of industry institutional advertising, there are the oil companies who are currently telling the public that they are using their revenues to explore for more oil, and there are the orange growers who are telling us that "orange juice isn't just for breakfast anymore," thereby encouraging us to drink their product any time during the day.

Worldwide Advertising

Perhaps the biggest problem advertisers face is that of writing an ad that appeals to the market. This can be a particularly difficult chore if the advertiser does not understand the customer, as is often the case when writing ads for a foreign market.

Oh sure, there are some ads that can be used worldwide. For example, in Hong Kong the hamburger clown, Ronald McDonald, looks about the same as he does in the states. And Merrill, Lynch, Pierce, Fenner & Smith use the bull as their trademark. However, these are the exceptions. Consider the Marlboro man, tirelessly riding his horse across the plain, pausing contemplatively atop his steed to survey the terrain. This goes over great in the U.S., but it doesn't sell cigarettes in Hong Kong. The Hong Kong Chinese, an affluent and urban people, don't see the joy of riding around

all day in the hot sun. So, today, the Marlboro man is still a cowboy but he's younger and better dressed than the original American counterpart. And he owns a truck as well as a horse, and a piece of Marlboro country, too.

Similarly, the Singer Sewing Machine Company recently proposed an outdoor ad campaign using bright Prussian blue. However, the firm's local distributor quickly pointed out that this shade of blue is known as the death color. The campaign was stopped, and just in time.

Of course, these are only a few examples of advertising problems. Many illustrations can be cited in the local and national, as well as international, markets. However, they all have one thing in common—they illustrate the importance of understanding the market to which the ad is directed.

All of these advertisements are designed to promote a quality image in people's minds. This image extends not to just one of a company's products but to all of them. In a manner of speaking, the firm is selling itself and its entire product line at the same time.

The major question for business, then, is how much money should we spend on each of the various forms of promotion, personal selling, and advertising? The answer will depend on two things. First, based on the job to be done, which form(s) of promotion will be most effective? Second, how much money is there available to spend on each?

8. If a company has a well-established product, What type of advertising will it do?

9. On what kind of advertising would you expect most firms to spend the bulk of their advertising budget: product or institutional?

"AT EASTERN, WE'RE SOLVING THE PROBLEM OF OVERCROWDING BY ADDING MORE PEOPLE."

—FRANK BORMAN, PRESIDENT, EASTERN AIRLINES.

As airfares have come down, airline traffic has gone up. And, too often, that's led to crowded terminals and long lines—a situation that's

A VIEW ON CROWDED AIRPORTS FROM EASTERN.

been particularly annoying to the most frequent fliers.

At Eastern Airlines, we don't think any of our customers should be inconvenienced just because there are more of them. And we're trying hard to see that it does not happen to you.

We've hired over a thousand new employees, specifically to work at airports. So, at Eastern terminals across the country, you'll find extra ticket agents and gate agents working to shorten lines. And more baggage handlers to speed you on your way.

But simply adding more people isn't enough. Because it's the quality of service our people provide that's really important. All of us at Eastern know that earning our wings every day is more than just a set of words. It's a commitment and a promise to give you good, personal service every time you fly.

No matter how frequently you fly with us. Or how many of you there are.

EASTERN
WE HAVE TO EARN OUR WINGS EVERY DAY.™

Advertising Ingredients

There are some ingredients or characteristics that an ad should have if it is to be effective. In general, these can be classified under the categories of layout, copy, typeface, and color.

Layout

Layout deals with what we see in an ad and where it is located. In the Eastern Airlines advertisement, for example, we see a headline, the name and title of the person in the ad, a picture, some additional written material, and the logo, name and slogan of the firm. These elements have been placed on the page in a particular order. The ad is designed to catch our attention and to interest us in reading it. If an advertisement is laid out properly, it will do this.

Copy

Copy is the reading matter in the ad. Almost all advertisements contain some copy. Many individuals feel that ads are read, either partially or totally, based on their copy. Certainly effective copywriters need to know something about the individuals to whom the ad is being directed so that they can make it interesting to these individuals. To a large degree this means writing a catchy headline. The one in the Eastern ad is effective because many people are interested in learning how the airline is solving the problem of overcrowding. They, therefore, read the rest of the ad to learn how Eastern is doing this. The material under the picture does this in an interesting, informative, and factual way—all important characteristics for effective copy.

Typeface

Some ads are set in one **typeface,** but most are set in several. The Eastern ad has five: the headline, the president's name and the text, the comment in the center of the far left-hand paragraph, the name of the firm in the lower right, and the slogan beneath the name. Naturally the typeface is chosen to attract attention. However, another consideration in this area is deciding how much white space to leave between the line of copy. In short, the format must be appealing.

Color

Finally, some ads use color, while some are strictly black and white. The Eastern ad was originally a multicolored magazine ad. Many advertisers like to use color. First, color advertisements attract more attention than do black-and-white ads. Second, they help in identification. When a buyer sees a product in a magazine and then goes to the store and sees one exactly like it, this helps sales. Third, some goods cannot really be advertised well in black and white. Food, automobiles, and cosmetic makeup are illustrations. Fourth, color adds strength to an ad. For example, yellow can be used to create a feeling of youth or spring; blue for coldness; red for bravery or passion. Of course, color ads cost more than black-and-white ones, so the firm has to decide whether the sales that are generated justify the cost.

10. Why do many people feel that ads are read, either partially or totally, based on their copy?

11. Why are color ads often superior to black-and-white ads?

Advertising Media

To communicate their ads to the public, advertisers have a number of media available. Some of the most commonly used ones include (a) newspapers, (b) magazines, (c) radio, (d) television, (e) direct mail, and (f) outdoor advertising (see Table 14.2).

Newspapers

Many businesses use **newspaper advertising.** The major advantage of newspaper ads is that they can cover a selected area extensively. They are particularly good for local advertising. Their major draw-

TABLE 14.2 ADVERTISING EXPENDITURES IN 1978

MEDIUM	TOTAL (IN MILLIONS)	PERCENTAGE OF TOTAL
Newspaper	$12,690	29.0%
National	1,810	4.1
Local	10,880	24.9
Magazines	2,595	5.9
Weeklies	1,165	2.7
Women's	670	1.5
Monthlies	760	1.7
Radio	2,955	6.8
Network	160	.4
Spot	610	1.4
Local	2,185	5.0
Television	8,850	20.2
Network	3,910	8.9
Spot	2,600	5.9
Local	2,340	5.4
Direct Mail	6,030	13.8
Outdoor	465	1.1
National	310	.7
Local	155	.4
Farm Papers	105	.2
Business Papers	1,420	3.3
Miscellaneous	8,630	19.7
National	4,495	10.3
Local	4,135	9.4
U.S. Grand Total	$79,925	100.0%

Source: *Statistical Abstract of the United States,* 1978, p. 595

back, however, is that not everyone who reads the paper will be interested in the product being advertised. Nevertheless, newspaper ads are widely used by business and currently receive the greatest percentage of the advertising dollar.

Magazines

Millions of Americans read magazines. As a result, advertisements in them will often be seen by many, many people. *TV Guide, Reader's Digest,* and *Time,* for example, command very large audiences. In addition, national magazines will often run regional issues so that a manufacturer whose goods are marketed in the Midwest can advertise in that area only and is not charged for national distribution. Still another advantage of **magazine advertising** is that the issue is often kept around the house for some time before being thrown out. This gives advertisers a better chance of having their ads read. Perhaps the biggest disadvantage is that magazines usually require advertisers to have their ads submitted to the publisher six to eight weeks before publication.

Radio

Radio advertising, especially on a local basis, is widely used today. One of its biggest advantages is that it allows the advertiser to select both the territory and the audience to whom the message is to be directed. Radio advertising has been very effective, especially during daylight hours. In the evening, however, many people switch their attention to TV.

Television

The amount of money spent on **television advertising** over the last five years has risen dramatically. In fact, we may see the day when more of the advertising dollar is spent on TV than any other medium. Perhaps the greatest advantage of television advertising is that it allows a product to be seen and demonstrated, at the same time as a verbal message is being delivered. In all, there are three types of TV ads: network, spot, and local. A **network ad** is directed at a major audience around the country. The viewers all see the same message at the same time. A **spot ad** or **announcement** is a message broadcast over one or more stations at various times; each station sends out the message separately. With spot ads advertisers can choose the station, time, and program for their message. **Local ads** are carried only in the immediate area. They are often used by local merchants and are cheaper than either network or spot ads.

Direct mail

Direct-mail advertisements are sent to people's homes. Illustrations include circulars announcing weekly grocery specials, a letter from an oil company offering a special price to credit-card holders on a set of tools, or a catalog announcing a sale. Many businesses like this approach because it not only helps them cover a wide territory but can also be directed at a particular market. For example, the catalog is sent only to the store's current customers. One of the problems with these ads, however, is that the receivers often throw them away without ever reading them.

Outdoors

Outdoor ads include printed billboards, painted signs, and electrical displays. These ads are directed at people who are passing by. As a result, they have to be simple and to the point. If they are placed in a locale where many people will see them, they can be effective. However, recent attempts to "beautify America" have led to restrictions on the kind and number of outdoor advertisements permitted.

Writing and Placing the Ad

Once a business decides to advertise, it is confronted with two major questions. One, how should the ad be written? Two, with which media should the ad be placed? One way of handling these questions is to turn them over to an advertising agency.

Advertising agencies

An **advertising agency** specializes in writing and placing ads. Large corporations, in particular, tend to use these professional organizations to help them advertise their products. Among the largest agencies are J. Walter Thompson, McCann-Erickson, and Young & Rubicam.

Advertising agencies can handle all phases of advertising for their clients, from writing the copy for the ad to creating the artwork and choosing the media. Just about all of the network ads we see on television, as well as those we read in national

Outdoor ads have to be simple and to the point.

"None of us likes to insult their intelligence, Bolton, but it just so happens that it pays to insult their intelligence."

From The Wall Street Journal; permission Cartoon Features Syndicate

magazines, are produced by professional agencies. For their services, the ad agencies are usually paid a 15-percent commission, although this has varied in recent years. The basic fee is usually based on either the size of the ad (in the case of newspapers or magazines) or its length (in the case of television and radio). For example, if an agency working on a 15-percent fee buys TV time for its client at a cost of $85,000, the agency bills the client $100,000, deducts its $15,000 fee, and turns the rest over to the television company.

The costs of these services, of course, can be quite high. As a result, it is common to find ad agencies used far more by large companies than by small ones. When a firm does decide to use an agency, it will usually ask a number of them to make a presentation on how they would handle the advertising account if it were turned over to them. After evaluating the proposals, the company will choose one agency. Often this choice is made by the firm's advertising manager, for it is this individual who will serve as the company's liaison with the agency. From then on the agency, working with this manager and her or his department, will be responsible for producing and placing all company advertising. Of course, if the firm does not use an ad agency, its own advertising department will be responsible for preparing and placing the company's advertising.

Do it yourself

Thousands of businesses, especially small manufacturers, wholesalers, and retailers, have little money to spend on an ad agency. For them, the preparation and placement of advertising copy is strictly a do-it-yourself proposition. This is not to imply that the ads are either unprofessional or ineffective; many of them are very good for the purpose for which they are created. One of the most common illustrations is the ad we see in our daily newspaper telling us about a sale being offered by a local merchant. Another is the flyer we find stuffed under our door, relating the latest prices and discounts at the nearby drugstore. These ads provide us with all the information we need in order to shop wisely. Thus, for these small businesses, personally prepared ads do the job quite well.

12. Why is TV such a popular advertising medium?

13. Will TV advertising expenditures ever surpass newspaper advertising expenditures?

14. When should a company consider using an advertising agency? When would it be foolish to use one?

The Real Story of "Heinz 57"

Say "Heinz 57" to someone and they are likely to reply "ketchup" or "steak sauce" or any of a hundred other food seasonings. And for years the products of Henry J. Heinz were advertised with the slogan "57 Varieties," leading most people to believe that this was the number of products the firm sold. Actually, when Heinz adopted this famous slogan in 1896 his firm was already making more than fifty-seven varieties of seasonings, many of which are still found, by the way, on the dining room tables of American homes--pepper, chili sauce, mustard, onions, and pickles, to name but a handful.

What Heinz had felt he needed was a catchy advertisement for promoting his products. One day while riding on the New York City elevated he saw an ad promoting twenty-one styles of shoes. Thinking over the gist of the advertisement, he realized that he needed a similar number, with poetic cadence, that everyone could remember. He decided that "57" was such a number and he began putting it everywhere--on bottles, jars, cans, and billboards. And soon, whenever people saw the slogan, they thought of his products. His idea proved to be a tremendous success. By the time his company dropped the "57" from its corporate symbol in 1969, it had over twenty times that number of products and was a multi-million dollar corporation. And a great deal of this success was directly attributable to the slogan that Heinz had chosen for his products.

How Effective Is Advertising?

Many people, especially those who are paying for the ads, would like to be able to judge the effectiveness of their advertisements. Are the ads resulting in sales or would people have bought the product even if they had not seen the commercial message? Unfortunately, it is difficult to answer this question. However, there are some techniques that are currently used to help measure, at least indirectly, the effectiveness of advertising.

One of these is the **consumer pretest,** in which consumers are asked to examine advertisng copy that has not been released for publication. They are asked to rank the ads along such lines as their effectiveness in getting and holding interest and their overall appeal or attractiveness. This method is used to prejudge the effectiveness of various ads.

A second method is the use of **readership reports.** This consists of asking readers of certain magazines and newspapers questions about ads that appeared in these media. The person conducting the study shows the readers some of the ads and tries to find out which ones they recognize, which they are able to associate with the company that ran the ad, and in which cases they read over 50 percent of the advertisement.

A third method, used to test radio and television advertising effectiveness, is to have telephone operators call homes at random and find out if the TV is on and, if so, what station is being watched. A fourth method, and perhaps the most controversial, is the **Nielsen Audimeter.** This is a mechanical device that is installed in a person's home and records on tape when a set is turned on and to which channel it is tuned. Each tape is replaced every two weeks and sent to the A.C. Nielsen Company for analysis. These Nielsen ratings are the ones that determine the fate of many of our TV shows. If Nielsen says they are being watched, the show is considered a hit; if they are not, the show is often canceled. The problem with the Nielsen ratings, in the opinion of many, is that only 1,050 households have audimeters and

The Persistent Advertising Agency

A local advertising agency recently contacted Ted Billings in an effort to gain his store's advertising account. Ted explained to the woman that the firm's annual advertising budget was only $12,000 and that therefore they simply could not afford an ad agency.

Two weeks later the woman called on Ted. With her she brought some of the ads Ted's store had been running in the local paper. She also had some similar advertisements created by her own agency. Placing the ads alongside each other, she tried to show Ted how her agency people had taken each of the store's ads and improved them. "If you let us handle your advertising," she told Ted, "we could increase the readership of your ads. This would result in more sales for you." Ted told the woman he'd get back to her in a week.

After discussing the matter with his staff, Ted turned down the agency. There were two reasons behind the refusal. First, Ted felt the agency's fee, which would be 20 percent of the store's total advertising budget in this case, was too high. Second, the personnel currently writing the store's advertising copy were unconvinced that the agency's ads would be any more effective than the present ones.

1. What are the advantages of using an advertising agency?

2. What bases should a company use in deciding whether or not to employ an advertising agency?

3. Was Ted right or wrong in turning down the agency? Explain.

3,000 more fill out weekly diaries of their television viewing. Is this a sufficient sample for accurately determining which programs (and the accompanying advertising, of course) people are watching?

All of these tests provide only an indirect measure of advertising effectiveness. We do not know for sure that ads that are read and/or remembered will produce sales. However, until someone designs a more direct type of test for evaluating advertising effectiveness, current procedures will have to do.

15. How does a consumer pretest work?

16. How are readership reports used to evaluate advertising effectiveness?

17. If you were going to evaluate an ad's effectiveness, how would you do it? Explain.

SUMMARY

Very few goods sell themselves; most need to be promoted in some way. When new goods first hit the market, customers need to be informed about them. As the products start to become established, buyers must be persuaded to both purchase and stay with these goods. As the products start declining in demand, promotional efforts must be directed at those who still want the goods.

What is the best way to promote a good? For those requiring some kind of explanation or demonstration, personal selling is often superior. This approach is commonly used in selling to industrial customers, wholesalers, and retailers. For selling to final consumers, however, it is more common to find a nonpersonal approach, such as advertising, heavily relied upon.

Personal selling involves two major activities: order getting and order taking. Meanwhile, in actually making the sale there are four major steps: (a) attention, (b) interest, (c) desire, and (d) action. Effective sales personnel know the value of each of these steps. They also know how to tactfully handle objections related to either the quality or the price of a product.

However, when personal selling is too expensive, a nonpersonal approach must be used. Advertising is the most common nonpersonal method. In essence there are two types of advertising: product and institutional. Product advertising is concerned with selling a product. Institutional advertising is designed to remind people of the name or reputation of a company or industry.

All advertising copy must be capable of catching a person's eye and getting him or her to read the message. This requires careful layout, interesting copy, attention-getting typeface, and appealing color. It also requires choosing the right advertising media for the message. Some of the more common media are newspapers, magazines, radio, television, direct mail, and the outdoors.

Writing and placing advertising copy can also be quite a chore. For this reason, many of our large corporations hire professional advertising agencies to do the job. However, for thousands of firms the cost of an ad agency is too high. For them advertising is a do-it-yourself proposition, and many of them have done very well working up their own ads. Yet there is one problem that still confronts advertisers. Is the ad effective? Measuring advertising effectiveness is difficult and to date we have tended to rely on indirect techniques such as consumer pretests and readership reports.

KEY TERMS FOUND IN THIS CHAPTER

QUESTIONS FOR DISCUSSION AND ANALYSIS

1. In what way is the adoption curve of a product tied to its life cycle?

2. To which group of customers is personal selling of importance: industrial customers? wholesalers? retailers? consumers?

3. What are the four steps involved in making a sale? Describe each.

4. What is product advertising? How does it differ from institutional advertising?

5. Exactly what is involved in advertising layout? What about advertising copy?

6. Why do you think newspaper ads receive the greatest percentage of the advertising dollar?

7. How do network television ads differ from television spot ads?

8. What benefits can be obtained from using an advertising agency?

15

It is not possible for this nation to be at once politically internationalist and economically isolationist. This is just as insane as asking one Siamese twin to high dive while the other plays the piano.

Adlai Stevenson

OBJECTIVES OF THIS CHAPTER

In the last three chapters we have been examining some of the important areas of marketing. One further, and very important, area is that of international marketing, or, as it is commonly known, international trade. No study of business would be complete without at least some attention to this topic.

The first objective of this chapter is to explain the reasons why nations trade with each other. The second is to discuss some of the traditional problems associated with international trade. The third is to examine the role of American business in this international trade arena. When you are finished reading this chapter you should be able to do the following:

a. identify the three major reasons for international trade;

b. define the principles of absolute advantage and comparative advantage;

c. describe some of the traditional problems faced by firms in the international arena; and

d. explain the role the United States has played in international trade.

International Trade

WHY DO NATIONS TRADE?

Most nations of the world **export** goods to other countries. Likewise, most **import** goods from other nations. Why do countries of the world engage in international trade? Why are they not self-sufficient, capable of living exclusively on the goods and services produced within their own borders? Various answers can be cited. In general, however, the reasons for international trade can be classified as (a) resource reasons, (b) economic reasons, and (c) political reasons.

Resource Reasons

Some nations of the world have certain conditions or resources that provide them with a basis for international trade. Illustrations include (a) favorable climatic conditions and terrain, (b) natural resources, (c) skilled workers, (d) capital resources, and (e) favorable geographic location and transportation costs.

Favorable climatic conditions and terrain

Some countries have year-round or seasonal weather conditions that make them ideally suited for the raising of particular crops. For example, Colombia and Brazil have just the right climate for growing coffee beans. The United States, with the exception of Hawaii, does not. Therefore, the United States must import coffee. On the other hand, our Great Plains states such as Kansas, Nebraska, South Dakota, and North Dakota, are major wheat-producing areas. The climate and terrain in these locales are ideal for raising this crop. In fact we grow so much wheat in the United States that we are able to export some, selling it to other nations abroad. Thus, climate and terrain help determine some of the goods a nation can produce and trade internationally.

Natural resources

If a country has an abundance of natural resources, it is common to find some of these resources being exported. Among less developed nations the raw materials may be sold before being processed. Tin from Bolivia and oil from some of the Middle East countries are examples. On the other hand, among highly industrialized nations the raw materials are often sold in finished form. For example, the United States sells its iron ore in the form of steel products such as automobiles and machinery. Yet regardless of how they are sold, raw materials play a major role in determining a country's involvement in international trade.

Skilled workers

If a nation has a great many skilled workers, it can produce sophisticated equipment and machinery, such as computers, jet aircraft, and electric generators. The United States, Japan, and Western Europe are illustrations. On the other hand, some nations have basically unskilled work forces and must confine their activities to the manufacture of simple products. India, Pakistan, and Indonesia are illustrations. The skill of a country's work force helps determine what it will be able to produce and trade with other countries.

Capital resources

Another important factor in international trade is that of capital resources. These include things such as plant, machinery, and equipment. The more capital resources a nation has, the better its chance to free its workers from menial jobs and allow them to work on more important tasks. In these countries, while the machines do the busy work people concentrate their attention on "think" jobs, such as developing technological breakthroughs that will result in a higher standard of living for the nation. Poor countries, of course, lack these capital resources and must rely heavily on manual labor in making goods for both domestic consumption and international trade.

Favorable geographic location and transportation costs

Nations located near each other tend to do more trading than those located thousands of miles apart.

The reason is quite simply that the transportation costs are less so the overall price of the goods is more appealing. Therefore, while raw materials are important to international trade, so too is geographic location.

1. Which of the resources listed in this section is the most important in raising a country's standard of living? Explain.

Economic Reasons

Another reason why nations engage in international trade is to secure some kind of economic benefit. However, this gain will be obtained only if they produce and sell the *right* good(s). In determining which good(s) these are, the businesspeople of the country must understand two important principles: (a) absolute advantage, and (b) comparative advantage.

Absolute advantage

A nation can have an **absolute advantage** if either of two conditions exist. First, the country must have something that cannot be obtained anywhere else. An example would be diamonds from South Africa. There are some countries that produce small amounts of diamonds every year, but for all practical purposes South Africa has a monopoly position in this field. For this reason, we say that it has an absolute advantage.

A second method of obtaining an absolute advantage is to produce a good more cheaply than anyone else. For example, Colombia grows coffee beans. So could the United States if it really wanted to. However, the expense associated with such a venture makes it uneconomical. It would cost a fortune to build huge indoor plantations for raising coffee. Therefore, we import our coffee and expend our efforts in other areas.

If nations are wise, they concentrate their efforts on the things they can do best and rely upon inter-

Colombian farmer feeding coffee cherries into the depulping machine.

national trade to make up the deficiencies. In this way they are able to improve their standard of living.

Comparative advantage

Comparative advantage takes place when a nation chooses to produce the product that yields it the *greatest advantage*. For example, a country may be capable of profitably producing both radios and cameras. However, it tends to specialize in radios and export the surplus to other countries in exchange for cameras.

In order to make this point about comparative advantage in international trade clearer, consider the case of two nations: Y and Z. Each can produce radios and cameras. Nation Y can make more of each than can Nation Z, as seen by the following data:

	Radios	Cameras
Nation Y	600,000	300,000
Nation Z	300,000	250,000

If neither trades with any country, nation Y will manufacture and use 600,000 radios and 300,000 cameras. Nation Z, meanwhile, will manufacture and use 300,000 radios and 250,000 cameras. How-ever, if each decides to specialize and then trade for the other product, both nations must determine the good that gives them the greatest comparative advantage. In the case of radios, nation Y has a 2:1 (600,000 versus 300,000) advantage. In the case of cameras this advantage is 1.2:1 (300,000 versus 250,000). Therefore, while nation Y has the advantage in both cases, it has the *greatest* comparative advantage in the case of radios. By concentrating all of its energies on this product, it can produce far more than 600,000 and trade the surplus to nation Z. Likewise, by producing only cameras, nation Z can turn out far more than 250,000 and trade the surplus to nation Y. Therefore, to restate the principle of comparative advantage, *a nation should concentrate its efforts on the production of those goods in which it has the greatest comparative advantage or relative efficiency.*

2. On which of the two above principles, absolute or comparative advantage, do you think the United States relies most heavily? Explain.

The global demand for U.S. produced airplanes is an example of comparative advantage.

Political Reasons

Some nations of the world trade with others for basically political reasons. For example, the USSR has traded with Cuba for two decades now because the Soviets want to support a government in that country that is in basic agreement with their political doctrine. The United States has traded with South Korea for similar reasons. In both cases, political objectives have outweighed economic considerations.

The reverse is also true: nations often refuse to trade with others because of political disagreements. For decades the United States had no trade involvement with mainland China and very little with the Soviet Union. Of course, now that America is moving closer to détente with China, trade is increasing between us; while because of the Soviet invasion of Afghanistan in 1980, the U.S. is moving to reduce its trade with Russia. And if relations between our country and Cuba should improve, we would find a similar situation there. Economically speaking, the United States would obtain an additional source of cigars and sugar. Meanwhile Cuba could use the American dollars to bolster her economy. However, realistically speaking there must be a mix of economics and politics in fashioning an international trade policy. As a result, at least at this writing, China and Russia are "in" and Cuba is "out."

3. In international trade, political considerations often outweigh economic considerations. Explain this statement.

UNIQUE PROBLEMS IN INTERNATIONAL TRADE

International trade is similar to domestic trade in several ways. For example, businesses must still offer goods and services that people want and are able to afford. Likewise, some kind of sales effort must be exerted to call the goods to the attention of prospective buyers and to bring about their sale. And, of course, there must be some profit in it for the business.

A Saudi Arabian engineer works on equipment that's part of a national telecommunications network Western Electric was contracted to establish for the Saudi Arabian Government.

However, there are also some unique problems in international trade and companies doing business overseas must be aware of them. In particular, these include (a) cultural problems, (b) monetary conversion, (c) trade barriers, and (d) the possibility of nationalization.

Cultural Problems

When companies do business overseas, they come in contact with people from different cultures. These individuals often speak a different language and have their own particular customs and manners. These differences can create problems.

Language

Language is important in international trade because buyers and sellers must be able to communicate and agree on many important matters, including the specific terms of the transaction. In countries that are non-English speaking, American businesspeople have tried to overcome this obstacle through the use of interpreters. This has helped a great deal. So too has the fact that over the last thirty years English has become the accepted language of international trade. Despite these developments, however, language remains a common cultural problem.

Customs and manners

Many countries also have different customs, of which foreign businesspeople should be aware. For example, in the United States an executive might bring a Japanese businessperson home for dinner. This would be one way they could get to know each other on an informal basis and overcome cultural barriers. Back home, however, the Japanese executive would never bring an American counterpart to his or her house for dinner. In Japan the home is not used for business entertainment; instead, businesspeople are taken out to dinner. Unless Americans are aware of this, however, they might feel they are being slighted by their Japanese host.

Manners are also important. In certain countries people are expected to behave in a particular way. For example, in France business meetings begin

Chemical Bank がほかの国際的銀行とちがうのは お金だけでなく、アイデアも提供できる点です」

"The difference between Chemical Bank and the other international giants isn't their money. It's their ideas."

More than money. In any language. CHEMICAL BANK

promptly at the designated time and everyone is expected to be there. Foreign businesspeople who are tardy are often left outside to cool their heels as a means of letting them know the importance of promptness. Unless Americans are aware of such expected behaviors they may end up insulting the people with whom they had hoped to establish international trade relations.

4. Why might the use of interpreters be insufficient when doing business in non-English-speaking nations?

Bribery and Foreign Trade

One common custom in international business not often discussed in textbooks is that of bribery or special payments. Recently this has become a major source of embarrassment for Lockheed Aircraft. Like it or not, however, only the most naive believe such payoffs are either unnecessary or useless. Officials in many foreign countries expect it and it has become a customary business practice in their nations.

In fact, in the last few years some Eastern European countries have actually begun to shake down Western firms doing business there. For example, the General Refractories Company of Balacynwyd, Pennsylvania, paid a Romanian military officer $250,000 for the release of an employee of an Austrian subsidiary who had been accused of "industrial espionage" in Romania. The government there called it a fine, but company officials called it ransom and linked payment to the firm's continued ability to do business in that country. Bulgaria and Poland are also regarded as having a high degree of business corruption.

However, American business firms have to be careful about assuming that all officials are on the take. In East Germany and the Soviet Union bribery is both rare and hazardous. One businessman who attempted to bribe a Soviet factory manager was recently sentenced to 15 years in prison. A rather harsh sentence, but not as great as that given to the factory manager--he was shot by a firing squad. All of which points out the importance of knowing the proper business practices and customs when dealing with foreign nations.

---

5. How can Americans doing business overseas deal with cultural problems such as customs and manners?

Monetary Conversion

A second traditional problem is that of **monetary conversion.** When companies conduct business with overseas firms, they often end up dealing in the currency of that country. For example, if an American business sells something to a firm in France, the latter will probably pay for it in francs. If a similar transaction is conducted with the Soviet Union, payment will be made in rubles. Of course, this currency is of little value to the American firm. It is, therefore, necessary to convert the foreign currency to American dollars. How much are these Russian rubles worth in terms of dollars? This conversion rate is determined every business day in international money markets, where the currencies of countries are bought and sold. Thus there is an established rate, although it will often fluctuate from day to day. For example, the ruble may be worth $0.75 on Monday and $0.72 on Tuesday because of an announced wheat shortage in Russia. This, of course, can create a problem for the business that receives 1 million rubles on Monday, valued at $750,000, and finds them worth only $720,000 on Tuesday because of the announced wheat shortage. In addition, there

From The Wall Street Journal; permission Cartoon Features Syndicate

Harassed currency dealer during hectic trading.

is the dilemma associated with converting at $0.72. Some financial institutions may be unwilling to pay this price, feeling that the ruble will sink much lower over the next week. As a result, conversion may finally come at $0.69. These "losses" must be accepted by the company as one of the costs of doing business overseas.

6. Given the fact that companies doing business overseas face monetary conversion problems, do you think most raise their prices to cover this risk?

Trade Barriers

A third unique problem is trade barriers. For one reason or another, all countries impose trade barriers on certain goods crossing their borders. Some trade barriers are directly related to exports. For example, the United States forbids trade with Cuba or North Korea and permits strategic military material to be shipped abroad only after government permission has been obtained. Most trade barriers, however, are designed to restrict imports. Two of the most common import barriers are quotas and tariffs.

Quotas

A **quota** is a quantitative restriction that is expressed in terms of either physical quantity or value. For example, a quota that states that no more than 50,000 Class A widgets may be imported from Europe each year is a restriction stated in terms of physical quantity. Meanwhile, a quota that restricts the importation of a certain type of Japanese glassware to no more than $1 million worth a year is stated in terms of value.

Tariffs

A **tariff** is a duty or fee levied on goods being imported into the country. These tariffs can be of two types: revenue or protective. A **revenue tariff** is designed to raise money for the government. These tariffs are usually low, often amounting to less than

twenty-five cents per item or pound. A **protective tariff** is designed to discourage foreign businesses from shipping certain goods into the country. The basic reason for a protective tariff is to keep out goods that will undersell products made in the home country. For this reason, protective tariffs are often very high, thereby forcing the foreign business to raise its prices to cover the tariff. This, of course, makes it easier for American firms to compete with these imported goods.

Tariff duties are of three types: specific, ad valorem, and compound. **Specific duties** are levied at the rate of so much per unit or pound. For example, the specific duty on one product might be $10 per unit, while on another it might be 25¢ per pound. Duties on imported foods are often levied on the basis of pounds or, in the case of liquids, gallons.

Ad valorem duties are levied on the basis of the product's value. For example, an ad valorem duty of 7 percent on a particular product valued at $100 would result in a $7 tariff. If a firm shipped in ten of these products, the tariff would be $70.

Compound duties are a combination of specific and ad valorem duties. For example, some products are taxed on both quantity and value. One example is suits. In the past the duty on them has been 37½¢ per pound and 21 percent ad valorem.

Why are there protective tariffs? Protective tariffs help domestic business, so they may be a good idea. However, what about our earlier discussion of comparative advantage? If other countries can produce goods with more relative efficiency than we, why establish trade barriers to keep out their products? Why does everyone not follow the principle of

Khaled Abu Su'ud

Talk about international business and it is almost impossible not to discuss the role of OPEC nations such as Kuwait. Although Kuwait is the fourth largest oil producer, behind Saudi Arabia, Iran and Iraq, it is considered to have the most sophisticated investment strategy of any Arab country. The individual who is in charge of these investments is Mr. Khaled Abu Su'ud.

Mr. Abu Su'ud has come a long way since he moved from Palestine to Kuwait over a quarter century ago. Working his way up the finance ministry, he became the financial advisor to the present ruler of Kuwait in 1977—no small task, given the fact that this country has billions of dollars to invest each year in foreign countries. It feels that it must do so, because its oil and gas resources will someday dry up and it needs something to fall back on.

Mr. Abu Su'ud is a great supporter of western economics. In fact, he has strongly argued against the purchase of gold, contending that such action represents nothing more than a lack of confidence in the country's economic system. What nation does he like best for investment purposes? The United States. In fact, about 65 percent of the $20 billion invested by Kuwait is in long-term U.S. investments; the balance is mainly in Europe.

At any one time Mr. Abu Su'ud has between $1 and $50 million in stock in almost every one of the top 500 U.S. firms. In addition, there are extensive U.S. real estate holdings, including part of an office complex in downtown Houston and resort property along the South Carolina coast. Recently he commissioned a Chicago bank to make a study that may lead to purchases of large U.S. farmland tracts. Mr. Abu Su'ud is also thinking of investing in developing countries, like Brazil and South Korea, and is currently discussing the takeover of a 25 percent interest in a Gulf Oil refinery in Seoul.

Does all of this responsibility worry Mr. Abu Su'ud? It sure does. In fact, he claims, "I'm losing my hair worrying about all that money." Nevertheless, he has faith that his investments are the right ones. Commenting on his support of the U.S. dollar, he holds that in the long-run the American economy will prove superior to those of West Germany and Japan because these countries will ultimately face a shortage of raw materials and energy. Of course, if he is wrong, it will be necessary to alter Kuwait's current investment strategy. However, one thing is clear. Mr. Abu Su'ud and his nation intend to remain active in the international trade arena.

comparative advantage? Following are some of the major arguments for a protective tariff.

Military-preparedness argument. Many people argue that any industry vital to our national defense should be kept alive at all costs. Otherwise, we would have to depend on other governments to provide us with defense materials. This argument seems to have a lot of merit, although some would argue that many of our national defense-related industries are inefficient and that such a tariff merely ensures their survival.

Home-industry argument. Some people believe that the consumer should always "buy American." This keeps our money at home and helps ensure the continued existence of American business. The argument against using protective tariffs for this purpose is that the American consumer will have to pay

---

CASE
Thanks, but No Thanks

Each year during the month of August, Ted Billings likes to get away for a few weeks with his wife and family. This past year they all went to Europe for three weeks. The trip was expensive but the family had saved for it for two years. In addition, they did not stay at any fancy hotels or eat many expensive meals. By the time they were ready to come home, they had managed to save $900 of their European budget. Just before leaving Europe, they went out and bought clothing. Ted purchased a conservative business suit. Everyone else opted for sweaters, shoes, and other accessories.

When he returned to his clothing store, a number of his salesmen congratulated Ted on his suit selection. A number of his customers liked it so well that they asked him why he did not get an okay from the home office to stock some of these suits. Just out of curiosity, Ted checked into the matter. He had paid $230 for the suit overseas. However, he estimated that with tariff duties and a markup for profit, the suit would retail stateside for approximately $300. At this price, none of his customers expressed much interest. As one put it, "Thanks, but no thanks."

1. What type of tariff duties might be levied on a suit? Explain.

2. What might be the reasons for such a tariff?

3. With which of these reasons do you agree? With which do you disagree?

higher prices for some goods. In addition, without some competition from efficient foreign producers, there is no way of forcing high-cost American manufacturers out of business.

Infant-industry argument. A third argument for using protective tariffs is to protect new industries until they are established. This argument has a great deal of merit as long as the tariff is discontinued when the industry reaches maturity. However, identifying when this occurs and then removing the protective barrier can prove difficult. In particular, many of the firms in the industry will argue for continued protection.

Favorable-balance-of-trade argument. A country has a **favorable balance of trade** when its exports exceed its imports. If the reverse is true, the country is said to have an **unfavorable balance of trade.** Many people believe a protective tariff should help ensure a favorable balance. Opponents of this argument, however, contend that the key area of concern should be the nation's standard of living and not the import-export position. This, of course, means that the country should be placing its emphasis on producing those goods it can make most efficiently and importing the others. Getting business to agree with this line of reasoning, of course, is another matter.

Ownership Problems

Another international trade problem revolves around the ownership of foreign enterprises. Many companies have set up overseas offices, branches, or factories to manufacture and market their goods. In recent years, however, some developing countries have started to become concerned over the fact that these firms are owned by "foreigners." As a result, there is a move today in many countries toward requiring all new businesses to be controlled by citizens of that country. This means that if an American firm wants to set up operations there, it may own no more than 49 percent of the company.

The rest must be held by nationals. This idea is unacceptable to many American businesses who feel that their investment is too great to allow operating control to be given away to another party. As a result, they refuse to do business there.

7. Why might an American firm refuse to relinquish operating control over a foreign operation?

THE UNITED STATES AND INTERNATIONAL TRADE

Despite the risks associated with international trade, the United States is the most active nation in this arena. Every year America exports and imports billions of dollars worth of goods to and from every area of the world (see Table 15.1). These goods take all forms, from machinery and transport equipment to beverages and tobacco (see Table 15.2). The firms that are active in this international trade arena are known as multinational corporations.

The Multinational Corporation

Multinational corporations are firms that have their base of operations in one country but carry on business in at least one other nation and have a management philosophy that is worldwide in nature. As a result, decision making in these firms is carried out on a global basis. Many of the largest multinational corporations are American owned (see Table 15.3). One of the reasons why American firms have moved into the international arena is to take advantage of new market opportunities that have developed there. Today American businesses own large percentages of the industries of *foreign* countries. For example, IBM holds about two-thirds of the computer market in

TABLE 15.1 U.S. FOREIGN TRADE, 1977 (IN MILLIONS OF DOLLARS

AREA OF THE WORLD	EXPORTS	IMPORTS	TRADE BALANCE
Canada	$ 25,749	$ 29,356	− 3,607
19 American republics	16,346	16,335	+ 11
Other Western Hemisphere	224	1,050	− 826
Western Europe	33,752	27,417	+ 6,335
Near East	11,020	12,981	− 1,961
Far East	21,219	36,405	−15,186
Australia	2,356	1,185	− 1,171
Africa	4,563	16,854	−12,291
Other	4,934	5,234	− 300
Total	$120,163	$146,817	−26,654

Source: U.S. Department of Commerce, Domestic and International Business Administration, as reported in Information Please Almanac, 1979, p. 71.

TABLE 15.2 U.S. EXPORTS AND IMPORTS OF LEADING COMMODITIES, 1978 (IN MILLIONS OF DOLLARS)

	EXPORTS	IMPORTS
Machinery and transport equipment	$ 59,270	$ 47,626
Other manufactured goods	22,657	46,299
Food and live animals	18,383	13,521
Crude materials, inedible, except fuels	15,553	9,297
Chemicals	12,618	6,427
Mineral fuels and related materials	3,878	42,105
Animal and vegetable oils and fats	1,521	511
Beverages and tobacco	2,293	2,221
Other transactions	5,030	4,018
Total	$143,660	$172,025

Source: U.S. Department of Commerce, Office of International Economic Research, as reported in *Information Please Almanac*, 1980, p. 72.

TABLE 15.3 SOME OF THE LEADING MULTINATIONAL CORPORATIONS IN 1979

NAME	SALES (IN THOUSANDS)	NET INCOME (IN THOUSANDS)	HEADQUARTERS
Exxon	$60,334,527	$2,763,000	United States
Royal Dutch/Shell Group	44,044,537	2,084,653	Netherlands-Britain
General Motors	63,221,100	3,508,000	United States
Ford Motor	42,784,100	1,588,900	United States
Mobil	34,736,045	1,125,638	United States
British Petroleum	27,407,620	853,057	Britain
Unilever	18,893,176	531,337	Britain-Netherlands
International Tel. & Tel.	15,261,178	661,807	United States
Volkswagenwerk	13,332,059	275,671	Germany
Toyota Motor	12,768,821	529,933	Japan

Source: *Fortune*, 1979.

One of the reasons why American firms have moved into the international arena is to take advantage of new market opportunities that have developed there.

both Italy and France, half of this market in West Germany, and around 30 percent of it in Great Britain. Other American-owned firms also have large holdings in foreign companies. No wonder some people feel that the United States is out to take over the world economically!

In all fairness, however, not all of the great multinational firms are American owned. While we have substantial foreign holdings, it is important to remember that foreign businesses in turn have invested in the United States. The Japanese and Germans, in particular, have bought into American industry. And the Arabs are looking to do the same, as a way of investing their oil revenues. When examining multinational corporations, therefore, it is necessary to remember that international trade is a two-way street. We have holdings in other countries and they have holdings in ours.

8. What might account for the fact that so many multinational firms are American owned?

The Business of International Business

The goal of the multinational business is no different from that of the domestic firm. It must work to improve the standard of living in the country where it operates. This is both a *social* and an *economic* responsibility. In examining the record, it is fair to say that American business and government have both done a great deal to stimulate worldwide economic development.

United States investment

United States investment abroad is currently in excess of $100 billion. And this does not include the

Here Come the Conglomerates

One of the biggest skirmishes between business and government today appears to be developing around the growing appetite of large conglomerates, who are taking over smaller businesses. The publishing industry is particularly affected by this trend. Some of the developments that have taken place recently include

CBS's purchase of Fawcett Publications,

Doubleday's acquisition of Dell Publishing,

Harper & Row's proposed purchase of J. B. Lippincott,

Time's take-over of Book-of-the-Month Club.

And then there was the move by Western Pacific Industries to take over Houghton Mifflin. Upon learning that Western was buying its stock, Houghton Mifflin announced that it was opposed to the secret purchase of an initially large block of its securities, and the take-over was eventually stopped. Western decided it was a bad idea after all.

Of course, some people support this trend, feeling that big firms have the money and marketing skills to turn these publishing houses into money-makers. And this development is impressive to many authors as well, who feel their royalties will increase. However, the Justice Department and the FTC are unimpressed with such arguments. In a surprise move recently, the Justice people brought suit against CBS, seeking to force divestiture of Fawcett Publications. The Department says that the acquisition eliminates competition between the two in mass-market paperback publishing because, prior to the merger, CBS was eleventh in the field and Fawcett was fifth. The suit says that mass-market paperback publishing is concentrated and there is a trend toward even further concentration. For its part, CBS has called the suit unjustified and says it will vigorously fight the action.

In any event, the government is determined to prevent the domination of small publishers by these big conglomerates. However, this is going to be quite a chore given the fact that RCA has just announced that its Random House division is for sale, and Allyn and Bacon are looking for a buyer. And who is most likely to purchase these publishers? The conglomerates, of course.

A Foreign Invasion

Foreign businesses are investing heavily in the U.S. In fact, the Commerce Department indicates that such investments in this country are in excess of $40 billion. How have these firms been spending this money? Following is a representative sample:

Royal Dutch/Shell (Netherlands/United Kingdom) owns 69 percent of Shell Oil and 100 percent of Asiatic Petroleum.

Anglo American (South Africa) holds 51 percent of Terra Chemicals, and 37 percent of Inspiration Consolidated Copper, and 30 percent of Englehard Mining & Petroleum.

British Petroleum has 26 percent of Standard Oil of Ohio.

Solvay & Cie S.A. (Belgium) owns 100 percent of Soltex Polymer and 8 percent of Allied Chemical.

British-American Tobacco holds 100 percent of Brown & Williamson.

Seagram Co., Ltd. (Canada) owns Joseph E. Seagram & Sons.

Nestle Alimentans (Switzerland) owns Nestle; Libby, McNeill & Libby; Stouffer Foods; and Alcon Labs.

Petrofina (Belgium) controls 70 percent of American Petrofina.

Sigma Ltd. (British Virgin Islands) holds 6 percent ownership of Diamond Shamrock.

---

money these firms made and reinvested in their overseas operations. These funds have been used to build factories and provide goods and services to the people of those countries. They have also provided jobs to the workers who made these goods. The result of such investments has been an increase in the standard of living of those nations.

Government assistance

In order to stimulate overseas investment by American firms, our government has provided a great deal of assistance. Some of the most important developments in the area of international trade have been (a) the General Agreement on Tariffs and Trade, (b) the Export-Import Bank, and (c) the International Monetary Fund.

General Agreement on Tariffs and Trade. Usually referred to as **GATT,** this international agreement has been signed by approximately one hundred nations. All have agreed to work together to reduce import tariffs and thereby promote international trade. Every few years the signatories get together to negotiate new agreements on import tariffs. Since its founding in 1947, the number of countries participating in GATT has increased dramatically, indicating that more and more nations seem to believe that reduced import tariffs are a key to the future of international trade.

Export-Import Bank. The **Export-Import Bank** is a federal lending agency that helps promote trade between the United States and other countries by making loans available to importers and exporters who are unable to obtain adequate financing from private agencies. The bank is also empowered to lend money to foreign governments to help them develop international trade.

International Monetary Fund. The primary objective of the **IMF** is to stabilize exchange rates between world currencies. In so doing this international association has helped build confidence in the currencies of many countries and reduce the fears often associated with accepting payment in any currency other than one's own. As a result, today American business does not have to worry about whether the Russian rubles paid to it on Monday can be converted into dollars on Tuesday.

9. How does GATT help promote international trade?

10. Do United States multinational corporations need the IMF? After all, the American dollar requires no stabilization in the world money markets, does it?

THE FUTURE OF INTERNATIONAL TRADE

What does the future of international trade look like? At present, all signs point to a continued vigorous growth of such trade between countries everywhere. Two reasons can be found in the emergence of economic unions and in the growth of internationalism.

Economic Unions

In the last twenty-five years a number of countries have formed **economic unions.** In essence, the nations in such a union work to reduce trade barriers between themselves so that they can take advantage of economic specialization. The best known of these is the European Economic Community (EEC), popularly called the **Common Market.** Founded in 1957 by the Treaty of Rome, it consisted of France, West Germany, the Netherlands, Belgium, Luxembourg, and Italy. Today, Ireland, England, Denmark, and Greece are also members. These countries have lowered, and in many cases eliminated, trade barriers between themselves so that some goods can be shipped from one to another without facing any quotas or tariffs. The results have been positive. Among the six original members, the standard of living has risen and most now enjoy unparalleled economic prosperity.

Another economic union is the **European Free Trade Association (EFTA).** The original members of Norway, Portugal, Sweden, and Switzerland. Since then, Iceland and Finland have joined while Great Britain and Denmark have withdrawn to enter the Common Market (see Fig. 15.1). EFTA's objective is to promote trade among its members, although some believe that these nations will eventually join the EEC. Obviously, such a development might well result in a stronger overall European economy.

Other nations have also formed economic unions. One of these is the **Central American Common Market.** It consists of Costa Rica, El Salvador, Guatemala, Honduras, and Nicaragua. This union was formed to enhance the economic growth of its members but, unfortunately, has made little progress because of disagreements between some of the participants. Another union is the **Latin American Free Trade Association (LAFTA).** The members include Argentina, Bolivia, Brazil, Chile, Colombia, Ecuador, Mexico, Paraguay, Peru, Uruguay, and Venezuela. The original goal of LAFTA when it was founded in 1960 was to establish free trade among the member nations by 1973. Although it had a promising beginning, the goal has not yet been attained. Today efforts are still under way to make this objective of free trade into a reality.

Economic unions such as the above hold a great deal of promise for the future. Where they have

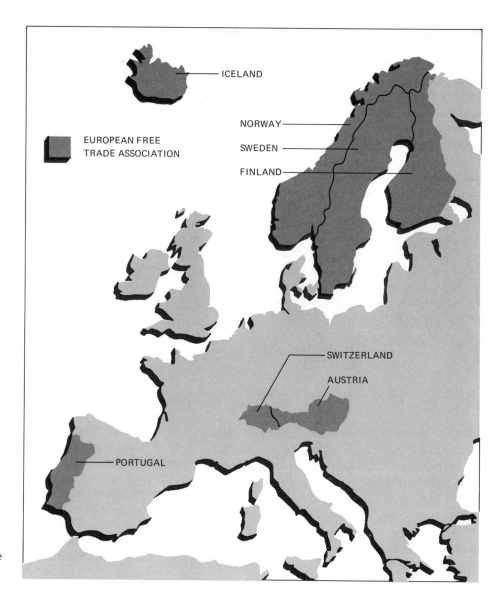

FIG. 15.1 *Membership in the European Free Trade Association*

worked well, as in the case of the Common Market, they have brought about economic prosperity. They are also viewed by many as a method of fighting off foreign economic domination. For example, France has often viewed the United States as an economic dinosaur that would like to swallow her up. The Common Market provides a basis, at least in France's view, for a united European economy capable of resisting advances by foreign nations, specifically the United States.

More Internationalism

Regardless of national fears, we are going to see more and more international trade. Nations of the world are no longer totally self-sufficient. Even countries like Russia, when it has a poor domestic crop, must import wheat from the United States. And how many countries of the world have sufficient oil and other resources to meet all the energy-related demands of their people? The only way to obtain these goods is to trade for them in the international marketing arena.

Will this mean the total abandonment of quotas and tariffs and strict adherence to the principle of comparative advantage? This is unlikely. However, it does indicate developments in this general direction. As a result, the field of international trade should prove to be an exciting one in the years ahead.

11. How has the Common Market helped countries such as France and West Germany?

12. Do economic unions support the principle of comparative advantage?

13. Why is the future likely to see more and more international trade?

CASE

A Matter of Protection

A few months after inquiring into the cost of a foreign-made suit, Ted Billings received a call from the manager of a competitive store. The man was quite upset over what he called "political developments." It seems that an American trade delegation had just returned from talking to the Common Market countries. The delegation was proposing a reduction, and if possible the total elimination, of the tariff on many articles of clothing manufactured in these nations. The manager expressed grave concern over these developments, noting to Ted that "If the tariff is reduced or rescinded, we are all going to be in a fight for our lives. We'll be flooded with clothing from overseas that will compete with our own lines. We need protection."

The man asked Ted to call his home office and ask them to contact their representatives and lobbyists in Washington. After he hung up, Ted sat back and thought about the other manager's comments. He would call the home office, of course, although he was sure they already knew the news. What he was not sure of was whether the tariff should be supported or opposed.

1. Is lowering the tariff good for international trade? Give your reasoning.

2. How might such a development help Ted's company?

3. Would you personally support or oppose the move?

SUMMARY

Nations of the world trade for any of three reasons: resources, economics, and politics. Of course, if all wanted to be as efficient as possible, they would adhere to the principles of absolute and comparative advantage. Often, however, political considerations outweigh economic ones.

In international trade businesses carry on many of the same activities they do at home. However, there are some unique problems that these firms also encounter abroad, including cultural problems, monetary conversion, trade barriers, and the possibility of nationalization. The most common of these is the trade barrier. For one reason or another, all nations impose quotas and/or tariffs on some of the goods crossing their borders. Quite often the reason given for such barriers is the need to protect industries operating in the home country. Sometimes this is a legitimate explanation, but many times it is just an excuse for keeping out foreign goods and promoting domestic production. Despite these problems and barriers, many business firms are active in the international trade arena. The largest, commonly known as multinational corporations, are headquartered in the United States and Western Europe. While some countries have misgivings about these corporations and feel they are out to dominate them economically, the multinational corporation appears to be here for the indefinite future. In particular, government treaties and international trade agreements are encouraging such activity. So too are economic unions such as the Common Market. As a result, we will find over the next decade that trade between nations is going to continue to increase.

KEY TERMS FOUND IN THIS CHAPTER

QUESTIONS FOR DISCUSSION AND ANALYSIS

1. What is the principle of absolute advantage? Comparative advantage? Put them in your own words.

2. In what way are political relations and international trade related?

3. What are the common cultural problems facing American firms doing business overseas?

4. How does a quota differ from a tariff?

5. What are the most common types of tariff duties? Describe each.

6. What kinds of ownership problems do firms doing business overseas face today?

7. What is a multinational corporation? Explain.

8. In what way do economic unions encourage international trade?

CAREERS
IN MARKETING

Marketing offers some very exciting career opportunities for the 1980s. Specific marketing areas include buying, selling, advertising, and marketing research, although as you saw in the previous four chapters, these represent only a handful of many such opportunities. The following paragraphs describe seven marketing careers, and the accompanying matrix relates to the latest employment figures, earnings, and employment outlook for each.

ADVERTISING WORKER

This individual can play many different roles because there are many facets to advertising. For example, some advertising jobs require the talents of a person who is creative, such as a writer, artist, or designer to develop and produce advertisements. Other opportunities are available for those who can handle the arrangement of broadcasting advertising messages on radio and TV, publishing them in magazines, mailing them direct to readers, or posting them on billboards. One of the most common occupations within this broad field is the advertising manager who directs the ad program of the business, determining the size of the budget, the type of ad and media to use, and whether or not to employ an ad agency. Another is the account executive who works for the ad agency in developing ad programs for client firms and individuals. A third is the research director who, with assistants, studies the market, reviews possible uses for the good or service being sold, and compares the advantages and disadvantages of competitive products in arriving at ways of reaching potential buyers.

BUYER

A buyer purchases goods for a retail store. Often the individual attends fashion shows or conventions where the latest products are being displayed. In order to purchase the best selection of goods for the store, the buyer must be familiar with the manufacturers and distributors who handle the merchandise. The individual must also be able to assess the resale value of goods after a brief inspection and make purchase decisions quickly. This individual works closely with assistant buyers and sales clerks in obtaining information about consumer likes and dislikes.

INSURANCE AGENT AND BROKER

An insurance agent or broker sells policies that protect individuals and businesses against future losses and financial pressures. The most common forms of insurance sold by the agent or broker are life, property-liability, and health insurance. The agent may be either an insurance company employee or an independent business person who is authorized to represent one insurance firm or more. Much of an agent's time is spent discussing insurance needs with prospective and existing customers, planning insurance programs that are tailored to the needs of the prospect, preparing reports, and maintaining records.

MANUFACTURING SALES WORKER

Virtually all manufacturers employ the sales worker. This person sells mainly to other businesses—factories, railroads, banks, wholesalers, and retailers,

SOURCE: *Occupational Outlook Handbook*, 1978–79 Edition, U.S. Department of Labor, Bureau of Labor Statistics

for example—in assigned sales territories. The individual usually sells nontechnical products, about which he or she must be well informed, and uses an approach adapted to the particular line of merchandise. A sales worker selling crackers or cookies will emphasize wholesomeness, attractive packaging, and variety of products. When selling machinery, the individual will stress the quality of the machine, and its ability to produce large amounts of goods at a low price. While most of the person's time is spent calling on prospective customers, the sales person also writes reports on sales prospects, plans his or her work schedules, draws up lists of potential customers, makes appointments, and studies literature related to the firm's product lines.

MARKETING RESEARCH WORKER
The marketing research worker helps the business make sound decisions on how to market its products. This is done by analyzing available data on products and sales and, if this is not sufficient, conducting marketing surveys to gather the needed data. This individual is concerned with customers' opinions and tastes and will design the survey to gather information about these things. The marketing researcher is often assisted by a statistician in selecting a group or sample to be interviewed or surveyed. Then, when the data has been gathered, the marketing research worker will analyze the information and draw conclusions that will be used to help the company decide how to market the particular good or service.

WHOLESALE TRADE SALES WORKER
The wholesale trade sales worker plays a significant role in moving goods from the factory to the consumer. This person will visit buyers and show sample pictures, or catalogs that list the items that the company stocks. Since there are many items being sold, the individual will push the entire line rather than any one particular good. Then, after sales are made, the worker will ensure prompt, dependable service so that buyers will become regular customers. The wholesale sales worker also performs important services for retailers, such as checking the store's stock and ordering items that will be needed before the next visit. Sometimes these workers will help the store personnel improve and update their systems for ordering inventory, as well as advise retailers about advertising, pricing, and window and counter displays.

PUBLIC RELATIONS WORKER
A public relations worker handles many different areas, from consumer relations to sales promotion to employee recruitment, to name but three. In business firms this individual can be found in the public relations department. Some of the responsibilities with which the individual need be concerned include putting together information that keeps the public aware of the employer's activities and accomplishments and keeps management aware of public attitudes. After preparing the information, the individual may contact people in the media who might be interested in publicizing the material.

CAREERS
IN MARKETING (continued)

Other functions include planning, researching, and making material ready for publication. In this job, the public relations worker brings together a blend of advertising and sales promotion activities.

RETAIL TRADE SALES WORKER
The job of the retail trade sales worker varies depending on the kind of merchandise being sold. For example, when selling furniture, electrical appliances, or clothing, the individual's primary job is to create an interest in the merchandise, answer questions about the article, demonstrate its use, and show various models and colors. On the other hand, when selling standard products, such as items in hardware or drugstores, the individual needs to do little more than wrap the purchases. Thus, the demands of the job vary with the nature of the work. Most retail sales workers, however, make out sales or charge slips, receive cash payments, give change and receipts, and often handle returns and exchanges of merchandise.

MEDIA DIRECTOR
Also called a space buyer or time buyer, the media director negotiates contracts for space advertising in newspapers and magazines, through direct mail, and buys air time on radio and television. For example, the media director determines the day and time when a television commercial will reach the largest group of prospective buyers at the lowest cost. To select the best medium for the advertiser, the media director must know the costs of using various media and the characteristics of the audience reached by specific publications, television, or radio stations.

TECHNICAL SALES WORKER
A technical sales worker or sales engineer sells very expensive, highly technical equipment such as computers, scientific instruments, generators, and missile guidance systems. In addition to having a thorough knowledge of their firms' products, they must be able to help prospective buyers with technical problems. Often sales engineers work with the research-and-development departments of their own companies to devise ways to adapt products to a customers' specialized needs. Technical sales workers sometimes train their customers' employees in the operation and maintenance of new equipment and make frequent return visits to be certain that equipment is giving the desired service. The technical sales worker usually has an undergraduate degree in engineering and a MBA in marketing.

CAREER	LATEST EMPLOYMENT FIGURES	EARNINGS	EMPLOYMENT OUTLOOK
Advertising worker	180,000	$11,000–$13,500	Faster than the average for all occupations
Buyer	109,000	$15,000–$25,000	More slowly than the average for all occupations
Insurance agent and broker	465,000	$12,000–$15,000	About as fast as the average for all occupations
Manufacturing sales growth	360,000	$ 6,000–$24,000 [a]	Faster than the average for all occupations
Marketing research worker	25,000	$13,000–$15,000	Faster than the average for all occupations
Wholesale trade sales worker	808,000	$12,000–$14,000	About the same rate as the average for all occupations
Public relations worker	107,000	$10,000–$13,000	Faster than the average for all occupations
Retail trade sales worker	2,700,000	$ 8,000–$10,000	More slowly than the average for all occupations
Media director	40,000	$11,000–$13,500	Faster than the average for all occupations
Technical sales worker	15,000	$17,000–$30,000 [a]	Faster than the average for all occupations

[a] Depending on experience

E

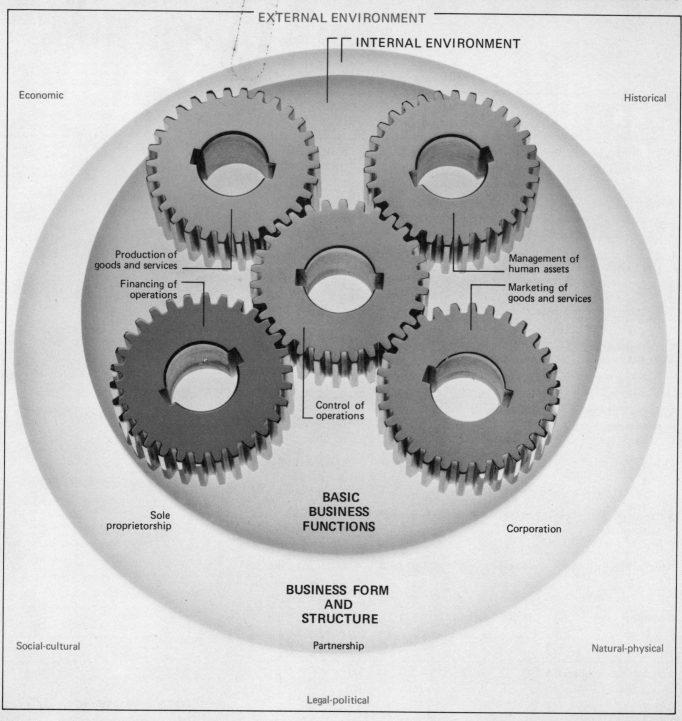

EXTERNAL ENVIRONMENT

INTERNAL ENVIRONMENT

Economic

Historical

Production of
goods and services

Management of
human assets

Financing of
operations

Marketing of
goods and services

Control of
operations

BASIC
BUSINESS
FUNCTIONS

Sole
proprietorship

Corporation

BUSINESS FORM
AND
STRUCTURE

Social-cultural

Partnership

Natural-physical

Legal-political

Financing the Firm's Operations

Thus far we have discussed some very important business activities, including, among others, organizing the firm, producing the desired goods and services, and moving them through the distribution channel to the ultimate user. The objective of this section of the book is to look at another critical area of business—the financing of operations. No firm can be successful for very long unless it has sufficient capital to take advantage of business opportunities. Sometimes a company needs short-run financing; other times it requires long-term capital. With these funds it can meet payroll deadlines and expand operations. Yet there is more to the subject of finance than the mere raising of capital. Managers also need to know how the securities markets work for this provides them information regarding how and when to float new stock and bond issues. They also need to understand how to manage risk—when to underwrite a risk and when to shift it (by, for example, using insurance). In this section we are going to be studying these three key areas of finance: short-term financing, long-term financing, and risk management.

In Chapter 16 the area of short-term financing will be examined. Short-term financing involves the raising of money for day-to-day operations. Sometimes a firm will find itself in a cash squeeze and will need to obtain some funds to tide it over; in this chapter we will be looking at some of the ways a business can obtain this money. Consideration will also be given to the impact of the Federal Reserve, a government agency, on the amount of short-term capital that is available for loans.

Chapter 17 focuses on long-term financing. Sometimes companies need money for an extended period of time. They can obtain these funds through long-term debt, bonds, preferred stock, and/or common stock. In this chapter, each of these sources will be examined in detail. Particular attention will also be given to the financial institutions that help businesses sell stocks and bonds.

Chapter 18 is devoted to an analysis of the securities market. How are stocks and bonds actually sold, and why do people invest in the market? These questions are answered in the chapter. Attention is also given to defining key stock market terms such as bull, bear, selling short, market order, and limit order, as well as to explaining how to read the stock and bond reports in the local newspaper. The latter part of the chapter discusses how to develop an investment strategy for the do-it-yourself investor.

Chapter 19 examines the area of risk management, with particular emphasis on insurance. At first glance, it might appear that this is not an area of finance. It is, however, in the sense that astute financing requires that the management know which risks to underwrite and which to shift to other people. Emphasis will be given to auto, fire, fidelity, surety, marine, public liability, health, and life insurance.

When you are finished reading this section, you should have a good understanding of how the firm finances its operations and handles the risks associated with these business activities. You should also be familiar with a number of key financial terms, including *cash flow, factoring, commercial paper, open-market operations, stocks, bonds, investment banking syndicates, growth stocks, bulls, bears, selling short, self-insurance,* and *whole life insurance.* Finally, you should have gained an appreciation for the role of finance in the world of business.

16

Bankers are just like anybody else, except richer.
Ogden Nash

OBJECTIVES OF THIS CHAPTER

Every firm needs to be concerned with financing its operations. In this chapter we are going to be studying the ways in which businesses raise money to meet short-run needs. Our first objective is to examine why firms need short-term financing. The second objective is to study the ways in which these funds are raised. The third is to point out the role of the Federal Reserve System in controlling the amount of money available in the economy for short-term use, and the fourth is to explain the purpose and role of the Federal Deposit Insurance Corporation. When you are finished reading this chapter you should be able to do the following:

a. state why firms will sometimes require short-term financing;

b. describe some of the most popular methods for raising short-term funds;

c. describe the Federal Reserve System, which helps monitor the country's money supply;

d. explain the three basic controls the Federal Reserve can use in regulating this money supply; and

e. explain the benefits associated with a bank being a member of the Federal Deposit Insurance Corporation.

Short-Term Financing

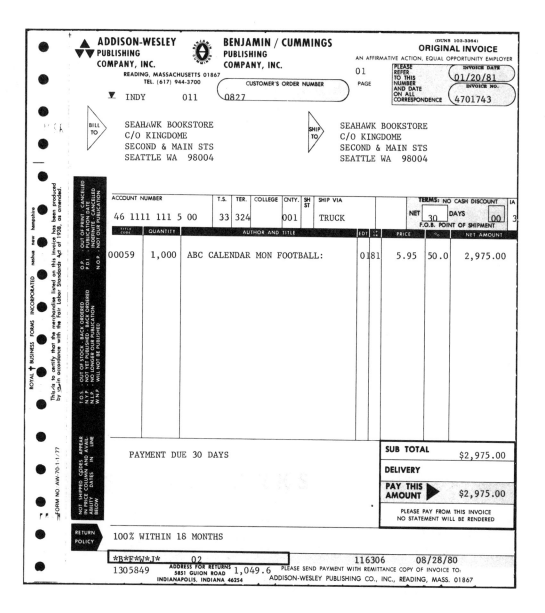

THE NEED FOR SHORT-TERM FINANCING

In our personal lives, we sometimes find ourselves caught in a cash squeeze. We would like to take a week to go fishing, but we do not have the money. We can often resolve our dilemma, however, by getting a short-term loan at the bank. If we have a good credit rating, for example, it should be quite easy to borrow $1,000 for ninety days. This is an illustration of short-term financing.

Many business firms frequently face the same type of problem. They are temporarily short of cash and need to do some short-term financing. What causes this problem? The easiest way to answer this question is to approach it from a **cash-flow** standpoint. The company has a cash balance at the beginning of the month. During this period it will be incurring expenses for things such as inventory and salaries. These represent *cash outflows*. At the same time it will be receiving payments from customers for goods purchased. These are *cash inflows* (see Fig. 16.1). If the outflows are greater than the inflows, the supply of cash from the beginning of the month will be depleted. As this happens the firm will estimate how low the balance will sink. If it approaches what the company considers a danger point, short-term financing will then be undertaken. In analyzing cash flows, keep in mind that short-term financing is used only when needed.

Remember also that a firm may have a cash-flow problem and still be highly profitable. For example, a company could take all of its cash, buy inventory, and sell it at a 50-percent profit. However, all of this might happen during one month, with none of these customer receivables due before the first of the next month. Thus the firm is out of cash, and needs financing to meet the payroll and any other expenses coming due, even though the business is profitable. When firms find themselves in a cash bind they turn to short-term financing. For the rest of this chapter we will discuss some of the most popular methods of obtaining such financing.

1. Why might a company that is making a profit end up needing short-term financing?

SOURCES OF SHORT-TERM FINANCING

There are various sources to which a firm may turn in obtaining short-term financing. The following examines some of the most common.

Family and Friends

For small firms, one of the easiest ways of raising short-term capital is to borrow it from *family and*

FIG. 16.1 *A simplified cash flow*

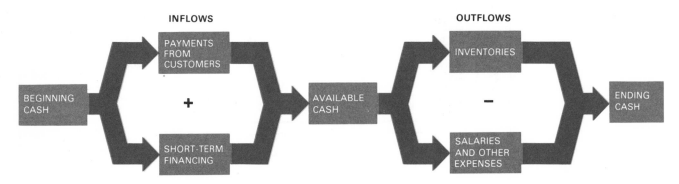

friends. Relatives and acquaintances are sometimes very happy to help out a fledgling business. In fact, many times these people will advance funds without charging any interest or stipulating repayment terms. On the other hand, there is no easier way to alienate relatives and lose friends than to borrow money and not repay it. A more preferred way is to use trade credit.

Trade Credit

The most popular form of short-term financing is **trade credit.** This is simply credit that is given to a company when it purchases goods from another firm. For example, if a retailer orders fifty watches from a wholesaler and receives delivery on June 1, there will be an invoice (bill) accompanying the merchandise. Commonly the invoice contains terms such as "2/10; n/30." These terms of "two-ten, net thirty" mean that the buyer can take a 2-percent discount if payment is made by the tenth of June. If the company does not take this discount, the entire bill is then due within thirty days.

The wholesaler is giving the retailer ten days of free credit and the chance for a discount. During this period, then, the wholesaler actually finances the retailer's purchase. This is easily seen in the case of the retailer who can sell all of these watches within ten days, for this individual has been able to secure the merchandise without putting out any money! Somewhere between 85 and 90 percent of all business transactions in the United States involve trade credit.

The question the business manager must answer is: should this discount be taken or is it better to wait and pay the bill at the end of the month? In most cases it is better to take the discount because the penalty for waiting is very high. In our illustration of 2/10; n/30, for example, the manager will pay a 2-percent penalty for waiting the extra twenty days. Assuming a 360-day year, this means that eighteen discount periods are lost. These eighteen periods times 2 percent add up to an annual expense of 36 percent. This is quite a penalty. As a result, most businesses will borrow money at the bank to meet these early payments. Short-term bank loans will

"*Getting back to those interests rates, could you be a little more specific than 'its going to cost a pretty penny?'*"

From The Wall Street Journal; permission Cartoon Features Syndicate

seldom exceed 12 percent. Keep in mind, however, that if the business is in poor financial condition and has borrowed its limit at the bank, it may be necessary to forego taking the discount.

Commercial Banks

Another important source of short-term funds are the *commercial banks.* These banks provide a number of financial services, including (a) loans and (b) lines of credit.

Loans

There are two basic types of loans, unsecured and secured. The needs of the situation will dictate which is to be used.

Unsecured loans. Many firms borrow money from banks on an **unsecured** basis. By this we mean that there is no security or *collateral* backing up the loan. In return for the funds, a company will sign a promissory note (see Fig. 16.2). The most common types require full payment of the loan within a year. These funds are often used to finance inventories or pay bills that will be coming due in the near future. Since these notes are unsecured, many banks require the

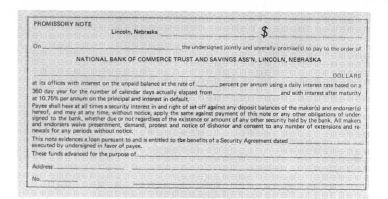

FIG. 16.2 *A promissory note (Reprinted by permission of the National Bank of Commerce, Lincoln, Nebraska.)*

A Budget for Five

One way to handle cash-flow problems is to live within a budget. In 1858 Horace Greeley, editor of the New York <u>Tribune</u>, published a weekly budget that he claimed would meet the needs of the average skilled workman and four dependents. It was the following:

Barrel of flour, $5, which will last eight weeks	$0.62
Sugar, 4 lbs. @ 8¢	0.32
Butter, 2 lbs. @ 31½¢	0.63
Milk	0.14
Butcher's meat, 2 lbs. beef a day	1.40
Potatoes, ½ bushel	0.50
Coffee and tea	0.25
Candlelight	0.14
Fuel, 3 tons of coal per year, $15; matches, etc.	0.40
Salt, pepper, vinegar, starch, soap, soda, yeast, cheese, eggs	0.40
Household articles, wear and tear	0.25
Rent	3.00
Bedclothes	0.20
Clothing	2.00
Newspapers	0.12

This certainly does not seem like a great deal of money, but Greeley received a lot of complaints from people who noted that they did not make $10.37 a week! In fact, the budget was high for everyone except blacksmiths, machinists, engineers, and skilled building tradesmen. Greeley, nevertheless, was unshaken, feeling that by following his budget everyone could make their way up the economic ladder.

company to get bank permission before borrowing money from anyone else, and in this way protect their own loan.

Secured loans. If asked to explain why the bank was willing to give an unsecured loan to a particular firm, the banker might well answer, "Oh, I know they're good for it." This same logic applies to us when we sign a ninety-day promissory note at the bank for $1,000 for a short vacation. If our banker knows from past experience that we can easily repay the loan, there is really no need to ask for collateral.

However, if a business wants a large loan the bank will often request **security.** This can be provided in several ways. In the case of small firms the banker might ask for a second party to sign the note as well. This can be any individual the bank regards as "acceptable," which means that the person is reliable and has a good credit rating. These two people will then sign the note. This also means, of course, that if the primary borrower does not pay the loan, the co-signer is liable. In this way the bank reduces its risk by getting another person to agree to accept responsibility in case of a default by the primary signer.

If the loan is extremely large, however, the bank may simply ask the firm to **"pledge"** part or all of its assets as security (see Fig. 16.3). This is particularly common when the business has tangible property. In the case of a railroad, for example, tangible property consists of locomotives, freight cars, and many other kinds of rolling equipment. If the bank lends the railroad $10 million and the line goes bankrupt, the bank may find itself waiting in line to collect. However, if the bank gets the railroad to pledge certain assets as security, then in case of financial failure

PROMISSORY NOTE WITH PLEDGE OF COLLATERAL ____________, ________ 19____ $ ________

The undersigned jointly and severally promise(s) to pay to the order of ________________

hereinafter called Bank, ________________________________ DOLLARS

at its offices with interest on the unpaid balance at the rate of ________ per cent per annum using a daily rate based on a 360 day year for the number of calendar days actually elapsed from ________________ with interest after maturity at 10.75% per annum on the principal and interest in default.

The said principal and interest shall be due as follows: ________________________

The Bank shall have at all times a security interest in and right of set-off against any deposit balances of the maker(s) and endorser(s) hereof, and may at any time, without notice, apply the same against the payment of this note or any other obligations of the undersigned to the Bank, whether due or not regardless of the existence or amount of any other security held by the Bank. All makers and endorsers waive presentment, demand, protest, notice of dishonor; consent to any number of extensions and renewals for any periods without notice and consent to any substitution, exchange or release of collateral, and to the addition or release of any other party or person primarily or secondarily liable. Nonpayment of an installment when due gives the holder the right to declare the entire balance due without notice.

Security Agreement: To secure the payment of this and any and all liabilities, direct or indirect, absolute or contingent, due or to become due, now existing or hereafter arising of any of the undersigned to the Bank or to the holder hereof (hereinafter called "obligations"), the undersigned grant to the Bank a security interest in the following property (which together with any substitutions and additions are herein called "collateral") to-wit:

____

The undersigned agrees to deliver to the holder additional collateral should the foregoing collateral decline in value or should the holder otherwise deem itself insecure.

At the option of the holder, all obligations shall become immediately due and payable without notice or demand upon the occurrence of any of the following events of default: (a) failure of the undersigned, with or without demand or notice, to promptly deliver additional collateral as above agreed; (b) default in the payment or performance of any liability or obligation of any of the undersigned, or of any maker, endorser or guarantor of any liability or obligation of any of the undersigned, to the holder; (c) failure to pay when due any premium on any life insurance policy held as collateral for the obligation of any of the undersigned to the Bank, (d) death, dissolution, termination of existence, insolvency, business failure, garnishment, or other levy against property or rights of, appointment of a receiver of any part of the property of, assignment for the benefit of creditors by, or the commencement of any proceedings under any bankruptcy or insolvency laws by or against any of the undersigned or any endorser or guarantor of the obligations of the undersigned. Upon the occurrence of any such event of default, and at any time or times thereafter, the holder shall have the remedies of a secured party under the Uniform Commercial Code. Unless the collateral is perishable or threatens to decline speedily in value, or is of a type customarily sold on a recognized market, the holder will give the undersigned reasonable notice of the time and place of any public sale thereof, or of the time after which any private sale or other intended disposition is to be made. The requirement of reasonable notice shall be met if such notice is mailed, postage prepaid, to the undersigned at the address given below, at least five (5) days before the time of the sale or disposition.

Right is expressly granted to the holder, at its option, to transfer at any time to itself or to its nominee, any collateral pledged hereunder, to exercise the rights of owner thereof, and to receive the income and proceeds thereon and hold the same as security for obligations, or in the case of money, apply it on the principal and interest on any obligations secured hereby.

The holder may, at its option, whether or not this note is due, demand, sue for, collect or make any compromise it deems desirable with reference to the collateral held hereunder. The holder's duty as to the collateral in its possession shall be solely use of reasonable care in its custody, and the holder shall not be bound to take any steps necessary to preserve any rights in the collateral against other persons, which the undersigned hereunder assumes to do.

No delay or omission on the part of the holder in exercising any right hereunder shall operate as a waiver of such right or any other right hereunder. A waiver on any occasion shall not be construed as a bar to a waiver of such right or remedy on any future occasion.

As used herein the word "holder" shall mean the payee or other endorsee of this note, who is in possession of it, or the bearer thereof if this note is at the time payable to bearer; and the word "undersigned" shall include both singular and plural. When signed by more than one party all references to the undersigned shall mean all or any one or more of them, and the obligations of the undersigned shall be joint and several.

The undersigned represents that at the time the collateral was deposited with the Bank, the undersigned has the right to transfer any interest therein and that the collateral is not subject to the interest of any third person; and the undersigned agreees to defend the collateral and its proceeds against claims and demands of all third persons.

This Agreement shall be binding upon the undersigned their heirs, assigns, and personal representatives.

These funds advanced for: ________________ ________________

Address: ________________ ________________

NBC 1053 Rev. 10/75 ________________

FIG. 16.3 *A promissory note with pledge of collateral (Reprinted by permission of the National Bank of Commerce, Lincoln, Nebraska.)*

these cars and equipment can be sold to recover the loan.

In the case of retail firms, banks will often accept accounts receivable as collateral. Of course, they will not advance the business the full value of these receivables. However, if the retailer has $100,000 due from customers, and past records show that 98 percent of all bills are collected, the bank might be willing to loan the company $80,000. If the business goes bankrupt, the bank can then hopefully collect the necessary receivables for repaying the loan.

Lines of credit

Some companies have an arrangement with their bank whereby a **line of credit** is made available to them. A firm with a line of credit of $250,000 can borrow up to this amount at any time it chooses. Whenever the funds are needed, the vice-president of finance, or some other authorized officer, can call the bank and have the money credited to the firm's account. This, of course, is very helpful to the company because it gives the business a ready source of funds when needed. And if over time the firm finds that it needs an extension of its credit line, this too may be possible. It will all depend on (a) the relationship between the bank and the company, (b) the banker's evaluation of how much the firm needs, and (c) how capable the firm is of repaying the debt.

2. What is trade credit? Put it in your own words.

CASE

Hamburgers, Anybody?

Three years ago Lucy White founded a hamburger chain. Starting with one retail outlet, within twenty-four months she had nine units in operation. All of these were owned by Lucy herself, with a local bank holding the mortgage.

The biggest problem Lucy has encountered recently is that of meeting her payroll and rent expenses. Three of her units are not making any money. However, Lucy believes that they will prove very profitable within a year. She is therefore reluctant to close them.

Her banker has agreed to step in and help out by extending a line of credit for $50,000. The banker has also provided some useful financial advice to Lucy by encouraging her to use trade credit in purchasing inventory. Lucy believes that with this new line of credit, and the accompanying financial advice, she will be able to handle her current cash squeeze and maybe even open another unit.

1. Is it possible that despite its cash squeeze, Lucy's company is making a profit?

2. How can the bank's line of credit help Lucy?

3. In what way can the use of trade credit help Lucy in overcoming her current cash squeeze?

3. If credit terms are 3/15; n/30, what percentage of interest is a firm paying if it never takes a discount?

4. If a business "pledges" its assets in order to obtain a loan, exactly what has the firm agreed to do?

Factors

A fourth method of raising short-term capital is to sell accounts receivable to collection agents, who are called **factors.** When firms have money owed to them by their customers, and they need cash for immediate operations, factoring can be a solution to their problem. The factor will pay the company a percentage of the face value of the accounts receivable. This percentage is determined by (a) the "quality" of the receivables, and (b) whether they are sold "with or without recourse."

Quality of the receivables

The quality of accounts receivable is judged on two bases. First, how long have the accounts been outstanding? If a firm has a policy of 2/10; n/30, then none of its bills should be outstanding for any longer than thirty days. However, what if an "aging" of these receivables reveals the following:

Days outstanding	Amount
1–30	$150,000
31–60	25,000
61–90	15,000
Over 90	10,000

A quick look at these statistics reveals that some of the firm's customers are not paying their bills on time. In fact, 25 percent of all receivables ($50,000/$200,000) are overdue. These, of course, are the ones the company will want to sell to the factor. In particular, the credit manager will want to unload the $10,000 of receivables that are over ninety days old, for these may well be uncollectable. Unfortunately, these old bills are those that the factor will probably consider to be poor-quality receivables.

Financial service companies also represent a possible source of financing.

David Rockefeller

Born in 1915, David Rockefeller is the youngest son of John D. Rockefeller, Jr. In 1936, the young Rockefeller graduated from Harvard University. After doing graduate work at both Harvard and the London School of Economics, he received a Ph.D. in Economics from the University of Chicago in 1940.

After World War II Rockefeller joined the Chase National Bank. His rise in the following years was dramatic. In 1949 he moved from assistant manager in the foreign department to a vice-presidency. The next year he was appointed to run Chase's Latin American operations. Then in 1952 he was named a senior vice-president for the economic research department and customer relations in metropolitan New York.

When Chase National and the Bank of the Manhattan Company were merged in 1955 into Chase Manhattan, David Rockefeller became executive vice-president in charge of the development department. Six years later, in 1961, he was named president of the bank. In March 1969 he became chairman of the board and chief executive officer. Today he continues as chairman and will until 1981.

Under his leadership Chase Manhattan has played a vital role in the growth of New York City and the nation. Rockefeller has been a strong advocate of both social responsibility and community development. Despite the fact that his personal wealth allows him a life of leisure, he is continually active in business and social affairs on both a national and international scale. For example, he frequently meets and discusses international finance problems with heads of foreign governments. And recently, under his direction, Chase Manhattan has opened an American bank in Russia and been named Correspondent for the Bank of China.

The second thing the factor will want to know is, what are the names of the firms who owe all of this money? If some of them include General Motors; Sears, Roebuck; or IBM, the factor knows that these accounts will be paid. There is virtually no risk involved here. Other firms, however, may be in financial difficulty (such as the Penn Central) and will constitute a great risk. After evaluating all of the receivables, a decision will be made regarding the collectability of the accounts.

The matter of recourse

When a factor buys a company's receivables, it can do so with or without recourse. If it buys them **"with recourse,"** the uncollected receivables can be returned to the firm. In this case the factor takes no risk for collection.

Sometimes, however, the factor is willing to take receivables **"without recourse."** In this case if the receivables cannot be collected the factor stands to lose whatever amount has been paid to the firm. As a result, factors not only give less for these receivables (for example, 50 percent of the value of a bill without recourse as against 80 percent with) but tend to accept only those it feels are definitely collectible.

Many customers are unaware of these factors. This is because factors seldom come into direct contact with the customer. Collection of the accounts receivable usually continues through the credit office of the firm from whom the merchandise was purchased.

Some industries or companies tend to use factoring more than others. In the furniture industry, for example, when merchandise is sold to the customer on a time-payment basis, factoring is common. It is also widely employed in the textile industry. However, this is not the only alternative available to a business seeking immediate funds from its installment contracts. Many retailers use sales finance companies.

5. How does a firm go about "aging" its receivables? Give an illustration.

6. If a company has some accounts that will probably never be paid by the customers, would it prefer to sell them to a factor with, or without, recourse?

7. Why do firms use factors? Of what value are they to businesses?

Sales Finance Companies

Sales finance companies will purchase installment sales contracts because their interest rate is high and, if the person does not pay, the merchandise can often be repossessed. Many appliances and automobiles are financed through installment contracts. And because these contracts are so lucrative, some manufacturing firms have established their own sales finance companies. These companies will buy the installment sales contract directly from the retailer. The retailer likes this because it provides an immediate inflow of cash. The manufacturer likes it because the interest rate on these contracts will range from 12 to 18 percent, while the cost of raising the money for their purchase often runs from a mere 9 to 12 percent.

In recent years sales finance companies have expanded the types of services they are providing to retailers. For example, some will send the goods to the retailer without requiring any payment. Then, as the merchandise is sold, the retailer will turn over the installment sales contract to the finance company. In turn, the retailer will receive the selling price minus the cost of the goods plus a service fee. Such an arrangement allows the retailer to operate with a minimum of cash because the inventory is never really purchased. Title to the goods always remains with the sales finance company. The risk is also reduced because the retailer never has to worry about getting stuck with merchandise that will not sell.

Commercial Paper

If the business is large enough, it can try selling **commercial paper.** In essence, commercial paper is simply an unsecured promissory note. These notes are usually sold in denominations ranging from $2,500 to $10,000. Businesses known as commercial paper houses will buy these notes from the company that issues them and then sell them to investors and other financial institutions. Commercial paper is very short term in nature, tending to mature within 60 to 180 days. The interest rate paid on this paper is higher than that which can be obtained in a savings account. Therefore, firms that have money sitting idle for a few months will often purchase commercial paper. Because the paper is unsecured, the creditors are, in effect, giving the company a loan without asking for any collateral. As a result, not everyone can sell commercial paper; usually the firm must have a good reputation and be considered a low risk. In addition, if one company defaults on its paper, other firms may find it difficult to sell very much of theirs in the near future. When the Penn Central defaulted on a couple of million dollars of commercial paper a number of years ago, the default had a dampening effect on the willingness of investors to buy commercial paper from other firms.

Government Sources

Other possible sources of short-term funds are agencies of the federal government. One of the best-known agencies is the Small Business Administration, which makes loans to small firms that meet minimum qualifications but are unable to get financing anywhere else. The Department of Defense is another source. On occasion this agency has granted cash advances to firms engaged in defense-related contract work.

Improved Credit Policies

Perhaps the best overall strategy to employ in dealing with short-term financing problems is to take steps that prevent them from recurring. One way is to **improve credit policies.** This often means establishing more stringent guidelines for determining who will, and who will not, be given credit. This, of course, usually results in a reduction in the firm's sales volume. However, there are also some very favorable advantages for the company. First, the people with whom it now does business will be those who pay more promptly. This means a reduction in the need for factors. Second, with less volume the firm can operate with a smaller inventory and less financial risk.

Keep in mind that as a company grows, there is continued pressure on the management to increase sales year after year. However, this can go on only so long before the market is saturated. At that point there will be no more customers—unless, of course, the firm is willing to change some of its current credit policies. One way to do this is to reduce the requirements for credit and sell to people who are poorer risks. A second is to give customers a longer time period in which to pay. In both cases, the firm may obtain new business. However, although this new credit strategy will sometimes lead to more sales and profit, other times it will result in a lot of unpaid accounts and a reduction in overall profits. In all cases, the amount of short-term financing needed to implement the strategy will go up. Sooner or later, a firm that is in a short-term financial bind will have to reevaluate its credit policies and decide whether or not to tighten up credit. This is where improved credit policies come in. Needless to say, many companies dislike this approach. On the positive side, however, it can be a rather simple remedy for a difficult problem.

8. How can a sales finance company help a retail firm with its short-term financing?

9. Exactly what is commercial paper? Why do small firms not use it as a means of solving their short-term financing problems?

10. How can improved credit policies lead to a reduction in a firm's overall sales volume?

THE FEDERAL RESERVE AND SHORT-TERM CAPITAL

In supplying short-term capital, there are a number of financial institutions that play a significant role. Perhaps the most important of these is the one that helps regulate the amount of money in circulation. It is called the Federal Reserve System.

Federal Reserve System

From the beginning of our nation's history until the early 1900s, banking was often a high-risk business. There was little banking legislation and almost no control over these financial institutions at the national or state levels. As a result, the country witnessed continual monetary panics and crises, resulting in many bank failures. Finally, in an effort to provide stability to our banking system, the Congress passed the Federal Reserve Act of 1913, which established the **Federal Reserve System.**

Members of the Federal Reserve Board, 1914 (seated clockwise around table, left to right): W. G. McAdoo, John Skelton Williams, A. C. Miller, F. A. Delano, H. Parker Willis, W. P. G. Harding, P. M. Warburg, and C. S. Hamlen.

The basic role of the Federal Reserve System is to control the nation's money supply. At the top of the system is the Board of Governors. The seven members of this board are appointed by the president and confirmed by the Senate. Each serves a fourteen-year, nonrenewable term. With these terms expiring at two-year intervals, presidents have the opportunity to appoint individuals with financial philosophies similar to their own. However, the board is virtually free from political pressure because the terms are so long and the individuals cannot be nominated to a second term. In addition, to ensure representation, the seven members of the board must all come from different Federal Reserve districts. In all, there are twelve such districts in the United States (see Fig. 16.4). Within each of these districts there is a Federal Reserve bank; these in turn operate twenty-four branch banks throughout the country. The Federal Reserve bank in each district is owned by the member banks located there.

Figure 16.5 presents an organization chart of the Federal Reserve System. The **Federal Advisory Committee** consists of one member from each of the twelve Federal Reserve banks. Its job is that of advising the Board of Governors. The Federal Open Market Committee also consists of twelve members.

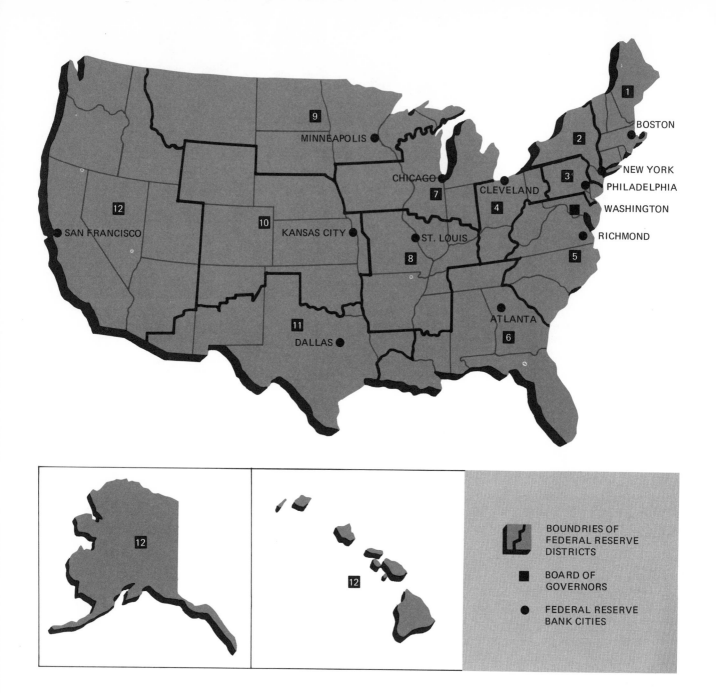

FIG. 16.4 *The Federal Reserve System*

Seven are members of the Board of Governors, one is always the head of the Federal Reserve bank in New York City, and the remaining four are representatives from other Federal Reserve banks. The rest of the system consists of member banks.

All banks in the United States are chartered under either federal or state law. At the present time there are around 4,500 nationally chartered banks and 9,500 state-chartered banks. All national banks *must* be members of the Federal Reserve system, while state banks can join if they wish.

Banks that are members of the system must purchase stock in their district reserve bank and keep reserves at this bank to cover checks written by their depositors. As members of the Federal Reserve System, these banks have a number of important privileges. Among other things, they may (a) obtain funds by borrowing or discounting from their district reserve bank, (b) make use of the funds-transfer and check-collection services provided by the system, (c) obtain financial advice and assistance, (d) vote in electing six of the nine board members of the district bank, and (e) receive a dividend on the stock they own in the district bank. At the present time there are approximately 6,000 banks that are members of the Federal Reserve System. In regulating the money supply in these banks, the Federal Reserve uses (a) the reserve requirement, (b) open market operations, and (c) the discount rate.

Reserve requirement

The most powerful tool available to the Federal Reserve System is the **reserve requirement.** All banks that are members of the system must maintain a certain percentage of their total deposits in the form of reserves. In the case of demand deposits such as checking accounts, this percentage ranges from 10 to 22 percent for large banks and 7 to 14 percent for smaller banks. On time deposits such as savings accounts this percentage ranges from 3 to 6 percent for all banks.

If the "Fed" decides to raise the reserve requirement, such a decision can, of course, result in a bank

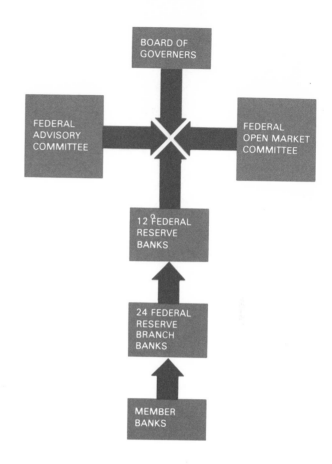

FIG. 16.5 *Organization chart of the Federal Reserve System*

having to call in some of its outstanding loans to meet the new reserve requirement. For example, a large bank with $10 million in demand deposits (checking accounts) might have $1.5 million in reserve to meet a 15-percent requirement. If the Fed increases this percentage requirement to 16 percent, the bank must put another $100,000 in reserve. If it does not have this amount available, it may have to ask for repayment of certain loans and cut back on making others in an effort to raise the money.

Open-market operations

Open-market operations involve the buying and selling of government securities. Federal Reserve banks can buy and sell these securities throughout the country, and by doing so they help transfer money from where it is available to where it is needed. For example, if there is a lot of money in one section of the country, the Federal Reserve banks will sell securities there and take the funds out of circulation. Meanwhile, if member banks in another location need money to lend, the Federal Reserve banks will buy their government securities, thereby pumping money into that area.

More importantly, the Federal Reserve uses open-market operations to control the overall money supply. If it feels there is not enough money in circulation, it will start buying government securities from the member banks. This will put more money into circulation. On the other hand, if the Federal Reserve feels that there is too much money out and wishes to reduce this amount, it will sell government securities to the member banks and draw down the supply of money.

In controlling this total money supply, the Federal Reserve tends to use open-market operations rather than changing the reserve requirement. It is easier to make small adjustments in the supply with open-market operations and such actions tend to escape the notice of the news media. This, in turn, reduces the psychological effect that can accompany a change in the reserve requirement or the Fed's other major instrument of monetary control, the discount rate.

Discount rate

When member banks want to raise additional money they can do so by borrowing at the Federal Reserve banks. This is why the Federal Reserve banks are often referred to as "bankers' banks." They lend money to member banks just the way the latter lend money to us.

When the member banks want to borrow, they will present either IOUs drawn against themselves or promissory notes from their borrowers. The interest rate charged by the Federal Reserve System on these loans to member banks is called the **discount rate.** Each district bank determines its own discount rate subject to approval by the Board of Governors of the entire system.

When the rate is lowered, member banks will be more likely to borrow from the Federal Reserve banks. When it is raised, such borrowing declines. This, of course, is the same pattern followed by you and me in transactions with our local bank.

Today, the discount rate is not as widely used as in the past. However, it does serve as an indicator to private bankers of Federal Reserve policy. When the Fed increases the rate, it indicates that there is too

The original Federal Reserve Board building, built in 1937.

A bank run in the early 1900s.

The Federal Reserve lends money to member banks.

much money in the system and member banks should start to slow down by restricting credit. Meanwhile, when the rate is decreased, this is a signal to the member banks to increase their credit efforts and expand the money supply. Table 16.1 illustrates how the Federal Reserve System's three tools for monetary control can be used to either stimulate or cool the economy.

TABLE 16.1 FEDERAL RESERVE SYSTEM'S TOOLS FOR MONETARY CONTROL

TOOL	TO STIMULATE THE ECONOMY	TO COOL OFF THE ECONOMY
Reserve requirement	Decrease	Increase
Open-market operations	Buy	Sell
Discount rate	Lower	Raise

A Lack of Credit

Lucy White received a call from her local banker last week informing her that the bank was reducing its line of credit from $50,000 to $25,000. Lucy was upset because during the past fiscal year she had borrowed the limit of her credit on three occasions. This reduction in the credit line would hamper her expansion plans.

Lucy's banker said he was sorry. However, the Federal Reserve had started to tighten up the money supply by raising the reserve requirement and selling government securities to the member banks. This, he explained, means that the bank has less money available to lend. To meet this new development, the board of directors voted to call in loans and cut outstanding lines of credit that were not currently being used. The banker again expressed his sympathy and said he hoped that the credit line could be restored within ninety days.

1. How can this reduction in the line of credit hurt Lucy's company?

2. In what way does a rise in the reserve requirement tighten up the money supply?

3. If Lucy needs more money for day-to-day operations, what might she now do?

FEDERAL DEPOSIT INSURANCE CORPORATION

Every bank that is a member of the Federal Reserve System must also subscribe to the **Federal Deposit Insurance Corporation (FDIC).** This corporation was established by Congress in 1933 to insure bank depositors. Banks that are not members of the Federal Reserve can also subscribe to the FDIC if they wish, and today there are very few banks that do not.

The FDIC guarantees deposits up to $40,000 in case of either bank failure or insolvency. If an insured bank needs a loan in order to remain open for business, the FDIC will step in. In turn, the FDIC establishes banking practices that must be followed if a bank wants to be insured, and examines all of the insured banks on a periodic basis to see that they are adhering to these practices. Along with the Federal Reserve System, the FDIC has done a great deal to provide stability and equilibrium in the United States banking and monetary system.

11. What are the benefits to a bank in being a member of the Federal Reserve System?

12. How does the reserve requirement help the Fed regulate the money supply?

13. What happens when the Fed engages in open-market operations?

14. How does the discount rate help regulate the money supply?

15. Why might a bank want to be insured by the FDIC?

SUMMARY

From time to time most every business finds itself in need of short-term financing. The firm needs money to conduct its day-to-day activities. These funds can be raised in a number of different ways.

One way is to borrow from family or friends. This approach is often used by small businesses. A second method, which is the most popular of all, is to use trade credit. A third is to borrow from a bank. For small amounts these loans are often unsecured, but for large sums banks often request security or collateral of some sort. A fourth way of raising short-term capital is to sell accounts receivable to collection agents, called factors. When these receivables are sold with recourse, they are returned if not collected. When sold without recourse, the factor assumes all risk for collection.

Some firms, especially retailers, are able to greatly overcome short-term financing problems by getting other companies to finance their inventory. Sales finance companies will sometimes do this because it gives them an opportunity to purchase lucrative retail sales contracts. Short-term financing can also be raised through the purchase of commercial paper or through various government sources.

Most of these above methods are available to the average firm. However, many businesses realize that they should be used only if needed. One way of reducing this need is to enforce more stringent credit policies. This can be a wise strategy, especially if the Federal Reserve starts to tighten up the money supply by means of the reserve requirement, open-market operations, and/or the discount rate.

KEY TERMS FOUND IN THIS CHAPTER

QUESTIONS FOR DISCUSSION AND ANALYSIS

1. When might a firm pass up the opportunity to take a 2-percent discount for early payment of a bill?

2. What is a line of credit? How does it help in meeting short-term financing problems?

3. How does a factor judge the quality of accounts receivable?

4. Would a factor pay more money or less money for receivables that are purchased with recourse?

5. What is a sales finance company?

6. In what way can the government be a source of short-term funds for a business?

7. If a firm imposes stricter credit policies, will it make more, or less, profit? Explain.

8. What is the basic objective of the Federal Reserve System?

That money talks/I'll not deny,/I heard it once:/It said, "Goodbye".
Richard Armour

OBJECTIVES OF THIS CHAPTER

Sooner or later just about every business needs to raise long-term capital. This money is used to purchase long-term assets such as plant and equipment. In this chapter we are going to be examining the ways in which long-term capital is raised. Our first objective is to study some of the methods of obtaining long-term debt. The second is to review the kind of stock, preferred and common, often sold to raise long-term capital. The third objective is to learn about the types of financial institutions that often help corporations raise this capital. By the end of the chapter you should be able to do the following:

a. describe what is meant by a long-term loan;

b. explain the importance of bonds in long-term financing;

c. identify the common characteristics of long-term debt;

d. describe preferred stock and its importance in long-term financing;

e. explain some of the basic characteristics of common stock; and

f. relate the role played by financial institutions in helping corporations raise long-term capital.

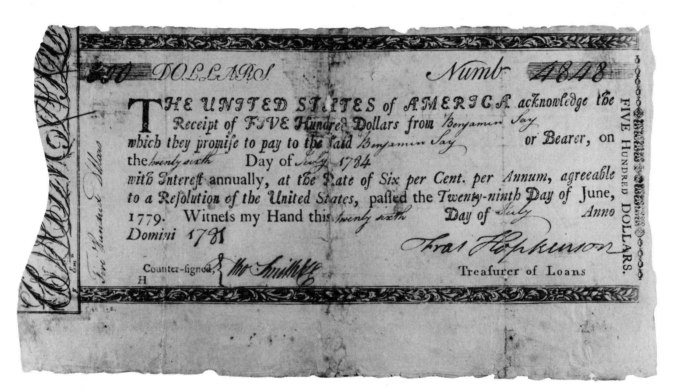

LONG-TERM DEBT

One major source of long-term financing is debt. Many companies rely heavily on this form of financing to obtain the necessary capital for expenditures such as plant expansion and the purchase of new equipment.

Long-Term Debt Financing

The most common methods of financing long-term debt are (a) through banks and other financial institutions in the form of long-term loans, and (b) through the sale of bonds.

Long-term loans

A **long-term loan** usually has a maturity date of one to five years. During this time the firm is required to pay interest on the debt and to abide by any other agreements associated with the loan. For example, it is common to find the lending institution requiring the company to seek its permission before doing any more long-term borrowing. In this way the lending firm protects its investment. If the loan is

extremely risky, the lending institution may even require the company to limit or eliminate dividends to the stockholders, as well as to pledge certain assets for security on the loan. Naturally, the conditions of the loan are heavily determined by the amount of protection the lending institution feels it must have. If they are too strict the firm may seek another lender and try for better terms. For companies in good financial condition, this is often possible. For marginal firms, however, it is usually not.

1. Do all long-term loans have accompanying restrictions requiring the firm to limit its dividends?

Bonds

Bonds are also long-term debts, but in contrast to loans they often have a maturity date twenty to thirty years into the future (see Fig. 17.1). Most carry a face value of $1,000 and pay a predetermined interest

FIG. 17.1 *A bond issued by AT&T (Reprinted by permission.)*

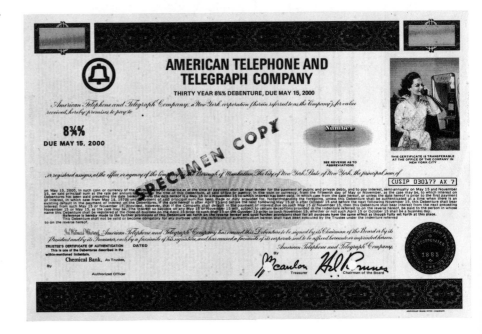

rate such as 8 percent. Investors who buy such a bond would receive $80 interest each year. This interest is paid quarterly (every three months), semi-annually, or annually, depending upon the terms of the particular bond issue. These terms are found in a corporate document known as the indenture agreement and help determine whether the bond will sell at a premium or a discount.

Indenture agreement. The **indenture agreement,** which is filed with each bond issue, sets forth all the features associated with the bonds. One of these is the interest rate. A second feature involves any specific assets that are pledged as collateral for the bonds. In the case of high-risk firms, pledging of assets may be the only way to generate interest among investors.

A third feature often found in the indenture agreement is a **call provision.** This provision covers the repurchase of bonds prior to maturity. For example, if a firm issued twenty-five-year, 8-percent, $1,000-par (amount stated on the face) bonds in 1977, the bonds would be redeemable in 2002. With a call provision, the company can retire them early. For this privilege, however, the firm will pay a small bonus, known as a **redemption premium,** to the bondholder. The following is an illustration of the type of premium that might be paid for calling in the bonds early:

Year	Redemption premium
1992	2.50%
1993	2.25
1994	2.00
1995	1.75
1996	1.50
1997	1.25
1998	1.00
1999	0.75
2000	0.50
2001	0.25

The above provisions indicate that the company cannot call in these bonds prior to 1992. After this,

it must pay a redemption premium to do so. If an investor's bond is called in 1994, for example, the person is entitled to the regular 8-percent interest plus a 2-percent premium, or a total of 10-percent interest that year. The closer the bonds are to maturity, of course, the less the redemption premium paid by the firm because the benefit to the company is smaller.

Another feature sometimes found in the indenture agreement is a **conversion privilege.** This allows bondholders to convert their investments to stock. For example, each $1,000 bond may be convertible to fifty shares of common stock. This privilege provides flexibility to the investor. If the price of the common stock goes to, say, $27 a share, the bondholder can convert and have an investment worth $1,350. If the stock price remains under $20, the investor can keep the bond and continue to draw the fixed interest. Many firms find that the conversion privilege makes a new bond very appealing to investors.

2. If the firm calls in a bond early, does the bondholder receive any special payment from the company?

3. Why do many bond issues have a call provision?

4. How is the conversion privilege a selling factor in making a new bond issue appealing to investors?

Premiums and discounts. Another feature of bonds that merits discussion is the selling price. When bonds are first issued, if they sell for more than face value we say they have been sold at a **premium.** Buying a $1,000 bond for $1,050 is an illustration. The investor has paid a premium of $50. Conversely, purchasing a $1,000 bond for $980 is an illustration of buying at a **discount.** When firms are viewed as very safe investments, their bonds may sell at a small premium. If a firm is believed to be a risky investment, however, investors may be unwilling to buy except at a discount.

Interest rates will also bring about changes in bond prices. For example, if a company issued twenty-five-year, 5-percent, $1,000-par bonds in 1968 and the current interest rate on new bond issues is 10 percent, investors will want to sell their old bonds and buy new ones. As this happens the price of the old bond will drop, because it is really overpriced given its low interest rate. The trading price will then stabilize at a lower level, such as $500. The investor who buys the bond at this $500 discount will still receive 5-percent interest on a bond that is redeemable for $1000 in 1993. This interest will be $50. However, since the investor paid only $500 for it, the current *effective* rate of interest is 10 percent (50/500)! Thus the selling price of bonds will fluctuate depending upon the amount of interest they pay. In the above illustration the price declined. On the other hand, if a firm issued 9-percent bonds in a market where everyone else was offering 8 percent, its bonds would probably sell at a premium. On a $1,000-par bond, the investor would receive $90 annually. If this bond was purchased at a premium of $100, however, the effective rate of interest would drop to around 8.2 percent (90/1100). Thus the selling price of a bond reflects current interest rates as well as the confidence people have in the firm.

5. When might a bond sell at a premium?

6. If interest rates continue to rise, would you expect old bond issues to sell at a premium or a discount?

Characteristics of Long-Term Debt

All forms of long-term debt have certain characteristics in common. These relate to (a) interest, (b) claim on assets, (c) prepayment, and (d) tax advantages.

Interest

All of the long-term debt instruments we have examined thus far are *interest bearing*. Some, of course, will pay higher rates of interest depending upon the degree of risk involved. In every case, however, this interest must be paid at stated intervals. If the company cannot meet these obligations, the creditors may well force it to declare bankruptcy.

Claim on assets

In the case of bankruptcy, all of the firm's creditors have a *claim on assets*. This claim is held not only by those who have sold merchandise to this company on credit, but also by those who have extended long-term loans to the firm and those who have purchased bonds. Naturally, a company that is forced into bankruptcy may be able to pay off its indebtedness at a rate of only 30¢ on the dollar. Nevertheless, these creditors are entitled to collect whatever is available. Furthermore, the stockholders receive nothing until all claims of all creditors are satisfied.

Repayment

Sooner or later all long-term debt instruments must be *repaid*. To ensure that these debts can be met, businesses will often set up separate accounts into which they will make periodic payments. Then when the loan or bond is due for repayment, the money is available. If the company is solvent, it may retire the debt and be done with it. In the case of bonds, however, the debt may come due just as the machines that were purchased with this money need to be replaced. When this happens, the firm will often repay the old bonds by issuing new ones. Then the money that was set aside for redeeming the old bonds can be used to buy the new machinery.

Tax advantages

All interest payments made on outstanding loans and bonds are tax deductible. By this we mean that a company can subtract these payments as part of their operating expenses. The result is a smaller tax bite on the firm. Let us consider an illustration. Assume

TABLE 17.1 PARTIAL INCOME STATEMENT ILLUSTRATING INTEREST EXPENSE

Sales		$1,000,000
Less: Interest expense	$100,000	
All other expenses	700,000	
Total expenses		800,000
Taxable income		$200,000
Taxes (48%)		96,000
Net income		$104,000

Table 17.1 to be a simplified income statement for a company. The company has taxable income of $200,000 and net income of $104,000. Note in the table that the interest expense is deductible *before* taxes are calculated and paid. If there were no interest expense, taxable income would have been $300,000 and net income would have been $156,000. This illustrates that because the company is in a 48-percent income-tax bracket, the government actually winds up paying 48 percent of the company's cost of debt financing! As a result of tax policies, interest-bearing debt is a very attractive source of funds for many firms.

7. If one investor has a million shares of common stock and another owns a $1,000 bond, who will have first claim on the firm's assets in the case of bankruptcy?

8. In what way does the government help a firm pay the cost of its debt financing?

EQUITY FINANCING

Another way to raise long-term funds is through equity financing. This involves selling part of the ownership or equity in the firm. This is most commonly done through the sale of preferred or common stock. The following examines both of these types of stock.

The Bankruptcy Line

During the last couple of years the nation's supermarket industry has been especially hard hit with bankruptcies. In particular there is the case of Food Fair, Inc., and Allied Supermarkets, Inc. Since October 1978 both have been forced to take shelter under the federal bankruptcy laws. They are now attempting to settle their multimillion-dollar debts—while other marginal grocery chains fret over who is going to be next in the bankruptcy line.

And they have good reason to be worried. The industry is beset by a host of problems including a declining national birthrate, competition from fast-food outlets, high labor costs, and slack productivity. Sales increases are lagging behind inflation and profit margins are very very small: 72¢ per $100. For a long time the supermarket industry attempted to adjust for this small margin with high turnover. However, now that turnover is slowing up, bankruptcies are increasing.

While it is still too early to say whether these firms will go under permanently, it is becoming obvious to the creditors and stockholders that unless there is a swift turnaround, they are going to have to get in line to recover a little of their investment.

Preferred Stock

Preferred stock is somewhat like a bond and somewhat like common stock in that it has characteristics of both. Some of the features of preferred stock that are worthy of note concern (a) dividend features, (b) claim on assets, (c) life of the issue, and (d) voice in management.

Dividend features

Preferred stock is like a bond in that it usually carries a **fixed dividend,** which is similar to the fixed interest rate on a bond. This dividend is often expressed as a percentage of par value. For example, a share of preferred that has a par value of $100 may have a stated dividend of 5 percent. If the stock does not have a par or stated value of $100, it is common to find the firm simply stating the dividend in dollars rather than as a percentage of par, such as $5 per share. In either case, the preferred stockholders are entitled to this dividend each year, and when dividends are declared the preferred stockholders *must* be paid before the common stockholders get anything. The preferred stockholders have first preference on dividends.

Some firms, in an effort to improve the marketability of a preferred stock issue, will add a few additional features. Two of the most common are the **cumulative feature** and the **participating feature.** Both are related to the firm's dividend obligations.

The *cumulative feature* deals with nonpayment of the preferred dividend. What happens if the firm is in such a financial bind that it cannot pay the

"It's a healthy company."

From The Wall Street Journal; permission Cartoon Features Syndicate

Stocks and bonds are long-term financing instruments that can help corporations grow even larger. However, from time to time companies will overextend themselves, find that they have to borrow a great deal of money and are unable to repay it. And this is exactly what happened to the Ling-Temco-Vought Corporation during the late 1960s, as it almost fell into bankruptcy. That is, until Paul Thayer came to the fore.

Taking over the controls of the near-bankrupt company, he pulled it out of its tailspin with some very nervy tactics and got it back on the road to economic recovery. Within two years he had gotten rid of unprofitable operations, opened up communication lines between the headquarters and the various subsidiaries, and concentrated on solidifying rather than diversifying the company. When he assumed control, LTV did not own 100% of any of its subsidiaries, had negative cash flows, and was in collateral default with the banks. Thayer immediately realized that LTV had to get 100% ownership

of what it had left. So he set out to buy total control of the Jones & Laughlin Steel Corporation, the LTV Aerospace Corporation, and Wilson & Company, the meat packing and food processing concern. In this three-year process, he disposed of several companies and some smaller assets.

The outcome has been a rousing success. By 1974, LTV was reporting record sales and earnings. This success picture has continued. For the three-month period ending June 1979, the company had consolidated net income of $40.3 million or $1.40 per share on consolidated sales of $2.03 billion. For the first six months of the year, the consolidated net income had been $80.8 million or $2.81 per share on consolidated sales of $4.02 billion.

How did Paul Thayer do it? By realizing that a good administrator must know not only how to raise money but also how to manage it. And the success of LTV illustrates that he can do both.

Paul Thayer

dividend to the preferred stockholders? If the stock has a cumulative feature the company must carry the dividend over to the next period and pay it then. Thus the firm cannot skip a preferred dividend; these obligations must be accumulated and eventually paid. And remember that until they are, the common stockholders receive no dividends. Of course, if the dividends begin to mount up over two or three years the firm may have to work out some kind of arrangement with the preferred stockholders. We will be talking about this later in the chapter; for

the moment, however, keep in mind that the cumulative feature requires dividends to accumulate rather than be cancelled.

The *participating feature* allows the preferred stockholders to share in dividends above the rate of their originally stated dividend. Usually, this participation is restricted to "extra" dividends given to the common stockholders. For example, if the usual dividend on common stock is $1.25 per year but the firm has had a spectacular year, it might declare an extra dividend of $1.00 per share. Usually these extra dividends are given only to the common stockholders. However, if the preferred stock contains the participating feature, these stockholders are also entitled to an additional $1.00 per share. Some firms are even more generous with their participation feature and allow the preferred stockholders to share in *all* dividends given to the common. Needless to say, this can be a very enticing feature that greatly improves the marketability of the preferred stock.

Claim on assets

As we noted earlier, in case of liquidation the creditors must be paid first. After they are paid, however, the preferred stockholders have the next priority claim on the assets of the corporation. They come before the common stockholders. Naturally, if the firm has to declare bankruptcy there may be very little money left. Nevertheless, if adequate funds are available the preferred stockholders are entitled to the par value of their stock. If anything then remains, it is available for distribution to the common stockholders.

Life of the issue

A third characteristic of preferred stock is related to the life of the issue. In contrast to common stock, which can never be called in by the firm, corporations sometimes make preferred stock **callable.** When this occurs, the stock is very much like callable bonds. If the firm wants to retire this stock, it will pay the owner par value plus a small premium, which usually comes to around 6 percent of par.

Voice in management

A fourth characteristic of preferred stock is its potential influence on management. This influence can be brought about by preferred stockholders in several ways. One is through **voting privileges.**

In some states preferred stockholders have the same voting rights as common stockholders. In these cases, except for the dividend policy and the call provision, there is really little difference between common and preferred stock. Not all states, however, give the preferred stockholders an automatic voice in the management of the firm; some spell out the voting rights of preferred stockholders in terms of the issue of the security. Quite often such terms allow the preferred stockholders to vote *only* if dividend obligations have not been met for a specified period of time. For example, if no dividend is declared on preferred stock for four consecutive quarters, these stockholders are entitled to vote on corporate matters. Because this can open the door to a lot of angry stockholders who might want to change the composition of the board of directors, there is a great deal of pressure on management to ensure financial stability and maintain the preferred dividend.

A second way in which preferred stockholders can secure a voice in management is through the *conversion privilege.* This feature was described earlier when convertible bonds were discussed. In essence, conversion allows the preferred stockholders to trade their preferred stock for a predetermined number of shares of common stock. This privilege often makes it easier to sell a new issue of preferred stock, because the investors know that if dividends are not paid or the board of directors provides inadequate leadership, they can convert their holdings to common stock and vote for a new board. If there are 10,000 shares of preferred and 100,000 shares of common outstanding, and the conversion rate is 10 to 1, by converting all of their shares, the preferred stockholders will hold 100,000 shares of common or 50 percent of the total common stock. Since this represents a substantial voting block, it provides the preferred stockholders with a large potential voice in the affairs of management.

9. Can the corporation declare a dividend on common stock if it has decided to pass up the dividend on the preferred stock?

10. If the preferred stock does not have a cumulative feature, what financial obligation

The Preferred Stock Proposal

By late last year Lucy White's hamburger franchise had increased to fifty units, half of which were owned directly by her. In order to acquire the capital necessary for this expansion, Lucy had borrowed quite a bit of money at her local bank. In fact, the bank told Lucy that it would be unwilling to advance her any more money. As a result, Lucy decided to issue stock. With some of the funds from this issue she planned on paying off her long-term bank loan; the rest she intended to put into further expansion.

After looking into the matter, Lucy thought she might try to obtain $5 million with an issue of preferred stock. She envisioned 50,000 shares of $100 par, 8 percent preferred. The preferred stock would be cumulative and participate in any "extra" dividends given on the common stock. In addition, if the dividend were not paid for four consecutive quarters, the preferred stockholders would be given the right to a voice in the management of the firm by being allowed to vote in the next election of the board of directors. For every preferred share held, an investor would receive two votes. Since there are already 200,000 shares of common stock outstanding, giving the preferred stockholders the right to vote would give them 100,000 votes, or one-third of all possible votes.

Finally, Lucy is thinking about also making this preferred stock convertible to common on a "one share of preferred for two shares of common" basis. Although she has not decided to go forward with this issue of preferred stock, Lucy is giving the matter serious consideration.

1. What are some of the characteristics possessed by preferred stock?

2. What does it mean if we say that this stock is "cumulative"?

3. If the preferred stockholders all convert their holdings, what effect will this have on their voice in the management of the firm?

does the firm have to these stockholders if it passes up their dividend?

11. What rights or benefits does the participating feature give to the preferred stockholders?

12. Why might the conversion privilege make a preferred stock issue more appealing to investors?

Common Stock

Most individuals who have an ownership position in a corporation hold **common stock.** This stock has four basic characteristics relating to (a) the right to share in the company's earnings, (b) a voice in management, (c) a claim on assets, and (d) permanent ownership.

Common stockholders are entitled to share in the earnings of the corporation.

Share in the earnings

Common stockholders are entitled to share in the earnings of the corporation. These earnings are distributed in the form of dividends. When the board of directors meets it makes a decision about whether or not to declare a dividend and how large it should be. For example, a corporation that pays an annual dividend of $4 per share will usually give $1 every three months. If the company's profits increase the board might vote a greater dividend such as $6, with $1.50 being paid each quarter. All common stockholders receive an identical dividend for each share they own.

Keep in mind, however, that a corporation is not required to pay a dividend. This is determined by the board of directors. As a result, if the firm is in financial difficulty it may pass up the quarterly dividend. If things do not improve, the company may even go so far as to reduce the dividend or eliminate it entirely. Corporations that have an excessive amount of debt or preferred stock often find themselves locked into high interest payments and "guaranteed" dividends, all of which must be paid before the common stockholders receive their dividends. As a result, in some firms the holders of common stock receive very little return on their investment in the form of dividends.

Voice in management

The common stockholders have a right to vote in corporate matters, including the election of the board of directors. Sometimes the voting method is **noncumulative.** This means that if there are thirteen people running for the board and only seven can be elected, you can cast one vote, for each share of common you own, for seven of these individuals. If you own one hundred shares, each of these seven will receive one hundred votes. The problem with noncumulative voting is that the stockholder who has 50 percent or more of the stock can *always* elect the total board. Minority stockholders end up having no voice.

For this reason some companies use **cumulative** voting. Under this method each stockholder is entitled to a number of votes equal to the number of shares owned multiplied by the number of directors to be elected. This total vote can be given to one individual, or divided up among more than one in any way the stockholder desires. Thus a stockholder with one hundred shares who is voting for seven directors is entitled to seven hundred votes. These can be distributed as the investor sees fit. This method of voting gives minority stockholders more of an opportunity to elect at least one or two members to the board of directors, thus assuring them some voice in the management of the firm.

In recent years many corporations with cumulative voting have voiced support for noncumulative voting. They argue that such a procedure reduces the power of dissidents and perpetual troublemakers. Supporters of cumulative voting, meanwhile, point to the importance of corporate democracy and minority representation. Actually, those supporting cumulative voting probably have the better argument because dissident stockholders are entitled to representation and it is unlikely that they ever really cause that much trouble, partly because the stockholders almost always vote for the proposed board of directors.

Of course, not everyone will be present at the board meeting when elections are held. Those absent, however, can vote by **proxy,** which is simply a legal document authorizing the treasurer or another top officer of the firm to vote on the stockholder's behalf (see Fig. 17.2). If the firm receives enough votes by stockholders attending the meeting

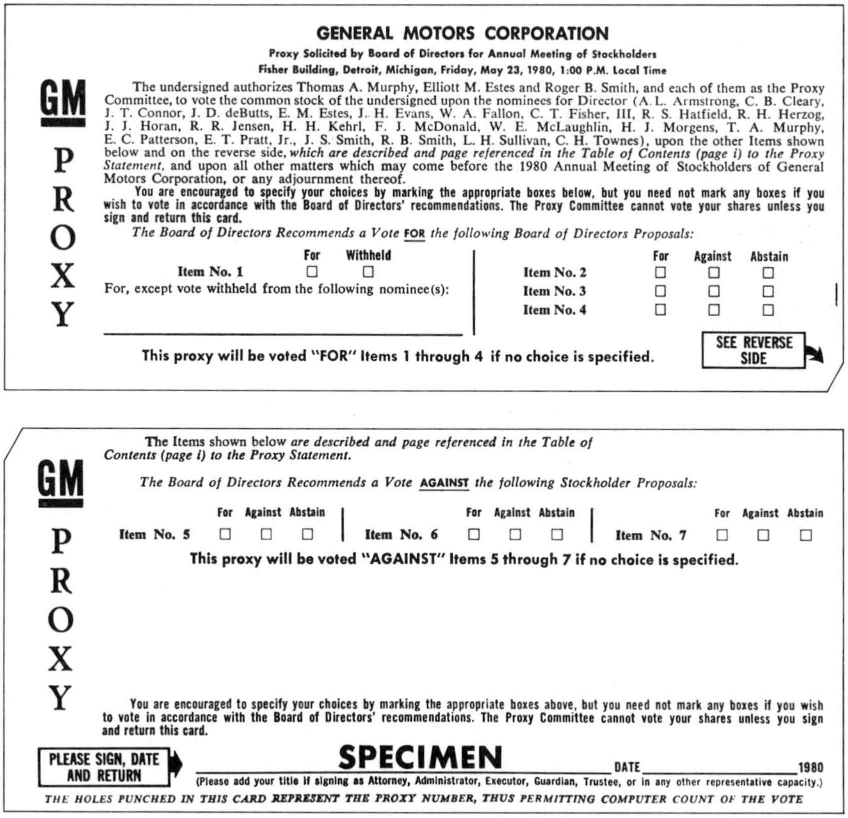

GM PROXY

GENERAL MOTORS CORPORATION

Proxy Solicited by Board of Directors for Annual Meeting of Stockholders
Fisher Building, Detroit, Michigan, Friday, May 23, 1980, 1:00 P.M. Local Time

The undersigned authorizes Thomas A. Murphy, Elliott M. Estes and Roger B. Smith, and each of them as the Proxy Committee, to vote the common stock of the undersigned upon the nominees for Director (A. L. Armstrong, C. B. Cleary, J. T. Connor, J. D. deButts, E. M. Estes, J. H. Evans, W. A. Fallon, C. T. Fisher, III, R. S. Hatfield, R. H. Herzog, J. J. Horan, R. R. Jensen, H. H. Kehrl, F. J. McDonald, W. E. McLaughlin, H. J. Morgens, T. A. Murphy, E. C. Patterson, E. T. Pratt, Jr., J. S. Smith, R. B. Smith, L. H. Sullivan, C. H. Townes), upon the other Items shown below and on the reverse side, *which are described and page referenced in the Table of Contents (page i) to the Proxy Statement,* and upon all other matters which may come before the 1980 Annual Meeting of Stockholders of General Motors Corporation, or any adjournment thereof.

You are encouraged to specify your choices by marking the appropriate boxes below, but you need not mark any boxes if you wish to vote in accordance with the Board of Directors' recommendations. The Proxy Committee cannot vote your shares unless you sign and return this card.

The Board of Directors Recommends a Vote FOR *the following Board of Directors Proposals:*

	For	Withheld
Item No. 1	☐	☐

For, except vote withheld from the following nominee(s):

	For	Against	Abstain
Item No. 2	☐	☐	☐
Item No. 3	☐	☐	☐
Item No. 4	☐	☐	☐

This proxy will be voted "FOR" Items 1 through 4 if no choice is specified.

SEE REVERSE SIDE

GM PROXY

The Items shown below *are described and page referenced in the Table of Contents (page i) to the Proxy Statement.*

The Board of Directors Recommends a Vote AGAINST *the following Stockholder Proposals:*

	For	Against	Abstain
Item No. 5	☐	☐	☐
Item No. 6	☐	☐	☐
Item No. 7	☐	☐	☐

This proxy will be voted "AGAINST" Items 5 through 7 if no choice is specified.

You are encouraged to specify your choices by marking the appropriate boxes above, but you need not mark any boxes if you wish to vote in accordance with the Board of Directors' recommendations. The Proxy Committee cannot vote your shares unless you sign and return this card.

PLEASE SIGN, DATE AND RETURN **SPECIMEN** DATE ______ 1980

(Please add your title if signing as Attorney, Administrator, Executor, Guardian, Trustee, or in any other representative capacity.)

THE HOLES PUNCHED IN THIS CARD REPRESENT THE PROXY NUMBER, THUS PERMITTING COMPUTER COUNT OF THE VOTE

FIG. 17.2 *A proxy statement for General Motors stockholders (Reprinted by permission.)*

and proxy statements mailed in by those who cannot be in attendance (and it almost always does), then the board of directors can be returned for another year. As a result, minority factions seldom succeed in overthrowing the old board. In fact, this has long been an argument used against boards of directors. Because they encounter little opposition, they can become self-perpetuating committees with little regard for the stockholders. To some degree, there is truth in the charge. After all, how many stockholders are willing to vote against the board if the firm is profitable and dividends are being paid on a regular basis?

Claim on assets

A third characteristic of common stock is that their owners have a claim on the company's assets in the case of liquidation. As noted previously, the creditors are first in line and the preferred stockholders are second. If anything remains after this, however, the common stockholders are entitled to it. For example, if the corporation has cash of $1,000,000 after selling all noncash assets, debts of $200,000, and 1,000 shares of $100-par preferred stock outstanding, there would be $700,000 left to divide among the common stockholders. If there were 100,000 shares of common outstanding, each share would be worth $7. Naturally, this stock might have sold for a great deal more before liquidation, but the common stockholders are at least getting something. Unfortunately for many such stockholders, the above illustration is not always the case. Quite often a firm that declares bankruptcy is so financially overburdened that the common stockholders will get nothing. Nevertheless, if there is something left they have a legal right to it.

Permanent ownership

A fourth characteristic of common stock is that of permanent ownership. Once a corporation issues common stock, it cannot be recalled from the market the way, for example, callable bonds or callable

preferred stock can. There are only two ways common stock can be "retired." The most obvious is for the corporation to repurchase it from the stockholders at the current market price. The other way is when the stockholders agree to a merger with another firm and their stock is traded in for ownership in the new company. If this is done on a "1 for 1" basis, the stockholders will receive one share of common in the new firm for each share they currently have. If the ratio is 3 for 1, they will be given three shares of common for each one they now have. The ratio is often determined by the current selling price of the company's common stock. For example, if corporation A, with a current stock value of $75 per share, is being merged with corporation B, which has a market value of $25 per common share, it is evident that the corporation A stockholders will want three shares of common for each one they now hold.

13. Is the corporation required to pay dividends on its common stock?

14. Why do some firms prefer noncumulative voting?

15. Do common stockholders have any claim on the firm's assets in case of liquidation?

FINANCIAL INSTITUTIONS FOR LONG-TERM CAPITAL

How does a business sell stocks and bonds so as to raise long-term capital? There are a number of ways, all of which involve financial institutions. The most important of these institutions are the investment banking companies. Other types include mutual funds, pension funds, and insurance companies.

Investment Banking Companies

Investment banking companies act as middlemen by purchasing and then reselling new issues of stocks and bonds. For example, if corporation A wishes to sell $10 million of new preferred stock in order to build a factory, it might have difficulty because it probably knows little about selling new stock issues. As a result, it will often go to an investment banking company and ask this firm to help out by buying the new issue. After analyzing the company's operations the investment bank will give its decision. In a case where the investment bank does decide to "underwrite" the issue, it will make an offer for the stock. For example, if it felt the stock would sell at $100 per share, the investment bank might offer $9.5 million for the entire issue. The difference between the selling price ($10 million) and what the investment bank is willing to pay ($9.5 million) is known as the *spread*. This spread, or margin, is used to handle the expenses involved in reselling the stock to other investors. There are many investment

CASE

A Common Issue

After serious thought Lucy White decided she would repay her long-term loan at the bank by issuing common stock. In addition to the 200,000 shares of common currently outstanding, which she has decided to keep herself, she is planning to issue another 200,000 shares of common for sale to outside investors.

Some analysts at a major investment banking house have told Lucy that they believe this new issue can be sold publicly for $50 a share. This would raise $10 million. The investment bank is willing to buy the issue for $9.5 million and assume the risk of reselling it. After giving the matter a great deal of thought, Lucy has decided to accept this offer and go ahead with the transaction.

Lucy believes that with this money she not only can pay off her loan at the bank but can expand her operations as well. With the increased profit she hopes to be able to pay an annual dividend of $2.50 per share. She also hopes to establish her firm as a solid, long-term growth company. In this way she believes it will be possible to finance future growth through more common stock offerings.

1. What are the characteristics of common stock?

2. To whom might the investment bank sell these 200,000 shares of common stock?

3. If Lucy has not yet decided whether this stock should allow for cumulative or noncumulative voting, what would you recommend? Why?

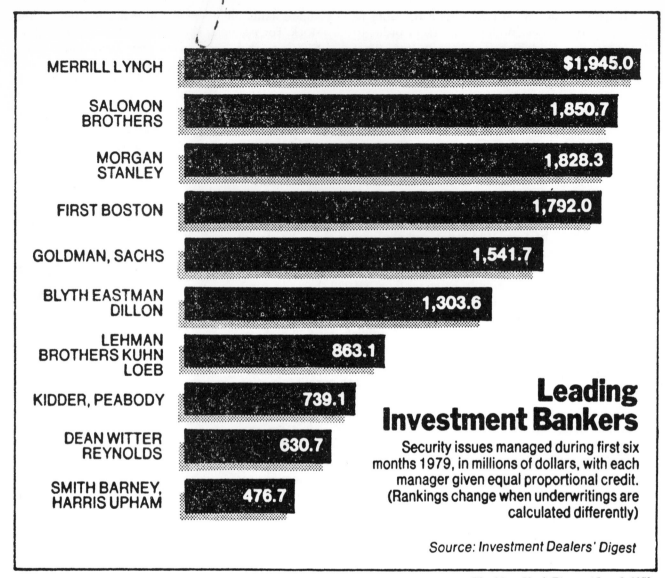

Leading Investment Bankers

Security issues managed during first six months 1979, in millions of dollars, with each manager given equal proportional credit. (Rankings change when underwritings are calculated differently)

Source: Investment Dealers' Digest

The New York Times / Oct. 8, 1979

MERRILL LYNCH — $1,945.0
SALOMON BROTHERS — 1,850.7
MORGAN STANLEY — 1,828.3
FIRST BOSTON — 1,792.0
GOLDMAN, SACHS — 1,541.7
BLYTH EASTMAN DILLON — 1,303.6
LEHMAN BROTHERS KUHN LOEB — 863.1
KIDDER, PEABODY — 739.1
DEAN WITTER REYNOLDS — 630.7
SMITH BARNEY, HARRIS UPHAM — 476.7

banks in America today. Some of the best known include Blyth Eastman Dillon Merrill Lynch, Pierce Fenner & Smith; and Bache, Halsey, Stuart, Shields, Inc.

Note that "investment banks" are neither investors nor banks. They are merely financial institutions that buy large blocks of stocks and bonds and then resell them in smaller blocks to other institutions and investors. Sometimes the cost of a new issue is so large that no one investment bank is willing to underwrite the entire issue alone. In this case two or more investment banks will form a **syndicate** and each will take so much of the offering. For example, five of them might take equal shares of a new $50-million bond issue. Each will then attempt to resell their respective block of bonds. One group to which they will often sell some of these securities is made up of investment companies, or, as they are commonly called, mutual funds.

Mutual Funds

Mutual funds, also known as **investment companies,** sell stock in their firms just the way other corporations do. However, these companies do not produce a product. Instead they take the money they receive for their stock and invest it in other corporations. Some large mutual funds will have substantial holdings in many high-grade or **"blue-chip"** stocks, such as IBM, AT & T, and General Electric.

Many investors like mutual funds because they are a way to invest in the market without having to worry about the day-to-day ups and downs of a particular stock. Usually the fund's holdings are so diversified that declines by one or two stocks may well be offset by increases in the others. Therefore, assuming that the stock market will go up over the next ten years, the price of the fund's stock will rise. This, in turn, will result in a profit for the investor. When one realizes that some of these funds have over $10 billion invested in the market, it becomes evident that they are a major source of long-term capital for business.

Pension Funds

Today millions of employees participate in pension plans. Sometimes the business firm makes the entire contribution; usually the worker and the company both put in a percentage of the worker's salary. In academic circles, for example, it is common to find the professors contributing 6 percent of their salary to a pension fund and the university matching this amount. What happens to all of this money? The answer is that it is invested by the insurance company or financial institution that is administering the retirement plan. Usually this firm will invest it in high-grade stocks and bonds that are likely to grow over the ensuing decades. In this way the investment should increase and the contributors be able to draw out enough money to cover their retirement. These pension funds are an important source of long-term financing for business.

Insurance Companies

Insurance firms receive billions of dollars in premiums from their policyholders each year. Even after paying out all claims, they still have a great deal of money left. This excess is invested in many things, including government and corporate bonds and, to a lesser degree, stocks. In fact, some insurance firms have so much money to invest that they are able to buy an entire security issue without having to go through an investment bank. As a result, insurance companies are an important source of long-term capital for many corporations.

16. What is an investment banking syndicate?

17. Why do so many investors prefer to buy mutual funds rather than put their money in one high-grade stock such as AT & T?

18. Why are insurance companies so important in raising long-term capital?

SUMMARY

At one time or another just about every corporation needs to obtain some long-term financing. One method of raising this money is through a long-term loan. A second is with a bond issue. Both of these illustrate the use of long-term debt, which has four common characteristics: it is interest bearing; in case of bankruptcy, it gives the creditors first claim on assets; it must eventually be repaid; and all interest payments are tax deductible.

Another method of raising long-term capital is with preferred stock. This stock is similar to a bond in that it carries a fixed rate of dividend; it is similar to common stock in that the investors are sometimes given the opportunity for a voice in management. In order to make an issue of preferred stock enticing to investors, some firms will add features to the issue such as making it cumulative and/or participating in regard to dividends.

The third basic method for raising long-term capital is to issue common stock. Common stockholders all have the right to share in the company's earnings, a voice in management, a claim on the assets in case of bankruptcy, and permanent ownership. Most individuals holding an ownership position in a corporation are common stockholders.

If the company decides to raise long-term capital with a loan, it will usually negotiate with a bank. If it decides to sell stocks and bonds, it will do so with the assistance of a financial institution that has experience in this area. The major institution is the investment banking company, which purchases and then resells new issues of stocks and bonds. Other important institutions in this area include mutual funds (also known as investment companies), pension funds, and insurance companies.

KEY TERMS FOUND IN THIS CHAPTER

QUESTIONS FOR DISCUSSION AND ANALYSIS

1. How does a bond differ from a long-term loan obtained from a bank?

2. What is contained in the indenture agreement filed with each bond issue?

3. What are the four basic characteristics of long-term debt?

4. How is preferred stock similar to a bond?

5. When might the preferred stockholders secure a voice in the management of the corporation's activities?

6. What does "voting by proxy" mean?

7. Can a corporation call in all of its outstanding common stock?

8. How does an investment banking company help a corporation raise long-term capital?

18

Don't gamble: buy some good stock, hold it till it goes up and then sell it. If it doesn't go up, don't buy it.
Will Rogers

OBJECTIVES OF THIS CHAPTER

In the previous chapter we studied long-term financing. However, our coverage of the area would be incomplete if we did not examine what happens to these long-term capital investments such as stocks and bonds. After they are sold, what do the investors do with them? Are they ever resold? What happens when they are? In order to answer these questions, we must study the securities markets. Our first objective in this chapter is to examine why people invest in the markets. The second is to study how security exchanges work. The third objective is to learn how securities are actually bought and sold and how to follow these transactions in the financial section of a newspaper. The fourth objective is to review some of the legislative acts that regulate security transactions. The final objective is to answer the question, Can you, an average citizen, get ahead in the markets? By the end of the chapter you should be able to do the following:

a. explain why people invest in the markets;

b. describe how security exchanges work;

c. relate how stocks are bought and sold;

d. define the following terms: bull, bear, selling short, market order, limit order, round lot, odd-lot;

e. explain how to read the stock and bond reports in the local newspaper;

f. describe some of the major federal acts used to regulate the sale of securities; and

g. develop an investment strategy for the do-it-yourself investors.

The Securities Markets

WHY DO PEOPLE INVEST IN THE MARKET?

There are millions of Americans who own stocks and bonds. Why do they invest their money here rather than put it into real estate, rare coins, or gold? Various answers can be given to this question but the four most common are speculation, growth, income, and yield.

Speculation

People who invest in stocks and bonds with the hope of making a large profit in a very short period of time are known as **speculators.** These individuals usually buy high-risk stocks that are selling very inexpensively ($1–$5) and hope that they will double or triple in a short time. Of course, there is very little likelihood that they will, but the speculator is usually not concerned. If the stock does not move, the individual will often sell it and buy a different speculative issue. For those investors who have very little money to invest, this approach is often appealing because they can buy a large amount of stock for very little money.

Speculating in bonds is a little different. What speculators do here is watch both the price of the bond and the return it is giving. If interest rates go up, as we noted in the previous chapter, the price of bonds will go down and vice versa. What the bond speculator does is try to buy the security prior to the time that interest rates decline. Thus, a $1,000 bond that is selling at $500 and pays 4 percent of the face value or $40 a year is returning 8 percent at its current price. If the speculator believes that interest rates will drop and the average bond will pay only 7 percent, a purchase of the bond is in order. After all, for the return to drop from 8 percent to 7 percent the price of the bond will have to rise to $571. You can check this arithmetic by merely dividing $40 by $571 to arrive at a return of 7 percent.

Growth

Investors who are interested in **growth** will seek firms whose stock prices are likely to rise. The dividend may not be very high because the money is being channeled back into the business to support expansion activities. However, this does not worry the investor because he or she believes this strategy will lead to increased sales and, ultimately, a higher stock price.

Many investors buy stock for growth believing that if they stay with a blue chip firm like IBM, General Motors, or Coca-Cola, the stock will rise faster than inflation and their investment will pay off handsomely. Others prefer to put their money in growth industries, regardless of the firm, because they believe that all these firms will evidence strong growth. In recent years companies in industries such as electronics, energy, and drugs have seen very strong growth. And regardless of which firm they invest in, these individuals intend to keep their stock for an extended period of time, in contrast to the speculator who will sell after the stock goes up three or four points.

"No, this is lover's leap, investor's leap is further up the hill."

From The Wall Street Journal; permission Cartoon Features Syndicate

Income

Some investors use **income** from stocks and bonds to supplement their other income. This is particularly true of people who are retired and living on fixed incomes. These individuals will pay very close attention to the dividends being paid. For this reason they are very likely to invest in conservative firms that should have no trouble paying their dividends. Banks and utilities are primary examples, as are insurance firms. One of the things the investor will look at is the company's track record. Has it ever failed to pay a dividend? When and why? The New York Stock Exchange reports that there are some firms that have never missed a dividend in over 100 years. Some of these are identified below:

COMPANY	YEAR IN WHICH DIVIDEND PAYMENTS BEGAN
Bank of New York Co., Inc.	1784
Citicorp	1813
J. P. Morgan & Co., Inc.	1840
Chase Manhattan Corporation	1848
Continental Corporation	1853
Singer Company	1863
Travelers Corporation	1866
Pullman Incorporated	1867
American Express Co.	1868
Cincinnati Bell, Inc.	1879

Such firms will rank high on the list of investors interested in income earnings.

Yield

Some investors are most interested in **yield,** which (while similar to income in that it considers the dividend) is measured by dividing income by stock price. For example, IBM at the time of this writing had a dividend of $3.44 and was selling for $70. This would be a better investment, if you were interested only in dividend, than a stock like Gulf Oil that was paying only $2.05. However, for the investor concerned with yield it is not as good an investment because the return is lower. In making this point clear, let us consider the following five stocks along with their dividend and selling price as of this writing.

STOCK	DIVIDEND	SELLING PRICE
IBM	$3.44	$70.00
Gulf Oil	2.05	31.00
Chase Manhattan	2.40	42.00
Texas Instruments	2.00	95.88
Xerox	2.40	67.13

By dividing the dividend by the selling price, the yield for each can be determined. Respectively they are 4.9, 6.6, 5.7, 2.1, and 3.6 percent. On the basis of yield, then, the best investment would be Gulf Oil. Keep in mind, of course, that the selling price can change and the dividend may be raised or lowered. If either or both of these things happen, the yield will change and the investor may find that Gulf Oil is no longer the preferable investment.

The Matter of Safety

Any one, or more, of the four guidelines—speculation, growth, income, yield—may be used in buying stocks and bonds. In fact, many investors prefer to use more than one of these. This is the case of those who put most of their money (60 percent) in growth stocks, some in dividend-yielding stocks (30 percent), and the remainder in speculative issues. Before we can say which approach is best, we would have to know something about the financial resources of the individuals and what their objectives are. Do they want to build a nest egg for retirement or are they very young and interested in long-term growth issues? Dropping speculation from consideration, Table 18.1 provides a handy reference for comparing investment objectives of income, growth, and safety with the three basic types of security: bonds, common stock, and preferred stock.

TABLE 18.1 INVESTOR'S OBJECTIVE

TYPE OF SECURITY	INCOME	GROWTH	SAFETY
Bonds	Very steady	Virtually none	The best
Common stock	Variable	Very good	The least
Preferred stock	Steady	Will vary	Good

CASE

A Family of Investors

Lucy White is president of her own corporation, which has 400,000 shares of common stock outstanding. Half of this is held by Lucy, herself, and the remainder is held by the general public including some of her relatives. For example, Lucy's niece owns 100 shares of stock and believes that it is a very good investment. "I bought it at 53 and it's now at 74. If it goes to 80, I'm going to sell. And at the rate it has been moving over the last month, I predict it will get there within three more months; then I'm going to sell out and take my money. After all a $2,700 gain in nine months is pretty good."

Lucy's aunt and uncle have a longer-run viewpoint. They bought the stock at its initial price of $50 and plan to hold it for the next three to four years. Meanwhile her grandfather likes the $3.00 dividend, an increase of 50¢ since it was first issued last year. Grandpa White bought 200 shares at 50 so the yield on his investment is 6 percent ($600/10,000) and he believes the dividend will be raised even higher in the next few years. "At the rate the company is making money it's only a matter of time," he recently said.

1. What are the investment objectives of Lucy's niece? What about Lucy's aunt and uncle?

2. How would you describe the investment objectives of her grandfather?

3. What type of an investor would be attracted to this company? Why?

1. What is the primary investment objective of the speculator?

2. Would a retired person be more interested in a growth stock or an income stock? Explain.

3. How is a stock's yield determined? Give an example.

4. If a person were most interested in safety, would they invest in bonds, common stocks, or preferred stock? What if they were most interested in growth?

THE SECURITIES EXCHANGES

When people buy stock, most do so through one of the **securities exchanges** or marketplaces for stocks and bonds. These marketplaces are commonly called "stock exchanges" and they provide a meeting place for both the buyer and seller. To understand why such securities or stock exchanges are important in the purchase and sale of stocks and bonds, consider what would happen if you, and everyone who wanted to buy (or sell) securities, had to find your own buyer (or seller). How would you know what a fair price for the security is? More importantly, how would you find out who is interested in selling that stock to you (or buying it from you)? In order to handle this marketing problem, securities exchanges sprung up. These exchanges are nothing more than locations where stocks are bought and sold. And since there is a common meeting place for these transactions, people interested in buying and selling go there (or send their representatives). The result is a very systematic market process, where transactions are handled in an orderly manner and the operations are both supervised and regulated by law. In this way, the buyer (or seller) is ensured that the best price is secured and they are not shortchanged or cheated in any way.

There are a number of security exchanges throughout the country. The two most famous are the New York Stock Exchange and the American Stock Exchange, which we will describe briefly.

The New York Stock Exchange

The **New York Stock Exchange (NYSE)** is located in Manhattan on Wall Street. Often referred to as the "Big Board" because of a large board on the stock exchange wall that used to be used to summon brokers from the floor and relay messages to them, it is the largest and best known of all the stock exchanges. In order to buy and sell securities on the NYSE, one must own a "seat" on the exchange. These seats (or memberships) are limited to 1,366 and to get one today it is necessary to buy one from

The New York Stock Exchange is located on Wall Street in the center of the financial district.

a current member. A few years ago the selling price for a seat had dropped to around $100,000 but today it is up to around $200,000. The individuals who fill these seats are permitted to buy and sell stock in the NYSE. Most of them do not personally own a seat, but as representatives of major stock brokerage houses such as Merrill Lynch and Bache Halsey (the real owners) they buy or sell stocks for the accounts of these brokerages.

Today around 1,600 stocks and 2,700 bonds are traded on the NYSE. These securities represent 90 percent of the market value of all outstanding stocks in the U.S. Many of the major firms with which you are familiar including Sears, McDonald's, Eastern Airlines, General Motors, and Westinghouse Electric are all traded there. In order for a company to be listed and traded on the NYSE, it must meet the following minimum standards:

1. Annual earnings for the most recent year must be at least $2.5 million before taxes, and for each of the preceding years it must have been at least $2 million.

2. At least 1 million shares have to be publicly held.

3. At least 2,000 investors have to hold 100 or more shares.

4. The outstanding common stock has to have a market value of at least $8 million.

5. The company has to have net tangible assets of at least $16 million.

The American Stock Exchange

The **American Stock Exchange,** commonly referred to as the AMEX, is also located in downtown Manhattan. It has approximately 500 full members and four hundred associate members. Some of the best known firms that are traded on the AMEX include Husky Oil, Bic Pen, Horn & Hardart, and The New York Times. While second in size and importance to the NYSE, the AMEX operates the same way as the Big Board when it comes to buying and selling stocks and has the same strict regulations regarding standards of conduct.

Other Exchanges

In addition to the two major exchanges, there are a number of regional and local exchanges as well as an over-the-counter exchange. The largest regional exchange is the Midwest Exchange in Chicago. Others include the Cincinnati Stock Exchange and the Pacific Coast Stock Exchange. Local exchanges operate in Boston, Pittsburgh, Detroit, and other large cities. The regional exchanges, which account for only about 7 percent of the annual volume of the organized exchanges, list about 500 companies each. The local exchanges, meanwhile, list around 100 companies each.

And then there is the **over-the-counter (OTC)** market. This market is difficult to describe because stocks trading on the OTC market is not done at any particular locale. Rather the trading of nearly 60,000 securities in this market is done between about 5,000 brokers who are scattered throughout the country and who buy and sell unlisted stocks and bonds by telephone. These brokers are in regular contact with each other, and the prices of the securities they trade are established by supply and demand, just as they are in the major stock exchanges. These OTC transactions are quoted on the electronic screens located in the offices of stock brokerage firms. Thus, if you have some OTC stock and want to get the latest price of your stock, a local broker could provide it to you right off the machine sitting on his or her desk. The OTC market includes trading in the shares of many insurance companies and banks and in the bonds issued by many city and state governments.

5. What is the purpose of a stock exchange?

6. What are the minimum requirements for being listed on the NYSE?

BUYING AND SELLING SECURITIES

The general approach in buying and selling securities, regardless of the exchange where they are purchased, is basically the same. We provide a general picture of how security transactions take place; and for a fuller understanding, we will discuss some of the important terminology and functions of security trading.

How Stocks Are Actually Purchased

How would you go about buying stock in a major corporation? It's really quite simple. First, you would decide what you want to buy—such as 100 shares of IBM. Then you would place a call to your stockbroker, who would enter an order to buy the 100 shares at the current market price.

Assuming your broker works for a major stock brokerage, the order would be telephoned directly to a company clerk on the floor of the New York Stock Exchange. The clerk would hand the order to a member of the Exchange who is a partner in the brokerage. This individual would then go to the appropriate locale on the trading floor and ask for the latest quote on IBM. Let us say it is "70 to a quarter." This means that someone is currently bidding $70 for the stock and another party is willing to sell at $70.25. If your broker wants, a sale can be struck at $70.25 since the order calls for a purchase at the current market price. More likely, however, your broker will bid $70.125 and hope to save you one eighth of a point or $12.50. And it is likely that another broker with an order to sell will show up and accept the bid of $70⅛. The two brokers will then initial each other's sales orders and see that the transaction is relayed to the exchange employee known as the reporter. The reporter sees that the sale is reported and a few minutes later it will come out on the ticker tape. In addition, both brokers will report the transaction back to their respective brokerage houses. Your own broker will then be able to tell you the final sale price. If you have an account with the brokerage, the sale price and commissions will be deducted from your cash on hand. Otherwise, your broker will ask you to send a check for the full amount since settlements must be made within five business days.

Bulls and Bears

If you have ever seen any commercials by Merrill Lynch, the largest of the brokerage houses, you have undoubtedly heard them claim that they are "bullish on America." You may even remember the herd of bulls that rampage across the plains as the person doing the voice-over explains why it is a good idea to use Merrill Lynch as your broker. What does "bullish mean? It is a term that is used to refer to investors who expect stock prices to rise. **"Bulls"** buy in anticipation of the market going up.

Of course, the market will not always rise. Sometimes stocks drop and remain low for extended periods of time. Those investors who expect stock prices to decline are known as **"bears."** During the Great Depression the bears made a great deal of money. While the bulls were "buying long" the bears were "selling short."

Buying long means buying stock for the purpose of reselling it at a higher price. If the market is going down the only way to recover your investment is to hang on to the stock and wait for it to come back. **Selling short** means selling stock that you do not own with the intention of replacing it later at a lower price. For example, if you heard that IBM was going to announce very low earnings and felt that the price would drop from $70 to $65 you could sell IBM short by telling your broker to borrow this stock from one of the brokerage's customer accounts and replace it when it drops to $65. Keep in mind, of course, that if the stock goes up instead of down, you will have to replace the stock at a higher price and will lose the difference between the selling and the replacement price. Thus, selling short can be a risky strategy. After all, the stock can drop no more than 70 points but can go up indefinitely. Thus, your gains are limited but your losses are not.

Types of Orders

When an investor decides to buy a stock, the individual often asks that the security be purchased at the current market price. This is called a **market order.** This is often done on a "best price" basis, with the investor notified of the purchase within a matter of minutes. However, investors do not always buy at market price. Sometimes they request that a stock purchase or sale be made at a specified price. This is called a **limit order,** in which case the transaction is made at this price or lower. For example, IBM is currently selling at $70 but you wish to pay no more than $68 for it. You can, therefore, put in a limit order at $68 and if the price drops to this level, assuming there is no one else ahead of you in line, you will get the stock at this price.

Round Lots, Odd Lots, and Commissions

Stocks are traded in quantities of 100 shares. These are called **round lots.** However, many people do not buy 100 shares of a stock but rather put in orders for 10, 25, and 50 shares. Their orders are filled through **odd lot** purchases, which are sales of fewer than one hundred shares of stock. The way in which the brokerage accommodates the odd-lot buyer is by purchasing a round lot and then breaking it up to accommodate the various odd-lot purchasers.

In addition to the price of the stock, the purchaser is charged a commission that goes to the brokerage firm for its services. Commissions vary among brokers and in recent years a number of discount brokers have sprung up. These individuals buy and sell for less than the standard commission charged by the major brokerages. In any event, commissions generally range from 1–2 percent of the total value of the stock transaction, although a slightly higher fee is charged when odd lots are traded.

Buying On Margin

Up to now we have given the impression that investors pay for their stock purchases by either having all of the money on hand or selling some of their current holdings to free up the necessary funds. However, this is not totally true. While many people do indeed pay the entire amount for their purchases, some **"trade on margin."** When they do so, they put up a percentage of the price of their stock and borrow the rest of the money. Interest is paid on this loan and the stock certificate remains with the broker as collateral. This investment strategy allows the individual to buy more shares of stock than would be possible should 100 percent financing be required. The margin requirement—the amount the customer can borrow—is set by the Federal Reserve Board and is changed periodically. The problem, of course, comes about when a person is fully margined and the Federal Reserve Board raises the margin. In this case the investor must either put up more money or have some of the stock sold and the funds be used to meet the new margin requirements. For example, if 100 shares of $100 stock are bought on margin of 40 percent, the individual will have put down $4,000 and borrow the other $6,000. Suppose the next day the Federal Reserve raises the margin rate to 50 percent. In this case, the individual must come up with another $1,000 or sell some of these shares so that only 50 percent of the sale price is financed on margin. This same logic applies when the price of the stock drops. If the $100 shares take a nose dive, the brokerage will immediately give the investor a "margin call" and tell the person to put up more money or have the shares sold. During the Great Depression when only a 10 percent margin was required, thousands of investors were unable to meet their margin calls and had to face the calamity of having all of their stock sold away. Today the margin requirement often ranges between 30 and 70 percent so the likelihood of such a problem is greatly reduced. After all, if a margin call cannot be met, the sale of the stock will result in some monies returned to the investor.

7. How does a bull differ from a bear?

8. What is a limit order? Is it different from a market order?

9. How does a round lot differ from an odd lot?

UNDERSTANDING THE FINANCIAL NEWS

Every day the newspapers carry the latest financial news. All major papers print the results of trading on the NYSE, the AMEX and, sometimes, OTC stocks. The following describes how to read the financial news.

Stock Prices

One of the most popular financial newspapers is the *Wall Street Journal*. Figure 18.1 is a partial reproduction of the stock sales as contained in the *Journal* on a particular business day. In order to learn how to read these stock reports, concentrate on FordM, which is Ford Motor. Notice that the price of the stock as of the close of trading was $42.75. This was the same price at which it had closed the previous trading day. During this particular day it had traded as high as $42⅞ and as low as $42⅝. In all 54,100 shares were traded (remember the 541 represents round-lot sales so you must multiply by 100). The price/earnings ratio is 3, the yield (dividend price) is 9.4 percent, and the current dividend is $4. For the

---

What Does It Mean?

S   IBM   X   DD   TXN   MOT   GO   CMB
  19   70   5s22 5/8   2s42   93 1/4   10s47 7/8   32 1/2   41

While you can read the results of the NYSE stock transactions in the local paper, if you went to the exchange itself you could see the ticker tape in action. However, in this case you would not see the name of the companies printed out. Instead each would be represented with a symbol or abbreviation. Look at the above display and see if you can interpret the ticker tape.

Do you know what each of these symbols means? How many shares of stock have been sold? How much has been paid? Your stockbroker would, but the average

person would not. Here is what the ticker tape means:

100 shares of Sears Roebuck at $19

100 shares of IBM at $70

500 shares of U.S. Steel at $22.625

200 shares of DuPont at $42

100 shares of Texas Instruments at $93.25

1,000 shares of Motorola at $47.875

100 shares of Gulf Oil at $32.50

100 shares of Chase Manhattan Bank at $41

52 Weeks High	Low	Stock	Div.	Yld %	P-E Ratio	Sales 100s	High	Low	Close	Net Chg.
46 5/8	39	FordM	4	9.4	3	541	42 7/8	42 5/8	42 3/4	+ 1/4
24 5/8	17 1/8	ForMK	1.56	6.4	5	102	24 1/8	24	24 1/4	+ 1/2
39 3/8	27 3/4	FMK	pf1.80	4.6	...	15	39 1/8	38 7/8	39	+ 1/4
14	12 1/8	FtDear	1.24	9.9	...	17	12 5/8	12 1/2	12 1/2	- 1/4
47 1/4	35 1/8	FrtHow	1.32	2.9	11	61	45	44 3/4	45	- 1/4
25 1/8	19 1/8	FosWh	s .64	2.4	8	1426	u26 3/4	24 3/4	26 5/8	+ 1 5/8
19 1/4	5 1/8	Fotomat	.25j	...	15	206	6 3/4	6 1/2	6 5/8	+ 1/8
44 3/4	24 1/8	FourPha		...	13	189	36 7/8	36 1/2	36 3/4	- 1/4
14 3/8	8 3/4	FoxStaP	.68	7.2	6	59	9 5/8	9 1/2	9 1/2	
44 3/8	29 1/8	Foxbro	1.20	3.0	11	109	40 3/4	40 1/2	40 5/8	+ 1/8
11 3/4	5 1/8	FrankM	.30	3.0	6	215	10	9 3/8	10	+ 1/4
45	30	FrptMn	s1.20	2.7	15	533	u45 5/8	44 3/4	45 1/4	+ 3/8
20	11	Frigtrn	.30	2.5	10	54	12 1/4	12	12 1/8	
40	25 5/8	Fruehf	2.40	7.2	5	114	34	33 1/4	33 1/2	- 3/8
14 5/8	7 1/8	Fuqua	.44	3.2	4	162	13 3/4	13 1/2	13 3/4	
15 1/2	12 1/4	Fuqa	pf1.25	8.5	...	7	14 5/8	14 1/2	14 5/8	+ 1/8

FIG. 18.1 *NYSE stock transactions*

Bonds	Cur Yld	Vol	High	Low	Close	Net Chg.
DukeP 8 1/8 03	9.5	8	85 1/8	85 1/8	85 1/8	
DukeP 9 3/4 04	9.9	12	99 7/8	98 3/8	98 3/8	- 3/8
DukeP 9 1/2 05	9.8	16	96 5/8	96 5/8	96 5/8	- 3/8
DukeP 8 3/8 06	9.6	5	87	87	87	- 1
DukeP 8 1/8 07	9.6	6	85 7/8	85	85	- 7/8
EGG 3 1/2 s87	cv	6	85	85	85	
ESvs 4 1/2 s92	cv	14	105	102	104	+ 2
EasAir 4 3/4 93	cv	2	54	54	54	+ 1/2
EasAir 11 1/2 99	cv	64	100 1/2	100 1/2	100 1/2	+ 1/4
Eaton 7.6s96	8.8	15	86 1/2	86 1/2	86 1/2	- 1/4
Eaton 5 1/2 92	6.5	7	85 1/4	85 1/4	85 1/4	+ 3/8
EatnCr 8 1/8 84	9.1	5	93 7/8	93 7/8	93 7/8	- 1/8
ElPas 8 1/2 95	cv	30	132	132	132	- 1
ElPas 6s93A	cv	4	125	125	125	- 1
Ens 9 3/4 s95	10.	1	96 1/4	96 1/4	96 1/4	- 4 3/4
Ens 8.95s99	9.6	4	93 1/2	93 1/2	93 1/2	- 1 3/4
EqtLf 6 3/4 90	cv	3	77 1/2	77	77	
Estrl 6 1/4 95	cv	1	90	90	90	+ 2
Exxon 6s97	8.0	29	74 3/4	74 3/4	74 3/4	+ 1/4
Exxon 6 1/4 98	8.3	17	78 3/4	78 1/8	78 1/8	- 1/2
ExxP 8.05s80	8.3	24	97 1/2	97 1/2	97 1/2	- 1/2
FMC 4 1/2 92	cv	2	77 1/2	77 1/2	78 1/8	+ 1/8
Frch 9 3/4 98	11.	1	92	92	92	
Feddr 5s96	cv	10	50 1/4	50 1/4	50 1/4	- 3/4
Filmwy 10s99	12.	2	83	83	83	+ 1/4
Finan 10 1/4 90	10.	4	98 1/2	98 1/2	98 1/2	- 7/8
FBkSy 8 3/4 83	9.0	5	97 1/4	97 1/4	97 1/4	+ 1/4
FstChi 6 3/4 80	7.0	30	96 1/2	96 1/2	96 1/2	- 1 1/2
FstChi 7 3/4 86	8.5	3	91 1/2	91 1/2	91 1/2	- 1/8
FintBn 9s83	9.2	25	97 1/2	97 3/4	97 1/2	+ 1/8
FtNBo 7.6s81	8.0	13	95 1/2	95	95	- 1/4
FtNBo 8s82	8.5	5	94 1/2	94 1/2	94 1/2	- 1/2
FtPenn 5s93	cv	32	59 3/4	59	59	- 3/4
FstSec 11s99	11.	19	102	102	102	+ 1/8
FtWis 8 1/2 96	9.9	1	86 1/4	86 1/4	86 1/4	- 1/4
FisbM 4 3/4 97	cv	50	65 1/2	65 1/2	65 1/2	- 1
FishF 6 1/4 94	cv	18	71	70 5/8	71	- 3/8
FlaECs 5s11	5.9	10	85 1/8	85 1/8	85 1/8	+ 1/8
FlaPL 8 1/8 80	8.3	30	98 1/4	97 25-32	98 1/4	
FlaPL 8 7/8 82	9.1	15	97 1/2	97 1/2	97 1/2	- 1/8
FlaPL 10 3/4 81	11.	40	100 3/4	100 1/2	100 5/8	+ 1/8

FIG. 18.2 *NYSE bond transactions*

Stock & Div.	Sales 100s	Bid	Asked	Net Chg.
Pabst Brw .40	743	16	16 1/2	- 7/8
PACCAr 1.80a	12	60	61	
PacerTech Rs	41	2 5/8	3 1/8	
PacersetCp .20	23	20	21	
Pacsetter .80g	3	12 3/4	13 1/2	
PcCst Hld .15d	5	18 3/4	19 1/2	
PcGamb 1.50g	46	21 3/4	22 1/2	+ 1/4
PacGold Uran	119	7/8	1 1/8	- 1-16
Pac Resource	42	19 1/4	20	+ 1/4
Pacific Std Lf	19	4 3/8	4 3/4	
Page Petrolm	9	15 1/2	16	
Palute Oil Mn	1232	5/8	3/4	- 3-32
Pako Corp .48	11	12	12 3/4	
PanAmBks .40	4	9 1/2	10	
PandickP .30b	137	9 1/2	10	+ 1/4
ParSystem Cp	34	10 3/4	11 3/4	

FIG. 18.3 *OTC quotes*

last 52 weeks the high and low were 46 5/8 and 39, respectively.

We can use the same approach to interpret most of the data in Fig. 18.1. However, there are a few items that we have not yet discussed. The letters "pf" refer to preferred stock, which was described in the previous chapter. The letter "s" indicates that there was a stock split. Such notations are identified in the explanatory notes that always appear at the end of the financial pages.

Bond Prices

Bond prices are read basically the same way as stock prices. Figure 18.2 provides a list of quotations from the Wall Street Journal. Notice that the first five bonds on the list are all from Duke Power, a large utility. The first bond pays 8 1/8 percent and matures in the year 2003. The current yield is 9.5 percent because the 8 1/8 percent is being paid on a bond that sells for $851.25 or $81.25/851 = 9.5 percent. There were eight bonds sold on this day with the high, low and close all being $851.25.

The second Duke Power bond pays 9 3/4 percent and matures in 2004. The current yield of this bond is 9.9 (97.50/983.75). There were twelve bonds sold on this trading day with the high being $998.50 and the low being $983.75. The latter was also the closing price and this was a drop of $37.50 or 3/8 from the day previously.

Looking further down the rest of the Duke Power bonds, notice that the current selling price is directly related to the interest on the bond. The higher the interest, the higher the current selling price. However, none of the bonds are selling at par; this indicate that interest rates have gone up since the time these bonds were first issued.

Over-The-Counter Stocks

OTC stocks are even easier to read because there is less information with which to be concerned. This is clearly evident in Fig. 18.3. We see that Pabst Brewing heads the list. This stock has a dividend of 40¢ per year; there were 74,300 shares traded this business day; the current bid price (what someone is

Bulls and Bears

The stock in Lucy White's corporation is traded over-the-counter. When first issued two years ago, it sold for $50. Since then it has risen to $84, although it has been as high as $88.

Lucy's niece bought the stock at $53 and sold it at $80. She then sold short for 200 shares, which she hopes to replace at $70. She has a limit order in at this price but will cover her losses if the stock goes to $90.

Lucy's aunt and uncle are hanging on to their stock. They bought it at $50 and believe it will continue to rise. As a result, they have purchased another 100 shares, this time on margin. However, Lucy's grandfather was happy with his current profits and sold his 200 shares of stock at $86 for a net gain of $36 per share.

Meanwhile Lucy's annual sales have increased dramatically reaching $80 million this past year. Of the 400,000 shares issued, half are held by a total of 3,725 people. In order to increase the number of stockholders, Lucy is thinking about issuing another 400,000 shares of common. This will dramatically increase her tangible net assets from the current level of $29 million and give her funds for additional expansion. However, she wants to wait until her current application for listing on the NYSE is accepted.

1. Is Lucy's niece a bull or a bear? If the stock drops to $70, will the niece make or lose money? What if it rises to $90? Explain.

2. Are Lucy's aunt and uncle bulls or bears? Also, what does buying on margin mean? Explain.

3. Does Lucy qualify for listing on the Big Board? Why or why not? Defend your reasoning.

willing to pay) is $16; and the asking price (what someone is willing to sell at) is $16.50. During this particular day the last price of the stock was ⅞ (87.5¢) lower than the previous trading day. Further down the figure is Pacific Gold Uranium. This stock is currently selling for $1.125 a share, which is a decline of 1/16 of a dollar (.0625¢) from its previous selling price. During this day of trading 11,900 shares exchanged hands and the current bid and asking price are ⅞ and 1⅛, respectively. As you can see, when stocks have very low prices they are traded in 1/16 of a dollar.

10. A stock had a high of 28, a low of 27, a closing price of 27⅞, and a net increase of ⅝. What does all of this mean?

11. If you saw that Duke Power had a "9¾ 09" bond that closed at "101," what would these two pieces of information in quotes tell you? Explain.

21. You have just called your broker for a quote on your OTC stock and learned that "the bid is 23 and the ask is 23½." What does this mean?

REGULATION OF SECURITIES TRANSACTIONS

In order to ensure that investors are not defrauded by unscrupulous individuals, federal and state governments have enacted legislation regulating the sale of securities. These early state laws were known as **blue-sky laws** because one state legislator remarked that some securities promoters would sell stock in the "blue sky," a term that quickly caught on and was applied to early state laws designed to regulate securities transactions. Over time every state except Nevada passed legislation to protect stock investors. In most cases these laws required that the securities being sold be registered with an appropriate state official, usually the secretary of state, and annual licenses were usually required for securities dealers and salespeople. These actions helped reduce intrastate problems. However, for interstate regulation it was necessary for the federal government to enter the picture.

Securities Act of 1933

The **Securities Act of 1933** is a federal law designed to protect investors by requiring full disclosure of all relevant financial information by firms desiring to sell new stock or bond issues to the general public. This information comes in one of two forms: (1) a registration statement containing detailed company information that is filed with the Securities and Exchange Commission, and (2) a condensed version of the registration in a booklet called a **prospectus** that must be given to each purchaser. In this way, investors know what the company does and how it intends to invest their funds. They can then judge the risk factor involved in making this type of investment.

Securities Exchange Act of 1934

The year after the Securities Act of 1933 was passed, Congress enacted the **Securities Exchange Act of 1934.** This law created the Securities and Exchange Commission (SEC) to regulate the national stock exchange. All firms listed on the NYSE or the AMEX are required to file registration statements with the SEC and to update them annually. Brokerage firms and individual brokers are also regulated by the SEC, and brokers who sell listed securities are required to pass an examination. The purpose of this Act is to keep a watchful eye on both the stock exchanges and the **brokerage houses,** thus preventing any practices that could result in investors being cheated in any way. The SEC will assess penalties and have legal action brought in the case of illegal activities. A typical problem with which the SEC deals is that of companies giving out false information regarding their financial strength, thereby misleading the average investor. Also, if a stock were to suddenly run up 20 points, the SEC would investigate to see if any of the company's officers, who had inside information, bought the stock. Use of inside information for the purpose of personal gain is prohibited. Investors who feel that they have been cheated in any way can appeal to the SEC for an investigation. As a result, the SEC is the watchdog of Wall Street.

Other Legislation

While the above two acts are the primary ones in regulating the securities markets, there are others. One is the **Maloney Act of 1938,** which is an amend-

Kirk Kerkorian

When you talk about the securities market and the buying and selling of stock, it is almost impossible not to think of Kirk Kerkorian who has made a great deal of money buying and selling business firms. The son of an immigrant Armenian farmer, he began buying and selling war-surplus airplanes after World War II. He then started a charter service and began replacing his propeller craft with jets. By 1962 his company, Trans-International Airlines, was doing just great and he sold it for $1 million. Buying it back the next year, Kerkorian took the firm public. In 1968, he sold the airline again, this time to Transamerica Corporation. The next year he took the stock he got for the airline deal and sold it for $104 million.

Kerkorian then started building a leisure-time financial empire. He purchased 30 percent of Western Airlines, bought the Flamingo Hotel-Casino in Las Vegas, and built the International Hotel there. He also started buying MGM. However, the setback in the stock market during the late sixties and early seventies forced him to sell much of what he owned at very low prices.

By 1976 he had bounced back. After selling his holdings in Western Airlines, he concentrated on MGM, building the MGM Grand Hotel in Las Vegas and another in Reno. Both are making money and he is now building another hotel-casino in Atlantic City. He has also acquired the Cal-Neva Lodge in Lake Tahoe and recently bought Columbia Pictures.

An individual who shuns public appearances and interviews, he spends his time collecting his $10 million a year in dividend income and looking for new business ventures. As one of his associates put it, "Whatever he does, it will probably raise eyebrows. That's what I like about working for him. You never do the same things twice."

---

ment to the Securities Exchange Act of 1934. This act authorized self-regulation of over-the-counter securities operations. The result was the creation of the National Association of Securities Dealers, which is responsible today for regulating all OTC business. Additionally, written exams are now required of all new brokers and dealers who are selling OTC securities. Another is the **Investment Company Act of 1940** that brought the mutual fund industry under SEC jurisdiction. Today mutual funds are required to register with the SEC. These developments have further helped in protecting investors from some of the security trading abuses and stock manipulations that occurred prior to the crash of 1929.

13. How did the Securities Act of 1933 help regulate the securities market?

14. What was the purpose of the Securities Exchange Act of 1934?

CAN YOU GET AHEAD IN THE MARKET?
The big question for stock and bond investors is, Can you get ahead in the market? This is no easy question to answer because there is more to investing

TABLE 18.2

COMPANY	PURCHASE PRICE	SALE PRICE	NET	DIVIDEND	TOTAL
Gulf Oil	$2,225.00	$3,100.00	$ 875.00	$205.00	$1,080.00
Texaco	2,212.50	2,925.00	712.50	216.00	928.50
Amerada Hess	2,325.00	4,212.50	1,887.50	140.00	2,027.50
Standard Oil of Indiana	4,875.00	6,800.00	1,925.00	300.00	2,225.00

than buying at a low price and selling at a high one. One must also consider how long the security has been held and how much of a return, including both dividends and net profit after commissions, has been realized. Today inflation is running in the range of 10–15 percent. Interest rates in banks are about 5½ percent. If the average investor bought dividend stocks, the interest rate would easily outrun that which could be obtained in banks. However, would the price keep pace with inflation? Also, there is the risk of the stock or bond price declining. This is why many investors try to get ahead by purchasing securities that offer a combination of dividend and growth.

While there are many stock and bonds that could fit into this category, let us consider a few oil company stocks as an illustration, namely Gulf Oil, Texaco, Amerada Hess, and Standard Oil of Indiana. If you had bought 100 shares of any of these at their low point between September 1, 1978 and September 1, 1979 and sold them on the latter day, your gain would have been as shown in Table 18.2. During this time period all of these stocks did well. Their dividend rates were 9.2, 9.8, 6, and 6.2 percent, respectively. All of these were far better than what the investor could have secured in the bank. Furthermore, if we take the total gain (minus commissions that we

Investing in Precious Metals

Because of the rate at which gold, silver, and other precious metals have been rising lately, some investors are kicking themselves for ever having put their money into the stock market. Moreover, Americans are becoming painfully aware of the connection between the rising price of these metals and their own economic lives. For example, the cost of a gold filling or crown has gone up dramatically, as has the price of gold jewelry. And with the rising price of silver, X-rays, camera film, and silver-

plate now all cost a great deal more than they did previously.

However, there is a "silver lining" in the cloud for those who have not invested in precious metals. The price of these metals has been rising and falling dramatically. In the case of gold, for example, the price has dropped as much as $125 an ounce in one day! So, for those who have a weak heart, or believe that the economy will remain strong during the 80s, the stock market offers a more rational approach to investing.

*Unless an investor has the time to manage his or her investments full time,
one is more likely to come out ahead by using a professional broker.*

have not yet subtracted but that would not represent more than about $50 in each case) the overall return would be 48.5, 42, 87, and 46 percent, respectively. Naturally, we assumed only the most advantageous position, namely, that you bought at its low point over the prior year and using a date at which these stocks were at or near their annual high. Nevertheless, the data do reveal that if the investor chooses stocks wisely he or she can indeed beat inflation.

Use of a Broker

Most people, unfortunately, do not have time to sit around all day long studying the ups and downs of the stock market. Most have full-time jobs that require their time. However, all of the major **brokerage houses** have research departments that study the market and make individual analyses of companies.

When they are finished they make recommendations to their brokers regarding which stocks to buy and which to sell. The brokers then communicate this information to their clients who are free to accept the advice or not. Of course, a broker cannot guarantee an investor that he or she will make money. However, there is a much greater likelihood of coming out ahead if one uses a professional than if one tries to randomly pick winners. Nevertheless, there are many people who believe that if anyone is going to lose their money, it is going to be they. These people subscribe to a do-it-yourself philosophy.

Do It Yourself

There are many subscription services and financial reports that will provide the do-it-yourself investor with information regarding which stocks, in the

opinion of experts, look like a good buy and which should be sold. If the individual has time to read all of these, he or she may be able to make a living out of playing the stock market. Most other people who do their own investing are content to find a good growth stock and ride with it for a while. *The Wall Street Journal* and *Business Week,* both of which are easily understandable to the average person, can provide a wealth of information on the strategies and expansion plans of business firms. For example, if you are convinced that the profits of the oil companies will keep going up, then any of the four stocks we just examined could be good buys. Or, if you are a movie goer and believe that you can tell a box-office smash from an average picture, you can buy the stock of a major movie producer prior to the time that the general public realizes the firm is going to make a great deal of money from this blockbuster. Paramount Pictures, which is owned by the Gulf & Western Corporation (G&W), has been especially successful in recent years in turning out money-makers. In fact, thanks largely to Paramount, the operating profits of G&W have increased dramatically. Figure 18.4 shows some of Paramount's great hits during the 1970s. If you had watched the firm make money during the early and mid-1970s and finally decided in late 1978 that the studio was going to go right on turning out winners, you could have investigated the stock of the major corporation and decided if G&W were a good buy for you. Had you bought it at its low point between late 1978 and 1979 and sold it at its high, you would have invested $1,125 for 100 shares and sold them for $1,825. This is a profit of $700 plus the $75 dividend resulting in a total return of 69 percent.

Naturally, you could just as easily have invested in some stock and lost money. However, the point to be remembered is that millions of Americans own stock because they feel it is the best way to increase their net worth. With some careful study of the market or the choice of a good broker, you can too.

15. How can an investor get ahead in the market? Outline a strategy.

FIG. 18.4 *Paramount's big winners*

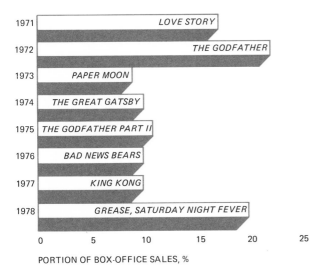

PORTION OF BOX-OFFICE SALES, %

SUMMARY

People invest in the market for many reasons, although their objectives can usually be reduced to one or more of the following: (1) speculation, (2) growth, (3) income, and (4) yield. Most use a combination of these.

When investors do buy securities, the transaction usually takes place at one of the established security exchanges such as the NYSE, the AMEX, a regional or local exchange, or the OTC market. In any event the process is basically the same. There is a bid and an asking price with someone prepared to buy at the former and sell at the latter. When the transaction is complete the investor is notifed of the sale price, and after the commission is computed a financial accounting is made.

These transactions are often made at market price although an investor can specify a purchase (or sale) price, in which case a limit order is used. The transaction is made in round lots, which are then broken up to accommodate odd-lot buyers and sellers. If the buyer is purchasing in the hopes of riding the stock up, the individual is called a bull. If the investor is selling because he or she believes the stock will go down, the person is called a bear. Furthermore, if the bear is selling borrowed stock in the hope of replacing it later at a lower price, the individual is said to be selling short. The progress of any security can be followed through the financial section of most major newspapers.

In the last fifty years both federal and state governments have enacted legislation to regulate the sale of securities. In addition to blue-sky laws there is the Securities Act of 1933, the Securities Exchange Act of 1934, and a host of others. All are designed to prevent security-trading abuses and stock manipulation.

Can the average investor make money in the market? Indeed, yes. Many do so by relying upon their stockholder's advice, but many more prefer to follow a do-it-yourself strategy.

KEY TERMS FOUND IN THIS CHAPTER

QUESTIONS FOR DISCUSSION AND ANALYSIS

1. When investing in the stock market, what types of stocks will be bought by those whose primary objective is (a) speculation, (b) growth, (c) income, (d) yield?
2. Of what importance is a security exchange in the purchase and sale of stocks and bonds? Be complete in your answer.
3. What are the minimum standards required for a firm to be listed and traded on the NYSE?
4. How does the OTC stock exchange work?
5. How are stocks actually bought and sold? Describe the process.
6. What do each of the following terms mean: bull, bear, selling short, market order, limit order, round lot, odd lot, trading on margin?
7. How can stock investors keep track of how well their securities are doing? Explain.
8. How did the Securities Act of 1933 help regulate the sale of stocks and bonds? What about the Securities Exchange Act of 1934?
9. How can an individual interested in investing in the market go about doing so? Outline a plan of action for the do-it-yourself investor.

19

Nothing is ever gained without risk. You can't steal second base and still keep one foot on first.
Anonymous

OBJECTIVES OF THIS CHAPTER

In the last two chapters we have been studying the ways in which business firms raise short- and long-term capital. We now want to turn to a final area of financial consideration —risk management. In very simple terms, every company must carefully examine the risks associated with doing business. Every company has to accept some risks, but to assume too many can result in great financial losses. The objectives of this chapter are to study this area of risk and then examine some of the ways of handling risk. Particular attention will be given to the importance of insurance, for individuals and businesses alike. When you are finished reading this chapter you should be able to do the following:

a. describe the four basic approaches used by businesses in handling risks;

b. understand how insurance firms are able to determine the possibility of a particular loss, such as a fire, occurring;

c. describe the important types of property and liability insurance that are available to businesses and individuals, including auto, fire, fidelity and surety, marine, workmen's compensation, and public liability;

d. explain the common forms of health insurance currently available;

e. describe the four basic types of life insurance; and

f. relate the most popular types of life insurance plans used by business firms today; and

g. discuss some of the common forms of special insurance needed by modern businesses.

Risk Management

BUSINESS RISKS

In its daily operations, every business encounters **risk.** Perhaps a new product line will not sell after thousands of dollars have been spent on research and development. Or a fire may burn down the plant and force the company to declare bankruptcy. Because of these and countless other possibilities, all firms have to decide carefully how much risk they are willing to undertake. In so doing, each firm will compare the total risk associated with a project against the total reward that can be attained.

Risk versus Reward

How much risk will a company be prepared to accept? The answer will differ from firm to firm. However, there are a few generalizations we can make about risk. First, the greater the risk a business assumes, the higher the reward, or profit, it will want. Second, the greater the amount of money it invests, the higher the firm will want the likelihood of success to be. Thus there are two important areas of consideration: (a) the amount of money invested, and (b) the probability of success.

Some firms are willing to take much greater risks than others. Individuals are the same. Some are big risk takers; others are very conservative. Figure 18.1 provides an illustration of the high- and low-risk taker, as well as the **personal risk preference curve.** The latter illustrates the average person's willingness to accept risk. This "S-shaped" curve shows that although people tend to accept high risks when there is only a small amount of money involved, when the stakes are very high, such as $1 million, people become very conservative and will take chances only if they think the probability for success is very high. This profile may apply to you person-

A floating restaurant presents a higher degree of risk to its owners than one located in a standard structure.

ally. If so, you are willing to risk small amounts of money without giving much consideration to the chance of winning but are unwilling to risk large amounts unless you feel you have a sure thing.

In evaluating a firm's willingness to assume risk, therefore, we would have to determine its risk preferences. We know, for example, that some managers are very conservative with their own money but are moderate- to high-risk takers when making decisions involving company funds. This is not to imply that they are reckless with company money; rather they are more willing to accept a risk if they feel after careful analysis that the rewards justify undertaking the project.

Sometimes the risk is too great, of course, and the firm will not proceed with the project. Other times the company will be unable to determine how much risk is really involved and will try to protect itself against a large loss by shifting the risk. Buying fire insurance is an illustration. If you have such insurance on your house and it burns down, you are covered. For this coverage, however, you must pay a premium to the insurance company. By purchasing fire insurance coverage you shift the risk to the insurance firm. If you had not bought such insurance but had put this money in a savings account for the life of the house, you might have accumulated a nice sum for retirement. The question, then, is whether the homeowner should buy fire insurance or not. Naturally the chance of a fire is small. However, so too is the premium, and if a fire occurs the homeowner may find that it was much wiser to have insurance than to try and save the premiums in the bank. In deciding how to handle risk, four basic approaches are used by business: (a) avoid the risk, (b) reduce the risk, (c) assume the risk, and (d) shift the risk.

FIG. 19.1 *Risk preference curves*

PROBABILITY OF SUCCESS

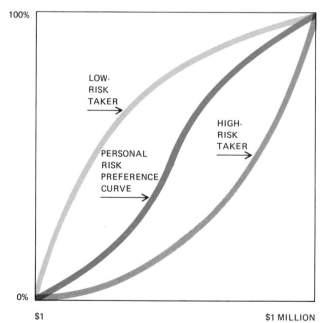

AMOUNT OF MONEY INVESTED

✿✿✿

1. What types of factors does a firm consider when it is deciding whether or not to undertake a particular risk?

2. In deciding how to handle risks, what are the four basic approaches used by business?

Avoid the Risk

Some risks are too high and must be *avoided*. For example, a firm may be willing to extend credit to customers it judges to be good risks, but will refuse those who are considered marginal. The company is simply unwilling to accept the risk associated with this latter group. The costs of extending them credit outweigh the benefits obtained from their business.

Another illustration is found in the case of new product lines. We know that only a small percentage of all newly proposed products ever actually reach the production stage. The rest are screened out because they are judged to be uneconomical. Of those that are finally produced and marketed, some still turn out to be losers. Because of the high risk involved in these new products, many firms prefer to market only those considered to be highly profitable. The rest are bypassed because the firm chooses to avoid the risk associated with them.

Reduce the Risk

When risks cannot be avoided, companies will often try to *reduce* them. In the case of extending credit, this will often be done by running credit checks on all customers. This allows the firm to decide who should and should not be given credit. In the case of a new product line, the company will often turn to marketing research. What do consumers want and how much are they willing to pay? Once answers to these questions are forthcoming, the firm can limit its scope of attention to those products most likely to be successful. A third common illustration, faced in the production area, is in the case of machinery breakdowns; this risk can be reduced through preventive maintenance. Meanwhile, in the case of worker safety, the establishment of "safety first" programs and the providing of safety equipment are very helpful in reducing risk.

Assume the Risk

Sometimes the best course of action is to *assume* the risk. This is done when the firm feels that the likelihood of something going wrong is very small or that if something does happen, the loss is "acceptable." One common example is found in the case of those companies that **self-insure.** These firms set up a special fund into which they put money every month. This money is used to cover losses associated with events such as fires, thefts, or accidents. If the company is large enough, it may be more profitable to self-insure than to purchase coverage from an insurance firm because the premiums charged by the insurance company will be more than the losses the firm sustains over a ten-year period. By self-insuring the company assumes the risk and saves money in the process.

Shift the Risk

Finally, it is sometimes best for a firm to *shift* the risk. There are a number of ways to do this, including hedging, subcontracting, and buying insurance. **Hedging** involves the purchase or sale of goods today with delivery scheduled for some time in the future. For example, a large baking corporation may need 50,000 bushels of wheat in six months. There are two ways of purchasing this wheat: (a) wait six months and buy it at the going price, or (b) make a deal today for delivery in six months. If the company agrees to buy the wheat today, the key question is how much it should pay. Since it is difficult to determine whether the price will be higher or lower in six months, the baking corporation takes a risk by entering into a contract today. It might agree to a price that ends up being 5¢ higher per bushel than the prevailing rate will be in six months. However, the company shifts the risk in that it is *guaranteed* the needed wheat at a predetermined price. The firm can then make plans based on receiving the wheat at this fixed price. Many corporations that need raw materials such as wheat, corn, and other produce often purchase them in the commodity market by entering into contracts today for future delivery.

A second method of shifting risk is to use **subcontracting.** An illustration is found in the case of the company that has agreed to build a telecommunications satellite but lacks the expertise to construct all the necessary systems in the satellite. As a result, this company will sign a contract with another firm that is capable of building these systems. This is called a subcontract, and it is widely used by businesses that either lack the expertise to carry out part of a contract or cannot do so profitably.

A third method of shifting risk, and the most commonly used, is through **insurance.** In exchange for the payment of a premium the insurance company will underwrite all or a part of many different types of losses, from fire and embezzlement to disability and accident. The challenge for the busi-

"My insurance company? New England Life, of course. Why?"

Of course, our mutual funds, variable annuities and investment counseling make a big hit with our customers, too.

ness firm is that of deciding which particular risks to shift and what types of insurance coverage to buy.

3. When will a firm attempt to avoid a risk?

4. How can a firm reduce risks?

5. In what way does hedging help a business shift risks?

WHAT IS INSURANCE ALL ABOUT?

Insurance is a topic we hear and read about a great deal. Most of us have "insurance policies" on our home, our car, and our lives. These policies provide coverage in the case of accident or death. How does insurance work? Put very simply, the insurance company charges a **premium** or fee to a

Insurance Strategies

While virtually every business needs insurance, recently some firms have started insuring themselves. There are three popular methods of doing so. One is to join together with other firms in the same industry, determine the premiums, put all of the monies into a pool, and pay claims out of it. At the end of every year, unused premiums can be returned, or, if losses were high, the deficit can be covered by a special assessment.

A second method is used by large corporations who have many subsidiaries. In this case the organization collects the premiums from all of the units and pays claims as they come due. It can be cheaper for the corporation to self-insure, thus eliminating the insurance company fee, than to place the coverage with an insurance broker.

Finally, there are some firms that find insurance coverage so high that they simply refuse to buy any. Instead they pay claims out of annual revenues. The big danger here, of course, is that the firm could suffer a large loss and have to declare bankruptcy.

Will the trend toward self-insurance increase? This depends. The Internal Revenue Service (IRS) currently is claiming that while insurance premiums are tax-deductible items, self-insurance payments are not. If the IRS wins its current suit, the self-insurance trend will be reversed. Otherwise, it should continue.

policyholder in return for protecting that policyholder against a particular risk.

How does the insurance company know how much money to charge for coverage? The answer is that the company relies on the **laws of probability.** For example, what is the likelihood that a person who is thirty years old will live to be thirty-one? Based on very accurate statistics, insurance companies can estimate the percentage of people in this country who will die in their thirtieth year. This statistic is slightly over 2 persons per 1,000, as you will see when we examine Table 19.1. As a result, if a life-insurance firm were to sell 100,000 males, each of whom was thirty years old, a one-year, $1,000 term policy, the company could estimate that approximately 200 of these people would die this year. It would not know which 200, of course, but it could forecast paying out around $200,000 in death benefits. It would therefore set the premiums for these 100,000 policies at a level that would return all death benefits and operating costs plus a profit.

This same approach is used by insurance firms in determining the likelihood of other events, from fire to accidents, and then in determining the premium for these policies. Keep in mind, however, that the insurance firms will not underwrite possible losses unless these risks have certain uniform characteristics. These characteristics are as follows:

1. The yearly loss has to be predictable. The insurance firm must be able to estimate accurately how many fires or accidents will occur annually.

2. The risk must be spread over a broad geographic area. Thus a serious fire in New York City may destroy some buildings insured by the firm but will not affect those in other cities. By insuring nationwide the company does not have all its eggs in one basket.

3. There must be a large enough number of people insured to allow the law of averages to work. If the firm insures only a small number of people, it is very difficult to scientifically determine premium rates.

4. Risks must be carefully selected. The firm cannot afford, for example, to insure only high-risk people, such as racing-car drivers, or those who are seriously ill. The company must try to obtain a cross sample of all types of people.

5. The cost of the policy must be low in relation to the insured's possibility of recovery. For example, there is no sense paying $5,000 a year for a fire-insurance policy on a building valued at $10,000. The premium is just too high, and people will seek a method other than insurance for protection against this risk.

6. How do the laws of probability help an insurance firm in setting policy rates?

"Mitch said I was self-assured, but not **insured** half enough."

"Nobody's knocking self-assurance. That and a lot of elbow grease helped me grab the brass ring. But sometimes too much self-assurance blinds you to pretty important concepts. Concepts like insurance.

I didn't think I needed more coverage. Mitch convinced me that I did. With a professional assessment of where I am today and where I want to be tomorrow.

Mitch dug in and boned up on my financial picture. Then he outlined a solid program tailor-made for me. It's going to work hard to secure my economic future."

The agents who sell life insurance for Ætna Life & Casualty. They're intelligent. Rigorously trained. And satisfied only when they arrive at the best plans for their clients' needs and financial goals.

Ætna
LIFE & CASUALTY

Ætna Life Insurance Company. 151 Farmington Avenue, Hartford, CT 06156.

CHAPTER 19

7. What uniform characteristics do risks have to possess for an insurance company to agree to underwrite them?

THE INSURANCE INDUSTRY

The insurance industry provides all sorts of coverage to individuals and business firms alike. Before we look at the types of insurance commonly provided, however, it is important to realize that there are public as well as private firms that provide insurance. **Public insurance companies** can be found operating in all fifty states as well as in the federal government. For example, federal law requires all states to have unemployment insurance. Every state also has workmen's compensation insurance, and many have their own retirement plans for state employees. Meanwhile, at the federal level all sorts of insurance are provided by the government. Sources include the U.S. Department of Agriculture, which insures farmers against various crop failures; the Federal Housing Administration (FHA), which insures private lending agencies against losses on FHA-approved home loans; the Federal Deposit Insurance Corporation, which insures bank deposits; and the U.S. Post Office, which insures mail.

Much of the insurance sold in this country, however, is handled by **private insurance firms.** Most of these companies tend to specialize in either (a) property and liability insurance or (b) life insurance, although both groups tend to be active in the sale of health insurance. While this categorization of insurance firms is overly simplistic, it does provide a framework for analyzing the various kinds of insurance that are available to businesses and individuals. The remainder of this chapter will be devoted to an examination of these types of insurance.

8. In what way is the federal government involved in the insurance business?

PROPERTY AND LIABILITY INSURANCE

Property and liability insurance fall into a number of major classifications. Some of the most important are (a) automobile, (b) fire, (c) fidelity and surety bonds, (d) marine, (e) workmen's compensation, and (f) public liability.

Automobile Insurance

Since automobile accidents are so common today, both businesses and individuals need to insure their autos. There are a number of important types of auto coverage. One is **liability insurance,** which is designed to protect the driver or owner against claims arising from auto accidents. There are two types of liability insurance: (a) **bodily injury liability insurance,** which provides coverage of anyone inside or outside the car who suffers personal injury because of the driver; and (b) **property damage liability insurance,** which provides protection against claims or damage to other people's property during an accident. Additionally, most drivers also have some form of **medical payments insurance,** which is designed to meet the medical needs of the individuals in the car. Medical payments insurance covers the occupants regardless of who was at fault in an accident. The coverage usually extends from $250 to $5,000 per person, depending upon how much protection is desired. However, most firms will sell this insurance only to those who have already bought the other types of liability insurance.

In addition to the above, there is also insurance available for protecting the owner's investment in the automobile. This is called **collision insurance** and covers the vehicle regardless of who was at fault in an accident. In providing this coverage, insurance companies offer collision insurance in two forms: (a) full coverage, and (b) deductible coverage. Under **full coverage** the firm will pay 100 percent of any loss or damage caused by a collision. Under a **deductible policy,** the owner assumes some of the expense by paying a stated amount, while the insurance company pays the remainder. For example, with a $100 deductible, the owner would pay the first $100 of a $675 repair bill and the insurer would pay the remaining $575. Of these two, full coverage is the most expensive. As a result, most drivers opt for deductible or 80-percent collision policies.

In the last few years there has been a move toward what is called *no-fault* auto insurance. Under this auto insurance plan, first enacted by Massachusetts in 1971, claim payments are made by the insurance companies to the policyholder without regard to who was at fault in the accident. Today nearly half of the states have these no-fault insurance plans. Some of their common features include (a) private automobile drivers must carry liability insurance to cover medical costs resulting from accidents involving themselves and other passengers in the car; (b) payment for losses, without regard to who was at fault, is made by the insurance company of the policyholder and not by the company of the person who is ruled to be at fault; and (c) victims are automatically limited in their right to sue.

Initial estimates by auto insurance firms indicated that no-fault policies would be cheaper. Unfortunately, many people now feel that no-fault is simply not that good. In particular, individuals who have been in accidents that were caused by another driver are upset over the fact that their right to sue

---

No-Fault Has Problems

Some people are saying, if you will pardon the expression, that no-fault auto insurance is not all it was cracked up to be. Under this insurance plan, in the case of an accident each party is paid by his or her own insurer with no attempt made to establish which driver was at fault. Proponents of no-fault felt it would lead to faster settlement of claims and lower insurance rates. The former has occurred but the latter has not. Many insurance companies report very high loss ratios.

For example, the Nationwide Insurance Company estimates that in the three years before no-fault became effective in Florida, it was paying out 70 percent of its premium income. Since then, however, it has paid out 81 percent of its premium income--and this occurred despite a rate hike. Other states are having similar problems. In Connecticut, this so-called loss ratio has jumped from 54 percent to 63 percent; in New York it went from 56 percent to 71 percent; and in New Jersey it soared from 76 percent to 112 percent.

What is causing these increases? Part of the answer is found in the rising cost of medical care and the fact that under no-fault the insurers must provide broader coverage, including such things as loss of income and medical rehabilitation. And while most states have a ceiling on medical coverage, Michigan, for example, requires insurers to pay all reasonable medical expenses without any ceiling. In the other states, meanwhile, people make it a point to use the maximum coverage for medical bills. As a result, no-fault insurance is becoming increasingly expensive. A great many people are disillusioned, and the future of this type of insurance coverage is highly uncertain.

is restricted. Furthermore, insurance rates for no-fault policies are beginning to rise. As a result, the future of no-fault insurance is still in doubt.

9. What are the basic types of automobile coverage available from insurance firms? Explain each.

10. Collision insurance comes in three forms. What are they?

Fire Insurance

Every ninety seconds a building in this country catches fire. This statistic illustrates why fire insurance is so important to individuals and businesses.

Fire insurance policies provide protection against loss suffered by fire. These policies pay either the loss at the time of the fire or the amount of the policy, whichever is lower. For example, if a firm has a building worth $1,000,000 and carries a fire policy for $900,000, the insurance company will pay $900,-000 if a fire destroys the structure. On the other hand, if the firm carried a policy for $1,100,000, the insurers would pay $1,000,000.

Naturally, few buildings are *completely* destroyed during a fire. A first-rate fire department can often save much of the structure and its contents. Therefore, many companies tend to **underinsure**, by carrying, for example, $500,000 of coverage on a $1,000,000 structure. In order to prevent gross underinsuring, the **coinsurance** clause was developed. This clause requires businesses to carry insurance equal to a certain percentage of the building's actual value —usually 80 percent. Most firms choose this approach because the insurance rates are lower.

Let us examine how fire losses are settled on these 80 percent coinsurance clauses. First, a company that has $1,000,000 of building and inventory and insures it for $800,000 can collect the full amount of all losses up to $800,000. If the firm chooses to insure above 80 percent, such as for $900,000, then its losses are insured to this amount.

Although this passerby seems unconcerned, you can bet the building's owner is checking his or her fire insurance coverage.

However, if it underinsures by taking coverage for only $600,000 then the insurance company will pay only a portion (three-fourths) of any losses. For example, on a loss of $200,000 the insurance firm would calculate the amount owed as follows:

$$\frac{\$600,000 \text{ (amount of insurance carried)}}{\$800,000 \text{ (amount of insurance required)}} \times \frac{200,000}{\text{(loss)}}$$

$$= \$150,000 \text{ (payment)}.$$

And regardless of the amount of the total loss, the insurance company will pay no more than $600,000, the amount of insurance provided.

If the business wants further insurance, this can be obtained through **extended coverage** in the form of a **rider** or addition to the policy. This insurance often covers such risks as storms, explosions, torna-

Fire in
Number Three

In order to provide fire insurance for three of her retail outlets, Lucy White had each appraised by a local insurance firm. The company informed Lucy that each store plus inventory was worth $120,000. Because the firm's coinsurance clause required all firms to carry insurance equal to 80 percent of the total value of the building and inventory, each would have to be insured for $96,000.

After analyzing the situation for herself, Lucy learned that two of the units were located some distance from the nearest fire department. In case of a fire, they could be totally destroyed. For this reason, she agreed to insure them for $96,000 each. However, the third unit was located only a block from a new fire department. Since a total loss of this unit was unlikely, Lucy decided to insure this one for only $72,000. Six weeks later this unit suffered a fire loss of $36,000.

1. How much will the insurance company pay toward this loss? Show your calculations.

2. If Lucy had insured the unit for $96,000, how much would the company have paid?

3. Instead of insuring for $96,000, suppose Lucy insured the unit for $120,000 and it was totally destroyed. How much would the insurance firm then pay?

---

does, cyclones, hail, and smoke damage. Some firms even have riders for **business interruption insurance** which replaces earnings that are lost because of such things as fire damage.

11. If the coinsurance clause requires that a firm carry insurance equal to 80 percent of a building's value, but the firm carries only 40 percent of this value, what percentage of the loss will the insurance company pay in case of a fire?

12. What is business interruption insurance?

Fidelity and Surety Bonds

Companies expect their employees to be honest. Sometimes, however, this is not the case and businesses find they have been embezzled for large sums. In order to protect themselves from such losses, firms can buy **fidelity bonds.** These bonds are usually written to cover people who hold jobs in which they have jurisdiction over funds. Sometimes the bond covers a specific person or group; other times it covers a particular position, such as the company treasurer. If there is a financial loss caused by the dishonesty of any bonded employee, the insurance company will pay the amount specified in the policy.

Other times a business will suffer a setback because of nonperformance of a contract. For example, a building contractor might fail to finish the structure by the agreed-upon time period. In order to protect itself from this risk the company can require the contractor to furnish a **surety bond** that the building will be erected according to the terms of the contract. If the contractor fails to finish the job, the insurance company will see that the project is completed.

Marine Insurance

Marine insurance provides protection for the transportation industry. **Ocean marine insurance** covers losses that occur on the high seas, such as loss of the vessel, loss of the cargo, and any other legal liabilities that may arise as a result of such a calamity. **Inland marine insurance** covers the hazards involved in shipping goods by rail, truck, airplane, steamer, or barge.

Workers Compensation Insurance

All fifty states have workers compensation laws. Under these laws, workers injured on the job are entitled to compensation unless the injury was deliberately inflicted or caused by intoxication. Some states require businesses to purchase **workers compensation insurance** from them, other states allow private insurance firms to compete with them for this business, while still others let private insurance companies handle the entire area themselves. The cost of this insurance is borne by the business, with rates depending upon the size of the payroll and the hazards of the industry. If a worker is injured, medical and hospitalization expenses are paid and the individual is given a weekly wage. This wage is commonly 50–70 percent of the usual weekly salary. In order to avoid paying for minor accidents, most plans call for a waiting period of two days to two weeks before any payments are made.

Public Liability Insurance

Public liability insurance is designed to protect from lawsuits individuals or businesses that own property. Quite often these arise when a person injures him-

" 'Lousy' isn't much of a symptom to go on."

From The Wall Street Journal; permission Cartoon Features Syndicate

self on someone else's property—for example, by breaking a leg falling down the front steps. Public liability insurance makes funds available for hiring lawyers to defend the insured as well as for paying any judgments against the individual.

13. What types of risks do fidelity bonds insure against? Surety bonds?

14. When is an individual entitled to workers compensation insurance?

15. Why is it a good idea for a business to have some form of public liability insurance?

HEALTH INSURANCE

Another major form of insurance is **health insurance.** Over 75 percent of all Americans have some form of health insurance. These policies often cover both accidents and sickness and, depending upon the specific type of policy, can take care of hospital and surgical expenses as well as any loss of income during the period of disability. Such policies usually carry a *deductible,* such as $100 per year, which is the amount of personal medical expenses the individual must have before the insurance company will pay any accident or sickness-related expenses. It is also common to find a maximum on the amount the insurance company will pay toward a hospital room. The coverage often pays for a double occupancy, so individuals who want a room of their own must pay the difference themselves. Other specific features of these policies are often related to how much the insurance firm will pay for specific services, such as ambulance, anesthesia, or amputation of a limb.

As noted earlier, many insurance outlets are involved in selling health insurance. Perhaps the best known association is Blue Cross and Blue Shield (this varies from state to state). Currently there are over a half dozen proposals before the Congress regarding national health insurance programs.

16. What kinds of risks does health insurance cover? Explain.

LIFE INSURANCE

Life insurance is widely used as a means of coping with risk. Today most Americans have life insurance. Annual premiums on these policies run into the billions of dollars! There is little wonder that this industry, as we pointed out in the last chapter, is so important as a source of long-term financing for business.

Life insurance is based on the law of averages. It is possible to predict with great accuracy the number of people who will die in any given year. From

Hank Greenberg

Have you ever heard of Hank Greenberg, President of the giant insurance firm? Probably not. Yet many people in the insurance industry consider him to be a true genius in the business. His former boss puts it this way: "He's the No. 1 insurance executive in the world today. I know, because I know most of them. When you talk to him, you're talking to the best." Competitors agree—although they hasten to add that Hank Greenberg is also abrasive, cocky, and shrewd. Commenting recently on his own appraisal of the competition, Greenberg remarked, "I wouldn't say they're all a bunch of dummies. They're not. Obviously there are some people out there who do pretty well. This is a big industry, and you can't just say that everybody in it is totally lackluster." When asked what his competitors do that really impresses him, Greenberg smiles, "You're being unfair," he protests.

Is he really *that* good? Perhaps the best way to answer this question is to look at the performance of his firm in last decade. Since he took over AIG, Greenberg has continually

aimed for earnings growth of 20 percent per year and has not once failed to achieve it. During the decade of the seventies, the compound annual earnings growth of AIG was 24.2 percent.

How does he manage it? The answer is found in risk management. By carefully studying the risks involved in the lines of insurance his corporation handles, he manages to pass on the major part of these risks while giving up a smaller portion of the premiums. Additionally, he has led the way in handling new kinds of insurance such as corporate directors' and officers' liability insurance, and kidnap and ransom insurance. Since few firms were initially in this area, his company set the rates and made the profits. And he is always on the lookout for new areas where insurance coverage is desired. He is an innovative packager. Because of his abrasive personality and high degree of success, his competitors do not care very much for him. However, this does not concern Greenberg. As he puts it, "I'd rather be respected than loved."

this information, life insurance firms can determine the annual premium that should be charged for each type of policy. The individuals who provide this information are known as **actuaries.** These people are experts in the areas of statistics and risk. With their help the firm is able to provide the greatest amount of insurance coverage at the most reasonable price. Table 18.1 provides a mortality table compiled by the National Association of Insurance Commissioners, an organization of state insurance commissioners, that shows the life history of ten million men

and women from birth until the age of ninety-nine. For example, the death rate for men who are twenty years old and women who are twenty-three years old is 1.79 per 1,000. From tables such as these, premiums for life insurance policies are determined.

Types of Life Insurance Policies
There are four basic types of life insurance: (a) term life insurance, (b) whole life insurance, (c) limited payment life insurance, and (d) endowment life insurance.

TABLE 19.1 COMMISSIONERS 1958 STANDARD ORDINARY TABLE OF MORTALITY (WITH DEATH RATE PER 1,000 AND "EXPECTATION OF LIFE")*

AGE M	AGE F	NUMBER LIVING	DEATHS EACH YEAR	DEATH RATE PER 1,000	EXPECTATION OF LIFE	AGE M	AGE F	NUMBER LIVING	DEATHS EACH YEAR	DEATH RATE PER 1,000	EXPECTATION OF LIFE
	0†	10,014,660	62,091	6.20	71.17	15	18	9,743,175	14,225	1.46	54.95
	1	9,952,569	16,621	1.67	70.61	16	19	9,728,950	14,983	1.54	54.03
	2	9,935,948	14,010	1.41	69.72	17	20	9,713,967	15,737	1.62	53.11
	3	9,921,938	13,395	1.35	68.82	18	21	9,698,230	16,390	1.69	52.19
	4	9,908,543	12,782	1.29	67.91	19	22	9,681,840	16,846	1.74	51.28
	5	9,895,761	12,271	1.24	67.00	20	23	9,664,994	17,300	1.79	50.37
	6	9,883,490	11,761	1.19	66.08	21	24	9,647,694	17,655	1.83	49.46
	7	9,871,729	11,352	1.15	65.16	22	25	9,630,039	17,912	1.86	48.55
	8	9,860,377	11,044	1.12	64.24	23	26	9,612,127	18,167	1.89	47.64
	9	9,849,333	10,933	1.11	63.31	24	27	9,593,960	18,324	1.91	46.73
	10	9,838,400	10,921	1.11	62.38	25	28	9,575,636	18,481	1.93	45.82
	11	9,827,479	11,007	1.12	61.45	26	29	9,557,155	18,732	1.96	44.90
	12	9,816,472	11,191	1.14	60.51	27	30	9,538,423	18,981	1.99	43.99
	13	9,805,281	11,472	1.17	59.58	28	31	9,519,442	19,324	2.03	43.08
	14	9,793,809	11,851	1.21	58.65	29	32	9,500,118	19,760	2.08	42.16
0†		10,000,000	70,800	7.08	68.30	30	33	9,480,358	20,193	2.13	41.25
1		9,929,200	17,475	1.76	67.78	31	34	9,460,165	20,718	2.19	40.34
2		9,911,725	15,066	1.52	66.90	32	35	9,439,447	21,239	2.25	39.43
3		9,896,659	14,449	1.46	66.00	33	36	9,418,208	21,850	2.32	38.51
4		9,882,210	13,835	1.40	65.10	34	37	9,396,358	22,551	2.40	37.60
5		9,868,375	13,322	1.35	64.19	35	38	9,373,807	23,528	2.51	36.69
6		9,855,053	12,812	1.30	63.27	36	39	9,350,279	24,685	2.64	35.78
7		9,842,241	12,401	1.26	62.35	37	40	9,325,594	26,112	2.80	34.88
8		9,829,840	12,091	1.23	61.43	38	41	9,299,482	27,991	3.01	33.97
9		9,817,749	11,879	1.21	60.51	39	42	9,271,491	30,132	3.25	33.07
10		9,805,870	11,865	1.21	59.58	40	43	9,241,359	32,622	3.53	32.18
11		9,794,005	12,047	1.23	58.65	41	44	9,208,737	35,362	3.84	31.29
12	15	9,781,958	12,325	1.26	57.72	42	45	9,173,375	38,253	4.17	30.41
13	16	9,769,633	12,896	1.32	56.80	43	46	9,135,122	41,382	4.53	29.54
14	17	9,756,737	13,562	1.39	55.87	44	47	9,093,740	44,741	4.92	28.67

* The "Expectation of Life" is the average number of years which a large number of persons of any given age have yet to live; that is, the sum of the years which all will live divided by the number of persons.
† Under six months.

AGE M	AGE F	NUMBER LIVING	DEATHS EACH YEAR	DEATH RATE PER 1,000	EXPEC- TATION OF LIFE	AGE M	AGE F	NUMBER LIVING	DEATHS EACH YEAR	DEATH RATE PER 1,000	EXPEC- TATION OF LIFE
45	48	9,048,999	48,412	5.35	27.81	75	78	4,129,906	303,011	73.37	7.81
46	49	9,000,587	52,473	5.83	26.95	76	79	3,826,895	303,014	79.18	7.39
47	50	8,948,114	56,910	6.36	26.11	77	80	3,523,881	301,997	85.70	6.98
48	51	8,891,204	61,794	6.95	25.27	78	81	3,221,884	299,829	93.06	6.59
49	52	8,829,410	67,104	7.60	24.45	79	82	2,922,055	295,683	101.19	6.21
50	53	8,762,306	72,902	8.32	23.63	80	83	2,626,372	288,848	109.98	5.85
51	54	8,689,404	79,160	9.11	22.82	81	84	2,337,524	278,983	119.35	5.51
52	55	8,610,244	85,758	9.96	22.03	82	85	2,058,541	265,902	129.17	5.19
53	56	8,524,486	92,832	10.89	21.25	83	86	1,792,639	249,858	139.38	4.89
54	57	8,431,654	100,337	11.90	20.47	84	87	1,542,781	231,433	150.01	4.60
55	58	8,331,317	108,307	13.00	19.71	85	88	1,311,348	211,311	161.14	4.32
56	59	8,223,010	116,849	14.21	18.97	86	89	1,100,037	190,108	172.82	4.06
57	60	8,106,161	125,970	15.54	18.23	87	90	909,929	168,455	185.13	3.80
58	61	7,980,191	135,663	17.00	17.51	88	91	741,474	146,997	198.25	3.55
59	62	7,844,528	145,830	18.59	16.81	89	92	594,477	126,303	212.46	3.31
60	63	7,698,698	156,592	20.34	16.12	90	93	468,174	106,809	228.14	3.06
61	64	7,542,106	167,736	22.24	15.44	91	94	361,365	88,813	245.77	2.82
62	65	7,374,370	179,271	24.31	14.78	92	95	272,552	72,480	265.93	2.58
63	66	7,195,099	191,174	26.57	14.14	93	96	200,072	57,881	289.30	2.33
64	67	7,003,925	203,394	29.04	13.51	94	97	142,191	45,026	316.66	2.07
65	68	6,800,531	215,917	31.75	12.90	95	98	97,165	34,128	351.24	1.80
66	69	6,584,614	228,749	34.74	12.31	96	99	63,037	25,250	400.56	1.51
67	70	6,355,865	241,777	38.04	11.73	97	100	37,787	18,456	488.42	1.18
68	71	6,114,088	254,835	41.68	11.17	98	101	19,331	12,916	668.15	.83
69	72	5,859,253	267,241	45.61	10.64	99	102	6,415	6,415	1000.00	.50
70	73	5,592,012	278,426	49.79	10.12						
71	74	5,313,586	287,731	54.15	9.63						
72	75	5,025,855	294,766	58.65	9.15						
73	76	4,731,089	299,289	63.26	8.69						
74	77	4,431,800	301,894	68.12	8.24						

Adjustable Life

It does what no single policy has ever done before!

- You may raise* or lower the amount of your coverage.
- You can raise or lower your premium payments at any time.
- You eliminate the need to choose between whole life or term protection.
- The amount of your coverage may be raised to help offset increases in the cost-of-living.

No other policy available today can match the ability of **Adjustable Life** to meet the changing personal and business needs that are a part of everyone's future. No longer is it necessary to cancel old, or add new, policies to bring your life insurance program up-to-date. You simply revise your original policy to best fit your needs at the moment. Not once, but as many times as necessary.

With an **Adjustable Life**' policy, you design it to meet your needs at the start. Then, at a later date when circumstances change—and they will—you may, within limits, make revisions in coverage or premium payments as your situation demands. Equally important, you are not tied to the basic restrictions of whole life or term types of coverage. You simply adjust your policy to emphasize the maximum amount of coverage or the accumulation of cash and loan values. The chart shows you how flexible Adjustable Life is in comparison with conventional forms of protection.

The cost? Probably less than other policies lacking its unique built-in flexibility. The Bankers Life of Des Moines is one of the lowest net cost companies in the industry, so we suggest you ask your agent to compare the **interest-** **adjusted cost** of this new policy with any others you may be considering. It's always good to check competitive life insurance quotations… and a way to save yourself some money.

	Five Year Renewable Convertible Term	Standard Whole Life Policy	Adjustable Life
1. Does the policy allow you to change the amount of coverage provided?			
Upward?	No	No	Yes*
Downward?	No**	No**	Yes
2. Does the policy allow you to change the amount of premium payments?			
Upward?	No	No	Yes
Downward?	No**	No**	Yes
3. Can one single policy provide for a growing life insurance program?	No	No	Yes
4. Is there a cost-of-living feature for most individuals which allows, within limits, increases in coverage without proving insurability?	No	No	Yes
5. Does the policy have cash and loan values?	No	Yes	Yes

*Subject to evidence of insurability.
**In some special instances it is possible to reduce premiums and amount of coverage.

For more information about why Adjustable Life has been called the most remarkable insurance development in fifty years, contact The Bankers Life of Des Moines office listed in the Yellow Pages. Or mail the coupon below.
¹Available in 49 states.

THE BANKERS LIFE

BANKERS LIFE COMPANY DES MOINES, IOWA 50307

Term life insurance

Term life insurance—for one, five, ten, or twenty years, for example—provides coverage for a limited period of time and the insurance company is obligated to pay only if the person dies. The greatest benefit of term insurance is that if offers inexpensive coverage.

The principles on which term insurance is based illustrate this. For example, if 100,000 men, all twenty years old, each buy a $10,000, one-year term policy, the firm can estimate from Table 19.1 that 179 of them will die. This will require paying a total of $1,790,000 (179 × $10,000) to the beneficiaries of these people. In order to operate profitably, then, the firm will have to charge each policyholder $17.90 plus costs for this one-year policy.

Term insurance is very useful for individuals who want inexpensive coverage for a limited number of years. An individual starting a new business, for example, may incur quite a few debts. If this person stays in operation for five years, these obligations can be repaid. If the individual dies before this time, however, the spouse will inherit the debts. Such a situation can be avoided through the purchase of term insurance with which the financial obligations can be repaid. Keep in mind, however, that the older a person is, the greater the annual cost of term insurance because the likelihood of death increases with age. Table 19.1, for example, shows that the death rate per 1,000 for fifty-year-old males is around five times that for twenty-year olds. Thus the premium would be much greater for older people. In fact, most insurance firms do not sell term policies to people over sixty-five years of age.

Whole life insurance

Whole life insurance, often called **straight life,** offers the policyholder a combination of protection and savings. The annual premium remains constant throughout the life of the policy and the individual continues to pay this amount as long as the policy is in force. Naturally, the earlier one buys such a policy the lower the premium will be. In any event, the insurance company pays the face value of the policy upon the death of the insured.

One of the biggest advantages of whole life insurance is that, with the exception of term insurance, it provides the greatest coverage for the lowest premium. In addition, as the policy remains in force it acquires a **cash surrender value,** which is payable upon cancellation of the policy. Or, if the owner wishes to borrow this money, he or she can do so at a low rate of interest (often 6–8 percent). On the negative side, the premium must be paid every year and this can be difficult when an individual retires and is living on a limited income. Also, some people object to an interest charge on loans made against the cash surrender value, claiming they are paying interest to borrow their own money.

Limited payment life insurance

Limited payment life insurance is similar to whole life insurance except that the individual pays premiums for only a limited number of years. The most common period is twenty years, and this policy is referred to as "20 pay life." The primary advantage of this type of policy is that because of this arrangement the individual can buy the policy during that period when his or her earnings are at a maximum. On the negative side, limited payment life insurance offers less protection for the premium than does straight life. As with all of these policies, of course, the face value would be paid if the insured died before the policy was paid up.

Endowment life insurance

Endowment life insurance provides both protection and savings, but tends to emphasize the latter most strongly. The premium for this type of policy is greater than that for either whole life or limited payment life, but the cash surrender value increases much faster too. In addition, at the end of a stated period, such as thirty years, the cash value of the policy is equal to its face value. For example, if a twenty-five-year-old man took out a $10,000 endowment policy for thirty years, the company would pay this amount to his estate if he died before fifty-five. If he lives thirty years he can then collect the face value of the policy or elect to receive annual payments. The biggest advantage of this type of policy is its saving feature. The greatest disadvantage is that the annual premium is higher than those for the other types of policies we have examined.

Business and Life Insurance

Business firms make use of various types of life insurance plans. Some of the most common include (a) group life insurance, (b) credit life insurance, (c) owner or executive insurance, and (d) retirement and pension plans.

Group life insurance

Group life insurance is very widely used by businesses. A group life insurance policy is simply a policy covering all individuals in the firm. Usually these policies are based on the earnings of the employees. Today it is common to cover the personnel for 1–2 times their annual earnings. These policies are often written on a one-year renewable term plan, with the employer paying most of the premium. The plans usually require no physical exam so everyone in the company, regardless of health, is covered. This can be a particular boon to personnel who, because of poor health, would be unable to obtain life insurance.

Credit life insurance

The use of **credit life insurance** has grown rapidly in recent years because of the increased amount of credit purchases and short-term borrowings by consumers. This insurance guarantees repayment of these installment contracts and personal loans in case the debtor dies. Today banks, finance companies, and retailers are particularly active in using this type of insurance. Often the policy is written on a one-year basis and covers all of the firm's credit customers, although the cost of this insurance is usually passed on to the latter. One great advantage of this form of insurance is that it reduces the risk of consumer financing for both lender and borrower.

Owner or executive insurance

If a sole proprietor dies, his or her business may have to be sold to pay funeral expenses and taxes. With the proceeds from an insurance policy, however, the widow or other heirs could continue operations. Similarly, if one partner in a partnership dies, the others may be unable to buy out his or her interest. To prevent dissolution, partnerships often take out policies payable to the surviving partners. With these proceeds the latter are then able to buy out the interest of the deceased partner. In the case of corporations, the death of a key executive could affect the company's profit. To help it absorb such a reduction in earning power, the firm will take out an

Some Insurance Proposals

Lucy White has been president and chairman of the board of her corporation for three years. At the present time the company has sales in excess of $10 million. There are also 450 full-time employees and another 200 part-timers. As the organization has grown, Lucy has found herself being confronted with more and more decisions relating to financial matters.

Recently an insurance executive called on Lucy to see if his firm could sell her an insurance package. There were three basic programs the executive talked about. The first was a group life insurance program that would cover all workers for $5,000 and all managers for $10,000. The executive pointed out that many firms make this type of program part of their wage and salary package, coming in the form of increased benefits. The second proposed program was a term life insurance policy on Lucy and the members of top management. These policies would extend $250,000 coverage on Lucy on down to $25,000 on some of the less important members of the management team. The third program was a retirement and pension plan that would provide all employees with income beyond that given by social security. Under its provisions, all employees could put up to 5 percent of their salary into this program and it would be matched by the company. These funds would then be returned to the individuals in the form of monthly payments upon retirement.

1. Of what value is a group life insurance program? What are its benefits?

2. Why would owner or executive insurance (the second program described above) be a good idea for Lucy and her top management team? Explain.

3. If social security is designed to provide people with retirement income, why is an additional retirement or pension plan necessary or desirable?

insurance policy on this individual's life. These funds can then be used to hire and train a replacement.

Retirement and pension plans

Many firms want to provide their people with retirement income beyond that given by social security. One of the most popular ways of doing this is to have an actuary or benefit consultant group come in and set up a **retirement and pension plan program.** Sometimes the actuary or consultant personnel work for a large insurance company, while in other cases they are independent firms. In any case, it is common to find these programs requiring the employer, and sometimes the employee, to put money aside every year into a retirement fund. From this fund money is then drawn out for retirement benefits.

There are many insurance firms that provide various types of coverage for business. Figure 19.2 shows an ad that features Independent Insurance Agent, an organization that offers many of the types of risk we have covered in this chapter.

17. What are the four basic types of life insurance? Describe each.

18. How does group life insurance differ from owner or executive insurance?

SPECIAL COVERAGE

In recent years there has been great attention directed to **special coverage insurance,** which is used for assuming risks other than those we have just discussed. One of the major areas of special coverage is that of **political risk.** A second is **director's and officer's liability.**

Political Risk Insurance

Many firms today are doing business overseas, thereby opening themselves up to all sorts of political risk. Three of the most common, for which coverage is available, are kidnapping/ransom, expropriation, and inconvertibility.

Kidnap/ransom insurance

Not much is heard about kidnap/ransom insurance because underwriting companies feel that the highest degree of confidentiality is needed when discussing rates and coverage. Some firms, in fact, use code names in their communications so that anyone reading the letter or listening in on a phone call is unaware that the parties are discussing kidnap or ransom insurance. Nevertheless, it is an important and growing area.

A typical policy, such as that issued by Lloyd's of London, will cover both losses, following the actual or alleged kidnapping of insured persons, or loss following a threat to kill, injure, or abduct insured persons. The losses include monies paid to those who are making the ransom or extortion demand, reward monies paid for information leading to the arrest and conviction of those responsible for these acts, and post-kidnap expenses for those engaged in negotiating the individual's release, as well as medical, legal, travel, and other associated expenses. With the increase in kidnapping of executives in foreign countries, this form of insurance is being purchased by virtually all multinational firms.

Expropriation

If a government confiscates, nationalizes, or expropriates the property of a foreign investor, in most cases it is obliged to offer that investor prompt, adequate, and effective compensation. However, sometimes no compensation is offered—or it is unsatisfactory. This is where expropriation insurance applies. Business firms can buy coverage for tangible assets such as plant, equipment, land, and inventories. Compensation is usually based on the difference between the value of the investment and the compensation received from the government that expropriates the assets. This coverage can be changed

FIG. 19.2

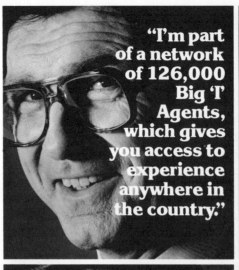

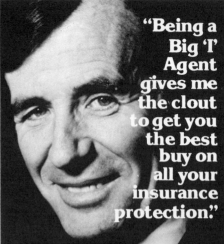

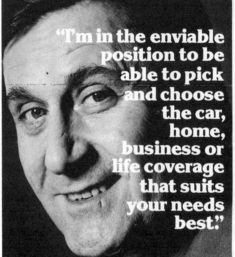

We're Independent Insurance Agents. We place insurance with any one of a number of fine companies. Which means we're in a position to negotiate in *your* behalf. A benefit you'll appreciate today more than ever.

We don't work for just one company. We work for you.

from year to year to reflect increases (or decreases) in the value of the insured assets. Particularly in third-world countries, many American firms are finding expropriation insurance to be an important hedge against the ever-changing political winds.

Inconvertibility

Another concern of foreign investors is the possibility that they will be unable to convert the local currency back into their own domestic currency. When this happens, dividends, interest, fees, and profits are tied up in the host country. Insurance can be purchased to protect the firm from this inconvertibility problem. In most cases, the coverage protects the insured from loss in two types of situations. The first is where the host country prevents the investors from converting for a period in excess of 30 days beyond the normal transfer period. The other is where, because of a failure of the host country to act on a proper application for local currency conversion for a period in excess of 90 days, investors are unable to convert their local currency. In these situations the insurance company will convert the monies into domestic currency at the exchange rates prevailing on the day the period of inconvertibility began. As a result of such coverage, business firms need not worry about having their money tied up in a foreign country for an indefinite period of time.

Directors' and Officers' Liability

When a business firm runs into problems, directors and officers of the company can find themselves open to a lawsuit, even though they personally may have done nothing to cause these problems. There are many cases of lawsuits brought against directors and officers. In one such suit, the board voted to sell a low-profit subsidiary to another firm. The latter turned it around and made a great deal of money. In turn, angry stockholders brought a lawsuit against the board charging that it was guilty of selling away a successful subsidiary and asked $5 million in damages.

In another case a company entered into a contract with another firm, and the latter made a great deal of money from the agreement. However, when some stockholders learned that members of the company's board of directors were also on the board of the other firm, they sued to have the contract terminated and asked for damages of $2 million. They eventually settled for $1.2 million.

In a third case, all board members had liability insurance. However, the insurance application had some untrue statements, which came to light only when a suit was filed and the directors sought protection under the terms of the policy. Then it was revealed that the chairman of the board was the one who had made the false statements. The other directors had nothing to do with this and insisted that they be covered by the terms of the policy. They were, but only after a long investigation that cleared them of any guilt.

These three examples illustrate why directors and officers need liability insurance. Any time there is a problem brought about because the board made a poor decision, or failed to make any decision, a stockholder lawsuit is likely. No one may be to blame, but just to be on the safe side should the issue wind up in court, liability insurance is a good idea. Depending on the size of the firm and the degree of risk, coverage into the millions of dollars can be purchased. And today, no astute director or officer will be without it. In fact, often the first question someone who is invited to join a board of directors asks is, "How much liability am I covered for?"

19. What kinds of firms would be interested in kidnap/ransom insurance? Expropriation insurance? Inconvertibility insurance?

20. Why do most directors and officers need liability insurance? Explain.

SUMMARY

Every business must decide very carefully how much risk it is willing to accept. As the amount of money it invests increases, the probability of the investment being successful must also go up. If it does not, the firm will then want to consider other ways of handling the situation, such as avoiding, reducing, or shifting the risk. In this chapter we looked very closely at some of the major ways of shifting risk, including hedging, subcontracting, and insuring. Major attention was given to the latter.

There are three important areas of insurance for individuals and businesses alike. One of these is property and liability insurance, which includes such major classifications as automobile insurance, fire insurance, fidelity and surety bonds, marine insurance, workers' compensation, and public liability insurance. A second major area is health insurance. A third is life insurance, including term life, whole life, limited payment life, and endowment life. Business firms also make use of various types of life insurance plans, including group life, credit life, owner or executive insurance, and retirement and pension plans as well as special coverage insurance for political risk and directors' and officers' liability. With these major types of insurance, individuals and businesses alike are able to manage risk more effectively.

QUESTIONS FOR DISCUSSION AND ANALYSIS

1. How does the personal risk preference curve help explain people's willingness to take risk?

2. What is meant by self-insurance?

3. In what way does subcontracting allow a business to shift risk?

4. How does auto liability insurance differ from collision insurance?

5. Why do most people choose to purchase collision insurance with a deductible?

6. How does the coinsurance clause prevent firms from underinsuring themselves on fire risks?

7. How does term life insurance work?

8. What are the benefits of buying whole life insurance?

9. When would business firms be interested in political risk insurance?

CAREERS
IN FINANCE

The field of finance has many fine career opportunities for those individuals who enjoy working in banks, stockbrokerage houses, insurance firms. The following summaries examine seven of the occupational careers available to those entering this field, although you should keep in mind that there are a great deal more than seven. These are designed merely to give you an idea of those types of jobs that make up the area of finance.

BANK OFFICER AND MANAGER
Virtually every bank in the country has a president who directs operations, one or more vice-presidents who act as general managers and are in charge of bank departments such as the trust department and the credit department, and a comptroller or cashier who, unlike cashiers in stores and other businesses, is an executive officer, generally responsible for all bank property. Large banks may also have treasurers and other senior officers, as well as junior officers, to supervise the various sections within different departments. Bank officers make decisions within a policy framework set by the board of directors and by existing laws and regulations. Loan officers, for example, evaluate the credit and collateral of individuals and businesses applying for a loan. Operations officers plan, coordinate, and control the work flow, update systems, and strive for administrative efficiency. Branch bank managers manage overall branch offices.

"Let me assure you that to us here at the First National, you're not just a number. You're two numbers, a dash, three more numbers, another dash, and another number."

From The Wall Street Journal; permission Cartoon Features Syndicate

SOURCE: *Occupational Outlook Handbook,* 1978–79 Edition, U.S. Department of Labor, Bureau of Labor Statistics

ACTUARY

Who determines how much you pay for your auto insurance or life insurance policy? In the final analysis it is the actuary, who is skilled in statistics and risk insurance and is able to assemble and analyze data to calculate the probabilities of death, sickness, injury, disability, unemployment, etc.; the insurance company bases its rates on the actuary's findings. In order to perform these duties effectively, this individual must keep informed about the general economic and social trends, legislative health, and other developments that may affect insurance practices. The actuary also must be prepared to testify before public agencies on proposed legislation affecting the insurance industry, for example, by explaining how intended changes in premium rates or contract provisions will impact on firms operating in an affected area.

CREDIT MANAGER

Many companies request credit, and this is where the credit manager comes in. The individual has final authority to accept or reject a credit application. In doing so, the credit manager analyzes detailed financial reports submitted by the applicant, interviews a representative of the company about its management, and reviews credit agency reports to determine the firm's record in repaying debts. The manager also checks at banks where the company has deposits, or previously was granted credit, in an effort to determine the credit worthiness of the firm.

ECONOMIST

Economists are concerned with how to use scarce resources such as land, raw materials, and human resources in providing goods and services for society. Economists who work for business firms provide the information management uses to make decisions on marketing and pricing the company's products, to analyze the effect of government policies on business or international trade, or to look at the advisability of adding new lines of merchandise, opening new branch operations, or otherwise expanding the company's businesses. They usually work for firms that carry on extensive operations abroad and may be asked to prepare both short- and long-term forecasts on both foreign and U.S. economies.

CLAIMS REPRESENTATIVE

When an insured person has a claim, the person who investigates it, negotiates the settlement, and authorizes payment is the claim representative. Often known as claim adjusters or claim examiners, this person's job is to ensure that the settlement is in line with the extent of the loss. Some claim adjusters work with all lines of insurance, while others specialize in areas such as property damage by fire, marine loss, auto damage, workers' compensation loss, or product liability. The claim examiner investigates the details surrounding questionable claims or those exceeding a specified amount. In so doing they may correspond with investigating companies, field managers, agents, or the family of the insured. And, like claims adjusters, they are sometimes called on to testify in court.

CAREERS
IN FINANCE (continued)

SECURITY SALES WORKER

When people want to buy or sell securities, they call on a security sales worker. In addition to performing buying and selling transactions, these workers relay orders through the firms' offices to the floor of a securities exchange and are responsible for notifying the customer of the completed transaction and the final price. Other services provided by security sales workers include advising clients, the devising of a portfolio for the investor, recommending the purchase and sale of securities, and providing information to customers about the advantages and disadvantages of each type of investment based on each investor's objectives.

UNDERWRITER

Insurance companies assume millions of dollars in risks each year by transferring the chance of loss from their policyholders to themselves. The underwriter appraises and selects the risks the firm will insure. This is done on the basis of an analysis of information gathered from insurance applications, medical reports, and actuarial studies coupled with the underwriter's own judgment. In deciding whether a policy is an acceptable risk, the underwriter may outline the terms of the contract and premiums. In doing so, however, it is common to find the individual corresponding with agents and managers about policy cancellations or requests for information. Most underwriters specialize in one of three major categories: life, property, or liability insurance.

BANK CLERK

In a small bank, one bank clerk may do several jobs including sorting of checks, totaling debit and credit slips, and preparing monthly statements for depositors. In a large bank, each clerk usually specializes and frequently has a special job title as well. Some bank clerks are sorters, who separate documents such as checks and deposit slips into different groups and tabulate each batch. Others are bookkeeping-machine operators who use conventional bookkeeping machines or electronic posting machines to record final transactions. Still others are accounting clerks who do routine calculating and posting.

BANK TELLER

A teller cashes checks and processes deposits or withdrawals. Large banks often have their tellers perform specialized functions such as selling savings bonds, accepting payment for customers' utility bills, or taking deposits for Christmas club accounts. The most common type of teller is the commercial teller who cashes customers' checks and handles deposits and withdrawals from saving and checking accounts. Regardless of the individual's specific function, however, most of them start their duties before banking hours begin and continue until after closing hours. The workday usually begins with the individual receiving and counting an amount of working cash, and ends with the person counting cash on hand, and balancing the day's accounts.

CAREER	LATEST EMPLOYMENT FIGURES	EARNINGS	EMPLOYMENT OUTLOOK
Bank officer and manager	300,000	$12,000–$16,000	Faster than the average for all occupations
Actuary	9,000	$12,000–$14,000	Faster than the average for all occupations
Credit manager	53,000	$11,000–$14,000	More slowly than the average for all occupations
Economist	115,000	$11,000–$13,000	Faster than the average for all occupations
Claim representative	155,000	$12,000–$15,000	About as fast as the average for all occupations
Security sales worker	90,000	$15,000–$35,000	About as fast as the average for all occupations
Underwriter	25,000	$18,000–$22,000	Faster than the average for all occupations
Bank clerk	456,000	$ 7,500–$ 9,000	Faster than the average for all occupations
Bank teller	310,000	$ 8,000–$11,000	Faster than the average for all occupations

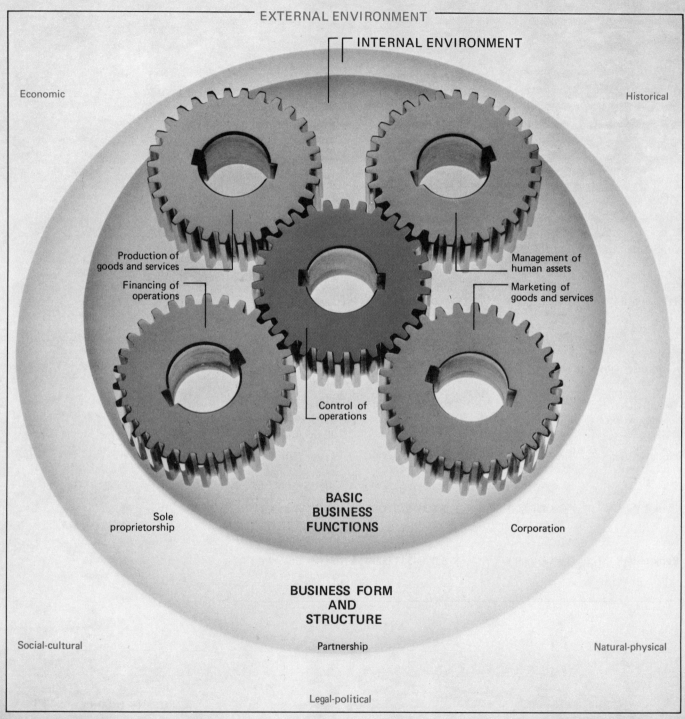

EXTERNAL ENVIRONMENT

INTERNAL ENVIRONMENT

Economic

Historical

Production of
goods and services

Management of
human assets

Financing of
operations

Marketing of
goods and services

Control of
operations

BASIC
BUSINESS
FUNCTIONS

Sole
proprietorship

Corporation

BUSINESS FORM
AND
STRUCTURE

Social-cultural

Partnership

Natural-physical

Legal-political

Controlling Business Operations

No matter what goods or services a firm produces and/or sells, sooner or later it must examine how well it is doing and draw up future plans on the basis of this evaluation. We call this evaluation procedure the control process, and in this section of the book our overall goal is to examine the methods used by business firms to control their operations.

In Chapter 20 we will take a close look at decision making and control, since these two activities are closely interrelated. For example, whenever we decide to control something, we have to make a decision; when we carry out this decision, we are again controlling. Careful consideration will be given to the steps in the decision-making process and to the types of conditions under which decisions are made. Attention will also be focused on the steps in the control process and how they can be used to maintain an efficient organization.

Then in Chapter 21 we will examine the area of accounting and financial control. In controlling operations, sooner or later we have to get down to dollars and cents. In this chapter we are going to be studying two of the most important financial statements for business: the balance sheet and the income statement. We will also be reviewing some of the most popular ratios used in analyzing balance sheets and income statements.

Chapter 22 focuses on the use of statistics for control purposes. In this chapter we are going to study what business statistics is all about and how it can be of value to the manager. Particular consideration will be given to the collection of primary and secondary data, some of the common statistical methods used to analyze this data, and a few of the most effective ways of presenting the results so that they are both clear and understandable.

Finally, in Chapter 23, the area of data processing will be studied. In this chapter we are going to place primary attention on how a computer works. Then we will shift our focus to the area of business and the computer and review some of the common uses companies make of the computer.

When you are finished reading this section you should have a good understanding of what the control process is all about and how firms use decision making, accounting information, statistics, and data processing to help them carry out this process. You should also be familiar with a number of key business terms, including *decision making, the control process, assets, liabilities, owners' equity, gross profit margin, index numbers, correlations, real-time processing,* and *time sharing.* Finally, you should have gained an appreciation for the importance of the control function in business.

20

It is the characteristic excellence of the strong man that he can bring momentous issues to the fore and make a decision about them. The weak are always forced to decide between alternatives they have not chosen themselves.

Dietrich Bonhoeffer

OBJECTIVES OF THIS CHAPTER

No business can exist for very long without some form of control process. Sooner or later it becomes necessary to check to see if everything is going according to plan. Based on this evaluation, corrective steps can then be taken where needed and further plans drawn up. This entire process consists of two parts: decision making and control. The first objective of this chapter is to study decision making from both a quantitative and a qualitative standpoint. The second is to analyze the control process and point out the importance of maintaining an effective control system. When you are finished reading this chapter you should be able to do the following:

a. define what is meant by the term decision making;

b. describe the five steps in the decision-making process;

c. identify the three types of conditions under which decisions are made;

d. explain how probabilities are used in making decisions that involve risk;

e. relate the steps in the creative thinking process;

f. describe how the control process works; and

g. explain the importance of this control process in maintaining an efficient organization.

Decision Making
and the Control Process

THE DECISION-MAKING PROCESS

Decision making is the process of choosing from among alternatives. Sometimes this process can be quite simple, with the "best" alternative easily determined. For example, a firm might have a rule that profit before taxes must be at least 10 percent of sales. Any product line that does not return at least this amount is judged to be unsatisfactory. Suppose a review of the financial records reveals the following percentage of profit before taxes/sales for the company's five product lines:

Product line	Profit before taxes/sales
A	22%
B	18
C	14
D	8
E	6

In this case it is evident that product lines D and E do not meet the minimum requirements of 10 percent and should be discontinued.

At other times, however, decision making is quite difficult. This is particularly true when the alternatives cannot be easily reduced to quantitative terms. For example, a board of directors is considering a mandatory retirement age for all personnel. One director suggests sixty-five, another says seventy. A third argues that some people are able to carry on their jobs until ninety, and that forced retirement is ridiculous. Each case must be judged on its own merits. How does one make a decision on the matter? In this case, it is usually by means of discussion, persuasion, and then, probably, compromise among the members.

The first example we presented is easy to handle because an objective decision can be made on the basis of quantitative data. Personalities and personal opinions play no role. The second example is more difficult because there are no clear-cut criteria for determining a mandatory retirement age. Opinions, biases, prejudices, and a host of subjective factors suddenly enter the picture to cloud things up. Yet whether one is dealing with objective or subjective decision making, there are some basic steps involved in the process.

Steps in the Decision-Making Process

Decision making consists of five steps. These are as follows: (a) defining the problem, (b) analyzing the situation, (c) developing alternative solutions, (d) selecting a course of action, and (e) implementing the decision.

Defining the problem

The first step in decision making is that of **defining the problem.** Exactly what is *causing* the dilemma? In this first phase it is important to differentiate between *symptoms* and *causes*. A symptom is a characteristic or development that first attracts our attention to the problem. For example, the company may be losing money. This is *not* the firm's problem; it is a symptom or effect of the problem. What, then, is the problem? There are numerous possible answers, including: (a) the company's product is poorly constructed, (b) the price is too high, or (c) the advertising program is being directed to the wrong market. In differentiating between the symptom and the cause one must ask *why* the firm is losing money. If the manager thinks the situation through very carefully, it should be possible for him or her to define the problem clearly. For example, the firm is losing money because sales are below the production break-even point.

Analyzing the situation

The next step is that of **analyzing the situation** by gathering all available information on the problem. Sometimes this process is a simple one because the manager has faced the situation before and knows exactly how to proceed. For those problems where past experience will not resolve the dilemma, however, it is necessary to obtain more information about the matter. Some of the more obvious steps would be to gather data related to the quality of the product, to compare the company's price with that of the

" 'Go ask your Mother', 'Go ask your Father'. When are we going to get some decisive management around here??"

From The Wall Street Journal; permission Cartoon Features Syndicate

competition, and to study the effectiveness of the firm's advertising program. When all of this has been done, the manager should have a fairly good idea of why sales are so low.

Developing alternative solutions

Having defined the problem and analyzed the available information, the manager is now ready to go to the third step: **developing alternative solutions.** We refer to these solutions or conclusions as **hypotheses** —possible answers to the problem. In arriving at these, heavy reliance is placed on past experience, judgment, and intuition, as well as on simple logic. The development of these alternatives is often regarded as the most important step in the decision-making process, for it is at this point that creative and original solutions to problems are formulated.

Selecting a course of action

Selecting a course of action is the step most often associated with decision making because it entails the actual choosing between two or more alternatives. In this step the manager must decide which of the formulated hypotheses is most likely to solve the problem. Two guidelines should be employed in making this decision. First, which hypothesis will solve the problem with the best cost/benefit ratio? The implementation of a decision is going to require the use of company resources such as money, manpower, and machinery; to find the cost/benefit ratio we must compare the expense associated with the use of these resources with the potential benefits to be derived from the solution. How much are we getting for our money? Remember, the astute manager tries to get a good return on investment. There is no sense spending $500 to solve a problem if it can be solved for half this amount.

The second important question in making a decision is whether the choice can be implemented effectively. In other words, is our alternative realistic or idealistic? Sometimes a hypothesis looks good on paper but does not work well when implemented. If the hypothesis passes both of the above requirements—a favorable cost/benefit ratio and realism—the alternative should be put into action.

Implementing the decision

The fifth and final step in the decision-making process is that of **implementing the decision.** This is sometimes the most difficult phase because it involves a commitment on the part of the manager. Implementation means more than just delegating part of the job to one's subordinates. Sometimes there will be questions that need to be answered; other times the personnel will require support or advice from the manager. Without this support even the best decision will sometimes prove unworkable.

Communication plays a key role in carrying out decisions. Sometimes subordinates will not understand what they are supposed to be doing. Other times they will have to be told why they are doing it and how important their efforts are in the overall success of the operation. The effective manager knows that group participation in decision making is a key motivational tool. People who understand what they are doing and why they are doing it are more likely to give 100-percent effort in implementing decisions. Thus decision making involves not only a quantitative analysis of alternative actions but also a solid understanding of human behavior.

1. What is the difference between a symptom and a cause?

2. What are the two guidelines that should be used in selecting a decision from among the available alternatives?

3. Why is "implementing the decision" often considered the most difficult step in the decision-making process?

Decision-Making Conditions

All decisions are made under one of three possible conditions: certainty, risk, and uncertainty. We can place these on a continuum as follows:

Certainty	Risk	Uncertainty
1.0	0.5	0.0
Full information about the alternatives	Some information about the alternatives	Little or no information about the alternatives

We will now examine each of these conditions.

Certainty

Certainty is present when a decision maker knows the outcome of a particular decision before it is made. We often refer to decisions under certainty as "sure things." A simple example is the investment of $10,000 in a government security at 7 percent for one year. We know that at the end of this time $700 in interest will be returned. There is, for all practical purposes, no risk involved.

The same is true when it comes to making decisions involving the allocation of resources. For example, suppose a company decides to take all of the machine parts it has in inventory and assemble as many units of a particular machine as possible. By simply computing the number of parts on hand, and determining how many of each will be needed per machine, the total can be ascertained. If it is a half dozen, the manager can order the assembly of six machines and know that this decision can be implemented with reasonable certainty.

Risk

Risk involves some degree of chance. However, enough information exists for the manager to predict the outcome of the decision with at least some degree of confidence. For example, if a fair coin is flipped into the air and allowed to drop to the floor, will the head or tail be facing up? We cannot say with certainty, but we do know that the chance of its being a head is 50 percent or .5 and the chance of its being a tail is also 50 percent or .5. This, then, is the information available about the outcome. As we will see, obtaining this information involves the use of probabilities.

Probabilities. Probabilities are of two types: objective and subjective. **Objective probabilities** are based on past experience. For example, by flipping a fair

coin 200 times we may get 100 heads and 100 tails. We can therefore assign a probability of .5 to each side of the coin. Or, on the basis of past production records we may learn that machinists who work over eight hours a day in the plant turn out 50 percent more rejects during the overtime period than during their regular work day. As a result, we can determine the probability of their work being acceptable or unacceptable.

Subjective probabilities are often made on the basis of "gut feel," hunch, or intuition. The manager may believe that strategy A is better than strategy B because of some previous experience with similar

Into the Vineyards

Most managers make decisions under conditions of risk, and the managers at Coca Cola are no exception. With 26 percent of the domestic soft-drink market under its control, the company has now expanded its horizons and moved into the wine industry.

Having expended $110 million to buy the Taylor Wine Co. of Hammandsport, N. Y., Coca Cola is currently in the process of applying to the wine business the same tools that have made Coke the biggest selling soft-drink in the world —money, muscle, and marketing. As one executive put it, "The same good merchandising principles that apply to any consumer packaged goods can be applied to wine as well." This calls for a consistent product backed by hard-sell advertising to create consumer awareness and win a preferred spot on the retailers' shelves. In short, the firm is trying to fit its newly acquired wine business to the soft-drink mold that has proved effective.

Can Coca Cola make this investment pay off? The firm is optimistic. For example, while Taylor grossed only $65 million the year it was purchased, Coca Cola executives believe it will gross over $1 billion by the end of the 1980s. This is nearly triple that of Gallo Wines' current sales and 15 times Taylor's current sales. On the other hand there are several things that Taylor has going for it. One is the Coca Cola money and management expertise that is available for this wine venture. The other is that while Taylor, in the past, dominated only the New York table wine business and produced sweeter wines that account for less than 10 percent of the domestic market for U.S. vintages (the bulk of such demand is for the drier California offerings), the Taylor wine brand was the most commonly recognized of all. Building on these assets, the management hopes to, via effective decision making, make Taylor wine almost as popular as Coca Cola.

strategies. Subjective probabilities often vary from one manager to the next. One manager may believe that a particular strategy has a 70-percent chance of success while another assigns it a 10-percent likelihood of occurring.

A great deal of probability assignment rests on a person's willingness to take a risk. We call this **risk preference.** As we saw in Chapter 19, some managers are great risk takers while others tend to be risk averters. In all cases, however, it is a fair generalization to say that as the amount of money being invested increases, the person's willingness to take a chance declines. Few managers are prepared to risk the fate of their entire firm on any decision lacking a high probability of success. In fact, most would demand a reasonably high degree of certainty.

Decision making with probabilities. After all alternatives are evaluated, the manager, using objective and/or subjective probability assignments, will determine the likelihood of success for each alternative. For example, assume that there are five strategies under consideration and each, if successful, will return $20,000 in profit to the firm. In this case, then, the choice can be made simply by deciding which has the greatest probability of success. In the guideline we set down in Chapter 6, when we discussed the planning process, we noted that a company should choose that alternative that provides it with the best payoff between profit and the probability of success. Let us now look at this in more depth by defining three key terms. The first is **conditional value,** which refers to the amount of money the firm will make if the strategy is successful. The second term is **success probability,** which refers to the likelihood that a particular strategy will succeed. The third is **expected value,** which refers to the net result when the conditional value is multiplied by the success probability. Applying these three terms to five strategies, each with a conditional value (expected profit) of $20,000 and varying success probabilities (such as .80, .50, .30, .30, and .10), gives us the results shown in Table 20.1. In this case the manager would

choose strategy A because it has the highest expected value.

TABLE 20.1 DETERMINING EXPECTED VALUES WITH IDENTICAL CONDITIONAL VALUES

STRATEGY	CONDITIONAL VALUE	SUCCESS PROBABILITY	EXPECTED VALUE
A	$20,000	.80	$16,000
B	20,000	.50	10,000
C	20,000	.30	6,000
D	20,000	.30	6,000
E	20,000	.10	2,000

In most cases, however, the conditional values will not be identical, a situation that is illustrated in Table 20.2. In this case strategy D is best. Note that although strategy E promises a greater profit, its success probability is very low in contrast to that of strategy D. Thus its expected value is not as good. So given the above information, the manager should choose alternative D.

TABLE 20.2 DETERMINING EXPECTED VALUES WITH DIFFERENT CONDITIONAL VALUES

STRATEGY	CONDITIONAL VALUE	SUCCESS PROBABILITY	EXPECTED VALUE
A	$10,000	.80	$ 8,000
B	20,000	.50	10,000
C	40,000	.30	12,000
D	50,000	.30	15,000
E	80,000	.10	8,000

Uncertainty

In some cases the manager may feel at a complete loss when it comes to assigning probabilities. The alternatives under analysis may present the manager with a brand new challenge and, unable to generalize from past experiences, he or she simply does not know what to do. Such a person is operating under **uncertainty.**

Mathematical techniques have been developed to help in these cases. These techniques will not be discussed here because they are too involved and complex. However, they do provide guidelines to the manager in assigning probabilities. For this reason, some experts say that there is no such thing as uncertainty. If there were, how could probabilities be assigned? We will not attempt to answer this question. Suffice it to say that when managers feel they are making decisions under uncertainty, there are methods that have been developed to assist them.

4. How do decisions made under certainty differ from those made under risk?

5. Under which condition do you think managers make most of their decisions: certainty, risk, or uncertainty?

6. In decision making, what is meant by the statement that "a company should choose that alternative that provides it with the best payoff between profit *and* probability of success"?

Creativity and Decision Making
So far we have been giving a great deal of attention to quantitative decision making. Yet the decision-making process consists of more than simply mathematical techniques. For example, qualitative inputs such as creativity also play a key role. No business can exist indefinitely without the implementation of some new ideas. A "follow the leader" strategy may work in the short run, but innovation is needed to survive in the long run. This is where the creative-thinking process comes in.

Steps in the creative-thinking process
Creative thinking and decision making actually go hand in hand. The steps in the **creative-thinking process** help carry out those in the decision-making process. The four steps in creative thinking are (a) preparation, (b) incubation, (c) illumination, and (d) verification.

"I've decided to vote for the candidate that bothers me the least for my vote!"

From The Wall Street Journal; permission Cartoon Features Syndicate

Preparation. Preparation is that stage when the decision maker gets mentally ready. During this period the individual gathers all the information available on the problem. In decision-making terms, we call this the definition and analysis of the problem. In creative thinking it is a mental process period during which the person becomes saturated with data. The more information the individual gathers and reviews, the more likely it is that the solution will be innovative or creative.

Incubation. After gathering these data it is often best to sit back and let one's subconscious mind work on the problem. Some of the world's greatest inventions have come as a result of the inventor's "dreaming" about the discovery. There in the individual's dream, cause-and-effect relationships came together. How is this possible? The answer is found in the brain, which rearranges all the data gathered in the preparation stage and presents them in a new, innovative way.

When applied to decision making, **incubation** can be very helpful both in developing alternative solutions and in choosing one of them. Often a person is able to come up with a new or fresh approach to a problem by merely relaxing and turning to other matters. Of course, this does not mean ignoring the problem indefinitely. It is wise to set a deadline such as ten days and, if no solution is forthcoming by this time, to go back to the preparation stage and review the data again.

Illumination. **Illumination** occurs when the individual suddenly realizes the answer to the problem. Often this solution seems to come like a "bolt out of the blue." The person may not even have been aware that any thought was being given to the problem—then, suddenly, there is the solution. In decision making this takes place in step 4, that of selecting a course of action.

Verification. The last step in creative thinking is **verification** of the solution. Will it work? In most cases there will be a need to refine or rethink some minor ideas. In an invention it is common to find some trial-and-error work being done to eliminate minor bugs. Modification and improvement take place in this phase. Verification is important in the implementation state of decision making.

Group participation and creative thinking. Creative thinking may be an individual process, but groups can use it as well. In fact, when individuals get together to exchange creative ideas, the results are often superior to those of people working alone. Two of the most famous approaches to group creative thinking are **brainstorming** and the **Gordon technique** (see Fig. 20.1).

Brainstorming. This technique was developed by Alex F. Osborn as a method of encouraging creative

thinking in an advertising agency. Since this time, however, the technique has been applied in many situations where it is desirable to obtain a large number of ideas for solving a problem.

The brainstorming session begins with the group leader telling the participating members the problem under analysis and encouraging them to be as imaginative and creative as they can in formulating their ideas. Criticism is usually forbidden, so the members can say anything they want. Emphasis is placed on quantity, and as people call out their ideas the others are allowed to combine some of them or improve them in any way they see fit. Free wheeling is encouraged.

Naturally many of the ideas will be of little value. Some will prove to be superficial, others too imaginative to be workable. However, those that remain are often very helpful. And without a creative-thinking session such as brainstorming, it is unlikely that these ideas would have been obtained in the first place.

Gordon technique. This technique, developed by William J. Gordon, is used for handling technical problems. It is similar to brainstorming in that free association is used, but with this method the participants are not told the problem under consideration. Instead they are given only a hint or stimulus, and they have to take it from there. For example, if the group leader wanted the participants to come up with ideas on auto engine designs that might lead to better mileage, the key phrase might be "better mileage." From there the members would toss out all sorts of ideas. Some ideas might be valuable in redesigning current engines, while others might be more useful on some other project in the future. In any event, the Gordon technique is an excellent method for obtaining creative ideas for solving technical problems. This technique and the Osborn brainstorming technique are summarized in Fig. 20.1.

Whether one uses brainstorming, the Gordon technique or some variation of these as presented in Fig. 20.1, creativity is vital to the decision-making

Osborn Brainstorming

Rules:

1. Judicial thinking or evaluation is ruled out.
2. Free wheeling is welcomed.
3. Quantity is wanted.
4. Combinations and improvements are sought.

Suggestions for the Osborn technique:

1. Length: 40 minutes to one hour, sessions of ten to fifteen minutes can be effective if time is short.
2. Do not reveal the problem before the session. An information sheet or suggested reference material on a related subject should be used if prior knowledge of the general field is needed.
3. Problem should be clearly stated and not too broad.
4. Use a small conference table which allows people to communicate with each other easily.
5. If a product is being discussed, samples may be useful as a point of reference.

Gordon Technique

Rules:

1. Only the group leader knows the problem
2. Free association is used.
3. Subject for discussion must be carefully chosen.

Suggestions for the Gordon technique:

1. Length of session: two to three hours are necessary.
2. Group leader must be exceptionally gifted and thoroughly trained in the use of the technique.

General Suggestions that apply to both techniques

1. Selection of personnel: a group from diverse backgrounds helps. Try to get a balance of highly active and quiet members.
2. Mixed groups of men and women are often more effective, especially for consumer problems.
3. Although physical atmosphere is not too important, a relaxed pleasant atmosphere is desirable.
4. Group size: groups of from four to twelve can be effective. We recommend six to nine.
5. Newcomers may be introduced without disturbing the group, but they must be properly briefed in the theory of creative thinking and the use of the particular technique.
6. A secretary or recording machine should be used to record the ideas produced. Otherwise they may not be remembered later. Gordon always uses a blackboard so that ideas can be visualized.
7. Hold sessions in the morning if people are going to continue to work on the same problem after the session has ended, otherwise hold them late in the afternoon. (The excitement of a session continues for several hours after it is completed, and can affect an employee's routine tasks.)
8. Usually it is advisable not to have people from widely differing ranks within the organization in the same session.

FIG. 20.1 *Summary of rules and suggestions for group sessions (From Charles S. Whiting, "Operational Techniques of Creative Thinking,"* Advanced Management, *October 1955, p. 28. Reprinted by permission.)*

process. This is particularly true when one approaches it from the standpoint of problem solving. Some problems require the development of new ideas; a creative, innovative twist is needed. And any technique the manager can use in obtaining this creativity is a step in the right direction. To many managers this may seem like a giant request. Actually, we know that the average human being's creative ability is seldom fully tapped under normal working conditions. How can this situation be changed? The answer is found in these creative-thinking techniques. Firms that continually use them find that they are able to develop conditions for creativity within the firm itself. People do not feel restrained or confined by the usual barriers to problem solving, and the result is an ongoing flow of creativity throughout the organization.

7. In the creative-thinking process, what happens in the illumination stage?
8. What happens in the verification phase of the creative-thinking process?
9. How does brainstorming help stimulate creative thinking?
10. How does the Gordon technique differ from brainstorming?
11. Of what value is creative thinking to the decision-making process?

A Try at Innovation

Johnson Manufacturing had hoped to increase its industrial sales by 18 percent last year, but it in fact achieved barely half of this. A thorough analysis of the problem revealed the cause as being ineffective advertising. The advertising department agreed with this analysis, but confessed that it was at a loss as to why current ads were not having the desired effect.

After thinking the matter over for a couple of days, however, the vice-president of advertising decided to bring together all members of his department for a brainstorming session. His reasoning was simply that a new, innovative approach to advertising was needed. Before the meeting he sent around copies of the advertisements being run by the competition to provide a basis for comparing these successful ads with those the company was running. The vice-president suggested that everyone look them over and then try to identify what the major differences between these and their own ads might be.

When the meeting opened, he said,

> All right, ladies and gentlemen, you have all had a chance to examine our problem. Now I want you to tell me how we might change our ads so that they are more effective. I want you to come out with as many ideas as you can during this forty-minute session. Right now I am more interested in quantity than quality. I want you to feel free to be as creative or imaginative as you can. Also, if you want you can add on ideas to those of other

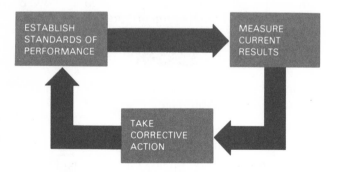

FIG. 20.2 *The control process*

THE CONTROL PROCESS

After decisions are implemented, there must be some form of follow-up to see that everything is going according to plan. We call this follow-up system the **control process.** The process consists of three steps: (a) establishing standards of performance, (b) measuring current results against these standards, and (c) taking corrective action. We can diagram these three steps as shown in Fig. 20.2. Note that in this figure the three steps operate in the form of a closed loop. After standards are set and results are measured, corrective action is taken. This then leads to the setting of new standards of performance. And so it goes, around and around this "closed loop." Now we will examine these three steps in greater depth.

people, or combine some of their suggestions to come up with a more complete idea. However, I do not want any criticism or cutting remarks. I want you to think only in terms of possible solutions to our problem.

When the forty minutes were over, the group had come up with over fifty ideas. Everyone seemed extremely excited about these suggestions. The vice-president then said, "Okay, now we have some ideas to work with. I want all of you to go back to your desks and, working either alone or in groups, formulate a basic ad to sell our industrial product line. We'll all meet here again in three days to examine the results and see if we can agree on a new ad campaign." With this the meeting adjourned.

1. What symptom would you expect of a problem such as ineffective advertising?

2. Which stage of the creative-thinking process do you think is most important in formulating a new, creative ad?

3. When the department again convenes with the new ads, what role will decision making play in solving the problem of ineffective advertising?

Establishing Standards

Standards for business are provided in the form of objectives. Some of the most common business objectives relate to profit, share of the market, and productivity.

Profit

Profit is simply the amount of money left after total expenses are deducted from total revenue. In the final analysis, profit spells the difference between a successful and unsuccessful business.

Share of the market

Share of the market refers to the number of units sold in relation to the entire market. For example, if a firm sells 10,000 units this year and there were a total of 250,000 units sold throughout the entire country, its market share can be computed as follows:

$$\frac{10,000}{250,000} = 4\%.$$

Many firms like to use share of the market rather than total sales as a standard because it forces them to compare themselves to the competition. For example, if a company increased its sales revenue from $50,000 to $75,000 in a given year, this might appear quite good. If every other firm in the industry tripled its sales, however, the company has really not done that well. By setting a share-of-the-market standard, the firm would realize this and could begin taking steps to recapture its market share.

Sir Lew Grade

Decision making and control are a matter of timing. And Sir Lew Grade has them both. A Jewish immigrant to Britain, he grew up on London's East end. He became a professional dancer and later one of Europe's most successful agents with clients including Jack Benny and Bob Hope.

In 1955 he made a momentous decision, collaring the commercial television franchise for the Birmingham area. Today his company, known as the Associated Television Network, controls an entertainment empire called Associated Communications Corporation. Its best known TV series is the internationally acclaimed and multi-award winning "The Muppet Show" featuring Jim Henson's famous Muppets and international guest stars. Major films include *The Boys from Brazil, The Muppet Movie, The Eagle Has Landed, The Return of the Pink Panther,* and *Raise the Titanic.* Besides TV and film production units, it runs a record company, a 14-theater chain, a music-publishing house that owns the rights to the Beatles' sheet music, a real estate firm, an insurance company, and a telephone-answering-device distributor.

However, Sir Grade (he was knighted by the queen) is best known for his decision making and control in the film-making industry. In fact, he has revolutionized the field with some previously unheard of tactics. Prime among these is the selling of film rights in lucrative markets all over the world *before* the film is ever made and distributed. This approach, widely used in Europe and Asia, allows him to sometimes collect up to 80 percent of the cost of a film before the first ticket is sold. Another Grade trademark is hiring big name stars and paying them a large sum of money for a relatively small amount of work. Throwing money away? Hardly. Grade believes that name stars like Sophia Loren, Charles Bronson, and Richard Burton help pack the movie theater and make his films financial successes. To date there are few who can argue with his business approach to film making. Of course some critics charge that his movies are memorable only because they are forgotten within minutes of the time the audience leaves the theater. However, Grade counters that the public likes his action films and that high salaries are justified. After all, he notes, "You can't get quality in a $3 million picture."

Best of all, however, he literally loves running his own show. "In Hollywood," he points out, "all the decisions are made by committees. I make the decision myself. If I read a book and love it, I say, 'Let's do it.' " His success to date shows that in an industry where decision making and control are key survival factors he truly understands the rules of the road.

Productivity

Productivity is measured by output/input. *Output* is the dollar volume or number of units produced. *Input* is the total cost of turning out these units as reflected in production and administrative expenses. By measuring output and input the firm can continually determine how efficiently it is operating. For example, if output goes up by 10 percent while input remains the same, productivity is increasing—the firm is getting more output for its input dollar. If the reverse is true, productivity is declining. In either event, it is possible to measure these factors of output and input and see how well the firm is doing.

In setting these standards the firm must balance current objectives with long-range goals. For example, it may be possible to obtain a profit this year of $150,000. However, this will require limiting salary raises to 2 percent and employee morale will drop. So too, therefore, will next year's productivity and profit. Meanwhile, if the firm gives 6-percent raises, which it feels are fairer, profits this year will be only $60,000 but employee morale will be high and performance next year will be good. Thus the company has a choice: extremely high profits this year and a big drop-off next year, or balanced profits both years. Since most firms have long-run objectives of survival and growth, they will select a balanced approach. In so doing they ensure that their short-run and long-run goals are in balance.

12. In what way is the control process like a "closed loop"?

13. How is share of the market computed?

14. If output increases and input remains the same, what happens to productivity?

15. Why is it important for a firm to balance its short-run and long-run objectives?

Measuring Results
The measurement of results involves collecting data on performance and comparing it to the previously established standards. Wherever possible these results should be quantifiable, thereby making it easier to compare them against the original objectives.

Techniques of effective measurement
Two of the most common methods used to measure results are financial statements and statistical techniques. **Financial statements** are prepared by accountants and provide information about a firm's operating performance and current holdings. From these financial data it is possible to obtain a great deal of insight into how well a company is doing. In particular, profits and losses can be determined and those areas in need of assistance can be ascertained. We will be looking at how this is done in Chapter 21, where accounting and financial information for control purposes is explained.

Statistical techniques are mathematical tools used to analyze quantitative data. With these techniques we can learn a great deal about the information under analysis. Common examples of such techniques include the computation of averages, trend lines, and correlations. More will be said about this in Chapter 22, where the use of statistics for control purposes is examined.

Characteristics of effective measurement
The measurement of results depends on more than the mere gathering of information. First, it is also important for the data to be *timely*. For example, if the firm is losing money on a particular product line, this should be known as soon as possible so the company can take immediate remedial action. Any delays in getting this information to management will mean increased financial losses for the firm.

Second, whenever deviations from standards are discovered, this information should be sent to the *proper authority*—in other words, the person who is authorized to take corrective action. Many firms fail to follow this procedure. Instead, the information is sent to some top executive and it takes weeks before the people who can act on the data actually receive the report. By now, of course, it may be too late to do anything except hurriedly try to correct the problem. Firms that have established effective control systems know who needs what type of information, and measurement results are immediately sent to the responsible person. From here the individual can quickly take the necessary action. Timeliness and the flow of control information to the proper authority are necessary characteristics of all control systems.

Taking Corrective Action

The taking of corrective action completes the control process. Without this step, nothing is done about deviations.

The big question in taking corrective action is: what specifically should be done? In answering this question it is necessary to examine the difference between symptoms and causes, and to realize the impact of personality on control.

Symptoms and causes

A **symptom** is the result of some problem. If an individual bumps his or her head, one of the common symptoms is swelling. Another is a headache.

CASE

Up, Up, and Away

Two months after initiating its new advertising program, Johnson Manufacturing found industrial sales going up. In fact, within ninety days orders were running 10 percent above expectations. By the end of four months, sales were up 42 percent over forecasts. At this time the president received a call from the vice-president of manufacturing.

The vice-president informed the president that she had been getting more and more orders for the firm's industrial products. However, while this was certainly good news for the sales department, it was creating a problem for manufacturing. The department had simply not been informed that the company was initiating a new industrial ad program, and had neither the parts nor the available machinery to meet these new orders. "At the present time," said the vice-president, "we are running 90 days behind on these orders. If the present rate continues we could be 120 days behind by the end of next month. We've got to do something about balancing sales and production. Unless I'm kept informed about ad programs, I have no way of knowing which product lines might be picking up and which will continue as before. As a result, everything in my department is getting out of control."

The president promised to call a meeting of marketing and production the following day. He also expressed concern that the vice-president had not been made aware of the new ad program and was not being sent the latest sales forecasts on product lines so that she could adjust her scheduling and production appropriately.

1. How would you define the problem in this case? Be specific.

2. At which step in the control process did things start to go wrong?

3. What recommendation would you make to the president to prevent a similar problem in the future?

Taking corrective action completes the control process.

The **cause,** of course, may be the fact that the person walked into something.

As we noted earlier in the chapter, when we discussed the steps in decision making, the symptom is the development that first attracts our attention to the problem. The cause is the factor responsible for the symptom. In a business setting, top management may be facing the fact that its sales forecast is 25 percent below expectations. This is a symptom. What is the cause? To answer this question an analysis of the problem area is necessary. The key question is: why are sales so low? Once this is determined, the necessary steps can be undertaken. Effective control is tied to overcoming causes!

Personality and control

In the final analysis, people control the organization. And since people have different personalities, they will do this in different ways. Some managers want to know about anything that goes wrong. They get so involved in petty details that they fail to spend enough time on major problem areas. Others are reluctant to hear bad news and tend to ignore these problem areas until it is too late. Managers with mature personalities try to put things into perspective. Minor problem areas are delegated to subordinates for action, while major problems are handled at their own level. If the situation is too complex or unwieldy for them to handle alone, support is sought from other organizational personnel. Corrective action is seen as a vital control step. As a result, it is given a high priority by the manager.

16. What takes place in the control process during the measuring of results?

17. How important is "timeliness" to an effective control system?

18. In what way does personality have an effect on control?

SUMMARY

Decision making is the process of choosing from among alternatives. This process consists of five steps: defining the problem, analyzing the situation, developing alternative solutions, selecting a course of action, and implementing the decision. All decisions are made under one of three possible conditions: certainty, risk, and uncertainty. Under certainty the manager knows the outcome of a particular decision before it it is made. Under risk the manager has some information about the outcome and can make predictions based on this knowledge. These predictions serve as a basis for setting objective and/or subjective probabilities. Under uncertainty the manager feels at a complete loss when it comes to assigning probabilities. Fortunately, however, mathematical techniques have been developed to help in this situation.

Yet decision making involves more than the mere use of quantitative methods. Subjective techniques such as creative thinking are also helpful. Creative thinking involves four steps: preparation, incubation, illumination, and verification. The creative-thinking process is often used by the individual working alone, although this need not always be the case. Groups can also employ creative thinking, as seen through the use of brainstorming and the Gordon technique.

The control process consists of three steps: establishing standards of performance, measuring current results against these standards, and taking corrective action. In this process objectives are compared to results for the purpose of correcting errors and then drawing up additional plans. One of the important characteristics of a control process is timeliness—errors or problem areas should be identified before they become critical. Furthermore, these deviations should be immediately reported to the individual charged with taking the proper action. If these things are done, the firm can implement a very effective control process.

KEY TERMS FOUND IN THIS CHAPTER

QUESTIONS FOR DISCUSSION AND ANALYSIS

1. What are the five steps in the decision-making process? Explain each.

2. How does an objective probability differ from a subjective probability?

3. What do we mean when we say that a manager is making a decision under uncertainty?

4. What is the first step in the creative-thinking process? Describe it.

5. How does the incubation stage of creative thinking differ from the illumination stage?

6. How does the control process work?

7. What are some of the common types of standards established by business for control purposes?

8. Why do we say that "effective control is tied to overcoming causes"?

To spend a dollar to protect 99 cents is not control. It is waste. "What is the minimum of control that will maintain the process?" is the right question to ask.
Peter Drucker

OBJECTIVES OF THIS CHAPTER

Business managers like to obtain quantitative feedback for the purpose of controlling their operations. They want to know exactly how well they are doing and where corrective action is needed. This is often accomplished through an analysis of the company's financial statements. The first objective of this chapter is to acquaint you with the two primary financial statements used by business firms: the balance sheet and the income statement. The second objective is to familiarize you with the types of ratios often used in analyzing these financial statements. By the time you are finished reading this chapter you should be able to do the following:

a. describe the major categories of a balance sheet;

b. explain the major components of an income statement; and

c. understand some of the most popular ratios used in analyzing balance sheets and income statements for control purposes.

Accounting
and Financial Control

ACCOUNTING AND THE CONTROL PROCESS

Every business must exercise some form of control over its operations. As illustrated in the previous chapter, this basic control process involves comparing actual performance to expected results in order to see how well the company has performed. This is then followed by the setting of new goals for the next time period. If the old objectives were attained, more ambitious ones can be set. If the old ones were not reached, lower performance targets can be established. To a large degree, an effective control process requires financial data. The firm wants to know *exactly* how much revenue it realized this year, what its profitable lines were, and what its unprofitable lines were. In arriving at quantitative answers to these questions, business relies heavily on its accountants and the information they furnish.

Accounting is the process of recording, classifying, summarizing, and interpreting financial information. With this information, management can better

"He's made himself indispensable. No one could figure out his system of keeping books in a million years."

Courtesy of Management Accounting, New York

control operations. In addition, accounting data are useful for record-keeping purposes, since the federal and state governments might want to examine the company's books at some time in the future to see if it has paid the proper amount of taxes. For these reasons accounting is very important to business.

FINANCIAL STATEMENTS

The two major financial statements used in providing accounting information to management, the government, the stockholders, and any other interested parties are the balance sheet and the income statement.

The Balance Sheet

The **balance sheet** is a financial statement used to display a firm's financial position at a specific point in time. This statement contains three major parts: (a) assets, (b) liabilities, and (c) owners' equity. **Assets** are those things the firm owns, such as machines, inventory, land, building, and cash. **Liabilities** are the firm's debts, such as money owed to creditors and taxes due the government. **Owners' equity** is the investment the owners have in the firm.

On a balance sheet, the assets are usually placed on the left side and the liabilities and owners' equity on the right, as follows:

Balance sheet

Assets	Liabilities
	Owners' equity

The reason for this division is that the total of the left side must *always* equal the total of the right side. This is known as the **balance sheet equation,** and can be stated in this way:

Assets = Liabilities + Owners' equity.

Any net change on one side of the equation will lead to a net change on the other. For example, if the

The Liability
of Accountants

The accountant's job is to record, classify, summarize, and interpret financial information. As such, this person is often in an excellent position to tell management where it is likely to have cash-flow problems, when its debt-equity ratio is too high, and whether it can afford to increase dividends by 10¢ per share. However, there are some things an accountant has trouble telling the management. One of these is when fraud is being committed.

Sometimes the accountant can examine the books and spot shortages immediately. Other times the thief is so clever that the accountant is unable to detect any irregularities.

For example, the accounting firm of Ernst & Ernst was sued by a group of Chicago investors. It seems that these individuals had invested more than $1 million over a period of twenty years in accounts they thought were providing backing for a small loan company. Actually the man in charge of the firm was pocketing the money and merely paying them yearly interest, ranging from 9 percent to 12 percent, on their invest-

ments. Ernst & Ernst certified the books of the company as being in proper order. When the loan company president committed suicide, however, he left behind a note admitting that the scheme was a fraud and the firm was bankrupt.

Were the auditors guilty of failing to spot fraud? Those arguing that they were said that the accountants should have uncovered the matter when they carried out their annual audit. Those who said the accountants were not guilty said that it is very difficult to spot fraud, and clues that seem so obvious once a fraud comes to light are often far less clear when the audit is being undertaken.

A Supreme Court ruling on the liability of public accounting firms has held that Ernst & Ernst was not guilty of negligence or liable for failing to spot the fraud. Many accountants welcomed the ruling, feeling that people expect too much from accounting firms. The lesson for businesspeople is that while accountants can help control financial operations, their value must not be overrated.

---

owner invested $50 more in the business, cash (assets) would go up on the left side and owners' equity on the right. If the company borrowed $5,000 to buy a new machine, assets (machinery) would increase on the left side and liabilities (accounts or notes payable) on the right.

The firm's balance sheet shows its assets, liabilities, and owners' equity as of a given point in time. Usually this is at the end of their fiscal year, which for most firms is December 31. Table 21.1 presents an illustration of a balance sheet for Johnson Manufacturing as of the end of its fiscal year. A quick look

TABLE 21.1 JOHNSON MANUFACTURING, INC., BALANCE SHEET (DECEMBER 31, 198–)

ASSETS				LIABILITIES AND OWNERS' EQUITY			
Current assets				**Current liabilities**			
Cash		$ 40,000		Accounts payable	$33,400		
Accounts receivable	$85,000			Notes payable	10,400		
Less: Allowance for				Accrued wages payable	19,500		
bad debts	5,000	80,000		Income taxes payable	60,700		
Notes receivable		15,000		Total current			
Inventory		105,000		liabilities		$124,000	
Total current assets			$240,000	**Long-term liabilities**			
Fixed assets				Mortgage payable	$36,000		
Machinery/equipment	$125,000			Notes payable	20,000		
Less: Accumulated				Long-term bonds			
depreciation	25,000	$100,000		outstanding	50,000		
				Total long-term			
Building	$ 60,000			liabilities		$106,000	
Less: Accumulated				Total liabilities			$230,000
depreciation	15,000	45,000		**Owners' equity**			
Land		55,000		Preferred stock	$ 10,000		
				Common stock	120,000		
				Retained earnings	80,000		
Total fixed assets			$200,000	Total owners' equity			210,000
				Total liabilities and			
Total assets			$440,000	owners' equity			$440,000

at this table shows that the financial statement is drawn up along the lines of the three major balance-sheet categories we just noted: assets, liabilities, and owners' equity. Within each of these there are various subcategories. The following discussion examines Table 21.1 in depth. A careful reading of this material should provide a good understanding of how the balance sheet is constructed and what is contained within it.

Assets

Assets, the economic resources the company owns, are usually classified into two categories: current assets and fixed assets.

Current assets. Current assets consist of cash and other resources that will be used or converted into cash within the next year. The most obvious of these, of course, is *cash* itself, which includes all the money the firm has in its checking and savings accounts. A second type of current asset is *accounts receivable*, which are all the debts owed the firm by customers. If any of these are judged uncollectible they are deducted under the heading of "allowance for bad debts." A third type of current asset is *notes receivable*, which are simply promissory notes from customers. A fourth current asset is *inventory*, which is the amount of money a firm has invested in raw materials, goods being currently processed, and finished goods waiting to be sold. Note that these current assets were discussed in the order presented in Table 21.1, which started with those assets that were cash or most easily converted to cash and continued on to less "liquid" assets. This is usually the format employed in listing current assets.

Fixed assets. Fixed assets consist of resources that will last for more than one year and are not intended to be sold; instead they are used in the operation of the business. One example is *machinery and equipment*. Whatever the firm paid for these assets is carried on the balance sheet less the *accumulated depreciation*. This is a term that refers to the decline in the book value of an asset due to wear and tear. For example, if a machine was purchased for $10,000 and has a useful life of five years, the company might depreciate it at the rate of $2,000 per year. The value after depreciation is carried on the balance sheet. The depreciation, meanwhile, is an expense that the government allows business to deduct from its sales revenue before calculating income taxes due. As a result, business gets back some of the money it invests in machinery and equipment through tax savings. A second fixed asset is the *building,* which is the structure in which the company does business. This too can be depreciated over its useful life. A third fixed asset is *land* that is purchased by the business. This asset is never depreciated because it is never really used up.

Office buildings and heavy machinery are common examples of fixed assets.

1. What is an asset? Put it in your own words.

2. How does a current asset differ from a fixed asset?

3. What is meant by the term accumulated depreciation?

Liabilities

Liabilities, or debts, are also usually divided into two categories: current liabilities and long-term liabilities.

Thomas L. Holton

When it is income tax time for most individuals, they either file their own return or have a friend help them out. However, business firms have much more complex returns and they need the advice of a professional accountant. In fact, all of the large corporations have public accounting firms go over their books, see that everything is in order, and provide them assistance in filing their tax returns and reporting their performance to the stockholders.

One of the largest, and most distinguished, public accounting firms is Peat, Marwick, Mitchell & Co. Thomas L. Holton is the Chairman and Chief Executive of the firm. After receiving his bachelor's and master's degrees in business at Baylor University, he went to work at the firm's San Antonio office and worked his way up to a managing partner. From here it was on to the Chicago office and then the executive office in New York City. And along the way he gathered both vital training and an impressive record. Some of the positions he has held include Chairman of Peat, Marwick's Auditing Procedures Committee and SEC Policy Committee and Chairman of the AICPA's Committee on SEC Regulations and the Committee on Auditing Procedures.

In late 1979 Mr. Holton was elected by the partners as Chief Executive of the firm, and many people in the field are delighted. They feel he brings an excellent reputation and dynamic personality to the job. And in an area like accounting, where integrity, honesty, and competence are of primary importance, they see the promotion as a big plus for both Mr. Holton and Peat, Marwick.

Current liabilities. Current liabilities are those obligations that will be due within the next year. The most common current liabilities are accounts payable, a term that refers to money owed by the firm to its suppliers and others who have extended credit. *Notes payable* usually consist of either promissory notes at the bank or current installments owed on long-term debt. For example, the company might have to pay $2,000 a year on a thirty-year, $60,000 mortgage. The $2,000 represents this year's installment, while the rest of the debt is considered a long-term liability. *Accrued wages payable* are those debts the firm has incurred for labor but has not yet paid. *Income taxes payable* are those debts owed to the government but not yet due. Business firms pay these taxes to the government on a quarterly basis and any taxes accrued during this period are considered "payable" until they are sent in to the Internal Revenue Service.

Long-term liabilities. Long-term liabilities consist of those debts that are not expected to be paid off during the next year. Common illustrations include (a) *mortgage payable,* which is the amount of money

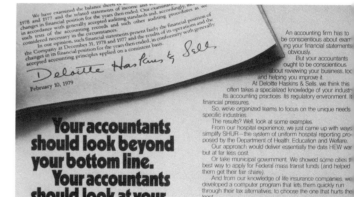

owed on land and buildings and is paid off a little each year; (b) *notes payable,* which are long-term debts owed to banks and other financial institutions; and (c) *long-term bonds outstanding,* which are bonds that have been issued by the company and are not due to be redeemed within the current year.

Owners' equity

Owners' equity often consists of three basic accounts. *Preferred stock* and *common stock* were discussed in Chapter 17 and you should be familiar with them. Whatever amounts of each the company sells would appear on the balance sheet under their respective entries. The third account, *retained earnings,* is a running total of the profits that have been earned and reinvested in the business.

The balance sheet can be very useful for controlling and decision-making purposes. In particular it reveals the solvency of a firm by showing a breakdown of all assets, liabilities, and owners' equity. Second, by comparing balance sheets from one year to the next, it is possible to measure how well the firm is performing over a given time period. It is also possible to make comparisons of these balance sheets with those of other firms on a year-by-year basis to see if the company is doing better, or more poorly, than the competition. Third, it provides the company with a financial statement that can be used by bankers and other lenders in determining the firm's credit worthiness. Fourth, it allows ratio analysis to be computed to pinpoint where the firm is doing well or poorly. We shall return to this area later in the chapter.

4. How does a current liability differ from a long-term liability?

5. What is meant by the term retained earnings?

6. Of what value is the balance sheet in the control process?

The Income Statement

The **income statement,** sometimes known as the profit-and-loss statement, presents a summary of the firm's operations over a period of time. An income statement for Johnson Manufacturing is presented in Table 21.2. This statement shows the change in the firm's position as a result of operations, as opposed to the balance sheet, which presents the firm's position at a particular point in time. The basic parts of an income statement include (a) revenues, (b) cost of goods sold, (c) expenses, and (d) net income. The following discussion explains these parts of the income statement using Table 21.2 as an illustration.

TABLE 21.2 JOHNSON MANUFACTURING, INC., INCOME STATEMENT FOR THE YEAR ENDED DECEMBER 31, 198–

Revenue from sales		
Gross sales	$1,410,000	
Less: Sales returns and allowances	10,000	
Net sales		$1,400,000
Cost of goods sold		
Beginning inventory	$ 130,000	
Purchases	975,000	
Total goods available for sale	$1,105,000	
Less: ending inventory	105,000	
Total cost of goods sold		1,000,000
Gross profit		$ 400,000
Expenses		
Selling expenses	$ 90,000	
Administrative expenses	110,000	
General expenses	60,000	
Total expenses		$ 260,000
Net income before taxes		$ 140,000
Federal income taxes		52,950
Net income		$ 87,050

Revenue from sales

The typical income statement begins with a listing of the revenue the firm has obtained from sales. This is often called **gross sales.** From this any merchandise that was returned is deducted. This figure is often called *sales returns and allowances.* The remainder is known as *net sales* and represents the total sales the firm made during that period.

Cost of goods sold

From sales revenue must be deducted the cost of the goods that were sold. This is usually done by determining the *beginning inventory* at the start of the period—these are the goods the firm had on hand from the start. To this are added all *purchases.* Then the *ending inventory* is subtracted. The remainder is the *total cost of goods sold.* When the total cost of goods sold is subtracted from net sales the firm obtains a *gross profit.* This is the "margin" between what it cost the firm to make the goods and the price for which the goods were sold.

Expenses

From the gross profit must be deducted all the expenses associated with selling the goods. These expenses fall into three categories: (a) selling, (b) administrative, and (c) general. **Selling expenses** are all the costs directly related to the product or service being sold—for example, commissions to sales people, advertising expenditures, and packaging costs. **Administrative expenses** are those costs incurred by the management and office personnel in running the company's operation. Management salaries, secretarial help, and office rent are examples. **General expenses** are those costs that are not charged to one department or unit because it is too difficult or time consuming to determine their proper allocation. Property taxes, insurance, and utilities, for example, are often grouped as general expenses on the income statement.

Net income

The final part of the income statement involves the computation of **net income.** This is done by sub-

tracting total expenses from gross profit to arrive at *net income before taxes.* The final step is to subtract *federal income taxes* to arrive at *net income.* In Table 21.2, taxable income is stated as $140,000. Using the current tax rate on corporations of 17 percent on the first $25,000, 22 percent on the second $25,000 and 48 percent on the remainder, we have the following calculations:

25,000	$25,000	$90,000
.17	.22	.48
175000	50000	720000
25000	50000	360000
$4,250.00	$5,500.00	$43,200.00

Together the three equal 52,950, leaving, as seen in Table 21.2, a net income of 87,050.

Like the balance sheet, the income statement can be a useful financial statement for control and decision-making purposes. First, the statement tells the firm if it is operating profitably or not. Second, by comparing income statements from one period to the next, the firm can see which expenses are rising too quickly and move to control them. Third, the statement allows bankers and other financial institutions to evaluate the credit worthiness of the business.

7. What are the four major parts of an income statement?

8. On the income statement, how is cost of goods sold computed?

9. Given the income tax data above, how much federal tax will a corporation pay on net income before taxes of $100,000?

10. Of what value is the income statement in the control process?

RATIO ANALYSIS OF FINANCIAL STATEMENTS

Preparing the balance sheet and income statement is only the first step in measuring a firm's performance and helping to control its operations. The

The New Machines

Johnson Manufacturing is thinking about selling $50,000 of common stock to raise money for new machinery. The firm believes that with this $50,000 it can increase sales by $200,000 a year and income before taxes by $20,000. The estimated life of the machinery is ten years and the firm intends to depreciate it at the rate of 10 percent a year for its useful life.

The top management at Johnson has examined the new stock proposal and given it their support. Now the proposal must go to the board of directors. One of the major questions the board is going to be concerned with is that of profitability. Will the new machinery really increase the firm's profit? A discussion with members of the board earlier this week revealed that they believe the company should be able to net at least $50,000 after taxes from this new machinery within the first five years. The firm's chief financial officer, the vice-president of finance, believes this objective can be attained. At the board meeting next week, it will be his job to present figures supporting his claim and then answer questions about them.

1. If the firm goes ahead with the sale of stock, what will be the accumulated depreciation on this machinery at the end of the first year? Fifth year? Tenth year?

2. How much will the company net after taxes from these new machines if it grosses $1,600,000 from all of its other operations?

3. Given the above answer, will the firm be able to net $50,000 after taxes from this new machinery within the first five years?

next phase requires using this information for evaluation purposes. Of course, a quick scanning of the two financial statements will tell us something about the company. We can see straight away whether or not the business made a profit, and we are able to determine the firm's cash balance at the end of the year. However, a closer and more in-depth look is necessary if management wants to spot problem areas before they become critical. One of the most popular methods of doing this is called **ratio analysis.** In this procedure items on the financial statements are compared to one another. A number of key ratios may be used as guidelines for monitoring business performance. Some of these deal with the balance sheet, some with the income statement, and others with items on both statements. The following examines key ratios in each of these three areas.

Balance-Sheet Ratios

In analyzing a balance sheet, there are some ratios that indicate the firm's current position, while others are more useful in evaluating the long-run position.

In analyzing a balance sheet, there are some ratios that indicate the firm's current position, while others are more useful in evaluating the long-run position.

In explaining these ratios we will again be working with the data provided in Tables 21.1 and 21.2.

Short-run position

The most common ratios used to measure a firm's current balance-sheet position are heavily concerned with the company's **liquidity.** This term refers to the ease with which an asset can be converted into cash. If a company has most of its assets in cash or "near cash" items, such as accounts receivable and government bonds, the firm is called "very liquid." If the company has most of its money tied up in assets that cannot be very easily converted to cash, such as inventory, it has a very low liquidity. The three most common measures of a firm's short-run position are (a) working capital, (b) the current ratio, and (c) the acid-test ratio.

Working capital. Working capital, which is not really a ratio but is widely employed as a measure of a firm's current fnincial position, is the excess of current assets over current liabilities. In Table 21.1, working capital would be computed in this way:

Total current assets	$240,000
Total current liabilities	124,000
Working capital	$116,000

This figure represents the capital the firm has available to carry on its day-to-day activities. By analyzing its prior needs and future plans the firm can determine for itself whether $116,000 is an adequate amount of working capital. If it is not, the company can negotiate a loan now rather than wait until it runs out of cash.

Current ratio. The **current ratio** is the ratio between current assets and current liabilities. For the Johnson Manufacturing firm in Table 21.1, the current ratio would be computed in this way:

$$\frac{\text{Total current assets}}{\text{Total current liabilities}} = \frac{\$240,000}{\$124,000} = 1.94 \text{ to } 1.$$

Because current assets are expected to be converted to cash sometime during the year and current liabilities are debts that will be coming due during this same period, the current ratio provides an indication of the firm's ability to meet its current liabilities. Is 1.94 to 1 a good ratio? The answer will depend on the industry. Utilities have a lower current ratio than manufacturing firms. For a typical utility, 1.0 to 1 is adequate. For most other kinds of firms, however, 2.0 to 1 or better is considered generally acceptable. Since Johnson Manufacturing has less than this, the management might be a little concerned. Since the ratio is almost 2.0 to 1, however, judgment should be withheld until the other liquidity ratio, the acid-test ratio, is computed.

Acid-test ratio. The **acid-test ratio,** also known as the *quick ratio,* is very similiar to the current ratio. However, it differs in one important way. The acid-test ratio compares only those assets that are "highly liquid"—such as cash and accounts receivable, notes receivable, and other assets easily converted into cash—against current liabilities; it does *not* include inventory because it will take a while to convert this asset into cash. For Johnson Manufacturing the acid-test ratio is calculated in this manner:

$$\frac{\text{Cash} + \text{Accounts receivable} + \text{Notes receivable}}{\text{Current liabilities}}$$

$$= \text{Acid-test ratio} = \frac{\$135{,}000}{\$124{,}000} = 1.09 \text{ to } 1.$$

A generally accepted acid-test ratio is 1 to 1, so the firm meets this guideline. As a result, the company should have no trouble paying its current liabilities.

Long-run position

Financial statement users are also interested in the long-run position of the firm. Three popular long-run position ratios are (a) the debt-asset ratio, (b) the equity-asset ratio, and (c) the debt-equity ratio.

Financial statement users are also interested in the long-run position of the firm.

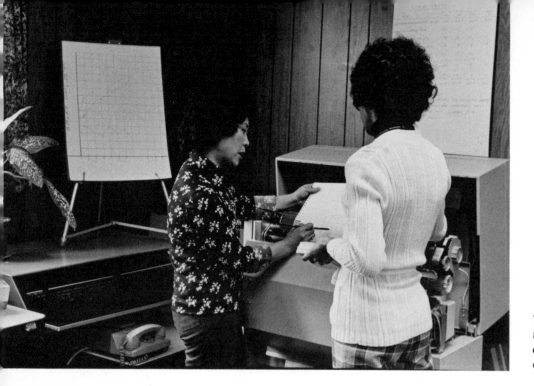

Three popular long-run position ratios are the debt-asset ratio, the equity-asset ratio, and the debt-equity ratio.

Debt-asset ratio. The **debt-asset ratio** expresses the relationship between the firm's total debt and total assets. For Johnson Manufacturing it is

$$\frac{\text{Total debt}}{\text{Total assets}} = \frac{\$230,000}{\$440,000} = 53\%.$$

This means that 53 percent of all assets were purchased with debt. This ratio is important to creditors for reasons of protection. In case of bankruptcy the firm will usually owe a great deal of money, but if the total owed is only a small percentage of all the assets, the chance of complete repayment is good. For Johnson Manufacturing 53 percent is probably high and creditors may be very reluctant to extend any more credit.

Equity-asset ratio. The **equity-asset ratio** is determined by dividing owners' equity by total assets. For Johnson Manufacturing it is

$$\frac{\text{Total equity}}{\text{Total assets}} = \frac{\$210,000}{\$440,000} = 47\%.$$

Owners are interested in this ratio because it indicates the percentage of assets on which they have a claim. Many individuals believe that the higher this ratio the better. This is not always true, because it is sometimes wiser to borrow money than to liquidate some ownership control by selling stock. Nevertheless, if the ratio of owners' equity to total assets is low, in case of liquidation there may be nothing left for the owners after the creditors are paid off.

Debt-equity ratio. The **debt-equity ratio** is calculated by dividing total debt by total equity. For Johnson Manufacturing it is

$$\frac{\text{Total debt}}{\text{Total owners' equity}} = \frac{\$230,000}{\$210,000} = 1.09 \text{ to } 1.$$

This indicates that more of the business is being financed by debt than by equity. This may not be the most advantageous approach to financing assets, for reasons explained above. As a result, it is likely that Johnson Manufacturing will try to lower its total debt and/or increase owners' equity over the next year in an effort to improve its financial picture.

11. What is meant by the term liquidity?

12. How is the current ratio of value to business for control purposes?

13. In what way does the acid-test or quick ratio differ from the current ratio?

14. Why would a business be interested in its debt-equity ratio?

Income-Statement Ratios

Income-statement ratios provide information on current operating performance and efficiency. Two of the most common are the (a) gross profit margin, and (b) net profit margin.

Gross profit margin

The **gross profit margin** is equal to gross profit over net sales. For Johnson Manufacturing it is

$$\frac{\text{Gross profit}}{\text{Net sales}} = \frac{\$400,000}{\$1,400,000} = 28.6\%.$$

This margin indicates the profit made on sales before deducting operating costs such as selling, administrative, and general expenses. By comparing the gross profit margin from year to year the firm can monitor the cost of goods sold and see that they do not get out of line.

Net profit margin

The **net profit margin** is equal to net income over net sales. For For Johnson Manufacturing it is

$$\frac{\text{Net income}}{\text{Net sales}} = \frac{\$7,050}{\$1,400,000} = 6.2\%.$$

The net profit margin shows the overall profitability of the company. By comparing this 6.2 percent mar-

gin with that of the last four to five years, the firm can obtain a trend line to see if profitability is improving or declining.

15. Which is more important, the gross profit margin or the net profit margin? Explain.

Combined Ratios

Some ratios show the relationship between items on the balance sheet and items on the income statement. Four of the most popular are the (a) inventory turnover, (b) accounts receivable turnover, (c) return on assets, and (d) return on owners' equity.

Inventory turnover

Inventory turnover refers to the number of times inventory is replaced during the year. Inventory that sits on the shelf and does not sell costs the firm money in the form of store space and possible obsolescence—to say nothing of the money the company has tied up in the purchase of the goods, money that could have been invested in something more profitable. Therefore, the business wants a good turnover.

Inventory turnover is computed by dividing cost of goods sold during the year by average inventory. *Average inventory* is equal to the amount of inventory on hand at the beginning of the year added to the amount on hand at the end of the year, divided by two. For Johnson Manufacturing, inventory turnover is computed in this way:

$$\frac{\text{Average}}{\text{inventory}} = \frac{\text{Beginning inventory} + \text{Ending inventory}}{2}$$

$$= \frac{\$130,000 + 105,000}{2} = \$117,500;$$

$$\frac{\text{Cost of goods sold}}{\text{Average inventory}} = \frac{\$1,000,000}{\$117,500} = 8.5 \text{ turns.}$$

Johnson is turning its inventory over 8.5 times a year. If we wanted to determine the average number of days inventory was on hand before being sold we could divide 8.5 into 365, the number of days in a year:

$$\frac{365 \text{ (days in a year)}}{8.5 \text{ (inventory turnover)}} = 43 \begin{array}{l}\text{(average number of}\\\text{days to turnover).}\end{array}$$

In order to determine whether 8.5 was a good inventory, we would have to find out what competitive firms were doing. If their turnover was 4.7, Johnson's 8.5 would be very good. If their turnover was 12.5, this would indicate that Johnson was not

"The controller is figuring out what the annual forecast should be."

Courtesy of Management Accounting, New York

doing as well and should take some steps to improve turnover. Dropping slow-moving lines and increasing credit sales to customers are some steps that might be taken.

Accounts receivable turnover

Accounts receivable turnover measures how quickly accounts receivable are being collected. If this turnover is small, it indicates that people are paying their bills very slowly. If it is very high, people are paying very quickly.

Accounts receivable turnover is computed by dividing net sales by average accounts receivable. In Table 20.1 there was no information given for beginning accounts receivable. However, if we assume that the beginning and ending accounts receivable were both the same, $80,000, then the calculation for determining accounts receivable turnover is

$$\frac{\text{Net sales}}{\text{Average accounts receivable}} = \frac{\$1,400,000}{\$80,000}$$
$$= 17.5 \text{ times.}$$

Going still further, we can determine the average number of days these accounts were outstanding by dividing the turnover into 365. That is

$$\frac{365 \text{ (days in a year)}}{17.5 \text{ (accounts receivable turnover)}} = 21 \begin{array}{l}\text{(average days}\\\text{receivables are}\\\text{outstanding).}\end{array}$$

If this firm is selling goods on terms of 2/10, n30, they are doing very well indeed. Those not taking the discount are still paying promptly. Of course, there may be some who are delinquent in their payments, but on average the firm is collecting its receivables every 21 days.

Return on assets

Return on assets is the ratio between profit and assets. For Johnson Manufacturing this is

$$\frac{\text{Net income}}{\text{Total assets}} = \frac{\$87,050}{\$440,000} = 19.8\%.$$

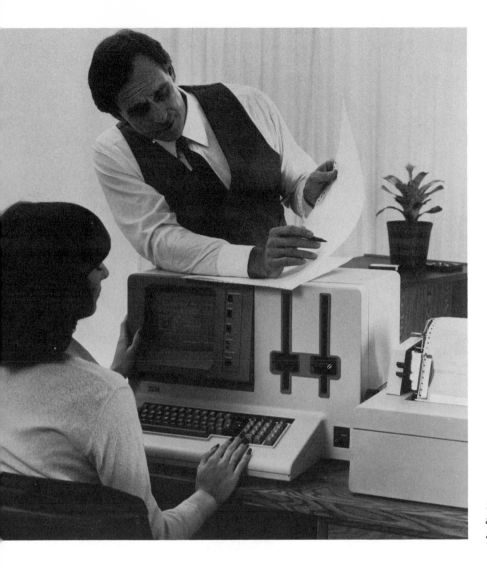

Return on assets measures how well a firm is doing with the assets available to it.

Return on assets, often referred to as *return on investment,* measures how well the company has performed with all of its assets. Some individuals believe that all a business should concern itself about is net income. However, if two firms each made $1 million net profit but one had total assets of $10 million while the other had assets of $100 million, the former has done much better than the latter.

Thus return on assets measures how well a firm is doing with the assets available to it. The greater the amount of assets, the more profit the firm should make. For a firm like Johnson, 19.8 percent is good.

Return on owners' investment
Another common ratio for measuring how well a firm is doing is the **return on owner's investment**

ratio. This is simply the relationship between net income and owners' equity. For Johnson Manufacturing it is

$$\frac{\text{Net income}}{\text{Total owners' equity}} = \frac{\$89,050}{\$210,000} = 41.4\%.$$

This is the amount of money earned for each dollar invested by the owners. Johnson has performed very well. It would not be possible to obtain a 41.4-percent return on our money if invested in a bank or government note. The investors have done very well this year.

Keep in mind that while this is the return on the owners' investment (ROOI), it is not the amount of money the owners will be receiving in dividends. Dividends may be $1.00 per share, with the remainder of the net income reinvested in the firm. If the company continues to average 41.4 percent over the next five years, however, these dividends will undoubtedly go up and the owners will start to realize a greater return on their investment. For the

---

CASE

The Proposed Credit Policy Change

The credit manager at Johnson Manufacturing has recently proposed a liberalizing of the firm's credit policies. His reasoning is that the change will lead to increases in sales, inventory turnover, and profit.

The firm's vice-president of finance opposes any such move. He believes that a liberalization of current credit policies will have a negative effect on the firm's profit. Put very simply, the vice-president feels that by lowering its credit standards the company will be selling to people who are poorer risks. This will increase the amount of uncollectible receivables, thereby reducing overall net profit. The result will be a decline in both return on assets and return on owners' investment. What we must remember," he recently told the board of directors, "is that all of these key financial ratios are interrelated. A drop in one of them can affect others."

The top management has promised to look into the matter and decide whether or not to change the current credit policy. A decision is expected in the near future.

1. If credit is liberalized, what will happen to inventory turnover?

2. If sales go up but accounts receivable turnover declines, how will this affect the firm's liquidity?

3. If sales were to go up by 10 percent but the net profit margin drop by 2 percent with the new credit policy, would you favor changing the current credit policy? Explain.

moment, ROOI is simply a gauge of how well the firm is performing with the money invested by the owners.

Industry Comparisons

The ratios we have just examined are those often used by business firms to measure performance. In and of themselves they provide only some of the information needed for control purposes, but they are useful in allowing firms to plot trends and see if they are doing better or more poorly than they have over the last few years. However, a word of caution is in order. All of these ratios must be compared to those of *comparable* firms. By this we mean that the return on assets of a particular business is only "good" or "bad" depending upon how similar firms of the same size and in the same industry are doing. If Ford Motor has a 15-percent return on assets this year, then General Motors should have something similar. A business can only judge its effectiveness on the basis of how well it is doing in relation to similar companies.

Industry ratios for all of the computations we have studied in this section are available in business and government reports. Table 21.3 presents a summary of return on owners' investment for selected industries. From these, companies can compare their results with those of the average firm in the industry. They can then take any necessary steps to control their operations by monitoring balance-sheet and income-statement accounts.

16. How is inventory turnover computed? What does it tell the manager?

17. Which is more important, a high inventory turnover or a high accounts receivable turnover?

18. What do we mean when we say that financial ratios must be compared to those of comparable firms?

"I've prepared this simple chart to give you a clear picture of our financial situation."

TABLE 21.3 RETURN ON OWNERS' INVESTMENT IN SELECTED INDUSTRIES IN 1978

INDUSTRY	PERCENTAGE
Broadcasting, motion-picture production and distribution	33.34%
Aerospace	28.22
Office equipment (includes computers)	20.87
Publishing, printing	20.39
Tobacco	17.09
Pharmaceuticals	12.31
Industrial and farm equipment	12.18
Petroleum refining	11.72
Motor vehicles	7.88
Soaps, cosmetics	5.33
Shipbuilding, railroad and transportation equipment	4.61
Food	3.24
Electronics, appliances	2.87
Mining, crude-oil production	1.67
Beverages	−4.39
Musical instruments, toys, sporting goods	−8.75
All industry composite	7.16%

Source: *Fortune*, May 7, 1979, p. 290.

SUMMARY

In controlling their operations business managers need to obtain feedback on how operations are progressing. One of the most popular ways of obtaining this feedback is from an analysis of the balance sheet and income statement. The balance sheet consists of three major parts: assets, liabilities, and owners' equity. Assets are economic resources the firm owns. Liabilities are the debts of the organization. Owners' equity is the investments the owners have in the firm. The reason this financial statement is referred to as a balance sheet is that assets *always* equal liabilities plus owners' equity.

The income statement presents a summary of the firm's operations over a period of time, usually one year. The income statement shows the change in a firm's position as a result of operations and contains four basic parts: revenues, cost of goods sold, expenses, and net income.

In analyzing these financial statements for control purposes many firms make use of ratio analysis. Some of the popular balance-sheet ratios include working capital, current ratio, acid-test ratio, debt-asset ratio, equity-asset ratio, and debt-equity ratio. With the income statement some of the most widely used include the gross profit margin and net profit margin. Meanwhile, some of the popular combined ratios, using items on both the balance sheet and the income statements, include inventory turnover, accounts receivable turnover, return on assets, and return on owners' investment. These ratios are all widely employed by business firms to measure performance. However, it is important to remember that they are useful only when compared to those of similar firms. If they are used in this way, they can be very valuable in helping a firm control its operations.

KEY TERMS FOUND IN THIS CHAPTER

QUESTIONS FOR DISCUSSION AND ANALYSIS

1. What is meant by the term accounting?

2. What is the balance-sheet equation? Put it in your own words.

3. Why do business firms depreciate a fixed asset such as a building but not land, another fixed asset?

4. How do selling expenses differ from general expenses?

5. How is a firm's working capital calculated?

6. Of what value is the debt-asset ratio for control purposes?

7. If the average time a firm's receivables are outstanding increased from twenty days to forty days, would this be good or bad?

8. What does the return on owner's investment ratio measure? Explain.

22

Do not put your faith in statistics until you have carefully considered what they do not say.

William W. Watt

OBJECTIVES OF THIS CHAPTER

In the last chapter we examined financial data that can be used for control purposes. Once we start getting into a systematic analysis of quantifiable business data, we enter the realm of business statistics, which is the systematic collection, presentation, and interpretation of data related to business problems.

Business statistics covers a broader field than accounting. The accountant is interested in the fact that the company made $1,000,000 in sales last year. The statistician, however, is also interested in who the customers were, where they live, and how they pay their bills, and thus is able to delve into problem areas in much greater depth. The goal of this chapter is to examine what statistics is all about and how it can be of value to business. We will study the four major areas of business statistics: (a) collecting, (b) analyzing, (c) presenting, and (d) interpreting data in the solution of business problems. By the end of this chapter you should be able to do the following:

a. define the term business statistics;

b. describe the difference between primary and secondary data;

c. explain why firms use sampling in the collection of primary data;

d. relate some of the common statistical methods used in analyzing data, including averages, index numbers, correlations, and time series;

e. identify ways of presenting statistical data; and

f. recognize the pitfalls involved in the interpretation of statistical information.

Statistics
for Control Purposes

DATA COLLECTION

In order to control operations, a business must first decide the types of information it will need. A manufacturing firm, for example, will be interested in knowing when to undertake preventive maintenance of its machines. The company knows it is cheaper to fix machinery before it breaks down; but to make repairs before they are needed can be very costly. As a result, business firms keep records on the dates each machine broke down and what went wrong each time. Management can then use this information to estimate when a machine is likely to break down again. In this way repairs can be made at the appropriate time. This, of course, is possible only because the firm has collected data on machine performance. Without such information the company would be unable to set up an effective cost-saving, preventive maintenance program.

At other times the business will need data that can be found in the library or in government reports. Statistics related to population growth, average income per person in the United States last year, or the latest consumer price index are all illustrations. When the firm gathers original information, it is known as **primary data.** When the information is already published and available for use, it is known as **secondary data.** Both types can be important for control purposes.

Primary Data

The most common form of primary data is *internal records*. By consulting its business records, a firm can obtain many valuable insights into its own operations. For example, a company might want to know in which section of the country the majority of its customers are located. It can secure this information by adding up sales in each major geographic area. Suppose the data reveal the following:

Area	Sales	Overall percentage
East	$2,500,000	50
South	750,000	15
Midwest	750,000	15
West	1,000,000	20

This statistical breakdown shows that the company's major sales are in the east. In controlling operations, therefore, primary attention should be devoted to this area. Much important information of this nature can be obtained from internal sources.

Sometimes, however, the company will want information from outside sources. For example, a firm that sells auto tires might want to know what its customers like and dislike about the product's performance. Using retail sales records, the business will call on some of these customers and ask them about the tires. The three most common methods of gathering external primary data are (a) mail surveys such as questionnaires, (b) personal interviews in which the interviewer records the customer's answers, and (c) telephone calls in which the caller writes down the customer's responses. If conducted properly, methods such as these can provide a business with a great deal of information about its products. For example, one tire manufacturer recently conducted a program that combined mail surveys and personal interviews to find out if its tires were as smooth riding as it believed them to be. The biggest complaint the firm received was from people who said they continually got rocks in the tire treads and wished the firm could do something about it. Further investigation revealed that the public's image of the firm's product was one of a rugged, long-wearing tire. As a result, farmers, ranchers, and truckers were buying them for use on gravel roads and out-of-the-way places! Given this information, the company changed its commercials so that they emphasized the durability and strength of the tires rather than their smooth ride. Sales began to climb almost immediately. Research was also undertaken into designing a tire tread that better met the needs of the customers.

The importance of sampling

Before concluding our discussion of primary data, it is important to point out that when a business decides to survey its customers or gather information from the general public, it will often poll only a percentage of the group because to try to survey every one of them would be too difficult and expensive. This process is known as **sampling.**

The theory behind sampling is that a small group can give responses that are representative of the whole. For example, 500 customers, if properly polled, could give replies that would be consistent with those of all 50,000 customers. Of course, to be sure that these 500 do indeed represent the entire group, it would be necessary to use **random sampling.** By this we mean that everyone in the group of 50,000 has an *equal chance* of being chosen as a member of the sample. One way of doing this would be to take the list of 50,000 customers, put each name on a card, put the cards in a giant fishbowl, mix them up, and then draw out 500 names. Statisticians would use much simpler, and specially devised, methods for obtaining a random sample, but the basic idea would be the same.

Most sampling carried out by business firms is **controlled sampling** in that the individuals who are contacted are representative of a larger group about whom information is wanted. For example, if a firm wants to know whether or not customers like the new line of shirts it is carrying, it will not want a random sample of the entire group of customers because not all of them buy, or are interested in, the new line. As a result, the statistician will want to reduce the list of customers to those who have an interest in this product and then poll a random sample of these people.

In order for a business to sample its customers and get a true reading of their opinions or desires, people skilled in the use of controlled sampling must be conducting the research. Some companies, especially large ones, have their own statistical staff gather the data, and over time these people will develop very effective sampling methods. The average firm, however, does not have such an expert staff available. Therefore, it will hire an outside agency to determine the sample. There are many private companies that do this, two of the best known being the Louis Harris and George Gallup firms, which conduct political polls. Using sophisticated statistical techniques, these companies make

"Do you realize that choice puts you in the 2% lunatic fringe?"

From The Wall Street Journal; permission Cartoon Features Syndicate

predictions about how the public will vote on given issues. They also poll people about how they feel on various issues from inflation to unemployment. In recent years their polls have proven to be very accurate, illustrating that sampling can be a highly valuable tool in gathering primary data for both general and business use.

Secondary Data

Secondary data are available in many forms. Some of the information is published by the government; other data can be found in newspapers and trade journals.

The U.S. Department of Commerce is one of the major sources of secondary data for business. This department publishes monthly information on the economy in its *Survey of Current Business* as well as the *Small Business Management* series. Another government department that provides important statistical information is the Bureau of the Census. This bureau issues the *Statistical Abstract of the*

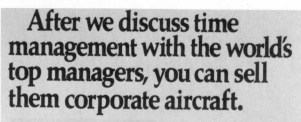

United States, which contains all types of general information data. It is also responsible for the Census of Manufacturers, which provides information on numerous types of industries, and the Census of Business, which classfies the channels of distribution on a geographic basis. A third important government department is the Bureau of Labor Statistics of the Department of Labor. This agency issues the *Monthly Labor Review,* which provides data on wages, employment, and price levels.

Nongovernment sources include publications issued by newspapers, magazines, trade journals, and institutions. The *Wall Street Journal* is an excellent source of secondary data, as is the business section of the *New York Times.* Magazines such as *Fortune, Forbes,* and *Business Week* also provide valuable business information, as do industry publications such as *Air Transportation* and the *Oil and Gas Journal.* Meanwhile, private agencies such as Dun and Bradstreet, Inc., and Moody's Investor Service publish secondary data that are very useful for those seeking financial information on other businesses. Institutional publications are issued by many different groups, including the National Industrial Conference Board, the Brookings Institution, and just about every major university. These publications provide a wide continuum of information ranging from the economic to the human side of enterprise. Because of the large amount of secondary data available to business firms, most will attempt to exhaust these sources before turning to the collection of primary data. Yet regardless of how it is collected, the next step is that of analyzing the information.

DATA ANALYSIS

Analysis of the data can be quite a chore if a great amount of information has been gathered. Calculators and computers may be needed to summarize all of the material. Once the data have been processed into usable summaries or tables, however, measurement and analysis can be undertaken. In addition to ratios and percentages, which we examined in the last chapter, other common methods of data analysis include (a) averages, (b) index numbers, (c) correlations, and (d) time series. We will now examine each of these in more detail.

1. In what way is business statistics a broader field than accounting?

2. How do primary data differ from secondary data?

3. What is meant by the term controlled sampling?

4. How useful are secondary sources in helping a firm gather data? What are some of the major government and nongovernment publications?

Averages

The word average has many different meanings. When we say an employee does an average amount of work, we mean one thing. When we talk about a baseball player's batting average, we mean something else. In statistical terms, the word *average* refers to *measures of central tendency*. It deals with values that are in the middle of the group. The three measures used most often are the (a) mean, (b) median, and (c) mode. Each provides a picture of

central tendency and, depending on what the company would like to know, can prove very useful.

Mean

The **mean** or **arithmetic average** is the most commonly used type of average. If a company is considering the sale of a particular product, it might be interested in learning the average price being charged by other firms. To calculate the mean price, the company would have to first list the prices charged by each firm. Some firms will charge the same price, of course, so the company will have to include a **frequency distribution** in the calculation of the arithmetic mean. Table 22.1 provides an illustration of how this can be done. By dividing the total points by the number of firms, the mean is obtained: $793 \div 80 = \$9.91$. If the company is interested in maintaining an average price for this product, it will price at $9.91.

TABLE 22.1 CALCULATION OF THE MEAN

PRICE	NUMBER OF FIRMS (FREQUENCY DISTRIBUTION)	TOTAL POINTS
$10.90	4	43.60
10.75	6	64.50
10.50	7	73.50
10.25	10	102.50
10.00	9	90.00
9.95	12	119.40
9.75	6	58.50
9.50	10	95.00
9.25	8	74.00
9.00	8	72.00
	80	793.00

Median

The **median** is the number that divides the group in half. Table 22.1 shows eighty firms. The median, therefore, is the price charged by the fortieth and forty-first firms, because there is no one firm in the middle of an even-numbered array. In this case both firms are charging the same price, so the median is $9.95. If one were charging $10 and the other $9.80, however, we would then have had to average the two, arriving at a median of $9.90. As you can see from these data, the mean and the median are not always the same. Yet both help measure central tendency. If the firm wanted to price its product exactly in the middle of all other prices, it would opt for the median.

Mode

The **mode** is that number that occurs most frequently in a distribution. In Table 22.1 it is $9.95; more firms are charging this price than any other. If a company wants to follow the leader and charge what most other businesses do, it will opt for the mode.

Which is best? Having now reviewed what is meant by mean, median, and mode, we must attempt to decide which of the three methods is the best one to use. Our answer must depend on the needs of the firm. Keep in mind that *all* provide some measurement of central tendency—each tells us something about what the other firms, on average, are doing. From here it is a matter of whether the company wants to price on the average (mean), in the middle of competition (median), or with those charging the most common price (mode). As a result, the statistician will find out what the company wants to do and then compare it to the data to arrive at a decision about how well the firm is actually doing. Any one, or more, of these three averages can be helpful in this undertaking.

Index Numbers

An **index number** is a tool for measuring the change that occurs in a group of related items over a specific period of time. Index numbers are widely used by business firms because they provide a basis for ex-

Joseph P. Kennedy

For many people statistics are just a bunch of numbers that have no real meaning. The daily stock-market reports are an illustration. However, for Joseph P. Kennedy these numbers had a great deal of relevance.

Born in Boston in 1888 to middle-income parents, Kennedy's rise in the financial world was spectacular. He enjoyed making money and he was good at it. His early successes came in the stock market, where he made millions speculating in all sorts of securities. He seemed to have a sixth sense when it came to predicting the trend of the market. Thus while he made a fortune during the 1920s, he realized that the market was overpriced and foresaw the giant crash of 1929. When it came, Kennedy was largely out of the market. "Only a fool holds out for the top dollar," he said at the time. And as the market plunged even lower, he made more money by selling stock short and repurchasing it at lower prices.

After World War II Kennedy turned his interests to real estate. His successes were dramatic. For example, he purchased one property in New York City for $600,000 that he sold for $3,970,000; a second for $1.7 million that he sold for $4,975,000; and a third for $1.9 million that he sold for $5.5 million. And he mortgaged each property to the hilt, thereby freeing up his purchase cash for investments in ventures such as oil, which gave depletion allowances for tax purposes.

Today business statistics is still a difficult area to understand. For many, playing the stock market or buying real estate is, at best, a gamble. For Joseph Kennedy, however, it was a science that could be mastered through hard work—and maybe a little luck.

amining the rise and fall of such things as wholesale prices, consumer prices, and stock prices. Of these, the one that probably receives the greatest amount of attention is the **consumer price index.** This index, which is issued monthly by the Bureau of Labor Statistics of the Department of Labor, measures changes in the retail prices of goods and services purchased by the average family. The index is expressed as a percentage of a base year. For example, Table 22.2 contains a list of average consumer price indexes for seven important commodities. The *base year* in this table is 1967, meaning that all price increases from 1970 to June 1978 are shown in relation to 1967. A look at the June 1978 statistics reveals that food prices increased 92.2 percent in this 11-year period, while apparel and upkeep rose 54.2 percent and the cost of housing 82.6 percent.

TABLE 22.2 CONSUMER PRICE INDEX BY GROUPS (1967 = 100)

COMMODITY	1970	1974	1978*
Food	114.9	161.7	192.2
Apparel and upkeep	116.1	136.2	154.2
Housing	112.9	150.6	182.6
Transportation	112.7	137.7	172.2
Medical care	120.6	150.5	202.4
Personal care	113.2	137.3	170.9
Reading and recreation	113.4	133.8	157.9

* As of June 1978.

Source: Bureau of Labor Statistics.

In determining changes in the *overall* consumer price index, the Bureau of Labor Statistics analyzes over four hundred commodities. In order to illustrate how this is done, we will take just four items—gasoline, eggs, bread, and milk—and show how the consumer price index would be calculated. First we must choose a **base,** or beginning, **year** and compare prices for the commodities then with prices for these same goods today. For purposes of the illustration we shall assume that the average family uses, on a weekly basis, ten gallons of gasoline, one dozen

eggs, two loaves of bread, and four gallons of milk. Converting these to annual expenditures and then comparing the totals of the base year with those of the current year, as shown in Table 22.3, gives us the change in the consumer price index.

TABLE 22.3 CALCULATING A CONSUMER PRICE INDEX USING FOUR BASIC COMMODITIES

BASIC COMMODITIES	BASE YEAR		CURRENT YEAR*	
	PRICE PER UNIT	TOTAL	PRICE PER UNIT	TOTAL
520 gallons of gas	$0.35	$182.00	$1.10	$ 572.00
52 dozen eggs	.60	31.20	1.00	52.00
104 loaves of bread	.34	35.36	.75	78.00
208 gallons of milk	1.10	228.80	2.00	416.00
		$477.36		$1,118.00

Index number: $ 477.36 = 100.0
$1,118.00 = 234.2

* The calculation for the index number of the current year is arrived at by taking the increase of the price of these commodities from the base to the current year, which is $640.64 ($1,118 − 477.36), and dividing it by the total amount paid for these same goods in the base year ($477.36) to arrive at a net increase of 134.2 percent ($640.64/477.36). Since the base year index number is 100.0, the current year index number is 234.2.

Although the total consumer price index is of course dependent on more than just the four commodities shown in Table 22.3, the basic calculation used is the same. Business firms like to use index numbers because they provide a quick way to measure percentage changes that have occurred between two periods of time.

5. How does the mean differ from the median?

6. Why do we say that the mean, median, and mode are all measures of central tendency?

7. How can the use of index numbers be of value in analyzing data?

Correlations

A **correlation** is a statistical term that refers to the degree of relationship that exists between two variables. For example, if a business firm invests $5,000 in advertising and this leads to an increase in sales of $10,000, there is a positive relationship between advertising and sales. Many companies that advertise attempt to determine the kind of relationship that exists between these two factors. How much of a sales increase can be obtained if advertising is increased from $5,000 to $10,000? What about from $5,000 to $25,000? By studying the correlation between these two factors a company can sometimes determine at what level of advertising it is obtaining maximum return on its investment.

This concept of correlation is useful in many ways. One of the most important is in forecasting changes in the economy. If we knew what was going to happen to business conditions over the next year, we would know whether to expand or contract our operations. For example, if the price of raw materials is going to double we could buy large quantities of these materials now and store them, thereby saving ourselves a great deal of money later on. Conversely, if the demand for one of our product lines is going to drop off dramatically, we could stop manufacturing that product now and avoid being caught with a lot of unsalable merchandise.

While it is impossible to answer such futuristic questions today, it is fortunate for business that much information is available about the factors that affect general economic conditions. And this data can be obtained from many sources, including the federal government. For example, the Bureau of the Census publishes a monthly report related to such important economic areas as prices, production, and labor. And the Department of Commerce publishes data on all sorts of information from staff-hours worked to business failures. Companies are continually analyzing such data to see if there are any correlations between these statistics and what is happening to their own individual companies. On an overall economic basis, business forecasters tend to put a great deal of faith in **lead indicators.** These are economic series or data that seem to indicate the direction in which the economy is moving. One of these is housing starts—if the number of new houses increases this is considered a positive sign. Other lead indicators for an upturn in the economy include increases in machine tool orders, increases in the number of hours worked per week, increases in common-stock prices, and new business formations. The **lag indicators,** which turn down after the economy starts to dip, include factors such as the unemployment rate, manufacturers' inventories, and bank rates on short-term loans.

Of course, this information will provide the firm with only a general idea of what is happening in the overall economy. However, by studying specific changes it is possible for the company to determine the net effect on their operations. For example, if net income after taxes for the average family increases, there is more money available for spending. The auto firms view this as a good development for they see a positive correlation between net income and car sales. Gasoline firms see a positive correlation between increased auto registrations and the demand for gasoline, for after all, people are going to have to buy fuel for their cars. And so it goes, with business firms trying to establish correlations among all sorts of statistical data for the purpose of planning and controlling their operations.

8. When analyzing data, why would a firm be interested in establishing correlations?

9. If a firm was trying to forecast economic conditions for the next couple of years, how could lead indicators be of value?

Time Series

Statistical data are often used to help a business identify how well it has done in the past. Comparing company sales and increases in share of the market to comparable figures for the competition are some ways of doing this. However, the firm needs information not only on past performance, but also on what the future holds. This is often obtained through a statistical analysis of three important types of economic conditions: (a) seasonal variations, (b) cyclical fluctuations, and (c) secular trends.

Seasonal variations

Seasonal variations are recurring economic fluctuations that tend to last only a short period of time. They are perhaps best illustrated by the month-to-month sales fluctuations of retail firms. A typical department store, for example, will find sales increasing sharply just prior to holidays such as Easter, Thanksgiving, and Christmas. At these times it is customary to find people buying merchandise to give as gifts. Immediately after most of these holidays, however, sales tend to drop off. As a result the store will have some months when sales are high and others when sales are low. And these peaks and troughs tend to occur at the same time, year after year.

Another illustration is found among new-car dealers (see Fig. 22.1). When the new autos first come out in October, sales usually go up. Then there is a slump from January to around May. However, with the warm weather of spring, sales again tend to pick up. Thus like those of the department store, the new-car dealer's sales will fluctuate depending on the month or season of the year. Most firms face seasonal variations and tend to meet them by adjusting their inventories appropriately, stocking up for peak periods and carrying little merchandise during slack periods.

Cyclical fluctuations

While seasonal variations tend to occur on an annual basis, **cyclical fluctuations** are economic variations that take place over a longer period of time. Sometimes these cycles last five to ten years, and they do not follow as predictable a pattern as do seasonal variations. Yet these cyclical variations are

PERCENTAGE OF SALES PER MONTH

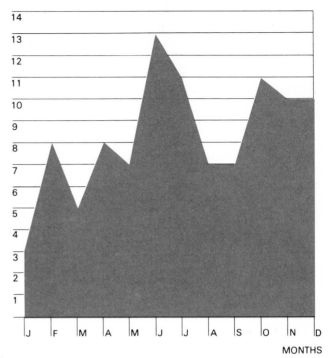

MONTHS

FIG. 22.1 *Typical auto sales on a monthly basis (Source: Paus Motor Sales, courtesy of Steven Paus.)*

well known to us because we hear so much about them in the news. There are four identifiable periods in all: (a) prosperity, (b) recession, (c) depression, and (d) recovery.

Prosperity is the cycle when the economy is moving upward. Sales are up, production is rising, wages are high, profits are good, and funds for expansion are available. When the economy starts to slip, however, the result is **recession.** During this period businesses often find that they have expanded too quickly and have an oversupply of inventory. Sales start to slow up and production must be reduced to prevent further excess inventory. Worker layoffs begin to occur because the company needs fewer employees to meet sales demands. If economic conditions do not stabilize the result can be a **depression,** such as we witnessed in the 1930s. During this period sales demand drops off drastically, production is cut back, unemployment rises dramatically, and wages are lowered. Depression is the trough of the economic cycle. As things begin to turn around, **recovery** takes place. Demand for goods starts to pick up again, production increases, people who were laid off are now rehired, and wages start to go back up. In contrast to the negative attitude that accompanies a depression, during recovery an attitude of optimism can be found almost everywhere.

The big question for business is: what cyclical variation will we see over the next two to three years? During the first half of the 1970s we saw the economy go into a recession. Some people were even predicting depression. By late 1975, however,

it appeared that economic conditions were stabilizing and the country was entering a period of recovery. Things began to improve as demand increased, production gradually started upward, and many of those who were laid off were recalled by their firms. Yet it is very difficult to predict these cyclical changes, and business is unable to control them. It must, therefore, be prepared for them and attempt to adjust operations accordingly. One of the primary ways this is done is through the use of lead and lag data, which were discussed previously. In addition, business relies heavily on government controls, and programs such as social security and unemployment insurance, to help smooth out the peaks and troughs of cyclical fluctuations.

Secular trends

Secular trends analysis covers a very long period of time and is used to reflect the long-term growth or decline of a particular company, industry, or nation. As applied to railroad passenger service, for example, secular trend analysis would reveal a pattern of decline. The number of people traveling by rail has dropped off dramatically over the last twenty-five years. Meanwhile, airline passenger service has increased greatly over this same time period. Thus we can draw conclusions as to the future of a particular industry by looking at its history over the past quarter century and identifying and studying the causes of its current growth or decline.

"What distribution do you want on this suicide note, Mr. Hinckel?"

From The Wall Street Journal; permission Cartoon Features Syndicate

10. Is it easier to forecast seasonal variations or cyclical fluctuations?

11. What are the four identifiable periods of a cyclical fluctuation?

12. How does business try to forecast cyclical fluctuations?

13. Of what value is secular trend analysis to business?

A Seasonal Forecast

Tom Markum, chief statistician for Johnson Manufacturing, recently reported some good news to his boss, Marion Collins. According to the economic data Tom has been receiving from the federal government, coupled with some statistical analyses he has conducted on industry conditions, this year's sales should be approximately 21 percent higher than last year's. Tom has been with the company for five years, and each year he has carefully studied correlations between external economic factors and company sales. He believes he has now worked up a statistical method for forecasting seasonal variations and annual sales. In particular, Tom has found lead factors to play a key role in his analysis.

Marion has expressed a great deal of enthusiasm with Tom's report. However, she is reluctant to send the report to the vice-president of manufacturing because last year the company was caught with a large amount of inventory and the president has cautioned against over-production. On the other hand, Marion does not want the company to lose sales due to lack of inventory. As a result, she has called the vice-president of manufacturing and set up a meeting for next Tuesday. At that time she intends to bring Tom over to the vice-president's office where the three of them can discuss the analysis and determine a plan of action.

1. Has Tom drawn his data from primary or secondary sources? Explain.

2. In addition to forecasting sales, how else can statistical correlations be used to help business?

3. If Tom's figures prove correct, could he expand the time frame from working with seasonal variations to forecasting cyclical fluctuations? What challenges and opportunities would this provide?

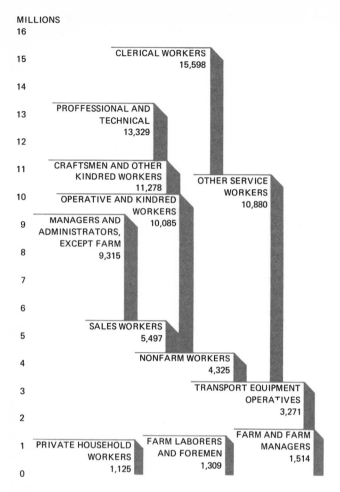

MILLIONS

CLERICAL WORKERS
15,598

PROFFESSIONAL AND
TECHNICAL
13,329

CRAFTSMEN AND OTHER
KINDRED WORKERS
11,278

OTHER SERVICE
WORKERS
10,880

OPERATIVE AND KINDRED
WORKERS
10,085

MANAGERS AND
ADMINISTRATORS,
EXCEPT FARM
9,315

SALES WORKERS
5,497

NONFARM WORKERS
4,325

TRANSPORT EQUIPMENT
OPERATIVES
3,271

PRIVATE HOUSEHOLD
WORKERS
1,125

FARM LABORERS
AND FOREMEN
1,309

FARM AND FARM
MANAGERS
1,514

FIG. 22.2 *Major occupational groups in the U.S.
(Source: Bureau of Labor Statistics.)*

DATA PRESENTATION

The presentation of data can take many forms. The important thing is that it be *understandable.* Does the reader or listener comprehend what is being communicated? Sometimes we will talk about a company increasing its sales from $1,370,655 to $1,644,786 for a net rise of 20 percent. However, for the average person this is rather difficult to follow. If put in the form of a table or graph, it would be much easier to understand. The following examines some of the most popular methods for presenting statistical information in easy-to-understand terms.

Summary Tables

A **summary table** allows a great deal of quantitative information to be presented in a very simple manner. Table 22.4 presents data related to the number of banks in the United States and the amount of deposits held by each major category. The table can be read quickly and easily, and provides people both within and outside the banking industry with useful information on the growth of United States banks.

Graphic Presentations

Some information is best illustrated by graphs or figures. One type is the **bar chart,** which allows the reader to quickly compare data between two or more groups. Figure 22.2 is a vertical bar chart showing major occupational groups in the United States. A quick look at the chart allows one to easily pick out those occupations that have the greatest number of people and those that have the least.

A second popular form of graphic presentation is the **pie chart.** This chart is commonly employed to present data related to dollar values or percentages. It is often used in annual reports to show the stockholders how the company spent its sales revenue, as is illustrated in Fig. 22.3.

A third popular type of graphic presentation is the **line chart.** Figure 22.4, which shows the United

TABLE 22.4 U.S. BANKS: NUMBER AND AMOUNT OF DEPOSITS

	NUMBER OF BANKS				TOTAL DEPOSITS (IN MILLIONS)				
	TOTAL OF ALL BANKS	NATIONAL	STATE	MUTUAL SAVINGS	OTHER	TOTAL OF ALL BANKS	NATIONAL	STATE	MUTUAL SAVINGS	OTHER
1960	14,006	4,542	1,675	513	7,276	$ 249,163	$116,178	$ 63,341	$ 35,316	$ 34,328
1965	14,295	4,803	1,432	504	7,556	362,611	171,528	88,215	50,980	51,889
1970	14,167	4,637	1,166	496	7,868	502,658	254,261	91,967	69,285	87,145
1975	15,108	4,741	1,046	475	8,846	897,101	447,590	143,409	110,569	195,533
1976	15,145	4,735	1,023	473	8,914	961,980	469,378	149,461	123,654	219,467
1977	15,174	4,664	1,014	467	9,039	1,074,426	520,167	163,443	134,916	255,898

Source: Federal Reserve System

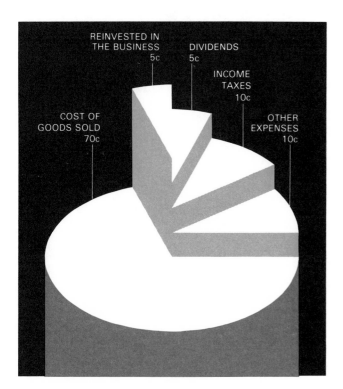

FIG. 22.3 *Breakdown of a firm's sales dollar*

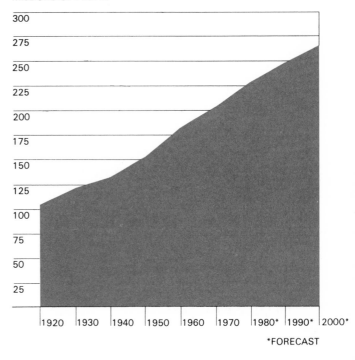

FIG. 22.4 *Actual and forecasted growth of the U.S., 1900–2000 (Source: Department of Commerce and Bureau of the Census.)*

States population growth since the turn of the century, is an illustration. A brief examination of the chart allows us to see this trend quickly and easily. Line charts are frequently used to display more than one type of data. For example, an auto manufacturer might plot both average consumer income after taxes and the number of new cars sold each year on the same chart—income on top and new cars underneath. Then a visual analysis can be made to see if there is a correlation between the two categories.

A fourth method for presenting data is the **statistical map.** This map is often used to convey sales information. A common method is to use colors on the map to represent current sales figures. For example, a map of the United States might be colored in, state by state, using the following legend:

Red	over $10 million
Blue	$1–$10 million
Green	$500,000–$999,999
Yellow	less than $500,000

By looking at the map one can immediately identify those states where the company makes its greatest revenue. If a salesperson in a "red" area quits, the manager knows that the position must be filled as quickly as possible because that is a high sales area for the firm. If the salesperson is from a "yellow" area, the situation may be less serious. In any event, the map helps the manager maintain control of sales operations because it identifies high and low sales revenue areas.

14. When is a summary table a useful method for data presentation?

15. In presenting data, when might a graphic presentation be a more effective method than a summary table?

16. Why do many firms use a statistical map for keeping track of sales information?

"The polls show we'll lose 12% of the vote if the speech preempts 'Quincy,' 20% if it preempts 'Lou Grant,' and 30% if it preempts 'Three's Company.'"

From The Wall Street Journal; permission Cartoon Features Syndicate

Take Me to Your Liter

What do Brunei, Burma, Liberia, Yemen, and the United States have in common? They are the only countries of the world not presently on the metric system. However, the United States is currently in the process of converting to this system. For years American companies doing business overseas have had to analyze and evaluate statistical data using the metric system. Now domestic data will also have to be evaluated this way, and many firms, including Chrysler, Ford, General Motors, Honeywell, IBM, Exxon, and Sears, Roebuck are moving toward total metric conversion.

Of course, this new system looks frightening to many people because it means a whole new way of expressing and thinking about measures. For example, when we go into a service station in the future we will be asking for gasoline in terms of liters. And if we are Camel cigarette smokers, we will now have to be willing to walk 1.6 kilometers for a smoke. And then some of our favorite cliches will have to be changed. For example, when we want to have nothing to do with something, we will have to say "I wouldn't touch it with a 3.02 metric pole." When one of our friends is sick, we will have to remind the person that 28.35 grams of prevention are worth .45 kilograms of cure. Finally, we will have to refrain from becoming overly excited when Rona Barrett tells us that a new starlet's measurements are 97-56-92. Ms. Barrett will be talking in centimeters not inches.

DATA INTERPRETATION

Once data have been gathered, analyzed, and presented, management is faced with the problem of *interpretation*. What conclusions can be drawn from the information? What actions should now be taken?

If management has carefully determined the types of information it needs for control purposes, and has designed its data collection procedures around these needs, interpretation of the information should be pretty clear cut. However, it is important to remember that errors can occur in even the best-designed studies. For example, arithmetic mistakes will lead to errors when the data are processed. Columns of numbers may have been added incorrectly and the conclusions that are drawn may well be wrong.

And then there is always the problem of bias. If the statistician who conducts the study is biased, data may be manipulated or interpreted to fit this person's views. For example, the statistician may have a personal bias against lenient credit terms. As a result, the individual reports to top management

"Another successful year, gentlemen. We broke even on operations and pulled a net profit on accounting procedures."

From The Wall Street Journal; permission Cartoon Features Syndicate

that uncollectible accounts have increased 100 percent in the last six months. Management, in turn, orders the enforcement of more stringent credit terms. Unknown to the managers, however, is that uncollectible accounts have risen from $5,000 to $10,000 while sales have increased from $1,500,000 to $2,000,000. By communicating only partial information, the statistician biases people's points of view.

To avoid such problem areas, management must be prepared to question and challenge some of the conclusions reached by its statisticians. In particular, astute managers find it helpful to ask how the statisticians arrived at their conclusions and what assumptions they made in their analyses. No statistician is perfect, and in analyzing data each will use his or her best judgment. Some will opt for the median as the best indicator of central tendency in a particular analysis. Others will use the mode. Still others will prefer the mean. The "best" measure may be a matter of opinion.

Finally, it is important to remember that statistics has limitations. The results of data analysis are often educated guesses at best. For example, if a

company has had sales over the last three years of $1 million, $2 million, and $3 million, what will the firm's sales be next year? A **straight-line extrapolation,** which is the extension of a trend line, would indicate $4 million. More sophisticated techniques that analyze internal factors (such as the company's ability to produce more goods) and external factors (such as changes in consumer demand) might point toward $3.7 million. Actual sales might be $3.4 million. In short, statistical analysis can help, but it is no guarantee of success. In the final analysis, the interpretation of statistical data is a managerial decision and there is no way of quantifying the role of intuition, experience, and judgment in the decision-making process.

17. How can a company protect itself against bias on the part of its statisticians?

18. What is meant by the statement that "the results of data analyses are often educated guesses at best"?

The Confused Vice-President

When Tom Markum, the chief statistician, learned that he and his boss Marion Collins were going to meet with the vice-president of production, he knew he had his work cut out for him. Tom's job would be to present his statistical analysis of next year's forecasted sales to the vice-president. The analysis was heavily mathematical, consisting of correlations between external economic factors and company sales. Tom believed his projections were accurate, but he knew the vice-president would be unwilling to increase production unless the presentation was first rate.

After thinking the matter over, Tom decided to put together a couple of summary tables showing his statistics. He had copies made for his boss and the vice-president. He also had a transparency of each made so he could project the numbers onto a screen, making it easier to follow the presentation.

Unfortunately, no sooner had Tom gotten into a description of the data collection and analysis than he realized that the vice-president was confused. The man appeared unable to follow all of the numbers in the table. This confusion resulted in the vice-president asking a lot of questions regarding how the data were collected—why Tom opted for correlations rather than some other form of statistical analysis, and how he arrived at the conclusions he did. After thirty minutes it was obvious that the presentation was not going to achieve its objectives. Marion, therefore, suggested that they all meet again on Friday. In the interim, Tom could rework his data presentation and be prepared to answer some of the questions raised by the vice-president. With this the meeting adjourned. On the way back to the office Marion suggested that Tom consider using a graphic presentation on Friday, specifically some line charts illustrating projected sales for the next year on a month-by-month basis. "This should be a lot easier to follow than your summary table," she said. Tom promised to do so.

1. In a presentation of sales data, why might a line chart be more effective than a summary table?

2. If Tom had made an effective presentation of his data, how might this have helped in persuading the vice-president that the statistical analysis was accurate?

3. Even if Tom's next presentation is well done, what kinds of questions would you still expect the vice-president to ask?

SUMMARY

Business statistics involves the collection, analysis, presentation, and interpretation of data in the solution of business problems. The collection of these data can be from either primary or secondary sources. Primary sources include business records, mail surveys, and personal interviews. In gathering this type of information it is common to find firms making use of sampling. Secondary data, meanwhile, are already published and are available in such sources as government reports, newspapers, and trade journals.

Data can be analyzed in a variety of ways. Some of the more common statistical tools for analysis include averages, index numbers, correlations, and time series. Each of these can be employed to analyze information in a particular way and, depending upon what the firm would like to know, can prove very helpful in providing the company with data for control purposes.

The presentation of this information can take numerous forms. The most common include summary tables and graphic presentations, such as bar charts, line charts, pie charts, and statistical maps. It is the responsibility of the presenter to choose whichever one of these will communicate the information to the listeners in the most easy-to-understand manner.

The fourth area of business statistics, data interpretation, is the responsibility of both the statistician and the management. Questions relating to what conclusions can be drawn from the information and what actions should now be taken are at the heart of this interpretation process. During this process, management must be particularly aware of bias on the part of the statistician and prepared to question both the method of data collection and the conclusions. Used properly, statistical information can prove very useful in the control process.

KEY TERMS FOUND IN THIS CHAPTER

QUESTIONS FOR DISCUSSION AND ANALYSIS

1. What are the four major areas of business statistics?

2. Why do firms sample their customers rather than poll every one of them if they want to obtain customer opinion on a given matter?

3. How does the mode differ from the median?

4. If the price of gasoline was 50¢ per gallon in the base year and $1.50 per gallon in the current year, what would the index number be for the current year?

5. How predictable are seasonal variations?

6. How does a secular trend differ from a cyclical fluctuation?

7. When is the pie chart an effective method for presenting data?

8. What are some of the limitations of statistical analysis?

23

Man is still the most extraordinary computer of all.
John F. Kennedy

OBJECTIVES OF THIS CHAPTER

The modern business firm is a hub of activity. Orders are coming in, merchandise is being shipped out, the plant is scheduling new production runs, and reports on all these activities are being written up. Obviously there needs to be some systematic method of processing the flow of the information or data from where they originate to where they are needed. We call this systematic procedure "data processing." It is one of the major keys to effective control, for without it information would never find its way to the manager who needs it.

The first objective of this chapter is to examine what data processing is all about. The second is to study the role of computers in processing data. The third is to point out some of the more common functions the computer performs for business. By the end of this chapter you should be able to do the following:

a. define the term data processing;

b. distinguish between analog and digital computers;

c. describe the binary number system used by computers;

d. relate the three basic units of a computer and tell what each does;

e. explain how flowcharts are of value to a computer programmer;

f. identify the two most popular symbolic languages used in programming; and

g. provide illustrations of some ways in which the computer is used in business operations.

Data Processing

METHODS OF DATA PROCESSING

In running a firm and controlling operations, modern business managers are often swamped with enormous quantities of data that have to be gathered, classified, recorded, stored, retrieved, and/or reproduced. In addition, the company needs to maintain all sorts of information, from financial records for tax purposes to personnel records for handling promotion decisions to inventory records for control reasons. How can a company handle the tons of data that flow throughout the organization every day and still manage to carry on operations efficiently? The answer is found in **data processing,** which is *an organized method of gathering, storing, and retrieving information.*

There are four basic ways of processing data. The simplest is through **manual data processing,** where the work is done by hand. A bookkeeper who makes accounting journal entries manually is an example.

A second method is through **electromechanical processing.** Examples would include business machines such as calculators, cash registers, and bookkeeping machines.

A third method of handling data is through **punched-card processing.** With this system, holes are keypunched on cards, which are then processed by a machine. Many of the bills we receive each month contain two parts: a statement and a stub. The part we send back to the company with our check is often a keypunched card that can be manually fed into a machine for processing. Credit-card companies and public utilities make wide use of this method.

A fourth way to handle information is through **computer data processing,** or, as it is often called, *electronic data processing.* The greatest advantages of the computer in processing data are its speed and capability. Since these machines work electronically, their speed is much, much faster than that of, for example, punched-card equipment, which depends upon gears and other mechanical parts. To illustrate, one business firm recently reported that it faced a data processing problem that would have taken ninety days to solve manually and forty hours to handle with punched-card equipment. The firm solved the problem in three seconds with the use of a computer. Because of their great value to business in processing data, our discussion in this chapter will be limited to computers.

1. What kinds of data processing problems would you expect a firm to handle with the use of electromechanical processing? Give two illustrations.

2. What kinds of data processing problems would you expect a firm to handle with computers? Give two illustrations.

"The instructions are pasted on the back."

From The Wall Street Journal; permission Cartoon Features Syndicate

TYPES OF COMPUTERS

There are two basic types of computers: analog and digital. The **analog computer** is used for scientific calculations and problems, such as translating physical conditions like pressure or voltage into related mechanical or electrical quantities. The National Aeronautics and Space Administration, for example, uses an analog computer to measure the speed, direction, and trajectory of manned space vehicles.

The **digital computer** counts numbers. And it can do so at a tremendous speed. It can also accept written instructions, make logical decisions, store information until needed, and then provide these data in the form of output. Since this type is the one most widely used by business, the remainder of our discussion about computers will be devoted to the digital computer.

3. What is the difference between an analog computer and a digital computer?

BINARY NUMBER SYSTEM

In understanding the role of the computer in business, it is important to have a working knowledge of how the machine processes data. This requires an understanding of the way in which the computer handles numbers.

In our number system there are ten digits: 0, 1, 2, 3, 4, 5, 6, 7, 8, and 9. By combining these digits in various ways we can write any number we want from a very small one such as two (2) to a very large one such as one million (1,000,000). The electronic computer, however, works with electrical switches that have only two positions: open and closed. As a result, the computer is limited to just two digits: zero and one. We call this a **binary number system.**

Of course, with just two digits it might appear that the computer can work with only a handful of numbers; but this is not true. The computer can perform all arithmetic functions from adding and subtracting to multiplying and dividing. However, it

Graphic display units make it easier for design engineers to communicate with a computer.

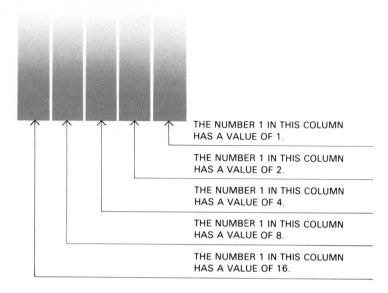

THE NUMBER 1 IN THIS COLUMN HAS A VALUE OF 1.

THE NUMBER 1 IN THIS COLUMN HAS A VALUE OF 2.

THE NUMBER 1 IN THIS COLUMN HAS A VALUE OF 4.

THE NUMBER 1 IN THIS COLUMN HAS A VALUE OF 8.

THE NUMBER 1 IN THIS COLUMN HAS A VALUE OF 16.

FIG. 23.1 *Binary number positions*

	16	8	4	2	1	
TO WRITE 5	0	0	1	0	1	THE VALUE OF 1 IN THE 1 POSITION PLUS THE VALUE OF 1 IN THE 4 POSITION EQUALS 5.
TO WRITE 11	0	1	0	1	1	THE VALUE OF 1 IN THE 1 POSITION, PLUS THE VALUE OF 1 IN THE 2 POSITION, PLUS THE VALUE OF 1 IN THE 8 POSITION EQUALS 11.
TO WRITE 27	1	1	0	1	1	THE VALUE OF 1 IN THE 1 POSITION, PLUS THE VALUE OF 1 IN THE 2 POSITION, PLUS THE VALUE OF 1 IN THE 8 POSITION, PLUS THE VALUE OF 1 IN THE 16 POSITION EQUALS 27.
TO WRITE 31	1	1	1	1	1	THE VALUE OF 1 IN ALL 5 POSITIONS— 1, 2, 4, 8, AND 16, EQUALS 31.

FIG. 23.2 *Determining binary code values*

has its own system for reading numbers. This system, often called a **binary code,** consists of combinations of the two digits: zero and one.

The computer reads these digits from right to left. In binary code the number 1 is written as 00001. The computer gives a 1 in the right-hand column the same value you and I do in our decimal number system. However, if the number 1 is found in the second column from the right the computer reads this as a 2; it doubles the value of the first column. Thus the number 2 in binary code is written 00010. If we move to the third column over, the value again doubles. Therefore, 00100 is equal to 4. Similarly, 01000 equals 8. The rule the computer follows can be diagramed as in Fig. 23.1. Using this simple number system, we can write any numerical value we want in binary code, as is illustrated in Fig. 23.2.

Use of the binary code is not restricted to numbers. It can also be employed for letters and symbols, as seen in Table 23.1.

TABLE 23.1 PARTIAL BINARY CODE FOR NONNUMERIC TERMS

LETTER OR SYMBOL	BINARY CODE
A	010001
B	010010
E	010101
I	011001
+	110000
$	111011
%	111100

The binary code is the language into which all data are translated. This language is then converted within the computer into electrical impulses. An analysis of how the computer works should make this clear.

4. In binary code, how do you write the number 7?

5. In binary code, how do you write the number 42? (Hint: use six digits in doing this.)

HOW THE COMPUTER WORKS

A computer consists of three basic components or units: (a) input unit, (b) central processing unit, and (c) output unit.

Input Unit

The purpose of the **input unit** is to allow the computer operator to communicate with the computer. The operator does this by feeding data and instructions into the machine. The data are the information that need to be processed; the instructions tell the computer how to do it.

These data may be contained on punched cards (see Fig. 23.3), punched paper tape, magnetic tape, drums, discs, and so forth. The input unit takes this information and converts it to an internal form for storage in the computer's memory unit. In the case of punched cards, for example, data are stored on the card in the form of punched holes. This information can then be sensed by a card reader and entered into the computer's memory. Figure 23.3 illustrates a card on which digits, the alphabet, and special characters have been punched. Note that there are eighty columns on a standard card and each time a number, letter, or special character is punched, one or more holes appear on the card. For example, the number zero results in a punch directly below it in the 0 column. The letter A results in two holes, one directly below it and the second further below in the 1 column. A comma results in three holes, in the 0, 3, and 8 columns directly below it. This same basic

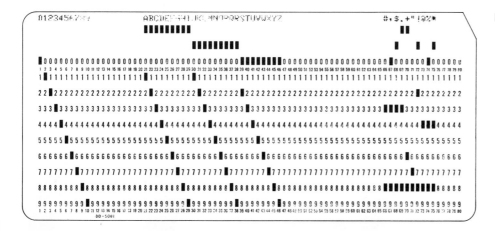

FIG. 23.3 *A punched card*

479

approach of translating input data and sending them to the computer memory is used in handling all other types of input.

Central Processing Unit

The **central processing unit** (CPU) consists of three parts: (1) the memory unit, (2) the arithmetic/logic unit, and (3) the control unit.

The Memory Unit

The **memory unit,** or storage unit as it is sometimes called, is the center of all computer operations. All data that are processed pass through this unit. Input data, program instructions for handling the information, the results of the calculations, and the final output that will be printed out are all held in the memory unit at some point in time.

There are several types of memory units commonly employed in computers. Many high-speed computers use the **magnetic core.** These magnetic cores are made of a ferro-magnetic material and shaped into circles or "doughnuts" the size of pinheads. Each of these can be magnetized in one of two directions. One of the directions stands for the binary 0, the other for the binary 1. Thus, using the binary code we just discussed, information can be stored in the magnetic cores.

Thousands of these magnetized cores are located in the computer, strung on crisscrossed wires like the strings of a tennis racket. In this case, however, they are strung inside square frames, which are then stacked on top of each other to make up a basic memory unit. This results in the magnetic cores being placed in columns. Each of these columns is given an *address* in the memory so that any information stored in the cores in that column can be easily retrieved. Large-scale computers have more than 25 million cores, so they can store a tremendous amount of information. In recent years, these cores have been replaced by semiconductor memories

A computer consists of an input unit, a central processing unit, and an output unit.

A portion of a field-effect transistor memory chip, enlarged 5,000 times.

consisting of memory circuits and support circuits etched on tiny silicon chips. It is expected that in the future the use of semiconductor memories will increase.

Arithmetic/logic unit

The **arithmetic/logic unit** performs operations such as adding, subtracting, multiplying, and dividing. This unit contains the circuitry that performs all mathematical/logical calculations. Years ago, in the **first-generation computers,** mathematical calculations were done with the use of vacuum tubes. In the late 1950s, **second-generation computers** arrived on the scene and vacuum tubes were replaced by transistors. These transistors were relatively small and inexpensive. They also generated less heat than vacuum tubes, required very little power, had a longer operating life, and rendered more reliable performance. Their speed could be measured in millionths of a second. In the mid-1960s, **third-generation computers** came along. These computers owe their development to the use of silicon chips, which replaced transistors. First used by the Radio Corporation of America in its RCA Spectra 70 series, the chips were smaller and less expensive than transistors. An entire electronic circuit could be mounted on a chip no larger than one-tenth of an inch square. This technology is called *integrated circuits,* and it has led to the development of more powerful and sophisticated computers. The speed of these machines is measured in billionths of a second and their storage capacity is almost infinite. Since the introduction of integrated circuitry in the mid-1960s the speed of computers has increased between 10,000 and 100,000 times, while storage costs have dropped off dramatically. In the 1970s a **fourth generation of computers** arrived on the scene. These computers are more evolutionary than revolutionary; circuits are now smaller than ever, storage capacity has been increased, two or more programs can be executed at the same time, and error techniques have been improved, just to name some of the improved capabilities of these new machines.

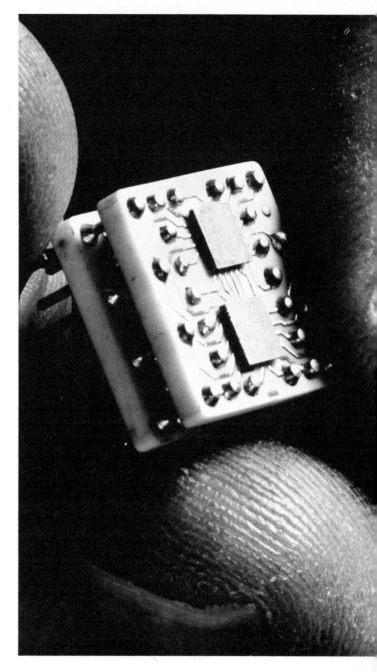

Modern computers owe their development to the use of these tiny silicon chips.

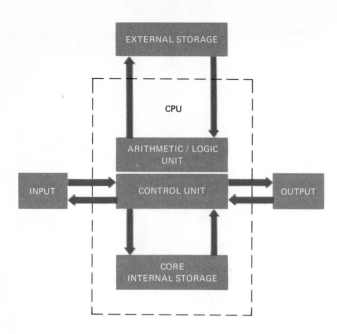

FIG. 23.4 *Basic components of a digital computer*

A typical computer room.

Control unit
The **control unit** interprets the program or instructions that are stored in the memory. It also issues commands to the computer circuits regarding the execution of instructions and sees that the orders are carried out properly.

Output Unit
The **output unit** prints out the information after it has been processed. Sometimes this output is in the form of punched cards or paper tape. However, for management information purposes the most important form of output is the printed page, or "computer printout" as it is often called. High-speed printers that are employed for this job are capable of printing up to 3,000 lines of numerical data per minute and somewhat less if the information is alphanumeric (both numbers and letters). Some of the important business information that can be produced by these printers includes financial statements, invoices, and checks.

An Overview
All three components in the computer are interrelated. The input unit passes data to the CPU. Here the data is processed. Then it is passed to the output unit for the purpose of translating the results. Meanwhile, the control unit monitors operations continuously. Figure 23.4 provides a diagrammatic illustration.

6. What is the job of the memory unit in the computer?

7. What technological breakthrough occurred between second-generation and third-generation computers that increased their speed so greatly?

8. Why is the computer printout regarded as the most important form of output for management information purposes?

Tomorrow's Promises

What will be the future of computers? Some of the predictions that have been made recently include the following:

1. Computer systems will become simpler to use.

2. The person using them will be trained to focus on problems and their solutions rather than on merely learning about processing techniques.

3. There will be less problems with the machines and if there is a shutdown of the system, it will be for a short time only.

4. There will be automatic error corrections so that if the user makes a mistake, the machine will pick it up and either adjust for it or call it to the person's attention, thereby reducing the amount of time spent trying to determine why the program did not run correctly.

5. It will be possible to get more work output per dollar of investment than at any time prior in computer history.

6. There will be improved system security so that people cannot tap into the system, find another person's program, and either copy it or destroy it.

7. Data processing hardware will become more specialized than it is today.

8. There will be less need for human intervention so that the individual using the machine will be able to interact directly with the computer and get feedback from it faster than ever before.

Summing up these expected developments, two trends are suggested: (1) No person or group will be in a position at any time to know what application the system is processing or for whom it is doing the processing. (2) Tasks that were never done before will be relegated to the computer, making the machine more and more a part of our lifestyle. To some degree the computer will become an extension of the human being, making our lives more enjoyable in the process.

FLOWCHARTS

Computers do what they are ordered to do—no more, no less. This may sound fine to those of us who have never used computers, but to those who have it often brings back memories of hours spent "debugging" program errors. What causes these errors? One major cause is incomplete instructions. When a programmer writes the computer program, the instructions must be complete. If there are any steps omitted the computer will either reject the program or perform the computations in a way other than that desired. One way of overcoming this problem is to first construct a flowchart.

A **flowchart** is a graphic representation of the operations or steps to be performed in solving a problem. For example, consider the case of a programmer who is writing a payroll program for hourly employees. This individual wants the computer to find out how many hours each of these people worked, multiply this by their respective

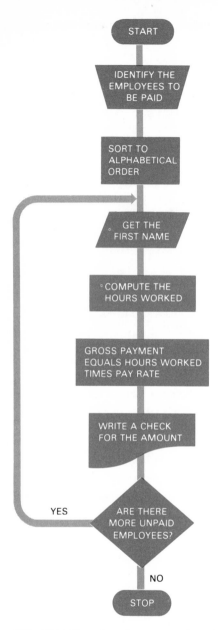

FIG. 22.5 *Flowchart for paying hourly employees*

hourly rates of pay, compute the total, and then issue checks to each of them. Figure 23.5 provides an illustration of a flowchart for this purpose.

Note in Fig. 23.5 that the programmer has first ordered the computer to identify all of the hourly employees who are to be paid. In this way the programmer has limited the amount of information with which the computer must work. Then the employees are listed in alphabetical order so that the computer can pay each one in turn. This is done by calculating the hours each worked and multiplying by their particular hourly rate of pay. As you can see in Fig. 23.5, each time the computer writes a check it then determines if there are any unpaid employees remaining. If so, it loops around and picks up the next of these. This process continues until all are paid. The logic in Fig. 23.5 holds for any number of employees from one to one million.

Keep in mind that the purpose of a flowchart is to help the programmer write complete instructions for the computer. Without such a chart, it is easy to make programming mistakes. For example, if the programmer tells the computer to pay all of the hourly people for the hours they worked, has the individual also told the computer to determine each one's hourly rate of pay? (Remember, without such information the computer cannot complete the assigned task.) And has the programmer given the computer logical instructions so that each person is paid but no one receives two checks? Without complete instructions, all of these can be problem areas.

9. In what way can a flowchart help a computer programmer?

COMPUTER LANGUAGE

As we noted before, the computer is capable of taking information from the programmer and converting it into binary codes. Thus we might say that

H. Ross Perot was born in Texarkana, Texas in 1930 and from a very early age gave indications of being a true salesman. For example, by the time he was twelve he had a paper route that was earning him $40 a week. And he wasn't afraid to take a chance. The paper route was located in the rough, slum area of the city, but rather than try to change the route Perot persuaded the newspaper to give him a 70-percent commission, in contrast to the standard 30 percent given to other news carriers.

In 1949 he went off to the U.S. Naval Academy, but by 1957 he was disenchanted with the Navy's promotion and seniority system and took his discharge. He then went to work for IBM as a computer salesman—and his success was phenomenal. In his fifth year with the firm, he made his annual sales quota by the third week in January!

In 1962 Perot left IBM to start his own firm, Electronic Data Systems. The goal of the company was to design, install, and operate electronic data processing systems for clients on a contract basis. Six years later, in 1968, the firm went public, offering its stock at an initial price of $16.50. This was 118 times earnings. Yet the public felt that the stock was worth this price. And in the two years that followed the price rose dramatically. By the late 1970s, however, the price had fallen to $25. Yet, earnings has grown dramatically, rising from $47 million in 1968 to $176 million in 1978.

Throughout all of this, Perot has steadfastly maintained that wealth has never been a major target for him. Rather, he feels that people are most important, something he demonstrated in 1979 when the Iranian government held two of his employees as hostages. Personally directing the rescue of the two by forming a unit led by the late Colonel Arthur D. Simons, the result was a successful jail break. Today he continues to prove that his philosophy of "money isn't everything" is one he lives by as well as expounds.

the computer takes input written in one language and translates it into another. However, the programmer does not write instuctions the way you and I do when we send someone a memo. Rather there are special types of computer language in which programs are written. Four of the most popular are **FORTRAN, COBOL, BASIC,** and **PL-1.** All of these are **symbolic languages,** in which the programmer writes instructions, using both English and algebraic symbols, in a special way.

FORTRAN is a contraction of the term *FORmula TRANslation.* This computer language was developed by IBM and is widely used by scientists and mathematicians for solving equations and scientific problems. It is basically a scientific computer language.

COBOL is a shortened version of the term *COmmon Business Oriented Language.* COBOL is widely used in solving business problems. In fact, it is currently the most common data processing language in the business world.

BASIC is an acronym for *Beginners Algebraic Symbol Interpreter Compiler* and is more sophisticated than either FORTRAN or COBOL. It is designed for ease of use in both input and output op-

The New Programmer

Aaron Whitcomb, vice-president of finance at Johnson Manufacturing, was recently contacted by Ralph Waite, the head of the computer department. Ralph wanted to know if there were any financial reports that Aaron would like to receive in addition to those already being provided on a weekly basis. Aaron said that there were, and proceeded to outline some financial ratios that he felt were important but that were not currently available. Ralph promised to have a computer programmer write a program for them and see that Ralph received this printout every Monday morning.

The assignment was given to Sandra Brown, a new computer programmer. It took Sandra only a few hours to write the program. However, on Monday morning Ralph received a call from Aaron. "I have this new computer printout," he said, "but it doesn't make any sense. The numbers are wrong or something." Ralph promised to look into the matter.

He began by calling in Sandra and telling her the problem. Sandra seemed shocked. "Well," said Ralph, "let's look at your program and flowchart." Sandra showed him the program but admitted that she had not worked up a flowchart. This made the job more difficult, but Ralph eventually found seven errors in the program. By the end of the morning the new program was running properly. It was then that Ralph gave Sandra some advice. "Listen, Sandra," he said, "don't ever write a new program around here without first constructing a flowchart and then looking at the computer printout to see if it's correct. Computers do what they are told, but they can't read your mind. If your instructions are wrong or incomplete, the printout will be wrong. Be more careful in the future."

1. Of what value is a flowchart to a computer programmer?

2. What did Ralph mean when he said that "If your instructions are wrong or incomplete, the printout will be wrong."

3. In the future, what steps do you think Sandra will take in handling new programs?

erations. Today its popularity in both business and academic institutions is growing.

PL/1 (*Programming Language 1*) is a very recent computer language that has been designed for use by both scientific and business organizations. It is a simple, concise language like FORTRAN, has the flexibility of COBOL, and can be quickly mastered by beginners.

The symbolic languages, FORTRAN and COBOL, require training on the part of the programmer. The individual must know how to write the program properly. For example, in FORTRAN a plus sign is the symbol for "add." In COBOL, however, the word "ADD" or the symbol can be used. From here, of course, the computer takes over, translating these words and symbols into the correct binary code·instructions. However, this is all impossible unless the programmer first knows how to program in these symbolic languages.

10. Which computer language is more widely used by business—COBOL or FORTRAN?

COMPUTERS AND BUSINESS OPERATIONS

Computers play a key role in helping business firms process their data and control their operations. There are numerous procedures for which the computer can be used, and the following examines some of the most common.

Payroll Processing

One of the biggest paperwork problems faced by business is **payroll processing.** Someone must determine how many hours all hourly employees have worked, compute their salaries, and issue checks to them. In addition, all salaried personnel must be paid. Years ago all of this was done by hand. People in the payroll department actually had to write out checks or pay the workers in cash. Today all of this payroll processing can be done by the computer.

Computers play a key roll in helping business firms process their data and control their operations.

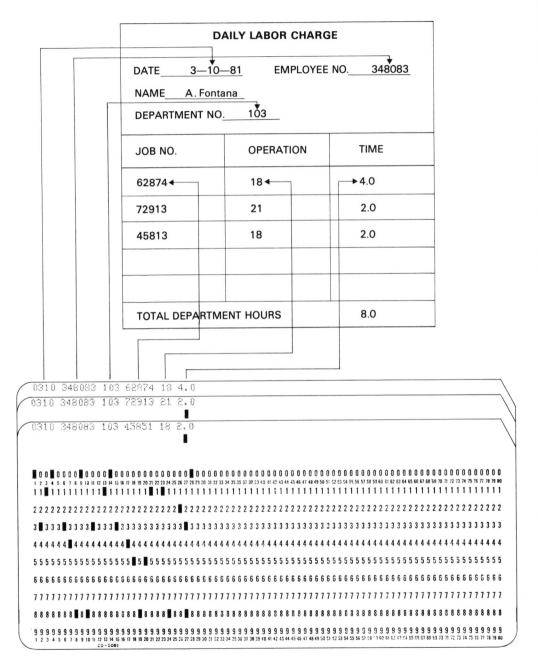

FIG. 23.6 *Gathering payroll data*

One way this can be handled is by taking the daily labor charge card of each hourly employee, showing the jobs on which the person worked and how long was spent on each, and transferring the information to punched cards (see Fig. 23.6). From here the computer takes over and processes the information appropriately. Note from Fig. 23.6 that the firm is not only collecting payroll data but also information on who did what and how long it took. The additional data can be used at a later time for examining such things as job costs and productivity on an individual and departmental basis.

In addition, the computer performs many other payroll-related processing chores. For example, it sees that a percentage of everyone's salary is deducted to meet income-tax and social-security payments. It also maintains a record of how much money each person earns throughout the year so that there will be an income-tax record to file with the Internal Revenue Service. And if employees buy group health insurance or life insurance, or want to purchase United States savings bonds through the payroll savings plan, this too can be handled by the computer.

Inventory Control

When a business is very small, the proprietor will often reorder inventory only when it is getting low. This may require a periodic physical inventory of perhaps 1,000 items. However, as a company increases in size it becomes very time consuming to physically keep track of how many units of every product are on hand. As a result, the firm will usually turn to the computer.

First, current inventory figures will be fed into the computer. Then a reorder level will be established. For example, there may be one hundred portable television sets on hand. When this stock level drops to twenty-five the firm will reorder. As customers buy these portable TVs, this information is fed into the computer and the current level of sets on hand is reduced appropriately. When the inventory level reaches twenty-five, the computer informs the purchasing department.

This sales information is often fed in by the clerk who rings up the sale. Many department stores, for example, have electronic equipment connected with the cash register, which communicates with the computer. Thus the clerk takes care of the sale and reports it to the computer at the same time. Such a procedure allows the firm to control large quantities of inventory with a minimum of time and expense.

"No, Baxter, you're not being replaced by a computer, only a silicone chip."

From The Wall Street Journal; permission Cartoon Features Syndicate

11. What types of payroll-processing jobs can computers do?

12. How can the computer help a firm with inventory control?

Bank Deposits and Withdrawals

The computer is also used for handling *bank deposits* and *withdrawals*. For example, if we go into a bank and deposit $10, the most common procedure is to fill out a deposit slip and give this and our $10 to the teller. The teller then uses a machine called a **computer terminal** to contact the computer and update our account. Likewise, if we withdraw $10 the teller will contact the computer and have our account reduced by this amount.

The computer that performs these functions provides an illustration of **real-time processing.** This term refers to the fact that the information is being processed immediately. There is at most only a split second between the time the computer receives the information and the time it acts on it. Real-time computer systems have three major characteristics. First, data are maintained **on-line.** By this we mean that the information and the instructions to be used in processing the data are either read in as required or are stored in the computer memory for immediate use. Second, based on these new data, the computer can update its records, such as changing the balance in a customer's bank account. Third, because the computer can be contacted from a number of remote terminals, more than one person can communicate with it. In a bank, for example, each teller will have a terminal for reporting transactions to the

FIG. 23.7 *Updating the customer's account with the computer*

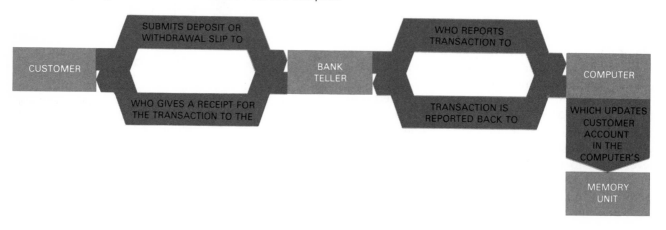

computer. For all practical purposes the response is immediate. Real-time processing is vitally important when dealing with customers who want an immediate response (see Fig. 23.7). After all, on one wants to sit around the bank for thirty minutes waiting for a computer to give an "okay" on a particular withdrawal.

Another new development in computers—very important to banks and other businesses using these machines in face-to-face dealing with customers—is **time-sharing.** In time-sharing a number of people can use the computer at the same time. This can be very important, for example, in bank operations, where five tellers may all be asking the computer to enter deposits to particular accounts at the same time. The computer can handle all of these in a matter of seconds, so that for all practical purposes each operator is receiving simultaneous feedback.

The same basic approach is used with bank credit cards that allow people to make deposits or withdrawals after banking hours. In this case, however, the customer personally operates the teller machine and communicates directly with the computer. All that is required is the bank credit card, an identification number, and an understanding of the proper procedures to use. The most common method is for individuals to (a) put their bank credit card into the machine, (b) type in their identification number so the computer knows that it is indeed their card, and (c) follow the instructions on the teller machine in communicating the transaction to the computer. If the individual attempts to withdraw more money than is in the account, the computer limits the withdrawal to that available. In addition, most of these machines are programmed to limit both the amount of any withdrawal (such as $50 each time) and the number of times an individual can use the machine in a twenty-four-hour period (such as three times). Meanwhile, if the amount of money on hand gets low, the computer is programmed to contact a bank manager and have more funds made available.

Many banks have electronic tellers to handle customer needs on a 24-hour basis.

13. Can a large bank process deposits and withdrawals without the use of a computer?

14. How is real-time processing of value to a bank? Does the bank really need this computer capability?

15. Do you think the future will see more, or less, use of bank-teller machines operated by the customer personally?

Airline Reservations

Computers are also used in making *airline reservations*. And like those used in the bank, these computers are illustrations of real-time, time-sharing systems. When an individual goes to a ticket counter to make an airline reservation, the ticket agent uses a console typewriter to communicate directly with the computer. In a matter of seconds the agent knows if there are any seats available on the desired flight. If the person decides to buy a ticket, the agent types in the individual's name and the computer reduces the number of available seats appropriately. Likewise, should someone cancel a reservation, the computer will increase the number of seats by one. And all of this can be done while the person is standing at the airline counter. If the individual goes through a travel agent, the latter will call in the necessary information to the airline and then contact the passenger to confirm the time and date of departure. In all cases, however, the computer handles reservations and balances the demand for each flight with the number of seats available in a matter of seconds.

16. In what way are computers that are used for making airline reservations illustrations of real-time, time-sharing systems?

Record Keeping

Another common use of the computer is for *record keeping*. Life insurance firms provide an illustration. Everyone who has a life insurance policy must pay a premium. This is usually done monthly and the computer must keep track of all payments. In addition, as the policy matures its cash surrender value increases; and the policyholder is entitled to borrow this cash value as long as he or she pays the annual interest on the loan. The computer must keep track of all this information.

It is easy to see that keeping records on a policy with a monthly premium of $50, a cash surrender value of $325, and a current outstanding loan of $100 can be quite a headache. And we realize how much more complex it must be when the policies pay annual dividends and the firm gives a status report on the policy to the policyholder each year. It might take someone thirty minutes just to handle the annual record keeping on one policy. And millions of Americans have more than one, so when they borrow $100 against their cash surrender value it is often $50 against one policy and $25 against two others. Finally, when they receive dividends they may apply them against the outstanding loans in any way they choose. Thus each transaction makes it more and more difficult to follow what is going on. This is why the computer is so invaluable.

The same is true, however, for many other types of businesses. For example, banks need computers to maintain records on deposits and withdrawals by their customers. Corporations need computers to keep track of the names and addresses of all stockholders so that dividends can be paid to them and proxies solicited. Finally, all firms that can afford it use computers to keep an account of their assets: cash, inventory, accounts receivable, and machinery. Without computers, accurate record keeping would be literally impossible for most businesses.

17. Can small and medium-size firms also profit by using computers for record-keeping purposes?

CHOOSING A DATA PROCESSING SYSTEM

There are many ways to process data. The most obvious, of course, is to do it by hand. As we have seen in this chapter, however, electronic methods such as computers are also available. The difficult problem for most firms is that of choosing the *right* data processing system. This becomes a matter of analyzing the costs and benefits associated with each particular piece of equipment. The total cost of a system is directly related to the amount of data being processed. If very little work needs to be done, manual operations are often the least expensive. However, as more and more information must be processed it pays to turn to more sophisticated equipment.

The major question for business firms is how much equipment is needed. Many companies have complained in recent years that they have purchased more data processing machinery than they can use profitably. For example, some have bought the latest giant computer when something smaller and less expensive would have been sufficient. By carefully comparing company needs with equipment capabilities, this problem can be avoided.

18. What is meant by the statement that "the total cost of a data processing system is directly related to the amount of data being processed"?

Without computers, accurate record keeping would be literally impossible for most businesses.

A New Computer Proposal

Seven years ago, Johnson Manufacturing bought a giant computer to handle its data processing problems. The computer took care of everything from payroll to inventory control. Since that time, however, more and more work has been assigned to the computer. Two months ago the head of the computer department, Ralph Waite, told the company president that the current computer would soon be inadequate. The firm would have to buy either some smaller additional data processing equipment or a newer, more powerful computer.

A number of representatives from computer firms called on the company to present proposals for handling Johnson's problem. The board of directors was split on the issue, but finally decided to opt for a new, giant computer. One board member who disagreed with the decision said that the firm did not need this new computer. "It has more capability than we require. The current computer and some smaller pieces of processing equipment are really all we need." Most of the others disagreed, saying that the firm's volume of data was so great that the new computer was absolutely necessary.

1. What types of data processing problems can a computer handle?

2. In choosing a computer, how do cost and volume of work to be done enter the picture?

3. How would you go about deciding whether or not Johnson should buy the new computer?

Here to Stay

There are two major reasons why computers are here to stay. First, they are capable of processing enormous quantities of data. Their storage capacity has greatly increased over the last twenty years, and the functions they can perform have been expanded tremendously. Second, computer costs have actually declined over the last quarter century. Today it is cheaper than ever to use computers. In the early 1950s it cost about $3 million for a computer. By the 1960s the cost was down to around $1 million and today it is less than $300,000. Furthermore, in 1951 $3 million was a great deal more than it is today given inflation and the rising cost of everything. What will the future hold? It seems that there will be even more computers being sold at a lower price than ever. The following provides some of the latest data regarding both past costs and future projections.

Year	Number of Computers Installed	Average Sales Price	Percent of 1951 Sales Price	Average Cost per 1 Million Calculations
1951	10	$3,000,000	100.0	$250.00
1953	50	2,750,999	91.8	250.00
1955	244	2,250,000	75.0	165.00
1959	3,000	1,225,000	41.8	20.00
1965	23,000	700,000	23.3	2.75
1971	82,000	375,000	12.5	.10
1975	155,000	300,000	10.0	.08
1980	300,000	265,000	8.1	.04
1985	500,000*	210,000*	7.0	.01

* Estimated figures

SUMMARY

In order to handle all of the information that flows throughout the organization, modern business firms have turned to data processing, an organized method of gathering, storing, and retrieving information. There are four basic ways to process data: manual processing; electro-mechanical processing; punched-card processing; and computer, or electronic, processing. The computer is the fastest method.

Computers are of two types: analog and digital. The digital is almost always used for business operations because of its ability to perform arithmetic calculations at a tremendous rate of speed. These calculations are carried out with the use of a binary number system consisting of just two digits: zero and one.

The computer itself consists of three basic units. The input unit feeds in the data to be processed and the instructions for carrying out these operations. The central processing unit includes the memory, arithmetic/logic, and control units. The memory unit stores the data and instructions until they are needed. The arithmetic/logic unit performs the mathematical calculations. The control unit issues commands to the computer circuits and sees that instructions are properly executed. The output unit generates the information after it has been processed.

It is important to remember that computers can do only what they are ordered to do. For this reason programmers often make flowcharts to help them write logical and complete computer programs. Then they convert the flowchart into a symbolic language such as FORTRAN or, in most business cases, COBOL. Finally the program is fed into the machine.

In business operations computers are used for performing many functions. Some of the more common include payroll processing, inventory control, the handling of bank deposits and withdrawals, airline reservations, and record keeping. Some of these jobs require a giant computer, others can be handled with a small computer. In choosing the right data processing system, from manual to computer, it is important for the company to compare its needs with the capability of the equipment under purchase consideration.

KEY TERMS FOUND IN THIS CHAPTER

QUESTIONS FOR DISCUSSION AND ANALYSIS

1. What are the four basic ways of processing data? Describe each.

2. How does a computer process large numbers if it is capable of working with just two digits: zero and one?

3. Why is the computer memory unit regarded as the center of all computer operations?

4. What job do magnetic cores perform in the memory unit?

5. Which symbolic language is more widely used by business—FORTRAN or COBOL?

6. Why do so many firms use the computer for payroll processing?

7. When is it important to a business to have a computer with real-time and time-sharing capabilities?

8. How should a firm go about determining the type of data processing system that best meets its needs?

CAREERS IN ACCOUNTING, STATISTICS, AND COMPUTERS

There are many career opportunities in accounting, statistics, and computers—in fact, far too many to be covered in just a few pages because there are many different occupational choices within each of these three major categories. For example, in the field of accounting there are public and private accountants. Additionally, there are accounting specialists in such areas as taxes, auditing, and management consulting. And among computer people there are programmers, systems analysts, statistical clerks, and computer operating people, to name but four. Thus the following represent only a handful of major categories in these three career fields.

ACCOUNTANT

The accountant prepares and analyzes financial statements that provide information for making decisions. There are three major accounting areas: public, management, and government accounting. Public accountants have their own businesses or work for accounting firms; management accountants handle the financial records of the company for whom they work; and government accountants examine the records of government agencies, private businesses, and individuals whose dealings are subject to government regulations. Most accountants specialize in a particular phase of accounting such as tax, auditing, or management consulting.

PROGRAMMER

The programmer writes detailed instructions for the computer to follow in solving a problem. This individual usually works from problem descriptions prepared by systems analysts who have examined the problem and determined the steps necessary to achieve the desired results. For example, a business applications programmer, dealing with developing instructions for billing customers, would first decide what company records the computer would need and would then draw a flow chart showing the steps the computer must follow to obtain old balances, add new charges, calculate financial charges, and deduct payments before determining a customer's bill. Using the flow chart, the programmer codes the actual instructions the computer will follow, checks the program to be sure there are no problems, and sees that an instruction sheet is prepared for the computer operator who will run the program.

STATISTICIAN

A statistician devises, carries out, and interprets the numerical results of surveys and experiments. In so doing, the individual applies knowledge of statistical methods to a particular subject area such as economics, human behavior, natural science, or engineering. These statistical techniques are often used to predict population growth or economic conditions, develop quality control tests for manufactured products, or help business managers make decisions. The statistician also decides where to get the necessary data, determines the type and size of the sample group, and develops the survey questionnaire or reporting form. Depending on the person's expertise and training, other common duties include designing experiments to test a theory, collecting data and summarizing the findings in tables, charts, and written reports, or using mathematical theory to improve statistical techniques.

SOURCE: *Occupational Outlook Handbook,* 1978–79 Edition, U.S. Department of Labor, Bureau of Labor Statistics

SYSTEMS ANALYST

The systems analyst is responsible for planning efficient methods of processing data and handling the results. The analyst begins an assignment by discussing the data processing problem with managers or specialists to determine the exact nature of the matter and to break it down into its component parts. Once a system has been developed, the analyst prepares charts and diagrams that describe the operation in terms that managers or customers can understand. If the system is accepted, the analyst translates the logical requirements of the system into the capabilities of the computer machinery. Because their work is so varied and complex, most analysts specialize in either business or scientific and engineering applications.

MATHEMATICIAN

All mathematicians can be grouped into one of two categories: theoretical and applied. Applied mathematicians are of most interest to business and government. These individuals use mathematics to develop theories, techniques, and approaches to solve practical problems in business, government, engineering, and the natural and social sciences. Their work ranges from analyses of the mathematical aspects of launching earth satellites to studies of the effects of new drugs on disease. While this work is all very broad in scope, modern applied mathematicians are basically concerned with applying mathematical knowledge to the solution of practical problems.

STATISTICAL CLERK

A statistical clerk prepares and ensures the accuracy and completeness of records. In all, there are four major groupings or categories in this field: (1) recording, (2) compiling and coding, (3) computing and tabulating, and (4) scheduling. The first collects and verifies the accuracy of information. The second ensures that the information is properly filed, verified or analyzed for data processing. The third gathers the information from records to present in a chart or table for analysis. The last schedules business activities that involve the movement of people and things, as in the case of the assignment clerk for a bus company who assigns drivers to meet riders' transportation needs.

COMPUTER OPERATIONS PERSONNEL

All data systems require specialized workers to enter data and instructions, operate the computer, and retrieve the results. Some of these people are keypunch operators who prepare input by punching patterns of holes into cards to represent different letters, numbers, and special characters. Others are console operators who examine the programmer's instructions for processing the input, make sure the computer has been loaded with the correct cards, etc., and start the computer. Still others are tape librarians who classify and catalog material and maintain files of current and previous versions of programs, listings, and test data.

CAREERS IN ACCOUNTING, STATISTICS, AND COMPUTERS (continued)

BOOKKEEPING WORKER

Every business needs systematic and up-to-date records of accounts and business transactions. Bookkeeping workers maintain these records in journals, ledgers, and on other accounting forms. They also prepare periodic financial statements showing all money received and paid out. In many small firms, general bookkeepers are the only bookkeeping workers. They analyze and record all financial transactions, such as orders and cash sales. They also check money taken in against that paid out to be sure accounts balance, and they calculate the firm's payroll. In large firms the bookkeepers often specialize in certain types of work. For example, some prepare statements on a company's income from sales or its daily operating expenses. Others may post payments and charges on cards using bookkeeping machines or feed information on accounts payable into the computer.

TECHNICAL WRITER

Technical writers put scientific and technical information into language that can be understood by people who need to use it. They research, write, and edit technical materials and also may produce publications or audiovisual materials. To ensure that their work is accurate, technical writers must be expert in the subject area in which they are writing—laser beams or computer science, for example. At the same time, their writing must be clear and easy to follow. Command of the language and an engaging writing style are tools of the trade that enable technical writers to convey information in a way that is helpful to people who use it—scientists, technicians, executives, sales representatives, and the general public.

CAREER	LATEST EMPLOYMENT FIGURES	EARNINGS	EMPLOYMENT OUTLOOK
Accountant	865,000	$15,000–$19,000 [a]	About as fast as the average for all occupations
Programmer	230,000	$12,000–$16,000	Faster than the average for all occupations
Statistician	24,000	$12,000–$15,000	Faster than the average for all occupations
Systems analyst	160,000	$15,000–$18,000	Faster than the average for all occupations
Mathematician	38,000	$12,000–$15,000	More slowly than the average for all occupations
Statistical clerk	337,000	$ 8,000–$12,000	About as fast as the average for all occupations
Computer operations personnel	565,000	$ 7,500–$11,000	About as fast as the average for all occupations
Bookkeeping worker	1.7 million	$ 8,400–$10,800	More slowly than the average for all occupations
Technical writer	22,000	$12,000–$19,000	About as fast as the average for all occupations

[a] But much higher for those with experience

Other Critical Dimensions

Thus far we have discussed the major operational activities of American businesses. However, there are some critical dimensions of the world of business which have not yet been examined. Among these are business-government relations and small business management. Since these do not fit directly within the two earlier sections of the book, we have saved it for now. Business and government constantly interact. As a result, students of business need to have an understanding of the relations that exist between these two institutions. In Chapter 24 the area of business law will be examined. Every firm has to operate within the law in carrying out its day-to-day activities. This means that the average businessperson needs at least a working knowledge of business law. Of course, the individual manager cannot hope to know as much as a lawyer. But the person should have some basic understanding of legal fundamentals. In this chapter we will study the law associated with contracts, negotiable instruments, agency, and bankruptcy. This will provide a good grasp of some of the legal aspects of business.

Next, in Chapter 25, the subject of government regulation will be examined. Because this area is so diverse we will concentrate our attention on just three primary subjects: federal regulation of competition, government taxation, and ethics. Antitrust and tax legislation are very important in determining the types of reactions that will exist between government and business. In this chapter we will look more closely at some of the best-known regulatory legislation, including the Sherman Antitrust Act, the Clayton Act, and the Federal Trade Commission Act. Then we will study the various types of taxes levied on proprietorships, partnerships, and corporations. Finally, consideration will be given to the role of ethics in business-government relations.

In Chapter 26 our attention will be focused on small business management. We will identify some of the major advantages and disadvantages of going into a small business and some of the major reasons for small business failure, as well as small business success. In addition the area of franchising will be examined. Then the role and scope of the Small Business Administration will be studied.

When you are finished reading this part you should know how the government goes about regulating business through legislation. You should also have a fundamental understanding of how such key areas as business law, ethics, taxation, and social responsibility affect business-government relations. And you should be aware of some of the major advantages and disadvantages of going into a small business. In addition, you should be familiar with a number of important terms, including *contract, negotiable instrument, blank endorsement, agent, principal, involuntary bankruptcy, interlocking directorate, progressive tax,* and *franchise.* Finally, you should have gained a solid understanding of the relationships that exist between business and government and the factors that help influence and change these relationships.

24

No man is above the law and no man is below it; nor do we ask any man's permission when we ask him to obey it.
Theodore Roosevelt

OBJECTIVES OF THIS CHAPTER

Every business must operate within the law. Therefore, it is vital that businesspeople have a fundamental understanding of some of the key areas of business law. There are two major objectives in this chapter. The first is to acquaint you with the American legal system, within which business functions. The second is to examine four of the most important areas of business law: contracts, negotiable instruments, agency, and bankruptcy. The first three are related to ongoing operations. The fourth deals with the way in which firms reorganize when they are unable to meet their debts or, if this is impossible, the manner in which a liquidation of assets occurs. When you are done reading this chapter, you should be able to do the following:

a. understand the American legal system;

b. know what the requirements are for a legal and enforceable business contract;

c. understand the requirements necessary for an instrument to be negotiable;

d. describe the four basic types of endorsements used to transfer negotiable instruments;

e. explain how a contract of agency is created; and

f. describe what bankruptcy is, and the types of action taken to either straighten out the firm or liquidate its assets.

Business Law

THE AMERICAN LEGAL SYSTEM

In order to understand the importance of business law, it is necessary to have a basic grasp of our American legal system. This system consists of laws that define "the rules of the game" within which individuals and businesses must operate.

In the United States there are two main sources of law: statutory law and common law. **Statutory law** is written law, consisting of formal enactments or statutes by various governmental bodies. The major form of statutory law is the Constitution. All federal and state statutes, as well as state constitutions, must conform to Constitutional law.

The second main source of law is **common law.** This is often referred to as *unwritten law,* and is based on court decisions that become precedents to be followed in future cases of a similar nature. For example, when confronted with a particular case, it is common for a judge to ask how other judges ruled in prior cases. By following the examples set by predecessors, the judge follows precedent. The source of many laws related to such business areas as contracts, property, and agency is common law. Our basic legal system can be diagrammed as in Fig. 24.1.

THE NATURE OF BUSINESS LAW

Business law is concerned with that part of the legal system that provides for both an orderly conduct of business affairs and also the settlement of any disputes that may arise in connection with these transactions. Many people believe that business law is

FIG. 24.1 *The basic U.S. legal system*

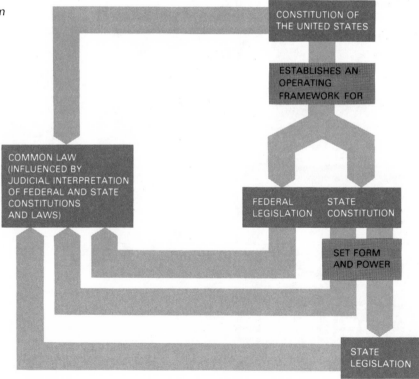

simply another name for business ethics. This is not so. Business law goes beyond ethics; specifically, by prescribing rules of conduct that *must* be obeyed.

Of course, the average business manager could call an attorney every time a legal problem arose. However, this would not only be very time consuming but would also lead to very costly legal fees. For this reason, managers need a basic understanding of business law and how it relates to day-to-day business operations. For example, in the case of contracts, what constitutes a binding agreement and when can the contract be legally set aside? Or, how should checks be endorsed in order to deposit them to the firm's bank account?

Sometimes these questions can get very involved and it becomes necessary to seek legal advice. However, the average manager can act properly in many cases if he or she has a good working knowledge of business law. This statement often evokes the following comment from business people: "How can I possibly remember all the business laws in all the states? If I'm transferred to another state, I'll have to start studying law all over again." Fortunately, this is not true.

In recent years there has been a trend toward accepting a single commercial code applicable to many kinds of business transactions. It is known as the **Uniform Commercial Code** and has been adopted by all the states except Louisiana. "The Code," as it is often called, covers many important business areas, including sales transactions, stock transfers, and negotiable instruments.

In this chapter we are going to be studying some of the most important areas of business law. We will begin with contracts, since no firm can escape entering into contracts in its everyday affairs.

1. How does statutory law differ from common law?

2. What is the Uniform Commercial Code?

"Harkness, I never want to hear from any employee of mine, 'it's not whether you win or lose, it's how you play the game'!"

From The Wall Street Journal; permission Cartoon Features Syndicate

CONTRACTS

A **contract** is a voluntary agreement between two or more competent parties in which, for consideration, one party receives the right to have the other carry out some lawful act. This definition, which can be diagrammed as in Fig. 24.2, is quite long, and it illustrates how detailed legal terms can be. They are designed to cover just about every eventuality. The following examines the terms used in the above definition, as well as other important contract-related information.

Voluntary Agreement

In order for a contract to exist there must be an *agreement* or *meeting of the minds* between the two contracting parties. This requires an *offer* and an ac-

FIG. 24.2 *Requirements for a legal and enforceable contract*

ceptance. The offer must be communicated in definite terms. For example, "I will sell you this brand-new suit at our sale price of $100." The acceptance must be made within a reasonable period of time, such as before the sale ends. Remember that the acceptance must conform to the *exact* terms of the offer. If the customer says "yes," there is agreement. If the customer says, "I'll give you $80," no contract exists—this is not an acceptance, it is a **counteroffer.** In order for a contract to now exist, the salesperson must accept the $80 offer.

The agreement must also be *voluntary.* Pressuring a person into signing a contract or tricking the individual in some way are grounds for setting aside the agreement.

Competent Parties
The individuals who are party to the agreement must be *competent to contract.* Insane persons, convicts, and drunkards are *not* regarded as legally competent. Nor are *minors,* who in most states are individuals under twenty-one years of age. If a merchant does business with a minor, the latter can *void the contract at his or her option.* For example, consider the case of a car dealer who sells a new Cadillac to a minor for cash. If the minor drives the car out of

the dealer's lot and drives it all around town, the young person can then return the vehicle and demand his or her money back. Thus there are times when parties are not competent to contract, and the manager must be aware of them.

Consideration
For a contract to be binding it is necessary for consideration to be present. **Consideration** is something of value received by one party or given up by another. For example, a business firm decides to expand its operations and build another plant. After looking over a number of available sites, the company finds one that seems to meet its needs. The firm thereupon offers the owner $1,000 for an option to purchase the land at a fixed price within sixty days. If the individual agrees, the payment of the $1,000 constitutes consideration. The firm gives up the money and the owner gives up the right to sell the land to anyone else for sixty days.

Another illustration of consideration would be when a person gives up a right in exchange for an agreed-upon sum of money. For example, a father promises his son $1,000 if the young man refrains from drinking until he is twenty-five years old. Giving up the right to drink constitutes consideration.

Lawful Act

A contract must involve a *lawful act*. An agreement to help restrain trade is a violation of the Sherman Antitrust Act and is, therefore, illegal and not binding. Likewise, in most states gambling is illegal. Thus if an individual loses money in a card game and he or she promises to pay, the agreement is not *legally* binding—and this is true even if the person puts it in writing. Nor can a lender collect more interest on a loan than that which is legally established. For example, if a company and a customer enter into a revolving credit contract whereby the individual agrees to pay an interest rate of 2.2 percent of any outstanding balance at the end of each month and the legal rate is 1.5 percent, the contract is not enforceable. In this case, as a general rule, the lender forfeits the right to any interest but the outstanding debt remains.

Required Form for a Contract

Many contracts are verbal in nature. The parties simply agree among themselves as to the terms and conditions, and that is that. However, there are times when it is helpful to have a contract in writing. Then if it becomes necessary to sue the other party for not complying with the agreed-upon terms, it is a lot easier to prove breach of contract.

There are situations when contracts *must* be in writing. One is for the sale of real estate. A second is for the sale of personal property valued at more than $500. A third is for agreements that cannot be completed within one year's time. A good general rule, however, is to put all important agreements in writing whether or not it is required by law.

3. In discussing the requirements for a legal contract, what is meant by a "meeting of the minds"?

4. What do we mean when we say that a contract must be communicated in "definite terms"?

5. Do all contracts have to be in writing?

Breach of Contract

When both parties fulfill their obligations, the contract is completed. Sometimes, however, a **breach of contract** will occur because one party fails to perform according to the terms of the agreement. If this party declares bankruptcy or can prove that some special problem exists, such as a serious illness, that prevented completion of the contract, the courts may excuse performance. Barring such events, the other party may bring legal action. The person(s) instituting the suit is known as the **plaintiff.** The person(s) against whom the action is brought is called the **defendant.**

After hearing both sides of the case, the court will reach a conclusion. If it feels the party bringing the suit is entitled to the payment of damages, the court will issue a *judgment* in favor of the plaintiff. In this case it may be necessary for the defendant to sell property and other valuables to pay the damages that have been awarded.

"I hate to tell you this but they just said on the radio that he's been indicted."

From The Wall Street Journal; permission Cartoon Features Syndicate

Sometimes the defendant will not have sufficient assets to pay the entire judgment. However, the matter does not always end here. In most states, if the person is a wage earner it is possible to force the employer to pay the amount owed by withholding part of the individual's salary each payday. This is known as **garnishment.** Based on a 1970 federal law, the percentage of garnished wages is limited to 25 percent of the worker's monthly income.

Statute of limitations

Every state provides that after a specified number of years have gone by, breach of contract claims are outlawed. This is called a **statute of limitations** and,

Xerography and Legality

Whenever we want a copy of something, we go to a photocopy machine (usually a Xerox machine) and make a duplicate. In fact, photocopying has become so prevalent in the United States that few people bother to copy anything longhand anymore. This has resulted in an epidemic known as "xeromania." In 1975 there were 2.3 million copying machines in this country emitting an estimated 78 billion copies. This is enough paper, if laid end to end, to girdle the globe 546 times at its widest point. And these copying machines are everywhere, from the local public library to the nearby business office. Furthermore, this xeromania seems to be going on worldwide. Even the Gosplan, Russia's state planning committee, reproduces many of its official documents on Xerox machines.

The problem currently confronting business firms, especially publishing houses, is that people are duplicating books, articles, sheet music, and so on—all of which are, in the view of the publishers, copyrighted material protected by law. Yet since the introduction of photocopying machines, nothing in printed form seems to be sacred anymore. Even expensive economic or stock-market newsletters that cost subscribers $500 a year are available for pennies if someone can get their hands on an original.

Many business firms and governmental organizations are viewing this problem very seriously and are taking steps to reduce, if not totally eliminate, the photocopying of copyrighted material. In those instances where an individual has access to the machine, this is very difficult. However, in those cases where there is a central photocopying department, the employees there are being instructed to return all copyrighted materials (or that seem to be copyrighted) to the person submitting them, along with a note relating why the work has not been done. This will not eliminate all copyright violations, but it is certain to reduce them substantially.

by its very title, limits the time period during which one may sue. This period begins at the moment the right to sue arises and varies in length depending on the nature of the claim.

Keep in mind that the statute of limitations does not discharge the contract. It merely provides a defense against a breach of contract claim. Thus, if legal action is brought against a party after the statute of limitations has run out, the person can plead the statute and defeat the action. Note, however, that if the party agrees either verbally or in writing to make good on the contract after the statute has run out, the entire obligation is once more revived and the period of limitation begins anew. In this case, the party again places itself in jeopardy should it fail to honor the contract.

6. What is a breach of contract? Can the party guilty of the breach be sued?

7. If the statute of limitations runs out and the party that failed to fulfill the contract then promises in writing to make good on the agreement, does this affect the situation in any way?

NEGOTIABLE INSTRUMENTS

A **negotiable instrument** is a form of business paper that can be transferred from one person to another as a substitute for money. The most common form of negotiable instrument is a check, which can be given to someone in the place of cash and then transferred from this person to others by simply endorsing it on the back.

Requirements for Negotiability

There are five requirements for an instrument to be negotiable. First, it must be *in writing and signed by the person who is drawing it up.* The instrument does not have to be on any kind of special material, nor does it have to be written with a special implement. A check, for example, can be made out in

Negotiable instruments come in a variety of forms.

pen, pencil, or even crayon. And it can be printed, handwritten, or typewritten. In most cases, of course, a check is drawn up on a special form printed by a bank (see Fig. 24.3). In all cases, the check is in writing and signed by the drawer.

Second, a negotiable instrument must contain *an unconditional promise to pay a specific amount of money.* By this we mean, first, that the promise or order to pay is not based on any condition. For example, to write a check "payable to Steven Mc-Dermott when he mows my lawn properly" is not negotiable. Any conditions written on the check destroy its negotiability, turning it from a negotiable instrument into a contract. Second, the amount must be clearly stated, such as $10.00.

Third, the instrument must be *payable on demand or at a definite future date.* In the case of a check, for example, the date is usually written in the upper right-hand corner. Sometimes a person will write a check but know that there will not be sufficient funds in the account for at least seven days. In this case, the drawer may postdate the check by, for example, making it out on March 3 but dating it March 10. In this way the check is not negotiable for seven days.

Fourth, the instrument must be *payable "to bearer" or "to order."* Note that the check in Fig.

24.3 contains such directions, ordering the bank to "pay to the order of."

Fifth, *the person receiving the instrument must be indicated with reasonable certainty.* This is usually done by writing in the name of the individual as opposed to making the check payable to "my good friend" or "my wife." If the drawer wants to cash a check on his or her own account, this too is possible. Rather than making the instrument payable to oneself and then signing it, the person can make it payable to "bearer" or "cash." In either case, the check is negotiable.

Transfer of Negotiable Instruments

Negotiable instruments can be transferred from one person to another by a process known as *endorsement.* In the case of a check, this simply involves the holder signing his or her name on the back of the instrument. The person who signs is known as the *endorser.* The individual to whom the check is transferred is called the *endorsee.* This latter person can then become a *holder in due course.* This is a term used to describe any individual who acquires a negotiable instrument through endorsement under the following conditions: (a) the instrument was filled out properly, (b) the individual gave something of value for it, (c) the person accepted it in good faith,

FIG. 24.3 *Illustration of a completed check (Reprinted by permission of the Metropolitan Bank and Trust Company, Melrose, Massachusetts.)*

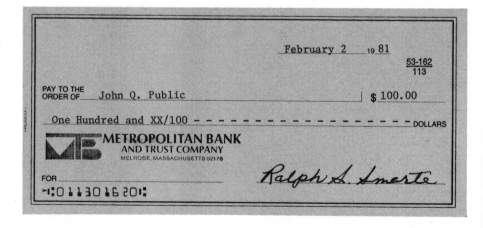

and (d) the individual had no knowledge of any problems associated with the instrument.

These conditions are comprehensive, and they are meant to be. A holder in due course is usually entitled to collect the value of the instrument. Therefore the law is strict regarding the conditions this person must meet. For example, if a check has some erasures on it and these are easily visible, a person accepting the check might not be a holder in due course. Or if part of the instrument is not complete, such as the date is missing or the person has not signed it, the individual receiving the check again would not be a holder in due course. Thus the law is very stringent on negotiable instruments.

Before we close our discussion of this topic, it should be noted that there are some *real defenses* against holders in due course. One of these defenses is *forgery*. If someone steals your checkbook and starts writing checks on your account, you could be out hundreds of dollars. In the case of a business firm, someone who stole some blank payroll checks from the company might cash thousands of dollars worth before the loss was discovered. In these cases, the thief would be very careful in completing the instrument. And the persons to whom the thief passed the checks would accept them in good faith, believing they were holders in due course. However,

because forgery is a real defense against such a holder, the person is not entitled to payment. Thus everyone who cashed these checks would be out their money.

This discussion should indicate that business law is very important to managers. Unless they have a basic understanding of some of the fundamentals of negotiable instruments, they can easily run into problems. One way of avoiding them is to understand the proper way to endorse negotiable instruments to other parties. In all, there are four basic types of endorsements: (a) blank, (b) restrictive, (c) special, and (d) qualified. All are illustrated in Fig. 24.4. Now we will examine each of these in detail.

Blank endorsement

When a person simply signs his or her name on the back of a negotiable instrument, this is called a **blank endorsement.** Because this is the simplest way to endorse such an instrument, it is also the most common. In the case of a check, all the person has to do is sign his or her name in the same way it appears on the face of the check. If the check has been made out to Jennifer Anne McDermott this is *exactly* how it should be signed on the back.

The major problem with a blank endorsement is that it turns the instrument into "bearer paper";

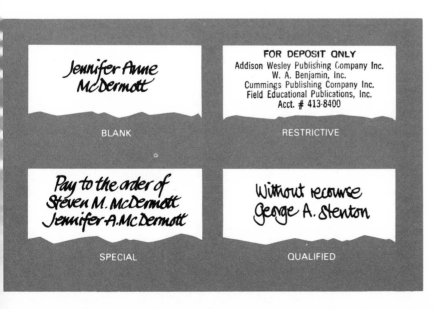

FIG. 24.4 *The most common types of endorsements on negotiable instruments*

Jennifer Anne McDermott

BLANK

FOR DEPOSIT ONLY
Addison Wesley Publishing Company Inc.
W. A. Benjamin, Inc.
Cummings Publishing Company Inc.
Field Educational Publications, Inc.
Acct. # 413-8400

RESTRICTIVE

Pay to the order of
Steven M. McDermott
Jennifer A. McDermott

SPECIAL

Without recourse
George A. Stenton

QUALIFIED

Is George Washington's check an example of blank endorsement, restrictive endorsement, special endorsement, or qualified endorsement?

the instrument becomes payable to the individual who holds or bears the paper. As a result, if Jennifer Anne McDermott writes a blank endorsement and then loses the check, the finder can cash it. Therefore, it is wise to use blank endorsements only when one is actually ready to transfer the check to someone else. For example, if Jennifer is cashing her payroll check at a bank, she should not put a blank endorsement on it until she is ready to give it to the teller.

Restrictive endorsement

A **restrictive endorsement** identifies the purpose for which the endorsement is made. The most common form of restrictive endorsement is for deposit or collection. In such a case the endorser writes "for deposit only" (or words to that effect) and then signs directly below it. In this way, if the check is lost the person finding it cannot cash it. Business firms often use a rubber stamp containing a restrictive endorsement so that they can handle a large number of incoming checks each day. An illustration of such an endorsement is presented in Fig. 24.4.

Special endorsement

When the endorser wants to specify the person to whom the instrument is being transferred, a **special** endorsement can be used. For example, if Jennifer A. McDermott wants to transfer a check to her brother Steven A. McDermott, she can endorse as shown in Fig. 23.4. The benefit of a special endorsement is that it provides protection against loss while allowing the payee to identify the next **holder in due course.**

Qualified endorsement

Sometimes an endorser wants to be relieved of any liability in case the person drawing up the negotiable instrument, such as a check, is unable to meet the obligation. This can be done with a **qualified endorsement.** The qualified endorsement shown in Fig. 24.4, for example, means that George refuses to accept liability if the check bounces. However, the party cashing the check is not totally out of luck. All those who endorsed the check before George, as well as the person who drew it up, are liable in order from last to first unless they too used a qualified endorsement.

Of course, very few people are willing to accept a qualified endorsement. If nothing else, such an endorsement implies that the person holding it believes the check will bounce. However, there are times when qualified endorsements are accepted. For example, the Acme Manufacturing Company is sending its lawyer, George Stenton, to purchase a particular patent process from another firm. Acme makes the check payable to George. Then, when the purchase is finalized and all the papers are signed, the lawyer endorses the check to the seller "without recourse." This endorsement releases George from any liability in case the check is returned marked N.S.F. (not sufficient funds). Since George is only an agent for his principal (Acme), a qualified endorsement is acceptable to the seller.

8. What are the five requirements for an instrument to be negotiable?

9. Why is it dangerous to make a blank endorsement of a check and then carry it around in one's pocket?

10. How does a restrictive endorsement differ from a special endorsement?

11. Why might someone refuse to accept a negotiable instrument from an endorser who has placed a qualified endorsement on the instrument?

AGENCY

Another important area of business law is that of **agency.** In conducting business relationships it is common for firms to assign people to represent them as agents. An agreement between two parties in which one is given the necessary authority to represent the other in business transactions with third parties is known as a *contract of agency.* The person who does the representing is known as the **agent.** The party represented by the agent is called the **principal.** We just saw an illustration of this when

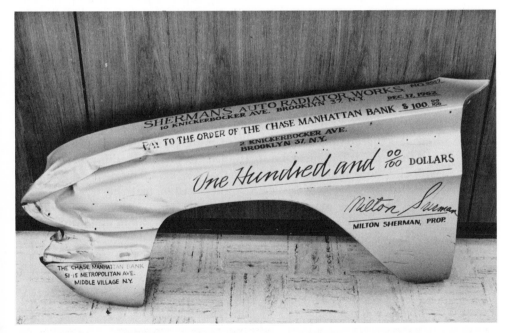

In all cases the check must be in writing and signed by the drawer.

George Stenton represented Acme Manufacturing in the purchase of the patent process.

When a company wishes to appoint an agent, it may do so either verbally or in writing. A formal written appointment is called a **power of attorney.** We saw an earlier illustration of this in Chapter 17 when the proxy was discussed. Another way of creating a contract of agency is through a written letter formally appointing the agent. If the period of performance will extend for more than one year, such a contract *must* be in writing.

Both parties, agent and principal, have obligations to each other. An agent is expected to obey the principal's instructions, act with reasonable care and skill in carrying out these orders, and maintain and render to the principal a true accounting of all transactions. The principal, meanwhile, is expected to reimburse the agent for all legitimate expenses and carry out all the terms of the agreement created by the agency.

12. What obligations does an agent have to his or her principal?

13. What obligations does a principal have to the agent?

CASE

And Not a Penny More

Annie Stockdale is an attorney for a large midwestern insurance firm. The company has just completed a new wing on its main office and is in the process of purchasing office equipment for the new facilities. Yesterday Annie was sent to a nearby office equipment and furniture store, Standard Office Furniture, Inc., to pay for the merchandise the firm picked out last Friday. The president gave Annie a check made out to her for $12,500. "I know the manager is asking $14,000 for the merchandise," the president told her, "but we are not going to pay that much. I am authorizing you to endorse this check to the store if they sell and deliver the goods to us for $12,500 and not a penny more."

When Annie entered the store, she immediately asked for the manager. She told the man that she had been given a check for $12,500 and that the company would pay no more than this for the equipment and furniture it had picked out. The two of them talked for ten minutes, with the store manager explaining that his company never discounted from list price. However, when Annie insisted that she was unable to pay list, the store manager placed a long-distance call to the New York office. After talking to someone there for a while, he hung up the phone and said to Annie:

> How much are you willing to pay for the equipment and furniture, including delivery?
>
> I will pay $12,500. I have a check here that I will endorse over to you if you agree.

CHAPTER 24

BANKRUPTCY

Bankruptcy occurs when a debtor's financial obligations are greater than his or her assets. The objective of bankruptcy laws is to allow debtors to straighten out the financial affairs of their business or to provide for the orderly and equitable distribution of the company's assets among the creditors. Of course, as we noted earlier in the book, when a firm declares bankruptcy most of the creditors (if not all) are able to collect only a portion of the debt owed to them. It is, therefore, better to try to straighten out the company if at all possible, thus avoiding the far-reaching effects of bankruptcy.

Working Things Out

One way to work things out is through an **extension agreement,** in which case the creditors give the firm an extension of payment terms. For example, they might allow the company one year as a grace period, during which time no debts come due. When the year is over, all obligations are again payable as scheduled. It is hoped, naturally, that during this year the firm can turn itself around.

A second approach used to avoid bankruptcy is for all the creditors to accept a **composition agreement.** This calls for everyone to take a reduction in the amount owed to them.

All right. You have a deal. Let me call in the secretary. We have a standard written contract for all sales, and I'll have to ask you to sign it. You can expect delivery by Friday.

Annie read over the contract and signed it. She then endorsed the check she had been given by the president over to Standard Office Furniture, signing "without recourse, Annie Stockdale." The store manager looked over the check, examined the endorsement, and thanked Annie for her business. The two shook hands and Annie left the store and immediately returned to the insurance company, where she phoned the president and told him that delivery of the merchandise could be expected by Friday.

1. Was Annie an agent for the insurance firm in this transaction? Explain.

2. Did the above agreement meet the requirements of a valid and enforceable contract? Explain why or why not?

3. Why did Annie endorse the check "without recourse"? Should not the manager have refused to accept such an endorsement?

Howard R. Hughes

When Howard Hughes was eighteen years old his father died, leaving him controlling interest in the Hughes Tool Company. Using this as a base of operations, Hughes moved into numerous enterprises—from RKO Pictures in the 1940s to TWA in the 1950s to Las Vegas casinos in the 1960s. In the last two decades of his life, however, his greatest accomplishment may well have been his ability to remain hidden from the public's view and outside the grasp of the law. For example, during all the legal maneuvering involved in his suit with TWA and the eventual sale of his holdings, he never made an appearance in court despite the fact that he was ordered to do so. In fact, he suffered a $137-million default judgment (later voided) rather than allow his isolation to be breached.

And throughout all Hughes's business transactions, competitors and the public alike were amazed at his ability to get his way. For example, he was the sole owner of seven Nevada casinos (Desert Inn, Sands, Frontier, Castaways, Silver Slipper, Landmark, Harold's Club) in a state where gambling is so regulated that no other individual owns even one resort casino. Yet Hughes was able to get special permission from the Nevada Gaming Commission and the U.S. Justice Department. And in Nevada, where applicants for casino licenses are normally required to be fingerprinted and to submit a recent photograph, Hughes had to do none of this for any of his seven licenses.

Furthermore, when Hughes decided to buy Air West Airlines,

the Civil Aeronautics Board also approved the acquisition without an appearance by him. And at the time Hughes happened to have a massive court judgment against him charging mismanagement of TWA.

Then it looked like the world might get to see Howard Hughes. On September 4, 1974, the United States consul in Nassau went to the Xanadu-Princess Hotel on Grand Bahama Island to serve Hughes, who was reportedly staying there, with a court summons growing out of his indictment on charges of stock-market manipulation in his acquisition of Air West Airlines. Such a summons requires a personal appearance, and without it one can be declared a fugitive from justice. The hotel management denied knowing of Hughes's whereabouts. The consul therefore served the summons on an individual who had been designated to accept mail for the billionaire.

Would Howard Hughes now appear? Nope. He got out of this one the way he did all others— with the help of top-notch attorneys. A week later the United States consul was informed by a Hughes lawyer that to serve the summons properly he would have to give it to Howard Hughes in person. And, of course, Mr. Hughes was inaccessible. As one federal court judge put it, "Attempting to apply orderly judicial processes to Hughes is like twisting with a ghost." Hughes's immunity from examination by government agencies and judicial systems remained an American phenomenon right up to his death in April 1976.

In either of the above cases, it is common for the creditors to demand some role in managing the business. For example, during the life of the extension agreement the creditors may require the owners of the firm to reduce the amount of money they are withdrawing for personal living expenses. It is also common to find creditor approval needed for raising employee salaries, increasing company debt, or making any large or unusual purchases. If the company is willing to agree to these terms, bankruptcy can be avoided (or at least delayed). If the firm is not prepared to agree, however, some form of bankruptcy is inevitable.

Voluntary and Involuntary Action

Bankruptcy can be either voluntary or involuntary. **Voluntary bankruptcy** occurs when the debtor files a petition of bankruptcy in the federal court. In the petition the debtor declares that liabilities exceed assets and that he or she (or the firm) wants the court to divide these assets equitably among the creditors and grant relief from further debt burden. If this is done the debtor is then given a new start, having been legally freed from all of these old financial obligations.

Involuntary bankruptcy occurs when the creditors file a petition in federal court alleging that the debtor has committed an act of bankruptcy. Some of the more common acts of bankruptcy include

1. transferring property for the purpose of defrauding the creditors,
2. failing to pay interest when it becomes due,
3. failing to pay principal when it becomes due,
4. concealing property, or
5. admitting in writing an inability to pay debts.

When the creditors bring the bankruptcy proceeding, the court notifies the debtor of the action. It is then the responsibility of the debtor to either deny or admit the alleged act of bankruptcy. If the debtor denies bankruptcy, the court can investigate the claim to determine if the creditors are correct. If they are not, of course, the matter is settled. If the

The objective of bankruptcy laws is to allow debtors to straighten out the financial affairs of their business or to provide for the orderly and equitable distribution of the company's assets among the creditors.

court finds that the debtor is indeed bankrupt, however, it will appoint a **referee,** who in turn will notify all the creditors to submit their claims to the court. The assets of the debtor will be turned over to a **trustee,** who will administer the assets or operate the business during the period of bankruptcy proceedings. If these assets are eventually liquidated, the trustee is the one who distributes the proceeds to the creditors. The order of claim against these assets is as follows:

1. all court costs, including the expenses of the trustee, lawyers, and all other people approved by the court;
2. employee wages earned within three months

prior to the start of the proceedings and limited to $600 per employee;

3. all reasonable expenses of those creditors who opposed the liquidation plan finally agreed to by the court, as well as all reasonable expenses incurred by creditors in obtaining evidence resulting in the conviction of any person violating the Bankruptcy Act;

4. all taxes; and

5. debts, in the order of priority determined by law.

✿✿✿

14. Why is it better to try and straighten out a company than to declare bankruptcy?

15. How does an extension agreement differ from a composition agreement?

16. What are some of the more common acts of bankruptcy?

Reorganization

Some corporations are so large that their liquidation would work a hardship on the general public. A large railroad such as the Penn Central is an illustration. In such a case the courts will prepare a plan of **reorganization** rather than of liquidation. In this case the trustee will be instructed by the court to prepare, with the assistance of a reorganization committee, a reorganization plan to keep the company in operation while providing an equitable settlement of creditor claims. This settlement will come not in the form of cash, but rather as stocks and bonds in the reorganized corporation. In such a situation the creditors frequently become part (if not total) owners of the corporation.

In order to be put into operation by the court, a reorganization plan has to be approved by two-thirds of each class of creditors and 50 percent of each class of stockholders. If a plan is rejected, another has to be formulated. This, of course, can take a long time, during which the trustee may have to raise money to continue the operation of the

Help

Some firms, rather than declare bankruptcy, seek government assistance. This is particularly true for grant corporations. The most recent example is the Chrysler Corporation.

The company's downhill slide began in 1975 with a net loss of $260 million, the largest in company history. To cope with the situation, Chrysler began selling off some of its subsidiaries and reorganizing others. In 1976 it sold the Airtemp Division to the Fedders Corporation and combined its South Africa Division with the Illings Group to form Sigma Motor Car Corp., the largest auto maker in South Africa.

In 1978 it sold Chrysler Europe to PSA Peugeot-Citroen for $230 million in cash and $200 million in stock. Later that year, it sold its 51 percent equity in Chrysler Argentina. Despite such maneuvers it had a $205 million loss.

In 1979 it sold its Venezuela assets to General Motors and one third of its equity in Chrysler Australia to Mitsubishi Motors. Second quarter losses were over $200 million, and by August layoffs were in excess of 23,000 workers and the projected loss for the year stood at $700 million. By the end of the year, Chrysler was enmeshed in discussions with the federal government regarding a loan of $1+ billion. While it initially was unclear as to how much money the government was willing to lend, it was apparent that Chrysler would not be allowed to go bankrupt. The impact on the economy would be too great. In early 1980 Chrysler received loan guarantees that permitted continued operation.

business. This is done through the sale of **trustee certificates.** In order to increase the salability of these certificates, their purchasers are given priority over all other existing creditors of the corporation.

Once the reorganization plan is finally agreed to by the creditors and stockholders, the court will order it put into action. At this point the corporation can begin a fresh start as a reorganized company.

17. Why are some companies reorganized rather than allowed to go into bankruptcy?

18. How much of a voice do creditors and stockholders have about how a bankrupt firm is reorganized?

Sixty Cents on the Dollar Beats Nothing

Standard Office Furniture, Inc., sold over $7,500 of furniture to Levalier Manufacturing three years ago. However, despite repeated phone calls, the manufacturing company never paid for the merchandise. Realizing that the firm was in financial trouble, Standard tried to strike a bargain in hopes of settling the bill. Standard asked for 70 percent of the outstanding amount. However, Levalier was in such financial trouble that it was unable to pay even this amount. It did offer to pay 30 percent of the bill, if Standard would accept this as full payment, but Standard rejected the proposal as "ridiculous."

Twelve months ago Standard and four other creditors decided to take legal action. The group filed a petition in the district court asking that the firm be declared bankrupt. The court notified Levalier of the action, and the firm admitted that it was unable to meet its debts and saw no way of doing so without liquidation of its holdings. However, Levalier did ask for more time to straighten out its operations.

The plaintiffs, on the other hand, felt that there was no way of getting their money if the firm was not dissolved. Therefore, they refused to accept any terms except liquidation. Two months ago the court appointed a trustee and, according to Standard's president, the store should receive about 60 percent of the outstanding bill. The firm hopes to have this money within six months. When asked why the plaintiffs insisted on a bankruptcy proceeding, the president explained that this was the only way of ever getting anything from the manufacturing firm. "Sixty cents on the dollar beats nothing," he said.

1. Was this a case of voluntary or involuntary bankruptcy?

2. What is the order of claims against the assets of Levalier? Where does Standard fall in this list?

3. Why did Standard opt for liquidation rather than letting Levalier try to work it out?

SUMMARY

Because every business must operate within the law, businesspeople need a basic understanding of the most important areas of business law. In this chapter we examined four: contracts, negotiable instruments, agency, and bankruptcy.

A contract is a voluntary agreement between two or more competent parties in which, for consideration, one party receives the right to have the other carry out some lawful act. In order for a contract to be binding, a number of prerequisites must be present: there must be a meeting of the minds between the parties; the individuals must be competent to contract; there must be consideration or something of value received by one party or given up by another; and the contract must involve a lawful act. In addition, the agreement must be in proper form. For example, some contracts have to be in writing.

In some cases a breach of contract will occur because one party fails to perform according to the terms of the agreement. If the other party brings a suit for damages and wins, the court will issue a judgment in its favor. This can result in the losing party having to sell its personal assets or having its salary garnished.

A negotiable instrument is a form of business paper that can be transferred from one person to another as a substitute for money. For an instrument to be negotiable, it must be in writing and signed by the maker, contain an unconditional promise to pay a specific amount of money, be payable on demand or at a definite future date, be payable "to bearer" or "to order," and indicate with reasonable certainty the person receiving the instrument.

Because negotiable instruments are transferred from one person to another, there are certain requirements for being a holder in due course. These are that the instrument is properly filled out and that the individual give something of value for it, accept it in good faith, and have no knowledge of any problems associated with the instrument. The actual endorsement of the instrument can take any of four forms: blank, restrictive, special, or qualified.

Another important area of business law is agency. A contract of agency occurs when a company appoints a party to represent it in business transactions. In such an agreement, both sides, the principal and the agent, have obligations to each other.

Bankruptcy occurs when a debtor's liabilities are greater than his or her assets. In order to salvage the situation it is common to find extension agreements or composition agreements being used. Or in the case of large companies, whose failures would work a hardship on the general public, a reorganization is common. Barring these eventualities, however, the court will appoint a trustee to liquidate the company's assets and distribute the proceeds to the creditors.

KEY TERMS FOUND IN THIS CHAPTER

QUESTIONS FOR DISCUSSION AND ANALYSIS

1. What do we mean when we say that all individuals party to an agreement must be competent to contract?

2. Is a contract requiring the performance of an illegal act a valid agreement?

3. How is the statute of limitations a defense against a breach of contract claim?

4. What are the four necessary conditions for an individual to be a holder in due course?

5. What is meant by the statement that "forgery is a real defense against a holder in due course"?

6. Does a contract of agency always have to be in writing? Explain.

7. What is the job of the trustee in bankruptcy proceedings?

8. If it takes years to get a plan of reorganization accepted by the creditors and stockholders, how does the trustee raise the necessary money to keep the firm going?

25

Government in the U.S. today is a senior partner in every business in the country.
Norman Cousins

OBJECTIVES OF THIS CHAPTER

In the last chapter we examined the importance of business law, which helps dictate rules of the road for business operations. However, there are other rules and regulations to which business must also adhere. We will be looking at some of these in this chapter, which involves a closer examination of the relations between business and government.

The first objective of this chapter is to study the key laws used to regulate competition. Included in this group are some with which you are already familiar, including the Sherman Antitrust Act and the Clayton Act. The second objective is to look at another key area of government regulation, namely taxation. In this discussion, attention will be given to the major types of taxes levied upon business. The third objective is to review the area of ethics and study the way in which ethics affect business-government relations. When you are finished reading this chapter you should be able to do the following:

a. identify the major goals of the important federal laws, including the Sherman, Clayton, Federal Trade Commission, Robinson-Patman, and Celler-Kefauver Antimerger acts;

b. describe the three major types of taxes: regressive, progressive, and proportional;

c. explain the difference between revenue and regulatory taxes; and

d. relate the importance of ethics to business-government relations.

Government Regulation
of Business

REGULATION OF COMPETITION

One of the most significant areas of business-government relations involves the regulation of competition. Over the last ninety years the federal government has enacted a number of important pieces of legislation in this area. These laws have established the guidelines within which business must operate. The most important of these include: (a) the Sherman Antitrust Act, (b) the Clayton Act, (c) the Federal Trade Commission Act, (d) the Robinson-Patman Act, and (e) the Celler-Kefauver Antimerger Act.

Sherman Antitrust Act

In 1890 the federal government passed the **Sherman Antitrust Act.** Its objective was to outlaw all contracts or agreements formed for the purpose of restraining trade in interstate commerce. At the heart of the law was the belief that "big is bad." The legislators of this era apparently agreed with this analogy, because the act was passed by both houses of Congress with only one dissenting vote.

As is commonly known today, the Sherman Antitrust Act was used to break up monopolies that were formed for the purpose of preventing free competition. The most famous early case was that involving the Standard Oil trust, headed by John D. Rockefeller. Starting out in the 1860s, Rockefeller managed, in twenty years, to build the Standard Oil empire to the point where its coffers were swollen with more than $40 million in cash and its market share of the nation's oil business stood at 90 percent. With the passage of antimonopoly legislation, however, the Ohio courts broke up the Standard Oil trust into twenty companies, thereby eliminating a major threat to free competition.

Today the Sherman Act is still being used to regulate commerce. The most famous current case is that of the federal government versus IBM. IBM is accused of violating the antitrust act by monopoliz-

An 1890 cartoon showing the greedy image of "King Monopoly."

ing the market for general-purpose digital computers. The government is also charging the firm with using its market power to extend and perpetuate this dominance. Supporters of IBM claim that the basic issue is merely one of size; IBM is larger than all of its competitors combined and so the government wants to break it up. Certainly there is still a great deal of support in the Justice Department for the belief that "big is bad," although there is undoubtedly more to the government's case than just this. For the moment, however, we will have to wait and see how the court finally rules in what promises to be a landmark antitrust case.

Clayton Act

By 1914 it was evident that the Sherman Act had too many loopholes. As a result, the Congress enacted the **Clayton Act,** which was much more specific than its predecessor. In passing this bill the government recognized that the problem with business trusts was more than just size; there was also the matter of illegal business practices.

As a result, the Clayton Act specified a number of illegal practices. One of these was **tying agreements,** whereby a buyer, in order to obtain merchandise from the seller, agreed to purchase other goods from the vendor as well. For example, a manufacturer of men's suits would refuse to sell to middlemen unless they also carried the manufacturer's line of shirts and ties. The sale of one product was thus tied to the sale of others. And in recent years computer manufacturers have been prevented from requiring companies that purchased their machines to also buy software, such as punched cards, from them.

A second outlawed practice was the use of interlocking directorates. An **interlocking directorate** occurs when a majority of the members of the board of directors of two or more competitive corporations, at least one of which has assets in excess of $1 million, are the same individuals. It is easy to see that under these conditions the board might well try to coordinate the activities of these corporations

in such a way as to drive out competitive firms in the industry.

The Clayton Act also forbade one corporation from buying up another corporation's stock if the purchase would result in a serious lessening of competition or in the creation of a monopoly. This part of the act has been particularly troublesome to business in recent years, and we have seen many newspaper headlines related to it. The most famous recent case involved the International Telephone and Telegraph Corporation (ITT). In early 1969, ITT announced its decision to acquire the Canteen Corporation, one of the leading manufacturers of vending machines. However, because ITT was already such a huge conglomerate, the Justice Department announced that it considered the merger of ITT with a giant vending-machine manufacturer to be a restraint of trade. Nevertheless, ITT went ahead and concluded the merger.

Shortly thereafter, the giant conglomerate announced two more pending mergers. The first was with the Grinnell Corporation, well known for its production and sales of fire-protection devices, industrial piping, and sprinkler systems. The other planned merger was with the Hartford Fire and Casualty Insurance Company, the nation's sixth-largest insurance firm. In both cases the Justice Department voiced its opposition.

In the final analysis, ITT was allowed to keep the Hartford Insurance Company. However, it was required to sell the Canteen Corporation and the fire-protection division of the Grinnell Corporation. The conglomerate also had to divest itself of some life insurance firms it owned as well as the Avis Rent-A-Car Company. Finally, ITT had to agree not to buy any large interest in a domestic automatic sprinkler company or in insurance firms whose assets exceeded $10 million.

This agreement, as you can see, meant that in order for ITT to acquire certain firms, it had to sell others. And this approach has become very common in recent years. The Justice Department feels that one way to prevent the formation of business trusts

If you've wondered what some of our earlier advertising meant when we said Ocean Spray® Cranberry Juice Cocktail has more food energy than orange juice or tomato juice, let us make it clear: we didn't mean ...d energy ...re. ...nt at ...may not ...energy, ...ean ...tail helps ...od energy ...drinks.

IMPORTANT NOTICE REGARDING THE FLAMMABILITY OF CELLULAR PLASTICS USED IN BUILDING CONSTRUCTION, AND LOW DENSITY CELLULAR PLASTICS USED IN FURNITURE

The flammability characteristics of cellular plastics used in building construction, and low ...

...Cranberry Juice Cocktail gives you and your family Vitamin C, plus a great wake-up taste. It's... the other breakfast drink.

The FTC keeps a watchful eye out for misleading or false advertising.

is to stop big companies from simply buying up smaller ones without having to divest themselves of any current holdings.

1. Why did Congress pass the Sherman Antitrust Act?

2. What kinds of business practices did the Clayton Act outlaw?

3. Why was the government opposed to ITT's purchase of the Canteen, Grinnell, and Hartford Insurance firms?

Federal Trade Commission Act

The **Federal Trade Commission Act** was passed in September 1914, a month before the Clayton Act. One of its key provisions was to create a Federal Trade Commission (FTC), which has helped enforce the Clayton Act. This commission was given the power to issue cease and desist orders wherever it felt a violation of the antitrust laws had occurred.

Over the years, however, the FTC's powers have been greatly expanded. Today it is very active in surveying business practices, often instigating "trade practice conferences" in which firms in a particular industry agree on what constitutes unfair competition. The FTC is also a vigilant watchdog in the area of business advertising. Newspapers continually carry reports about firms under FTC investigation for false or misleading advertising. In recent years the FTC has investigated all sorts of advertising claims, from those made by aspirin manufacturers to those by tire makers. In one of the most famous cases, the commission persuaded a bread manufacturer to change part of its television commercial on diet bread. The company claimed that its bread had less calories than a regular slice of its competitors' bread. In fact, this occurred because the diet bread was sliced thinner, and in actuality the difference in total calories was very small. In its future commercials the firm began to point this out.

The FTC has been called "the policeman of the business world." Certainly in recent years it has taken on new dimensions and has begun to play a more active role not only in helping to enforce the Clayton Act but also by investigating all sorts of deceiving or misleading business practices.

Robinson-Patman Act

In 1936 Congress enacted the **Robinson-Patman Act,** the purpose of which was to eliminate unfair price competition. In essence, the act prevents a vendor from selling to one buyer more cheaply than others, unless the price differential is based on cost or the need to meet competition. Thus a manufacturer cannot discriminate against its customers by arbitrarily deciding to charge some people more than others.

The act forbids sellers involved in interstate commerce from engaging in price discrimination or terms of sale between customers purchasing goods of similar quality and characteristics. It also prohibits sellers from giving advertising allowances or other special services unless these concessions are granted to all buyers on "proportionately equal terms." In the case of price discrimination, the act sets the burden of proof on the seller.

One of the best-known cases involved the Borden Company, which was charged with selling evaporated milk at different prices to different buyers. This was done with the use of "dual branding," in which the company sold milk under its own brand at one price and under private brands to retailers at different prices. The milk, in all of these cases, was identical; only the brand names differed. The company was found guilty of violating the Robinson-

Thomas J. Watson, Jr.

Is there such a thing as being too successful? If so, IBM is a perfect illustration, and it owes much of this success to Thomas J. Watson, Jr.

Born in 1914, Watson attended private schools and then entered Brown University, where he majored in geology. During these early years his father had moved the family to New York, where he assumed the presidency of the Computing-Tabulating-Recording Company. In 1924 the firm's name was changed to International Business Machines.

Upon graduation from Brown in 1937, young Watson reluctantly agreed to become a salesman for his father's company. And following his discharge from the military after World War II he returned to IBM, where he was named assistant to the vice-president in charge of sales. Over the next six years he continued to move up the organizational ranks, becoming president of IBM in 1952. In 1956 he became the chief executive officer, and board chairman in 1961.

During the 1950s and 1960s Watson built IBM into a formidable computer giant. He reorganized the corporate structure and launched a vigorous investment program designed to keep IBM in the forefront of computer technology. Remington Rand had brought out the first commercially successful computer in 1951, and Watson was determined that IBM would not be bested again. During the mid-sixties IBM brought out its 360 computer and followed in 1970 with its 370. These computers gave IBM undisputed leadership in the field. At the same time IBM continued to emphasize the versatility of its machines for handling business problems, and the quality of its service to the customer.

The results were dramatic. From the time Watson assumed the presidency until his retirement in 1971, sales had zoomed from $133 million to $8,273 million. And IBM rose to fifth place on the list of industrial firms. Today the results of Watson's leadership are still evident in IBM's performance. In fact, IBM has been so successful in the computer field that it is currently under attack by the antitrust division of the federal government, leading one to wonder if it is a crime to be too successful.

Patman Act. Labels alone, the Supreme Court has held, do not justify different prices for the same basic product.

Celler-Kefauver Antimerger Act

The Clayton Act had restricted corporations from buying up large amounts of stock in competitive firms. However, there are ways of purchasing firms other than by simply buying their stock. One is to purchase the assets of the firm, such as the plant, equipment, machinery, and inventory. Thus the Clayton Act had a loophole. In 1950 the government closed this loophole through the **Celler-Kefauver Antimerger Act.**

This act prohibits any firm from acquiring the assets of competitors where the effect would be to substantially reduce competition. As a consequence, companies that are major competitors are no longer allowed to merge under *any* conditions. For example, General Motors and Chrysler would not be allowed to merge. Nor would United States Steel and Bethlehem Steel. The act also forbids giant firms from merging with small ones in the same industry, no matter how small the market share of the latter. Finally, small and intermediate-size firms are forbidden to merge if the consolidation will result in their holding 30 percent or more of the market.

The Celler-Kefauver Act also amended the Clayton Act by giving the FTC and the Justice Department jurisdiction over merger cases. Under the terms of the law, both of these federal agencies have the right to approve merger plans before the merger actually

---

CASE

The Problem with Success

Last year the stockholders of Standard Office Furniture, Inc., voted to go along with a proposal by the company's board of directors. The board had proposed buying out their largest competitor, National Furniture, for $20 million. However, no sooner was the stockholders' decision made known than the president of Standard received a call from the Justice Department. It seems that the government felt such a purchase would be dangerous to free competition. The government spokesman put it this way:

> At the present time your firm sells over 10 percent of all the office equipment and furniture in a six-state region. If you are allowed to merge with or buy out a competitor you will control even more. For example, in the case of National, you will now have over 16 percent of the total market in this region. This is going to hurt many of your smaller competitors. You will be able to buy furniture and office equipment in larger quantities and pass these savings on to your customers. The result will be bankruptcy for many of these small competitors.

Company lawyers expressed regret with this line of thinking. One of them said, "It appears the government believes that highly efficient companies are bad for the economy because they drive less efficient ones out of business. What ever happened to the old saying about hard work leading to success? Apparently the government doesn't mind if we are successful, but they don't want us to become too successful."

---

occurs. Therefore the companies are at least aware of any impending law suits. This does not mean that merger plans cannot proceed, but it does mean that the firms involved may be in for a long court battle if they decide to go against the expressed opinion of the FTC and the Justice Department.

4. Why did Congress enact the Federal Trade Commission Act?

5. What kinds of practices did the Robinson-Patman Act outlaw?

6. Why does the Celler-Kefauver Antimerger Act forbid the merging of giant corporations?

TAXATION

Another important area of business-government relations is taxes. Article 1, Section 8 of our Constitution states, in part, that "Congress shall have the power to lay and collect taxes, duties, imports, and excises to pay all the debts and provide for the common defense and general welfare of the United States." Over the past 200 years government services at the federal, state, and local levels have risen dramatically. With this has come an increase in taxes to pay for these services. At the present time there are a variety of taxes now levied by all three levels of government.

We will present this area of taxes by first reviewing the types of taxes that are levied on both individuals and business firms. Then revenue and regulatory taxes will be examined. Keep in mind that when we

After giving the matter serious thought, the board voted to move ahead with its purchase plan. However, two weeks later the Justice Department went to court and asked for an injunction preventing the company from completing the purchase until its own lawyers had had a chance to explain to the court why such a move was in violation of the antitrust laws. When the company saw how seriously the Justice Department regarded the purchase, it decided to drop its plans. This decision was not an easy one for the board members, but after consulting with an outside legal firm they concluded that the government would win the case. "Why spend all of this money for a legal fight," the president said, "if you're eventually going to lose. We'd rather back off now."

1. In what way is the company purchase plan dangerous to free competition?

2. What antitrust law do you think the company was violating? Explain.

3. Do you think the government was right in threatening the firm with a lawsuit? Explain.

The Government versus Business

The number of laws regulating business is increasing and this is resulting in more and more business–government legal battles. One of these is shaping up in the cereal industry where the federal government is attempting to break the hammerlock that the Kellogg Company has established with such products as Corn Flakes, Frosted Flakes, Raisin Bran, and Rice Krispies. These four cereals hold first, third, fourth, and fifth place, respectively, in the industry.

Of course, Kellogg's has more than just cereals. Since 1969 some of its major acquisitions include Salada Tea, Mrs. Smith's pies, Fearn International, Inc. (soups, sauces, and other foods for institutions), and Pure Packed Foods, Inc. (nondairy whipped toppings and coffee whiteners). And today its interest in acquisitions increases. For example, although unsuccessful in its efforts, the company tried to buy Tropicana Products Inc. (the orange juice producer) and Binney & Smith Inc. (the maker of Crayola crayons). The firm is also increasing the number of breakfast cereals it is offering, having introduced five new ones in just the last year.

All of this worries the Federal Trade Commission (FTC), which feels that Kellogg is becoming too big and too powerful. In fact, its dominance in cereals has made the firm the industry's profit leader with a net return on capital of 21.5 percent compared with an industry average of 13.5 percent. As a result, Kellogg currently ranks sixth in pretax return on investment among the country's 200 largest manufacturers. What does the government want to do with Kellogg? It wants to break their cereal division into five competing companies. However, Kellogg is having none of this. The firm recently has hired a new law firm that has filed suit in federal court, seeking to set back the FTC's suit. At the same time, Kellogg is looking for other acquisitions and expanding the markets of its current holdings. As a result, if the federal government wants to stop Kellogg, it is first going to have to catch the firm.

---

discuss the subject of taxes a great deal of consideration must be given to individual taxes. This is because proprietors and partners, as we noted in Chapter 4, pay taxes as individuals, and these two groups represent the most common types of business forms.

Types of Taxes

Taxes are usually classified by their economic impact on the individuals or firms that have to pay them.

In essence, there are three major types of taxes: (a) regressive, (b) progressive, and (c) proportional.

Regressive tax

A **regressive tax** is one that hits poor people harder than rich people. An illustration is a food sales tax. If a state has a tax of 4 percent on food, the tax burden is greatest on the poor because they are paying a larger percentage of their income in taxes.

For example, if a poor family has an annual income of $8,000 and spends $2,400 for food, it pays a sales tax of $96. This means that 1.2 ($96/8,000) percent of its total income goes to pay this tax. An upper-class family making $50,000 a year will undoubtedly eat much better and may spend $500 a month for food. This will put its annual food sales tax at $240 ($6,000 × .04), far higher than that of the poor family. However, as a percentage of its total income, the rich family is paying less than ½ of 1 percent ($240/50,000 = .48) in taxes.

Another illustration of a regressive tax is social security. Every month, wage earners have money deducted from their paychecks for social security. The amount of tax they pay is based on the size of their paycheck. The total annual tax, as of 1980, was 6.13 percent of the first $25,000 of income. This means that a person making $12,500 a year paid $766.25, an individual making $25,900 paid $1,587.67, and anyone making more than $25,000 also paid $1,587.67. Thus the more one grosses, the lower the percentage of their salary that goes for social security payments. Of course, the rate and the base on which these payments are computed are both scheduled to go up. At the time of this writing the percentage in 1981 is supposed to be 6.65 percent on the first $29,700 and 6.7 percent on the first $31,800 in 1982. However, the tax will still be regressive because the more money one makes, the smaller the percentage tax bite caused by social security payments. We can draw a general graph of a regressive tax as shown in Fig. 25.1. Regressive taxes are often regarded as "unfair" because they place a heavy burden on those least able to pay.

Progressive tax

A second type of tax is the **progressive tax,** which is based on the principle of "ability to pay." With this tax people who make the greatest amount of money should pay the largest amount of taxes. In its ideal form, a progressive tax can be graphed as in Fig. 25.2. The more someone makes, the greater the tax burden.

Perhaps the most commonly cited illustration of

TAX AS A PERCENTAGE OF INCOME

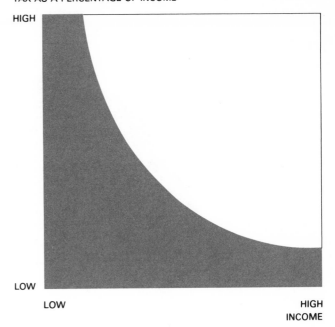

FIG. 25.1 *A regressive tax*

FIG. 25.2 *A uniform progressive tax*

TAX RATE

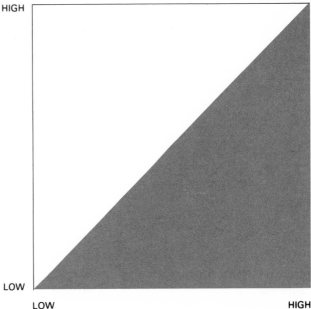

TAX RATE

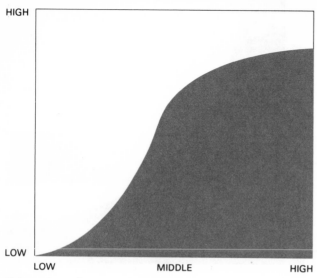

FIG. 25.3 *Federal income taxes paid by individuals*

a progressive tax is our federal income tax. To some degree, it is a progressive tax. However, tax statistics reveal that many rich people pay less to the federal government than do middle-income people. Tax loopholes account for much of this, resulting in a structure very similar to that shown in Fig. 24.3 At the present time Congress is reviewing the income-tax structure for the purpose of closing many of these loopholes. In particular, it appears that everybody may soon be required to pay a minimum percentage of their annual income to the federal government. Such a development would end the cases we often hear about of wealthy persons who make $1 million a year and end up paying taxes of less than $10,000.

Proportional tax

A **proportional tax** is one in which the rate remains the same, regardless of the base. For example, a

The figures would be higher today with the increase in personal and dependent deductions allowed by the government.

HOW TO PAY NO TAXES

1. Don't work.
2. Have ten children. (With parents this deduction totals $9,000.00.)
3. Support your aged relatives and lazy brother-in-law (an additional $750.00 each).
4. Hire babysitter for ten children while your wife works and deduct sitter's wages.
5. Use a room in your house for business purposes. (I know you can't work with ten kids in the house. That's your problem.) Deduct portion of rent, typewriter, file cabinet, supplies, dues for professional organizations.
6. With all those people in the house, you must be moonlighting. Deduct union dues.
7. Rejoice and be glad and don't eat apples. If someone gets sick, you can deduct all medical expenses beyond 3 percent of your adjusted gross income.
8. Save all of your sales slips. All of them. Sales taxes are totally deductible. If you lose them, you can still deduct according to an optional tax table.
9. Try to be a million-dollar football player on second job. You should be able to average your income with the pittance you made in prior years.
10. Try to get to be age sixty-five as soon as possible. With your schedule, it shouldn't take long. Social Security receipts are not taxable.
11. Last resort. Let government pay you. If you make $4,000 or less, government will pay you up to $400 or 10 percent in a negative income tax. Also, deduct mortgage interest, mortgage real estate taxes, all interest on installment buying, car expense if you are a traveling salesman, uniforms if you are a hairdresser, interest on all of your other loans.

school tax of 1.5 percent on all earned income would require an individual earning $10,000 to pay a $150 tax and a person earning $50,000 to pay $750. The latter individual made five times as much money as the former, and so paid five times as much in school taxes. We can therefore graph a proportional tax as in Fig. 25.4.

Many states also have a proportional real-estate tax. A person pays a fixed percentage of the assessed valuation of the land (such as 2 percent). The higher the value, the greater the tax bill.

Purpose of Taxes

Thus far we have examined the area of taxes from the viewpoint of who bears the burden. This, however, is only one way of approaching the issue. Another way is to evaluate taxes by studying the reason behind the levying of the tax. When this is done, we find that taxes were created for two purposes: (a) to raise revenue for the government, or (b) to limit or regulate the use of certain products or services.

7. In what way does a regressive tax put a heavier burden on the poor than on the rich?

8. How does a progressive tax work?

9. With a progressive tax, who pays more—the rich or the poor?

10. In what way does a proportional tax treat everyone equally?

Revenue taxes

Revenue taxes are designed to raise money to finance government programs and services. The largest of these is the income tax, which brings hundreds of billions of dollars into the United States treasury each year. Figure 25.5 shows how important income taxes are as a source of federal revenues.

Except for a short period of time around the Civil War, the United States had no income tax until

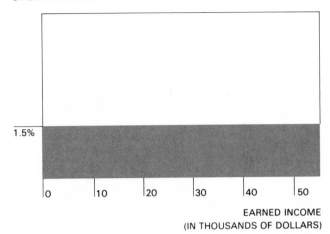

TAX AS A PERCENTAGE OF EARNED INCOME

1.5%

0   10   20   30   40   50

EARNED INCOME
(IN THOUSANDS OF DOLLARS)

FIG. 25.4 *A proportional tax*

FIG. 25.5 *Estimated revenues for 1979 (Source: Office of Management and Budget.)*

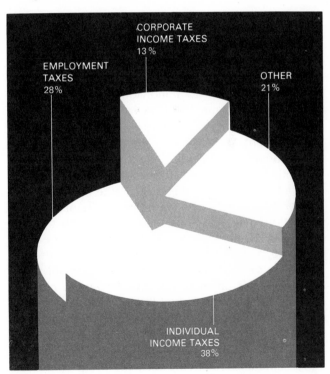

CORPORATE INCOME TAXES
13%

EMPLOYMENT TAXES
28%

OTHER
21%

INDIVIDUAL INCOME TAXES
38%

"I first suspected something was wrong when the 1040 tax form made sense to me."

From The Wall Street Journal; permission Cartoon Features Syndicate

1913. And even then the tax rate was very low. Today, of course, all of that has changed. Income tax is a major expense for both individuals and businesses alike.

As seen in Fig. 25.5, individuals pay the greatest amount of income tax. However, corporations are also a very important source of revenue for the government. In fact, when one realizes the number of companies that pay income tax versus the number of individuals who do, it becomes evident that the corporations are carrying a very large portion of the federal tax burden. As we noted in Chapter 4, corporations pay a tax rate of 17 percent on the first $25,000, 22 percent on the next $25,000 of earned income, and 48 percent on everything thereafter. In the case of giant corporations such as GM, IBM, and GE, this adds up to an effective tax rate of close to 50 percent—almost half of the total earnings of multimillion-dollar corporations are paid to the government!

Other important revenue taxes are the sales tax, the estate and inheritance tax, and the property tax.

Of these, the only one that has a direct effect on business is the property tax. As we noted previously, this tax is a proportional one. It is levied on the value of the property at some fixed rate, such as 2 percent. For this reason it is common to find communities attempting to lure business firms to their locales by offering a waiver of property taxes for a fixed period of time, such as five years. This, of course, can be quite a saving. For example, a corporation with property valued at $2,000,000, facing a tax rate of 2 percent, will save $200,000 over five years if the taxes are waived. This money can then be used to cover other operating expenses and improve the firm's profitability.

Regulatory taxes

Regulatory taxes are designed to regulate or restrict certain types of business practices. One of the most common is the excise tax. An **excise tax** is a tax on the manufacture, use, or consumption of a particular product. The primary reason for such a tax is supposed to be regulation; the secondary reason is supposed to be the raising of revenue. In practice, it sometimes appears that these two end up in reverse order.

Excise taxes are often levied on goods having a high stable demand. At the state level, cigarettes are an illustration. Supposedly the tax is designed to discourage smoking. To some degree it does (in that the higher the price the more reluctant people will be to buy the product), but on the other hand, demand for the product is very high. Therefore, the tax can be very great and cigarette consumption will still remain fairly high. As a result, the government increases its revenue dramatically.

Excise taxes are also levied on other high-demand products. Gasoline is an illustration. A large percentage of the price of this product is tax. People who drive must have gas, and therefore they pay the levy without hesitation. Since the Arab oil embargo of 1973 there has been a great deal of talk about raising the excise tax on gasoline to discourage excessive consumption. In this regard, the tax is being used as a regulatory device. At the same time, however, it still remains a large source of government revenue at both the federal and state levels.

Another type of excise tax is that levied on imported goods. Often known as **import duties,** these taxes are good illustrations of how government levies can regulate consumption or use. The purpose of import duties is to discourage foreign competition and promote a "buy American" philosophy. One illustration is found in the case of foreign cars such as Volkswagens. These autos are subject to an import duty that is eventually paid by the purchaser. The tax, therefore, performs a number of important functions. First, it helps regulate the number of Volkswagens sold in America by making them less competitive with domestically produced automobiles. The manufacturer must raise the price to cover the cost of the import duty, thereby reducing the price difference between the Volkswagen and competitive American cars. Secondly, the tax protects the jobs of many American workers simply by discouraging the importation of many more foreign-produced automobiles. Third, it raises revenue for the government.

11. What is the basic objective of a revenue tax?

12. On earned income of $80,000, how much would a corporation pay in taxes? (Use the tax rate given in this section.)

13. What is the purpose of a regulatory tax?

14. Upon what types of goods would you expect to find excise taxes levied?

ETHICS

The relationship between business and government is a complex one. And it is continually changing. For example, years ago Congress saw the problem in allowing big corporations to buy up their competitors or squeeze them out with illegal business tactics. As a result, legislation to break up the trusts

was enacted. Today, however, we see the case of IBM, which, in the view of many, is under government attack simply because it has become so large. While this may be a simplified view of the situation, it is true that the computer giant is regarded by the government as dangerous to competition. Does this mean that our modified system of capitalism encourages moderate success but is opposed to a firm being "too successful"? The fact that we can even raise this question today indicates that business-government relations in the area of competitive regulation are changing.

The same is true in the area of taxation. As the public begins to demand new or different goods and services, taxes will rise or fall. Usually they go up—and one of the main groups required to pay the bill is business. Thus once again, business-government relations are in a state of flux.

Yet when we look at the relationship between these two institutions, it is important to realize that there is more here than simply a list of government regulations. A great deal of the interaction between the two is influenced by the values, beliefs, and attitudes of the individuals on both sides. We call this area "ethics."

What Are Ethics All About?

Ethics are often defined as "standards that govern the moral conduct of individuals." In a practical setting, we call this "doing the right thing." Government employees are expected to be honest in their dealings with business and not accept bribes or favors in return for special treatment, and vice versa. This high level of conduct is expected of both groups regardless of whether the parties believe they can get away with unethical practices (see Fig. 25.6).

Ethics and Businesspeople

Ethics can be quite a challenge to people in the business world. For example, in large stock brokerage houses there are research departments that specialize in investigating firms for the purpose of determining whether or not their stock is a good buy. This information is then passed on to the brokers so they can recommend appropriate stock purchases to their clients. To whom should the brokers give the information? This is an ethical question.

Many brokers feel that those customers who have listened to them in the past and lost money should be given first chance at any of the latest issues that look good. Other brokers will use this information to lure in new customers under the sales pitch of "invest with my brokerage firm and let us show what we can do for you." Still other brokers wait for these "hot tips" and then recommend the stock to their friends and relatives, while buying some for their own account.

At what point is such conduct unethical? In the case of a broker, this is not an easy question to answer. However, most people would agree that the

FIG. 25.6 *Ten commandments for corporate directors (Adapted from John D. Donnell, "Sixteen Commandments for Corporate Directors," Business Horizons, February 1976, pp. 45–58.)*

TEN COMMANDMENTS FOR CORPORATE DIRECTORS

1. Don't join the board of directors of a corporation that competes with one on whose board you now serve.

2. Never buy or sell securities of the corporation based on inside information you might have but that has not yet been disclosed to the public.

3. Don't discuss plans or prospects of the corporation with anyone except other directors and top officers.

4. Always attend board meetings regularly and participate actively.

5. Require the corporation to establish a thorough and effective antitrust compliance program.

6. Insist upon the establishment of a system for providing information to directors appropriate to their needs.

7. Read every word of a prospectus prepared for a security issue and any proxy statement designed to solicit stockholder votes.

8. Before voting on a dividend declaration, get an opinion from the general counsel and auditors stating that such distribution is permissible under the applicable corporate law.

9. Be aware of the liabilities imposed on the directors by the corporation laws of the state where the firm is incorporated.

10. Never allow the corporation to exceed the powers granted to it in its articles of incorporation.

A Continuing Challenge

Everyone in the business community believes that high ethical standards are important. However, one of the key questions often asked about the area is, What brings about high standards and what leads to low ones? A survey by the Harvard Business Review reports that those factors that help bring about higher standards include the following:

    public disclosure

    publicity

    media coverage

    better communication

On the other hand, those factors that cause lower standards include

    lower societal standards

    a more permissive society

    loss of church and home influence

    desire for less quality and more quantity

In summary, the Review reports that its readers believe (1) public disclosure and concern over unethical business behavior are the most powerful forces for improvement in ethical standards; (2) hedonism, individual greed, and the general decay of social standards are the factors that most influence a decline in ethical standards; and (3) the elements that influence shifts in ethical standards are ones over which they have little control. Does this mean ethics will decline? Not at all. What it does mean, however, is that business people will have to realize that ethical issues will continually confront them and these issues will often have no totally satisfactory resolution. Business people of the 1980s are simply going to have to learn to live with the continuing challenge of ethical behavior in the world of work.

Source: Steven N. Brenner and Earl A. Molander, "Is the Ethics of Business Changing?" Harvard Business Review, January–February 1977, pp. 57–71.

third illustration—selling the stock to relatives, friends, or oneself—constitutes unethical conduct.

Analogous situations exist in all business firms. Consider the banker who gives his or her friend at the country club a short-term note at 8¾ percent interest, while all other customers are charged 9 percent. Or the head of the purchasing department of a large corporation who buys certain supplies from one company and, in turn, is given a token of the supplier's thanks in the form of a new car each year. And then, of course, there are those firms that have given bribes to foreign officials to smooth the way for their international operations.

The above represent common illustrations of poor ethical practices. Yet all these practices have two things in common. First, although they may be questionable they are not outright illegal. Second, they are carried out in secrecy with the hope that uninvolved parties will not hear about them. This raises the question: are all businesspeople unethical? Fortunately, the answer is no. In fact, most managers refuse to go along with such practice.

The greatest influence on businesspeople to make ethical decisions is their **personal codes of ethics.**[1] Parental training and a basic belief in the importance of Judeo-Christian values are very important in helping to shape the ethical practices of today's managers. And research shows that the level of business ethics is rising.[2]

A second influence is industry and, more importantly, company **codes of conduct.** For some firms these codes are strictly window dressing. There is ample evidence, however, to show that most codes really do have a positive influence on business practices. In particular, managers in highly competitive industries like them because they provide something to hide behind when the pressure for unethical practices becomes extremely great. For example, consider this dialogue between a client and a salesman.

> You know, Chuck, I've bought quite a bit of merchandise from your firm this year.
>
> You sure have, Andy, and we appreciate it.
>
> Yeah, but how much? Now my other suppliers are all giving me extra discounts of 3 percent, under the table of course.
>
> Andy, you know that's unethical and I won't do it.
>
> Why not? Everyone else does.
>
> Sure, but we have a policy against extra discounts. Why last month one of our district managers was fired for violating the policy. The company says this gives us a bad reputation and the accounting department is watching us like a hawk. I couldn't help you out even if I wanted to.

Note that Chuck cited company policy when Andy refused to accept his personal comment about the practice being unethical.

While it is difficult to generalize about overall business ethics, it is accurate to say that the public is demanding higher levels of ethical practices. Re-

"Mr. Holcomb, were you expecting a lynch mob?"

From The Wall Street Journal; permission Cartoon Features Syndicate

cent revelations of illegal corporate contributions to presidential campaigns give clear evidence that shady business practices continue in many firms. However, it is also important to note that most managers not only believe ethics are important to business but also welcome the establishment of ethical standards for industry. For them, high levels of moral conduct are vital to the success of a business. As a result, when we talk about business and government relations, we must remember that these relations are formed and maintained by individual conduct. And ethics play a key role in this relationship.

❧❧❧

15. In what way are business-government relations continually changing?

16. What is meant by the term ethics?

17. Why are ethics so important to the business world?

18. Why do most businesspeople favor the establishment of an industry code of ethics?

---

[1] George A. Steiner, *Business and Society*, 2d ed. (New York: Random House, 1975), p. 214.

[2] Raymond Baumhart, *Ethics in Business* (New York: Holt, 1968), p. 216.

Profit versus Reputation

Two months ago, Standard Office Furniture, Inc., was looking forward to a highly profitable year. Then out of the blue two major developments occurred. First, property taxes on the company's largest store were raised from 1.5 percent to 2.5 percent. The board of assessors explained that with the cost of everything rising so quickly, it had become necessary to increase taxes. Several methods of taxation were available to them, but they opted for a proportional tax because they felt it was fairer to everyone involved. Since the taxable property value of this store was $6 million, the profit picture suddenly began to look bleaker.

The second development was an increase in the import duty of some furniture that Standard was bringing in from the Far East. This furniture had sold very well in the past year, but with the new import duty the demand suddenly slowed up and Standard estimated that it would be lucky to sell the rest at cost.

And, as if this were not enough trouble, yesterday one of the store managers called headquarters and said that her largest customer was demanding a special discount. It seems that the customer had done over $200,000 worth of business with Standard in the past year and felt that he was entitled to an "extra" discount. The company president explained to the store manager that in past years the firm had sold a lot more than $200,000 to customers without giving any special discounts, and they were not about to start now. Furthermore, the president said that this type of conduct was immoral and the company would rather pass up the business than get a reputation for making special deals under the table. The store manager explained this to the customer, who thereupon cancelled his latest order. When the president learned of this, he said, "We're better off without his business. I'd rather lose a little profit than the goodwill and trust of the rest of my customers."

1. How much of an increase in property taxes will Standard's largest store now have to pay? Show your calculations.

2. In what way does an import duty affect the demand for a particular product?

3. Was the president's action in handling the request for an "extra" discount wise or foolish? Explain, incorporating the topic of ethics into your discussion.

SUMMARY

One of the most important areas of business-government relations is that related to the regulation of competition. Over the past ninety years a number of important laws have been enacted. The Sherman Antitrust Act was passed to outlaw all contracts or agreements formed for the purpose of restraining trade in interstate commerce. The Clayton Act closed many of the loopholes in the Sherman Act, including tying agreements and interlocking directorates. The Federal Trade Commission Act created the FTC, which is empowered to issue cease and desist orders whenever a violation of the antitrust laws occurs. The Robinson-Patman Act was passed to eliminate unfair price discrimination. The Celler-Kefauver Antimerger Act was enacted to restrict large corporations from merging with each other.

Yet business-government relations consist of more than just laws designed to regulate competition. There is also the area of taxation. Taxes can be divided into three major types: regressive, progressive, and proportional. Regressive taxes hit poor people harder than rich. Progressive taxes are based on ability to pay. Proportional taxes are those in which the rate remains the same, regardless of the base. Another way to examine the area of taxes is to study the reason behind the levying of the tax. In essence, taxes are created for two purposes. The first is to raise money. This is done through the use of revenue taxes. The second is to limit or regulate the use of certain products or services. Excise taxes are an illustration.

A third important area of business-government relations is that of ethics. These are standards that govern the moral conduct of individuals. Individuals working for both government and business are expected to have high ethics. Unfortunately, in practice this is not always true. However, in recent years it has become evident that business-people not only think ethics are important to business but also welcome the establishment of ethical standards for industry.

KEY TERMS FOUND IN THIS CHAPTER

QUESTIONS FOR DISCUSSION AND ANALYSIS

1. How does an interlocking directorate work?

2. In what way is the FTC the policeman of the business world?

3. What is the purpose of the Celler-Kefauver Antimerger Act?

4. In what way is the federal income tax an illustration of a progressive tax?

5. What are some of the most important revenue taxes levied by the government?

6. Why does the government levy import duty taxes?

7. What are some of the common ethical problems faced by business managers?

8. Are business ethics higher or lower than they were ten years ago? Explain.

26

To be a success in business, be daring, be first, be different.
Marchant

OBJECTIVES OF THIS CHAPTER

The previous chapters in this book have presented a great deal about the world of business. However, there is one topic we have not addressed, namely that of going into business for oneself. The overriding objective of this chapter is to study small business management. Particular attention will be devoted to an examination of small business in the economy, its advantages and its disadvantages. We will also study why small businesses fail and how these failures can be avoided. Finally, consideration will be given to franchising, how it works, and why it is a popular approach to getting into small business. By the end of this chapter you should be able to do the following:

a. define the term small business;

b. identify some of the major advantages and disadvantages of going into a small business;

c. cite some of the major reasons accounting for small business failure;

d. explain some of the success factors in small business;

e. define the term franchising and explain how it works;

f. discuss the advantages and disadvantages of franchising; and

g. relate the value of the Small Business Administration to small firms in the economy.

Small Business Management and Franchising

WHAT IS SMALL BUSINESS?

Small businesses are often referred to as the backbone of our economy. Without them our economy would suffer greatly. While this sounds like a cliché, it is true. Seventy-seven percent of all the businesses in this country have sales and assets of less than $1 million and fewer than 20 employees. In short, most businesses in this country are small businesses! Of course, we hear much more about big businesses like IBM, Sears Roebuck, General Motors, and Chase Manhattan than we do the smaller ones, but that is because the large ones are more in the public eye.

Exactly when is a company a "small" business? The Small Business Administration (SBA) feels that a manufacturing firm with less than 250 employees is a **small business,** while a wholesaling firm with less than $15 million in annual sales and a retailing or service firm with less than $5 million in annual sales are small businesses. This *quantitative* measurement helps provide us a general picture of small business.[1] Meanwhile, the Committee for Economic Development has set forth four standards that are more *qualitative* in nature. If a business is characterized by *two or more* of these features it is a small business: (1) the owners are also the managers, (2) the capital for running the business is supplied, and ownership held, by one individual or a small group, (3) the area of business operations is mainly local, and (4) when compared to the large firms in the field, this business is small.[2]

1. In your own words, what is a small business?

SMALL BUSINESS IN THE ECONOMY

There are small business opportunities in all sectors of the economy. However, there are three areas of business activity where these firms seem to be present in great numbers: manufacturing, merchandising, and service enterprises. The following examines each.

Manufacturing

There are many types of small manufacturing firms. Typical illustrations include bakeries, toy factories, machine shops, clothing manufacturers, ice cream plants, and job printing shops. All, however, perform the same basic function. They take a raw material and convert it into a useful end product for either the final customer or some other manufacturer who, in turn, performs further processing.

Large firms tend to dominate in manufacturing, but there are still many small firms that have less than five employees. One of the major reasons for the survival of the small companies is that the large ones depend on them. For example, the giant auto makers, radio manufacturers, and aircraft manufacturers all rely on small subcontractors to build some of the parts that go into the final products. It has been estimated that there are probably no more than 500 firms in the mass-production industry that employ more than 1,000 workers each. Meanwhile, there are over 300,000 firms in this industry that have less than 500 workers. The latter support the former.

Other small manufacturing firms that do not depend heavily on subcontracting tend to make things for the local market. In this category are some of those companies we mentioned earlier: bakeries, job print shops, and machine shops. These firms are found all over America and as the local community grows, they do too. Their success or failure is greatly dependent on the economic conditions in the nearby area.

Merchandising

Merchandisers are middlemen in the channel of distribution who either sell products to the final consumer (as in the case of retailers) or buy goods for resale to retailers (as in the case of wholesalers).

---

[1] *SBA Business Loans* (Washington, D.C.: Small Business Administration, 1973).

[2] *Meeting the Special Problems of Small Business* (New York: Committee for Economic Development 1947), p. 14.

There are more retailers than wholesalers in this country and typical illustrations of retail establishments include food stores, gasoline service stations, restaurants, and drug stores. Most of these businesses are very small. In fact, around 70 percent of them have less than four paid employees. Furthermore, of the approximately 1.2 million retail establishments in this country, 95 percent are small-scale independents.

Most wholesalers are larger than the average retailer and have from four to ten employees. However, in recent years the growth of wholesale establishments has not kept pace with that of the general population. The reason for this decrease in the growth rate can be traced principally to such developments as the rise of chain stores and department stores that perform the wholesale function for themselves. Nevertheless, wholesale establishments remain an important part of the economy, accounting for well over $500 billion in sales annually.

Service Enterprises

In the last three decades, service enterprises have increased dramatically. Some of the most common include hotels, motels, auto repair, recreation services, and personal services (dry cleaning, barbers, etc.).

Many of these establishments are small, require a minimal investment to get started, and rely heavily on close personal supervision. Their growth has been made possible by the increase in the purchasing power of the average consumer, who now demands more business and personal services. For example, with the increase in the number of families in which both spouses work, there has been an increase in the amount of money spent for dry cleaning and household services. Working people do not have time to do all of these household chores so they have others do it for them.

Another reason for the growth of the service industry is the large increase of funds spent on leisure time activities. Now, more than ever, people are bowling, skiing, boating, or doing something relaxing with their leisure time.

"Can you write me a fast, off-beat, 10-second routine for my telephone answering machine?"

From The Wall Street Journal; permission Cartoon Features Syndicate

Finally, the service industry is not highly mechanized. A waiter can serve only a limited number of tables and if more customers show up, more waiters must be hired. Likewise, a ski instructor can instruct only a limited number of skiers and a barber can give only a limited number of haircuts. As a result, as more money is spent on services, the number of business opportunities increases. Of all industries, in fact, service enterprises offer one of the finest opportunities because (1) there is a relatively low initial investment needed for getting into many of these businesses, and (2) there is the opportunity for greater self-expression and personal contacts.

2. How do small manufacturers manage to survive in an industry dominated by giant firms?

3. What kinds of services do merchandisers provide? Which types of merchandisers seem to be doing better today: retailers or wholesalers?

4. Why have service enterprises increased so dramatically during the last three decades?

Many small business owners like knowing that their success depends heavily on their own abilities rather than someone else's and if they succeed, the rewards are theirs.

ADVANTAGES OF A SMALL BUSINESS

Some of the many benefits associated with owning a small business include (1) independence, (2) financial opportunity, (3) challenge, and (4) job security.

Independence

Many small business owners admit that they like being their own boss. They enjoy doing things their own way. Furthermore, they like knowing that their success depends heavily on their own abilities rather than someone else's and if they succeed, the rewards are theirs. Many of them have worked for others and have seen decisions made and operations carried out which, in their opinion, were either wrong or inefficient. Believing " I can do this better than they can," these individuals set out to start their own firms. Service enterprises are a good illustration. Certain persons will work in a restaurant or a repair shop for awhile, watch the way things are done, and realize that by going off independently and setting up a business of their own, they can enjoy all the advantages associated with being the boss while not having to worry about how to run the operation. They have all the experience they need.

Financial Opportunity

Another major reason for going into business is the financial opportunity. Obviously, most owner-managers make more money than the people who work for them and the latter would not be working there if they could get better salaries elsewhere. Thus, the reasoning is simple: owner-managers make more money from their efforts than do the workers.

Of course, the big questions are, What kinds of businesses are most likely to return a good profit and which are poor investments? The insert story entitled "The Ten Best" provides some guidelines as of the late 1970s. A close reading of the list of the ten reveals that there are two things that are very important to financial opportunity. First, there must be a growth factor. The sales must be increasing year after year. Second, if there is competition, there must be something the owner-manager can do to make the business unique, such as providing home delivery or quality service.

The Ten Best

Interested in going into business for yourself? Then you will want to know what types of businesses have the greatest chance for success. A recent survey by Money magazine was conducted among bankers, business school professors, officials of the Small Business Administration, and other individuals likely to know these things. The group selected the following ten businesses as those most likely to succeed.

1. Building Materials Store. Increased residential construction and do-it-yourself repairs should boost sales 10–15 percent this year.

2. Auto Tire and Accessories Stores. Car owners are doing more and more repairs themselves. The result should be an annual growth rate of approximately 9.7 percent this year.

3. Liquor Stores. Industry growth is expected to run around 11 percent, so a hard-working owner-manager should be able to obtain about 3 percent profit on each sales dollar.

4. Sports and Recreational Clubs. Exercise is becoming of greater importance to Americans so these clubs should do well. Although a large initial investment is required to build such a club, annual membership fees of $1 million should produce profits of $26,000.

5. Funeral Homes and Crematories. Small establishments make around 9 percent profit on every $100,000 they earn. While the death rate is decreasing, the annual number of deaths still remains around 1.9 million.

6. Seed and Garden Supply Stores. The profit rate is about 2.6 percent and growth is expected to increase by 8–9 percent annually.

7. Sporting Goods Manufacturers. Increased participation in outdoor sports is producing growth ranging from 8 percent for bicycles to 19 percent for snow and water ski manufacturers.

8. Engineering, Laboratory, and Scientific Equipment. Engineering equipment sales should grow at about 12 percent annually and scales and lab equipment at 11 percent.

9. Hardware Stores. Do-it-yourselfers are helping these stores succeed. For every $1 million in sales, the store should net $45,000.

10. Office Supplies and Equipment. This type of business is very recession resistant and profits are substantial. Growth is about 18 percent annually and profits are about 4 percent of sales.

Source: Money Magazine, March 1978, p. 50.

Challenge

Another advantage of going into business for oneself is the challenge. In every enterprise there is a chance that one will fail. There is also the psychological reward that accompanies facing such a challenge and winning. Research reveals that small business managers like to feel there is a chance of both winning and losing and the final outcome depends on them. In fact, when small business owners are asked why they have gone into business, many admit that the money is important but there is only so much they need for living. The rest is used as a measurement of how well they have met the competitive challenge and succeeded.

Do you have this desire for facing challenge and succeeding? One way of answering this question is by considering whether you would take a grade of "C" in this course or study hard for the final exam and try for a "B" or better. If you are the type of person who would study for the exam rather than take a guaranteed average grade, you have high achievement drive like that possessed by the small business entrepreneur.

Job Security

When one owns a business, job security is ensured. The individual can work as long as he or she wants. And there is no mandatory retirement. The owner can go on for as long as he or she wants. Many people like this because it means there will always be a chance for them to contribute. They need never have to face the question, What will I do with the rest of my life?

5. How important is a desire for independence to the success of a small business?

6. What kinds of businesses should an enterprising individual be looking at today? List at least four.

7. In what way is challenge important to the small business owner? What does the term challenge mean to the owner?

8. How important do you think job security is to the small business owner when contrasted with financial opportunity? Explain.

DISADVANTAGES OF A SMALL BUSINESS

There are also a number of disadvantages of going into a small business. Some of the most important include (1) financial loss, (2) increased responsibility, (3) employee relations, and (4) laws and regulations.

Financial Loss

While a successful small business can make the owner a lot of money, an unsuccessful venture can lose the individual a great deal of money. Furthermore, as we studied earlier in the book, most small businesses are proprietorships or partnerships and the owner(s) usually have unlimited liability for all debts of the business. Furthermore, this liability extends to personal assets as well as business assets, so the owner(s) are risking just about everything.

Earlier in the chapter we looked at some businesses that are likely to be successful during the next decade. Are there any that are not likely to do very well? There certainly are, and the story "The Ten Worst" describes some of these. As you read that story, note that some of the common characteristics include slow growth, and/or increased competition. These two factors result in lower profit and make it difficult for the average business to survive.

Increased Responsibility

A second disadvantage of owning one's business is the increased responsibilities. And there are many of them. For example, the typical owner-manager is often a bookkeeper, accountant, salesperson, personnel manager, janitor, and maintenance repairman all rolled into one.

Furthermore, there are many decisions that need to be made and all of the responsibility for the ultimate decision rests on the owner-manager's head. Sooner or later the individual is bound to make a bad decision. This, of course, will reflect itself in a

The Ten Worst

Earlier in the chapter the ten best types of small businesses were identified. Unfortunately, there are many businesses that do not do well. In fact, 30 percent of all small enterprises fail within the first year and less than 50 percent survive two years. The following list represents the ten types of companies with the poorest chances of survival.

1. <u>Laundries</u> <u>and</u> <u>Dry</u> <u>Cleaners.</u> Improved home laundry systems and the increasing use of synthetic fabrics have slowed the growth of these businesses. Many of the old, more established firms have survived by providing additional services such as rug cleaning.

2. <u>Used-car</u> <u>Dealerships.</u> Banks have soured on loans to these firms because of the high risk involved. The future does not show much growth.

3. <u>Gas</u> <u>Stations.</u> Competition and thinning profits have hurt these businesses. Gross sales of $1 million often produce sales of less than $15,000.

4. <u>Local</u> <u>Trucking</u> <u>Firms.</u> Growth here is sluggish. The high costs of unionized labor and government regulation make these businesses risky ventures.

5. <u>Restaurants.</u> This type of business attracts more prospective entrepreneurs than any other. Growth is good, running about 10 percent; and, profits are a respectable 3.5 percent. However, the success rate is low because a lot of these people lack management know-how. And then there is the competition from the fast-food franchises such as McDonald's and Burger King.

6. <u>Infant's</u> <u>Clothing</u> <u>Stores.</u> The birth rate is slowing up and these stores particularly the independents are encountering stiff competition.

7. <u>Bakeries.</u> Independents are having a tough time surviving against the supermarket bakery departments. Those that do make it are the ones providing specialized services.

8. <u>Machine</u> <u>Shops.</u> The large number of stores makes this a very competitive business. Each $100,000 in sales yields approximately $3,300 in pretax profits, not a very large return.

9. <u>Grocery</u> <u>and</u> <u>Meat</u> <u>Stores.</u> The return here is very low, except among those stores that offer special services.

10. <u>Car</u> <u>Washes.</u> Because of the high rate of turnover, strong competition, and high capital investment, this business is not a very attractive one.

Source: <u>Money</u> Magazine, March 1978, p. 50.

financial loss. The successful small business owner makes mistakes but, unlike the unsuccessful counterpart, they are either few in number or small in magnitude. Decision making is no easy chore, however, especially if the owner-manager is in a very competitive business where fast decisions must be made.

Another factor that most small business owners say is difficult to deal with is sales fluctuations. Some months are big sales months and others are small ones. Yet the bills must be paid regularly. This requires the owner to balance inflows with outflows and make sure that there is enough working capital to keep the business afloat. Wages must be paid, utility bills met, and a sufficient inventory kept on hand. Some owner-managers say that at the end of a busy day they ask themselves why they ever gave up their old 9–5 job.

Employee Relations

In addition to worrying about financial and product-service line problems, the owner needs to be concerned with employee relations. If the workers are not content, the firm's sales will suffer. This is where the manager's human-relations skills come in. The individual has to know how to delegate authority and assign jobs; how to hire and when to fire; and most important of all, the proper way to discipline employees and resolve conflicts among them.

In the beginning these problems are not very serious. However, as the firm increases in size and the number of employees grows from three to five and then ten, the number of employee-relations problems increases dramatically. Furthermore, the owner-manager is likely to face financial-compensation problems. There is the question of not only how much to pay the help, but also how much of a raise to give to each. And then there are the benefit-related issues such as medical insurance, retirement programs, and other fringe benefits. If the business does not adequately address these issues, it is likely to find itself being unionized. Fortunately, these developments can be resolved with an effective, employee-relations program.

Law and Regulations

A final drawback to owning a small business is dealing with all of the laws and regulations to which the enterprise is subjected. For example, in addition to keeping federal income tax records, one has to file social security taxes for all employees, collect state taxes on all sales and remit them to the appropriate state agency, obtain any licenses required for operation, maintain the requisite standards of safety and health on the premises. And these are only a handful of all the regulations with which the firm must deal. No wonder some managers feel that they are overregulated and overtaxed!

9. What types of businesses offer the poorest chances for success during the 1980s? List at least five.

10. Do small business owners really have that much responsibility? Explain.

11. What kinds of employee-relations problems do small owner-managers face?

12. How regulated are small businesses? Explain.

WHY DO SMALL BUSINESSES FAIL?

Research shows that most small businesses fail within the first five years. Dun & Bradstreet, which keeps records on business failures, reports that approximately 68 percent of all small businesses have been in existence for less than five years, 19 percent have been around for 6 to 10 years, and only 13 percent have survived more than 10 years. Of course, some businesses have a lower failure rate than others. For example, furniture stores have a higher failure rate than drug stores, and textile firms have a higher failure rate than lumber firms. Nevertheless, for each industry or firm, there seems to be some common causes of small business failure. The following examines some of the most common.

When Dr. An Wang started Wang Laboratories there was only one employee—An, himself. In 1951 he hired a half-time person, increasing total employment by 50 percent. However, that was over thirty years ago, and it did not take Wang Laboratories much time to start growing.

Almost from the start, Dr. Wang was recognized in the scientific community for his invention of the magnetic pulse controlling device, a device that remained a basic component of modern computers for over twenty years. As his small company began building computers, it started to grow. By 1964 there were 35 people working in a 20,000 square foot plant in Tewksbury, Mass. Since then, the firm has grown to the point where it has close to 2 million square feet of plant space and over 7,000 employees.

During these last fifteen years, Wang Laboratories has joined the prestigious list of *Fortune 500* with sales in excess of $300 million and over 125 offices worldwide. Today it is recognized as a leader in computers and word processing. The future looks like more of the past. Cur-

rently, the company is hiring an average of 50 people per week and projects annual growth in the 25 to 35 percent range. Sales are expected to hit a billion dollars by the middle of the 1980s.

Dr. Wang is very excited about these developments. In the past the industry has had word processing systems and computer systems, but the two were not interchangeable. However, Wang Laboratories are now working toward that goal and believe they will attain it. How do the personnel feel about working for Dr. Wang? One key executive puts it this way: "It probably sounds like a cliché but morale here is very high. Individuals here work hard and that's the reason for the success of this company. Dr. Wang is a leader, but not a flag carrier saying 'Follow me'. The respect for him among the employees is enormous. That relationship has added to the success of the company. Success is also due to the management team he's developed." No wonder when it comes to success stories in small business so many people see Dr. Wang a classic example.

Incompetence

The major reason, year after year, why businesses fail is **incompetence.** The owners simply do not know how to run the enterprise. They make mistakes that an experienced well-trained entrepreneur would quickly see and easily sidestep. One of the most common is that of entering into contracts that are not favorable to the firm, such as agreeing to manufacture 20 specialized items for $1,000 each when the cost of manufacturing is $1,990. The profit is minimal and a competent owner-manager would

have performed the necessary calculations, realizing that the return would not justify the risk, and turned down the contract.

Unbalanced Experience

Another common problem is **unbalanced experience** in which case the owner does not have well-rounded experience in the major activities of the business. For example, the owner-manager who is an outstanding salesperson but does not know much about manufacturing is going to have a difficult time making a go of it as a subcontractor for a large manufacturing firm. The individual may be able to obtain a contract from the latter but will be unable to fill it because of a lack of manufacturing experience. Or consider the many small business people who go broke each year because they know a little about construction work but do not have any purchasing or finance experience before getting into the contracting business. The result: they bid too low on some contracts and too high on others. The ones they get require them to spend more money to fulfill the contract obligations than they are taking in. The result, of course, is financial failure.

In each of these cases the owner-manager had some experience in business but it was not well balanced. The person knew one thing well but did not understand the others. The successful small business owner needs to be a jack-of-all trades.

Lack of Managerial Experience

A third common cause of business failure is **lack of managerial experience.** The owner simply does not know how to manage people. The owner-manager often tries to do too many things and ends up overworked, while making decisions in areas that he or she does not really understand. In other cases the person delegates authority to subordinates, but these individuals have not been carefully selected or trained. As a result the latter make many mistakes, all of which are costly to the business. If the owner understood management fundamentals and knew how to get things done through people, these problems could have been averted.

Other Causes

Other common causes of business failure include neglect, fraud, and disaster. **Neglect** occurs whenever the owner-manager does not pay sufficient attention to the enterprise. The owner has someone else working the store while he or she is off fishing or holding down a second job.

Fraud involves intentional misrepresentation or deception. One of the most common situations in small business is when the bookkeeper purchases materials or goods for his or her own account and has the company pay for them. Another is when the individual systematically steals money from the firm. In either case it may take a while before the irregularities are discovered by the accountant who does the books, and by that time the business may already be on the verge of bankruptcy.

Disaster refers to some unforeseen happening or act of God. For example, a hurricane may hit the area and destroy some of the company's materials that are sitting out in the yard. Or a thunder storm may start a fire that burns down the store. Or the company may be burglarized by thieves who break in and steal most of the inventory. All of these events can be covered with a proper insurance policy but the owner may feel the business cannot afford the luxury of such coverage. In this case, bankruptcy may be the only alternative.

13. How likely is it for a small business to fail because of incompetence of the owner-manager(s)?

14. What is unbalanced experience? When is it present in a small business?

15. In what way can managerial experience be a cause of small business failure?

16. What is neglect? Fraud? How can they lead to small business failure?

SUCCESS FACTORS IN SMALL BUSINESS
How can small businesses improve their chances for success? Four of the most important success factors are (1) the existence of a business opportunity, (2) management ability, (3) adequate capital and credit, and (4) modern business methods.

Existence of a Business Opportunity
The primary factor in the success of a small business is the existence of a real business opportunity. There must be some customers in the marketplace who

are willing to buy the good or service being offered. As we noted earlier in the chapter, one of the biggest problems faced by those businesses that are not doing well is the existence of competition and the failure of the business to distinguish its goods and services from those of these other firms. How can an organization do this?

The best way is to take a **marketing-oriented** approach. First, do some marketing research to determine the needs of the customers. Unfortunately, research reveals that most small businesses work in the opposite direction. They proceed under the philosophy that there is always going to be a demand for a good product or service. What they do not realize is that there may already be enough good products or services being provided and no one is interested in new ones. When a business is founded under the belief that there is room for another good product in the market, we call this **production orientation.** The product creates its own demand; people will buy it when they learn of its existence. This is the wrong way to do things, however, as illustrated by the story entitled "Mouse, Trap and All." Rather than naively believe that people will buy the product, the owner-manager should conduct some marketing research to see if there is a real business opportunity in making this good. In general, relying on one's intuition is not the best way to measure market demand. Just because the owner would buy this particular good or service does not mean there is a demand in the market place for it. One cannot generalize from personal needs to the market. This is a dangerous approach to starting a new business, and it helps account for many of the annual failures.

Management Ability

A second success factor is **management ability.** The owner must know how to handle money, machinery, manpower, and materials. Also, the person must be able to manage others. Additionally, the owner-manager should know quite a bit about the business line, or at least a closely related line. Otherwise the individual is likely to be at a loss regarding how to conduct operations.

Mouse, Trap and All

Will the world beat a path to your door if you build a better mousetrap? Will a better product always outsell an older, inferior one? A few years ago the Woodstream Corporation, manufacturers of all sorts of animal traps, decided to build a mouse trap. Specially designed and much more efficient than the older, wooden ones, this new trap was made of aluminum. While it cost a little more than the old trap, there was one feature that Woodstream thought would help it sell—the trap could be cleaned and reset instead of being thrown out, as was the case with the old wooden traps.

After manufacturing a large number of traps, the company sent them out to their dealers all across America. What happened? Nothing! No one wanted to buy them. Why not? Because, while the trap may indeed have been better designed and more efficient than the old one, people preferred the wooden trap. Why? Because nobody wanted to throw out the dead mouse and then clean and reset the trap. They liked the old method of throwing out the mouse trap with the mouse. By starting from the assumption that a better product will always outsell a less efficient one, the corporation got into trouble. It failed to plan for the one major variable in all sales activity —the consumer.

Adequate Capital and Credit

A third success factor is adequate **capital and credit.** If the owners do not have enough money when they start the business, they are likely to find that their capital is soon exhausted. This will require a further investment of capital or the borrowing of funds. However, since few banks will lend a small business more money than the owners themselves have invested, the ratio of loans to capital is seldom greater than 1:1. The way to avoid this pitfall is to have enough money on hand to carry the business through its first year of operations.

Additionally, it is important to open lines of credit with suppliers and keep these lines available by paying for merchandise and supplies within the 30–60 day credit terms. In this way, the business is able to buy materials and repay the credit when its own customers pay.

Modern Business Methods

The other success factor is **modern business methods.** Firms should use the most efficient equipment and procedures available for two reasons. First, it keeps the cost of business down. Second, it allows the firm to remain price competitive.

Modern business methods ensure intraorganizational efficiency: output is maximized and costs are minimized. Of course, a small business must be careful not to overspend on equipment and machinery. As noted earlier in the book, some firms tend to

---

CASE

Aaron's Decision

Aaron Wilson has been at Standard Office Furiture for the last twenty years working his way from the stock room to general manager of the business. Aaron has a high salary and qualifies for the annual bonus whenever the firm has a good year. Bonuses have been given during eight of the last ten years, and it looks as if there will be a bonus again this year.

However, Aaron is in his early forties and is beginning to realize that if he does not make a career move now he will have to remain at Standard for the rest of his working days. In particular, Aaron has been thinking about going into business for himself. He has talked to the company president about opening a new outlet on the south side of town. The city has been growing very fast and Aaron has noticed that quite a few of their new customers have offices on the south side. He believes that it would be easier and cheaper to set up another store away from the main location for selling and servicing the product line. However, the president has turned down his request.

After looking into the matter, Aaron believes that he can get an office furniture and supply store started in the Southwest part of the city for approximately $50,000. This capital would take him through the first three months of operations. He also believes that, thanks to his contacts in the business, he can get sufficient credit to carry him another nine

---

buy more office equipment and computer power than they need. However, as long as the owner-manager strives to maximize efficiency, this pitfall can be avoided.

17. What is the primary factor in the success of a small business?

18. Which is more important, management ability or adequate capital and credit?

19. How can a small business ensure that it is using modern business methods? Explain.

FRANCHISING

When we discuss going into small business for one-self, you may immediately think of raising money, opening a store, and having a first-rate marketing plan designed to attract customers to the locale. However, while much of the information we have studied in this chapter can help you in starting your own small business, it is not always necessary to begin from scratch. There is another way of getting into a small business. It is known as franchising.

A **franchise** is a system of distribution that enables the person selling the franchise (the franchisor) to arrange for a dealer (the franchisee) to handle a product or service under certain mutually agreed upon conditions. While a franchise can be given for

months. Thus, he can remain in operation for one year without selling very much merchandise. His experience in the field, however, has convinced him that he should be able to start making money within six months. Of course, all of these calculations have been done in his head only. He does not know for sure whether the business will prove profitable. That is why Aaron has decided that he will take the first week of his vacation and investigate the possibilities. His greatest concern is that he might lose everything he has worked for all of these years. If he leaves Standard at the end of the year, he will have a pension plan that he can cash in for $27,500. He will also have a bonus of $11,000. In addition, Aaron estimates that he can raise $25,000 from his personal savings.

1. What are some of the advantages that can accrue to Aaron if he starts his own business?

2. What are some of the disadvantages associated with being a small business owner?

3. What advice would you give to Aaron in helping him decide whether or not to go into business for himself.

"I NEVER THOUGHT WE'D FEEL REALLY INDEPENDENT!"

"It takes *money* to feel really independent – and I never thought we'd have enough to give us at least a little sense of security. Then we discovered Amway."

Craig & Laurie Shreeve
Amway distributors

"Now we're earning extra income as independent Amway distributors. We started part-time, just like more than 500,000 other independent Amway distributors. Most of them are husband-and-wife teams like us.

"We serve our friends and neighbors with more than 150 Amway® home-care, personal-care, nutrition and diet, and housewares products. And we help people start their own Amway businesses – some of them are in these photos with us.

"We're building our Amway business *our* way. *We* run it. *We're* the boss. And that freedom makes us feel so good!"

When someone wants to tell you about Amway – listen! But don't wait for your Amway distributor to call. Talk to him or her today. If you need help in finding a distributor, dial toll-free (except in Hawaii and Alaska, write from there) 1-800-253-4463. (Michigan residents dial 1-800-632-8723). Do it now. Amway Corporation, Ada, MI 49355; Amway of Canada, Ltd., London, Ontario, N6A 4S5.

Get the <u>whole</u> story.

Amway
SHOP WITHOUT
GOING SHOPPING

a particular product, such as General Electric appliances or Whirlpool washers and dryers, the word is most commonly used today to refer to the management of an *entire* business enterprise; for example, McDonald's, Pizza Hut, and Burger King. When you buy a franchise, the people who own it provide you with many of the things you need to get started as well as the right to use their name. In turn, you pay a fee for this privilege.

How Franchising Works

A franchise can be used for either goods or services. In each case it generally works the same way. The franchisee, an independent business person, contracts for a "package" business. This requires the individual to do such things as

1. pay a franchise fee for the right to run the operation;

2. obtain the equipment and inventory needed to run the business from the franchisor;

3. maintain a specified quality of performance;

4. follow the specified operating procedures and promotional efforts of the franchisor;

5. pay a percentage of gross revenues to the franchisor;

6. engage in a continuing business relationship.

Put very simply, the franchisee buys a business unit from the franchisor. Of course, one would be foolish to buy, at least for very much money, the rights to a franchise unless the venture looked like it would be profitable. This is why a well-known fast-food franchise such as Sambo's, Hardee's, or Wendy's would be much preferable to "Uncle Charlie's Hot Dogs," which you could buy from a local merchant who wants to franchise his company, "Uncle Charlie's Hot Dogs." When a person does buy a franchise, there are certain responsibilities that the franchisor has toward the buyer. Some of the most common include the following:

1. use of the company name (such as McDonald's) and its symbols (the golden arches), which, of course, provide "drawing power" in terms of customers;

2. professional management training for the unit's staff;

3. the sale of specific merchandise to the unit at wholesale prices, as well as the equipment to run the operations;

4. financial assistance of various types in order to ensure that the unit is run as efficiently as possible;

5. continuing assistance throughout the contract.

If the individual buys this kind of franchise from an established and successful franchisor, the investment can be a very profitable one. One reason is the current popularity of these units. For example, consider how many times during the last year you have gone to a fast-food franchise. Remember that franchising is not restricted to the fast-food business. There are many other types of franchises from auto dealerships and auto services to hotels, motels, dry cleaning services, rental services, and soft drink bottlers. The thing they all have in common, however, is that the owner has entered into a franchise agreement with the company that is providing the assistance in running the operation and, in turn, is receiving a fee.

The Growth of Franchising

In recent years franchising has proven to be a very popular vehicle for getting into business. In 1969, as seen in Table 26.1, there were almost 400,000 franchise establishments in the U.S. Today that number is approximately a half million. Note also from the table that many of these units are owned by the franchise. In recent years some franchisors have be-

TABLE 26.1 NUMBER OF FRANCHISE ESTABLISHMENTS, 1969–1979

YEAR	TOTAL NUMBER OF ESTABLISHMENTS	COMPANY-OWNED ESTABLISHMENTS	FRANCHISE-OWNED ESTABLISHMENTS
1969	383,908	68,863	315,045
1970	396,314	71,934	324,380
1971	431,169	74,721	356,448
1972	445,281	77,539	367,742
1973	453,632	78,850	374,782
1974	440,701	78,680	362,021
1975	434,538	80,561	353,977
1977	463,482	87,127	276,355
1979	492,379	89,367	403,012

Source: Department of Commerce, *Franchising in the Economy,* 1977–1979 (Washington, D.C.: U.S. Government Printing Office, 1979), Table 3, p. 34.

gun buying back their units and/or refusing to sell any more. Instead they are operating franchises themselves. Pizza Hut is buying their's back while Denny's has been opening only company-owned units. Others like Burger King prefer to franchise through existing restaurant or retail chains by looking for establishments that are not doing well and getting them to start a Burger King there. The Horn & Hardart Company of New York City, pioneer in fast foods during the early part of this century, found that its cafeteria concept died when fast-food chains moved in. Today it has a Burger King franchise in Manhattan and is in the process of replacing its old outlets with Burger Kings. Meanwhile, McDonald's is selling units only to those current franchisees who have proven that they can run a store successfully. Thus, the new small business owner who wants to buy a franchise may find that he or she is unable to get one from some of the big-name fast-food franchisors. However, there are many more opportunities available. All the individual needs to do is check the *Wall Street Journal* or specialized publications such as *National Franchise Reports* to obtain infor-

mation on franchise opportunities, exhibitions, and trade shows being held by franchisors from time to time in various cities. Finally, one can always turn to franchisors themselves to get information on specific opportunities and then go out and talk to the franchisees themselves to see how well they like the arrangement. In doing so, one must be sure to evaluate the advantages and disadvantages of franchising.

Advantages of Franchising

There are numerous advantages associated with franchising. One of the most important is the training and guidance that is given by the franchisor. One of the best known training programs is that offered by McDonald's, which sends the owner to "Hamburger U." Here the individual learns how to make hamburgers, control inventory, keep records, handle human relations problems, and manage the unit.

Another advantage is the customer appeal associated with buying a well-known name. Many of these franchisors advertise on television and radio and have catchy jingles that attract customers to the unit. Just think of some you have heard during this past week from Pizza Hut, Holiday Inn, and Kentucky Fried Chicken.

A third advantage is that the franchise, assuming it is an established one, is a proven idea. There is no need to worry about whether people will like the food being sold or the auto service being provided. There are many other successful franchised units selling the same goods and services.

Finally, there is the financial assistance angle. Some bankers will not be willing to lend money to get a small business started but will change their mind when they find that it is an Aamco franchise, a Holiday Inn, or a Jack-in-the-Box.

Disadvantages of Franchising

On the other hand, one must be careful to weigh the above-mentioned advantages against the accompanying disadvantages of franchising.

One of the biggest drawbacks is that of paying a high franchise fee only to find the business does not succeed. The investment must be carefully weighed. Does the gain justify the risk?

The fact that the franchisor has some degree of control over how the business is managed presents another drawback. We know that in franchise units such as Holiday Inns the buildings and decor are similar wherever their location. The franchisor wants this. The company also wants the units operated the same way, using the same management procedures. If the entrepreneur decides not to follow the franchisor's direction and starts raising prices or changing the menu in the restaurant, it is possible that the individual will not have the franchise license renewed when that time arrives. In short, the franchisor has a great deal of control over how the franchise is run.

A third drawback is unfulfilled promises. The franchisor may promise to provide training, which is never given, or may provide overly optimistic profit forecasts, which never materialize, or sell supplies at wholesale prices that are much higher than they should be. All of these unfulfilled promises can result in eventual bankruptcy for the entrepreneur.

Look Before You Leap

In deciding whether franchising is a good way to get into business, the best advice is to *look before you leap*. This can be done by following three simple steps.

First, find out the franchise opportunities that are available. Look through business newspapers and check your local library. Also, talk to any friends you have who own their own franchise operation and have them tell you about the advantages and drawbacks.

Second, investigate the franchisor. Anyone who is going to sell you a franchise is going to want to know about you—if they are on the level. You should do the same. If the franchisor does not make a vigorous effort to check you out, there is something wrong. At the same time, ask the franchisor to tell you the names and address of individuals who have purchased franchises in the local area. Talk to these people about the type of treatment they have received from the franchisor. Find out if there are any promises that have been made but not fulfilled.

Finally, seek professional help. Go to your lawyer with a copy of the franchise contract and have this individual look it over. Find out what problems, penalties, or restrictive clauses there are that you should know about. Of major importance are the contract provisions related to cancellation and/or renewal of the franchise. If it is cancelled, how much of your initial investment will you get back? Also, talk to an accountant and run through the numbers with this individual. How much should you be able to gross during the first couple of years? What return on investment can you expect?

If things look good, franchising might be an ideal approach. If things do not look good, walk away from the deal. There are many people who have bought franchises from lesser-known franchisors and wound up losing their entire investment. The astute business person knows that not every deal will look as good after investigation as it did at first glance. The person also knows that if an investigation reveals problems, it is best to go no further. There are many good business opportunities out there; thorough research will ensure your choice of franchise is one of them.

20. How does a franchising arrangement work?

21. What are some of the advantages and disadvantages of franchising?

22. How can one investigate a franchising opportunity? Explain.

Forewarned Is Forearmed

Aaron Wilson has been thinking of going into business for himself. His experience at Standard Office Furniture, Inc., has provided him with a wealth of knowledge about managing an office furniture-equipment store. However, just as he decided that he would quit his job at Standard and open his own store, Aaron learned that a large national office equipment franchisor was looking for a franchisee in the local area. Aaron contacted their representative and has a meeting with the man later tomorrow afternoon.

Although Aaron was thinking of investing approximately $50,000 in his own venture, the franchise fee is only $10,000 and the franchise representative has told him that if he gets the franchise they will help him with financing. This is all very good news to Aaron.

Between now and tomorrow, however, he has decided to look more closely into the area of franchising. He really does not know too much about how a franchise operation works nor what will be expected of him. Most importantly, he is unsure of what types of assistance he can expect from the franchisor. Additionally, he knows that this company has a franchisee located about 200 miles north and he is thinking of calling the individual and to discuss the advantages and disadvantages of

THE SMALL BUSINESS ADMINISTRATION

As noted earlier in the chapter, small business is the backbone of the economy. In order to help small businesses, the federal government in 1953 established the **Small Business Administration (SBA).** This agency is the principal government group concerned with small U.S. firms. Small companies can seek assistance from the SBA if they encounter problems.

Most of the SBA's time is spent providing financial assistance to small businesses, helping with government procurement matters, and offering management training and consulting. Of primary interest to small businesses is the first of these functions, namely, financial assistance. The SBA has several loan programs. However, the initial step is to have the business first seek a loan through a local bank.

If the company has a good credit rating, then the SBA need not get involved. However, if the loan is extremely large or the bank is reluctant to grant it, the SBA may step in and guarantee the loan repayment. The agency also seeks to bring together individuals with venture capital and small business entrepreneurs who need financing.

The SBA also helps small firms secure government contracts. In an effort to support small business, the federal government tries to contract with small firms for some of the things it purchases annually. When one remembers that the government spends hundreds of billions of dollars annually, it becomes obvious that any effort by it to support small business can provide a giant financial shot in the arm for these firms.

entering into a franchising arrangement with this franchisor. Later today Aaron is going to talk to his accountant and try to get an idea of the types of questions and issues with which he should be concerned. Aaron believes that a franchise approach to getting into business can be a very good one. However, he is concerned about being sold "a bill of goods." He has heard of many reports where franchisees have wound up losing all of their investment or have not received all of the benefits that they have been promised. By carefully investigating the nature of franchising, he will be in a better position to talk to the franchise representative tomorrow. "After all," he told a friend of his earlier today, "forewarned is forearmed."

1. How does a franchise arrangement work? Explain.

2. What are some of the advantages and disadvantages of getting a franchise? Discuss three of each.

3. In addition to what Aaron is currently doing, what other steps would you recommend he take? Explain.

Finally, the SBA provides management advice to small businesses. This is done in two ways. One is through the distribution of publications related to effective small business management procedures ranging from how to write more effective advertising to the important steps in selling a product or service. Additionally, the agency has a variety of management consulting programs including the following:

1. The Active Corps of Executives (ACE) and the Service Corps of Retired Executives (SCORE). These two groups have volunteer management consultants who assist small businesses with their problems.

2. The Small Business Institute (SBI). The SBI sends out senior and graduate business students from nearby colleges to act as consultants on small business problems. There is no cost to the firm requesting the help. At the present time the SBI program operates under faculty supervision at almost 400 schools across the United States.

3. Business Development Centers. These centers are part of a program aimed at using qualified faculty personnel and others to help small firms through research and consulting activities. In this case fees are charged to offset the costs that are involved.

23. How does the SBA help small business? Cite some examples.

SUMMARY

Small business is the backbone of our economy. And most businesses in this country are small if measured by such criteria as (1) less than 250 employees, (2) less than $5 million in sales, or (3) owner-managed.

While there are many business opportunities in all sectors of the economy, three of those where small business are present in large numbers are manufacturing, merchandising, and service enterprises. Each was discussed in this chapter.

Why do people go into business for themselves? Some of the main reasons include independence, financial opportunities, job security, and challenge. However, there are also disadvantages that must be considered, including financial loss, increased responsibility, employee relations, and laws and regulations.

Research shows that most small businesses fail within the first five years. Some of the most common causes of failure are incompetence, unbalanced experience, lack of managerial experience, neglect, fraud, and disaster. However, there are ways that small business owners can increase the probability of success, including ensuring the existence of a business opportunity, developing management ability, having adequate capital and credit, and using modern business methods.

Starting a business from scratch is one way of getting into business. Another is by purchasing a franchise, such as a Wendy's or a Holiday Inn. Under a franchise arrangement, the franchisee pays a fee and agrees to operate the business in accord with the terms of the contract. The franchisor allows the franchisee to use its name and symbol and usually provides assistance in managing and operating the unit. However, an individual must take careful steps before getting into a franchise arrangement. One should first investigate franchising opportunities, then check out the franchisor, and seek professional help in making the final decision. Once this is done, the individual should know whether or not the franchise opportunity is a good one.

KEY TERMS FOUND IN THIS CHAPTER

QUESTIONS FOR DISCUSSION AND ANALYSIS

1. In your own words, what is a small business? Be complete in your answer.

2. What are the advantages of going into business for oneself? Explain at least three.

3. What are the disadvantages of going into business for oneself? Describe at least three.

4. Why do small businesses fail? Cite at least three reasons.

5. How can small businesses ensure themselves success? Describe at least three success factors.

6. In your own words, what is a franchise? How does it work?

7. What are some of the advantages of franchising? What are some of the disadvantages? Explain.

8. How should a prospective small business owner go about investigating franchising opportunities? Be complete in your answer.

CAREERS IN GOVERNMENT, LAW, AND SMALL BUSINESS

There are many careers in law, government, and small business administration. To a large degree, we have noted them in earlier career sections of the book. Obviously, careers in law and government require more than mere training in business. A lawyer has to have attended law school and passed rigorous exams that measure the individual's grasp of legal concepts. Meanwhile, for careers in government work it is common to find people needing experience and training in such areas as engineering, chemistry, or some field of science. However, for the individual who is interested in studying business and then going into the field directly, there are many small business opportunities. A necessity in many cases is that the person first study the area, for example, by taking a job as a hotel manager and then, after learning the ropes, opening up a hotel. What does this job involve? In order to answer the questions for yourself, go back to the section on careers in management and read the descriptions, for they were used to provide an example of a management career. There are some careers we have not yet mentioned that also fit within the realm of small business. We will discuss two that are popular with many people who get into business for themselves today: (1) the travel agent and (2) the real estate agent, or real estate broker. These are not the only ones available; they are set forth only as examples.

LAWYERS

Lawyers are very important to the business world. Perhaps the most fundamental activity they perform for business firms is helping write and interpret legal contracts. Additionally, if they work exclusively for a particular business firm or specialize in a specific area such as patent law, they must stay abreast of their field in both legal and nonlegal matters. In particular, their work involves contacting people, consulting with their clients to determine the detail of the specific problems, advising them of the law, and suggesting actions that might or must be taken.

It should be noted that not everyone who has legal training works as a lawyer. Sometimes these people need additional training for work in such areas as journalism, management consulting, financial analysis, insurance claims adjusting, and credit investigating.

REAL ESTATE AGENT AND BROKER

A real estate agent or broker represents property owners who are interested in selling or renting their properties. A broker is an independent business person who not only sells real estate but also rents and manages properties, makes appraisals, and develops new building projects. In closing sales, the broker usually arranges for loans to finance the purchase, for title searches, and for meetings between buyer and seller when details of the transaction are agreed upon and the new owners take possession. This individual also manages his or her own office, advertises properties, and handles business matters. A real estate agent, meanwhile, is generally an independent sales worker who contracts his or her services with a licensed broker. The agent shows and sells real estate, handles rental properties, and obtains "listings" (owner agreements to place properties for sale with the firm). Since obtaining listings is an important part of the job, the agent spends a lot of time

SOURCE: *Occupational Outlook Handbook*, 1978–79 Edition, U.S. Department of Labor, Bureau of Labor Statistics

on the telephone exploring leads gathered from advertising and personal contacts. The individual also answers questions about properties and interviews potential buyers regarding their needs.

GOVERNMENT HEALTH AND REGULATORY INSPECTORS

Health inspectors work with engineers, chemists, and health workers to ensure compliance with public and safety regulations governing food, drugs, and various other consumer products. They also administer regulations that govern the quarantine on people and products entering the U.S. from foreign countries. The major fields of health inspectors are food and drug, meat and poultry, and agricultural quarantine. Regulatory inspectors ensure compliance with various laws and regulations that protect the public welfare. Regulatory inspectors are active in the field of immigration, customs, aviation safety, mines, wage-hour compliance, alcohol, tobacco, firearms, and occupational safety.

TRAVEL AGENT

A travel agent makes arrangements for individuals who are seeking assistance in getting from one place to another. Most of the travel agent's time is devoted to checking fare schedules and the arrival and departure times for various modes of transportation. Additionally, the individual will often be required to provide accommodations for the traveler and so it will be necessary to inquire about hotel rates and rental car charges. In making these arrangements the travel agent consults fare schedules published by regulatory bodies and refers to guides and fact sheets for hotel ratings and other tourist information. Travel agents who have traveled extensively can base their recommendations on their own travel experience, and their personal observations can strongly influence the clients. The person also needs to do considerable promotional work, such as informing local business firms of the travel agency's existence and encouraging the companies to take advantage of the agent's services. Thus, the travel agent often meets with business managers and social groups that could benefit from the services of a travel agent.

FBI SPECIAL AGENTS

To be considered for appointment as an FBI special agent, applicants are usually required to have either law or accounting degrees. Under the direction of the U.S. Department of Justice FBI special agents investigate violations of Federal laws in connection with bank robberies, kidnappings, white-collar crimes, thefts of Government property, organized crime, espionage, and sabotage. Because the FBI is a fact-gathering agency, its special agents function strictly as investigators, collecting evidence in cases in which the U.S. government is or may be an interested party. Special agents conduct interviews, examine records, observe the activities of suspects, and participate in raids. Because the FBI's work is highly confidential, special agents may not disclose any of the information gathered in the course of their official duties to unauthorized persons, including members of their families. Frequently agents must testify in court about cases that they investigate.

CAREERS IN GOVERNMENT, LAW, AND SMALL BUSINESS (continued)

GOVERNMENT CONSTRUCTION INSPECTORS

Federal, State, and local government construction inspectors ensure that recognized standards of construction are observed in public and private construction. They inspect the construction, alterations, or repair of highways, streets, sewer and water systems, dams, bridges, buildings, and other structures to ensure compliance with building codes, zoning regulations, and contract specifications. Construction inspectors generally specialize in one particular type of construction work, such as building, electrical, mechanical, or public works. Building inspectors inspect the structural quality of buildings from the planning stage through completion of the structure. Electrical inspectors inspect the installation of electrical systems and equipment to ensure they comply with electrical codes and standards. Mechanical inspectors examine plumbing systems, the installation of mechanical components of kitchen appliances, heating and air-conditioning equipment, gasoline and butane tanks, gas piping, and gas-fired appliances. Public works inspectors ensure that government construction of water and sewer systems, highways, streets, bridges, and dams conform to detailed contract specifications.

DENTIST

Nine out of ten dentists are either self-employed or part of a cooperative with other dentists or medical teams. A license to practice dentistry is required in all States and the District of Columbia. Dentists examine and treat patients for oral diseases and abnormalities, such as decayed and impacted teeth. Most dentists are general practitioners with ten percent specializing in areas such as orthodontics or oral surgery. Those who are self-employed must hire assistants to help with patients. In addition, personnel is required for the scheduling of patients, keeping records, receiving patients, and ordering dental supplies. Sound business policies must be practiced by a dentist to run a successful small business.

CAREERS	LATEST EMPLOYMENT FIGURES	EARNINGS	EMPLOYMENT OUTLOOK
Lawyer[a]	396,000	$16,000–$25,000	Increase at a slower rate than for all occupations in general
Real estate agent or broker	450,000	$15,000–$30,000 [b]	Expected to increase at a faster rate than for all occupations in general
Government health and regulatory inspector	115,000	$16,000–$19,000	Expected to increase at a faster rate than for all occupations in general
Travel agent	15,000	$11,000–$16,000	Decrease at a slower rate than for all occupations in general
FBI special agent	8,600	$16,000–$28,000	About as fast as the average for all occupations
Government construction inspectors	22,000	$10,500–$13,000	Faster than the average for all occupations
Dentist [c]	112,000	$17,000–$31,600	About as fast as the average for all occupations

[a] Law degree required
[b] Depending on experience and effort
[c] State dental license required

Business and You

Now that you have almost finished reading this book, the time has come to ask a key question. Do you think you might like a career in business? Of course, it is a little early for you to give any more than a general answer, such as, "I think so, but I'm not positive." After all, you have had only a brief survey of the major areas of business. You do, however, know a lot more now than you did before you began. Therefore, it is not too early to at least look into the area of business career opportunities.

The goal of this part of the book, which consists of only one chapter, is to provide you with some general insights into how you can go about deciding whether a business career is for you. You will first learn some of the basic aids that can be of value in choosing an occupation. Then those areas of business where career opportunities are available will be discussed. Finally, important guidelines on how to conduct yourself during a job interview and draw up a resumé will be reviewed.

When you are finished reading this section of the book you should have a good understanding of (a) how to go about deciding whether you are interested in a business career, and (b) how to pinpoint those areas you would like to further investigate. You should also be familiar with a number of important terms, including *mental ability, aptitude, vocational literature, public accounting, job interview,* and *resumé.* Finally, you should have gained important insights into how to investigate and pursue a career in the modern world of business.

Every calling is great when greatly pursued.
Oliver Wendell Holmes

OBJECTIVES OF THIS CHAPTER

Having completed a survey of all the major areas of business, we now want to examine how you can go about deciding on a business career for yourself. The first objective of this chapter is to review some of the aids useful in choosing an occupation. The second objective is to review the areas of career opportunities. The third objective is to prepare you for the job interview by providing general pointers on how to conduct yourself. When you have completed this chapter you should be able to do the following:

a. understand the importance of mental ability, aptitude, interest, and personality in choosing a career;

b. know those areas of business where career opportunities are available;

c. understand how to conduct yourself during a job interview; and

d. draw up an effective resumé.

Career Opportunities
in Business

AIDS TO CHOOSING AN OCCUPATION

In deciding whether or not a business career is for you, there are a number of aids that can be of value to you. The first is a personal evaluation of your own abilities and interests. Others include work experience, college courses, and vocational literature. In this section we will examine each of these.

Personal Evaluation

In choosing a career, the first place to begin is with yourself. Your own abilities, aptitudes, interests, and personality should be the primary factors in deciding on an occupation.

Larry, baby, I see you going to work for a free wheeling maverick steel company.
A steel company that pioneers, innovates and does the unexpected.
A steel company that's growing, with a billion dollar expansion program.
A steel company that's making money.
A steel company that's one of the best managed businesses in the country.
A steel company that needs managers in greater number than ever before in its history.
I see you going to work for this mellow steel company and I see you working your tail off, earning great bread, rising like the sun in management and batting .340 for their softball team.

Mental ability

Some career opportunities are available to just about anyone who wants them. Others require a high degree of **mental ability.** If you have not done so, you can have your intelligence measured via an IQ test. While these tests require interpretation by skilled people (since they are prepared and validated on white middle-class Americans and may contain a bias against other cultural and ethnic groups), they can tell you areas where you are strong. For example, if you have high quantitative ability, accounting, finance, or statistics are areas that may prove rewarding to you. On the other hand, if you score well in the qualitative areas such as English, you might try advertising or personal selling.

Aptitude and interest

While mental ability is important, **aptitude** and **interest** are also key elements in choosing a career. *Aptitude* refers to a person's ability to do something. Aptitude tests, for example, can measure an individual's manual dexterity and eye coordination. In turn, these tests can be used to screen out people who do not have the particular skills for performing certain types of jobs. No matter how much you may want to do something, if you lack the necessary aptitude you will never do it well.

Of greater importance, however, is *interest*. It is very difficult to succeed unless you really want to. Without a strong interest in something, the average person usually gives it up. Remember, success requires hard work and perseverance. Without an initial interest in a business career, you will probably never see it through.

How do you know you have such an interest? One way is simply to make a personal appraisal of yourself. Do you think you might like a career in business? A second, and complementary approach, is to take an interest test. The best-known interest tests are the *Kuder Preference Record* and the *Strong Vocational Interest Blank*. These tests are available at most testing centers, private counseling agencies, and universities around the country. And there are people there who can interpret them and help you identify your own interests. Sometimes there is a fee involved, especially if it is a private agency. However, the cost of the service can be well worth the investment if it helps you identify a future career path.

Personality

Another important characteristic is **personality.** Are you able to get along well with others? Business often involves interaction with superiors, subordinates, suppliers, and customers. In addition, one needs to possess other personality traits such as initiative, judgment, and emotional stability. Are you a "self starter" or do you generally rely on others to tell you what needs to be done? Really successful businesspeople possess high initiative, good judgment, and emotional stability. When something drastic occurs they remain calm and try to determine how the situation should be handled. Their tempers are under control as they think through the next action step.

It would be nice if there were personality tests that could tell you if you possessed these traits. Unfortunately, there are not. To a large degree, you must judge for yourself whether you have the necessary personality to succeed in a business career.

1. In what type of business career do you think mental ability plays a key role?

2. Which is more important to success in business—aptitude or interest? Explain.

3. What are some of the personality traits possessed by successful people in business?

Work Experience

A second useful aid in choosing a career is your **work experience.** You probably have already had a part-time job, such as a newspaper route or a cashier's job at a local supermarket. And during the summers you may have worked in a factory or an office. These work experiences are useful in that

they give you an insight into the world of work. There are some things you now know from first-hand experience that you like (as well as dislike). This will help you in choosing a career. For example, did you find that as a youngster you often got involved in door-to-door selling for the purpose of raising money for school or club projects? Did you like it? If so, you might have been motivated by the financial aspects of the undertaking, in which case a career in finance or accounting may be for you. And it is important to remember that if you liked these projects, in which you go out and sell the product *your* way, you may do well in a proprietorship or partnership.

College Courses

Now that you are near the end of this book, you have learned a great deal about how the world of business operates. Is there some special area that particularly interests you? If so, follow it up with a formal *college course.* For example, if you liked Chapters 12–15 on marketing, look into a basic marketing course. If you enjoyed Chapters 16–18, register for a basic finance course. By using this approach, you can obtain more in-depth information on all the areas in this book.

If you are currently a business student, of course, these courses will be required in your program. You will have to take basic marketing, management, finance, accounting, and statistics. However, there are other offerings that are undoubtedly available but are optional. After looking through your college catalogue and comparing the courses to those areas we covered in this book, you may hit upon some that are not required but are of interest to you. For example, were you intrigued by the discussion in Chapter 4 and Chapter 26 where sole proprietorship, partnerships, and small business management were discussed? If so, you should see if your college offers a course in small business management or entrepreneurship. Did you enjoy Chapter 14 and the discussion of advertising? Then a course in this area is in order. Or how about Chapter 15 and international trade? If you liked this discussion, a course in inter-

Henry Ford II

As a grandson of Henry Ford and chairman of the board of the Ford Motor Company, Henry Ford II really never had to work a day in his life. Nor did he have to play an active role in providing job opportunities to millions of Americans. However, a cursory review of Ford's life reveals that he has been a leading social activist and prime initiator behind Ford Motor's drive to provide job opportunities to everyone who wants them.

In particular, Ford organized the National Alliance of Businessmen to help, at least initially, in finding jobs for minorities. By 1974 this organization was placing well over half a million adults on the job annually. The large majority of these individuals were voluntarily absorbed by business firms, with no government subsidies involved. In fact, five out of every six placements made by the Alliance have been at no public sector expense. And in recent years the Alliance has expanded its programs from minority hiring to finding jobs for veterans and youths. In the latter program, which begins with summer jobs, the individual can move on to work-study, with a guided view of career opportunities and counseling on educational requirements tailored to the person's own interests.

Meanwhile, within the company itself, Ford Motor is promoting equal opportunity for all of its employees, while trying to do even more for minorities such as blacks. Commenting on this strategy, Ford noted, "What we're doing now is to hire black college graduates in a higher proportion than their numbers in the population. Then we're going to spend more money to train them and watch their upward mobility closely."

Yet Ford's greatest contribution to job opportunities has undoubtedly been his willingness to get involved and lead the way with such social action programs, both within his firm in particular and American industry in general. As someone once remarked about Ford, "It is not his power alone that gives him his importance. Rather, it is his willingness to use that power for causes in which he believes." Today, with a large personal fortune, he could retire and do just about anything he wants. However, Ford continues to remain at his post and push for those ideas he believes will help create a healthy business environment and a better America.

national management, marketing, or economics may prove highly rewarding for you. And if you want to find out more about computers and their role in business, why not register for a course in electronic data processing or management information systems? In short, there are many business activities and functions that may appeal to you. Before settling on a career in this area, however, investigate it further through more formal study.

Vocational Literature

Another helpful aid in choosing a business career is **vocational literature**—literature written about various jobs or occupations. One of the most helpful sources, available in many libraries, is the **Dictionary of Occupational Titles,** prepared by the United States Training and Employment Service. This book contains over 20,000 occupations with more than 35,000 occupational titles. These titles and descriptions pro-de excellent insights into the work performed by eople in the business world. The following are me illustrations.

Cost Accountant. Applies principles of accounting and statistics to install and maintain systems for providing establishment with detailed cost data not ordinarily supplied by accounting systems: Plans, sets up, and directs cost finding and reporting system regarding cost records of items, such as raw material purchases, labor, and machinery depreciation, to determine unit cost. Analyzes changes in design, raw materials, manufacturing methods, or wages for effects upon production costs. Provides management with reports which can be used as basis for decisions regarding matters, such as setting prices and retaining or discontinuing items in company's line of product.

Financial Analyst. Conducts statistical analyses of information affecting investment program of public, industrial and financial institutions, such as banks, insurance companies, and brokerage and investment houses: Interprets data concerning investments, their price, yield stability, and future trends, according to daily stock and bond reports, financial periodicals, securities manuals, and personal interviews. Constructs charts and graphs regarding investments. Summarizes data setting forth current and long term trends in investment risks and measurable economic influences pertinent to status of investments. May perform research and make analyses relative to losses and adverse financial trends and suggest remedial measures. May transmit buy-and-sell orders to broker based on securities analysis.

Production Superintendent. Coordinates, through subordinate supervisors, all activities of production departments or subdivisions, applying knowledge of plant layout, and production capacities of each department: Consults with plant executives and analyzes economic trends, sales forecasts, and marketing and distribution problems to plan and develop production procedures and time and cost estimates. Interprets company policies and production procedures to subordinate supervisors, and directs their activities. Confers with department heads to formulate programs regarding availability

of raw materials, maintenance of plant equipment and physical structure, product quality control, related production records, labor and materials costs, and equipment depreciation, to insure that operating costs are maintained at budgeted level. Reports production figures and job completion dates to plant executives. Originates or assesses measures designed to improve production methods, equipment performance, and quality of product, and recommends changes in working conditions and modifications in machines and equipment. Plans surveys, such as those designed to determine effectiveness of manpower utilization, and projects manpower requirements. Negotiates with workers'

Everyone wants you... but, what do you want?

Career Challenge?
Individual Growth?
Opportunities?
Good Income?
Job Diversification?
Responsibility?

Barber-Colman offers all of these to you.

Our greatest need right now is engineers ...Design, Application, Sales, Electrical, Mechanical, Industrial.

Barber-Colman is a growing, successful, world-wide organization that is diversified. We are involved in the textile industry, aviation, electronics, specialized machinery, specialized tooling, controls for the building environment and controls for industrial processes.

Our diversification offers a variety of ways to challenge your personal growth.

If you want a challenge and are serious about your future, contact Al Seals, 815-877-0241 and get started now!

Barber-Colman Company
1300 Rock Street, Rockford, Illinois, U.S.A., 61101

An Equal Opportunity Employer — M/F

representatives in connection with grievance procedures, and reports unsettled grievances to plant executives.

By looking up the titles of the occupations you feel might be of interest to you, it is possible to obtain a working knowledge of what the job actually involves.

4. How can the *Dictionary of Occupational Titles* be of value in choosing a career?

AREAS OF CAREER OPPORTUNITIES

If after using the aids in the previous section you decide a business career is what you are seeking, you should work on narrowing down your scope of interest. Exactly which areas appeal most to you? Then you will want to find out what career opportunities exist in each. When we boil down all of the areas discussed in this book, we come up with six general classifications: (a) going into business for yourself, (b) production, (c) personnel, (d) marketing, (e) finance, and (f) accounting, statistics, and computers. The following examines each of these. In addition, Table 27.1 presents some of the forecasted manpower needs between now and the mid-1980s.

Going into Business for Yourself

In Part II we discussed the firm's structure and management. Particular attention was given to organizing a sole proprietorship and partnership. And in Part III small business management was discussed. If you think you have the drive and willingness to work hard, *going into business for yourself* is a distinct possibility. The rewards associated with this effort can be very great. First, there are the financial rewards. Success in your own business can often lead to early financial independence. Second, there is the freedom of action. In a sole proprietorship you yourself decide how to run the business. In a partnership you have less freedom than in a sole

TABLE 27.1 FORECASTED MANPOWER NEEDS TO 1985

OCCUPATION	AVERAGE ANNUAL OPENINGS
Accountants	51,500
Bank clerks	36,000
Bank officers and managers	28,000
Bank tellers	21,000
Bookkeeping workers	95,000
Economists	6,400
Hotel managers and assistants	7,000
Insurance agents, brokers and underwriters	27,500
Lawyers	31,900
Office machine operators	7,700
Personnel and labor relations workers	23,000
Psychologists	5,600
Public relations workers	8,300
Purchasing agents	13,800
Real estate agents and brokers	44,500
Retail trade sales workers	155,000
Wholesale trade sales workers	41,000
Sociologists	800
Statisticians	1,500
Systems analysts	7,600

Source: *Hammond Almanac*, 1979, p. 207

proprietorship, but a lot more than you will have in a big company—at least until you attain a high position with the corporation, which will probably take years.

On the other hand, going into business for yourself can present a large number of headaches. First, you have to raise the necessary money to finance operations. Second, you must be willing to work hard and persevere in the face of discouragement. Third, if you or your partners go bankrupt, you stand to lose all your personal assets. Thus you could find yourself wiped out financially.

When you compare the benefits and penalties of going into business for yourself, you may feel the negative side outweighs the positive. However, re-

The Mandatory Retirement Issue

Many people have spent a lifetime in a particular career. Today, that lifetime ends for most of them when they become seventy years old because many business firms have forced retirement at this age. This has raised a great deal of controversy in both the business world and Congress.

On the one hand, there is probably some truth to the fact that older people cannot do at least certain jobs as well as younger people. Manual labor occupations, in particular, fit into this category. In addition, in the past most corporate pension plans and health insurance plans are predicated on retirement at sixty-five.

On the other hand, many people, including those who have reached this retirement age, oppose mandatory retirement. It is something that the individual should decide, they argue. And there are plenty of illustrations of people over seventy who can do just as good a job as ever. This has led some firms to either change or eliminate mandatory retirement policy.

Will everyone follow suit and abolish mandatory retirement? It is really too early to tell. One thing is certain, however; many people want to work past sixty-five or seventy and there will be continued pressure on business firms to accommodate them.

---

member that just because you have read this book does not mean you are ready to go into business. You still need to do further research and find out more about the particular career you are thinking of pursuing. When you do, you will greatly reduce the risks involved, and the benefits of going into business for yourself may easily outweigh the drawbacks.

5. What are some of the key advantages and disadvantages of going into business for yourself?

Production

Approximately 23 percent of all employees in the United States work in production-related jobs. Career opportunities are very numerous indeed. At the lower level there are openings for *supervisors or foremen*. These jobs involve the planning and scheduling of work loads, the administering of safety rules, and the control of overall work progress. A college degree is not required for these jobs although it certainly helps.[1] Recent statistics indicate that the average salary for new supervisors who have majored in business administration or industrial relations is

[1] Much of the data in this section related to opportunity and salary are based on government statistics from the late 1970s.

around $15,000 a year. Success at this level can mean promotion to department head and then to plant manager, and government projections indicate that there will be a slow but steady increase in demand for supervisors and foremen through the early 1980s.

Another key production area offering career opportunities is purchasing. Many of the people in this area are *purchasing agents,* who process company orders, contact vendors, negotiate contract terms, and see that delivery is on time and as promised. For this job, a college degree is very helpful but not mandatory. Salaries usually start around $12,000 and, with experience, personnel can work themselves up to the $15,000–$20,000 range. And, of course, advancement up the ranks toward vice-president of purchasing will carry further salary increases. Government forecasts show a good increase in demand for purchasing agents between now and the early 1980s.

Personnel

The personnel area offers a number of career paths depending upon the individual's interest and training. At the lowest level are **personnel clerks,** who gather and file information. This job requires only a high-school education. However, one's advancement is limited as the highest attainable position is usually that of supervisor and beginning salaries are only around $9,000.

Other areas offer greater opportunity. For example, medium-size and large banks, insurance firms, manufacturing firms, and mercantile enterprises all have personnel departments that perform a number of important functions for the company. Many of them have a **testing** or **counseling director** who helps screen applicants and match personnel interests with job requirements. Some firms also have a **wage and salary administrator** who helps develop wage and salary scales and administer federal regulations related to these areas. In factories there will often be a **safety director** who designs and administers safety programs. And in unionized firms there will be an **industrial or labor-relations director** who handles

management relations with the union. All of these jobs require some college education and a degree is going to be very helpful. Depending upon the size of the firm, salaries will range from about $11,000 for those just starting out to around $17,500 for a seasoned veteran. In most cases there is opportunity for advancement up the ladder to such jobs as personnel director, and the latest forecasts show that the entire area of personnel will undergo a very rapid increase in demand between now and the early 1980s.

6. What types of interests should a person interested in a career in the production area possess?

7. How is a personnel department vital to a bank? What types of aptitudes would a person need to do well in such a department?

8. To which types of firms would you apply if you were interested in a career in labor relations?

Marketing

The field of marketing offers a wide variety of occupations. One of the most exciting is that of advertising. Jobs in this area cover a broad range. One is **copywriting,** which involves the writing of descriptive ad copy from the information provided by marketing research. The salary range for this job is currently between $7,500 and $30,000 depending on education, experience and, most of all, the success one has had with one's past ads.

A second challenging career is that of **account executive.** This is an employee who works for an advertising agency and serves as the liaison between the agency and the client. This individual helps develop ad campaigns that meet the needs of the client. Account executive jobs are usually held by college graduates who have majored in advertising and have had some years of work experience in the field. At the present time, the typical salary range for this job is $22,000–$35,000.

The person with whom the account executive works very closely is the company **advertising manager.** This person represents the firm in its dealings with the ad agency. Advertising managers are usually college graduates and all have spent many years in the advertising business. Most of them command very large salaries. The current range for advertising managers is between $25,000 and $75,000, depending upon the company and the requirements of the job.

A second major area of marketing is selling, which has two major occupational avenues: wholesale and retail. **Wholesale salespersons** are the middlemen that operate between the manufacturers and the retailers or buyers. For these positions junior college training is usually all that is required. At the present time beginning salaries are around $12,000 and experienced personnel go as high as $45,000 (not including the company car and travel expense account). Individuals who do well as wholesale persons can look forward to being advanced to sales supervisor and/or regional manager, depending on the needs of the firm. The government reports a slow steady demand from now until the mid-1980s for people in this occupation.

Retail selling offers two occupational areas. One is that of *buyer.* This individual purchases merchandise from manufacturers and wholesalers for the retail store. Some college training is desirable for entry to this job. Beginning salaries are around $10,000 and one can work up toward $35,000 depending upon the size of the store and requirements of the particular job. The top position in the department is usually that of merchandise manager. The government reports that from now until the mid-1980s there will be a slow increase in the demand for people in this occupation.

Retail salesworkers are those people who do the actual selling of the merchandise to the customer. These individuals seldom need much more than a high-school education and can work their way up to department manager and possibly even store manager. Current salaries usually begin around $8,000

and, depending upon whether one is on commission or straight salary, can go as high as $15,000.

9. What are some of the major occupations available to a person seeking a career in marketing?

10. How would the interests of a person considering a career in advertising sales differ from those of an individual wanting to work in retail sales?

Finance

The field of finance offers a wide range of vocational opportunities. One of these is in the area of credit management. Businesses need people to manage their credit area, deciding who should be given credit and how much. This person is usually called the **credit manager.** The job involves authorizing customer credit purchases, analyzing financial reports to see who has not been paying his or her bills on time, and following up to see that collection is made. The requirements for such a job usually include some college education, especially in the accounting and finance areas. At the present time credit managers can expect to start around $11,000 if they have had little or no experience and, if they have had a great deal of experience, can command salaries of $30,000–$40,000. Recent statistics indicate that career opportunities in this area will increase slowly between now and the mid-1980s.

A second career opportunity in the finance area is in the field of insurance, particularly as an **insurance agent.** Most agents represent one company, although "independent" agents do not. They will shop around for their clients and see which firm offers the best coverage at the lowest price. In either case, the agent's job is to sell insurance to his or her clients. Although a college degree is not mandatory, it is very helpful. In addition, most states require the agent to pass a licensing exam. It is very difficult to estimate salaries for these jobs because most agents

work on a commission. However, typical agents will start out earning between $12,000 and $15,000 annually. Those selling a great deal of insurance, of course, like a life insurance salesperson who does $2 million a year, can expect to gross upwards of $55,000. In terms of advancement, for those agents who want to leave the field and go into the home office, home manager and district sales manager positions are always opening up. The government reports that there will continue to be a moderate increase in demand for people in the insurance field.

A third major career opportunity is in the securities area as a **stock broker.** The job of the broker is to execute orders from customers by buying and selling stock. The broker also furnishes the clients with information about potential investments. In recent years it has become increasingly important to have a college degree if one wants to enter this area because the demands of the job require one to be familiar with accounting and finance. In addition, there are licensing tests that one must pass. Beginning brokers will often make around $15,000, while experienced brokers will make upwards of $35,000 when the stock market is good. Remember, however, that when the market is bad most brokers will either sell out the holdings of their customers and have them remain on the sidelines with their cash, or just ride out the market. During these periods the broker will be doing little buying or selling for the customers because market conditions are not favorable. This means that commissions will drop off dramatically and brokers who made $50,000 one year may be lucky to bring in $20,000 the next.

A fourth major career opportunity is commercial banking. One of the banking areas where a rapid increase is expected between now and the early 1980s is that of loans. A **loan officer's** job is to evaluate the credit and collateral of individuals and businesses applying for a loan and decide how much money the bank can afford to lend them. Today such a position usually requires a degree in business administration with special emphasis in accounting and finance. In addition, it is common to find the bank training new people further via a short on-the-job

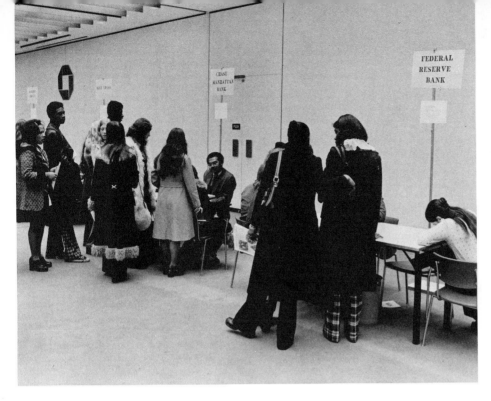

Job fair for high-school students.

training program. Beginning salaries usually range between $10,000 and $14,000, but with experience one can eventually earn up to $20,000–$25,000. In addition, if the individual is successful as a loan officer, he or she can look forward to becoming a senior officer of a department and/or vice-president.

11. What types of interests should a person thinking about a career in finance possess?

12. How does the work of a stockbroker differ from that of a loan officer?

Accounting, Statistics, and Computers

Accounting is a large field containing three major subdivisions: public, private, and governmental. **Public accounting** is a profession and most individuals in it usually strive to become a Certified Public Accountant (CPA). This requires passing a rigorous exam and, in some states, having experience in the field. The typical CPA works for an accounting firm, which specializes in providing accounting information (usually related to taxes) to its clients, verifying that the company's books are in proper order and that the financial statements released to the public and/or the government conform to the commonly accepted principles of accounting. Today it is virtually impossible to become a CPA without having a college degree in accounting and many firms are encouraging their prospective employees to get a master's degree. Salaries usually begin around $16,000 for those with a bachelor's degree and no experience, but one can expect to double this within five years. In addition, in many public accounting firms one can expect to eventually be made a partner in the concern.

Private accounting encompasses accounting activities in all types of business. Private accountants

Career opportunities are dependent upon one's educational background.

perform a number of important functions, depending upon their area of expertise. For example, *cost accountants* determine the cost of a firm's operations and devise and supervise cost control systems. *Tax accountants* prepare tax returns for the firm and study new tax rulings by the courts. *Internal auditors,* who review the company's accounting system, check to see that there are no funds missing, and verify that the books do indeed represent the firm's financial status. All of these jobs require a bachelor's degree in accounting and a special emphasis in the particular field in which the individual is working. Beginning salaries usually start around $14,000 and with experience one can work up to $25,000 depending upon the size of the firm and the job requirements.

Governmental accounting opportunities exist in many branches of state and local government. Most of these jobs involve work on the financial records of a governmental agency or a business that is subject to government control. Entry into these jobs requires a college degree in accounting, and recent reports indicate that there will be a continual rapid increase in the demand for governmental accountants. One can expect to start at about $13,000 and with experience work up to around $22,000.

Career opportunities in the area of statistics are expected to be favorable between now and the mid-1980s. Salaries, however, will be dependent upon educational qualifications, which will open the door to specific jobs in the area. For example, with a college degree in statistics or an applied field such as economics, one could become a **survey statistician.** This individual specializes in preparing questionnaires and supervising the collection of data. This job has a beginning salary today of around $11,000–$13,000. With an advanced degree (M.A. or Ph.D.) one can become an analytical statistician or a mathematical statistician. An **analytical statistician** applies standard statistical methods to particular subject areas such as economics, population, or engineering. The starting salaries for these people are in the $15,000–$18,000 range. The **mathematical statistician** studies and improves on statistical theory, principles, and methodology. While this is more theoretical than the other two occupational areas, the beginning salary is also higher, ranging in the area of $17,000–$20,000.

Career opportunities in the computer area are dependent on the specific job. For example, *keypunch operators,* who operate typewriter-like machines that punch holes in computer cards, which are then fed into the computer, usually need a high-school degree along with some keypunch training. The beginning salary for this work is around $8,000. However, between now and the mid-1980s there will be a decreasing demand for these people. Other computer-related areas look much more promising. For example, *console operators,* who load and start the computer and adjust machinery if the computer stops or an error is detected, require a little college training but are in an area of rapid demand growth. Beginning salaries are around $8,000 and with experience one can work up to around $11,000. And then there are *systems analysts,* who study business data processing and information system flows to determine if everyone is getting the information they need to make effective decisions. Their job requires a college degree with concentration in data processing and business-related courses. Beginning salaries for these jobs are around $16,000 and with experience one can work up to the high twenties. The government has forecasted a good increase in demand between now and the mid-1980s for people in this area.

13. How does a public accountant differ from a private accountant?

14. Why is it likely that career opportunities in the computer area will increase over the next decade?

PREPARING FOR THE JOB INTERVIEW

Once you have decided on a business career, you will have to take that all-important step—getting the job. This process begins with the **job interview.** Generally, the interview lasts no more than thirty minutes, and during this time you will have to present yourself in such a manner that the recruiter believes you have the qualifications his or her firm is seeking.

Unfortunately, many interviewees are unable to create the right impression with the interviewer. Some are so nervous that they cannot answer even the simplest questions; they simply freeze up. Others are just the opposite. They are so casual in their approach that the recruiter believes that they are really not interested in the job and are just going through the interview to get an idea of what is available in the job market.

General Information

To overcome these problems and present yourself in the best possible light, there are a few useful guidelines worth noting.

First, you should know exactly when and where the interview is to take place. No interviewer is going to be impressed by an applicant who shows up late for the first meeting. If you are in a major city, plan on getting to the locale where the interview is scheduled at least ten minutes early. Then, if you have some trouble finding the street or the office, you have time to ask directions. If you are too early, and do not want to give the impression of being overly anxious, go have a cup of coffee at a nearby coffee shop and wait.

Second, know something about the firm with whom you are interviewing by doing some research on the company. How old is it? What products does it manufacture and sell? Where are its headquarters? Who are its major competitors? How successful has it been in the last five years? Recruiters are often impressed by interviewees who have done their homework. They feel that the individuals are truly interested in their particular firm.

"My ultimate goal? Retirement."

From The Wall Street Journal; permission Cartoon Features Syndicate

Third, dress neatly and appropriately. Do not wear anything that is too "far out." Let good taste be your guide. Use your research on the firm to help you decide on your choice of clothing. If you are interviewing with an insurance firm or a bank, you should dress more conservatively than in the case of an engineering firm, where it may be typical for people to shed their coats and work with their sleeves rolled up.

GETTING THROUGH THE INTERVIEW

It is really impossible to anticipate everything that is going to happen during an interview. Therefore, you must be prepared to "play it by ear." Keep in mind, however, that you should never lose your composure. Rely on your own courtesy and good sense to get you through even the tightest spots. Some recruiters may throw you a curve ball by putting you under pressure. The objective of such a tactic is to see how you react. The job for which you are being considered may require an individual who does not get rattled very easily. Therefore, by remaining calm and handling the situation as best you can, you are showing the interviewer that you are worthy of fur-

ther consideration. The following presents other suggestions for getting through the interview.

General Information

First, relax! The interviewer knows that you are going to be nervous at the start, but remember that the company has not sent this person out to scare off prospective candidates. The interviewer is there to hire people. And if you fit the bill, this is exactly what will happen.

Second, when you meet the interviewer, let this person lead the way. Shake hands only if the individual makes the first gesture. And wait until you are offered a chair before sitting down. Do not chew gum, and smoke only if you are invited to do so.

Third, be prepared for a general opening remark, such as, "Tell me about yourself." Another common opening is, "Why are you interested in our firm?" Other frequently asked questions, for which you should be prepared, are:

1. What college courses did you like the best? The least?
2. What are your hobbies?
3. What books have you read lately?
4. Why do you think you might like to work for our company?
5. What type of boss do you prefer to work for?
6. In what kind of position are you most interested?
7. Do you prefer any particular geographic locale? Why?
8. Are you willing to go where the company sends you?
9. What do you consider to be your best talents?
10. In terms of a career, where do you hope to be in ten years? By retirement?

These questions are designed to tell the interviewer something about you. They are also aimed at helping identify whether you are really interested in the firm or just out looking for a job and talking to a number of firms along the way. If you have prepared some answers in the back of your mind, you should be able to handle these questions without much problem. In responding, be as specific as you can. Let the interviewer know that you are familiar with the company and have a particular career path in mind. Of course, you may change your mind over the next five years, but for the moment at least you know what you want and should be prepared to convey this information. In so doing, make a mental note of the important ideas you want to express and then go through them, leading from one to the next. Once again, this requires some initial preparation. However, it will help you present your ideas smoothly and easily.

15. How can a person go about doing research on a firm before actually interviewing with the company?

16. Which three of the ten questions listed above do you think are most important? Why?

Handling Recruiter Questions

Most recruiters will use questions like those listed above in handling the interview. Your goal should be to answer these queries as fully and consistently as possible. Whether or not you have anticipated a particular question, guard against giving contradictory answers. Do not let the recruiter sway you to a particular line of reasoning unless you feel the individual is correct. Otherwise, stand your ground. And if you feel you do not know the answer to a question, say so. Be frank and honest. Do not try to bluff your way through.

After you have answered a particular question, if you think you may have gotten off on a tangent or sidestepped the issue, pitch the question back to the recruiter. "Have I covered all aspects of that question, or is there something else you would like to know?" Don't be afraid to put the person on the spot. Remember, the individual has probably interviewed hundreds of people and used these questions over and over. If you have not suffi-

How To Interview A Company.

When you sit down with industry recruiters, you're going to talk about a big chunk of your future. So while they're interviewing you, interview them.

Look beyond the smile and the handshake. Probe. If you stick to simple questions about salary and fringe benefits you could get stuck in a job you hate.

Ask about their ideas, and what they've done with them.

Some companies lead in new ideas and product applications. Others follow. Look for the leaders. Generally, they're the guys who are willing to listen, cut through management layers, and give your ideas a chance to grow.

At Phillips, for example, we took an idea about petroleum by-products and turned it into the first unbreakable plastic bottle. Since then we've developed an underlining to protect asphalt highways from harsh weather, an additive that helps multi-grade motor oils stand up to severe operating conditions, a surgical web that reduces postoperative complications, and much more.

Ask what they're working on now. Today.

Some companies break a lot of ground, then sit back and rest on their laurels. Make sure their efforts are continuing.

Right now, Phillips has more exciting projects than we can cover in a single page, or a single publication. We're developing a new seismic system that is expected to significantly improve methods for gathering basic seismic data in difficult environments like the Tropics and the Arctic.

We're looking at a new way to produce much-needed protein for this hungry planet by growing yeast on methanol. We have a new design for heat exchangers that cuts the vibration problem. It not only costs less to maintain, it also takes less energy to operate.

Last year Phillips ranked first among oil companies in the number of U.S. patents issued. We've built a company on ideas and innovations. We're not about to change now.

Ask about the future of the industry.

No matter how forward-thinking a company may be, if the industry is dying, they're in trouble. Look for an industry that is looking toward the future.

Right now the future depends on what happens in the energy field. Phillips is in the forefront. We're searching the world for new oil and gas fields, developing new ways to produce more oil and gas from old fields. And we're looking into alternative, or "exotic" energy resources.

Ask where you fit in.

In a growing, responsive company, there's no limit to growth for all sorts of people. Phillips needs graduates in: Administration and Service; in Management Information and Control; (management, accounting, and computer services) in Engineering and Services; (chemical, mechanical, electrical and architectural design and construction) in Natural Resources; (worldwide exploration, production and plant operation) in Petroleum Products and Chemicals; (refinery and chemical plant operations, transportation and marketing) Applied Automation and Research and Development.

Now ask about the nitty-gritty.

If you'd like to talk to Phillips, we'd like to talk to you. Contact W. M. Hutchison, Coordinator of Recruitment and College Relations, Phillips Petroleum Company, Bartlesville, Oklahoma 74004.

Phillips is an equal opportunity employer.

The Performance Company.

ciently answered the question, the interviewer will know how to follow up and rephrase the question.

Also keep in mind that many interviewers ask a lot of questions and it is easy to follow their lead. Some, however, ask very few and depend upon the interviewee to carry the ball. This is the most difficult situation you will confront. It can be turned to your advantage, though, in that it gives you an opportunity to sell yourself to the recruiter. Use the time for getting across your good points. If you are active in a fraternity or sorority, say so. This indicates a willingness to assume managerial responsibility. If you are the treasurer let this be known. It shows that you can handle financial responsibility. However, be careful about coming on too strong. Blow your own horn, but do not give the impression that you believe you are the greatest human being alive. For example, if the recruiter asks you what position you think you will hold by retirement, you should shoot high but not too high. The vice-presidential level indicates high drive, but to say that you will be president may be going too far. Likewise, if you are asked how much money you would like to be making by the age of forty, a response of $1 million is too high. Instead you should state a figure that is both reasonable and attainable. One recent survey of top businesspeople indicated that executives on the move earn approximately $1,500 per year of age up to the time they reach forty. Therefore an answer of $60,000 to this question would be within the range of possibility. Or you might allow for the inflation factor and estimate $70,000, along with an explanation of how you arrived at this particular figure.

17. If you answer an interviewer's question and are told "you are wrong," what should you do?

General Pointers
In addition to the above, there are several general pointers that should prove useful to you. First, no matter how greatly you impress the interviewer, it is highly unlikely that you will be offered a job on

---

CASE
Ready for Anything

Al Ferris, a marketing student at State University, is now in his last semester of course work. Al has a 3.1 grade-point average on a 4.0 scale. In marketing, his grade-point average is 3.5 and he had straight A's in the three international marketing and management courses he took. In addition to having a high grade-point average, Al can speak German and Spanish fluently and has a working knowledge of Portuguese. Al has decided that he would like to go into the area of international marketing.

Two weeks ago Al went to the University Placement Office and looked over the list of firms that would be interviewing on campus this semester. He picked out three that were looking for overseas personnel. During the next ten days Al found out all he could about these firms, from the type of goods and services they market to the latest financial report issued by each.

Later today Al has an interview with the first of these firms. To prepare for it, he has thought through answers to some of the questions he feels he will be asked. In particular he has been reviewing in his

the spot. Rather, the firm will contact you within ten days or two weeks and, if interested, will invite you for a follow-up interview and a tour of the facilities before making you an offer.

Second, if you do receive an offer and have a couple of prospective employers who have still not responded, ask for a week to think things over. Then contact these other firms and tell them that you have a job offer and would appreciate hearing from them as soon as possible. Never accept an offer and then, if you receive a better one a week later, drop the first one. Consider all your alternatives before you choose one.

Third, know what competitive salaries are for the job you are considering. Otherwise you will be ill prepared to know whether a particular offer is good or bad. Some firms will ask you how much you want. If you are really interested in the firm you might pass the buck back by indicating that you are more interested in the job and will rely on them to be equitable in determining the salary. In the case of large corporations, there is usually a standard of-fer for entry positions and no negotiations are un-dertaken. However, if you check into the matter and find out that the firm is flexible, do not be too quick to let them set the salary. If you know they generally pay $13,000 but occasionally go higher, ask for $13,500. Remember, there is no sense taking less than you can get, and if the company is unwilling to go another $500, all they have to do is say so.

THE RESUMÉ

A **resumé,** or **data sheet** as it is often called, is a short biographical sketch of yourself. Some firms ask job applicants to fill out a standard data sheet so they can gather all the important information they need about the individuals. However, it is helpful to have one of your own already made up. Figure 27.1 provides an example.

The self-prepared resumé should be neatly typed and should bring the reader up to date on your activities. If you are going to be visiting with a large number of firms, it is helpful to have a number of copies available.

mind responses to three queries: (a) **Why do you want to work for our firm?** (b) **In what kind of position are you most interested?** and (c) **Where do you hope to be in your career in ten years?** Although his research and preparation may not be complete on all points, Al feels that he is more than ready to meet the interviewer.

❧❧❧

1. Based on what you know about Al and his background, do you think he possesses the training needed by individuals in international marketing?

2. What information should Al have gathered about these companies in his research?

3. In addition to the three questions listed in the case, what others might the recruiter ask him? Cite at least four.

FIG. 27.1 *Resumé illustration*

There is no universally accepted format to use in drawing up a resume. The sample shown in Fig. 27.1 is divided into five major areas: personal, education, extracurricular activities, work experience, and references. These represent those areas most often covered in resumes. It is also common to start the resume with some personal information about yourself and close it with a list of your references. Aside from this, the organization of the data sheet is up to you. Remember, however, that the information should not be crowded onto the page. Space it out so that it looks orderly and neat. Also, stay away from gimmicks. Do not use a fancy typeface. And if you are including a picture of yourself in the upper right-hand corner, make it a conservative-looking one. In addition, since you are just starting out, you really will not have that much information on your data sheet. Therefore, keep your resumé short—usually no more than two pages. And do not use glossy paper if you are having the data sheet reproduced by a printer. You are looking for a job in business, not a Hollywood movie career. Flashy paper and long resumés telling the reader how great you are tend to detract from the image you should be projecting.

Finally, a word on references is in order. You should include a list of individuals who can say something positive about you. If you have worked for someone who knows that the quality of your work is high, you can use that person as a reference. Teachers in courses where you did well are another source. In all cases, however, *always* check with these people before putting their names on the resume. If someone is not prepared to give you a good recommendation, you can often tell by that person's reaction and can quickly remove his or her name from the list of possible references. And in the case of a teacher, the person may not remember you very well, especially if you were in a class of 150 students. As a result, the professor will often take out the grade book for that semester and write a recommendation tied exclusively to your class performance. If you want something more personal said about you, drop by and ask him or her to serve as a reference. If the person says yes, leave a copy of your resumé or a typed index card with your name on it, as well as the names of any firms with whom you will be interviewing. This helps the individual place you when he or she receives a letter from a company asking for personal comments. Remember, even if you visit an individual and get a personal promise of a reference, there may be forty other students doing the same thing. As a result, the professor may still have trouble identifying you without some reference form from which to work. The resumé provides this.

18. How should a person go about deciding whom to ask for a reference?

Not Quite Prepared

When Al Ferris went to interview for a position in international marketing last week, he thought he was prepared for just about any questions the recruiter would throw him. After some initial "get-acquainted" talk, the recruiter began telling Al about the company. Having done some research on the firm, Al asked some questions of his own. For a while things seemed to flow smoothly. Then the recruiter asked him in which country he would like to work. Al said Germany, and began to explain why.

However, it was not long before it became evident that the recruiter knew a lot more about the customs and culture of the Germans than did Al. In fact, at various times during the interview she corrected false impressions Al had about these people. It was evident that Al had not done sufficient research on the background and social customs of the Germans. He was embarrassed for having allowed himself to talk for so long on a subject on which he was not fully prepared. What upset him most was that he had done so much research on the firm and should have stayed with what he knew best.

If Al was upset, the recruiter certainly was not. In fact, she seemed quite pleased that Al had chosen to interview with her firm. As the interview drew to a close she said, "Well, Al, I'd like to thank you for visiting with me and we'll be in touch with you in a few weeks. In the interim we'd like to look into your resumé some more and check your references." Al thanked the woman and left. It was then that he remembered that he had failed to ask one of the people on his list for a reference. He therefore hurried over to the professor's office and got approval from the individual.

Ten days later Al received an offer in the mail. It was $500 less than that being offered to his fellow students who had interviewed with competitive firms. Al was unsure of whether to take the offer or try to negotiate a better one with the company.

1. How could Al have avoided the problem he encountered when talking about the background and social customs of the Germans?

2. What mistake did Al make in regard to his references?

3. Should Al accept the company's offer or should he negotiate? Explain.

SUMMARY

There are many career opportunities in business. If you feel you might be interested in a business career, the first thing you should do is make a personal evaluation of yourself. Do you think you have the mental ability, aptitude, interest, and personality for such a career? Other aids to choosing a business career include work experience, college courses, and vocational literature.

If you decide a business career is what you are seeking, you should work on narrowing down your scope of interest. Examine the career opportunities that exist in each. Business careers can be boiled down into six general areas: going into business for yourself; marketing; production; personnel; finance; and accounting, statistics, and computers.

Once you have decided on one of these areas, you will have to go about getting the job. This process begins with the job interview. In the short time this interview will take, you will have to convince the recruiter that you are the right person for the job. In addition to dressing properly and employing good manners, keep in mind a few other general pointers that can be very helpful. First, do research on the firm so you know something about its line of business. This not only shows the recruiter that you are interested in the job but also helps you formulate questions of your own for the recruiter to answer. Second, if you are asked a question and do not know the answer, say so. Be frank and honest.

Finally, when looking for a job it is a good idea to have a resumé, or short biographical sketch of yourself, prepared. While there is no universally accepted format to use in constructing a resumé, typical major areas that should be covered include personal, education, extracurricular activities, work experience, and references. For someone just starting out, a resumé ought to be no more than two pages. It should be orderly, neat, and well typed. Finally, anyone who has been listed as a reference should know about it and have agreed to write a recommendation on your behalf. Leaving a copy of your resumé with this person will help the individual remember you when it comes time to write the letter.

KEY TERMS FOUND IN THIS CHAPTER

QUESTIONS FOR DISCUSSION AND ANALYSIS

1. What do we mean when we say that a person has an "aptitude" for a particular job?

2. In what way is work experience helpful in choosing a career path?

3. What type of training do you think a person interested in a production career should have?

4. What types of interests would you expect to find in a person who is considering a career in advertising?

5. What is the purpose of a job interview?

6. How would you decide whether or not to try negotiating a salary offer?

7. If you do not know the answer to a recruiter's question, should you bluff a response or admit you do not know? Why?

8. Why is it a good idea to stay away from using gimmicks on a resumé?

PHOTO CREDITS

270. Courtesy Allstate Insurance Companies

271. Marshall Henrichs

275. Marshall Henrichs

277. Courtesy TWA

281. Marshall Henrichs

284. Courtesy The Singer Company

288. Courtesy ITT

287. Courtesy Nina Cohen

291. Courtesy Eastern Air Lines Inc.

294, 301. Marshall Henrichs

303. Courtesy Columbian Information Service

304. Courtesy Boeing Commercial Airplane Company

305. Courtesy Western Electric

306. Courtesy Chemical Bank

308. Wide World Photos

309. Dick Brehl for TIME, Inc.

310. Courtesy Khaled Abu Su'ud

314, 326, 329. Marshall Henrichs

335. Courtesy Bankers Trust Company

336. Jan Jachneiwicz/Chase Manhattan Bank

339, 342, 343. Courtesy Federal Reserve System

344. (top) Library of Congress; (bottom) Jan Jachneiwicz/Chase Manhattan Bank

349. Chase Manhattan Bank

355. Courtesy Paul Thayer

358. Arthur Lavine/Chase Manhattan Bank

362. ©1979 by The New York Times Company. Reprinted by permission.

367, 371. Marshall Henrichs

379. Courtesy Kirk Kerkorian

381. Marshall Henrichs

382. Courtesy Merrill Lynch Pierce Fenner & Smith Inc.

387. Marshall Henrichs

388. Boston Globe Newspaper Company

391. Courtesy New England Mutual Life Insurance Company

392. Courtesy Aetna Life & Casualty

395. Marshall Henrichs

397. Courtesy Marsh & McLennan Companies

398. Courtesy Fireman's Fund, American Life Insurance Company

399. Hank Greenberg; Chel Dong/Institutional Investor

402. Courtesy Bankers Life Company

406. Courtesy Independent Insurance Agents of America, Inc.

414, 417. Marshall Henrichs

428. Courtesy Lord Grade, Associated Communications Corporation Limited

431. Courtesy The Stanley Works

435. Marshall Henrichs

439. (top) Courtesy E.I. DuPont De Nemours & Company; (bottom) Courtesy Bethlehem Steel Corporation

440. (top) Courtesy Thomas L. Holton; (bottom) Courtesy Deloitte Haskind + Sells

444. Ellis Herwig/Stock Boston

445. Courtesy IBM

446. Tyrone Hall/Stock Boston

449. Courtesy IBM

455. Marshall Henrichs

458. (left) Courtesy Harvard Business Review/Doremus & Company; (right) Courtesy Macmillan Book Clubs, Inc.

460. John F. Kennedy Library

475. Marshall Henrichs

477. Courtesy Western Electric

480–482. Courtesy IBM

485. Courtesy H. Ross Perot; Karsh, Ottawa

487. Courtesy IBM

491. Courtesy Citibank, N.Y.

502, 505. Marshall Henrichs

511, 514, 515. Chase Manhattan Bank

518. UPI

519, 525. Marshall Henrichs

526. New York Historical Society/American Heritage

529. Courtesy Thomas J. Watson, Jr.

545, 548, 549, 551. Marshall Henrichs

553. Courtesy An Wang

558. Courtesy Amway Corporation

570, 573. Marshall Henrichs

574. Courtesy Inland Steel Company

576. Courtesy Ford Motor Company

577. Courtesy Barber-Colman Company

581. Created and produced by McFrank and Williams Advertising Agency Inc., New York/Houston

583. Courtesy Raymond Juschkus/Chase Manhattan Bank

584. Anna K. Moon/Stock Boston

587. Courtesy of Phillips Petroleum Company

Glossary

GLOSSARY

This glossary contains definitions of many of the key terms and ideas found in this book. For the most part, these definitions correspond to those in the text itself, but in some cases they have been expanded for purposes of clarity. If, after looking up a term in this glossary, you would like to know more about the area, consult the index and locate that portion of the book in which the term is more fully discussed.

absolute advantage An economic theory that explains the economic advantage one country has over others when it can produce products that the others cannot duplicate.

accounting The process of recording, classifying, summarizing, and interpreting financial information.

accounts receivable turnover A financial ratio that measures how quickly accounts receivable are being collected, determined by dividing net sales by average accounts receivable.

acid-test ratio Also known as the quick ratio, it is the relationship between highly liquid assets and current liabilities.

ad hoc committee A committee formed for a particular purpose and then disbanded when the objective is accomplished.

ad valorem duty A tariff duty levied on the basis of a product's value, such as 7 percent of the good's monetary worth.

advertising agency An organization that specializes in creating, writing, and placing advertisements.

agency shop A shop in which all employees, union or not, must pay union dues.

agent A person who is authorized to represent another.

American Stock Exchange Commonly referred to as the AMEX, it is second in size and importance to the NYSE and has the same strict regulations regarding standards of conduct as does the NYSE.

analog computer A computer used primarily as a measuring device and widely employed by scientists for solving problems such as translating voltage into electrical quantities.

analytic process A production process in which a raw material is reduced to its component parts for the purpose of extracting one or more products.

arbitration A technique for settling a labor dispute that involves bringing in an arbitrator to act as the sole umpire in resolving the disagreement.

assets Those economic resources that a firm owns, such as machines, inventory, and land.

authority The right to command.

balance sheet A financial statement used to display a firm's financial position at a specific point in time.

balance sheet equation The accounting equation that states that assets equal liabilities plus owner's equity.

BASIC A symbolic computer language designed for ease of use in both input and output operations.

bear An individual who believes that the stock market is going to go down.

binary number system A two-digit number sytem, consisting of the digits 0 and 1, used by the digital computer to perform calculations.

blue-sky laws State laws regulating the sale of securities.

board of directors Those individuals elected by the stockholders to oversee the operations of the corporation.

bonds Long-term debts that carry a fixed rate of interest and a stipulated maturity date.

boycott A technique used by unions in which members refuse to buy a company's goods, thereby bringing economic pressure against the firm.

brainstorming A technique widely used in creative thinking that involves the encouragement of imagination and creativity in the formulation of problem-solving approaches.

brand name A name used to help a person identify a specific product.

break-even point That point at which revenues equal total fixed and total variable costs.

broker An individual who brings buyers and sellers together.

bull An individual who buys stock in the anticipation of the security going up.

business An organized approach used by individuals for the purpose of providing goods and services to mankind.

business cycles Economic fluctuations in the economy, evidenced by such developments as recessions, recoveries, and growth periods.

business statistics The systematic collection, presentation, and interpretation of data related to business problems.

buying A marketing function that involves the selection of both the type and amount of goods to be purchased.

buying long Buying stock in the hope of selling it later at a higher price.

call provision A provision, found on some bonds and preferred stock, that allows the company to retire the security prior to its maturity date.

capital Often used as another name for money, this term also includes machinery, equipment, and any other physical labor-saving devices that will help people do a job better or faster.

capitalism An economic system in which individuals are basically free from government control in determining all kinds of goods and services that will be produced and distributed.

cash discount A discount given to buyers who pay cash.

Celler-Kefauver Antimerger Act An act designed to restrict corporations from buying up large amounts of stock in competitive firms, or merging with them where the result would be a substantial reduction in competition.

centralization A system of management in which most decision making takes place at the upper levels of the hierarchy.

certainty A condition that exists when a decision maker knows the outcome of a decision before it is made.

chain store Two or more stores in the same general line of business that are controlled and operated by the same firm.

channels of distribution Those routes that goods take in moving from producer to consumer.

Civil Rights Act An act that forbids discrimination in employment on the basis of race, color, creed, sex, or national origin.

Clayton Act An act designed to regulate competition that was passed to close the loopholes that existed in the Sherman Antitrust Act.

closed shop A union-management agreement whereby the company agrees not to hire anyone who is not a member of the union.

COBOL An acronym standing for Common Business Oriented Language, COBOL is a computer language widely used in solving business problems.

collective bargaining The process in which the union and management come together to negotiate a labor contract.

commercial good A good that is used by business in the form in which it is purchased and is not intended for use in making other goods. Illustrations are typewriters, filing cabinets, and office furniture.

commercial paper An unsecured promissory note.

committee organization An organization consisting of individuals from different areas who are brought together to study organizational problems and either recommend or order solutions to them.

common law Unwritten law based on court decisions that have become precedents to be followed in future cases of a similar nature.

common stock The most basic type of corporate ownership.

communication process. The process of conveying meanings from sender to receiver.

communism An economic system in which the government decides how resources are to be allocated.

comparative advantage The theory of international trade that holds that a nation should concentrate its production in those areas where it has the greatest comparative advantage or relative efficiency.

competitive advertising Advertising that encourages buyers to purchase the company's products over those of the competition.

composition agreement A method of avoiding bankruptcy that involves all of the creditors taking a reduction in the amount owed to them.

compound duty A tariff duty that is a combination of specific and ad valorem duties. For example, a compound duty of 25¢ per pound and 15 percent ad valorem on a good weighing 10 pounds and worth $100 would be $17.50.

conceptual skills Those skills that help the manager see the whole enterprise as well as the relationships between the various parts.

conciliation A method for settling labor disputes that involves inviting in a third person (the conciliator) to help both sides rethink their positions and work toward a solution of the problem.

consumer good A good destined to be used by the final consumer.

consumerism A movement currently under way in America in which buyers are demanding more and better goods and services for their dollar.

consumer pretest A test used for judging an ad's effectiveness that involves asking consumers to examine advertising copy that has not yet been released for publication and rank the ads along such lines as attention-getting ability, appeal, and attractiveness.

continuous production A production sequence characterized by a constant flow of raw materials, as seen in the case of mass-production work such as automobiles.

contract A voluntary agreement between two or more competent parties in which, for consideration, one party receives the right to have the other carry out some lawful act.

contract of agency An agreement between two parties in which one is given the necessary authority to represent the other in business transactions.

control process The process of establishing standards of performance, measuring current results against these standards, and taking corrective action.

convenience good A good that consumers like to purchase quickly and with a minimum of effort, such as cigarettes, newspapers, and candy.

conversion privilege A feature sometimes found on bonds or preferred stock that allows the holder of the instrument to convert it to a predetermined number of shares of common stock.

coordination Synchronization of effort in cooperative pursuit of organizational objectives.

corporation A legal entity created by law and endowed with certain characteristics as specified in its charter. These entities can only be created with permission from the state.

correlation A statistical term that refers to the degree of relationship that exists between two or more variables.

critical path The longest path in a PERT network.

cumulative voting A method of voting for members of the board of directors in which each stockholder is entitled to a number of votes equal to the number of shares of stock owned multiplied by the number of directors to be elected.

current assets Those company holdings that are cash or expected to be converted into cash within the next year.

current liabilities Those financial obligations that will be due within the next year.

current ratio The ratio between current assets and current liabilities.

cyclical variation An economic fluctuation that tends to last a long time such as five to ten years.

data processing An organized method of gathering, storing, and retrieving information.

debt-asset ratio The ratio between a firm's total debt and its total assets.

debt-equity ratio The ratio between a firm's total debt and its total equity.

decentralization A system of management in which a great deal of decision-making authority rests at the lower levels of the hierarchy.

decision making The process of choosing from among alternatives.

decoding process That part of the communication process in which the receiver interprets the message.

defendant A party against whom a legal action is brought.

depression An economic period characterized by mass unemployment, low wages, and extremely poor economic conditions.

Dictionary of Occupational Titles A book prepared by the United States Training and Employment Service that provides titles and descriptions of thousands of jobs.

digital computer A computer, widely used by business firms, that works primarily with numbers.

directing The function in which management supervises and guides the subordinates.

directors' and officers' liability Insurance designed to cover directors and officers of a corporation against liability stemming from decisions they make as managers of the business.

disaster An unforeseen happening or act of God such as a tornado, hurricane, or fire, it is one of the most common causes of small business failure.

discount rate The rate charged by the Federal Reserve district bank to member banks that wish to sell it securities.

domestic corporation A corporation that is operating in the state in which it was incorporated.

dormant partner A partner who neither plays an active role in the operation of the business nor is known to the public as a partner.

ecology A term that refers to the relationship between an organism and its environment.

economic environment That environment that is characterized by buyers, sellers, and competition. For business firms, this is usually the most important of all the environmental forces.

economic order quantity formula A formula used to help a manager determine how often to reorder inventory and how many units to reorder each time.

economics The allocation of scarce resources for the purpose of fulfilling society's needs.

empathy The process of putting oneself in another's shoes and trying to see things from that person's point of view.

employment tests. Tests designed to help measure a potential employee's intelligence, interests, personality, and so on.

encoding process That part of the communication process in which the sender converts his or her ideas into some form of written message or picture for the purpose of conveying it.

enlightened self-interest A doctrine that holds that by helping society business actually helps itself.

entrepreneur A French word that, in English, means a person who has founded his or her own business or made a great deal of money through ingenuity and business skill.

environment Those forces that surround and affect business, including the historical, natural-physical, social-cultural, political-legal, and economic environments.

Equal Pay Act An act that forbids salary discrimination on the basis of sex for jobs that require equal skill, effort, and responsibility and are performed under similar working conditions.

equity-asset ratio The ratio between a firm's total equity and total assets.

ethics Standards that govern the moral conduct of individuals.

exception principle A management principle that states that the manager should be concerned only with significant deviations and exceptions and not worry about minor differences between expected and actual results.

extension agreement A method of avoiding bankruptcy that involves the creditors giving the firm an extension of payment terms, such as a one-year's grace period.

fabrication The combining of a host of materials or parts in such a way as to form a finished product.

factor A collection agent who purchases accounts receivable either with or without recourse.

favorable balance of trade. A situation that occurs when a country's exports are greater than its imports.

Federal Deposit Insurance Corporation A federal agency that insures bank deposits up to $40,000 in case of either bank failure or insolvency.

Federal Reserve System The central banking system of the United States, developed to provide control and stability of the country's monetary system.

Federal Trade Commission Act Legislation that was passed to help enforce the Clayton Act and also created the Federal Trade Commission.

financing A marketing function that involves obtaining credit or paying cash for goods.

fixed assets Those company resources that will last for more than one year and are intended to be used in the operation of the business rather than sold.

fixed costs Those expenses that remain the same in the short run regardless of how many units the firm manufactures.

flat organization structure An organization structure with a wide span of control.

flexible pricing The selling of merchandise to different buyers at different prices.

flow chart A graphic representation, widely used by computer programmers, of the operations or steps to be performed in solving a problem.

formal organization The officially designated organization structure as reflected by the company's organization chart and job descriptions.

FORTRAN An acronym standing for FORmula TRANslation, it is a computer language widely used in solving scientific problems.

franchise A system of distribution that enables the person selling the franchise (the franchisor) to arrange for a dealer (the franchisee) to handle a product or service under certain mutually agreed upon conditions.

fraud Intentional misrepresentation or deception on the part of business employees, which is one of the most common causes of small business failure.

freedom of choice The right of individuals in business to choose whatever good or service they want to produce rather than to be told by the government.

functional organization An organization in which specialists are placed in line positions.

Gantt chart A chart widely used for production control purposes that shows work progress and time.

general partner A partner who is usually very active in the firm's operation and who has unlimited liability.

general partnership A partnership in which all partners have the right to act in the firm's name and all have unlimited liability.

Gordon Technique A creative thinking technique widely used in handling technical problems.

grading A marketing function that involves the sorting of goods into classes, or grades, on the basis of quality.

grapevine The informal communication channels in the organization through which rumor and gossip and sometimes fact are passed.

Gross National Product The total value of all goods and services produced in the economy in one year.

hedging The purchase or sale of goods today with delivery scheduled for some time in the future.

human resources philosophy The belief that the workers are an important human resource of the organization and must be treated at least as well as, if not better than, the physical resources such as machinery and equipment.

human skills Those skills that help a manager work effectively with others on a person-to-person basis.

hygiene factors As described by Frederick Herzberg, things that will not motivate people but will lead to a lack of motivation if they are not present. Illustrations include money, security, and good working conditions.

income statement Also known as the profit-and-loss statement, a financial statement that presents a summary of the firm's operations over a period of time.

incompetence Inability to understand or run an operation properly, which is a common cause of failure among small business people.

indenture agreement An agreement that sets forth all the features associated with a bond issue.

industrial good A good used by industry or business to produce commercial, consumer, or other industrial goods.

inference An assumption made by the receiver of a message.

informal organization The unofficial organization structure that emerges from the social interaction of the people in the organization.

injunction A court order forbidding a particular action. This tactic is often used by a company against a union, in which case the injunction forbids the union from interfering with the company's operations.

institutional advertising Advertising designed to remind people of the name or reputation of a company or industry.

interlocking directorate An outlawed practice in which a majority of the members of the board of directors of two or more competitive corporations, at least one of which has assets in excess of $1 million, are the same individuals.

intermittent production A production sequence in which goods are produced in batches or are "one of a kind." Commonly used by firms producing goods for specific customer orders.

inventory control A method of balancing inventory levels and carrying costs.

inventory turnover A financial ratio that measures how often a firm is selling its inventory, computed by dividing cost of goods sold by average inventory.

investment banking company A middleman in the purchase and resale of new issues of stocks and bonds.

job enlargement Attempting to overcome job boredom by giving workers more operations to perform or moving them from one job to another.

job enrichment Changing a job so as to build in the things that really motivate the workers, such as increased responsibility, challenging work, and the opportunity for advancement and growth.

joint venture A partnership that is created for a particular purpose and, when the objective is accomplished, is then dissolved.

labor In economic terms, the human effort that is available to produce goods and services for consumption.

Labor-Management Relations Act An amendment to the National Labor Relations Act, this enumerated many specific unfair labor practices and helped swing the legislative pendulum away from labor and back toward management, so that there was a more equal balance of power between the two.

Labor-Management Reporting and Disclosure Act An act that required reporting and disclosure of union activities so as to eliminate racketeering and financial irresponsibility in some unions.

laissez-faire A French term that can be translated to mean that government should not interfere in the affairs of business.

land A term that refers to a nation's natural resources.

leadership The process of directing people toward the attainment of predetermined objectives.

liabilities The debts of a firm, such as money owed to creditors and taxes due the government.

limit order An order to buy or sell a stock at a predetermined price.

limited partner A partner whose liability is limited to the amount of money he or she has invested in the firm. This individual usually does not have the right to make any contracts in the name of the partnership.

line organization An organization in which there is a direct flow of authority from the top of the organization to the bottom.

line and staff organization An organization in which staff specialists are used to help out those directly responsible for attaining organization objectives.

list price The recommended retail price, usually placed on a good by the manufacturer.

lockout A management tactic consisting of simply refusing to allow the workers to enter the company's facilities.

long-term liabilities Those financial obligations that are not expected to be paid off during the next year.

long-term loan A loan with a maturity date of more than one year.

loss leader A product priced either at or below cost for the purpose of getting customers into the store with the hope that they will buy other goods as well.

macroeconomics That branch of economics concerned with the overall economy.

management The process of getting things done through people.

management functions The duties of a manager—namely planning, organizing, directing, and controlling.

management science Mathematical tools and techniques used in the decision-making process.

market order An order to buy or sell a stock at current market price.

marketing The process of identifying the goods and services the consumer wants and then providing them where they are needed, when they are desired, and at a price the purchaser is willing to pay.

marketing information Data upon which marketing decisions can be made.

marketing research The conducting of research on consumer buying habits for the purpose of marketing goods more effectively.

mean Another name for the arithmetic average.

median The number in a mathematical array that divides the group in half.

mediation A method for settling labor disputes that involves bringing in a mediator to make suggestions for resolving the problem.

message channel The means used to convey a message from sender to receiver.

microeconomics The branch of economics concerned with the individual firm.

middle management Plant managers, department managers, chief engineers, and others who report directly to top management and whose job it is to see that the long-range objectives set by top management are carried out.

mixed production sequence A combination of continuous production and batch (intermittent) production.

mode The number in a mathematical array that appears most frequently.

modification A synthetic process in which raw materials are changed into a product by being altered in some way.

modified capitalism Modern-day capitalism, in which the government regulates business activity to some degree.

monopolistic competition A market in which there are many firms in the industry with each producing only a small share of the total output being demanded.

motivation The process of creating the organizational conditions that will result in employees striving to attain company goals.

motivators As described by Frederick Herzberg, factors directly related to the work itself that result in high motivation and job satisfaction. Illustrations include recognition, responsibility, and advancement.

multinational corporation A corporation that has its base of operations in one country but carries on business in at least one other and has a management philosophy that is worldwide in nature.

National Labor Relations Act A federal act that gave workers the right to organize and required management to bargain collectively with the union.

natural-physical environment God-given resources such as air, water, land, and minerals.

neglect The condition of not paying sufficient attention to the enterprise, which is a common cause of business failure.

negotiable instrument A form of business paper that can be transferred from one person to another as a substitute for money.

network ad A television advertisement that is directed at a major audience around the country and that viewers all see at the same time.

New York Stock Exchange The best-known stock exchange, where 90 percent of the market value of all outstanding stocks in the U.S. are traded.

Nielsen Audimeter A mechanical device installed in a person's home for the purpose of determining which television programs are being watched. These devices play a key role in determining the fate of many of our television shows.

nominal partner A partner who lends his or her name to the enterprise but who invests no money in the firm and plays no role in its management.

noncumulative voting A method of voting for members of the board of directors in which each stockholder can cast one vote for each share owned for each available seat on the board. A stockholder voting for seven board members who holds 100 shares can cast 100 votes for seven candidates.

Norris-LaGuardia Act A federal act that expanded many of the provisions of the Railway Labor Act to include all workers.

objectives Goals the organization wishes to attain.

odd lot Less than 100 shares of stock.

odd pricing A pricing system, also known as psychological pricing, that involves pricing at an odd number such as $9.95 rather than $10.00.

oligopoly A market in which there are a few dominant firms.

one-way communicators Individuals who give orders but do not allow any feedback for the purpose of asking questions or clarifying meanings.

open corporation A corporation whose stock is available to anyone in the general public who is willing to pay the asking price.

open-market operations Operations that are used by the Federal Reserve to control the money supply and involve the buying and selling of government securities.

open shop An organization in which individuals can decide whether or not they wish to join the union. Union membership is not compulsory.

operating management Foremen, supervisors, and unit heads who report directly to middle managers and whose jobs consist of seeing that day-to-day operations are carried out.

opportunity cost of capital A term that refers to the theoretical cost of forgoing one investment in favor of another.

order getting The seeking out of potential buyers with a well-organized sales presentation.

order taking The completion of a sale to a customer who has expressed an interest in the product.

organizing A process in which the individuals and resources of a company are brought together for the purpose of attaining the enterprise's objectives.

owners' equity The investment the owners have in the firm.

partnership An association of two or more persons to carry on as co-owners of a business for profit.

partnership contract An agreement between partners that delineates such things as how profits will be distributed, the duties of all individuals, and how assets will be divided in case of dissolution.

penetration pricing A pricing strategy characterized by a low price designed to capture a large share of the market.

perception A person's view of reality.

picketing A union practice in which members march at the entrance to the company, usually carrying or wearing signs that identify their complaints against the firm.

pioneering advertising Advertising used to inform people of some new product or service.

place That part of the marketing mix that is the locale in which a product is available for sale.

plaintiff A party who brings a legal action.

planning The process of setting objectives and deciding how they are to be attained.

PL/1 A symbolic computer language designed for use by both scientific and business organizations.

political-legal environment Those laws and regulations that restrict business activity.

political risk insurance Insurance purchased by firms doing business overseas, to cover risks such as kidnapping, ransom, expropriation, and inconvertibility.

preferred stock A form of stock that gives its owner preference in dividends, prior claim on assets in case of dissolution, or both.

preventive maintenance Fixing something prior to its breaking down.

price That part of the marketing mix that is the amount that a company asks for a particular good or service.

primary data Data collected from original sources.

primary needs Physiological needs such as food, clothing, and shelter.

principal A person who is represented by an agent.

principle of clarity A communication principle that states that messages should be framed in such a way that they are clearly understood by the receiver.

principle of conciseness A communication principle that states that messages should be brief and to the point.

principle of delegation of authority A management principle that states that the manager should delegate authority to competent individuals at the lowest level of the hierarchy.

principle of the efficient use of the informal organization A management principle that holds that in receiving and transmitting information, managers should use the informal organization to supplement formal communication channels.

principle of equality of authority and responsibility A principle of management that holds that authority must be equal to responsibility.

principle of flexibility A management principle that states that an organization must be capable of adapting to changing conditions, such as upturns or downturns in the external environment.

principle of minimum levels A management principle that states that a firm should have as few levels in the hierarchy as possible.

principle of open communication A communication principle that states that employees will be motivated to achieve results if they are informed about what they are doing.

principle of work similarity A management principle that holds that it is most efficient to group together people who are doing the same kinds of work.

private enterprise The right of individuals to set up and operate their own businesses without having to share this ownership with the government.

private property The right of individuals to own land and other physical assets.

probability The likelihood of a particular event occurring.

process layout A type of work-flow layout in which the machines and equipment are grouped by function.

product Part of the marketing mix, this is the physical item and accessories that a company offers to the consumer.

product advertising Advertising that is directly concerned with the sale of a product.

production The process of transforming inputs such as raw materials into outputs such as goods and services.

productivity Another name for efficiency, this is measured by dividing output by input.

product layout A type of work-flow layout in which all the machines and services are set up along a product-flow line such as the assembly line used in producing automobiles.

program evaluation and review technique An operations research method used to manage and control complex projects.

progressive tax A tax based on the principle of ability to pay.

promotion That part of the marketing mix that refers to the methods used to stimulate demand for the company's product. Common methods include packaging, advertising, and personal selling.

proportional tax A tax in which the rate remains the same regardless of the base.

prospectus A booklet containing detailed company information, which is issued whenever a firm wants to sell new stock or bond issues to the general public.

prosperity An economic period during which the economy begins to move upward.

protective tariff A tariff designed to discourage foreign businesses from shipping certain goods into the country.

pure capitalism A form of capitalism in which the government practices laissez-faire.

pure competition A market in which there are many independent sellers, each offering a standardized product in a highly organized manner.

pure monopoly A market in which there is only one seller or producer and there are no substitutes for the good or service being provided.

quantity discount A discount based on the amount of merchandise purchased. The more someone buys the greater the discount.

quota A quantitative restriction expressed in terms of either physical quantity or value.

Railway Labor Act An early piece of labor legislation in the railroad industry that required employers to bargain collectively with their employees.

random sampling A method of sampling in which everyone has an identical chance of being chosen as a member of the sample.

readership reports A method of judging an ad's effectiveness that involves asking readers of certain magazines and newspapers about ads that appeared in these media to see which ones were remembered.

real-time processing A term that refers to a computer's ability to process information as soon as it is fed in.

recession An economic period during which the economy begins to slip or move downward.

recovery An economic period during which the economy begins to move out of a recession.

redemption premium A small bonus paid by a company when it exercises its right to call in a security prior to its maturity date.

regressive tax A tax that hits poor people harder than rich people.

regulatory tax A tax designed to regulate or restrict certain types of business practices.

reliable test. A test that consistently and accurately measures what it is designed to measure.

reminder advertising Advertising designed to keep a product's name before the public.

reserve requirement The percentage, established by the Federal Reserve System, of all bank deposits that must be maintained in the form of reserves.

resumé A short biographical sketch of oneself, also known as a data sheet.

retailers Those middlemen who sell goods and services to the final consumer.

return on assets A financial ratio that measures how well a company is performing with all of its assets, computed by dividing net income by total assets.

revenue tariff A tariff designed to raise money for the government.

risk A condition that exists when a decision maker does not know with certainty the outcome of a decision before it is made.

risk taking A marketing function that involves taking a chance when purchasing merchandise. Common illustrations of chance include the possibility that the goods will be stolen, destroyed by fire, or be obsolete before they can be sold.

Robinson-Patman Act An act designed to eliminate unfair price competition.

round lot One-hundred shares of stock.

safety stock A protective cushion used by a firm to prevent its running out of inventory.

seasonal discount A discount given to buyers who purchase merchandise before the season begins.

seasonal variation An economic fluctuation that tends to last only a short period of time such as one year.

secondary data Data that have already been collected and can be found in published sources.

secondary needs Psychological needs such as love, the need to feel wanted, and the desire to associate and interact with other people.

secret partner A partner who plays an active role in running the business but is not known to the public as a partner.

secular trend An economic fluctuation that covers a very long period of time and reflects the long-term growth of a particular company, industry, or nation.

secured loan A loan for which collateral is given.

Securities Act of 1933 A federal law designed to protect investors by requiring full disclosure of all relevant financial information by firms desiring to sell new stock or bond issues to the general public.

securities exchange A market place where stocks and bonds are bought and sold.

Securities Exchange Act of 1934 The law that created the Securities and Exchange Commission.

selling A marketing function that involves a transaction in which a buyer pays money for a good and the seller hands over the item.

selling short Selling stock in the hope of replacing it at a lower price.

semantics A common barrier to communication that involves the same word having different meanings for different people.

Sherman Antitrust Act An act designed to outlaw all contracts or agreements formed for the purpose of restraining trade in interstate commerce.

shopping good A good that the consumer buys only after comparing what competing stores have to offer in the way of such things as price, style, and quality.

silent partner A partner who is known as an owner in the business but who takes no active role in managing the operations.

sitdown strike A strike in which the workers go to their jobs but refuse to do any work.

skimming A pricing strategy that involves setting a high price on a product for the purpose of capturing the top of the market demand.

slowdown strike A strike in which the employees simply reduce their work tempo so that very little gets done.

small business An enterprise in which two or more of the following features are present: (1) the owners are the managers, (2) the capital for running the business is provided by one individual or a small group, (3) business operations are mainly local, and (4) the business is small in contrast to the large firms in the field.

social-cultural environment That environment consisting of the beliefs, attitudes, customs, and practices of everyone in the society.

socialism An economic system in which certain primary industries such as steel, utilities, and transportation are controlled by the government.

social responsibility The moral obligation business has to assume concern for the welfare of the society in which it operates.

sole proprietorship A business owned and controlled by one individual.

span of control principle A management principle that states that managers can effectively handle only a limited number of subordinates.

specialty good A good for which consumers are willing to spend extra effort to locate and buy, such as a particular type of car or a specific kind of specialty cheese.

specific duty A tariff fee levied at the rate of so much per unit or pound, such as $10 per unit or 25¢ per pound.

Speculator A person who invests in stocks and bonds with the hope of making a large profit in a very short period of time.

spot ad A television ad broadcast over one or more stations at various times, each station sending out the message separately rather than all at once.

standardization A marketing function that involves the establishment of specifications or categories for products.

standard of living The measure of a nation's wealth, usually determined by dividing production by population.

standing committee A committee formed on a permanent basis.

static product layout A type of workflow layout in which the workers are brought to the product rather than vice versa. This layout is common in the production of bulky or heavy goods that cannot be moved around the plant.

statutory law Written law consisting of formal enactments or statutes by various governmental bodies.

storage A marketing function that involves holding the goods in either company-owned facilities or public storage warehouses until they are demanded by the consumer.

strike A temporary refusal by workers to continue doing their jobs until their demands are met by management.

structured interview An interview in which the interviewer follows a prepared, prearranged format.

synthetic process A production process in which a number of different raw materials or parts are converted into a finished product.

system 1 A term used to describe a manager who has very little confidence in the subordinates.

system 2 A term used to describe a manager who is heavily benevolent.

system 3 A term used to describe a manager who consults with subordinates before making decisions.

system 4 A term used to describe a manager who has complete confidence and trust in subordinates.

tall organization structure An organization structure with a small span of control.

tariff A duty or fee levied on goods being imported into a country.

technical skills Those skills that allow a manager to use techniques, methods, and equipment in performing specific tasks.

technology The application of knowledge to production as evidenced by the development of new machines that reduce the time and expense associated with producing goods.

term life insurance A form of life insurance that provides coverage for a limited period of time, with the insurance company obligated to pay only if the person dies.

Theory X A list of assumptions managers often have about the workers, including beliefs such as (a) the average person dislikes work, (b) to get people to work it is necessary to use constant pressure, and (c) people actually like to be directed, controlled, and supervised very closely.

Theory Y A list of assumptions about workers which holds that (a) work is a natural activity, (b) close control and threats of punishment are not the only ways to get people to do things, and (c) commitment to objectives is determined by the rewards associated with their achievement.

time sharing A new computer development whereby a number of people can use the computer at the same time.

top management The board of directors, president, vice-president, and other key company officers who help set the long-range objectives of the firm.

trade credit Credit given to a company when it purchases goods from another firm.

trade discount A price reduction given to people who help move a good through the distribution channel. A common illustration is a 20-percent discount given to retail stores by publishing houses on the price of all books.

trade on margin The purchase of securities on credit.

Truth in Lending Act An act that requires banks and other lending agencies to tell the borrower exactly how much money is being loaned and what the interest rate is on the entire loan.

Truth in Packaging Act An act that requires that the consumer be told the volume and contents of the package.

two-way communication The transmission of information and ideas both up and down the hierarchy.

tying agreement A contract in which a buyer agrees to purchase other goods from the seller as part of a "package" deal.

unbalanced experience The condition of not having well-rounded exposure in all of the important areas of operations, which is a common cause of failure among small business people.

uncertainty A condition that exists when a decision maker feels completely incapable of estimating the outcome of a particular decision.

unfavorable balance of trade A situation that occurs when a country's imports are greater than its exports.

union shop A union-management agreement whereby the individuals in the firm must join the union after a prescribed period of time.

unity of objective principle A management principle that holds that each department in a company must assist in attaining the overall objectives of the firm.

universality of management functions A management principle that holds

that all managers perform the same basic functions.

unlimited liability The responsibility for all debts and financial obligations. This is one of the greatest disadvantages of both sole proprietorships and general partnerships.

unsecured loan A loan for which no collateral is given.

valid test A test that measures what it is supposed to measure.

variable costs Those expenses that change in relation to output.

vestibule training Training given to an individual in an environment that duplicates the on-the-job situation.

whole life insurance Also known as straight life, this is a form of insurance in which the annual premium remains constant throughout the life of the policy and the individual is required to pay this amount as long as the policy is in force. The face value of the policy is payable upon the death of the insured.

wholesalers Middlemen who purchase goods and sell them to buyers for the purpose of resale.

working capital The difference between current assets and current liabilities.

yellow-dog contract A written pledge not to join the union.

Yield The return obtained from a stock, which is computed by dividing income by stock price.

Index

Index